PRINCIPLES AND TYPES OF SPEECH

fifth edition

For this edition, Keith S. Montgomery, Purdue University, provided substantial revisions in the text and exercises as well as many new short illustrative examples and sample speeches.

Douglas Ehninger, State University of Iowa, suggested changes throughout the book and also was chiefly responsible for the revisions of Chapters 1 and 22 and the analyses of speeches in Chapters 20 and 22.

A. H. M.

PRINCIPLES AND TYPES OF SPEECH

Fifth Edition

ALAN H. MONROE
Purdue University

SCOTT, FORESMAN AND COMPANY
Chicago, Atlanta, Dallas, Palo Alto, Fair Lawn, N. J.

Preface to the Fifth Edition

This fifth edition, like the earlier ones, presents a functional approach to the problem of effective speaking. Its basic philosophy is that the purpose of speech is to communicate and that its effectiveness must be judged by the reaction of the audience. Therefore, it constantly stresses audience analysis and adaptation to the listener; and, in discussing the problems of delivery and composition, it emphasizes the relationship between the technics and the end for which they are designed—effective communication. The familiar devices of speech composition—reference to subject, illustration, causal reasoning, summary, contrast, and the like—are presented not as arbitrary means of building a speech but rather as methods of securing a particular audience response. Thus the first half of this text, while considering in detail the classic principles of speech preparation and delivery, always points to their eventual application in actual speech situations.

In Parts Four and Five, which discuss specific types of speech, the emphasis upon audience reaction is even more direct. To clarify the dynamic relationship between speaker and listener, the names of the conventional divisions of a speech (introduction, body, and conclusion) are dropped in favor of ones emphasizing the function of each part in securing a particular audience reaction. The speech structure is thus divided into five steps—attention, need, satisfaction, visualization, and action—which together form a motivated sequence: the sequence of ideas which, by following a normal process of human thinking, motivates the audience to respond to the speaker's purpose. (The chart on page 328 indicates the parallel between steps in the motivated sequence and the conventional divisions of a speech.) Depending upon the general end of a speech, the sequence may be used in its complete form, or modified by omitting, expanding, or combining certain steps. Whether used in a complete or abbreviated form, however, the motivated sequence serves as a constant reminder that the function of speech is communication.

The book is divided into six main parts. Part One, with its two chapters on the essentials of effective speaking and backgrounds and fundamental concepts, provides the student with valuable help for his first speeches and a perspective for his approach to the study of speech. The four chapters in Part Two explain the fundamentals of speech delivery—physical behavior and vocal quality, variety, and intelligibility. Part Three is concerned with specific problems of speech preparation, such as audience analysis, attention and motivation, selection of subject matter and wording, and the adaptation of speech organization to purpose and audience.

In the second half of the book, the principles and technics elaborated in the first three parts are applied to the various types of speech. Part Four considers in detail the special problems involved in building the basic kinds of speech, with the general ends to entertain, inform, stimulate, and convince. Part Five contains a series of chapters on more specialized types of public speech, such as introductions and courtesy speeches. Part Six takes up the technics of discussion, concluding with a chapter on parliamentary law for informal groups.

A brief appendix provides (1) "A Guide to Effective Listening," which shows how the principles of good speech elaborated in the text (clarity, logic, motivation, word meaning, and the like) may be applied in developing ability to listen with greater comprehension, appreciation, and critical judgment; (2) an abridged version of the International Phonetic Alphabet; and (3) a chart showing the adaptation of the motivated sequence to audience attitudes.

For this edition, incidental changes have been made throughout the book. For example, modifications have been made in Chapters 14 through 17 to point up more clearly that Chapters 14 and 15, taken together, provide the traditional method of organizing a speech; and Chapters 16 and 17, building on these two chapters, demonstrate the functional speech structure—the motivated sequence—that integrates speech composition and audience psychology. In addition, the text and exercises throughout the book have been brought up to date with many new short illustrative examples and sample speeches.

Major changes have been made in Chapter 1, where greater emphasis has been placed on the importance of the speaker's integrity and more help has been given to the student in preparing his first speeches; in Chapter 22, which has been considerably expanded to include several common variations of the speech to convince; and in Chapter 30, where at least two ways of organizing a discussion plan are provided. Another feature of the revision is the two sample analyses, one for a speech to inform and one for a speech to convince. It is hoped that these analyses will provide students with helpful suggestions for studying speeches for themselves.

Two further changes include the deletion of the chapter on the after-dinner speech, which seemed amply considered in other chapters. In keeping with the ever-increasing seriousness of purpose and emphasis on stricter standards of college curricula in general, the picture program has been limited chiefly to purely functional illustrations—to necessary charts and diagrams in sections such as the one on mechanics of speaking and to photographs for sections on physical behavior and on the use of visible supporting materials. In addition, to supply dramatic contrast and interest, Robert J. Billings has provided sketches for the six part openings.

The author is deeply indebted to Professor Keith Montgomery of Purdue University for much of the detailed revision and for seeking out new examples and speeches, and to Professor Douglas Ehninger of the State University of Iowa for his many critical suggestions, the revision of Chapters 1 and 22, and analyses of speeches in Chapters 20 and 22. In addition, he appreciates greatly the permission of speakers and publishers to use selections for illustrative purposes.

If the students using this fifth edition learn more fully to appreciate the value of effective speech, to improve their own speaking, and to listen to the speech of others with greater comprehension and critical judgment, its purpose will have been fulfilled.

A. H. M.

West Lafayette, Indiana
January 20, 1962

acknowledgments

28–29   Original drawing by Arnold W. Ryan.

40   (top) Courtesy of Bell Telephone Laboratories; (bottom) Courtesy of Purdue University.

57   (left to right, top to bottom) Courtesy of *U.S. News & World Report;* Wide World Photo; United Press International Photo; *Look* Magazine Photo; Henry Grossman; Courtesy of *U.S. News & World Report;* Courtesy of University of Kansas; *Newsweek*—Curtis G. Pepper.

70–71   Original drawings by Arnold W. Ryan.

75   Courtesy *Life* Magazine. Copr. 1940 Time Inc.

159   (top) Courtesy of Elmhurst College; (center left) Photograph by Carl Purcell, National Education Association; (center right) United Press International Photo; (bottom) Courtesy of A.T.&T. Photo Service.

164   (top) Courtesy of General Electric Company; (bottom) Charles Phelps Cushing.

208   (top) Nate Fine Photo; (bottom) Courtesy of Florida State University.

209   (top) Courtesy of Purdue University; (bottom left) Courtesy of Indiana University; (bottom right) Courtesy of Purdue University.

210   (top left) Wide World Photo; (top right) Courtesy of University of Kansas; (bottom left) Courtesy of Indiana University; (bottom right) as published in *Educational Screen and Audiovisual Guide,* October 1960.

215   Chart prepared by Arnold W. Ryan.

285   Courtesy of the United Nations.

contents

— Triteness — Slang — Connective
phrases—Building a vocabulary

Part 4 Basic Types of Speech

19. The speech to entertain

Typical situations requiring speeches
of entertainment — The purpose: to
entertain the audience—Some characteristics of delivery and content—
The use of humor—Organization—
Sample speech

20. The speech to inform

Types of informative speeches—The
purpose: to secure understanding—
The manner of speaking—Characteristics of content — Organization —
Sample speeches

**21. The speech to stimulate
(or to actuate through emotional stimulation)**

Typical situations requiring speeches
which stimulate—The purpose—The
manner of speaking—Characteristics
of content—The types of imagery—
Organization—*Sample speech*

**22. The speech to convince
(or to actuate through conviction)**

Situations requiring speeches to convince—The purpose: to secure belief
or action based on belief—Analysis of
propositions — Organization — The
manner of speaking—Content of the
speech to convince—Technics of the
speech to convince—Adapting organization to audience attitude—*Sample
speeches*

xii   *Contents*

part one

Basic
Viewpoints
and
Beginning
Steps

Essentials of effective speaking   •   Backgrounds and fundamental concepts

Integrity without knowledge is weak and useless. . . .
Knowledge without integrity is dangerous and dreadful.
Samuel Johnson

CHAPTER 1 / *Essentials of Effective Speaking*

PRESIDENT SPEAKS TO NATION 8:30 TONIGHT. This newspaper headline, often appearing at a time of national crisis, always arouses strong interest. Why does the President *speak* instead of merely issuing a statement? Obviously he feels that by speaking he can make a more personal appeal for unified national support. Because of the great prestige of his office, the President's speech is always front-page news. Every day, however, over one hundred eighty million other citizens of this country speak. They order groceries, discuss the neighbor's new car, sell life insurance, teach school, hold conferences and committee meetings, argue on the street corners, pay compliments to their sweethearts. Their speech is not headline news, but to each of them it is a necessary part of daily life.

Speech is probably the most important activity at your college. Think of the dozens, perhaps hundreds, of lectures that are delivered every day; the countless classroom demonstrations and discussions; the conferences between students and instructors; the faculty committee meetings; the informal conversations and bull sessions; the oral examinations and quizzes; the school radio or television station sending forth its steady stream of news and information; the debates at fraternity and sorority meetings; the public lectures, plays, and programs. How many words, do you think, are spoken during a typical day on your campus? Clearly they run into the millions.

Not only are millions of words spoken every day, but speech itself is a concern of colleges. Many departments are actively engaged in trying to learn more about human communication and how to increase its effectiveness. The physicist and engineer seek improved means of transmitting speech sounds; the physiologist endeavors to learn more about the vocal mechanism and the structure of the ear; the psychologist studies the role of speech in human behavior; the historian investigates the part the spoken word has played in great social and political movements. In the speech and hearing clinics deficiencies of speech production or reception are diagnosed and treated. In voice and diction courses students learn to speak more clearly and pleasingly; in oral interpretation courses they learn to interpret and communicate to others the ideas contained on the printed page; in public speaking, discussion, and debate, they learn to select and organize material for presentation to a group.

Both in its dependence on speech in carrying out its daily functions and in its concern with the effectiveness of oral communication, a college is typical of most human institutions. Publishing houses, government agencies, industrial plants, railroads, air lines, even hospitals and research laboratories—here, too, millions of words are spoken every day, and here, too, the concern with effective communication is high.

Just talking, therefore, is obviously not enough; people also need to talk *well*. Make a list of the ten or fifteen most influential people in your community—those who are leaders in business or the professions or who hold public office. Isn't it true that nearly all of them are effective speakers? The importance of speaking ability becomes even more apparent if you expand your list to include the names of those prominent in state, national, or world affairs. The simple truth is that in a democratic society such as ours, and in a world that increasingly seeks to talk out its differences rather than fight them out, the ability to express ideas is just as essential as the capacity to have ideas. Even in your own circle of friends and acquaintances, you will find that the impression you make depends largely upon the ease and vigor with which you talk, the tact with which you advance and defend your convictions, and the attractiveness of your habitual speaking manner.

IMPORTANCE OF THE SPEAKER'S INTEGRITY

What has just been said does not mean, of course, that acquiring the skills and technics of good speech will overnight make you a leader of men. Such hasty miracles seldom occur except in novels or movies. Nor will skills and technics by themselves make you a truly effective speaker. More than two thousand years ago, Aristotle emphasized a truth that was then already old and widely recognized. Success as a public speaker, he said in his treatise *The Rhetoric,* depends upon more than a ready vocabulary, pleasing diction, and coordinated gestures. An effective speaker must first of all be an effective person. He must be intelligent and well-informed, not only about his immediate subject but about human affairs in general, and he must possess a high degree of poise and self-control. But above all, if a man is to win acceptance of his ideas, he must be respected as a man of character and moral worth by those who hear him.

This emphasis upon character as an essential element in effective speaking has been echoed by major writers on the subject from Aristotle's time to our own. In order to communicate ideas to others, one must first express himself; and *self-expression* is a two-part term. It involves not only the mechanical processes of sound production and transmission but also—inevitably—the expression of some*thing* by some*body*. People never listen merely to a speech; they always listen to a *person* speaking. And because a man's words and manner mirror what he is, the *self* and the *expression* can never be divorced.

The man who has a reputation for knowing the facts and speaking the truth will be listened to because people believe in his integrity. On the other hand, the man who is not respected can seldom, even with the strongest arguments or most subtle appeals, win lasting adherence to his views. People are quick to see through insincerity and to recognize a speaker for what he really is.

Traditionally, this persuasive force which resides in the character or reputation of the speaker is called "ethical proof," after the Greek word *ethos,* meaning character. Of all the modes of persuasion, it is perhaps the strongest and most permanent. Certainly, when actions contradict words we lose faith in what is said. The speaker who habitually cheats in school or business can hardly hope to persuade others to be honest and fair. Requests for objectivity or open-mindedness fall upon deaf ears if the one who makes them is known as a bigot. The speaker whose character contradicts his message may win a temporary success, but if he becomes known as a person who seeks unfair personal advantage, who suppresses or warps evidence to prove his case, he will soon lose his ability to convince an audience. The currency of his speech is recognized as counterfeit and his influence is lost.

When Winston Churchill took over the British government during the Second World War, he offered his countrymen only "blood, sweat, and tears" in the struggle with Nazi Germany. Yet this very rugged honesty captured their support far quicker than rosy promises could have. The British people believed in his integrity because earlier, when the policy of appeasing Hitler had been popular, he had courageously opposed it. To the British people during the war, Winston Churchill became the symbol of their courage and their faith. His mastery of the art of speech made people listen, but it was confidence in his integrity that made them follow him.

In order to be listened to and believed, then, you must have a deserved reputation for integrity. Effective speaking calls for skills and technics, but first of all it requires that you develop as a person. Learning to speak well is not an art to be mastered during the course of a single semester nor to be comprehended within the covers of any textbook, no matter how long or profound. It is a lifelong task which calls for an individual's best efforts.

Remembering that integrity and moral worth are the basis of the personal persuasiveness we call *ethos,* let us turn to the other requisites for effective speaking—knowledge, self-confidence, and skill in the use of voice and body. Without knowledge even the most honest and sincere speaker will be empty; without self-confidence he will stumble and lack impressiveness; without skill he may be unheard or misunderstood. Read Alot

DEVELOPING A BACKGROUND OF KNOWLEDGE

When Daniel Webster was asked how he was able to prepare his famous reply to Senator Robert Y. Hayne on such short notice, he replied that the ideas came to him like thunderbolts which he had only to reach out and seize, white hot, as they went smoking by. But this store of "thunderbolts" was not an accident. Over many years a constant study of law, politics, and literature had filled his mind with an abundant supply of facts, illustrations, and arguments. When faced with a specific speaking situation, he had only to call these forth.

You, too, will find it important to read widely and carefully to broaden your background of knowledge and understanding. Through such study your speaking should grow in depth and maturity. Of course you will not need to wait until you have reached middle age before you dare speak in public. The very process of selecting and organizing material for a speech often tends to clarify your thoughts, and the background you already have, when properly reconsidered and supplemented by additional study, will provide sufficient material for your early speeches.

As you grow in skill and confidence, you will, of course, want to reach out beyond immediate and familiar topics—to learn and speak about subjects in new fields. You may want to investigate topics related to the business or profession you intend to enter, since most of your speeches after college will be on subjects closely related to your vocation. Doctors usually speak on problems of health or disease; history teachers, on current events; football coaches, on football. Why not begin now to correlate your vocational objective with your development as a speaker by occasionally talking on subjects related to that vocation? The more you learn about these subjects, the better lawyer, engineer, or merchant you will be—and the better you will be able to speak intelligently about your profession in years to come.

But a thorough knowledge of your own field of interest is not sufficient if you wish to become an accomplished speaker; you must know about more than this single subject. You should certainly keep abreast of current events and make a habit of reading at least one daily newspaper and some current magazines and of listening to authoritative news broadcasts. You should also have several topics besides your profession which particularly interest you and about which you are eager to learn more. Are you interested in the theater? See as many plays as possible; study the development of drama from ancient to modern times; read about recent trends in costume design, make-up, lighting, and scenery. Do you like good literature? Find out as much as you can about current books and authors while you also continue to study the classics. In short, try to become well-informed on current events and on at least three or four subjects other than your own vocation. Remember, too, that in order to relate your ideas to persons without your specialized knowledge, you will need a wide variety of illustrative material. This may be acquired by wide reading and careful listening. Perhaps you will even want to build up a file of pertinent notes and clippings.

In speaking, as in any other activity, there is no substitute for knowledge that is thorough and varied. The list of topics at the end of this chapter may suggest subjects for your first classroom speeches; but as you go further, choose subjects which will develop your store of knowledge and force you to extend the range and depth of your understanding. In the proportion that you do this, you will be on your way to becoming a truly successful speaker.

INCREASING SELF-CONFIDENCE

What traits characterize a poised and self-confident speaker? Among other things, an erect but comfortable posture free from dependence on chairs, tables, or other supports; easy movement free from fidgeting or jerkiness; direct, eye-to-eye contact with the audience; earnestness and energy in the voice; and an alertness of mind which enables him to think on his feet.

Many factors help determine the amount of nervousness a speaker may feel—including the amount of sleep he had the night before and the quantity of mince pie he ate for dinner. But the observance of the following simple rules will almost certainly increase your poise and self-control.

Pick an interesting subject. Have you ever noticed how a shy youngster loses his bashfulness when you get him to talk about what really interests him: his new skates, the rabbit his dog was chasing, or the proposal to build a bonfire with the leaves on the front lawn? The more a speaker thinks about his subject and the less he thinks about himself, the less self-conscious he becomes. Avoid, therefore, topics to which you yourself are indifferent; choose material that compels your attention. Don't talk about something merely because you think it might make a good subject for a speech; take something that will make you want to talk—an idea that you are eager to communicate to others. A fairly sound test is to ask yourself what subjects habitually interest you; what do you normally think and talk about when your work is finished? On such subjects you will usually be able to talk freely and confidently.

Know your subject thoroughly. Compare the way you feel when called on to recite after you have thoroughly studied your lesson with the way you feel when you are unprepared. The man who knows his subject is always more confident than the one who does not. But how can you gain an adequate knowledge of your subject? There are two ways: (*a*) you may study in order to find out more about your subject than anyone in your audience will know; or (*b*) you may pick a subject from your own experience upon which your knowledge is already direct, personal, and reasonably complete. Normally, you will choose subjects you already know about for your first few speeches and later on select subjects that require more research. In either case you will be wise not to choose too broad a subject. You will feel more confident if you talk about living conditions on the campus or in your home town, situations with which you are familiar, than if, with a smattering of information hastily obtained from reading, you try to discuss the American standard of living in general.

Learn thoroughly the sequence of the ideas you intend to present. As long as the highway is straight or the turns are clearly marked, the motorist is confident of reaching his destination; but if he gets off on a lonely, unmarked road, he is less certain of his direction and hesitates at every turn. Similarly, you will feel more confident if you have the direction of your speech firmly in mind, if you have memorized the sequence of main points. Do not, however, memorize your speech word for word. When you memorize verbatim, you usually become more concerned with the words than with the ideas; and if you forget one phrase, you are likely to confuse the entire sequence of your speech.

Speak as often as you can. The first time a person drives a car or flies an airplane alone, he is likely to be tense and unsure of himself; but with each successful attempt, his confidence grows. In the same way, each successful speech you make will strengthen your self-assurance.

Focus your attention on your audience. When you step up to a soda fountain and ask for a malted milk, do you worry about how you are standing, sitting, or speaking? Of course not; you are concerned only that the clerk understands you correctly. Public speaking is no different from ordinary conversation in this respect. There is, of course, a difference in degree—just as driving a railroad spike differs from pounding a carpet tack—but the fundamental process is the same: in any kind of speaking you are trying to communicate an idea to someone else. So concentrate on Tom, Bill, and Sally in your audience; watch to see whether they are getting your point. If not, say it over again in a different way or explain it more completely; but be thinking of them and talking to them while you do it. Of course, there are times when you need to be concerned with your manner of speaking; everyone has his weak points, and nearly everyone can improve himself by special drill upon them. As you proceed with your course of study, you will want to single out one or two things at a time to practice on in detail. But practice on your weak points in private so that your technic becomes habitual and you will be unconscious of it while speaking to your audience. Forget yourself as much as possible when you are giving a speech; think only about getting your audience to understand and to agree with you.

Be physically active while you speak. Just as the athlete is nervous because of the tension of his muscles before the gun is fired to start the race, so the speaker who stands before an audience with taut muscles feels the strain; but the athlete loses all trace of nervousness as soon as the race begins and his muscles are put to use, and the speaker can accomplish the same result by moving about and gesturing while he speaks. Such movements tend to stimulate energetic thought and speech. If you reinforce the strength of what you have to say with gestures of your hands and arms, you will speak more vigorously and will feel the assurance and confidence which come naturally to an active person. Walk from one part of the platform to another as you begin to present a new idea; go to the blackboard and draw a diagram or write down the points you want the audience to remember; show your listeners the object you are talking about and demonstrate how it is used; imagine you are on the scene you are describing and use your arms and hands to point out where each thing is as you tell about it. In this way you will increase both your own confidence and the vitality of what you say.

Remember that some nervous tension is both natural and good for you. Even in the deepest sleep our muscles are never completely relaxed; there is a certain amount of tension in them which physiologists call "muscle tonus." When we are awake, this tonus is higher; and it increases when we are keyed up and getting set to do something. Naturally, then, when you stand up to talk to a group of people, the tonus of your muscles will rise, and you will literally be more alive. Much of the sparkle and punch that we admire in good speakers comes from this physical verve and energy. Thus, if you feel tense just before you start to speak, regard this as a good sign; it means that there is little chance of your making a dull and listless speech. If your tension is so high as to hamper you, pause and move around a bit. (In fact, many good speakers do this at the beginning of every speech; they stand up, walk out slowly, let their eyes pass easily over the audience for a moment, then take another step forward and begin to talk.) But instead of worrying because you feel a bit keyed up, be happy that your nerves and muscles are alive enough to put vigor into your speaking.

Never allow yourself to give up. Each time you meet a situation and master it, the more confident you become; each time you acknowledge yourself beaten or evade an issue, the harder you will find it to face the next time. Avoid setting yourself too difficult a task in your first few speeches—that is, avoid subjects which are too complex—but once you have begun, go through with the job. Confidence, like muscles, develops by overcoming resistance.

One final word on this matter of self-confidence. Do not infer from the amount of space devoted to the subject here that your instructor expects you to be completely lacking in assurance. The fact that you have reached your present age and have been able to enter college gives him the right to expect from you a reasonable ability to speak and a reasonable degree of confidence in that ability. You will be given speech assignments, at first simple but later increasing in difficulty, and you will be expected to do them. Do not expect your instructor to coddle you along; stand on your own feet and add to the confidence you now have with each successive well-prepared and effective speech you make.

DEVELOPING SKILL

Although success as a speaker depends upon more than a ready tongue, well-modulated vocal inflections, and appropriate gestures, these skills are of great importance. Combined with moral integrity, sound knowledge, and the poise that comes from merited self-confidence, skill in delivery increases a speaker's effectiveness immeasurably by helping him display to best advantage his inner traits of mind and character.

You have already developed considerably in each of the skills or abilities necessary to good public speaking—fluency, control of the voice, and purposeful use of the body. For the past sixteen to twenty years you have been speaking many thousands of words every day. As a result, you are better able to express yourself today than you were at the age of five or six; your vocabulary is larger, and you are able to put ideas into words more clearly and readily. Through training and casual practice, your control of voice and body has also advanced steadily since babyhood. But over the years you may have developed bad speech habits as well as good ones; moreover, no matter how skilled a speaker is, further improvement is always possible. The task which lies before you as you begin a course in public speaking, therefore, consists of sloughing off whatever bad speech habits you may have unthinkingly acquired and of developing further the desirable skills and habits you already possess. As this process takes place day by day, your effectiveness as a public speaker will gradually increase. As new skills and correct habits become fixed—so much a part of you that you do not even need to stop to think about them—speaking will become an enjoyable and stimulating experience.

Fluency

By a "fluent" speaker we do not mean one who possesses a large vocabulary of exotic words which he delights in parading at every opportunity. Of course, knowing many words is helpful since it enables one to express a wide variety of ideas more precisely and economically than would otherwise be possible. But more important than the size of your vocabulary is an intimate acquaintance with the meanings and nuances of the words you do know and the ability to use these words readily and smoothly, without distracting pauses or the frequent intrusions of "ers," "ahs," and "uhs." Such ability is developed by wide reading of the best authors, by frequent reference to a good dictionary or thesaurus, and, above all, by constant practice in writing and speaking. In this practice always aim to express ideas as simply and clearly as possible—to make the substance of each thought or argument stand out vividly. Other things being equal, speaking in which language facilitates full and ready comprehension is always good speaking; speaking in which language hides or draws attention away from the thought is always bad.

The conversational mode

In practicing to gain skill in the use of your voice, you must take care not to develop artificiality. Superficial skill, without sincerity of purpose, makes speaking a mockery. Many an awkwardly delivered speech has proved eloquent simply because of the enthusiastic sincerity of the speaker. On the other hand, a speaker may be completely sincere and yet fail to communicate because he seems to withdraw into a shell; he mumbles his words and appears to be talking primarily to himself. The pattern of speaking which falls between these two extremes, and which you should seek to develop, is known as the *conversational mode*. The name is derived from the fact that this type of speech is based upon the best elements of conversation, stepped up to meet the demands of the public or larger audience situation. Good conversational speaking is distinct and lively. It does not strive for artificial effects but is decidedly informal. Yet it commands attention and is forceful because of the speaker's earnest desire to communicate important ideas to others. Good public speaking should have these same characteristics. In fact, many effective public speakers seem merely to be conversing energetically with the audience. Although the larger number of listeners and the acoustics of the auditorium may require increased volume and more pronounced inflectional patterns from a speaker, he should retain the essential spirit of animated conversation.

Types of speakers who lack the conversational manner The following paragraphs describe some types of public speakers who do not employ the conversational mode and hence lack the earnest, animated communication which springs from it:

(*a*) The *elocutionist* allows himself to get carried away by the sound of his own voice at the expense of the thought behind it. He talks for display rather than for communication. His voice drips tears; there is a studied care about every pause and inflection; and he bows when he is through, waiting expectantly for applause. Such a speaker usually lacks both energy and substance; and while the audience may applaud him as an accomplished actor, they will seldom be moved by what he says.

(*b*) The *oracle*, by his voice and manner, conveys the impression that he knows everything. The simplest statement is solemnly intoned; the speaker's whole attitude seems to say, "When I talk, let no dog bark!" Like the elocutionist, the oracle fails to communicate because he is parading himself rather than honestly attempting to convey worth-while ideas to others. Although he is very much aware of the audience, he is more interested in applause than in securing an honest response of understanding, belief, or action.

A third type of speaker, (*c*) the *hermit*, fails to communicate because he ignores or fears the audience—he seems to be mumbling to himself. The hermit may have a wealth of sound ideas, well organized and developed, but he talks in a weak, monotonous voice and makes no effort to be understood. He gives the impression of not caring whether anyone hears him—and usually, no one does. Then there is (d) the culprit—the speaker who seems ashamed of what he says. He shrinks from his hearers and refuses to raise or vary his voice, on the apparent assumption that the fewer persons who hear him the fewer mistakes he will make. Sometimes he apologizes verbally; but his manner is always apologetic and tentative. He is never forthright in his statements because he seems hesitant to believe them himself. Neither the hermit nor the culprit employs the conversational mode. While they avoid the display in which the elocutionist and oracle delight, they lack the distinct and lively speech so necessary to good communication.

One final type of speaker should be mentioned—(e) the gibberer. He emits a continuous stream of words with little or no apparent thought behind them. He fails to communicate because he has no single compelling thought which he seeks to convey. He wanders aimlessly from one idea to another until both he and his audience are dizzy from meandering; then he usually stops by saying, "Well, I guess that's all I have to offer on the subject now." So far as the timing and melody patterns of his voice are concerned, the gibberer may be employing the conversational mode. In reality, however, he is unconversational because he, like the elocutionist and oracle, has no important idea to communicate. The conversational mode is dependent upon the presence of thought as well as upon the natural use of inflection, rate, and pause. It requires sound sense no less than earnest, energetic expression.

Physical behavior on the platform

Just as the natural pattern of conversation furnishes the ideal basis for a speaker's vocal delivery, so does a completely natural and unobtrusive use of the body furnish the ideal basis for that part of delivery which an audience sees rather than hears—for what might be termed bodily delivery or the speaker's physical behavior on the platform.

When a friend is trying to communicate some important idea to you in conversation, you seldom are aware of how he is standing, the position of his head, the slant of his shoulders, or the gestures and facial expressions he is using to help convey his thoughts. All of these aspects of bodily delivery are completely natural and hence completely unobtrusive. But put your friend on a platform in front of an audience and ask him to communicate the same idea to a group of one, two, or three hundred persons. Unless he has had some training or experience as a public speaker, one of two things may happen: (*a*) he will "freeze" into a tense and rigid posture with hands held stiffly at the sides or clasped hard together and with face immobile and expressionless; or (*b*) he will assume a completely artificial or exhibitory manner, marked by those exaggerated traits of posture, gesture, and facial expression that we call oratorical.

For obvious reasons, neither of the foregoing manners is desirable. Both the speaker who becomes stiff and rigid and the speaker who adopts an oratorical manner violate the first rule of good bodily delivery: they lack the naturalness of the conversational manner. They split attention away from the ideas being expressed and center it upon the *manner* rather than upon the *matter*. When an audience is more aware of how a speaker looks than of what he says, it can hardly be hoped that they will either understand or believe his ideas. The important guiding principle in your physical behavior on the platform, as in the use of your voice, therefore, is to be natural. Concentrate on the ideas and arguments that are to be communicated; present these in such a way that the audience's attention is always focused upon your speech rather than upon your delivery.

One common mistake should be carefully avoided: Do not attempt to imitate the manner of some older, highly skilled speaker. What is perfectly natural for persons of long training and experience often seems strange or affected in the novice. No speaker is ever at his best unless he is genuinely and completely himself. Your instructor will help you overcome any specific difficulties that you face; the course of training you are entering upon is designed to develop your speaking ability in easy and natural stages; and Chapters 3 through 6 offer many practical suggestions for improving your voice and platform manner. Depend upon these means to improvement rather than upon apish imitation.

Moreover, as your first step toward becoming a good speaker, resolve right now always to be guided by these three basic rules, which summarize much of what has been discussed in the earlier pages of this chapter:

1. Have something important to say.
2. Want someone else to understand or believe it.
3. Say it as simply and directly as you can.

The more experience you get in speaking, the more you will come to understand the reasons underlying these rules and to appreciate their importance.

CLASSROOM DISCUSSION

In nearly every class you will be called upon to do various kinds of speaking, including simple recitations, informal discussions, or short oral reports. Discussion procedures will vary from answering rapid-fire questions to giving fairly long explanations, comments, or demonstrations. Sometimes, instead of conducting a formal recitation period, your instructor may present a topic for general discussion by the class, or he may outline a problem and ask you to discuss its solution. In some classes, you will speak sitting down; in others, standing at the blackboard or before the class. (If you use the blackboard, be sure you stand to one side so that the class can see what is written on it; and guard against talking to the blackboard instead of to the audience.) In every instance, however, these rules apply:

Be prepared. There is no substitute for knowledge. If you study your assignments daily, you will have little trouble.

Act alert. Sit or stand erect; even when not speaking, avoid a slouched position. Keep awake, mentally as well as physically.

Listen to what is being said and keep close track of the discussion. Don't plan what you will say next while another speaker is talking. Effective listening is just as important as effective speaking.

Talk loudly enough to be heard. Do not mumble or swallow your words; remember that everyone should be able to hear you. If what you say is not worth being heard, don't say it at all. But if you are asked a question, at least answer, "Yes," "No," or even "I don't know," with alertness and vigor.

Do not remain silent when you have something worth while to say. Avoid giving the impression that the discussion is beneath your dignity or that the subject is uninteresting. At least show your interest by facial expression, and if possible express that interest by participation. Ask sensible questions and add useful comments. Of course, this does not mean that you must talk when you have nothing to say.

Speak to the point; do not ramble. In most discussions time is valuable. Don't waste it by saying something unimportant or by using five minutes to express an idea that could be stated in one. Be definite. Avoid vague statements, uncertain opinions, and equivocal answers. Do not stretch the facts, but be as conclusive as possible with your information.

Do not try to show off. Sarcasm, flamboyant statement, the continuous suggestion that "I know it all"—any of these will irritate your listeners. Do not try to efface yourself completely—self-assurance is desirable—but avoid the appearance of arrogance.

Accept criticism with dignity. Avoid irritating replies to criticism. If you think criticism justified, accept it graciously; if not, refute it politely or ignore it.

Above all, remember that you are part of a group and that every member of it has as much right to consideration as you have.

THE FIRST SPEECHES

In your speech course your instructor will probably require you to begin making classroom talks almost immediately—before the more detailed suggestions contained in later chapters of this book have been studied. How should you go about preparing these first speeches? What principles should you keep in mind when delivering them? The following recommendations are discussed more fully in later chapters. They are given here in order to provide you with a starting point—a foundation upon which to build.

1. *Select for your speech a subject that fits you, your audience, and the occasion.*

(*a*) A subject fits you if it is one you already know something about and are eager to learn more about. Indeed, you will do well to begin by talking about subjects drawn from your own personal experience. The student whose speech is printed on pages 20–22 had, like most of us, often compared dreams with her friends and had developed a lively curiosity about their significance. She therefore decided to talk about dreams when she discovered an interesting magazine article on dream research.

(b) A subject fits your audience if it is suited to their level of knowledge and adapted to their interests and needs. Since the audience for your beginning speeches will be your fellow students, you probably can safely assume that their knowledge and interests will be similar to your own.

(c) A subject fits the occasion (1) if it is consistent with the prevailing mood or tenor of the speaking situation (humorous when humor is called for, serious when the occasion is serious, etc.); (2) if it fulfills the specific requirements of the assignment; and (3) if it can be handled adequately within the time limit.

2. Determine the precise response you wish to win from your hearers as a result of your speech. Your teacher will usually specify the general purpose of the speech you are to make— whether it is to be a speech to entertain, to inform, or to persuade. It will be up to you to decide upon the exact idea or proposal to which you want your audience to respond. When you have decided upon the specific purpose of your speech, frame it into a short, simple, clear sentence. The thesis sentence of the speech on dreams was: "Scientific study has revealed amazing facts about the interpretation, universality, and necessity of our dreams." You should keep your thesis sentence constantly in mind, and use it as a master guide to the selection and organization of the material for your speech.

3. Find out as much as you can about your subject. Even though your talk is based on personal experience and observation, you may be able to increase your information by discussing your subject with other people and by reading about it in newspapers, books, magazines, and so on.

4. Select the main ideas of your speech and arrange them according to a clear and coherent plan. Among the common types of plans are: (a) a time sequence, in which events or developments are presented chronologically, just as they occurred; (b) a space sequence, in which the parts of a whole are described systematically, beginning at the left and working toward the right, or from

top to bottom, east to west, etc.; (c) a cause-effect sequence, which moves from a study of causes to a consideration of the results produced; (d) a problem-solution sequence, which moves from evils or deficiencies to solutions or remedies; (e) a special topical sequence, which follows an order dictated by the nature of the subject matter being presented. (For a fuller discussion of these plans, see pp. 235–239.) The girl speaking on dreams decided to discuss her subject under four main points:

I. The impermanence of dreams.
II. The interpretation of dreams.
III. The universality of dreams.
IV. The importance of dreams.

Her talk as a whole followed a topical sequence, moving from a brief introductory discussion of the impermanence of dreams to a consideration of their importance to us. (Some of your first speeches may be organized around a single point. For suggestions regarding the development of a one-point speech, see pp. 212–219.)

After you have selected and arranged the main points of your speech, be sure you develop an attention-getting introduction and also a conclusion that will not simply stop but will round out your talk. (For suggestions on beginnings and endings, see pp. 261–276.)

5. *Explain or prove each of your points with ample facts, figures, examples, quotations, or comparisons.* Note how the main points in the speech on dreams have been explained and substantiated (pp. 20–22).

6. *Talk through your speech a number of times aloud to make sure you can express the ideas clearly and in the proper order.* Talk it through, not by parts, but from beginning to end. You may need to refer to your outline at first, but put it away just as quickly as possible, and of course do not use it in your actual speech. With each repetition you will become increasingly sure of yourself. Do not attempt to memorize the exact words you will use in delivery. The purpose of these rehearsals is to master the ideas, not the language. During rehearsal, time your speech to be sure that it does not exceed the assigned time limit.

7. *When speaking, maintain an alert but relaxed posture, look directly at your audience, and keep your hands and arms free*

so that you can make gestures that will be helpful in explaining or supporting your ideas.

SAMPLE SPEECH

As you read the following sample speech, decide how well you think the student speaker has followed the suggestions for preparing beginning speeches. Do you think the speech would have been interesting to her audience? In what ways do you think the speech could be improved?

TO SLEEP—TO DREAM

I had the strangest dream last night, but now I can't remember any of it." How many times have you said this to yourself or perhaps to a friend?

According to Dr. William Dement, a physiologist at Mount Sinai Hospital in New York, this is the usual pattern. We forget much of what we've dreamed five minutes after a dream is completed, and in another five to ten minutes we've forgotten almost all of it. So unless we wake up in the middle of a dream or soon after, we won't remember much, if any, of it in the morning.

If dreams disappear so fast, you wouldn't think that they would be worth serious study—or, for that matter, that they *could* be studied. Many scientists, though, are convinced that dreams are a vital part of human behavior, and they've found some pretty accurate ways to study the process of dreaming.

Over sixty years ago, Sigmund Freud, the Viennese doctor, came up with some very important observations about the meanings of dreams. From information derived from his own dream experiences and from those of his patients, he formulated the psychoanalytic theory of dreams. According to this theory, the dream is a type of wish fulfillment. All of our wishes that are not acceptable to our conscious self are repressed into the unconscious and appear symbolically in our dreams.

Recent investigators, however, think dreaming can occur in relation to any emotional upset, unresolved conflict, or disturbing problem. My father, for example, dreamed the other night that our house was on fire. I don't know how Dr. Dement would explain this dream, but my father thought he might have dreamed it because several days before he had received an insurance notice for the house. Dream researchers do seem to agree that whatever disturbs us during the day may be carried over in some form into our dreams.

But, you may say, these theories about dreams may be very interesting to those who dream, but I don't dream. Oh, but you do. Dr. Dement and others feel they have proved that all of us dream on the average about eighty or ninety minutes a night, in three to five cycles of ten to thirty minutes each.

What is the proof? Well, countless scientific experiments have been performed by men such as Nathaniel Kleitman, a physiologist at the University of Chicago; Dr. Dement, once Dr. Kleitman's graduate assistant; and Charles Fisher, Dr. Dement's psychiatrist colleague. They have tested hundreds of volunteers. One of the most valuable aids in their dream research is the electroencephalograph, a machine which makes EEG's—recordings of brain-wave patterns—and also detects and records eye movements. Here is a rough sketch of the electroencephalograph and the way the electrodes are attached to a person's head [displays sketch].

But, you may be thinking, how can it be proved, even with the aid of this machine, that we all dream? It so happened that Dr. Kleitman, knowing that the eyes of sleepers sometimes moved rapidly during periods of sleep, had a hunch that these movements might indicate dreaming. Using the electroencephalograph, he would waken sleeping volunteers when the machine indicated a period of rapid eye movements. Invariably, the volunteers could give detailed accounts of what they had just been dreaming. If they were awakened after these periods of rapid eye movements, they would be able to recall nothing or only fragments of their dreams.

Thus the researchers could always determine when a volunteer was dreaming, and if they woke him up during his dream, they could get a pretty detailed account of it. Later (attention all those who claim they don't dream), two other investigators, Dr. Donald Goodenough and Dr. Arthur Shapiro, worked with two groups of volunteers, including one group of people who insisted that they never dreamed. The tests revealed conclusively that the supposed nondreamers dreamed just as much as those who said they dreamed.

Well, you may be thinking, so I dream. So what? One of Dr. Dement's most important conclusions was that dreaming with reasonable regularity is essential to mental and physical health. He based his conclusion on a series of dream-deprivation experiments. After the volunteers had settled down for a good night's sleep, they were awakened just as soon as the electroencephalograph indicated they were beginning to dream. After five nights of this, the volunteers were tense, irritable, and foggy. I know without taking part in the experiment that I'd feel the same way!

But why couldn't this just be the result of being deprived of sleep? This same question occurred to Dr. Dement. He found no such signs in volunteers who were awakened the same number of times but always during sound sleep, *not* during dreams. Further experiments showed that the folks who had been deprived of their dreams for five nights dreamed an abnormal length of time the first time they had a chance for an uninterrupted night of sleep and that they continued to dream more than usual for several nights after.

Therefore, as you turn out your lights tonight, I bid you all pleasant dreams; but if worse comes to worse and they're nightmares instead, remember it's necessary.[1]

PROBLEMS

1. After rereading the second and third paragraphs of this chapter, list as many additional ways as you can think of in which speech is used in the instructional, research, and extracurricular programs of your college.

2. Describe in detail the part that speech plays in carrying on the work of one or more of the following: a commercial air line, a manufacturing plant, an insurance company, a newspaper.

3. Give two or three examples from your own experience of men who exerted influence over others because of their strong ethical appeal.

4. With the aid of your instructor, select for detailed study a speech that has become historically important. Prepare to answer as accurately and completely as possible these questions concerning it:
    A. What had the speaker done prior to the delivery of the speech to establish confidence in his personal integrity?
    B. How did the speaker bring his general background of knowledge and experience to bear in developing the subject?
    C. What specific skills of voice, language, and body did the speaker employ to help achieve his end? (In the case of voice and body, you will, of course, have to depend on reports of observers.)

5. Attend a speech or lecture given by some prominent person in your own community—a minister, teacher, public official, etc.—and insofar as possible attempt to answer the questions asked in Problem 4.

6. Compare two nationally known persons whom you have recently heard speak on television as to knowledge, self-confidence, and skill.

7. Make a list of five subjects drawn from your own personal background or experience which you think would prove interesting and informative to your classmates.

8. Analyze your background of knowledge and interests as a speaker:
    A. What business or profession do you intend to enter, and how much do you know about it first-hand or through reading or

---

[1] Most of the data for this speech came from the following articles: Edwin Diamond, "The Science of Dreams," Special Science Report, *Newsweek*, April 6, 1959, p. 69 ff. and Jerome Ellison, "Dream and Stay Sane," *The Saturday Evening Post*, April 1, 1961, p. 21 ff.

talking with others? Make a list of subjects connected with this vocation on which you would like to speak but on which you need more information.

B. List several principles or proposals which you sincerely believe in and would be willing to defend vigorously.

C. On the basis of this analysis, prepare a list of eight or ten topics upon which you might talk in class during the semester. Do not include any topic in which you are not vitally interested.

9. Gather as much information as you can concerning the vocational and avocational interests of the other members of the class. Record this in a systematic fashion and use it as a guide to the selection of the subjects upon which you will speak during the semester and as an aid in adapting these subjects to your hearers.

10. Give a short oral report telling about some speaker you have heard recently who fits one or more of the categories listed on pages 13–14 (the elocutionist, the culprit, the oracle, etc.). Imitate his manner of speaking so that the class will know exactly the sort of speaker you are describing. Then point out specifically how his manner impairs effective communication with his hearers. Finally, demonstrate how you think he should have spoken in order to achieve maximum communication.

11. Analyze as carefully as you can some situation other than a speaking occasion in which you were highly tense and nervous—your first day in the army or on a new job, before an important final examination, while participating in an athletic contest, etc. To what extent do you believe the causes of nervousness discussed in this chapter also applied in this nonspeaking situation? Did you try any of the remedies suggested in this chapter? With what success? Did you try any other remedies?

12. Take critical notes of any class discussion in which you participate during the next few days. As objectively as possible, rate yourself on your performance and contribution. Refer to the rules on pages 16–17.

13. Review the program of speech preparation outlined on pages 17–20. Be prepared to explain why each step is important and usually must be carefully carried out if you are to make a good speech, and why the steps should usually be carried out in the order indicated.

14. Prepare a two-minute speech in which you introduce yourself to the class. Cover briefly such topics as the following: where you come from; your major in college; your vocational objective; your extracurricular activities; your hobbies; trips you have taken; jobs you have held, etc. Make a rough outline of the points you are going to cover and talk this outline through aloud until they have become firmly fixed in your mind. Take care, however, not to memorize the exact words you are going to use in delivering your speech. Let these come to you extemporaneously as you stand before your listeners.

15. Following the same method of preparation and practice, present a two-minute speech in which you illustrate from your own personal experience the truth of some well-known adage or proverb: Haste makes waste; Look before you leap; A penny saved is a penny earned, etc.

16. Again following the same method of preparation and practice, present a two- or three-minute speech on one of the following topics, or on a topic suggested by one of them:

What I expect from college.
In defense of popular music.
High-altitude flying.
Television advertisements I dislike.
Initiation into a chemistry (biology, home economics, etc.) lab.
Weather prophets.
Hunches.
Deep-sea fishing.
Candid-camera techniques.

*It is reason and speech that unite men to one another;
there is nothing else in which we differ so entirely from
the brute creation.*

Cicero

CHAPTER **2/** *Backgrounds
and
Fundamental
Concepts*

Before going deeply into the detailed problems involved in the
improvement of his speaking ability, the careful student will
want to capture a broad view of the whole subject. He will want
to know something of the history and development of the principles to be studied and to gain some insight into their rhetorical
and psychological foundations. In this way he will be able to attack the more specific problems with some perspective. While a
comprehensive and thorough treatment of these matters is far
beyond the scope of this book, a brief survey of some of them
should prove useful. Let us begin with the origin of language itself as an illustration of the social function of speech.

THE SOCIAL FUNCTION OF SPEECH

Many interesting theories about the origin of language have
been suggested. Some scholars believe that the automatic cries of

alarm, the screams of pain, the snarls of rage, and other emotional expressions formed the basis of language. As human beings recognized these sounds and the finer distinctions among them, a means of communication developed which became more and more specific in its meaning until a language developed. A different suggestion is that as men found it necessary to work or fight together in groups for their common good, they discovered the utility of audible signals to coordinate their effort. Thus, in lifting or pulling heavy objects, the rhythmic grunt which naturally occurred became the signal for all to heave together. (This theory is often called the "Yo-He-Ho!" theory.) Another theory suggests that language began with man's attempt to imitate the sounds of nature (like the child saying "choo-choo" for train) in order to tell about his experiences; and still another theory is that language resulted from the movements of the tongue, jaw, and lips which accompanied the facial expressions (scowls, grins, etc.) used to express friendly and unfriendly attitudes. Of course none of these theories can be proved because we have no records of those primitive ages; but a study of the known history of language changes and of certain common elements in language systems does lend partial credence to some of them.

We can, however, directly observe the development of speech in children. Beginning with simple emotional cries of hunger, pain, and pleasure, the child soon reaches the "babble" stage—that is, he plays with sounds, making all sorts of noises apparently just for the fun of it. He gradually finds that certain of these noises produce reactions: his mother responds to some of his sounds but not to others. Then he associates the sound with the response it secures and begins to use the sound consciously for this purpose: he has discovered a "word." His parents meanwhile talk to him, and he notices similarities between their sounds and his own; through imitation, and with encouragement from his parents, he thus learns additional words and their meanings. Later, words are put together into simple sentences ("Bobby bye-bye," etc.), and gradually this process is extended to more complex phraseology and more accurate pronunciation as it keeps pace with the growing complexity of his own thoughts and actions.

Note that speech develops in the child, as in the race, in order to meet a social need. It serves a communicative function. The child at first cries and gurgles merely to express his own emotions, but his speech develops only as he discovers how to use these sounds *to get responses from other people.* As he grows older, he uses speech on the playground and in the schoolroom, at home and at the store, in the club and at work—but he always speaks to a listener, always to someone else.

This communication of ideas to impart knowledge and to secure cooperative action is what we mean by the social function of speech. By means of this tool we cease to be isolated individuals, relatively weak in the face of the forces of nature. We join forces to control our environment, developing the great strength of our industrial and political organizations. We hold these joint enterprises together and direct their course of action through language, written and oral.

By learning to think and to speak in language symbols, the human race has speeded greatly the rate of its own development. In his interesting book *Human Destiny*,[1] published in 1947, Lecomte du Noüy, the biologist, points out: "The incomparable gift of the brain, with its truly amazing powers of abstraction, has rendered obsolete the slow and sometimes clumsy mechanisms utilized by evolution so far. Thanks to the brain alone, man, in the course of three generations only, has conquered the realm of air, while it took hundreds of thousands of years for animals to achieve the same result through the processes of evolution. Thanks to the brain alone, the range of our sensory organs has been increased a millionfold, far beyond the wildest dreams . . . we see the infinitely small and we see the infinitely remote; we hear the inaudible; we have dwarfed distance and killed physical time. We have enslaved the forces of the universe, even before we have succeeded in understanding them thoroughly." He then goes on to explain the importance of language in this process: "Thousands of young dogs and cats and tens of thousands of chickens and other animals have been run over on the roads since the invention of automobiles. This will continue for a long time simply because the experiences of the parents who have survived by chance cannot be transmitted to the young for lack of speech and tradition. Articulated speech

---

[1] From *Human Destiny* by Lecomte du Noüy (Longmans, Green and Company, Inc., N.Y., 1947), pp. 120–122.

alone has already considerably shortened the time necessary for certain adaptations. What we call the education of young children can be considered as an extraordinarily quick short-cut, replacing the biological process of adaptation, and obtaining in one generation results better than those which required ages amongst the animals at the cost of innumerable deaths."

Thus, in the evolution of man, social processes involving speech have replaced the slower biological processes of adaptation. This social function, the communication of knowledge from one individual to another, is the most important role of speech. As we study speech, therefore, we must be careful not to think of it as an isolated thing; we must think of speech in its functional setting, as a means of communication, as something going on be-

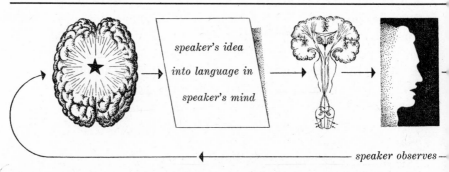

speaker's idea
into language in
speaker's mind

speaker observes

Here is a diagram of the circular response. Notice that each step is required to make the process complete. An idea forms in the speaker's mind, where it is translated into language symbols; reacting to impulses from the nervous system, the muscles used in speech convert these language symbols into audible speech; the sounds are carried as wave patterns in the air until they strike the eardrums of the listener; as

tween a speaker and a listener. We shall then be less concerned by what speech is than by what it *does;* its form and beauty will be important only in terms of the response it secures from those who hear it.

THE NATURE OF THE SPEECH ACT

What is the chain of events involved in this process of communication that we have just considered? What happens when one person speaks to another?

Speech as a circular response

We must realize first that the act of speaking is not a one-way process: it involves a series of interacting elements. Thus the sound of my voice reaches my own ears as well as my listener's and causes me to talk louder, perhaps, or more slowly. Likewise, my listener, if he cannot hear, may cup his hand behind his ear; seeing him do so will cause me to raise my voice. A frown of perplexity on my listener's face may impel me to clarify my explanation, or a look of doubt may cause me to offer added proof. This interaction is most obvious in the give and take of conversation and group discussion, but it is also present and important even when only one person is speaking and the rest are listeners. Not only does the speaker cause his audience

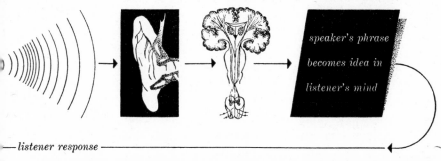

speaker's phrase becomes idea in listener's mind

listener response

nerve impulses, they travel to the brain, where they again become language symbols which convey meaning to the listener's mind; the listener reacts to what he has heard; the speaker observes this reaction and responds to it. Thus we see that the process of communication depends not only on the speaker's saying something to a listener but also on his constant awareness of the listener's reaction to what he says.

to react, but the listeners' reactions constantly influence the speaker's speech; and since he also listens to himself, the speaker constantly reacts to his own efforts. This continuous interaction, often called a *circular response*, is a fundamental characteristic of the act of speaking.

For the sake of simplicity, however, let us break this chain of interaction at some point and describe the process of speaking as if its various elements occurred in a direct sequence. (1) We shall begin with an idea in the speaker's mind which he wants to communicate to a listener's mind. How he got the idea—through observation, reading, or listening to others—is of no concern to us at the moment, nor is the reason why he feels impelled to transmit that idea to another. We begin at the point where he has the idea and wants to communicate it. (2) He must translate the idea into language symbols of some kind: words, phrases, sentences—in English or some other language. As yet, however, these language symbols are mental concepts only; they have not emerged from the speaker's mind. To make these symbols audible, (3) nerve impulses from the central nervous system must actuate and control the complex systems of muscles used in speech—the breathing muscles, the muscles of the larynx and jaw, the tongue, the lips, etc.—and (4) these muscles must react in a coordinated movement to produce the proper sounds.

But these sounds are now no longer words and sentences; they are merely disturbances in the molecules of air surrounding the speaker, a wave pattern of compressed and rarefied particles of gas. (5) The outward movement of these wave patterns through the air transmits the sounds the speaker has made until they strike the eardrums of a listener. (The use of telephone or radio, of course, introduces additional steps by changing sound waves to electronic waves and back again to sound waves.) (6) In the ear of the listener, the waves of compressed and rarefied air are again translated into nerve impulses and (7) are carried to the brain by the auditory nerve. When this happens, the listener has "heard" the sounds, but he has not yet understood the speaker. He must (8) recognize these nerve impulses as language symbols—words and sentences—and he must (9) attach meaning to these symbols. (10) Finally, the listener reacts at this point, and the speaker, observing his reaction, responds to it, thus continuing the circular response. The process of communication is complete only when these ten steps have occurred. (See diagram on pp. 28–29.)

From this description it is easy to see why speakers are so often misunderstood. A break or distortion *anywhere* along this chain of events between speaker and listener will result in the listener receiving an idea different from that intended by the speaker. Poor choice of language by the speaker (step 2), poor articulation (steps 3 and 4), interfering external noise (step 5), partial deafness (steps 6 or 7), possession of an inadequate vocabulary or misinterpretation of the meaning by the listener (steps 8 or 9), failure of the speaker to observe his listener's reaction (step 10)—a break at any one of these points will result in distorted or incomplete communication.

Speech as habit

If each step in this process of oral communication required the conscious effort of the speaker and listener, talking to one another would be slow and painfully laborious. Yet in spite of the complexity of the process described above, speech is, for most of us, easy, natural, and spontaneous. This is true because so much of the act of speaking and of listening to the speech of others is automatic. By practice, we have reduced much of the total process to the level of habit. Thus, when we see a certain animal, the word *cat* automatically occurs to us; and if we wish to talk about that animal, habit has established appropriate neuromuscular patterns so that our speech mechanism produces the sounds of the word *cat* without much conscious effort. Even the sentence structure we use and to some extent the arrangement of the larger units of thought we express are profoundly influenced by our habits of thinking and speaking. To the extent that the various steps in the act of speaking become habitual through practice, the easier speaking becomes for us. By the same token, however, the more our speech becomes a matter of habit, the less conscious we are of it *regardless of whether our habits are good or bad*. "Practice makes permanent"—but not necessarily perfect. As students of speech, we may profit by examining our habits of speech at each stage of the communicative process described above to see whether our habits contribute to the clarity with which our ideas are transmitted or whether they are likely to distort or prevent easy communication.

THINKING AND EMOTION IN SPEECH

Behind the actual process of communication we have just examined lie the thinking processes of the speaker and of the listener and the patterns of emotional reaction which they possess. Leaving the details of their practical application in speech composition for later study, let us here consider a few aspects of their fundamental nature.

Thinking consists essentially of *The thinking process* *identification, classification, determining relationships,* and *solving problems.* We begin by observing the environment around us. A certain object catches our eye and we note its shape, color, and size; we feel its texture, and perhaps lift it to note its weight; we may smell or taste it as well. This combination of impressions is remembered and serves to *identify* that object for us if we are confronted by it again. Suppose later in the day we come across another object similar in every respect except that it is a little larger. In spite of this difference, we note how similar our impressions of this new object are to our memory of the first one, and we say to ourselves, "This is the same sort of thing." Later, we repeat this process as we encounter more and more similar objects, until we become aware that all of them may be thought of together as a *class of things* having similar characteristics. At this point we are likely to coin a name for our classification— we say to ourselves, "Let us call these things *rocks.*"

From this point on as we observe new objects, we say, "This is a rock," or "This is *not* a rock," depending on whether they have the same characteristics. Similarly, we classify other objects, events (falling—not falling), and qualities (hot—cold, black—white). As our thinking proceeds, we subdivide our classes into smaller units (limestone, gravel, etc.) and combine them into larger classes (rocks + dirt + humus, etc. = land), giving each new group a name. We even note intangible similarities in qualities and behavior and group them together in such categories as "beautiful" and "friendly." This form of thinking enables us to arrange our impressions in an orderly way; we are able to deal with relatively few *classes* of things instead of an infinite number of slightly different *individual* things. On the other hand, we run the risk of forgetting the differences which always exist between individual objects in a class and at times of mistaking the *name* we have given a class of things for the things themselves. (Just what, for example, is "New York State"?) The study of logic and of semantics is concerned with these problems.

Another type of thinking deals with relationships other than mere classification. We note, in the objects around us and in the events which occur, certain connections and sequences that are regular. One type of event *follows* another; one type of object is *larger* than another; qualities A and B always occur together, *except* when quality C is present. We note these relationships and use our knowledge of them to analyze our experiences and predict the results of our actions. Thus we think *back* and think *ahead* in terms of related phenomena.

Much thinking of the types described above would be purely academic were it not for its application to another form of thinking which we do, namely, problem solving. Suppose a man is separated from his dinner by a high board fence which he cannot scale. If he does not *think about the problem,* he may waste his energy in aimless running back and forth and fruitless efforts to jump high enough to get over; failing in his effort, he sinks down exhausted and hungry. But if he thinks about the problem, he does his running and jumping *in his mind;* by analyzing the situation and reviewing his experiences with similar problems, he concludes that he cannot jump over the fence and that he must build a platform or ladder of some sort, and he goes about doing so. This type of thinking, then, is creative and imaginative. By manipulating and combining mental concepts, one puts together a pattern of action in his mind before actually expending any energy.

In all these thinking processes, you will note the important part played by language, for it is the names of things we manipulate in our thinking that saves us the effort of manipulating the things themselves. Thus the speaker uses language in his own thinking and in leading the thinking of his audience. In general, it may be said that clear thinking and sloppy language do not occur together.

Emotion and its effects   From our discussion of the thinking process, it might be inferred that human beings are ruled by reason. This, however, is not the case. A very large part of human behavior is emotional in nature or at least colored by emotion. Ages ago, in the struggle for survival, the human race developed certain patterns of reaction to the dangers that beset it. The basis of these patterns still persists in what we now call anger, fear, and the like. These reactions have a strong physiological foundation: when we become angry or afraid, adrenalin is secreted, sugar pours into the bloodstream, the heart beats faster, and our breathing rate is changed. Our bodies prepare, as men's bodies did in past ages, to meet the emergency—to run or to fight. Civilized man has largely substituted words for deeds, the language symbol for the act. Thus we become angry when we are struck by a word just as much as if we were struck by a fist, and we strike back in the same symbolic way. But the physiological processes go on just as they did in the past—and we feel angry! The thinking processes described above may serve to modify and direct our behavior, but the basic emotional patterns are automatic to a large extent and beyond our conscious control.

Emotion varies in intensity. Most psychologists agree that a *mild degree of emotion* is nearly always present and serves a beneficial purpose. Such emotion exhibits itself in a feeling of pleasantness and controlled enthusiasm or in mild irritation which stirs us to improve our lot. (A speaker, for example, who does not feel somewhat stimulated when confronted by an audience is likely to speak poorly as a result of his apathy.) A second level of emotion, which we may label *strong emotion,* tends to differ in type as well as degree. Usually, strong emotion has a focal point: we are angry *about* something or *at* somebody, or we are afraid *of* something. Moreover, strong emotion usually (though not always) is of a definite type—fear, anger, love, etc.—rather than being a vague and general feeling. The physiological changes are greater than in mild emotion, and we are prepared to exert strong effort. We find it difficult to keep from doing something since our energies demand release, but we can still direct them in an organized fashion. The extreme degree of emotion, however, is a *disrupting emotion.* When emotion is very strong, we may lose control of ourselves entirely. We may "freeze" as some animals do when startled, unable to move or speak, or we may break out in random and unintegrated movements having no value whatsoever. The level of emotion at which disruption sets in varies from person to person, but it is rarely reached in situations where previous experience has established appropriate action to solve the problem. Thus the trained soldier may be deathly afraid, but he does not go to pieces under fire because he has practiced what to do in such a situation.

The speaker may use his knowledge of emotion both to manage his own emotional reactions and to stir the feelings of his listeners. He may increase the vigor of his own speaking, and minimize his fear of criticism, by talking about subjects which arouse his own enthusiasm or strong feeling. He may arouse his listeners to action by describing emotion-provoking situations to them. Although he uses his own and his listeners' thinking processes to give sensible direction to his proposals, it is his knowledge of emotion that he uses to give power and exhilaration to his own speaking and to elicit an active response from his audience.

The theories and concepts of speech and the facts about it which we have examined so far in this chapter are drawn from existing knowledge of the subject. Let us turn now to examine some of the sources from which that knowledge comes.

SOURCES OF KNOWLEDGE ABOUT SPEECH

The scientist attempts to discover truth by carefully controlled observation. The artist, however, seeks not so much to discover truth as to express it in a creative manner. The scientist sets out to test the truth of a clearly stated hypothesis: he devises a systematic and unbiased method for collecting and analyzing data bearing on this hypothesis. Then he draws his conclusions from these observations, limiting his assertions strictly to what the data clearly show. The artist, however, projects himself into his work: he applies a sensitive and creative imagination to his observation until he has conceived a design which embodies the true essence of the thing he has observed or felt. He then applies his artistic skill in molding this raw material into a complete and beautiful expression of that design. And if he is engaged in one of the practical arts, such as architecture, his design and execution will be concerned with usefulness as well as beauty.

The study of speech employs both of these methods: the scientific and the artistic. Thus by studying speech scientifically, we may learn a great deal about its phenomena, and we may test many of its basic hypotheses in an objective manner. And since speaking, like writing or painting or designing bridges, is a form of creative expression, we may learn a great deal about how to do it by studying the creative methods recommended by experts and by studying the great masterpieces themselves. We must not expect all the principles we study to be capable of scientific demonstration, for creative expression is an individual act and varies from person to person. But we must also realize that people are sufficiently alike biologically and psychologically and that sound waves and language symbols behave with sufficient consistency to make possible the scientific study of many of the basic aspects of speech. Let us consider, then, some sources of knowledge about speech phenomena and about the creative act of speaking.

Don't Assume

A priori assumptions   To begin with, certain facts and principles have to be accepted *a priori:* at face value. Like the axioms of mathematics, they are accepted because they are self-evident and any variation from them is obviously absurd. For example, consider the following: "The ability to speak depends upon the possession of the physical organs of speech (tongue, vocal cords, etc.) and the ability to use them properly." Obviously, a person with a paralyzed tongue or cleft palate or damaged vocal cords will have difficulty speaking well if at all. Or consider this statement: "Speaking requires the use of language." Presumably one could communicate vocally to some extent without using words, but he would be sharply limited in the number and variety of ideas he could express. As soon as his grunts and groans and hisses began to have specific meanings, he would actually have coined a new set of words and have created a sort of language. From self-evident assumptions like these, we derive logical corollaries such as, "The proper choice of words is necessary for effective speech," or, "Flexible and energetic use of the tongue and lips is important for distinct utterance." The truth of such corollaries will depend both on the basic assumptions on which they rest and on the logic with which they are derived. Learn to test the validity of such statements as you study them.

Another type of assumption you will encounter in the study of speech is "intentional" in nature—that is, it expresses a point of view or purpose. Your acceptance of this kind of assumption will depend upon whether you agree with the viewpoint expressed.

For example, consider the following statements: (*a*) "the purpose of speech is to communicate ideas from one person to another," and (*b*) "the purpose of speech is to express one's ideas well." If you accept statement (*a*), the effectiveness of speech is determined by its success in *transmitting* ideas; but according to statement (*b*), effectiveness consists *merely in expression*. According to (*b*), you could make an excellent speech all by yourself with no one to listen, as long as you expressed yourself to your own satisfaction; but according to (*a*), the perfectly expressed speech is no earthly good unless someone else hears it and understands what you mean. Assumptions of this type are not accepted as obvious truth by everyone, nor can they be proved universally true or false. Acceptance depends upon each individual's intention or purpose. One must determine his own point of view and then make whatever assumptions of this kind are consistent with it. The author, for instance, agrees with the first assumption (*a*) stated above, and for elaboration of it you may want to refer to the opening sections of this chapter. Many of the later suggestions in this book are also based on that assumption, and your acceptance of these suggestions will depend somewhat on whether or not you agree with it.

Expert opinion

The fact that a great many people say a thing is true does not make it so, and even experts can be wrong in their opinions. Nevertheless, when there is substantial agreement on the truth of a principle among those who have devoted careful study to it, or when those who have used a given method agree on its value, there is at least a strong presumption that they are right. Many of the principles and methods included in the study of speech come from this source. Indeed, adaptations of statements by Aristotle and Quintilian on rhetoric will be found in many books on speech composition today. The successful application of these principles over so long a period is evidence of their essential soundness. Of course, success may have come in spite of following some of these principles rather than because of them; but until proof to the contrary is presented, we are safe in accepting these principles and methods as valid and well worth applying.

Direct observation A great deal can be learned about speech simply by observing others speak, analyzing the methods they use, and noting the results. Most of us make such observations in a random fashion all the time. By going about it systematically, we can improve the soundness of our judgments. Thus we may select in advance the type of speaking we wish to observe and what aspects of speech we intend to concentrate upon; we may devise a systematic way of recording our observations so that their bearing upon the principle or method we are studying can be easily summarized and a judgment made. Essentially this was the method used by Charles Darwin in preparing his great biological study *Origin of Species*.

To a large extent, you will find that direct observation is also the method used by most experts on speech. We know, for example, that Aristotle used this method on nearly every subject about which he wrote; indeed, even in the natural sciences, it is interesting to note that modern scientists disagree with Aristotle chiefly on those points where the technics of observation and the apparatus used have been improved. These facts suggest that the more completely expert opinion is based on systematic observation, the more credence can be given it. If we can verify the conclusions by our own observations, we can be doubly certain that they are valid.

Two mistakes should be avoided in making observations of this sort. One must be careful not to project his preconceived ideas into his observation. It is quite easy to see what we *expect* to see. While the observer cannot entirely divorce himself from his observation, he can guard against subjective judgment. The other mistake consists in jumping to the conclusion that what one observes in a particular situation is typical of *all*, or in trying to generalize from an insufficient number of situations. Thus, what is observed to be effective speaking in the United States Senate might not be effective in a business conference and what was a good speech in Cicero's time may not be today. Likewise, conclusions based on observing the speech of a few good speakers cannot be accepted as universally true of all. If these mistakes are avoided, a great deal can be learned about speech by observing it directly.

Historical evidence

Men and women have been speaking for a long time. Although speech through the centuries obviously cannot be observed directly, careful study of historical and linguistic source material can disclose a great many facts about speech. Development and change in the English language and in its pronunciation are disclosed in this way. The written reports of contemporary observers give us information about the lives, the manner of speaking, and the influence of great speakers of the past. Biographical material sometimes explains the influence of environment and education upon these men and in some instances even tells us their methods of speech preparation. Moreover, a study of history provides background on the economic and social conditions existing when they lived and on the issues (many of them still pertinent today) about which they spoke.

Of course, knowledge derived from this source is always incomplete, and conclusions must therefore be limited and tentative. Moreover, care must be taken to evaluate the thoroughness and freedom from bias of the source material used. For instance, all sorts of conflicting reports were printed in the newspapers of the day regarding Lincoln's now famous speech at Gettysburg, and it is still not clear just how effective it was *as a speech* on that day. In addition, one must be careful to seek out primary (original) source material, because a second- or third-hand written report about what happened is just as likely to be inaccurate as hearsay oral evidence.

Textual analysis,
pictures, and
recordings

The texts of important speeches are often recorded in written form. In modern times even the voice is frequently recorded, and sometimes newsreels preserve the visible as well as the audible record of speech. These records are made not just of great speakers but of speakers of all kinds. Such records provide a useful source for a great deal of knowledge about speech, especially since a careful and leisurely study can be made of them. Vocabulary, sentence structure, types of logic and emotional appeal, intonation, pronunciation, appearance, movement —all these can be studied from appropriate types of records, and many such studies have been made. One word of caution: printed

In recent years, various scientific studies have greatly increased our knowledge of speech. The top picture shows the focusing effect of an acoustic lens on sound waves emitted from the horn at the left. This technic is expected to prove useful in the study of communications equipment. In the bottom picture a young woman's respiratory movements, blood pressure, and skin reflex action are being checked to learn how the voice changes under varying emotional conditions.

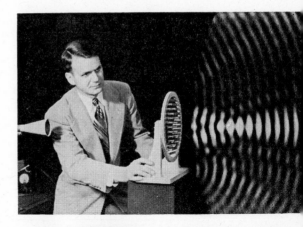

texts of speeches are often unreliable because speakers sometimes edit their remarks before printing so that the record shows what they wish they had said rather than what they actually did say.

Experimental studies   Certain aspects of speech may be subjected to experimental study. Here the observer controls not only his observation but also the phenomenon itself. In order to simplify and narrow his field of observation, and to rule out complicating influences, he sets up a set of conditions under which he permits or causes an event to occur. Many times he uses apparatus to secure accurate and objective data. An increasing amount of knowledge about speech is being gathered from this source, including information about such widely different questions as how the vocal cords vibrate, what effect emotion has on the voice, how important humor is in influencing opinion, how to build loud-speakers for reproducing the voice with maximum intelligibility, and what mannerisms of speakers annoy audiences most.

Experimental evidence provides us with the most reliable information possible about those aspects of speech which can be studied in this way. We must remember, however, that the very controls necessary for conducting an experiment tend to destroy the spontaneity with which people usually speak in normal situations. Thus I may not speak quite the same into a microphone in a laboratory with a pneumograph around my chest as I would before a live audience and without this apparatus. One must be careful not to overextend the conclusions reached in an experimental situation. Nevertheless, this source of knowledge about speech is very important, and a growing number of experimental studies are being made each year. You would be well advised to keep abreast of this kind of information in such publications as the *Quarterly Journal of Speech, Speech Monographs,* and the *Journal of Speech and Hearing Disorders.*

Inferences drawn from other fields of knowledge   Perhaps no other field of study leans so heavily on other areas of knowledge for added information as does the study of speech. Speech performs so important a function in both personal and social life and depends upon the interplay of so many forces—biological, physical, and psychological—that it seems like the hub of a wheel, dependent upon the support of a great many radiating spokes. Thus the physiologist tells us a great deal about how our vocal apparatus works. The psychologist gives us insight into problems of memory and emotion. The physicist helps explain the nature of the sound waves our voices make. The linguist traces the sources of our language. Historians, economists, journalists, and students of literature and the arts— all present to the student of speech a large body of information and varied methods of study. From all of these, inferences may be drawn which relate to problems in speech. You will find that many of the principles set forth in this book are based upon such inferences.

THE INFLUENCE OF CLASSICAL RHETORIC

At this point we may well pause to remember the strong influence which classical rhetoric has had on the study of speech, particularly on public speaking. Too often we tend to think of the study of speech as something new and different, whereas actually it is one of the oldest branches of academic study. The great scholars of Greece and Rome gave particular attention to the study of rhetoric (literally in Greek: "the art of speaking"), and their systematic writings on the subject are among the world's great scholarly works.

Rhetoric, of course, covers the use of written as well as spoken language, and the classic scholars included the art of writing in their studies. But the printing press had not yet been invented, and books were scarce; therefore, reading and writing were far less important than speaking, dramatic presentation, and poetic declamation. The principal emphasis in classic rhetoric was thus on language in its spoken form.

After the Dark Ages, the revival of learning in western Europe centered upon the Greek and Roman manuscripts that had been preserved. Classic rhetoric thus became the basis of later study in the field, and its influence was carried across the Atlantic with the establishment of American schools and colleges. Indeed, allowing for changes in terminology and emphasis, the range of subject matter and most of the basic principles included in modern textbooks on public speaking are similar to what is found in the writings of the classic scholars. If the persistence of these principles of rhetoric were only the result of historical tradition, we could well be skeptical of their value; but the fact that they have been *successfully used* by speakers through the ages suggests that the initial formulation of these principles by the classical rhetoricians was based on keen observation and insight on their part.

Let us consider briefly, then, five men who lived in Greece and Rome whose names should be familiar to every student of speech.

The principles of speech formulated centuries ago by such men as Plato, Aristotle, and Cicero are still used by speakers today.

Corax

Corax, a Sicilian Greek, lived during the fifth century B.C. Law courts had been set up in Syracuse to settle the claims of returning exiles whose land had previously been taken from them by the tyrants whose rule had now been overthrown. Rival claimants appeared in these courts to argue their respective titles to the land. Corax made a study of these arguments in court and worked out a plan for the arrangement of the subject matter in speeches of this sort. He also made a study of the use of evidence to establish *probability* in those cases where certainty could not be proved. His treatises on speech organization and on the nature of probability are generally considered to be among the first systematic presentations of the principles of public speech.

Plato

Primarily, Plato (427–347 B.C.) was a moral and political philosopher. His interest in rhetoric arose from his dislike of the use made of it by the orators of Athens, where he lived. He felt that too much emphasis in the rhetoric of his day was placed upon verbal trickery rather than upon careful logic and thorough knowledge of the subject. In his *Dialogues* he emphasized this point, and outlined what he considered the "true" rhetoric based on truth and moral purpose. In so doing, he also recognized the importance of a speaker's knowing the nature of the human "soul"—by which he meant what we now call psychology—in order to adjust his speaking to the understanding of his audience. Besides his emphasis on truth and morality of purpose, his chief contribution to classical rhetoric was his further development of the principles of speech composition.

Aristotle

Aristotle (384–322 B.C.) studied under Plato and was strongly influenced by him. His work reflects a marked ability to classify and organize all of the existing knowledge of his times in a systematic fashion. His *Rhetoric* was the first comprehensive and systematic presentation of the subject. He discussed the speaker and his training, the speech and its development, and the audience to which speech must be adapted. His treatise is distinguished not so much by what was new in it as by its thoroughness and its practical usability. For this reason, the *Rhetoric* has had tremendous influence, actually providing the basis for nearly every subsequent work in the field.

Cicero

Cicero (106–43 B.C.) is known primarily as a great Roman orator. His speeches have served as models of oratorical art down to the present day. Yet his oratory was no accident. He studied its principles carefully and wrote about them from the viewpoint of one who was concerned with their practical use. He was interested in the proper training of the orator and recommended a breadth of education far wider than the study of rhetoric alone. His writings differ in principle very little from those of Aristotle except that he gives more emphasis to style of composition and delivery. His best known works on this subject are *The Orator* and *On Oratory*.

Quintilian

Quintilian (A.D. c35–c95) was a Roman educator rather than a speaker. His great treatise, *Institutes of Oratory*, consisting of twelve books, presents an entire course of study for the education of the speaker. Like Cicero, he believed that the orator must have knowledge and character as well as skill. To him, the great orator was always the good and able man speaking well. The principles of rhetoric presented by

Quintilian lean heavily on Aristotle, but he added to them the educator's advice on how to master the use of them. He also covered the entire range of subject matter, including everything he felt a speaker should know.

From the writings of these five men have come most of the principles of public speaking, tested through long experience and modified by more recent psychological study but essentially the same in both extent and substance. The serious student of speech will gain interest and breadth of understanding by reading from the works of these men, all of which are available in English translation.

At the beginning of this chapter, we set out to review the fundamental concepts that serve as background for the study of speech. We have considered briefly the social function and purposive nature of speech and how the action of nerve and muscle, the transmission of sound through the air, and the sensitive reaction of ear and brain are all correlated in the total act of communicative speech. We also noted how language, thinking, and emotion are intimately related. The last part of the chapter emphasized the sources of our knowledge about speech and the influence of classical rhetoric upon its study.

Although only a brief review of these concepts has been possible here, the perspective gained should clarify our study of the more specific problems of effective speaking. For the latter, we turn now to the following sections of this book, where the basic principles involved in the development of speaking skill, and some of their applications, are more fully discussed.

PROBLEMS

1. What is the social function of speech? Discuss its dependence upon the *circular response*.

2. At what stage do you believe the circular response is broken or distorted most frequently? Compare your answer with those of others in the class. (Watch for examples in the class discussion that support one of the viewpoints.)

3. List as many of your good and poor speech habits as you can. Compare your habits with those of some experienced speaker you have recently heard.

4. In speeches you have heard or in articles or editorials you have read, find examples of each kind of thinking described in this chapter. Be prepared to discuss in class the relationship between *thinking* and *language* as employed in these examples.

5. From your own experience, select occasions when you have experienced each of the three degrees of emotion (mild, strong, disrupting) described in this chapter. As accurately as you can remember them, write a brief description of your feelings and outward reactions.

6. Describe to the class an instance you have observed in which a speaker aroused the emotions of his listener (or listeners). Did this emotional response help or hinder him in achieving the purpose for which he spoke?

7. From each of the other courses in which you are enrolled during this school term, select one important "fact" or principle recently studied. Determine which one (or ones) of the "sources of knowledge" discussed in this chapter is the basis for each of these "facts" or principles.

8. Begin gathering information on one of the classical rhetoricians mentioned in this chapter. Plan to use the material soon for an informative speech in class.

part two

Basic
Principles
of
Delivery

Physical behavior on the platform ● Improving voice quality ●
Developing vocal variety ● Making the voice more intelligible

There was language in their very gesture.

Shakespeare

CHAPTER *3 / Physical Behavior on the Platform*

The effectiveness of your speaking depends both on what you say and on how you say it. These two—the content and delivery of your speech—work together to help you communicate your ideas to others. Without clearly developed substance, you will have nothing to say; without effective delivery, you cannot clearly and vividly convey your thoughts to others.

In this chapter and in the three following, your attention will be focused on delivery: your physical behavior and your voice. Just as the pitcher by the way he throws the ball gives it direction and power, so the speaker can give his speech strength and vitality by the manner of his delivery.

The best assurance of effective speaking, however, is straightforward sincerity. The point of view of this chapter and of those which follow is not that you should develop a mechanical set of arm movements and vocal manipulations. Such artificiality is to be abhorred. In fact, effective delivery cannot be learned merely by applying a set of fixed rules; effectiveness comes from long and continual practice under the direction of a competent instructor who can help you smooth out the rough spots and encourage you to develop your individual points of strength.

There are, nevertheless, a few principles and suggestions which good speakers have always found effective. An understanding of these principles will help you make the most of your instructor's individual criticism. While practicing some of the technics suggested, you may at first feel a slight awkwardness; do not let this discourage you—many valuable technics seem awkward until they become habitual. If you feel uncertain, consult your instructor; he will show you how to apply these suggestions to your own individual problems.

Roughly speaking, there are two aspects of delivery: that which people see and that which they hear. We may speak of the former as the speaker's *physical behavior on the platform* and of the latter as his *use of the voice*. We shall consider the first of these points in this chapter and discuss the second in the next three chapters.

That this physical aspect of delivery is important becomes apparent after a moment's thought. The eyes are quick to see any discrepancy between the attitude of the speaker and what he says. Through visual impressions the audience makes its first estimate of the speaker—of his sincerity, his friendliness, and his energy. They read these things in his facial expression, in the way he stands and walks, and in the things he does with his arms and hands. Many times a slight shrug of the shoulder or an expressive movement of the hand is more revealing than a hundred words could be. A speaker's effectiveness may therefore depend as much upon what the audience sees as upon what it hears.

CONTACT WITH THE AUDIENCE

The first thing a speaker must do when he addresses an audience is to make them feel that he is talking to them personally. Audiences do not like to feel that the speaker is merely broadcasting a speech to which he graciously permits them to listen.

They want to feel a sense of personal relationship, to feel as if the speaker were engaging them in a conversation.[1]

Visual directness Nothing is quite so important a means of establishing personal contact with the audience as the simple device of looking directly at them. For this reason, reading a speech or even using notes too closely invariably reduces the effectiveness of the speaker. Of course, it is impossible to look in the eyes of each member of the audience at the same time; such an attempt would result in either a vacant gaze or crossed eyes. Do as you would in a conversation: pick out one person and talk to him personally for a short while, looking him in the eye as you do so; then shift to someone in a different part of the audience. Be careful that you pick out people in various parts of the audience and that you stay with each of them long enough to avoid the appearance of simply wagging your head. Whether you are able to look in the eyes of everyone in the audience during the course of your speech is unimportant; the fact that you have talked personally with some of them will show that you have made the attempt and that your attitude toward them is personal.

Mental attitude To achieve audience contact, you must have the proper mental attitude. You must be interested in your audience and keep thinking of them as you speak. Develop the habit of watching their reactions to what you say. Know the content of your speech so well that you do not have to spend all your mental energy remembering the sequence of your ideas but can concentrate more on your audience.

POSTURE

Posture, or the speaker's stance, is an important factor in his physical behavior. How do you stand when you talk to people? Are you erect? Comfortable? Alert? Although there is no one way to stand that is best for everyone, there are several things which

---

[1] See discussion of the conversational mode in Chapter 1.

all speakers should avoid. In general your posture should be comfortable without being slouchy, erect without being stiff. Avoid hiding behind the speaker's table or stand. Ordinarily, keep your hands out of your pockets, and do not put them on your hips as if you are about to perform gymnastic tricks. Beware of the stiffness of a military posture and the widespread legs of a sailor in a bad storm. Let the weight of your body fall on the balls of your feet rather than on the heels, but do not jiggle up and down on them. Your bearing should give the impression that you are alert, at ease, and in command of yourself and the situation.

To insure good posture when you speak, you need to develop good habits of posture when you are not speaking. If you sit humped over at your desk or slumped down on the small of your back when you read, you will find it harder to stand erect before an audience. If you usually walk with your chin out, your shoulders drooping, your chest down, and your abdominal muscles relaxed, the attempt to stand erect on the platform is likely to be overdone; you are likely to overcompensate by puffing out your chest and pushing back your hips too far, by squaring your shoulders and drawing back your head too stiffly. The better way is to maintain good posture always, so that you will naturally stand erect when you speak. Stand tall; sit tall; walk tall. Without being stiff about it, develop the habit of reaching up with the top of your head. If you do this, the rest of your body—shoulders, chest, abdomen, hips—will tend to assume their proper positions. Not only will you appear better, but you will also feel more vigorous and confident.

MOVEMENT

There are two kinds of movement: that of the whole body as the speaker walks across the platform and that of parts of the body as the speaker uses them to gesture. Technically, however, the term *movement* refers only to the first.

One effect of the speaker's movements is to attract the audience's attention. The eye instinctively follows moving objects and focuses upon them. A sleepy audience can often be awakened by the simple expedient of moving from one part of the platform to the other. So long as your movement is natural and easy, it is valuable, but you must beware that it does not become a distraction to the audience. Continuous or aimless pacing back and forth will no doubt attract attention, but that attention will be directed to the pacing and not to what you are saying. Such random movement should be avoided.

On the other hand, movement properly employed can assist in conveying your thought. Transitions from one main point in the speech to another can often be indicated and made emphatic by merely shifting the weight from one foot to the other or by a lateral movement of a step or two. Such a movement is literally a signal that "I am done with that point; now let us turn our attention to another." Always start lateral movements with the foot that is on the side toward which you are going (that is, your left foot if you move to the left) in order to avoid awkwardly crossing your feet, and then walk a step or two naturally in that direction. Forward or backward movements usually serve to imply the degree of importance attached to an idea. A step forward implies that you are coming to a more important point which you do not wish your audience to miss. Backward movement suggests that you are willing for them to relax a bit to let the last idea take root before you present another important one.

But, you may ask, how much movement is desirable? How often should one move around while speaking? The basic principle to remember here is moderation: don't remain glued to one spot, but don't keep on the move all the time. If you avoid these two extremes, your natural impulses will be apt to take care of the rest. In general, the more formal the occasion, the fewer your movements should be; and the larger the audience, the more steps you should take when you do move. In the beginning you will be better off with too much movement than with too little. Even random movement is better than none, for it serves to release pent-up energy and to reduce muscular tension. If your movements are purposeful—in the manner indicated above or for more specific ends, such as walking to the blackboard or window to point out something—so much the better. As your skill and experience increase, you will find your movement becoming at the same time less obvious and more meaningful, and you will learn to modify it to suit the size of your audience and the formality of the occasion.

The speaker's movement does not begin or end with his appearance on the platform. The way he walks to the platform and the way he leaves it are also important; the audience's first and last impressions of the speaker are gained from these movements. Instead of walking up in a slovenly, meandering fashion, walk briskly and purposefully. Let your manner breathe confidence; do not tiptoe forward timidly as though you were afraid the audience would see or hear you. Avoid also the exaggerated swagger of the bully, the pompous strut of artificial dignity, and the high-strung, nervous walk of one who lacks emotional control. On reaching the platform, don't rush into your speech. Take time to get a comfortable stance and to look out over the audience; *then* begin to talk. And when you are through speaking, don't rush off too abruptly or relax on the way as if to say, "Well, that's over." Pause at the end long enough to let your final words sink in; then walk firmly back to your seat.

GESTURE

A gesture may be defined as the movement of any part of the body to convey some thought or emotion or to reinforce its oral expression. The difference between gestures and random movement should be kept clear. Speakers often fidget with coat buttons, pencils, beads, handbags, and the like. Some even play games of arranging books, papers, watch and chain, and other objects on the speaker's table. Such movements are not gestures, because they are not purposive; they do not help convey the speaker's idea but ordinarily distract the audience's attention. Nevertheless, keeping still without appearing stiff is difficult. The best way to avoid both stiffness and random movement is to practice until you have become proficient in the use of meaningful gestures.

A warning is in order here. The impulse to gesticulate should come from within rather than from without. Gestures should never be "laid on." It is fatal to decide ahead of time that at a certain sentence in your speech you are going to point at your audience and a moment later point dramatically at the heavens above. Gestures arise naturally from a stirred-up state, from enthusiasm, excitement, emotion. Practice gesturing all you please at home—the more the better—until you can feel the easy swing, the abandon, the punch in it; but when you stand before an audience to speak, do not force your arms to move. If you have practiced the movements at home and feel enthusiastic about your subject, then let yourself go, and the gestures will come naturally and effectively.

The value of such gestures is threefold: they increase the speaker's energy and self-confidence; they assist in the communication of his ideas; and they help hold the audience's attention. By providing an outlet for his pent-up energy, gestures tend to relieve the muscle tension in the nervous speaker. To the lethargic speaker, on the other hand, the use of vigorous gestures is stimulating, quickening his pulse and making him more lively and animated. (See also Chapter 1.)

That gestures aid in the communication of ideas is the testimony of nearly all great speakers. A simple experiment should convince you of the importance of gestures: try to direct a stranger to a place several blocks away and notice how necessary it is for you to point the way and show him every turn he must take. Observe two persons in a heated argument and notice how often their hands come into play to emphasize the points they are trying to make.

The attention value of gesturing is equally apparent. Just as we will watch the moving automobile rather than the stationary one, so will we give our attention to the active speaker rather than to the quiet one. One reason for this is that people tend to project themselves into situations they observe. When we watch a race or a football game, we are likely to tense the muscles of our legs and back—literally, though incipiently, to run and plunge with the athletes. Were you ever pushed along with the surge of the crowd in the stadium as they, together with the halfback, carried the ball over for a touchdown? This tendency to do what we see being done, to react as we see someone else reacting, is an important factor in controlling our attention. Unless he compensates for the lack in some other way, the speaker who uses no gestures will seem sluggish and apathetic, and his audience may respond with sluggishness and apathy. But a physically active speaker will stimulate in his listeners a lively, attentive attitude.

Roughly speaking, there are two types of gestures: *conventional* and *descriptive*. Let us consider these two types as they are made with the hands and arms, the principal agents used in gesturing, and then give brief attention to the uses made of other parts of the body.

Conventional gestures of the hands and arms — There are six basic movements which have been used so universally that almost everyone recognizes what they mean. These gestures have become a sort of generalized sign language.

Pointing. The index finger has been used universally to indicate direction and to call attention to objects at which it is pointed. You might, for example, point at a map hanging on the wall as you say, "That map you see is already out of date; the boundaries have been changed since it was made." Or if you were to say, "The whole argument rests upon this one principle: . . ." you might use the index finger to point in front of you as if that principle were there in tangible form before you. An accusation or challenge can be made doubly forceful and effective by pointing your finger directly at the audience or at some imaginary person assumed to be on the platform beside you.

Giving or receiving. If you were to hand someone a sheet of paper or were to hold out your hand to accept one given to you, you would find that the palm of your hand would be facing upward. This same movement is used to suggest the giving of an idea to the listeners or the request that they give you their support. This gesture indicates "This is the information I have discovered," or "The ideas I am holding before you are worth your attention," or "I appeal to you to give me your help in this matter." Because of the variety of uses to which it can be put, no other conventional gesture is used quite so much as this one. Sometimes it is even combined with the pointing gesture described above— the idea is, as it were, held out in one hand while the other hand is used to point at it.

Rejecting. If a dog with dirty paws were to jump up on your clean clothes, you would push him down and to one side with your hand. In the same way you can express your disapproval, or rejection, of an idea. This movement with the palm of the hand turned down can be used to reinforce such statements as, "That proposal is absolutely worthless," "We must put that idea out of our heads," "It can't be done that way."

Clenching the fist. This gesture is reserved for use with expressions of strong feeling such as anger or determination. The clenched fist may be used to emphasize such statements as, "We must fight this thing to a finish!" or "We must put every ounce of our energy behind this plan!" or "He is the worst scoundrel in the community!"

Cautioning. If you wished to calm a friend who had suddenly become angry, you might do so by putting your hand lightly on his shoulder. A similar movement of the hand as if on an imaginary shoulder before you will serve to caution an audience against arriving at too hasty a judgment or against making too much noise. This gesture is often used with such statements as, "Don't take this thing too seriously," "If you'll just keep quiet a moment, I think I can make the point clear," "Before you make up your mind, look at the other side of it." By using this gesture you check your hearer's thoughts and get him ready to listen to another idea.

Dividing. By moving the hand from side to side with the palm held vertically, you can indicate the separation of facts or ideas into different parts. You might, for instance, appropriately use this gesture while saying, "We must be neither radical in our ideas nor ultraconservative"—moving your hand to one side on the word *radical* and to the other on the word *conservative.*

These are the six basic movements of conventional gesturing. From what has been said about them, you must not infer that they are set and invariable. No two persons will make them exactly alike or on exactly the same occasions. They are general in meaning and are primarily useful in emphasizing the expressions they accompany. Moreover, they do not always start from the same position; frequently one gesture begins at the point where another ends, so that the effect is one of continuity. Only practice will make your use of these gestures smooth and effective; and that practice will be doubly valuable if carried on under the supervision of your instructor.

Study the gestures being made by Douglas Dillon, Albert Gore, Charles de Gaulle, Maxwell Taylor, David Ben-Gurion, Robert McNamara, a college student, and Enzo Ferrari. Which gestures seem the most effective?

Descriptive gestures   Many other movements of a more descriptive nature are also quite effective. Descriptive gestures are imitative. The speaker describes the size, shape, or movement of an object by imitation. You may show how vigorous a punch was by striking the air with your fist, the height of a younger brother by holding the hand high enough to rest on his head, the speed of an automobile by a quick sweep of the arm. A complicated movement may be shown by performing it in pantomime as you describe it. Because they are spontaneous and imitative, descriptive gestures cannot be cataloged. Some suggestions can be obtained by watching other speakers, but the best source is your own originality. Ask yourself, "How can *I show* my audience this?"

Gestures of the head and shoulders   In addition to the arms, other parts of the body may be used for gesturing. Conceivably, any part of the body can be so used—the legs and feet, for instance, may be employed to demonstrate how a football should be kicked. Practically speaking, however, the head and shoulders are the only other members with which gestures are frequently made. Shrugging the shoulders and shaking the head have the same implication in public speech as they do in conversation, and vigorous nods of the head are frequently used for emphasis.

Facial expression   Our facial expressions also help carry our thoughts to the audience. Of course, to attempt mechanically to put on an effective expression is not wise. Too often this results only in an artificial grimace or a fixed smile. A better way is to work on your facial expression from the inside. If you have a cordial feeling for your audience, are interested in the subject of your talk, and are enthusiastic about speaking, your face will reflect your attitude. Some people, however, seem to have extremely immobile faces; if you are one of them, limber up your facial muscles by practicing before a mirror until they respond to your feelings—but don't practice on the actual audience. Moreover, concentration tends to make many people frown; as a result, the audience may believe that the frown comes from the speaker's dislike for them, and they will be inclined to frown back. If you have the habit of frowning, cultivate a pleasant expression by learning to concentrate pleasantly.

Pantomime and impersonation
Sometimes a speaker may want to make his story more vivid by acting and talking as if he were the person described. In this imitative process the speaker's posture, movement, gesture, and facial expression all combine. Effective pantomime is selective, however; it does not present a photographic picture but, like a cartoon, picks out the most significant and characteristic details. The shoulders are perhaps allowed to droop and the walk develops a slight limp; the hand trembles as it knocks on the door and the face shows surprise at what is seen when the door opens. All together, these few vivid details present a character and tell what he is doing without cluttering the picture with too many details. In general, the speaker's pantomime, which only suggests the character and the action, will be more restrained than the actor's.

In moderation, pantomime and impersonation are useful devices for a speaker to use. They serve to enliven any narrative. For the beginner especially, they may serve to break tensions and develop freer movement and gesture.

CHARACTERISTICS OF GOOD GESTURES

Gestures can be made well or poorly. The only way to perfect your use of them is through practice, but that practice will be more effective if you keep in mind the qualities characteristic of good gestures.

Relaxation
When the muscles which move the human skeleton are held in tension, jerky, awkward movements result. Paradoxical as the advice may seem, the best way to relax is to move. Warm up as the athlete does by taking a few easy steps and making a few easy gestures with your arms. Avoid stiffness; before you start to speak, let all the muscles of the body slacken. Avoid awkwardness by relaxing.

Vigor Gestures, however, should not be insipid and lifeless. Put enough whip and punch into them to make them convincing. A languid shaking of the clenched fist will not support a threat or challenge. On the other hand, sledge-hammer pounding of the table to emphasize minor points or continuous violent sawing of the air is monotonous and often ludicrous. Vary the degree of vigor you use, but in the main use enough vigor to suggest reality.

Definiteness If you point out the window, make the movement so distinct that there will be no doubt where you are pointing. This is especially important when several gestures follow each other rapidly. Too often the effect is merely a blur. Be careful to avoid jerkiness, but be sure that each of your movements is definite and clean-cut.

Timing The stage comedian gets many a laugh from his audience merely by making his gestures a little late. The effect of making a gesture after the word or phrase it was intended to reinforce has already been spoken can be nothing else but funny. The stroke of the gesture should fall exactly on, or slightly precede, the point it is used to emphasize. If you practice using gestures until they have become habitual and then use them spontaneously as the impulse arises, you will have no trouble with timing. Poor timing usually comes from the attempt to use "canned" gestures—gestures planned out and memorized ahead of time for a particular word. Avoid this practice; use gestures of all kinds when you rehearse your speech so that when you stand before the audience your gestures will be spontaneous.

ADAPTING GESTURES TO THE AUDIENCE

Just because one type of gesturing is effective with one audience is no sign that it will suit all occasions. You will need to modify your gestures with reference to both the size and the nature of your audience.

The *size of the audience* will govern the sweep of the gesture. Generally speaking, the larger the audience, the wider the arc through which your arm should travel. Remember the effect of perspective: what would seem a wild swing of the arm to a person with whom you were conversing close at hand will appear quite moderate before an audience of two hundred. Conversely, small gestures of the hand hinged at the wrist, while effective in conversation, would seem weak and indefinite to the larger audience.

The *nature of the audience and occasion* will govern the number and degree of vigor of the gestures. People who are young or who are engaged in vigorous physical activities are attracted to a speaker who uses vigorous gestures. Older, more conservative persons are likely to be irritated by too strong or too frequent gestures. Moreover, some occasions such as formal dedication exercises call for dignity of movement as well as expression, while others such as athletic rallies require more violent and enthusiastic activity.

To make the most effective use of gesture, you must consider all these elements. The immediate task of most student speakers is to break loose from their hesitancy and begin using gestures freely and often. Begin by using as many gestures as you can. Get your arms out from your body and let the swing be complete. If some classmate tells you that you are using too many gestures, make sure that the criticism is not really that you are using too many of the same kind of gesture. Instead of cutting down the number, increase the variety. Leave the final judgment on this point to your instructor.

And remember: good posture, adequate movement, contact with the audience, and effective gestures can be just as natural and easy as combing your hair or handling a knife and fork. You were not born doing them either; but practice made them habitual and natural. Practice, practice, practice until good posture, movement, and gesture also become habitual and natural. Then you can forget them as most good speakers do; they will automatically obey your impulse and effectively reinforce your ideas.

PROBLEMS

1. Be ready to discuss the following questions in class: When should the speaker move on the platform? How? In what ways do gestures aid the

speaker? How do conventional and descriptive gestures differ? What qualities characterize good gestures? How do the size and nature of the audience affect the speaker's physical reaction?

For developing freedom of movement and gesture. (While working on problems 2–5, do not worry about the kind or quality of your actions; be concerned only with the amount. Let yourself go, and purposely overdo.)

2. Imagine yourself in the following situations—picture in detail all that has led up to them—and react spontaneously with whatever physical behavior your impulse suggests. Speak out also if you feel the urge to do so.

A. Someone has fired off a shotgun right behind you.

B. A child just in front of you is in the path of a fast-moving car.

C. Someone has just slapped your face.

D. There is a prize for the student who can get to the blackboard and write his name there first.

E. You catch a grounder and throw to first base; there are two outs with a runner on second.

F. Someone shouts to warn you of a heavy object about to fall on the spot where you are standing.

G. A pickpocket steals your purse and tries to dodge away through the crowd—you catch him, or you fail to catch him.

H. Your roommate is in bed asleep; the house is on fire.

I. You are marooned on an island and are trying to catch the attention of people on a passing boat.

J. A mob is bent on destruction; as the crowd goes past, you try to turn it in another direction.

3. Remembering to get your elbows well out from your body, to keep your wrists flexible, and to use a vigorous excess of energy, do the following things in sequence:

A. Shake your arms and hands vigorously as if trying to get something loose from your fingers. Do this with your arms far out at the sides, up over your head, out in front of you; continue until all stiffness is eliminated.

B. While you are doing this, begin repeating the alphabet over and over—not in a monotonous rhythm but as if you were actually talking in highly colored language. Continue this "talking" throughout the remainder of this series.

C. Let one hand at a time fall to your side and continue shaking the other.

D. Gradually change from mere shaking of the arm and hand into varied gestures: that is, clench your fist, point your finger, reject the idea, drive home a point, etc. (See pp. 55–57.) During this change, be sure to continue the vigor and complete abandon of the arm movement.

E. Get a partner. Harangue each other (alphabetically), keeping up a vigorous flow of violent gestures all the while. Both of you talk and gesticulate at the same time.

F. In a group of four or five, all talking simultaneously at the front of the room, harangue the rest of the class in the same way you did your partner in (E). See which one of you can keep the attention of the class away from the others in the group.

4. Think of something which arouses your fighting spirit—campus injustices, favoritism, cruelty, unnecessary red tape, thoughtlessness, unsympathetic officials or teachers, unfair requirements or restrictions, dangerous demagogues—something which makes you genuinely angry, excited, indignant. Make a short tirade on this subject. Urge your audience in no uncertain terms to "Turn the rascals out!" Let yourself go vocally and physically.

5. In your own room, before a mirror, stretch and manipulate your facial muscles in the following ways: (A) raise your eyebrows, (B) wink one eye, then the other, (C) wink one eye while raising the other eyebrow, (D) pucker your nose, (E) wiggle your ears—if you can! (F) draw down the corners of your mouth, (G) stretch your lips in a wide grin, (H) pucker your lips, (I) move your lips as far as you can to one side of your face and then the other, (J) drop your jaw as far as it will go, (K) wrinkle your forehead in a frown, (L) combine the movements listed above two, three, four at a time, (M) assume an *exaggerated* expression of horror, surprise, anger, excitement, laughter, etc. Remember that these exercises are for the sole purpose of developing facial flexibility; you cannot prepare facial expressions to be assumed at given points in a speech. Genuine facial expression must reflect genuine feeling.

For developing a sense of values regarding physical behavior through observation of it. (You will have to be keenly alert in your observations of the things suggested in problems 6–11 because much of the most effective action is unobtrusive, blending naturally with what is expressed in words.)

6. Go to hear some speaker and write a brief report on your observations regarding his platform behavior. Note both good and bad qualities in his audience contact, posture, movement, and gesture. A good way to proceed is to make a brief outline of the suggestions and warnings contained in this chapter before you go and then to check the speaker on these points while he is speaking.

7. While observing some speaker, note what statements he emphasizes or clarifies by gestures. Write the statement in one column, and in the opposite column note the type of gesture used. Indicate also whether he lacked any of the characteristics of good gestures discussed on pages 59–60.

8. Observe ten different types of people as they walk down the street. From their manner of walking, make as shrewd an estimate as you can of their temperaments and of the nature and urgency (or lack of it) of their errands. Write a paragraph apiece on two or three about whom you feel most sure, justifying your conclusions.

9. During the next half-dozen purchases you make in retail stores, pay particular attention to the degree of eye contact maintained by the clerks who wait on you. Which one seemed most interested in you? In what other way did he make you feel that he was personally concerned with helping you?

10. Attend a motion picture or play or watch a play on television and report on the physical behavior of the actors. Comment on such points as these: (A) What impression of the character was conveyed by the actor's posture and manner of walking? (B) How was movement used to help hold attention? (C) Did you at any time find yourself "participating" in the action you were observing? (D) What special meanings were conveyed by facial expression and by movements of the head or shoulders? (E) What conventional gestures and what descriptive ones were especially effective? (F) What relation did you notice between comedy effects and the characteristics of good gesture—energy, relaxation, definiteness, and timing?

11. After hearing some speaker, prepare to talk before the class, first paraphrasing parts of his speech and imitating his platform behavior as closely as possible and then criticizing his weaknesses and showing what you think he should have done.

For increasing communication through physical action.

12. Observe some well-known type of character performing an act and convey to the class without words a clear picture of the character and what he does. For example:

  A. Nervous pedestrian crossing a street through heavy traffic.
  B. Irate motorist changing a tire on a hot day.
  C. Mother getting dinner and setting the table while trying vainly to keep the two-year-old out of mischief.
  D. High school boy or girl getting home late and trying to keep from waking his parents.
  E. Christmas shopper trying to carry too many parcels, some of which slip out of his grasp.
  F. Panhandler asking several different people for a dime for a cup of coffee.

13. Show the class how to perform some action, such as driving or putting a golf ball, preparing a cherry pie, doing a sleight-of-hand trick, playing a musical instrument, etc. Without talking, see how clearly you can make your audience understand you.

14. Make a demonstration similar to the one suggested above, but for a more complex operation, such as assembling a model airplane, making a party frock, breaking in a horse, performing a laboratory experiment, or the like. This time, however, accompany your action with verbal description.

15. Try to communicate the following ideas silently by means of physical action alone:
   A. "Get out of here!"
   B. "I'm so glad to see you; won't you come in?"
   C. "Why Tom (or Mary)! I haven't seen you for ages!"
   D. "You people on that side, sing the first line, and we'll sing the second."
   E. "Right in front of me was a big field with a brook running straight through the middle of it."
   F. "If we're going to get what we deserve, we'll have to fight for it, and fight hard!"
   G. "Quiet down a little, won't you? Give him a chance to explain."
   H. "At that price, I wouldn't even think of buying it."
   I. "Come here a minute, Jim, will you?"
   J. "Every penny I had is gone."
   K. "Now the first thing to remember is this: . . ."
   L. "If you think it was easy, you're all wrong."
   M. "What a hot (cold, windy, or rainy) day it is!"
   N. "In a sweeping spiral the plane went up, and up, and up, until it disappeared in a cloud high above us."

16. Express these same ideas orally, accompanying your words with appropriate gestures.

17. Memorize or paraphrase a part of one of the speeches printed in this book and develop appropriate platform behavior, especially gestures, to reinforce what you say.

18. Make a short speech describing some exciting event you have witnessed; use movement and gesture to make the details clear and emphatic. Try to make your description so vivid and your action so dynamic that your listeners will tend to project themselves into the situation. Remember that to succeed in doing this you will need to imagine yourself back in the situation while you describe it; you must feel the excitement in order to communicate that feeling.

There is no index of character so sure as the voice.

Benjamin Disraeli

4/*Improving Voice Quality*

S omeone has said, "Let me hear his voice, and I can tell you what sort of a man he is." Although this generalization is exaggerated, its essential truth is borne out both by common experience and by scientific experiments. The tone of a person's voice varies from normal when he is, for example, angry, excited, sleepy, or terrified. Habits of temperament, such as nervousness, irritability, or aggressiveness, also seem to be reflected in one's habitual speaking voice; people are inclined, therefore, to judge one's personality largely on the sound of the voice. A woman whose tones are sharp and nasal is often thought of as a nagging person. A man whose voice is harsh and guttural is judged to be crude and rough. Weak, thin voices suggest weakness in character. These judgments may be absolutely contrary to fact, but often they are close to the truth. Whether true or false, such judgments are important in that they color the listener's attitude toward all that the speaker does or says. They are often a major factor in determining an audience's first impression of a speaker.

But the development of a good speaking voice is important for another reason. With a well-controlled voice the speaker can put much more meaning into what he says. Have you listened to children at church or school programs say pieces which were rattled off so that, even though you heard the words, you could not understand the meaning? Or recall the various announcers you have heard over the radio giving a play-by-play account of a football game; was not a great deal of the difference in the vividness of their descriptions due to the way they used their voices? After all, our meaning is carried to the audience not only by what we say but also by the way we say it.

How, then, can you acquire an effective speaking voice? First, last, and always—by practice. Only by using your voice can you improve it. But unintelligent practice may do as much harm as good; repeatedly doing the wrong thing merely fixes a bad habit more firmly. To make your practice worth while, you must know something about the mechanics of voice production, the qualities which characterize a good voice, and the methods by which these qualities are acquired. Although this chapter and the next two contain a discussion of these things, the printed page alone is hopelessly inadequate for conveying detailed voice instruction. These pages cannot produce a pleasing tone for you to hear nor judge the quality of tone which you produce. Moreover, individual differences are great. Your difficulty may be of one kind, while that of your classmate may be of quite another. You must, therefore, take your individual problems to your instructor. He is trained to pick out flaws which your untrained ear may not detect, and his experience qualifies him to suggest specific remedies. His criticisms and suggestions, however, will be more fruitful if you have first acquired a knowledge of the underlying principles of voice production and have become acquainted with the terms employed in discussing it. This knowledge can be acquired by reading and is presented here. Practice material to be used according to your instructor's directions is appended to these chapters.

Accurately speaking, there is no such thing as a speech mechanism or vocal mechanism. We shall use these terms, however, to include those parts of the body which are used in speaking. All those muscles, bones, cartilages, and organs have, as you know, other functions which are biologically far more important than producing the voice. The tongue, for example, even though so vital a part of the speaking mechanism, is far more important in eating. Even the vocal cords have as their chief function the protection of our lungs from cold air, smoke, and other forms of dangerous irritation. Indeed, the very fact that speaking is a secondary function of these organs makes a program of vocal training doubly important, for although we were born instinctively prepared to eat and to breathe, we had to learn how to talk. This fact explains why so many of us use our voices badly. We have established bad habits of speaking.

But even though we may have poor speech habits, we have all learned in childhood how to use these organs together in some form of speaking. Let us therefore forget for the present their primary biological functions and consider them together as a single mechanism, the instrument of speech. We may, for discussion, conveniently divide this mechanism into four parts: the motor, the vibrator, the resonators, and the modifiers. The following discussion will be more clear if you refer constantly to the diagrams on pages 70 and 71.

The motor

For the purposes of speech, the motor is essentially a pump for compressing air. It consists of (*a*) the *lungs*, which contain space for the air; (*b*) the *bronchial tubes*, which converge into the windpipe, or *trachea*, thus forming a nozzle out of which the compressed air is released; (*c*) the *ribs*, and other bones, cartilages, and tissues, which serve to hold the motor in place and give leverage for the application of power; and (*d*) the *muscles*, which alternately expand and contract the space occupied by the lungs, thus serving alternately to draw air into the lungs and to compress it for expulsion afterwards. To detail the large number of muscles used in this process is beyond the scope of this book. One thing should be noted, however. This air pump works in two ways: certain muscles draw the ribs down and in when we exhale so as to squeeze the lungs after the fashion of a bellows, while others—the strong abdominal muscles—squeeze in below to exert pressure up against the bottom of the lungs after the manner of a piston. Likewise, air is drawn into the lungs by double action: one set of muscles pulls the ribs up and out to expand the horizontal space, while the diaphragm—a layer of muscles and flat tendon tissue—expands the vertical space by lowering the floor of the chest cavity; this two-way expansion creates a suction, drawing air into the lungs. Thus, both inhaling and exhaling can be done in two ways: by movement of the ribbed walls of the chest and by raising and lowering its floor. For efficient operation both sets of muscles must work in harmony so that the bellows and the piston are synchronized; otherwise the pressure created by one set of muscles is dissipated by the action of the other.

The vibrator   The air compressed in the lungs is directed through the trachea into the *larynx,* which contains the vibrating unit. The larynx is situated at the upper end of the trachea and is attached, above and below, to muscles which shift it up and down. (Have you ever seen a tenor's Adam's apple move up and down when he sings? That is his larynx.) The larynx itself consists of a group of small cartilages joined together so that they can move. The position of these cartilages is changed by a number of small muscles which are delicately intertwined. Within the larynx, stretched between the cartilages, are the *vocal cords*— the vibrators proper. These are not really cords but a pair of membranes very much like thin lips. When a tone is to be produced, they come together until there is only a very small slit between them. The compressed air from the lungs, pushing against and between the vocal cords, causes a vibration which forms the original speech tone. This tone may be changed in pitch, up or down the scale, by the muscles which control the tension of the cords and the size of the opening between them. The position of the larynx as a whole is adjusted to a proper relation with the air cavities above by the action of the larger outside muscles which

Skillful use of the voice is one of the most important assets of the speaker. Good tone quality, distinct articulation, and variety of pitch, rate, and force are all essential. In order to understand the mechanics of voice production refer to these diagrams often as you study this section.

THE VOCAL MECHANISM

(anatomy involved in speech)

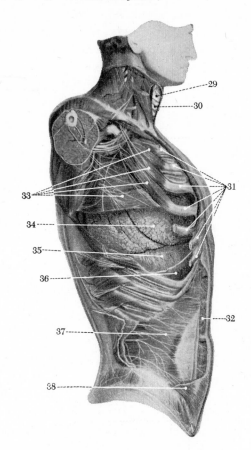

THE VOICE: A WIND INSTRUMENT

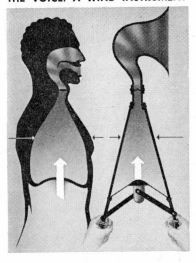

This diagram shows how the speaking mechanism functions as a wind instrument. The motor, by both a piston and a bellows action (indicated above by arrows), compresses the air in the lungs; this compressed air is sent through the vibrator, which produces the original speech sound; the speech tone next enters the resonators of the throat, mouth, and head to be amplified and modified in quality; finally, the tone is affected by the modifiers, which alter the quality further and produce the consonant sounds.

THE VOCAL CORDS

(laryngoscopic view of the vocal cords in relaxed position during normal breathing)

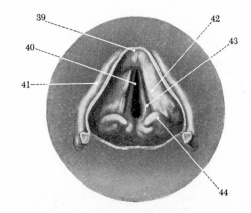

1. Frontal sinus
2. Upper nasal bone
3. Middle nasal bone
4. Nasal cavity
5. Lower nasal bone
6. Hard palate
7. Upper lip
8. Upper teeth
9. Tongue
10. Lower lip
11. Lower teeth
12. Lower jaw
    (mandibula)
13. Soft palate
14. Base of the tongue
15. Hyoid (tongue)
    bone
16. Epiglottis
17. Thyroid cartilage
18. False vocal cord
19. True vocal cord
20. Cricoid cartilage
21. Thyroid gland
22. Windpipe (trachea)
23. Gullet (esophagus)
24. Sphenoidal sinus
25. Region of the pharynx
26. Vertebrae of the neck
27. Spinal cord channel
    (cord removed)
28. Cranial cavity
    (brain removed)
29. Larynx
30. Windpipe (trachea)
31. Rib bones
    (numbers 6, 7,
    and 8 cut away)
32. Abdominal
    muscles
33. Chest muscles
34. Lungs
35. Diaphragm
36. Peritoneum
37. Abdominal
    muscles
38. Rectal sheath
39. Base of epiglottis
40. Rima glottidis
41. Thyroid cartilage
42. False vocal cord
43. True vocal cord
44. Arytenoid
    cartilage

SPEECH SOUNDS ARE FORMED HERE

*(sagittal section of the head and neck
—tongue drawn out for clearer view)*

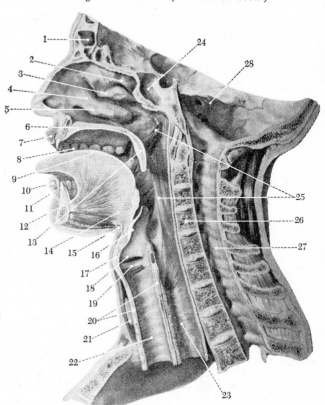

DETAIL SHOWING STRUCTURE OF THE LARYNX

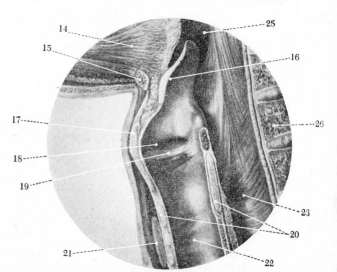

hold it in place. The action of these two sets of muscles, particularly the small internal ones, is largely automatic—that is, they cannot be controlled individually. We can, however, operate these laryngeal muscles as a group to control the pitch of our voice.

The resonators

The sound originating in the larynx would be thin and weak were there not some means of building it up. This function is performed by a group of air chambers in the head and throat. Of these, the principal ones are the upper part (or *vestibule*) of the *larynx,* the throat (*pharynx*), the *nasal cavities,* including the *sinuses,* and the *mouth.* These cavities act much as the resonating parts of musical instruments do: they amplify the sound, making it louder; and they modify its quality, making it rich and mellow, or harsh, or whining. Moreover, by a proper manipulation of the size and shape of some of these cavities, various tone qualities are formed which we recognize as the different vowel sounds.

The modifiers

The *tongue, lips, teeth, jaw,* and *palate* act as modifying agents in the production of speech sounds. These agents form the movable boundaries of the resonators mentioned above, and by moving them we modify the shape of these resonators and affect the quality of the tone. Another function of the modifiers, quite as important as this, is the formation of consonantal sounds. The stops, hisses, and other interruptions to the steady flow of vowel tone are an important part of our spoken language; it is the *p, m, k, s* sounds and their companions that serve to make words out of what would otherwise be mere vocal tones. Precision and sharpness of articulation come from active use of these modifiers.

PHYSICAL REQUIREMENTS FOR A GOOD SPEAKING VOICE

To what has been said about the speech mechanism, we may add a few simple requirements for its effective use. These suggestions, as indicated earlier in the chapter, must be general; for more specific suggestions to fit your individual problems, you must seek the advice of your instructor.

Control of breathing
Singing tones are often sustained, but speech sounds are not. They are short and precise. Therefore, you do not need a big lung capacity to speak well; what you need is control over what you have. By controlling the pressure exerted on the vocal cords by the air in your lungs, you may vary the strength of your voice and give your utterance power or delicacy as you will. Lack of control, on the other hand, results in lack of power, jerkiness, or a breathy, wheezing tone. Exercises such as panting like a dog, expelling the breath slowly with a long, slow whistle or hum, counting from one to ten with increasing force— these and other similar exercises help increase breath control.

Relaxation of the throat and neck
In addition to causing strain and soreness, tension in the throat and neck results in harshness and a loss of tone flexibility. Pleasing voice quality comes from a relaxed condition of the throat coupled with the breath control mentioned above. Letting the head hang limp, yawning, singing vowel tones softly—these are good ways to practice relaxation before you speak.

Flexible and energetic use of the modifiers
If the jaw remains frozen tight or the tongue and lips fail to move in a lively fashion, the result is a jumble of unintelligible sounds. Mumbling speakers can seldom be heard clearly and, even when heard, are not given full credit for what they say. Sharp, precise utterance comes only from an energetic use of the modifiers. Keep your jaw, lips, and tongue moving, and moving with precision. For practice, exaggerate these movements, watching yourself in a mirror to make sure the movements are as vigorous as they feel. Practice saying words that are difficult to pronounce, and develop ability in saying tongue twisters (such as "She sells sea shells," etc.) rapidly without mistake.

If you establish sufficient control over your vocal mechanism, what results should you then strive to achieve with it in order to make your speech effective? For a voice to be considered good, it should be clear, pleasant, varied, and understandable, and it should be free from tension in the throat, lack of breath control, or inadequate use of the resonating cavities. Leaving the discussion of variety, emphasis, and precise utterance until later, let us consider here in more detail the problem of voice quality—the development of a pleasant, clear, and vibrant tone of voice.

VOCAL QUALITY

When you describe someone's voice as being harsh or mellow or guttural or nasal, you are describing its quality. Quality is often referred to as timbre or tone color. It is determined by the combination of resonances in the voice. Just as the quality of tone produced by one violin differs from that produced by another, so does the quality of one person's voice differ from that of another. In the human voice the quality is determined in part by the initial tone produced in the larynx and in part by the influence of the resonating air chambers above. (See drawings on pp. 70 and 71.)

A proper balance between oral and nasal resonance results in a normal quality, that which occurs in normal conversation when all the resonators are used in balanced proportion and when excessive tension and breathiness are avoided. You should use your "normal" voice quality because it will be the most pleasant for your listeners and will permit the greatest flexibility. If your instructor says you are not doing so, take special note of the next few pages.

Unpleasant vocal qualities

Let us consider a few of the more common types of poor vocal quality and see what causes them.

Thin, weak voices lack carrying power. More often found in women than in men, this type of voice is faint and flabby. The voices of people who have been sick a long time are usually of this type. A number of causes may combine to result in such a voice: the muscles of the tongue and palate may be so inactive that inadequate use is made of the resonating cavities; the pitch level may be too high—even a falsetto—so that the lower resonances are not used (similar to what happens when you tune out the

 *th* ese

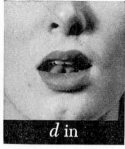 *d* in

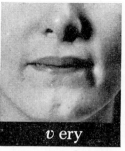 *v* ery

 *w* ool

Clear speech depends on distinct consonant sounds and requires a vigorous use of both tongue and lips. Notice the positions of these organs in pronouncing th, d, v, and w, as shown in these pictures.

Many small children—and even adults who are not careful—have difficulty with the v sound; failure to bring the lower lip back near the upper teeth makes their pronunciation of very sound like "wery."

 k *ee* p

 *ee* overdone

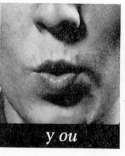 y *ou*

 l *et*

While the position of the lips is important in producing the right vowel sound, the position of the tongue is even more important. Say "keep" and "car," and notice the difference in your tongue and jaw positions.

Certain vowels require a rounding of the lips while others require a wider opening produced by lowering the jaw. Compare the pictures above with those below and with those in the opposite column.

 c *a* r

 h *a* t

 j *aw*

 f *a* ther

New Englanders say "car" with an a vowel very seldom heard in the Midwest. Compare the pictures above with those in the next column.

The positions of the lips in the two pictures above are those normally taken in saying the vowels in such words as jaw and father.

lower partials on your radio); or the power given to the voice originally by the breathing muscles may be inadequate. Of these causes, the last two are the most common. If your voice is thin, try lowering the pitch of your voice (come down the musical scale a bit) and at the same time talk a little louder. Say "bound" as if projecting it from deep in your chest and bouncing it upon the back wall of the room.

Huskiness and harshness result either from tension in the throat or from forcing too much air through the vocal cords. An irritated or diseased condition of the throat may have the same effect. If a throat examination fails to disclose any pathological condition, you can be sure that the huskiness can be eliminated by proper breathing and relaxation. Let the neck muscles become slack; then say such words as *one, bun, run,* very quietly, prolonging them almost to a singing tone. Work at this until you are sure the tone is clear and free of all breathiness; if you have trouble, use less breath. When you are sure the tone is clear, gradually increase the volume until you can produce a strong tone without tension or huskiness.

Nasality, contrary to popular notion, is more often the result of too little nasal resonance than of too much. (Persons with cleft palates usually have too much nasal resonance; a consideration of their problems is beyond the scope of this book.) Most nasality results from failing to open up the nasal passages enough. Say the word *button* or *mutton.* Notice what happens to your soft palate; did you feel it tighten up just before the explosion of the *t* and then relax to allow the explosion to carry the *n* sound out through the nose? For the explosive consonants, such as the *t, p,* etc., the palate has to close tight; but if this tension is continued during the production of the vowel sounds, a flat, nasal sound is likely to result. To correct this difficulty, begin by working on those sounds which must be produced through the nose—*m-m-m-m* and *n-n-n-n.* Hum these sounds, prolonging them until you can feel the vibration in your nose. At the same time, keeping the lips closed, drop the jaw somewhat and let the sound reverberate in the mouth cavity. When you can feel a "ringing" sensation in both these places, open your lips and let the *m* become an *ah* thus: *m-m-m-m-m-a-a-ah.* You should still feel some vibration both in the mouth and nose; continue until you do. Once you have this feeling for nasal resonance, practice using it on other sounds. You will be wise, however, to have your instructor listen to you because, while the chances are slight, it is possible to relax the palate *too* much so that you give the tone an excess of nasal resonance.

These are by no means the only types of unpleasant quality nor the only causes that produce poor quality. In the main, the best thing to do is to ask your instructor for a frank criticism of your voice and for suggestions to guide you in practicing to improve it. The exercises beginning on page 78 at the end of the chapter should also prove helpful.

Effect of emotion on vocal quality

Changes in quality of tone are closely related to emotion. Indeed, our voices automatically register any strong feeling. To tell an angry man or an enthusiastic one by the tone of his voice is not difficult. Ordinarily, if you really feel what you are saying, your voice will change of its own accord to suit your feeling. But to attempt artificial variation in quality in order to suggest emotion is usually unwise—it puts the cart before the horse; you will be better off to let the emotion affect the tone naturally. Only in mimicry and impersonation can most people purposely make a change of quality without suggesting insincerity; when the speaker is obviously impersonating someone else, then an effective imitation of that person's voice quality even to the point of suggesting its emotional tone is perfectly in order. As a vocal exercise, or for variety, such impersonation is useful; be careful, though, that you do not get into the habit of playing with emotional tone merely for effect, or you will become the elocutionist type of speaker described in the first chapter and will lose your direct conversational contact with the audience. On the other hand, if you allow the depth of your feeling to fill you and let your voice ring out freely without restraint, you will find the quality of your voice vibrant with that feeling—not in a superficial way but with the subtle and varied shadings which will carry conviction to your audience.

In brief, gain control of the mechanics of your speech. Learn to control your breathing, to relax your throat, and to develop energy and flexibility in your jaw, tongue, and lips. Develop a pleasing quality in your voice, and let your voice respond easily and naturally to your feelings. Do all these things under the supervision of your instructor so that your practice can be focused on your own individual problems.

PROBLEMS

To increase your knowledge of the structural mechanics of speech.

1. Make a set of drawings of the organs used in speech—the so-called "speech mechanism." (A good set of drawings may also be found in *The Bases of Speech,* third edition, by G. W. Gray and C. M. Wise; more detailed drawings may be found in such books as *Gray's Anatomy.*)

2. Make a tabulation of the muscles used in inhaling, exhaling, raising and lowering the larynx in the throat, changing the position or tension of the vocal cords, manipulating the jaw, tongue, soft palate, and lips. (Refer to the same sources as for Problem 1.)

3. Make a set of diagrams showing the position of the articulating organs—tongue, palate, jaw, lips, etc.—in the production of each of the vowel and consonant sounds. (Consult such books as *Phonetics,* revised edition, by C. E. Kantner and Robert West.)

To improve your control of breathing.

4. Practice expelling the air from your lungs in short, sharp gasps; place your hand on your abdomen to see that there is a sharp inward contraction of the muscle wall synchronous with the chest contraction on each outgoing puff.
   A. Then vocalize the puffs, saying "Hep!—Hep!—Hep!" with a good deal of force.
   B. In the same way, say "bah, bay, bee, bo, boo," with staccato accents and considerable vigor.

5. Fill your lungs; then exhale *as slowly as possible* until the lungs are empty. Time yourself to see how long you can keep exhaling without a break. (Note that the object here is not to see how much air you can get into the lungs but how slowly you can let it out.)
   A. Then, filling your lungs each time, vocalize the outgoing breath stream first with a long continuous hum, second with an *oo* sound, and then with other vowel sounds. Be careful not to let the sound become "breathy"; keep the tone clear.
   B. Place a lighted candle just in front of your mouth and repeat the series outlined above. The flame should just barely flicker.

6. On the same breath alternate the explosive and the slow, deliberate exhalations outlined in the preceding two problems. Practice until you can shift from one to the other easily both in silent breathing and in vocalized tones.

To induce relaxation of the throat.

7. Repeat the following sequence several times in succession:
   A. Turn the head slowly and tensely to the right as far as possible; to the left; backward; forward. In each direction, *stretch*.
   B. Break the tension, letting the head fall inertly forward on the chest; let the jaw drop open and the eyes close; move the jaw from side to side with the hand to be sure the jaw muscles are relaxed; let the facial muscles become lax as if you were asleep.
   C. With the muscles in this relaxed condition, allow the head to roll around slowly, making a complete rotation in each direction; repeat two or three times.
   D. Keeping your eyes closed and your neck and jaw muscles as relaxed as possible, raise your head easily to an upright position and then yawn with your mouth open as wide as possible.
   E. While your mouth is thus open, inhale deeply and exhale quietly two or three times; then intone "a-a-a-ah" very quietly.
   F. Each time nodding the head forward quietly and without tension, say "m-m-a-a-ah" several times slowly.
   G. Keeping the same degree of relaxation, count aloud slowly from one to twenty and then continue in the same relaxed manner, saying several times over:

   > And may there be no moaning of the bar,
   > When I put out to sea.
   >   *Tennyson*

To improve the quality of tone.

8. Intone the following words quietly at first, then louder, and louder; try to give them a ringing quality; put your fingertips on the nose and cheekbones to see if you can feel a vibration there. Avoid breathiness due to the use of too much air.

one	home	tone	alone	moan
rain	plain	mine	lean	soon
ring	nine	dong	moon	fine

9. Read aloud the following passages in as clear and resonant tones as you can. Be sure that you open your mouth wide enough and that you use only enough air to make the tones vibrate. Do not force the tone. If you notice any tension in your throat or harshness in your voice, go back to the preceding exercises until the tension and harshness disappear.

Roll on, thou deep and dark blue Ocean, roll!
                                    Byron

Alone, alone, all, all alone,
Alone on a wide, wide sea!
And never a saint took pity on
My soul in agony.
                              Coleridge

The day is cold and dark and dreary;
It rains, and the wind is never weary;
The vine still clings to the moldering wall,
But at every gust the dead leaves fall,
    And the day is dark and dreary.
                                    Longfellow

I have raised my head,
And cried, in thraldom, to the furious wind,
"Blow on!—This is the land of liberty!"
                                    Knowles

God of our fathers, known of old,
    Lord of our far-flung battle-line,
Beneath whose awful Hand we hold
    Dominion over palm and pine—
Lord God of Hosts, be with us yet,
Lest we forget—lest we forget!
                              Kipling

Selected passages for further practice.

Some of these selections are included because of the emotional tone
they portray; others because of the vocal control they require. All of
them, however, call for a clear, resonant quality for the best expression.
Study them first for their meaning so that you are sure you understand
what the author is saying. Then absorb the feeling; allow yourself to follow the mood of the writer. Finally, read the passages aloud, putting as
much meaning and feeling into the expression as you can.

    from *The Congo* [1]

Fat black bucks in a wine-barrel room,
Barrel-house kings, with feet unstable,
Sagged and reeled and pounded on the table,

---

[1] From Vachel Lindsay: *The Congo and Other Poems.* Copyright 1914 by
The Macmillan Company and used with their permission.

Pounded on the table,
Beat an empty barrel with the handle of a broom,
Hard as they were able,
Boom, boom, BOOM,
With a silk umbrella and the handle of a broom,
Boomlay, boomlay, boomlay, BOOM.

Vachel Lindsay

from *The Man with the Hoe* [2]

Bowed by the weight of centuries he leans
Upon his hoe and gazes on the ground,
The emptiness of ages in his face,
And on his back the burden of the world.
Who made him dead to rapture and despair,
A thing that grieves not and that never hopes,
Stolid and stunned, a brother to the ox?
Who loosened and let down this brutal jaw?
Whose was the hand that slanted back this brow?
Whose breath blew out the light within this brain?

Edwin Markham

from *The Barrel-Organ* [3]

There's a barrel-organ carolling across a golden street
    In the City as the sun sinks low;
And the music's not immortal; but the world has made it sweet
    And fulfilled it with the sunset-glow;
And it pulses through the pleasures of the City and the pain
    That surround the singing organ like a large eternal light;
And they've given it a glory and a part to play again
    In the Symphony that rules the day and night.

Alfred Noyes

from *Apostrophe to the Ocean*

Roll on, thou deep and dark blue Ocean, roll!
    Ten thousand fleets sweep over thee in vain;
Man marks the earth with ruin—his control
    Stops with the shore;—upon the watery plain
    The wrecks are all thy deed, nor doth remain
A shadow of man's ravage, save his own,
    When for a moment, like a drop of rain,

[2] Copyright by the author and used by permission.
[3] From *Collected Poems* by Alfred Noyes, J. B. Lippincott Co., Philadelphia, 1947.

Problems **81**

He sinks into thy depths with bubbling groan,
Without a grave, unknelled, uncoffined, and unknown.

Byron

Death, Be Not Proud

Death, be not proud, though some have called thee
Mighty and dreadful, for thou art not so;
For those whom thou think'st thou dost overthrow
Die not, poor Death; nor yet canst thou kill me.
From rest and sleep, which but thy picture be,
Much pleasure; then from thee much more must flow;
And soonest our best men with thee do go—
Rest of their bones and souls' delivery!
Thou 'rt slave to fate, chance, kings, and desperate men,
And dost with poison, war, and sickness dwell;
And poppy or charms can make us sleep as well
And better than thy stroke. Why swell'st thou then?
One short sleep past, we wake eternally,
And Death shall be no more: Death, thou shalt die!

John Donne

Wind in the Pine [4]

Oh, I can hear you, God, above the cry
   Of the tossing trees—
Rolling your windy tides across the sky,
   And splashing your silver seas
     Over the pine,
     To the water-line
   Of the moon.
Oh, I can hear you, God,
   Above the wail of the lonely loon—
When the pine-tops pitch and nod—
   Chanting your melodies
Of ghostly waterfalls and avalanches,
Swashing your wind among the branches
   To make them pure and white.

Wash over me, God, with your piney breeze,
   And your moon's wet-silver pool;
Wash over me, God, with your wind and night,
   And leave me clean and cool.

Lew Sarett

---

[4] From *Covenant with Earth* by Lew Sarett. Edited and copyrighted 1956 by Alma Johnson Sarett. Gainesville: University of Florida Press.

God's Grandeur

The world is charged with the grandeur of God.
  It will flame out, like shining from shook foil;
  It gathers to a greatness, like the ooze of oil
Crushed. Why do men then now not reck his rod?
Generations have trod, have trod, have trod;
  And all is seared with trade; bleared, smeared with toil;
  And wears man's smudge and shares man's smell: the soil
Is bare now, nor can foot feel, being shod.

And for all this, nature is never spent;
  There lives the dearest freshness deep down things;
And though the last lights off the black West went
  Oh, morning, at the brown brink eastward, springs—
Because the Holy Ghost over the bent
  World broods with warm breast and with ah! bright wings.
                                    Gerard Manley Hopkins

By the Bivouac's Fitful Flame

By the bivouac's fitful flame,
A procession winding around me, solemn and sweet and slow—but first I
    note,
The tents of the sleeping army, the fields' and woods' dim outline,
The darkness lit by spots of kindled fire, the silence,
Like a phantom far or near an occasional figure moving,
The shrubs and trees, (as I lift my eyes they seem to be stealthily
    watching me,)
While wind in procession thoughts, O tender and wondrous thoughts,
Of life and death, of home and the past and loved, and of those that are
    far away;
A solemn and slow procession there as I sit on the ground,
By the bivouac's fitful flame.
                                    Walt Whitman

from *Fern Hill* [5]

Now as I was young and easy under the apple boughs
About the lilting house and happy as the grass was green,
    The night above the dingle starry,
        Time let me hail and climb
    Golden in the heydays of his eyes,
And honoured among wagons I was prince of the apple towns

---

[5] From *The Collected Poems of Dylan Thomas.* Copyright © 1957 by New
Directions. Reprinted by permission of the publishers, New Directions, N.Y.,
and J. M. Dent & Sons, Ltd., London.

And once below a time I lordly had the trees and leaves
        Trail with daisies and barley
   Down the rivers of the windfall light.

And as I was green and carefree, famous among the barns
About the happy yard and singing as the farm was home,
   In the sun that is young once only,
        Time let me play and be
   Golden in the mercy of his means,
And green and golden I was huntsman and herdsman, the calves
Sang to my horn, the foxes on the hills barked clear and cold,
        And the sabbath rang slowly
   In the pebbles of the holy streams.

All the sun long it was running, it was lovely, the hay-
Fields high as the house, the tunes from the chimneys, it was air,
   And playing, lovely and watery
        And fire green as grass.
   And nightly under the simple stars
As I rode to sleep the owls were bearing the farm away,
All the moon long I heard, blessed among stables, the nightjars
   Flying with the ricks, and the horses
        Flashing into the dark.

                             Dylan Thomas

Doom Is Dark and Deeper Than Any Sea-Dingle [6]

Doom is dark and deeper than any sea-dingle.
Upon what man it fall
In spring, day-wishing flowers appearing,
Avalanche sliding, white snow from rock-face,
That he should leave his house,
No cloud-soft hand can hold him, restraint by women;
But ever that man goes
Through place-keepers, through forest trees,
A stranger to strangers over undried sea,
Houses for fishes, suffocating water,
Or lonely on fell as chat,
By pot-holed becks
A bird stone-haunting, an unquiet bird.

There head falls forward, fatigued at evening,
And dreams of home,
Waving from window, spread of welcome,

Kissing of wife under single sheet;
But waking sees
Bird-flocks nameless to him, through doorway voices
Of new men making another love.

Save him from hostile capture,
From sudden tiger's spring at corner;
Protect his house,
His anxious house where days are counted
From thunderbolt protect,
From gradual ruin spreading like a stain;
Converting number from vague to certain,
Bring joy, bring day of his returning,
Lucky with day approaching, with leaning dawn.

Wystan Hugh Auden

Accent is the soul of talk: it gives it feeling and verity.
Jean Jacques

CHAPTER 5 / *Developing*
Vocal
Variety

Police radio calls are usually clear and understandable, but the announcer's tone of voice is often monotonous. The variety and animation so necessary for effective speech in most situations are lacking. The men in the squad car have to listen, but your audience does not. Nothing is so likely to put an audience to sleep as a monotonous voice. It is like a drug that dissipates attention and enervates the mind. On the other hand, the sparkle and vitality that accompany vocal variety do as much to stimulate the attentive interest and enthusiasm of a listener as does any other one factor. The preceding chapter emphasized the development of a clear and pleasing voice; this chapter is concerned with its flexibility and expressiveness. For the sake of attention value alone you will be repaid for every minute you spend increasing this flexibility.

Furthermore, through the variations in your voice you convey a great part of your meaning. Take a simple sentence such as "John stole my watch." Notice the different shades of meaning conveyed by placing the emphasis first on *John*, then on *stole*, on *my*, and on *watch*. The first way points out the thief; the second tells what he did; the third calls attention to the rightful owner; and the fourth names the article stolen. All of these ideas are contained in the sentence, but the way you say it conveys to your listener which one is uppermost in your mind. Indeed, a single word can be made to mean several different things by varying the inflection of your voice. You can speak the name *Tom* as a question (meaning "You are Tom, aren't you?"), as a command (meaning "Stop that!"), as a request for attention (meaning "Listen a minute."), as a cry for help ("Come here quickly!"), or as conveying any one of a number of other meanings. But a flexible voice makes possible the expression of more than just the exact intellectual meaning of what you say; it enables you to transmit to the audience the full depth of feeling behind it. The greater the flexibility of your voice, the more clearly will you be able to transmit fine shades of feeling to your listeners and the more vigorous and colorful will be your remarks.

THE VARIABLE ATTRIBUTES OF VOICE

When the physicist describes a tone, he refers to the frequency and amplitude of the sound wave and to the distribution of energy in the partials that compose it. The psychologist describes the sensation of sound in terms of pitch, timbre, and loudness. Most writers on voice production refer to these variables, as produced in the speaking voice, by the terms *pitch, quality,* and *force;* and they add another term, *rate,* to describe the speed of successive syllables. For convenience we shall follow this terminology here.

Thus you can vary your voice by the rate at which you speak, the force with which you speak, the pitch of your voice, and its quality. Vocal *quality* has already been defined as the resonance pattern of the tone. By *rate* we mean the speed of utterance—that is, the number of syllables uttered per minute. *Force* is the loudness of utterance, varying from the softest whisper to the full-throated shout. The location of the sound on the musical scale is its *pitch;* varying the pitch means going up or down on this scale.

Since variation in quality of voice was discussed in the preceding chapter, here we shall consider the many ways in which the voice may be varied by each of the other three attributes: rate, force, and pitch. Remember, however, that no amount of reading about these matters will improve your voice one bit unless you practice, and practice often. Remember, too, that the aim of this study and practice is to help you establish natural habits of flexibility in your voice and not to provide you with tricks for elocutionary display. The exercises at the end of this chapter are helpful. Use them. Practice the technic of vocal manipulation until the ability to vary your voice becomes automatic and unconscious; then when you speak, your emphasis and melody will vary naturally in accordance with your meaning.

RATE

The normal speed of utterance for most speakers averages between 120 and 180 words a minute; however, this rate is not maintained with a continuous clocklike regularity. In general, the speed of talking ought to correspond to the thought expressed. Weighty or complex matters should be presented slowly so that the audience may have time to digest them properly. On the other hand, when you are attempting to present a rapid sequence of events or a quick cumulation of ideas, your speed should be more rapid. Observe how fast the sports announcer talks when he is describing a quick play in a football game; in contrast, notice the slow, dignified rate with which one repeats the Lord's Prayer. A fairly rapid rate is usually essential in narrative—nothing spoils a story so easily as to have it drag; but whenever you wish to drive home an important point or to emphasize some major fact, the rate of your speaking should be reduced materially. An enthusiastic or excited person talks rapidly; a poised or a lethargic person talks more slowly. But while an excited person talks fast *all* the time and a stolid one talks *always* in a slow drawl, the person who is both enthusiastic and poised varies his rate; he tells his story, lays out the facts, and cumulates his argumentative points at a lively pace, but he is careful to present his main ideas slowly and emphatically in order to let them sink in. Audiences are quick to note the difference between sheer excitement or apathy and the energetic self-control that shows itself in a varied rate.

Variation of rate, however, involves more than mere speed or slowness, for the rate of speaking depends on two elements: *quantity*, or the length of time used in the actual utterance of sound within a word, and *pause*, or the length of time spent in silence between words. Thus one may say "ni-i-ine fo-o-o-our three-ee-ee," using long quantity, or "nine four three," using short quantity; or he may say "nine————four————three," using long pause, or "nine, four, three," using short pause. The longer the quantity or pause or both, the slower the rate; the shorter the quantity or pause or both, the faster the rate. Besides affecting the general rate of speaking, quantity and pause in themselves help convey the speaker's meaning.

Quantity

Quantity varies primarily to suit the mood or sentiment expressed. Beauty, solemnity, dignity, peacefulness, serenity, and the like call for long quantity. If you say the beginning of Lincoln's famous address at Gettysburg ("Four score and seven years ago, our fathers brought forth on this continent a new nation, . . .") with sharp staccato quality, the result is obviously absurd; such sentiments require sustained tones. On the other hand, excitement, wit, gayety, surprise, vivacity, and the like require the use of short quantity. Imagine listening to the following play-by-play account of a basketball game given in a slow drawl: "Jones passes to Schmidt—he's dribbling down the floor—back to Jones—back again to Schmidt—over to Lee— and it's in! Another basket for. . . ." Like the game itself, such a description needs snap; short quantity provides it.

A good way to develop a feeling for quantity values is to practice reading aloud selections in which some particular type of sentiment prevails or in which there is a definite shift from one sentiment to another. A number of the passages of poetry and prose at the end of this chapter are of this type. Notice in reading them that vowel sounds are usually longer than consonant sounds, and that some consonants and vowels are longer than others. The word *roll*, for example, contains sounds that are intrinsically longer than those in *hit*. In this way many words suggest their meaning by the very duration of the sounds in them. Writers know this and use such words, either consciously or because of an unconscious sensitivity to these values, to help convey their feelings. By absorbing the feeling expressed in these selections and then reading them aloud with as near an approximation to the writer's feeling as you can induce in yourself, you will develop something of that same sensitivity to quantity values, and the expressiveness of your voice will be increased.

Pause   Pause is primarily an intellectual device serving to punctuate the spoken thought. Just as commas, semicolons, and periods separate written words into thought groups, so pauses of different length separate the words in speech into meaningful units. Haphazard use of pause, therefore, may be just as confusing to the listener as the injudicious use of punctuation would be to the reader. Be sure that your pauses come between thought groups and not in the middle of them. Moreover, in reading aloud remember that written and oral punctuation differ; not every comma calls for a pause, nor does the absence of punctuation always indicate that no pause is required. And when reading poetry, do not always pause arbitrarily at the end of each line; convention may require that the poet write his words to fit a given metric pattern, but his thought frequently runs on into the next line.

Pauses may also be used for emphasis. Placed immediately before or after an important statement, they serve to suggest to your audience, "Let this idea sink in." A pause just before the climax of a story sometimes helps increase suspense; a dramatic pause at the right moment may express the depth of the speaker's feeling much more forcefully than any words could.

Many speakers are afraid to pause. Fearing that silence will focus attention on them personally, they rush on with a stream of words, or, failing to find words readily, they substitute such sighs and grunts as "and-er-ah." Remember that a pause seldom seems as long to the audience as it does to the speaker and that the ability to pause for emphasis or to clarify a thought is an indication of poise and self-control. Audiences respect speakers who are able to think on their feet, and the proper use of pause is a good sign of this ability. On the other hand, do not stop purposelessly just to let the time pass; concentrate on the thought or emotion you are trying to emphasize. Thoughtful pauses are dynamic; empty ones are merely silly.

Meaningful variety of rate through the effective use of quantity and pause is one of the easiest ways of achieving flexibility of expression; practice will help you develop it.

FORCE

The first requirement any audience places on a speaker is that he talk loud enough to be heard easily. In addition, a certain amount of force is needed if the speaker is to give the impression of confidence and vigor. Continuing to talk too softly may suggest that you are not sure of yourself or that you don't care whether your audience hears you or not. Sometimes, of course, making an audience strain for a moment to hear what you say is desirable because it serves to break through a passive attitude. But such a strain continued for too long wears the listener out; his attention wanders, and he moves about restlessly in his seat, wishing the ordeal were over. On the other hand, beware of continuous shouting. This, too, wears out an audience and dissipates attention. People become quite as bored by a continuous loud noise as by a continuous soft one. With respect to force, as with rate, keep in mind that variety should be your objective.

The force with which you speak may be varied in degree and in form. *Degree* refers to the *amount* of force applied; a whisper or an undertone is uttered with a low degree of force, while a shout takes a high degree. *Form*, on the other hand, refers to the *manner* in which that force is applied; we may apply the force abruptly and explosively, or we may increase it with a gradual swell. The relative amount of force applied to different syllables in a word, or to different words in a phrase, is called *stress*. The effect of stress, however, is as often obtained by a change of pitch or rate as by an increase of force—in fact, all three variables usually combine to create stress—but since stressing a sound usually makes it louder, we may conveniently consider stress as a third type of force variation.

Degree Force is varied in degree primarily for emphasis. Either by increasing the loudness of a word or phrase or by pointedly reducing its loudness, you may make that word or phrase stand out as if it had been underscored. Moreover, changing the degree of force is an effective way to reawaken lagging interest. A drowsy audience will sit up quickly if you suddenly project an important word or phrase with sharply increased force. Remember, however, that the effect is produced not by the degree of force applied but by the *change* in degree; a sharp reduction is quite as effective as a sharp increase. A man sleeping in a noisy room, for example, may be awakened by a sudden silence.

While you are practicing to develop control of the degree of force you use, you will do well to observe what happens to the pitch and quality of your voice. The natural tendency for most speakers is to raise their pitch when they try to increase their loudness; you have probably noticed that when you shout, your voice is keyed much higher than when you speak in a conversational tone. This happens because the nerves which control the speaking mechanism tend to diffuse their impulses to all the muscles in that mechanism; the resulting general tension is apt to produce high pitch as well as more force. Sometimes this tension is so great in the throat that a harsh quality is produced as well. A little practice, however, will enable you to overcome this tendency. Just as you have learned to wiggle one finger without moving the others or to wink one eye without the other, so you can learn to apply force by contracting the breathing muscles without tightening the muscles of the throat or unnecessarily raising the pitch of your voice. A good way to begin is by repeating a sentence such as "That is absolutely *true!*" Hit the last word in the sentence with a greater degree of force and at the same time lower your pitch. When you have mastered this bit of vocal control, say the entire sentence louder, and LOUDER, and LOUDER, until you can shout it without your pitch going up too. Keep a fairly sustained tone; use rather long quantity; and try to maintain a full resonance. By developing control over the degree of force in your voice, you will have done a great deal to make your speaking more emphatic and to convey to your audience an impression of reserve power.

Form

The manner, or form, in which force is applied generally indicates the underlying sentiments of the speaker. If force is applied gradually and firmly, in what is called the *effusive* form, it suggests deep but controlled sentiment; generally, effusive form is used to express grandeur, dignity, reverence, and the like. When the *expulsive* form is used, force is applied firmly but more rapidly and energetically; this form is used to express decisiveness, vigor, and earnestness. The sudden and *explosive* form of applying force suggests violent or uncontrolled feeling; it is associated with extreme anger, sudden fear, or other strong emotions that burst out abruptly.

Obviously the form of force used is closely related to the quantity or duration of the words spoken. The effusive form, for instance, demands longer quantity than the explosive form. Thus the elements of quantity and force combine in the expression of feeling. The suggestion made on page 89, therefore, applies equally well here: to acquire skill in expressing feelings through the form of force, practice reading aloud passages of prose or poetry laden with these feelings, first absorbing the feelings and then giving free play to their expression. The selections at the end of the chapter are useful for this practice, and your instructor can give you helpful criticism and advice. Remember that the form of force should be the natural response to inner feeling; sheer vocal manipulation is bound to sound artificial and hollow. Only by a certain amount of conscious drill, however, can you develop sufficient flexibility and control over your voice to provide these feelings with a free and easy means of expression.

Stress

To be understood, a word must be correctly accented, according to accepted standards of pronunciation. Consider the change of meaning produced by shifting the stress from one syllable to the other in the word *content*. The rules of stress, however, are by no means inflexible when words are used in connected speech. Emphasis and contrast often require the shifting of stress for the sake of greater clarity. For example, notice what you do to the accent in the word *proceed* when you use it in this sentence: "I said to proceed, not to recede." Many words completely change in sound when they are stressed; especially is this true of short words such as pronouns, articles, and prepositions. If you are speaking normally, you will say, "I gave 'im th' book." But if you stress the third word, or the fourth one, you will say, "I gave *him* th' book," or "I gave 'im *the* book." Thus both conventional accent and the requirements of contrast and emphasis influence the placing of stress in words. Effective use of stress is essential for intelligible utterance and for vigorous, animated expression.

PITCH

Just as singers' voices differ, some being soprano or tenor and some contralto or bass, so do people in general vary in the normal pitch level at which they speak. Except in the impersonation of characters, the wisest plan is to talk in your normal pitch range; otherwise there is danger of straining your voice. You will find, however, that there is considerable leeway within that normal range. Few beginning speakers use enough variation even within their normal range of pitch; they tend to hit one level and stay there. We will therefore discuss not only the *key*, or general level of pitch, but also changes of pitch—both abrupt changes called *steps*, and gradual changes called *slides*, together with the *melody pattern* thus produced. Nothing improves the animation and vivacity of speech so much as effective variation in pitch.

Key

The general pitch level, or key, varies considerably from person to person; but most of us have a wider range of pitch than we suspect. Nearly everyone can easily span an octave, and many people have voices flexible enough to vary more than two octaves without strain. We normally speak at a general key-level, taking excursions above and below this key-level, and within it, to vary our expression. The key-level at which we speak creates a very definite impression; ordinarily, a pitch that is continuously high suggests weakness, excitement, irritation, or extreme youth, while a lower key-level suggests assurance, poise, and strength. For that reason, your customary pitch should normally be in the lower half of your natural range; but your voice must not remain there all the time—break away and come back. Be particularly careful when you are applying increasing degrees of force not to let your voice get out of control, going to a higher and higher key until it cracks under the strain. If you notice tension, pause for a moment and lower your pitch. At times, of course, you will be excited, and your voice will rise to a high pitch to match your emotion. Remember, however, that somewhat restrained emotion is much more impressive to an audience than emotion which has gone beyond control.

Steps and slides — There are two ways in which pitch is changed in connected speech—by steps and slides. For example, suppose someone had made a statement with which you agreed completely and you answered by saying, "You're exactly right!" The chances are that you would say it something like this:

$$\text{"You're ex-}\qquad\overset{\text{actly}}{\qquad}\qquad\text{ri-}_{\text{i}}\overset{\cdot}{\underset{\text{ight!}}{}}\text{"}$$

Notice that a complete break in pitch level occurs between the first and second syllables of the word *exactly*—that sort of abrupt change in pitch is a *step;* on the word *right,* however, a more gradual pitch inflection takes place during the actual production of the sound—such a continuous change of pitch within a syllable is a *slide.* Both steps and slides may go upward or downward depending on the meaning intended; slides are sometimes double, the pitch going up and then down or vice versa, as when one says,

$$\text{"O}\sim^{\text{o}}{}^{\sim\text{O}}\sim^\text{o}\sim\text{oh!"}$$

to express the meaning, "I didn't realize that!" In general, an upward step or slide suggests interrogation, indecision, uncertainty, doubt, or suspense, while a downward inflection suggests firmness, determination, certainty, finality, or confidence. Thus if you were to say, "What shall we do about it? Just this . . . ," a rising inflection on the question would create suspense, while a downward inflection on the last phrase would indicate the certainty with which you were presenting your answer. A double inflection, as indicated by the example above, suggests a subtle conflict or contradiction of meaning; it is frequently used to express irony or sarcasm and to convey all sorts of subtle innuendo. Steps and slides are primarily useful in carrying the thought content rather than the emotional content of speech. By mastering their use, you will be able to make your meaning more obvious.

All this does not mean that when you arise to speak you should say to yourself: "This sentence requires an upward inflection; I shall use a step between these two words and a slide on that one." Such concentration on the mechanics of utterance would destroy the last vestige of communicative contact with your audience. Rather, in private and in class exercises, you should practice the technic, reading aloud selected passages which require pitch inflection, until the habit of flexibility grows on you. Then, when you speak, these habits will show themselves in the increased variety and greater expressiveness of your utterance.

Melody patterns
In all kinds of speech the rhythm and swing of phrase and sentence weave themselves into a continuous pattern of changing pitch. As the thought or mood changes, this melodic pattern should also change. Sorrow or grief are not well expressed by the quick, lilting melody of playfulness and wit. A monotonous melody pattern, however, is just as deadly as staying in one key all the time. Beware particularly of seesawing back and forth in a singsong voice. Avoid also the tendency of many inexperienced speakers to end every sentence with an upward cadence; assertions become questions when so uttered, and you may sound doubtful even though you feel certain. A monotonous downward cadence is almost as bad, though, since it suggests certainty when you may want to express uncertainty. If you develop flexibility of pitch inflection as suggested in the paragraph above, your melody pattern will normally adjust itself to the thought and mood you intend to express, but be careful not to get into a vocal rut, unconsciously using the same melody for everything you say.

EMPHASIS

Obviously, all forms of vocal variety help provide emphasis. Any change of rate, or of force, or of pitch serves to make the word, phrase, or sentence in which the change occurs stand out from those which precede or follow it. This is true regardless of the direction of the change; whether the rate or force be increased or decreased, whether the pitch be raised or lowered, emphasis will result. And the greater the amount of change or the more suddenly it is applied, the more emphatic will the statement be. Furthermore, emphasis is increased by pause and contrast: the former by allowing the audience to get set for the important idea or to digest it afterwards, and the latter by making the change seem greater than it otherwise would.

Two warnings, however, should be given: avoid overemphasis, and avoid continuous emphasis. If you emphasize a point beyond its evident value or importance, your audience will lose faith in your judgment; if you attempt to emphasize everything, nothing will really stand out. Be judicious. Pick out the things that are really important and give them the emphasis they deserve.

VOCAL CLIMAX[1]

Frequently a speaker expresses a thought or feeling that rises steadily in power until it reaches a point where the strongest appeal is made. Such climaxes of thought or feeling require climactic use of vocal expression. Roughly, there are two methods of expressing vocal climax. The first involves increasing vocal power; the second, decreasing vocal power coupled with increasing intensity of emotion. The first method requires that each successive thought unit, whether it be word, phrase, or sentence, be said with a successive increase in force, with a more rapid rate, with a higher level of pitch, or with any combination of these changes. When the second method is used, the force is successively decreased, the rate slowed down, or the pitch lowered; but coupled with these changes is an increasing intensity of feeling expressed by the speaker's movement, gesture, facial expression and by the emotion evident in his voice. Notice that the second method involves much more than merely letting the voice run down; the power is there, but it is kept under control—the audience is made

---

[1] Not to be confused with *rhetorical* climax, which is the arrangement of ideas in order of increasing importance.

to feel the tremendous strength of feeling which the speaker is holding in check. The former method is easier and more frequently used; the latter requires more skill but is often more effective.

There are times when the two types of climax may be combined or contrasted. The speaker may build up a climax of vocal power and then swing rapidly and positively into one of emotional intensity; or he may show an increased intensity of controlled emotion followed by a climax of vocal power. When such a shift of direction is motivated by genuine feeling and enough time is given to the climactic movement in each direction, the contrasting swing gives an added momentum to the second climax that can rarely be achieved by moving in one direction alone. The reaction of the audience is like the action of a pendulum which is given an added increment of power on the return stroke. You must be careful if you use this method not to make the shift too sudden— allow a slight pause—nor to make the climactic movements too short. Give the climax time enough to build, and keep it building steadily.

Some immature speakers try to have too many climaxes in one speech. The effect of climax is lost by repetition; if climaxes become too commonplace, they are no longer climactic by the end of the speech. One good climax has more power to move an audience than five mediocre ones, and frequently even more than five good ones. Save your vocal climaxes for the places where they will be most effective, usually near the end of the speech, or at the ends of really major thought units.

Beware also of anticlimax. When successive stages of climactic power begin to follow one another, audiences expect them to continue until the peak of interest has been reached. If before the real climax has been reached the added increments of power begin to lessen or the climactic movement stops, the audience feels let down. Start slowly enough, or quietly enough, or at a low enough pitch, so that you can keep on building till the end has been reached. Furthermore, if a vigorous and effective climax has been completed, don't continue talking on in a normal manner; pause, or shift your manner of speaking and mood completely, or stop talking altogether; above all, don't say the same thing over in an ordinary way.

Effective vocal climax requires considerable skill. To develop that skill, nothing is so effective as to select climactic passages from the speeches of great speakers and to practice reading them aloud or speaking them from memory. Digest the meaning and the mood of the passage before you start in order to get the feel of it; then use all the power and control you have.

In this chapter we have covered a great deal of ground. We have talked about variety of rate, and of force, and of pitch. The relation between these variables of vocal expression and the meaning and emotional intent of the speaker has been considered. Comment has been made on the usefulness of variety in holding the attention of the audience and on the methods of securing emphasis and building climaxes. Do not expect to master all of these technics in one day, or one week, or one month. The greatest artists often spend years to perfect the details of their art so that the technic becomes almost unconscious when it is applied in the creation of a masterpiece. Take time to digest the ideas explained in this chapter; practice on the material provided for exercise; return to this practice again and again, even after your expressive powers have materially improved, so that your technic does not become clumsy from disuse. And above all, remember that all technic, before it becomes natural and effective with an audience, must become so much a habit with you that you are able to forget it when you actually arise to speak. Only in this way can you improve your expressive powers and retain a sincere communicative spirit.

PROBLEMS

1. Be ready to discuss the following questions in class: How does each of the variable attributes of voice contribute to a more interesting and effective voice? How are the variables used to produce emphasis and vocal climaxes?

To develop flexibility in vocal manipulation.

2. While repeating the alphabet or counting from one to twenty, perform the following vocal gymnastics (being careful throughout to maintain good vocal quality and distinctness of utterance):

A. Beginning very slowly, steadily increase the speed until you are speaking as rapidly as possible; then, beginning rapidly, reverse the process.

B. Stretch out the quantity of the vowel sounds, speaking at a slow rate but allowing no pauses between letters or numbers; then shift to short quantity with long pauses. Shift back and forth between these two methods with every five or six letters or numbers you say.

C. Begin very softly and increase the force until you are nearly shouting; reverse the process. Then practice shifting from one extreme to the other, occasionally changing to a moderate degree of force.

D. Keeping the loudness constant, shift from an explosive application of force combined with a staccato utterance to a firm, smooth application of force.

E. Stress alternate letters (or numbers); then change by stressing every third letter, every fourth, etc.; then change back to alternate letters again.

F. Begin at the lowest pitch you can comfortably reach and raise the pitch steadily until you reach the highest comfortable pitch; reverse the process. Shift back and forth suddenly from high to low to middle, etc.

G. Practice slides with the vowel *o*. Try upward slides, downward slides, and those which are double—going up and down or down and up.

H. Using a half dozen letters or numbers, practice similar pitch changes in steps; then alternate steps and slides.

I. Combine the above gymnastics into as many different complex patterns as your ingenuity and patience will permit. (Mathematically, there are several hundred different permutations and combinations.)

3. Vary the *rate* with which you say the following sentences in the manner indicated:

A. "There goes the last one."
 1) Use long quantity, expressing regret.
 2) Use short quantity, as if excited.
 3) Use moderate quantity, merely stating a fact.

B. "The winners are John, Henry, and Bill."
 1) Insert a long pause after *are* for suspense; then give the names rapidly.
 2) Insert pauses before each name as if picking them out.
 3) Say the whole sentence rapidly in a matter-of-fact way.

C. "If you come one step nearer, I'll . . . End the sentence with the following words:
 1) punch your nose!"

2) scream!"
3) never talk to you again."
4) show the picture to you."
5) well, I'm not sure just what I will do."
(See how many shades of meaning you can make these statements express.)

4. In the manner suggested, vary the *force* with which you say the following sentences:

A. "I hate you! I hate you! I hate you!"
1) Increase the degree of force with each repetition, making the last almost a shout.
2) Say the second *hate* louder than the first, and the last one *sotto voce*.
3) Shout the first statement; then let the force diminish as if echoing the mood.

B. "What kind of a thing is this?"
Repeat the question, stressing a different word each time. Try not to raise the pitch, but to emphasize by force alone.

C. "I have told you a hundred times, and the answer is still the same."
1) Make the statement a straightforward assertion, using expulsive form.
2) Speak explosively as though uncontrollably angry.
3) Speak as with deep but controlled emotion, applying force gradually and firmly.

5. Practice varying the *pitch* with which you say the sentences below, following the directions given:

A. "I certainly feel fine today;—that is, except for my sunburn. Now don't slap me on the back! Ouch! Stop it! Please!"
Begin confidently on a low key, successively raising the pitch level until the *Please* is said near the top of your range. Repeat several times, trying to begin lower each time.

B. "Oh, yes. Is that so."
In the following notation, diagonal lines indicate slides; horizontal ones indicate a level pitch; differences in height between the end of one line and the beginning of the next indicate steps. Each line represents one word. Say the sentence in the following ways:

1) __ ‾ __ ‾ __

2) __ ╱ __ ‾ ╲

3) ⌐ \ _ _ ∕

4) _ ∧ _ _ ∧

5) ⌐ — _ ⌐ \

What are the different meanings conveyed?
C. Say the sentence given in Problem 4B with varied pitch inflections so that it will mean as many different things as possible.

6. Practice reading aloud sentences from prose and poetry that require emphasis and contrast to make the meaning clear. Vary the pitch, rate, and force in different ways until you feel you have the best possible interpretation of the meaning. Here are some examples for practice:

A. One of the most striking differences between a cat and a lie is that a cat has only nine lives.

Mark Twain

B. So, Naturalists observe, a flea
Has smaller fleas that on him prey;
And these have smaller still to bite 'em;
And so proceed ad infinitum.

Jonathan Swift

C. I have waited with patience to hear what arguments might be urged against the bill; but I have waited in vain: The truth is, there is no argument that can weigh against it.

Lord Mansfield

D. Gentlemen may cry, peace, peace!—but there is no peace. The war has actually begun! I know not what course others may take; but, as for me, give me liberty, or give me death!

Patrick Henry

E. Some books are to be tasted; others to be swallowed, and some few to be chewed and digested; that is, some books are to be read only in parts; others to be read but not curiously, and some few to be read wholly, and with diligence and attention.

Francis Bacon

F. "Beauty is truth, truth beauty,"—that is all
Ye know on earth, and all ye need to know.

John Keats

7. Read the following passages so as to give the effect of climax: first practice the climax of increasing force, and then that of increasing intensity of feeling with diminishing force.

A. There is no mistake; there has been no mistake; and there shall be no mistake.

Duke of Wellington

B. Let us cultivate a true spirit of union and harmony . . . let us act under a settled conviction, and an habitual feeling, that these twenty-four States are one country. . . . Let our object be, OUR COUNTRY, OUR WHOLE COUNTRY, AND NOTHING BUT OUR COUNTRY.

Daniel Webster

To increase vocal expressiveness of thought and emotion.

8. Clip a paragraph from a newspaper story describing some exciting incident and read it with appropriate vocal variety.

9. Memorize a section of one of the speeches printed in this book, as assigned by your instructor, and present it in such a way as to make the meaning clear and the feeling behind it dynamic, through the use of your voice.

10. Find an argumentative editorial or magazine article with which you vigorously agree or violently disagree. In your own words attack or defend the point of view presented, and do so with all the emphasis, contrast, and vocal variety of which you are capable. If you cannot find some issue on which you are genuinely aroused, find a mock issue and burlesque the professional spellbinder: point with pride or view with alarm!

11. Select a short bit of dialogue from a play, involving at least three characters, and read it in such a way that your voice indicates the identity of each character. Here are a few suggestions:

Shakespeare: *As You Like It*
                Taming of the Shrew
                Merchant of Venice
Goldsmith: *She Stoops to Conquer*
Pinero: *The Second Mrs. Tanqueray*
Rostand: *Cyrano de Bergerac*
Ibsen: *An Enemy of the People*
Galsworthy: *Strife*
Shaw: *Arms and the Man*
       Pygmalion
O'Neill: *The Hairy Ape*
Miller: *Death of a Salesman*

Williams: *A Streetcar Named Desire*
Fry: *The Lady's Not for Burning*
Chayefsky: *Marty*

12. Practice reading aloud (or speaking from memory) the selected passages printed on the next few pages, attempting to express completely and vividly the thought and feeling contained in them. (Refer also to the passages at the end of Chapter 4.)

Selected passages for practice in vocal expression.

Before you begin to practice on any one passage, study it carefully to understand its full meaning and allow yourself to drink in the dominant mood. Some of the selections are light and fast moving; others are thoughtful and serious; some contain sharp contrasts of tempo or mood or character; a few are climactic. Avoid mere superficial manipulation of voice; read so as to make the meaning clear and the feeling contagious to your listeners. Effective reading of this sort requires that you practice enough in private so that before an audience you will not have to keep thinking of vocal skill but can concentrate on the ideas and feelings you are trying to express.

Hamlet's Advice to the Players

Speak the speech, I pray you, as I pronounced it to you, trippingly on the tongue; but if you mouth it, as many of your players do, I had as lief the town crier spoke my lines. Nor do not saw the air too much with your hand, thus; but use all gently; for in the very torrent, tempest, and, as I may say, whirlwind of your passion, you must acquire and beget a temperance that may give it smoothness. O, it offends me to the soul to hear a robustious periwig-pated fellow tear a passion to tatters, to very rags, to split the ears of the groundlings who, for the most part, are capable of nothing but inexplicable dumb-show and noise; I would have such a fellow whipped for o'er-doing Termagant; it out-Herods Herod; pray you, avoid it.

Be not too tame, neither, but let your own discretion be your tutor; suit the action to the word, the word to the action; with this special observance, that you o'erstep not the modesty of nature; for anything so overdone is from the purpose of playing, whose end, both at the first and now, was and is, to hold, as 'twere, the mirror up to nature; to show virtue her own feature, scorn her own image, and the very age and body of the time his form and pressure. Now this overdone or come tardy off, though it make the unskilful laugh, cannot but make the judicious grieve; the censure of which one must in your allowance o'erweigh a whole theater of others. O, there be players that I have seen play, and heard others praise that highly, not to speak it profanely, that neither having the accent of Christians nor the gait of Christian, pagan, nor man, have so strutted and bellowed, that I have thought some of nature's journeymen had made men, and not made them well, they imitated humanity so abominably.

Shakespeare

The Disagreeable Man

If you give me your attention, I will tell you what I am:
I'm a genuine philanthropist—all other kinds are sham.
Each little fault of temper and each social defect
In my erring fellow-creatures, I endeavor to correct.
To all their little weaknesses I open peoples' eyes,
And little plans to snub the self-sufficient I devise;
I love my fellow-creatures—I do all the good I can—
Yet everybody says I'm such a disagreeable man!
    And I can't think why!

To compliments inflated I've a withering reply,
And vanity I always do my best to mortify;
A charitable action I can skillfully dissect;
And interested motives I'm delighted to detect.
I know everybody's income and what everybody earns,
And I carefully compare it with the income-tax returns;
But to benefit humanity, however much I plan,
Yet everybody says I'm such a disagreeable man!
    And I can't think why!

I'm sure I'm no ascetic; I'm as pleasant as can be;
You'll always find me ready with a crushing repartee;
I've an irritating chuckle, I've a celebrated sneer,
I've an entertaining snigger, I've a fascinating leer;
To everybody's prejudice I know a thing or two;
I can tell a woman's age in half a minute—and I do—
But although I try to make myself as pleasant as I can,
Yet everybody says I'm such a disagreeable man!
    And I can't think why!

William Schwenck Gilbert

There's a Certain Slant of Light

There's a certain slant of light,
On winter afternoons,
That oppresses, like the weight
Of cathedral tunes.

Heavenly hurt it gives us;
We can find no scar,
But internal difference
Where the meanings are.

None may teach it anything,
'Tis the seal, despair,—
An imperial affliction
Sent us of the air.

When it comes, the landscape listens,
Shadows hold their breath;
When it goes, 'tis like the distance
On the look of death.

Emily Dickinson

Sonnet XXIX

When, in disgrace with fortune and men's eyes,
I all alone beweep my outcast state
And trouble deaf heaven with my bootless cries
And look upon myself and curse my fate,
Wishing me like to one more rich in hope,
Featured like him, like him with friends possess'd,
Desiring this man's art and that man's scope,
With what I most enjoy contented least;
Yet in these thoughts myself almost despising,
Haply I think on thee, and then my state,
Like to the lark at break of day arising
From sullen earth, sings hymns at heaven's gate;
    For thy sweet love remember'd such wealth brings
    That then I scorn to change my state with kings.

Shakespeare

When I Heard the Learn'd Astronomer

When I heard the learn'd astronomer,
When the proofs, the figures, were ranged in columns before me,
When I was shown the charts and diagrams, to add, divide, and measure
    them,
When I sitting heard the astronomer where he lectured with much ap-
    plause in the lecture-room,
How soon unaccountable I became tired and sick,
Till rising and gliding out I wander'd off by myself,
In the mystical moist night-air, and from time to time,
Look'd up in perfect silence at the stars.

Walt Whitman

Storm-Fear [2]

When the wind works against us in the dark,
And pelts with snow
The lower chamber window on the east,
And whispers with a sort of stifled bark,
The beast,
   "Come out! Come out!"—
It costs no inward struggle not to go,
Ah, no!
I count our strength,
Two and a child,
Those of us not asleep subdued to mark
How the cold creeps as the fire dies at length,—
How drifts are piled,
Dooryard and road ungraded,
Till even the comforting barn grows far away,
And my heart owns a doubt
Whether 'tis in us to arise with day
And save ourselves unaided.
                  Robert Frost

Richard Cory [3]

Whenever Richard Cory went down town,
  We people on the pavement looked at him:
He was a gentleman from sole to crown,
  Clean favored, and imperially slim.

And he was always quietly arrayed,
  And he was always human when he talked;
But still he fluttered pulses when he said,
  "Good morning," and he glittered when he walked.

And he was rich—yes, richer than a king—
  And admirably schooled in every grace:
In fine, we thought that he was everything
  To make us wish that we were in his place.

So on we worked and waited for the light,
  And went without the meat, and cursed the bread;
And Richard Cory, one calm summer night,
  Went home and put a bullet through his head.
             Edwin Arlington Robinson

---

[2] From *Complete Poems of Robert Frost*. Copyright 1935 by Holt, Rinehart and Winston, Inc. Reprinted by permission of Holt, Rinehart and Winston, Inc., New York, and Laurence Pollinger, Ltd., London.
[3] From Edwin Arlington Robinson: *Collected Poems*. Reprinted by special permission of Charles Scribner's Sons and Macmillan & Co., Ltd.

from *The Cestus of Aglaia, VI:* The Fly

I believe we can nowhere find a better type of a perfectly free creature than in the common house-fly. Nor free only, but brave; and irreverent to a degree which I think no human republican could by any philosophy exalt himself to. There is no courtesy in him; he does not care whether it is a king or clown whom he teases; and in every step of his swift, mechanical march, and in every pause of his resolute observation, there is one and the same expression of perfect egotism, perfect independence and self-confidence, and conviction of the world's having been made for flies. Strike at him with your hand; and to him, the mechanical fact and external aspect of the matter is, what to you it would be, if an acre of red clay, ten feet thick, tore itself up from the ground in one massive field, hovered over you in the air for a second and came crashing down with an aim. That is the external aspect of it; the inner aspect, to his fly's mind, is of quite a natural and unimportant occurrence—one of the momentary conditions of his active life. He steps out of the way of your hand, and alights on the back of it. You cannot terrify him, nor govern him, nor persuade him, nor convince him. He has his own positive opinion on matters; not an unwise one, usually for his own ends; and will ask no advice of yours. He has no work to do—no tyrannical instinct to obey. The earthworm has his diggings; the bee her gathering and building; the spider her cunning network; the ant her treasury and accounts. All these are comparatively slaves, or people of vulgar business. But your fly, free in the air, free in the chamber—a black incarnation of caprice—wandering, investigating, flitting, flirting, feasting at his will, with rich variety of choice in feast, from the heaped sweets of the grocer's window to those of the butcher's back-yard, and from the galled place on your cab-horse's back to the brown spot in the road, from which, as the hoof disturbs him, he arises with angry republican buzz—what freedom is like this?

Ruskin

from *The Training of the Intellect* [4]

. . . The fault of our age is the fault of hasty action, of premature judgments, of a preference for ill-considered action over no action at all. Men who insist upon standing still and doing a little thinking before they do any acting are called reactionaries. They want actually to reach to a state in which they can be allowed to think. They want for a little while to withdraw from the turmoil of party controversy and see where they stand before they commit themselves and their country to action from which it may not be possible to withdraw.

The whole fault of the modern age is that it applies to everything a false standard of efficiency. Efficiency with us is accomplishment,

---

[4] This excerpt from Woodrow Wilson's Address, published in the *Yale Alumni Quarterly*, is reprinted by permission.

whether the accomplishment be by just and well-considered means or not; and this standard of achievement it is that is debasing the morals of our age, the intellectual morals of our age. We do not stop to do things thoroughly; we do not stop to know why we do things. We see an error and we hastily correct it by a greater error; and then go on to cry that the age is corrupt.

Woodrow Wilson

from *A Letter to the Corinthians*

Though I speak with the tongues of men and of angels, and have not charity, I am become as sounding brass, or a tinkling cymbal. And though I have the gift of prophecy, and understand all mysteries, and all knowledge; and though I have all faith, so that I could remove mountains, and have not charity, I am nothing. And though I bestow all my goods to feed the poor, and though I give my body to be burned, and have not charity, it profiteth me nothing. Charity suffereth long, and is kind; charity envieth not; charity vaunteth not itself, is not puffed up, doth not behave itself unseemly, seeketh not her own, is not easily provoked, thinketh no evil; rejoiceth not in iniquity, but rejoiceth in truth; beareth all things, believeth all things, hopeth all things, endureth all things. Charity never faileth: but whether there be prophecies, they shall fail; whether there be tongues, they shall cease; whether there be knowledge, it shall vanish away. For we know in part, and we prophesy in part. But when that which is perfect is come, then that which is in part shall be done away. . . . And now abideth faith, hope, and charity, these three; but the greatest of these is charity.

Paul, the Apostle (1 Corinthians, 13)

I Will Be Heard

I am aware that many object to the severity of my language; but is there not cause for severity? I will be as harsh as Truth and as uncompromising as Justice. On this subject I do not wish to think, or speak, or write with moderation. No! No! Tell a man whose house is on fire to give a moderate alarm; tell him to moderately rescue his wife from the hands of the ravisher; tell the mother to gradually extricate her babe from the fire into which it has fallen—but urge me not to use moderation in a cause like the present. I am in earnest—I will not equivocate— I will not excuse—I will not retreat a single inch—and I will be heard.

William Lloyd Garrison

from *Oration on Lafayette*

And what was it, fellow-citizens, which gave to our Lafayette his spotless fame? The love of liberty. What has consecrated his memory in the hearts of good men? The love of liberty. What nerved his youthful arm with strength, and inspired him, in the morning of his days, with sagacity and counsel? The living love of liberty. To what did he sacrifice power, and rank, and country, and freedom itself? To the horror of licentiousness,—to the sanctity of plighted faith,—to the love of liberty protected by law. Thus the great principle of your Revolutionary fathers, and of your Pilgrim sires, was the rule of his life—*the love of liberty protected by law.*

Edward Everett

from *Lincoln* [5]

There was a darkness in this man; an immense and hollow darkness,
Of which we may not speak, nor share with him nor enter;
A darkness through which strong roots stretched downwards into the
   earth,
Towards old things;

Towards the herdman-kings who walked the earth and spoke with God,
Towards the wanderers who sought for they knew not what, and found
   their goal at last;
Towards the men who waited, only waited patiently when all seemed
   lost,
Many bitter winters of defeat;

Down to the granite of patience
These roots swept, knotted fibrous roots, prying, piercing, seeking,
And drew from the living rock and the living waters about it,
The red sap to carry upwards to the sun.

John Gould Fletcher

from *The Leader of the People* [6]

The morning flies buzzed close to the ground and the ants dashed about in front of the steps. The heavy smell of sage slipped down the hill. The porch boards grew warm in the sunshine.

Jody hardly knew when Grandfather started to talk. "I shouldn't stay here, feeling the way I do." He examined his strong old hands. "I feel as though the crossing wasn't worth doing." His eyes moved up the side-hill and stopped on a motionless hawk perched on a dead limb. "I tell those old stories, but they're not what I want to tell. I only know how I want people to feel when I tell them.

"It wasn't Indians that were important, nor adventures, nor even getting out here. It was a whole bunch of people made into one big

---

[5] From *Breakers and Granite* by John Gould Fletcher, The Macmillan Company, New York, 1921. Reprinted by permission of Mrs. Fletcher.
[6] From *The Portable Steinbeck*, copyright 1938, 1943 by John Steinbeck. Reprinted by permission of The Viking Press, Inc., New York, and Curtis Brown, Ltd., London.

crawling beast. And I was the head. It was westering and westering. Every man wanted something for himself, but the big beast that was all of them wanted only westering. I was the leader, but if I hadn't been there, someone else would have been the head. The thing had to have a head.

"Under the little bushes the shadows were black at white noonday. When we saw the mountains at last, we cried—all of us. But it wasn't getting here that mattered, it was movement and westering.

"We carried life out here and set it down the way those ants carry eggs. And I was the leader. The westering was as big as God, and the slow steps that made the movement piled up and piled up until the continent was crossed.

"Then we came down to the sea, and it was done." He stopped and wiped his eyes until the rims were red. "That's what I should be telling instead of stories."

When Jody spoke, Grandfather started and looked down at him. "Maybe I could lead the people some day," Jody said.

The old man smiled. "There's no place to go. There's the ocean to stop you. There's a line of old men along the shore hating the ocean because it stopped them."

"In boats I might, sir."

"No place to go, Jody. Every place is taken. But that's not the worst— no, not the worst. Westering has died out of the people. Westering isn't a hunger any more. It's all done. Your father is right. It is finished." He laced his fingers on his knee and looked at them.

Jody felt very sad. "If you'd like a glass of lemonade I could make it for you."

Grandfather was about to refuse, and then he saw Jody's face. "That would be nice," he said. "Yes, it would be nice to drink a lemonade."

Jody ran into the kitchen where his mother was wiping the last of the breakfast dishes. "Can I have a lemon to make a lemonade for Grandfather?"

His mother mimicked— "And another lemon to make a lemonade for you."

"No, ma'am. I don't want one."

"Jody! You're sick!" Then she stopped suddenly. "Take a lemon out of the cooler," she said softly. "Here, I'll reach the squeezer down to you."

John Steinbeck

The Moth and the Star [7]

A young and impressionable moth once set his heart on a certain star. He told his mother about this and she counseled him to set his

[7] Reprinted by permission from *The New Yorker*, February 18, 1939. Copyright 1939 by The New Yorker Magazine, Inc.

heart on a bridge lamp instead. "Stars aren't the thing to hang around," she said; "lamps are the thing to hang around." "You get somewhere that way," said the moth's father. "You don't get anywhere chasing stars." But the moth would not heed the words of either parent. Every evening at dusk when the star came out he would start flying toward it and every morning at dawn he would crawl back home worn out with his vain endeavor. One day his father said to him, "You haven't burned a wing in months, boy, and it looks to me as if you were never going to. All your brothers have been badly burned flying around street lamps and all your sisters have been terribly singed flying around house lamps. Come on, now, get out of here and get yourself scorched! A big strapping moth like you without a mark on him!"

The moth left his father's house, but he would not fly around street lamps and he would not fly around house lamps. He went right on trying to reach the star, which was four and one-third light years, or twenty-five trillion miles, away. The moth thought it was just caught in the top branches of an elm. He never did reach the star, but he went right on trying, night after night, and when he was a very, very old moth he began to think that he really had reached the star and he went around saying so. This gave him a deep and lasting pleasure, and he lived to a great old age. His parents and his brothers and his sisters had all been burned to death when they were quite young.

Moral: Who flies afar from the sphere of our sorrow is here today and here tomorrow.

James Thurber

Speak clearly, if you speak at all;
Carve every word before you let it fall.

Oliver Wendell Holmes

CHAPTER 6 / *Making the Voice More Intelligible*

The first duty of the actor or speaker is to make sure he is heard easily and accurately. He may speak with a voice of pleasing quality and with all the variety that could be desired, but if he speaks so softly or indistinctly that his listeners have to strain to understand what he is saying, they will soon tire of the effort. In the two preceding chapters we have considered the development of pleasant voice quality and of interesting and meaningful variety in pitch, rate, and force; here we are concerned with the very practical problem of making our speech intelligible to those who hear it.

LOUDNESS

Probably the most important single factor in vocal intelligibility is the loudness with which you speak in relation to the *distance* of the listener from you and the amount of *noise* surrounding him.[1] Obviously, the farther away your listener is, the louder you must talk for him to hear you well. All of us do this unconsciously at extreme distances; when we call to someone a block away or across the field, we have learned that we must shout in order to be heard. What we often forget is that the same principle applies to shorter distances. You must realize that your own voice will always sound louder to you (unless you are deaf) than to your listeners—even if they are only ten or twenty feet away—since your own ears are closer to your mouth than the ears of your listeners are.

The sound of your voice diminishes rapidly as it travels away from you; and if it were not reflected from surrounding surfaces, listeners only a short distance away would hear only a small portion of its initial loudness.[2] This fact explains why it is important to hold a microphone or the mouthpiece of a telephone fairly close to your mouth or, if the microphone is of a type which picks up sounds at a little greater distance, why you should be careful not to vary your distance from it. The effects of distance on the loudness of your voice cannot be too rigidly stated, however, since the surface of the room—whether acoustically treated or made of smooth plaster—and the number of people present whose clothing absorbs the sound will largely determine how loud you must talk.

In addition to distance, the amount of surrounding noise with which you must compete should also affect the loudness of your voice. It is important to realize that even in normal circumstances some noise is always present. For example, the noise level of rustling leaves in the quiet solitude of a country lane (10 decibels [3])

---

[1] The term *loudness* is here used synonymously with *intensity* because the former term is clearer to the average speaker. Technically, of course, loudness, a distinct function in the science of acoustics, is not strictly synonymous with intensity. To explain the exact relation between the two terms is beyond the scope of this book, since it involves many complicated psychophysical relationships. See *Hearing: Its Psychology and Physiology* by Stanley S. Stevens and Hallowell Davis (John Wiley, N.Y., 1938), p. 110 ff.

[2] The loudness of your voice—strictly speaking, its intensity—varies inversely with the square of the distance from your lips. (Expressed mathematically, $I \propto 1/D^2$.) Thus, if it were not reflected from the walls and ceiling, your voice would be only one sixteenth as loud twelve feet away as at a distance of three; and the listener fifty feet away would hear only a very tiny fraction of the original sound.

[3] Loudness is expressed in *decibels* (*db*). Within certain acoustic limits, one decibel is roughly equal to the smallest difference in loudness which the ear can detect. Standard measurements for loudness are at distances of three feet unless otherwise noted.

is louder than a whisper six feet away. The noise in empty theaters averages 25 decibels, but with a "quiet" audience it rises to 42. In the average factory a constant noise of about 80 decibels is likely to be maintained. This is just about the same level as very loud speaking at close range.

The table below will make these comparisons more clear.[4]

Loudness of Speech vs. Noise *(At distances of three feet, except as noted)*		
Speech	*Loudness*	*Noise*
Loud shout (at 1 ft.)	110 db.	Hammer on sheet steel (at 2 ft.)
Loud speech	80 db.	Very loud radio in home
Average conversation	60 db.	Noisy office
Faint speech	40 db.	Interior of house in large city
Whisper (at 4 ft.)	20 db.	Interior of very quiet country house

You cannot merely equal the noise about you if you expect to be understood; your voice must be loud enough for your listeners' ears to distinguish the speech sound above this noise.[5] Of course, shouting at your listeners in a quiet room is not necessary and may even distract them from what you are saying. What is necessary is a degree of loudness strong enough to be clearly heard above whatever noise is present.

The obvious question now is: how can you determine for yourself the proper strength of voice to use in order to achieve sufficient loudness for the distance and noise conditions of a particular speech situation. While apparatus is available to measure these

---

[4] For more detailed information on this point, see *Hearing and Deafness* by Hallowell Davis (Murray Hill Books, N.Y., 1947), pp. 43–45; and *Man's World of Sound* by John R. Pierce and Edward E. David, Jr. (Doubleday & Co., Garden City, N.Y., 1958), pp. 202–206.

[5] See "The Effect of Very Loud Speech Signals upon Intelligibility" by Harry M. Mason in Speech Monographs, Vol. 13, No. 2 (1946), pp. 19–23, which reported that *actual* loudness of speech sounds was less important to a listener than their *relative* loudness to surrounding noise. That is, when speech and noise were both decreased or increased proportionately, the listener understood more at the lower loudness levels. This relative loudness of the speech sounds to the interfering is called the *speech-to-noise ratio* (S/N). Interesting studies on other aspects of speech intelligibility may be found in current issues of *Speech Monographs*, the *Quarterly Journal of Speech*, the *Speech Teacher*, the *Journal of Speech and Hearing Disorders*, and the *Journal of Speech and Hearing Research*.

sounds accurately, most of us do not have it and would not want to carry it around with us if we did. You can, however, use your eyes to see if those in the back row appear to be hearing you or, even better, ask if they can hear you. Get your instructor's advice on this point. Ask your friends to report on the loudness of your voice as you talk in various-sized rooms and under varying noise conditions. In all these situations, listen to the sound of your own voice so that you begin to correlate your own sensations with their reports. You will soon learn to gauge the volume you must use in order to be heard.

The proper loudness for talking into a microphone introduces a different problem. Here the loudness of your voice will be affected by the type of microphone, the amplifying system, and the loudspeaker. No invariable rule can be given since the equipment varies so much. It is important, however, to try out the equipment before your scheduled appearance. Ask the announcer or technician in the radio or television studio to advise you and find out what signals he will use to tell you to talk louder or to move closer to the microphone. Similarly, test out any public address system you plan to use and, if possible, arrange some similar signals with the technician in charge.

SYLLABLE DURATION

Another factor affecting your listener's ability to understand what you say is the duration of sound within the syllables you utter. Generally, a slower rate of speaking is more easily understood than a fast one, but merely slowing down is not enough. The previous chapter pointed out that rate of speaking depends on two elements: quantity, or the duration of the actual sound within the syllable, and pause, or the silent periods between sounds. Experimental evidence seems to show that the intelligibility of speech—how much the listener hears accurately—depends more on syllable duration than on the overall rate of speaking. Thus a slow staccato utterance is not much more intelligible than a faster staccato utterance, but talking at a moderate rate while prolonging the sounds uttered improves intelligibility a great deal.

This does not mean that everything you say should be uttered in a slow drawl; it *does* mean that a "machine-gun" utterance is often hard to understand. When the rapid sweep of a fast-moving narrative is more important than exact comprehension of every word you say, naturally you will want to speak with some speed. But when you want to be sure your listeners understand precisely what you are saying on some important point, take time to dwell on every significant word long enough to be sure it will be understood.

Syllable duration is of special importance when you are talking in a large hall, when you must be heard above a great deal of noise, or when the acoustics of the room in which you speak produce a noticeable echo effect. Those who speak to mass meetings out-of-doors, or make announcements at a banquet where there is a clatter of dishes, have found they must stretch out their syllables if they are to be understood. Even unaccented syllables (such as *-ing* in *going*) are drawn out longer than usual. The ringmaster at a circus and the announcer at a prize fight are not just trying to be different when they sing out, "L-a-a-d-i-e-s and ge-e-n-tle-m-e-en"; they have learned through experience that they have to prolong the sounds if they are to be understood. Similarly, pilots, in talking on the plane intercom and in radioing the control tower, have found that sustained and slightly drawn-out syllables are much more easily understood above the airplane noise. You will find the same thing true in talking over the telephone in a noisy office or shop.

Practice, then, until you can prolong your syllables without losing the rhythm and emphasis of your sentences; but be careful not to overdo it when neither noise nor distance requires you to do so. Remember that the suggestions made in the previous chapter for giving emphasis and variety to your speech through change of rate are the *normal* principles to follow; employ longer syllable duration than you usually do only when your normal utterance cannot be easily understood.

DISTINCTNESS

For people in the back row, louder speaking is not always so necessary as greater distinctness. Nor is adequate syllable duration all that is required to make your speech clear and crisp. Good articulation is the job of the modifiers, especially the jaw, tongue, and lips. Only by using the muscles which manipulate these members with skill and energy can clean-cut speech be achieved. Do not be satisfied with sloppy articulation. Bite off your words in an exaggerated fashion for a time until you find you are developing the habit of precision.

There are four faults responsible for most of the indistinctness in speech. By eliminating them you will have done a great deal to improve the understandability and precision of your utterance. These faults are (a) the "immovable jaw," (b) the "idle tongue," (c) "lazy lips," and (d) too much speed.

Some oriental peoples move their jaws very little in speaking; so much of the meaning in their language is conveyed by variation in vocal pitch that scarcely any jaw movement is necessary. In the English language failure to open the jaws adequately is a serious fault because so much meaning is conveyed by consonant sounds, which cannot be made effectively unless the tongue is given enough room to move vigorously. Even the vowel sounds are likely to be muffled if the jaws are kept nearly closed. As you talk, therefore, remember to move your jaws freely.

The tongue has more to do with the distinct formation of speech sounds than does any other organ. Even when the jaw is opened adequately, the sounds produced cannot be sharp if the tongue lies idle or moves sluggishly. All the vowel sounds depend partly on the position of the tongue for their distinctive qualities. Try saying "ee, ay, ah, aw, oor" and notice how the highest point of the tongue changes its position. A great many consonant sounds, such as d, th, ch, g, and k, also depend upon the active movement of the tongue.

The lips, too, are important to distinct speech. If the lips are allowed to become lazy, the result will be a mumbled articulation, particularly of such sounds as p, b, m, and f, which demand vigorous use of the lips. Of course, when talking directly into a microphone, violent explosive utterance of consonant sounds should be avoided. But in ordinary speaking, and especially in public speaking, most of us should use our lips more decisively to cut and mold the sounds we make.

There is a limit, however, to the speed with which the jaw, tongue, and lips can move. A great deal of indistinctness could be avoided if speakers took time enough to get the sounds out clearly instead of being in such a hurry just to get them out. Take time to speak distinctly; as your jaw, tongue, and lips develop more flexibility and precision, you can speed up. For the present, though, avoid rushing.

Briefly, then, when you are talking, open your jaw wide; move your lips energetically; whip your tongue into vigorous activity; and don't talk too fast. Practice the exercises for distinctness at the end of this chapter repeatedly, and see that the effect of this practice is carried over into your daily conversation. It is possible to be so precise as to seem affected, but the chances are ten to one that your fault lies in the other direction. There is nothing which will create so much unconscious respect for you as crisp and decisive speech.

ACCEPTABLE PRONUNCIATION

Spoken words are the sound symbols of meaning. If you fail to pronounce them correctly, your listener may not understand what you are saying. Even if the words are recognized, any peculiarity of pronunciation is quickly noticed by the audience and may distract attention from the thought or even discredit the speaker.

It is sometimes difficult to know what pronunciation is acceptable, because standards differ. The best criterion to follow is the usage of the educated people of your community. For most words, a dictionary provides a helpful guide. But with respect to a few words, dictionaries are likely to be out of date, so they should not be followed too slavishly. Moreover, most dictionaries do not take sufficient notice of regional differences in dialect. A native of Louisiana pronounces words differently from a man who lives in Montana. And a Chicagoan is easily distinguished from a Bostonian by his speech. Nevertheless, a dictionary will provide you with helpful guidance on most words. The dictionary standard, modified to agree with the usage of educated people in your community, should be the basis of your pronunciation.

Be careful not to misplace the accent in words. An obvious error is saying "genu-*ine*," "*de*-vice," "the-*ay*-ter," "pre-*fer*-able," instead of the more accepted forms, "*gen*-uine," "de-*vice*," "the-ater," "*pref*-erable." Other errors arise from the omission of sounds (such as "guh'mnt" for *government*), from the addition of sounds (such as "athalete" for *athlete*), and from the substitution of sounds (such as "set" for *sit*). The way words are spelled is not always a safe guide to pronunciation, for English words contain many silent letters (of*t*en, i*s*land, mor*t*gage), and many words containing the same combinations of letters require different pronunciations (b*ough*, r*ough*, thr*ough;* call*ed*, shout*ed*, gasp*ed*). In addition, the formality of the occasion exerts considerable influence; many omissions acceptable in conversation become objectionable in a formal address. In radio and television broadcasting, careful pronunciation is particularly important. Because many programs are heard throughout the nation, broadcasting is tending to minimize regional differences in pronunciation and to develop a common standard across the country. In general, however, what is good pronunciation elsewhere is also good "on the air."

Do not be so labored and precise as to call attention to your pronunciation rather than to your idea; but do not take this warning as an excuse for careless speech. Avoid equally pronunciation that is too pedantic or too provincial. Use your ears; listen to your own pronunciation and compare it with that of educated people in your community. If your pronunciation is faulty, keep a notebook in which you list the words you miss, and practice them frequently.

CHOICE AND SEQUENCE OF WORDS

This is not the place to discuss the choice of words in terms of their rhetorical or persuasive value; that will be covered in a later chapter. We are concerned here with the sounds words contain,[6] and the errors in understanding which occur because one word is mistaken for another. Experiments have shown that the word *fox* is more than twice as hard to understand as *dog* and that six times as many errors of recognition are made on the word *nuts* as on *limeade*. And if the listeners in these experiments had never heard of foxes or nuts, the percentage of error would have been even greater since strange words are usually harder to understand than familiar ones. The English language contains many words with

---

[6] See *Speech and Hearing* by Harvey Fletcher (Van Nostrand, N.Y., 1929), pp. 273–278.

different meanings but the same, or very similar, sounds: words such as *one* and *won, for* and *four, sick* and *six,* and the like. Moreover, the acoustic difference between certain individual sounds is often too small for clear differentiation if all the other sounds in the word are the same. Thus it may be hard to understand the rapid utterance of such a phrase as "nine fine swine."

Careful articulation and lengthening the duration of syllables will help reduce misunderstandings of this sort. Especially when you talk on unfamiliar subjects requiring the use of terms—particularly technical terms—which are strange to your listeners, you must talk more slowly, prolong your syllables, and articulate more carefully. Wherever possible try to avoid this difficulty by using words which cannot be mistaken in context. In particular, be careful about using similar sounding words close together in sentences where the meaning of the first word may carry over to the second.

)terms

The story is told of a reporter who interviewed a farmer by telephone and reported in his newspaper that the farmer had just purchased "2008" pigs. The farmer had actually told him that he had bought "two sows and eight pigs." A difference of only one sound resulted in an error of 1998 hogs. Although errors of this magnitude do not often occur, a listener is frequently confused until something is said later in the discussion to clarify the point, and in the meantime the effectiveness of the intervening remarks may have been reduced. Be careful, therefore, to think of words in terms of the way they *sound* and not the way they look in print. Remember, it is what the listener thinks he heard that counts.

· To be clearly understood, talk loud enough in terms of distance and noise level, give adequate length to the duration of your syllables, use your speaking mechanism vigorously to improve the distinctness of your utterance, give due attention to your pronunciation and to your choice of words. Practice on the following problems under the critical supervision of your instructor; if possible, record your speaking so that you can listen to the sound of your own voice. And in speaking, keep a close eye on your listeners in order to judge how they are reacting to your vocal intelligibility.

PROBLEMS

1. Be ready to discuss the following questions in class: What factors determine the necessary loudness of voice? How does syllable duration affect intelligibility? What faults most commonly cause indistinctness of speech? How is audience understanding affected by the speaker's pronunciation of words? By the speaker's choice of words?

To test the intelligibility of your speech.

2. The following lists of phonetically balanced words are taken from tests constructed by the Psycho-Acoustic Laboratory of Harvard University.[7] They may be used in class to test whether your speech is intelligible to others. Your score will not be so accurate as if these tests were conducted under scientifically controlled conditions, but they will provide a measure of the relative intelligibility of your speech as compared with your classmates' and will show you what happens under various conditions. Proceed with the test as described on page 123.

A		B		C	
bat	muff	at	muss	aid	map
beau	mush	barn	news	barge	nap
change	my	bust	nick	book	next
climb	nag	car	nod	cheese	part
corn	nice	clip	oft	cliff	pitch
curb	nip	coax	prude	closed	pump
deaf	ought	curve	purge	crews	rock
dog	owe	cute	quack	dame	rogue
elk	patch	darn	rid	din	rug
elm	pelt	dash	shook	drape	rye
few	plead	dead	shrug	droop	sang
fill	price	douse	sing	dub	sheep
fold	pug	dung	slab	fifth	sheik
for	scuff	fife	smite	fright	soar
gem	side	foam	soil	gab	stab
grape	sled	grate	stuff	gas	stress
grave	smash	group	tell	had	suit
hack	smooth	heat	tent	hash	thou
hate	soap	howl	thy	hose	three
hook	stead	hunk	tray	ink	thresh
jig	taint	isle	vague	kind	tire
made	tap	kick	vote	knee	ton
mood	thin	lathe	wag	lay	tuck
mop	tip	life	waif	leash	turn
moth	wean	me	wrist	louse	wield

[7] Printed also in *Hearing and Deafness* by Hallowell Davis, pp. 475–476.

D		E		F	
awe	nab	ache	muck	bath	neat
bait	need	air	neck	beast	new
bean	niece	bald	nest	bee	oils
blush	nut	barb	oak	blonde	or
bought	our	bead	path	budge	peck
bounce	perk	cape	please	bus	pert
bud	pick	cast	pulse	bush	pinch
charge	pit	check	rate	cloak	pod
cloud	quart	class	rouse	course	race
corpse	rap	crave	shout	court	rack
dab	rib	crime	sit	dodge	rave
earl	scythe	deck	size	dupe	raw
else	shoe	dig	sob	earn	rut
fate	sludge	dill	sped	eel	sage
five	snuff	drop	stag	fin	scab
frog	start	fame	take	float	shed
gill	suck	far	thrash	frown	shin
gloss	tan	fig	toil	hatch	sketch
hire	tang	flush	trip	heed	slap
hit	them	gnaw	turf	hiss	sour
hock	trash	hurl	vow	hot	starve
job	vamp	jam	wedge	how	strap
log	vast	law	wharf	kite	test
moose	ways	leave	who	merge	tick
mute	wish	lush	why	move	touch

A. Choose one of the fifty-word lists above and rearrange the words on a sheet of paper in some different and random order. (Subsequent students should use different lists to avoid immediate repetition.)

B. Stand in a corner of the room with your back to the class and read aloud one word at a time, saying, "Number one is ———." Then pause long enough for your classmates to write it down (3–5 seconds) before proceeding to the next word.

C. The rest of the students will write down in a numbered column the words they understood you to have said.

D. To determine your score, add together the number of words understood correctly by each listener and divide this total by the number of listeners times fifty (the number of words spoken); the result will be your percentage of intelligibility on this test.[8]

---

[8] Dr. Davis says, "It is a very convenient property of these lists that the volume at which 50% of the words is correctly understood is a little above that at which we can easily understand ordinary connected speech." *Ibid.*, p. 151.

E. Repeat this test, using a different list, under each of the following conditions:

    1) Listeners' ears plugged with cotton (in order to simulate distance).

    2) Relatively loud phonograph music playing while the list is read.

3. A somewhat more difficult test may be conducted in a manner similar to that described in Problem 2 with the word series listed below.[9] Listeners should keep their books closed while listening to the speaker and writing down the words they understand him to say. In this test the speaker should read four words consecutively—long pause; read four more—long pause; etc., until he has completed one of the series. Score as in Problem 2.

A. Three, flap, switch, will——resume, cold, pilot, wind——chase, blue, search, flight——mine, area, cleared, left.

B. Iron, fire, task, try——up, six, seven, wait——slip, turn, read, clear——blue, this, even, is.

C. Nan, flak, timer, two——course, black, when, leave——raise, clear, tree, seven——search, strike, there, cover.

D. List, service, ten, foul——wire, last, wish, truce——power, one, ease, will——teeth, hobby, trill, wind.

E. Flight, spray, blind, base——ground, fog, ceiling, flame——target, flare, gear, low——slow, course, code, scout.

F. Tall, plot, find, deep——climb, fall, each, believe——wing, strip, clean, field——when, chase, search, select.

G. Climb, switch, over, when——this, turn, gear, spray——black, flare, is, free——runway, three, off, red.

H. Thing, touch, marker, sleeve——find, top, leave, winter——skip, free, have, beach——meet, aid, send, lash.

I. Try, over, six, craft——green, victor, yellow, out——trim, X-ray, ramp, up——speed, like, believe, sender.

J. Dim, trip, fire, marker——wave, green, rudder, field——climb, to, plot, middle——speed, like, straight, lower.

K. Smooth, mike, four, catch——strip, park, line, left——leg, wheel, turn, lift——time, baker, orange, look.

L. Wake, other, blue, been——size, wish, black, under——field, down, empty, what——ship, strip, land, fire.

---

[9] From a test used by Gayland L. Draegert in an experiment reported in *Speech Monographs*, Vol. 13, No. 2, p. 50 ff. With noise interference, military personnel averaged 38.2% of the words understood correctly in the initial test, and 46.3% after training. For scientific purposes, this test is not so accurate as the list in Problem 2 or a similar test developed by C. Hess Hagen at Waco, Texas, Voice Communication Laboratories, which is described in OSRD Report No. 5414, issued by the Office of Technical Services, Department of Commerce. For classroom purposes, however, it is sufficiently accurate for determining relative intelligibility among members of a group.

M. Leg, on, strip, leave——ground, trip, plot, area——speed, blue, will, ramp——wheel, blind, sector, nan.

N. Tail, when, through, at——climb, off, tower, rain——time, gear, cloud, pass——loaf, three, crash, direction.

O. Station, left, reply, read——final, blue, field, out——wind, west, marker, fire——tower, ground, gear, time.

P. Sighted, toward, finder, search——red, blind, each, weather—— tall, after, while, wide——close, hole, mark, signal.

Q. Neat, warm, beam, where——side, leader, bell, map——view, face, trap, well——seem, feed, clutch, vine.

R. Circle, beach, up, that——port, even, catch, pad——reach, heat, break, safe——still, put, enter, iron.

S. Chamber, wait, hair, open——wind, keep, sector, free——light, home, take, will——base, eleven, headphone, by.

T. Service, flat, have, on——bay, wait, fade, cold——tire, horn, bill, sad——feel, cave, set, limit.

To develop an adequate degree of loudness and syllable duration.

4. Practice saying the words in the above lists with a voice loud enough—

A. to be barely understood (score below 50%) in a quiet classroom.

B. to be perfectly understood in a quiet classroom.

C. to be understood in a quiet classroom with your listeners' ears plugged with cotton (to simulate distance).

D. to be understood above the noise of two, three, or four other students who are all reading aloud from different pages of the textbook.

5. Practice saying the words in the lists above with varying degrees of syllable duration under the conditions listed in the problem above.

6. Devise variations of these conditions with whatever recording or public address systems are available to your class.

7. Prepare sentences requiring precise understanding of the component words and practice saying them with the loudness and syllable length required for:

A. a small group in a small room

B. a class in a fairly large lecture room

C. an audience in your college auditorium

D. a crowd in your football stadium

Here are a few sample sentences to use:

"Just ten minutes from now, go in single file to room 316."

"In 1985 the population of Panama may be one and two fifths what it was in 1948."

"Hemstitching can be done by machine operation using strong thread."

"Oranges, nuts, vegetables, and cotton are raised on the Kingston ranch."

8. Prepare a two-minute oral report on one of the topics in this chapter and present it to the class from the back of the room in a voice that can be clearly understood.

To increase distinctness of articulation.

9. Stretch the muscles of articulation:
   A. Stretch the mouth in as wide a grin as possible; open the mouth as wide as possible; pucker the lips and protrude them as far as possible.
   B. Stretch out the tongue as far as possible; try to touch the tip of the nose and the chin with the tongue tip; beginning at the front teeth, run the tip of the tongue back, touching the palate as far back as the tongue will go.

10. With vigorous accent on the consonant sounds, repeat "pah, tah, kah" several times. Then vary the order, emphasizing first *pah,* then *tah,* then *kah.* In the same way practice the series "ap, at, ak" and "apa, ata, aka." Work out additional combinations of this sort, using different combinations of consonants and vowels.

11. Experiments have shown that the words grouped in fours below are easily mistaken for one another under conditions of noise interference.[10] Practice articulating them distinctly and precisely. Then with your back to the class and with three or four other students creating a noise by reading aloud from the textbook at the same time, read down one column or across one row, choosing one word at random out of each four. Announce before you start which column or row you are going to read from, pause briefly after each word, and have other members of the class put a check by the word they understood you to say. (Used in this way, the following list is not an accurate *test* of intelligibility, but it should provide interesting material for practice.)

	A	B	C	D	E	F
1	system	firm	banner	puddle	carve	offer
	pistol	foam	manner	muddle	car	author
	distant	burn	mother	muzzle	tarred	often
	piston	term	batter	puzzle	tired	office

[10] Taken from answer sheets for standardized tests developed by C. Hess Hagen, printed in *Intelligibility Measurement: Twenty Four-Word Multiple Choice Tests,* OSRD Report No. 5567 (P.B. 12050), issued by the Office of Technical Services, Department of Commerce, p. 21.

2	heave	detain	scream	porch	fable	cross
	heed	obtain	screen	torch	stable	cough
	ease	attain	green	scorch	table	cloth
	eve	maintain	stream	court	able	claw

3	roger	pure	petal	vision	bubble	thrown
	rupture	poor	battle	bishop	tumble	drone
	rapture	tour	meadow	vicious	stumble	prone
	obscure	two	medal	season	fumble	groan

4	art	sponsor	game	cape	texture	eye
	heart	spotter	gain	hate	lecture	high
	arch	ponder	gage	take	mixture	tie
	ark	plunder	gang	tape	rupture	hide

5	comment	exact	made	process	glow	single
	comic	retract	fade	protest	blow	jingle
	cannon	detract	vague	profess	below	cycle
	carbon	attack	may	possess	low	sprinkle

6	bumper	cave	pier	divide	kitchen	baker
	number	cake	pierce	devise	mission	major
	lumber	cage	fierce	define	friction	maker
	lover	case	spear	divine	fiction	banker

7	gale	glamour	ward	leap	second	rich
	jail	slimmer	wart	leaf	suction	ridge
	dale	swimmer	wash	lease	section	bridge
	bail	glimmer	war	leave	sexton	grip

8	danger	enact	hold	crater	seaport	joy
	feature	impact	old	traitor	keyboard	going
	nature	relax	ode	trainer	piecework	join
	major	intact	hoed	treasure .	eastward	dawn

12. Make a list of as many tongue twisters as you can find and practice saying them rapidly and precisely. Here are a few short examples to start on:

A. She sells sea shells on the seashore.

B. National Shropshire Sheep Association.

C. "Are you copper-bottoming them, my man?" "No, I'm aluminuming 'em, mum."

D. He sawed six long, slim, sleek, slender saplings.

E. Dick twirled the stick athwart the path.

F. Rubber baby-buggy bumpers.

G. "B—A, Ba; B—E, Be;
B—I, Bi; Ba Be Bi;
B—O, Bo; Ba Be Bi Bo;
B—U, Bu; Ba Be Bi Bo Bu!"

13. Read the following passages aloud in a distinct and lively fashion; move the tongue, jaw, lips, etc., with energy:

> To sit in solemn silence in a dull, dark dock
> In a pestilential prison, with a lifelong lock,
> Awaiting the sensation of a short, sharp shock,
> From a cheap and chippy chopper on a big black block!
>
> *Gilbert and Sullivan*

> "You are old," said the youth, "and your jaws are too weak
>   For anything tougher than suet;
> Yet you finished the goose, with the bones and the beak—
>   Pray, how did you manage to do it?"
> "In my youth," said his father, "I took to the law,
>   And argued each case with my wife;
> And the muscular strength which it gave to my jaw
>   Has lasted the rest of my life."
>
> *Lewis Carroll*

> How does the water
> Come down to Lodore?
>   My little boy ask'd me
>   Thus, once on a time;
> And moreover he ask'd me
> To tell him in rime.

> The cataract strong
> Then plunges along,
> Striking and raging
> As if a war waging
> Its caverns and rocks among;
>   Rising and leaping,
>   Sinking and creeping,
>   Swelling and sweeping,
> Showering and springing,
>   Flying and flinging,
>   Writhing and whisking,
>   Spouting and frisking,
>   Turning and twisting,
>   Around and around . . .

> And rushing and flushing and brushing and gushing,
> And flapping and rapping and clapping and slapping,
> And curling and whirling and purling and twirling,
> And thumping and plumping and bumping and jumping;
> And dashing and flashing and splashing and clashing;

And so never ending, but always descending,
Sounds and motion forever are blending,
All at once and all o'er, with a mighty uproar,
And this way the water comes down at Lodore.

Robert Southey

To encourage acceptable pronunciation.

14. Make a list of words which you have heard pronounced in more than one way. Look them up in the dictionary and come to class prepared to defend your agreement or disagreement with the dictionary pronunciation. Here are a few words on which to start:

abdomen	creek	gauge	indict	route
acclimated	data	gesture	inquiry	theater
advertisement	deficit	grievous	recess	thresh
alias	drowned	humble	research	vagary
bona fide	forehead	idea	roof	yacht

Passages which require careful speech to convey their meaning.

15. The whole meaning of each of the passages below depends on a clear understanding of the words and phrases used in it. Be sure you understand the significance of an entire passage before you begin practice on it. Practice reading it as you would before a small, quiet audience; then as you would need to do if the audience were large or there were considerable noise interference. Remember that *exaggerated* precision, loudness, syllable duration, etc., beyond the amount clearly required for easy intelligibility under the actual situation will sound artificial and is not good speech. (In a similar way, practice again the passages at the end of Chapter 5.)

from *The War Song of the Saracens* [11]

We are they who come faster than fate: we are they who ride early
or late:
We storm at your ivory gate: Pale Kings of the Sunset, beware!
Not on silk nor in samet we lie, not in curtained solemnity die
Among women who chatter and cry, and children who mumble a prayer.
But we sleep by the ropes of the camp, and we rise with a shout, and
we tramp
With the sun or the moon for a lamp, and the spray of the wind in our
hair.

James Elroy Flecker

[11] From *Collected Poems* by James Elroy Flecker. Reprinted by special permission of Mrs. Flecker and Martin Secker & Warburg, Ltd.

from *Essay on Self-Reliance*

A foolish consistency is the hobgoblin of little minds, adored by little statesmen and philosophers and divines. With consistency a great soul has simply nothing to do. He may as well concern himself with his shadow on the wall. Speak what you think now in hard words and tomorrow speak what tomorrow thinks in hard words again, though it contradict everything you said today—"Ah, so you shall be sure to be misunderstood."—Is it so bad, then, to be misunderstood? Pythagoras was misunderstood, and Socrates, and Jesus, and Luther, and Copernicus, and Galileo, and Newton, and every pure and wise spirit that ever took flesh. To be great is to be misunderstood.

Emerson

from *The Sea Around Us* [12]

For the sea as a whole, the alternation of day and night, the passage of the seasons, the procession of the years, are lost in its vastness, obliterated in its own changeless eternity. But the surface waters are different. The face of the sea is always changing. Crossed by colors, lights, and moving shadows, sparkling in the sun, mysterious in the twilight, its aspects and its moods vary hour by hour. The surface waters move with the tides, stir to the breath of the winds, and rise and fall to the endless, hurrying forms of the waves. Most of all, they change with the advance of the seasons. Spring moves over the temperate lands of our Northern Hemisphere in a tide of new life, of pushing green shoots and unfolding buds, all its mysteries and meanings symbolized in the northward migration of the birds, the awakening of sluggish amphibian life as the chorus of frogs rises again from the wet lands, the different sound of the wind which stirs the young leaves where a month ago it rattled the bare branches. These things we associate with the land, and it is easy to suppose that at sea there could be no such feeling of advancing spring. But the signs are there, and seen with understanding eye, they bring the same magical sense of awakening.

Rachel L. Carson

---

[12] Rachel Carson, *The Sea Around Us*, Oxford University Press, 1961, pp. 28–29.

part three

Basic Principles of Speech Composition

The process of preparing a speech • Determining the subject and purpose of the speech • Analyzing the occasion and the audience • Selecting the basic appeal • Where to go for speech material • Supporting main points • Choosing material that will hold attention • Arranging and outlining points of a speech • Beginning and ending a speech • Adapting speech organization to the audience: the motivated sequence • Outlining a speech using the motivated sequence • Wording the speech

Before beginning, prepare carefully.

Cicero

CHAPTER 7/*The Process of Preparing a Speech*

B ecause of the apparent ease with which good speakers talk, some people mistakenly believe that such men spend little time in preparation. Nothing could be further from the facts. The very ease with which a speech is given often indicates the thoroughness of its preparation. A careful study of the methods used by great speakers, from the times of Demosthenes and Cicero to Wilson and Roosevelt, reveals the painstaking care with which they all made ready for the occasions when they spoke.

The actual method of preparation has varied from speaker to speaker. Some of them have written out their remarks word for word and then committed the entire speech to memory. Others have spent most of their time thinking through the ideas carefully, writing down only the barest skeleton of an outline. But quite significantly, the greater the speaker, the more careful has been his preparation.

If, then, there is no magic formula for successful speaking, how can a thorough preparation for it be made? This question involves two things: the general preparation of the speaker as an individual and his specific preparation for a particular speech. Some of the elements in the general preparation of the speaker have already been discussed in the preceding chapters. If you have followed the suggestions offered in them, you should have developed an increasing degree of self-confidence and a reasonable amount of physical and vocal skill. Your background of knowledge is an especially important part of your general preparation. This background will develop, as suggested in Chapter 1, as you give increased attention to contemporary man and events and to the literature in your vocational field. But even though your general preparation is excellent, you will usually need to make a special study of each subject upon which you choose to speak. You will also need to organize and adapt this material to suit your purpose and your audience, and you will need to practice it for oral presentation. It is to this specific process of preparation that we now turn.

FOUR METHODS OF SPEAKING

Regardless of your general knowledge or the vocal skill which you have developed, a new problem will confront you each time you speak, and you will need to prepare specifically for each occasion. There are four principal methods of speaking, differing primarily in the degree and type of preparation they involve. These are the *impromptu* method, the *extemporaneous* method, the method of *memorizing,* and the method of *reading from manuscript.*

The impromptu method   The impromptu method means speaking on the spur of the moment. No specific preparation is made for the particular occasion; the speaker relies entirely on his general knowledge and skill. The ability to speak impromptu is useful in an emergency, but its use should be limited to emergencies. Too often the moment arrives without the "spur." Whenever possible, it is better to plan ahead rather than to risk the rambling, incoherent speech which the impromptu method so often produces. Of course, practice in organizing and presenting speeches will help you develop orderly habits of arranging material and maintaining coherence in its presentation, and these habits will assist you in meeting those situations where specific preparation is not possible and you are forced to speak impromptu. You will find the principles of speech composition and discussion discussed in later chapters helpful in developing your skill for rapid adaptation to impromptu speaking situations.

Memorization   The method of memorizing goes to the other extreme. The speech is not only planned but written out and committed to memory word for word. Some speakers can use this method effectively, but too often it results in a stilted, inflexible presentation. The speaker tends to hurry through his speech, saying the words without thinking of their meaning. Besides, with this method it is difficult to make the changes so often needed to adapt a speech to the reactions of the audience.

Reading from manuscript   A third method is reading from a manuscript on which the speech has been written out verbatim. This method is just as inflexible as the method of memorizing and is even more apt to erect a barrier between the speaker and his audience. Since the speaker's eyes must be on the manuscript, he cannot look at his listeners except in hasty glances. Unless he is a skillful reader, he is not likely to use sufficient emphasis and vocal variety to give life to his remarks. In short, he may sound as though he is doing exactly what he is doing—reading a speech—and not as though he were speaking to his audience. This weakness can be minimized with practice; and the more speaking *without* a manuscript one does, the more likely he is to develop effective vocal habits which will carry over into reading *from* a manuscript. On occasions where extremely careful wording is required —such as the President's messages to Congress, where a slip of the tongue could seriously affect domestic politics or even foreign diplomacy, or in the presentation of precise scientific reports, where accuracy and time limits require exact and briefly stated exposition—the speaker usually reads from a manuscript. In such instances, however, the speaker is wise to practice his reading in advance—if possible, to record his reading and listen to himself—in order to improve the emphasis and variety of his delivery. Many radio and television speeches are also read from manuscript because of the strict time limits imposed by broadcasting schedules; more will be said about this problem in Chapter 28. Since few people write in the informal style required for most speech occasions, reading from manuscript is probably the least effective method of speaking and should be avoided except in the special situations indicated above.

The extemporaneous method

The extemporaneous method is the one usually employed by most good speakers. This method takes a middle course. The speech is very carefully planned and outlined in detail, and sometimes a complete draft of it is written out; but the wording is never specifically committed to memory. Instead, after preparing the outline or manuscript, the speaker lays it aside and practices saying his speech aloud, choosing his words anew each time he goes through it. He uses the outline to fix the sequence of ideas firmly in his mind, and by practicing a variety of wordings he develops flexibility of expression. If the extemporaneous method is used too sketchily, the result will be as slipshod as the impromptu method—a fact which sometimes leads to a confusion of these two terms; but a thorough and careful use of it will result in a speech nearly as polished as a memorized one and certainly more vigorous, flexible, and spontaneous.

THE SEVEN ESSENTIALS OF SPEECH PREPARATION

The following seven steps comprise the essential items in thorough preparation for a speech:

1. Determining the Purpose of the Speech.
2. Analyzing the Audience and Occasion.
3. Selecting and Narrowing the Subject.

Surveying the problem

4. Gathering the Material.
5. Making an Outline
   of the Speech.
6. Wording the Speech.

*Building
the
speech*

7. Practicing Aloud.

Oral practice

It will not always be possible, or perhaps even advisable, to arrange your work in just this order. Ordinarily you will want to survey the problem before you start building the speech, and you will have to build a speech before you can practice it; but other than this, the sequence should remain flexible. Of the seven items listed, you will often want to do two or more at the same time or alternate from one to the other in order that your preparation may be properly integrated. For instance, surveying the problem involves the consideration of three things: purpose, audience, and subject. To deal with any one of these adequately without noting its relation to the other two is difficult if not impossible. Sometimes you will be asked to talk on an assigned subject. When this occurs, you will have to narrow it to fit the audience, and you will need to determine the purpose of your speech with that subject and audience in mind. On the other hand, you may sometimes begin your preparation by determining your purpose—let us say, to entertain and amuse your audience. You will then need to select your subject with this purpose in mind and with constant thought to the type of audience which is to be entertained. But regardless of the order in which you consider the seven items listed, a thorough preparation will include them all. We will now consider each of them briefly.

*Determining the
purpose of the speech*

Too often a speaker arises to "say a few words" with no idea what his purpose in speaking is. When this happens, the net result is merely the consumption of time. It is not enough merely to center the speech about a definite subject; the speech should always be thought of in terms of the response desired from the audience. You may want the audience to be entertained, or to understand a difficult point, or to believe a proposition, or to become emotionally aroused, or to take some definite action. In any event you must think of your speech as an instrument of utility—a means of getting a reaction. If you determine your purpose for speaking and keep in mind the response you seek, you can save a great deal of time.

Analyzing the audience and occasion
If your speech is to achieve its maximum effect, you must have, early in the process of preparation, a clear picture of the conditions under which you are to speak. Many audiences have been lulled to sleep by speakers who seemed to be addressing imaginary listeners. People like to feel that they are being talked to directly—that they are at least silent partners in the conversation. Further, they do not like to have too heavy a diet of thought forced upon them at a jovial gathering, nor are they pleased by facetious comments on a solemn occasion. Whenever possible, therefore, find out ahead of time what sort of gathering you are to address.

You should also make a point of finding out what kind of people will make up the audience, what brings them together, what their age and social position are, who else is going to speak to them, and what will be their probable attitude toward you and your purpose. Sometimes, of course, you will not be able to learn all these things in advance, and you will have to adapt yourself to conditions as you find them when you speak; but the more accurately you can picture the audience and occasion beforehand, the easier this adaptation will be when the time comes for you to deliver your speech.

Selecting and narrowing the subject
As you know, your subject will sometimes be chosen for you. But whether you are given a subject or choose it yourself, you must narrow it down to fit the time limits of your speech and the interest and capacity of your audience. Moreover, your own interest and knowledge must be considered: whenever possible, talk about something with which you have had personal experience and about which you can find out more than your audience already knows. Try to speak on a subject in which you are vitally interested and on which you can make a real contribution.

Gathering the material   Having completed your survey of the problem by considering the purpose, audience, and subject, you are now ready to begin building your speech. Ordinarily you will begin by drawing together what you already know about the subject and deciding roughly what points you want to include in your speech. Almost always, however, you will find that what you already know is not enough. You will want to gather additional information—facts, illustrations, stories, examples, and so on—with which you can develop your speech. It is often necessary to inquire from those who know more about the subject and to investigate written sources. Newspapers, magazines, books, reports—these form a valuable storehouse of information which is readily available in the library. Gradually, what you already know and the new material you find can be brought together, sifted, and made ready for the detailed building of the speech.

Making an outline of the speech   Although you will make a rough sketch of the points in your speech even before you look for material to develop it, you cannot prepare a detailed outline until you have most of the information you need. With this material at hand, you will first set down the main points you expect to make in the order you expect to make them. Then under each main point you will fill in the detailed items, being careful that these details are germane to the point under which they are included. This outline should be worked out in considerable detail in order to insure unity and coherence in your speech; later you can make a skeleton outline to use in fixing the points in your memory.

Wording the speech   With the detailed outline before you, there are two ways in which you may develop the wording of your speech. You may write the speech out word for word, or you may want to lay the outline before you and say it through several times, composing your sentences orally in a variety of ways until you find the most effective way of stating them. Which of these methods is better will depend on the individual speaker and the type of occasion, though the method of oral composition is recommended because of its greater flexibility. On this point, however, you will do well to seek the advice of your instructor.

Practicing aloud You are now ready for the final step in your preparation—the actual practice for oral presentation. The best method for most speakers is to take the outline or manuscript and, in the privacy of a room, to talk aloud, following the sequence of ideas as written. You should do this several times until you have the sequence of ideas clearly in mind. You can then lay aside the outline or manuscript and think through your speech silently, point by point, until you are sure the ideas are really fixed in your mind. Finally, get up and go through the speech aloud without looking at the written speech. The first time through you will probably leave out a good deal, but do not let this worry you. Go over the speech again and include what you left out. Continue doing this until not only do the ideas come in an orderly fashion but the words flow easily as well. Put into practice the suggestions made in the last four chapters: work for variety and expressiveness in the pitch, rate, and force of your voice, and give adequate play to movement and gesture. Throughout this practice, preserve a mental image of the audience you expect to face. Decide whether the situation which will confront you can best be handled by a vigorous, lively presentation or by a quiet, dignified one; whether you should be jovial or serious; whether the situation will call for straight talk or a tactful approach. Above all, practice making your manner of speaking seem personal; remember that you will be speaking *to* people, not *at* them.

The amount of oral practice you will need depends entirely on your ability, experience, and knowledge of the subject. Although it is not wise to practice a speech so often that you become stale, you must be sure that you have the material well in mind. As a general rule, the less experience you have had in speaking, the more oral practice you will require. Students are more apt to practice too little than too much.

It is hard to force the development of a speech; speeches grow. Therefore, begin thinking about your subject and the desired audience response as soon as you know you are to speak. In this way you can best utilize your background of knowledge and fill in the gaps with additional material. Work on the speech as frequently as possible, even if only for a few minutes at a time. Your confidence will increase in direct proportion to your mastery of the speech. To postpone beginning the preparation of even a classroom speech until the night before it is to be given is folly. The wise speaker will start to prepare as early as he can.

This chapter has presented in summary form the method by which speech preparation may be conducted in an orderly fashion. The succeeding chapters will consider in more detail all of the essentials mentioned so briefly here. In studying the following chapters remember that the problems they treat must not be considered in isolation, but rather as related parts of an integrated process of preparation.

PROBLEMS

1. For each of the four methods of speaking, list several speech situations for which you believe that method would be appropriate or necessary. What factors determined your selection?

2. Keep a "log" on the preparation for your next speech. Note in what order you take up the various steps of speech preparation and the amount of time you spend on each.

3. What differences in the order of preparation and in the time allotted to each of the seven steps would be required by these different situations:
   A. You are told at noon that you are to speak to the freshman class for five minutes that evening about campus traditions.
   B. You are asked a month in advance to speak to the seniors in the high school from which you graduated on a subject of your own choice.
   C. You are vigorously opposed to the existing rules regarding absence from classes and have been given an opportunity to represent your classmates at a meeting of a joint faculty-student committee scheduled five days hence.
   D. You have just returned from a summer's travel in Europe and have been invited to talk about it before the local Rotary Club three weeks from now. You are informed that you will be given twenty minutes unless the district officer, who is also scheduled to speak, fails to come—in which case you will be expected to talk for forty minutes.

E. You would like a place on the college debate team. At the try-outs which will be held in two weeks, you must make a five-minute speech on the debate question.

4. Make a brief report to the class on the methods of preparation and speaking used by some famous speaker of the past or present. (*A History and Criticism of American Address* [Volumes I and II edited by W. N. Brigance; Volume III edited by Marie Hochmuth] provides interesting studies of orators of the past.)

When a wise man chooses a fit subject he always speaks well.

Euripides

CHAPTER 8/*Determining the Subject and Purpose of the Speech*

The first step in your speech preparation is to decide what you are going to talk about and what reaction you want from your audience. Subject and purpose are thus intimately related, the former having to do with the central theme and substance and the latter with the response you plan to get from the audience by discussing this theme.

Sometimes a predetermined purpose governs your choice of subject. For instance, if your purpose is to get people to vote for John Smith in the next election, your subject must concern John Smith, his experience, his policies, and his party's platform. On the other hand, a predetermined subject frequently governs your determination of purpose. For example, if you have been asked to talk on the subject of bass fishing, your purpose must be limited to getting some reaction from the audience toward this subject. In spite of their intimate relation to one another, however, subject and purpose are two different things. Your analysis must be *subjective* in that it must consider the topics you expect to discuss; it must be *purposive* in considering the audience and the reaction desired from them. Neither one is adequate alone.

THE SUBJECT AND TITLE

The most common mistake of young speakers is either to pick a subject that is so profound that neither they nor their audiences know anything about it or to pick one that is so old and overworked that the audience describes it as "the same old stuff." Students frequently attempt to speak on subjects that are too broad for their grasp or for the time limits of their speech. What is more absurd than an attempt once made by a student to discuss "The Causes and Results of the Russian Revolution" in a five-minute speech. The usual result of choosing too broad a subject is a thin, sketchy discussion which tells the audience nothing new. How much better it would have been for the student to have limited himself to a description of a typical collective farm in Russia after the revolution or to an explanation of village government under the soviet system. To avoid this and other faults, test the subject you pick by the following rules:

Select a subject about which you already know something and can find out more. Knowledge is power in speech as it is elsewhere.

Select a subject that is interesting to you. Unless you are interested yourself in what you talk about, you will find preparation a dull task, and your speaking is likely to be listless and ineffective.

Select a subject that will interest your audience. The more interest your listeners already have in the subject, the less you will have to worry about holding their attention when you speak. A subject may be interesting to the audience for one or more of the following reasons:

1. Because it vitally concerns their affairs.
2. Because it concerns the solution of a definite problem.
3. Because it is new or timely.
4. Because there is a conflict of opinion on it.

Select a subject that is neither above nor below the intellectual capacity of the audience. A talk about the value of a savings account in the local bank would be appropriate for an audience of grade school children, but a discussion of the Federal Reserve System would be beyond them. It is equally unwise to underestimate the capacity of an adult audience and to select a subject that makes you seem to be talking down to them.

Select a subject that you can discuss adequately in the time you have at your disposal—an important rule, as we have already observed.

In the event that your subject is chosen for you, you can apply the preceding rules to narrowing the subject. Subjects chosen for you are usually stated broadly, and you have the right to limit your discussion to some particular aspect of the subject which fits the requirements of the particular occasion.

Closely related to the subject of the speech is its *title*. The *subject* denotes the content of the speech: the problem to be discussed, the objects or activities to be described. The *title* is the label given to your speech—usually announced by the chairman—for the purpose of arousing the audience's interest. The title is a sort of advertising slogan, dressing up the subject in an attractive form. Thus, when St. Clair McKelway, then editor of the *Brooklyn Eagle,* discussed the importance of discarding outworn creeds and foolish dogmas in order to make way for progressive thinking, he gave his speech the title, "Smashed Crockery," in order to arouse the interest of the National Society of China Importers, before whom he was speaking. A college orator wishing to condemn the practice of expending huge sums of money in political campaigns called his speech, "Our Gold-Plated Democracy," while another labeled his discussion of the modern tendency to condone successful crime with the provocative title "The Eleventh Commandment."

What, then, are the requirements of a good title? There are at least three: it should be *relevant;* it should be *provocative;* it should be *brief.* To be relevant, a title must have something to do with the subject or with some part of the speaker's discussion of it. Thus, the relevancy of the title "The Eleventh Commandment" was made clear when the speaker pointed out that the commandments "Thou shalt not steal" and "Thou shalt not kill" had been supplemented by a new one, the eleventh, "Thou shalt get away with it." In this example you will notice that while the title was not a prosaic and academic statement of the subject, it definitely had something to do with it. No audience likes to be misled by the speaker's title; people do not enjoy false advertising.

To be provocative, the title should make the audience sit up and listen. Sometimes the subject of the speech is of such compelling interest in itself that no effort is required to make the title impelling: a mere statement of the subject is provocative enough. In most instances, however, the speaker must find a more vivid or unusual phrasing. Moreover, care must be taken at times not to give away the whole speech in the title. Especially if the audience is hostile to his purpose, the speaker must not let that purpose be too obvious in the title of his speech. To entitle a speech for a fraternity group "Why Fraternities Should Be Abolished" is provocative enough, but undiplomatic in the extreme.

Obviously the title of a speech should be brief. Imagine the effect of announcing the title of a speech as "A Graphical Description of the Various Methods of Chimney Construction and Their Effects upon the Economical Use of Fuel." Such a title can only be excused when the discussion is a technical one to be made before a professional audience having a specialized interest. Here the precise denotation of the subject matter may be of greatest importance. Even so, the title should be as short as possible.

Usually the phrasing of the title can best be left until the speech has been completely built. To word a title that is both relevant and provocative will be much easier then. The phrasing of titles has been discussed in this chapter because of its close relation to the subject and purpose of the speech and not because it is done early in the process of speech preparation.

Regardless of the subject or title, the aim of every speech is *to get a reaction from the audience*. This point must never be lost sight of, for it is the basis of the entire process of speech preparation. The question immediately arises, then: What *kinds* of reactions does one try to get from his hearers?

THE GENERAL ENDS OF SPEECH

There can be no doubt that the reaction sought by the after-dinner speaker at a social banquet differs materially from the one desired by a legislator urging the adoption of a bill, or that both of these differ from the response a college professor seeks in a class lecture. The first speaker wants his audience to enjoy themselves; the second seeks action, a vote of "aye"; the third is trying to secure understanding.

Writers on practical speaking, from the time of the classical rhetoricians to the present, have grouped the purposes of speech into a few fairly definite types, and for the last two centuries they have described them in terms of the audience reaction sought by the speaker. Many such classifications, varying in size and detail, have been used. The following one, listing five general ends of speech, will be found quite workable:

The Five General Ends of Speech		
General End	*Reaction Sought*	*Class of Speech*
1. To Stimulate.	Inspiration (emotional arousal)	
2. To Convince.	Belief (intellectual agreement)	Persuasive
3. To Actuate.	Definite Observable Action	
4. To Inform.	Clear Understanding	Instructive
5. To Entertain.	Interest and Enjoyment	Recreative

A general end, as the term is used here, denotes a general class of speech purpose in terms of the reaction the speaker wants from his audience. Merely because your purpose falls within one of the five general ends, it does not follow that you will have no concern with any of the others. You will sometimes need to entertain during your speech in order to inform; you must usually inform in order to secure belief; you will need to convince or stimulate in order to actuate; and you may even, on rare occasions, actuate in order to cause enjoyment. But one of these five will be your general end, and the others means to that end; one will be your objective, and the others only contributory. For this reason you must take care that the secondary purposes do not run away with the speech —that they are included only when they advance the principal aim of the speech, and only for as long as they do so. The following discussion treats each general end in its capacity as a *primary* aim.

To actuate   The aim of your speech will be to actuate when you desire to obtain some definite observable performance from your audience. This performance may be to vote "yes" or "no"; it may be to contribute money, to sign a petition, to form a parade and engage in a demonstration; or it may be any one of a hundred types of observable public acts. The basis of this action may be the creation of a strong belief, or it may be the arousal of emotion, or it may be both. For this reason the development of the speech which aims at action will follow closely the methods suggested for speeches which aim to convince or to stimulate. The only distinguishing feature of the actuating speech is that it goes further than the other two; in it you definitely ask your audience to do something at a specified time which others can observe. This relationship can be diagramed as follows:

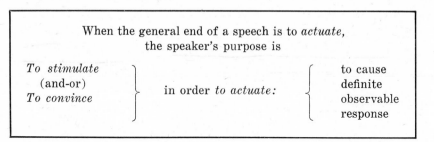

When the general end of a speech is to *actuate,*
the speaker's purpose is

| To stimulate (and-or) To convince | in order *to actuate:* | to cause definite observable response |

The actuating speech differs from the other two, therefore, only in the *degree* of reaction sought from the audience. The method of development will closely parallel that used for one or the other of them, or it will be a combination of both. There are times, of course, when speeches are made to stimulate or convince alone, with no specific action desired. The next two sections, therefore, may be considered as means by which action may be secured as well as discussions of independent general ends.

To stimulate	Your general end will be to stimulate when you are trying to inspire, to arouse enthusiasm, or to deepen

a feeling of awe, respect, or devotion on the part of your audience. Speeches commemorating great events, such as Memorial Day or Veterans Day, and those given at rallies, pep sessions, and as keynotes to conventions usually have stimulation as their general end. Seldom is the attempt made to change the attitude of the audience, but rather the aim is to strengthen it. Rarely does the speaker try to prove anything; but such a speech is full of striking statements, vivid descriptions, and strong emotional appeal. No specific performance is demanded of the audience.

To convince	The general end of your speech will be to convince when you attempt to influence the beliefs or intellectual

attitudes of your audience. A very large share of present-day speeches have this as their general end. Political speakers urge their constituents to believe in the principles and performances of their respective parties; attempts are made to create belief in the superiority of certain products, principles, or forms of government; the truth of scientific and philosophical hypotheses is debated pro and con. But in all these cases, if the general end is only *to convince* (and not to actuate through conviction), no specific performance is asked of the audience. They are merely asked to agree with the speaker.

In fact, many times listeners are incapable of taking definite action, since the authority for it lies with some other group. But they can form opinions by which to judge the actions of those who are in authority. For example, a great many speeches are made to public audiences, even in nonelection years, about the foreign policy of the administration. The actual authority for controlling these policies lies with the President and with Congress, yet speakers outside the administration attempt to influence the beliefs of the ordinary citizen. Why? Because these beliefs will ultimately affect government policies through the influence of public opinion. The immediate purpose of the speakers, however, is not performance, not action in the form of voting, but agreement in belief. Later, of course, the candidates for President and Congress will talk on these same subjects in the attempt to actuate—to get people to exert a direct influence on foreign policy by voting in the fall elections. In the former case, the attempt is made merely to convince the audience; in the latter, to secure definite action through conviction.

The essential characteristic of a speech made to convince is that it attempts to prove something; hence, it is usually filled with arguments supported with facts, figures, and examples. New situations are referred to old beliefs, and evidence is presented to substantiate the speaker's assertions. In this way the attempt is made to establish or change the convictions of the audience.

To inform

The object of your speech will be to inform when you try to make the audience understand something or to widen the range of their knowledge. This is the purpose of the foreman who is showing a workman how to operate a new machine. The teacher lectures to his class primarily to inform, and the county farm agent desires chiefly that his audience understand when he explains the results of tests carried on at the agricultural experiment station. What has been said, however, does not mean that clear explanation is useful only in a speech in which information is the general end. In a speech to convince, for example, belief can rarely be secured unless an understanding of the proposition is first established. But in a speech which aims to inform, the speaker does not want to urge any particular belief or advise action of any kind; his purpose is only to have his audience understand and to provide them with the information needed for this understanding. To do this, he must relate his ideas to the existing knowledge of his audience; he must be sure that the structure of his speech is clear; and he must present enough concrete examples and specific data to avoid becoming abstract and dry.

To entertain

The general end of your speech will be to entertain when your primary concern is to have your audience enjoy themselves. This is a frequent purpose of after-dinner speakers, but this type of purpose is by no means limited to such speakers. The popular lecturer may attempt to inform; but more frequently, even though he presents information of a type (usually of an unusual and striking character), his chief aim is not to create an understanding of the subject but rather to entertain his audience. Humor, of course, is the primary means of entertainment, but curious bits of information serve the same purpose if the people are not asked to exert effort to understand them. There will be many occasions when your legitimate object in speaking will be to show your audience a good time. You will then need to avoid heavy discussion and controversial issues; if you present facts and figures, they must be striking and unusual ones; vividness and originality of statement will play an important part in achieving your goal. Above all, you must not have an ax to grind in a speech of this sort.

But choosing the general type of purpose for your speech is not enough. Your general purpose must be narrowed to a more specific one before you proceed with building your speech.

THE SPECIFIC PURPOSE—LIMITING FACTORS

We may define the specific purpose of a speech as the *specific response* desired from the audience by the time the speaker has finished talking. It is the exact thing that he wants the audience to do, feel, believe, understand, or enjoy. The following example will illustrate the relationship between the subject, general end, and specific purpose of a speech:

Subject: Health Insurance for Students.
General end: To actuate.
Specific purpose: To get members of the student council to vote in favor of the group policy offered by the ABC Health Insurance Company.

Or consider this example:

Subject: Space Travel.
General end: To inform.
Specific purpose: To make the audience understand how the physiological problems of man's travels in space are solved.

Before going very far with the preparation of a speech, then, you must determine not only the type of reaction you want from your audience but also the exact response you want. While making this decision, you will need to keep in mind the following factors.

Authority or capacity of the audience

To demand of a group of college students that they "abolish all required courses" is foolish; they do not have the authority to do so since curricular requirements are in the hands of the faculty. But students do have the right and ability to bring pressure on the faculty toward this end. A more logical demand for the speaker to make, therefore, would be that the student audience "petition the faculty to make all courses elective." Limit your request to something that is within your listeners' power and ability. Do not ask the audience to do something which they couldn't do even if they wanted to.

Existing attitude of the audience

A group of striking workmen who believe that they are badly underpaid and unfairly treated by their employer would probably be hostile to the suggestion that they return to work under these same conditions; but they might approve submitting the dispute to arbitration by some disinterested person whose fairness and judgment they respect. A hostile audience might be influenced in one speech to the point of agreeing that "there may be something to the other side of it," but to get them to take positive action might prove impossible. Your purpose, then, must be reasonable. Do not ask your audience for a response that you cannot reasonably expect from persons with their attitudes and beliefs.

The occasion

To ask people to contribute money to a political campaign fund might be appropriate at a pre-election rally, but to do so at a church dinner would be decidedly out of place. The celebration of a football victory is hardly the occasion to secure an understanding of Einstein's theory. The members of a Little Theater Association do not want to listen to a discussion of the financial statement between the acts of a play on a program evening, though they may respond to a brief announcement urging their attendance at a business meeting where it will be discussed. Be sure that your purpose is modified to fit the spirit of the occasion at which you are to speak.

Personal or ultimate aim of the speaker

Suppose that a plant superintendent is presenting a reorganization plan to his executive committee or board of directors. His immediate purpose is to secure the adoption of his plan; but his ultimate personal aim is probably to increase his own reputation, authority, or salary, and he must do nothing which will ruin his chances in that direction. Keeping this in mind, he may modify his plan somewhat, or he may strive to get someone else to urge its adoption so that the responsibility for it will not be entirely his own. Failure to consider the ultimate aim can sometimes be disastrous. For example, a campaign was started to raise funds for a Union building for the student body of a large university. At a mass meeting of the senior class the members were asked to sign pledges to contribute a specified amount each year after graduation. High-pressure methods were used, and the students were even told that they would not be allowed to leave the meeting until they had signed. The next morning the college paper announced that the senior class had pledged itself 100 percent—the immediate purpose had been attained. But less than a third of these signers ever paid any money, and so much opposition was created by the high-pressure methods that it became difficult to secure money from anyone else; as a result the entire project was delayed several years. The *ultimate* objective was delayed by the attempt to secure too great an *immediate* response. Do not try to get from the audience an immediate response which will have a negative effect upon your ultimate objective.

Time limit of the speech

You may be able in a few sentences to induce a hostile majority to postpone action until a later time; but you will probably need a full discussion in order to change their attitudes so completely that they will favor your proposal. Moreover, if your subject is complex, you may be able *to inform* your audience, to get them to understand your proposal, but you may not have time *to convince* them of its desirability. The time may even be too short for you to give them an understanding of the subject. In an hour you may be able to get an audience to understand the working of the Federal Reserve System in expanding and contracting credit; but if you have only five minutes, you had better limit your efforts to an emphasis of the importance of this function and to suggestions for finding out more about it. Do not attempt to get a reaction which the time limits of your speech would make impossible.

If you keep these five limiting factors in mind when you determine the specific purpose of your speech, you will make a successful beginning to speech preparation. And once determined, the specific purpose should be continually referred to throughout the entire preparation of your speech. Only those things which will advance this purpose should be included in it; everything else must be rigidly excluded. To insure this, write down your specific purpose in a simple sentence and fix that sentence in mind. The following are a few sample purpose sentences:

Get the audience to
—vote for Johnson on November sixth.
—work harder getting members for our club.
—believe in private ownership of electric utilities.
—understand exactly how safety matches are made.
—laugh at the absurdities of puppy love.
—appreciate the excitement of deep-sea exploration.

Observe that each of the specific purposes listed is stated in terms of the reaction you desire from your audience. Rarely will the audience be told this purpose in so many words in the speech itself; certainly no such didactic statement will be made at the beginning of the speech. But whether the purpose is obviously revealed to the audience or not, it should remain in the focus of your thoughts while you prepare and present the speech.

A study of this chapter should have made clear the importance of defining your objective early in the process of speech preparation and the considerations which govern your choice. Remember that the following questions should be answered soon after you begin preparing to speak and that no one question may be answered without simultaneous consideration of the others:

1. What subject shall I talk about, and to what aspect of it shall I limit myself?
2. What general end shall I try to attain?
3. What specific response shall I seek from my audience; that is, what is my specific purpose in speaking to this group?

And after you have finished building your speech in detail, be prepared to answer the fourth question:

4. How shall I phrase a title for my speech which will make my audience want to hear it?

PROBLEMS

1. With the other members of your class, select three speeches from a recent issue of *Vital Speeches of the Day;* then, independently, write your opinion as to the subject and specific purpose of each speech. Compare your judgments and see if agreement can be reached. Do the printed titles seem appropriate to these subjects and purposes?

2. Supposing the class to be your audience, select a subject, and phrase five sentences stating a specific purpose, each one appropriate for a different general end but all concerned with the chosen subject. Check to make sure the specific purposes seek responses within the capacity or authority of the class.

3. List five subjects upon which you could talk in your class, and make up a title for each one that would command attention.

4. For each of the five general ends, list one occasion which has occurred in your experience during the past year at which a speech for that general end would have been appropriate.

5. Prepare a two-minute speech intended to convince the class of the values of some campus organization to which you belong. What changes would you make to secure some definite observable action from your audience?

The wise man, before he speaks, will consider well what he speaks, to whom he speaks, and where and when.

St. Ambrose

CHAPTER *9/Analyzing the Occasion and the Audience*

U nless there were someone to listen, speech would merely be a verbal exercise. Talking to hear one's own voice may be helpful in bolstering up courage on a dark night, but it is hardly communicative speech. Yet it is a curious fact that, without meaning to, many a speaker has done this very thing. Too often we become so engrossed in our own interests, so impressed by what seems important to us, that we forget we are talking to other people whose knowledge and interests may differ widely from our own. It is a fairly safe assertion that more speeches fail to achieve their purpose for this one reason than for any other.

The most important lesson a speaker can learn is to see things from the viewpoint of his audience. He must continually ask himself, "How would I feel about this if I were in their places? Would I understand this point with the background they have? Would this sound reasonable if I had been through their experiences?

Would it be interesting to me if I were they?" This ability to project ourselves into the lives of our hearers and to hear ourselves as others hear us is not quickly gained, but it is essential. It must influence our choice of purpose, guide our selection of subject and subject matter, modify the building of our speech, and actively control our behavior during its actual presentation.

To do this effectively, we must thoroughly analyze the audience and the occasion at which the speech will be given. The object of this chapter is to outline a method for this analysis.

THE INFLUENCE OF THE OCCASION

As we have already pointed out, tact and good taste require the speaker to consider carefully the nature of the occasion at which he is to speak. Comments that would be quite appropriate at a pep session might be in decidedly poor taste at a chapel or convocation program. To be able to adjust yourself adequately to the occasion, you must be able to answer at least four questions about it.

What is the purpose of the gathering? Are you to address the regular meeting of some organized group, or has the audience come together for some special reason, or is the gathering merely a chance one? Have people come primarily to hear you talk, or is your speech merely incidental to their object? Is the subject and purpose of your talk in line with their reason for meeting, or do you mean to make use of their presence in order to secure some response not connected with it?

What rules or customs will prevail? Will there be a regular order of business or a fixed program into which you will have to fit? Is it the custom of this group to ask questions of the speaker? Is formality the prevailing custom, or does this group prefer informality in the speaker's manner? Is the speaker expected to extend gracious or complimentary remarks to some person or to display respect or reverence for some traditional concept? A knowledge of these facts will help you avoid feeling out of place and will prevent you from arousing antagonism by some untactful move.

What will precede and follow your speech? At what time of day will your speech be given? Immediately after a heavy meal? After a long and heavy program? Just before some other important event? What other events (music, business, other speakers) are on the program besides your own speech? All these things will influence the interest the audience may have in your talk. In some instances you may make use of other events on the program to increase interest or belief in your own remarks; sometimes they will work against you. In any event, you must always consider what effect the program as a whole may have on your speech.

What will the physical conditions be? Will the speech be given out-of-doors or in a good auditorium? Is it likely to be hot, cold, or comfortable? Will the audience be sitting or standing; and if sitting, will they be crowded, comfortable, or scattered around a large room? How large a room will the speech be given in; will a public-address system be used; can the speaker be seen and heard easily? Are there likely to be disturbances in the form of noise or interruptions from the outside? All these things and many other physical factors have their effect on the temper of the audience, their span of attention, and the style of speaking you will find necessary.

DIAGNOSIS OF THE AUDIENCE

In addition to analyzing the occasion at which the speech is to be made, the speaker must consider the people who will make up the audience. It is obvious that an argument which will convince some people will leave others unmoved and that what will be highly interesting to one audience will be dull to another. But how are you to find out these things? The best way is to ask some of the people who you know will be in your audience; or if you do not know any such persons, you can learn a great deal from others who have spoken to this, or a very similar, group. Even this method is sometimes impossible, and you will then be forced to infer the attitudes and beliefs of your audience from what general knowledge you can gather about their education, occupation, age, and the like. In any event, there are a number of facts about an audience that you should know, the most important of which we shall briefly consider.

General data Some general facts about the audience should be determined early in your analysis. They include:

The size of the audience. As we discussed earlier, your vocal and physical delivery should be adapted to the size of the audience: the larger the audience, the greater the need for broader gestures and movement and for distinctness in articulation.

The age of those making up the audience. It is important to know whether the audience is of the same age level or of widely divergent ages. Age will affect their ability to understand you and will determine how far back their experience runs. For example, World War II events are only second-hand experiences to most students. In general, older persons are less impulsive and more conservative than younger ones.

The sex of members of the audience. Is it a mixed audience or not? Men and women differ in their interests, though these interests often overlap. Some subjects suitable for discussion before one sex are unsuitable for the other or for a mixed audience.

The occupation of the members of the audience. Occupation tends to suggest what interests and type of knowledge people will have. A talk to University Club members will doubtless differ from one before the local labor union. A fair index of income level can also be gained from this information.

The education of those in the audience. Both formal education and that education which comes from experience are important. A Chicago cab driver may not have a broad formal education, but his knowledge of the ways of human nature and of the conditions in that city may be profound. Remember to consider both schooling and experience.

Membership in social, professional, and religious groups. Memberships in special groups often indicate both interests and prejudices. Rotary Club, Knights of Columbus, Sigma Chi, Forest Hills Tennis Club, Young Republican Organization, American Association of University Women, Elks—what do these organizations mean to you? They should represent types of people, points of view, interests, and special abilities. Whenever you find out that a

*Pictured above are an outdoor college commencement,
a breakfast meeting to instruct volunteer lobbyists,
a group of men beginning their Peace Corps training,
and an A.T.&T. stockholders meeting. How do you
think the speaker should adapt to each of these audiences and occasions?*

sizable part of your audience is affiliated with some special group, you will have gained a valuable clue for your analysis.

Audience's knowledge of the subject

Through either the general data about the audience or some special information which you have secured, you should be able to infer what the members of your audience know about the subject of your speech. Will they understand technical terms without explanation? Will an elementary discussion of the subject seem boring and trivial to them? What facts will be new to them, and what material will be old stuff? For a speaker to imply by his remarks that he thinks his listeners ignorant or for him to assume a condescending manner toward them is decidedly tactless; but it is equally bad policy to talk over their heads. A fairly successful plan generally is to aim the speech at a level of knowledge characteristic of the average listener.

Audience's primary interests and desires

Any speaker should be concerned about the primary interests and desires of his audience. In analyzing your audience you should ask yourself: What do the people in this audience want most, and in what are they chiefly interested? How are their wants and desires related to my subject and the purpose of my speech? These questions are of such importance that they will be considered in detail in the next chapter.

Audience's fixed attitudes and beliefs

As soon as a child begins to receive impressions of his environment, he starts to form opinions and attitudes about it. These opinions and attitudes are modified by his later experience, but by the time he has grown up, some of them have, through habit and repetition, become the fixed bases for his conduct. Some people, for example, believe firmly in the value of science; others (though they may not admit it openly) believe in hunches, jinxes, and the like. A man may be fixed in his belief in a high tariff, or in the law of supply and demand, or in the superiority of a certain race. Such proverbs as "Honesty is the best policy" and "Spare the rod and spoil the child" are but traditional ways of stating rather common fixed beliefs.

The speaker who knows what beliefs and attitudes are the fixed bases of his hearers' thinking can avoid arousing needless hostility and can often use these beliefs as pegs upon which to hang his proposal. If you can show how your idea fits in with one already fixed in the minds of your audience, or how your proposal applies some of their existing principles, your battle is won.

Attitude of the audience toward the speaker If your general diagnosis of the audience covering the points mentioned above has been accurate and comprehensive, you will be in a position to estimate their probable attitude toward you and your speech. Ask yourself first of all what will be their attitude toward you personally and toward your qualifications to address them on the chosen subject. Two things must be considered: (*a*) the degree of their *friendliness* toward you and (*b*) the degree of their *respect* for you or your knowledge of the subject. These two phases of their attitude may vary extremely and sometimes in opposite directions. For instance, a father may love his small son deeply, but he may not respect his son's judgment very much. On the other hand, the son may have the greatest respect for a neighborhood policeman but hate the ground that man walks on. Respect and friendliness are two different things, but they both must be taken into account.

Adaptation to personal hostility. When your analysis predicts that your audience will be hostile toward you, your first job as a speaker is to try to overcome this attitude. You can hardly accomplish your purpose in speaking without doing so. The method will vary, of course, with the cause of that hostility, and your job will be easier if their respect for you is high. In any case, try in some way to establish common ground with your audience. This can often be done by one of the following methods:

1. By showing a friendly attitude toward your audience.
2. By maintaining an attitude of fairness, modesty, and good humor.
3. By pointing out your own agreement with some of their cherished attitudes or beliefs.
4. By referring to experiences held in common with them.
5. By tactfully complimenting their abilities, accomplishments, or friends.
6. By using humor that is in good taste, especially that which is at your own expense.

Adaptation to an attitude of condescension. The thing not to do when an audience has a condescending attitude toward you is to assume a conceited or antagonistic attitude yourself. Of course, you must appear self-confident, but this confidence must be tempered with a large measure of modesty. Gain the respect of your audience by the soundness of your thinking and the grasp you show of the facts about the subject rather than by parading yourself. Avoid saying "I think . . ."; instead, present the evidence which makes that conclusion evident. If you have occasion to call attention to your own accomplishments in a pertinent connection, do so in a matter-of-fact, unassuming way. Remember that real personal worth does not advertise itself with a brass band but by its real accomplishment.

Attitude of the audience toward the subject — Ordinarily, people are either *interested* in a subject or they are *apathetic* toward it. The latter attitude is usually present if they see no connection between the subject and their own affairs. When your diagnosis indicates that this will be their attitude, you will need to show the audience some connection with their affairs which they had not realized, or you will need to arouse their curiosity in some novel aspect of the subject. Utilize all the methods for holding attention that you can. Of course, you cannot neglect doing these things even if the audience is already interested—as you must be careful not to lose that interest; but when an audience is apathetic, you will find that more effort is required to hold their attention.

Attitude of the audience toward the purpose — If, with no preliminaries at all, you told the audience the specific purpose of your speech, what would be their attitude toward it? The answer indicates the meaning of "attitude toward purpose." It is not the attitude you hope for at the end of your speech but rather what it is before you begin. Of course, only rarely will you actually state your purpose at the start. Yet, to build a speech that will get the proper response, you must try to determine the audience's attitude toward your purpose assuming you had baldly stated it. Since an audience is never a homogeneous group, it will represent many differing shades of attitude. It is usually best, therefore, to determine what attitude is predominant and to adapt your speech to that predominant viewpoint while making allowances for any marked variations you expect. The following outline suggests the principal attitudes which may prevail toward the speaker's purpose.

Possible Attitudes Toward the Purpose

I. When the general end is *to entertain* or *to inform:*
  A. The attitude toward the purpose will be governed largely by the attitude toward the subject.
  B. Hence, it will be one of the following:
    1. Interested.
    2. Apathetic.
II. When the general end is *to stimulate, to convince,* or *to actuate:*
  A. The attitude toward the purpose will be governed largely by the attitude toward the specific feeling, belief, or action to be urged.
  B. Hence, it will be one of the following:
    1. Favorable but not aroused.
    2. Apathetic to the situation.
    3. Interested in the situation but undecided what to do or think about it.
    4. Interested in the situation but hostile to the *proposed* belief, attitude, or action because the audience
      a. doubts its workability or soundness, and/or
      b. fears its possible bad effects, and/or
      c. favors some other belief, attitude, or action.
    5. Hostile to any change from the present situation.

The attitudes listed in the first section of this outline are closely related to the audience's attitude toward the subject, which has already been explained. The five attitudes listed in the second section require brief illustration. Let us assume that property taxes in your college community are high and that fraternity property is tax-exempt. Under these conditions, suppose your purpose were to start a movement for the removal of this exemption so that fraternity houses would be placed on the assessment sheet. An audience of local property owners (provided they were not fraternity alumni) would most likely be favorable, but they would need to be aroused before they would take any concerted action. Nonfraternity students would ordinarily form an apathetic audience since they would not see what connection the proposal had with them. The university administration and faculty on the whole would be

Study the audiences in these pictures. The one above is a group of sales engineers; the one below is a group of workers in a plant. How do you think they might differ in their interest and attitude toward a given subject? How might their reactions be influenced by their education and occupation and by the occasion?

interested in the situation because of its connection with both students and community but would be undecided whether to support the plan or not (excepting those who were influenced by owning property themselves or were fraternity alumni). Property owners who were also fraternity alumni or sympathizers would be interested in the situation and desirous of some way to relieve themselves of the heavy property tax, but they would probably be opposed to this particular way of doing it because of their fraternity connections. Student fraternity men, on the other hand, would be frankly hostile to any change from the present situation under which they were obtaining a distinct advantage. Thus, a knowledge of the proportion of each of these groups in your audience would give you a good estimate of its complexion.

Having determined the prevailing attitude or combination of attitudes of your audience toward your purpose, you will need to adjust the method of approaching your audience, and the structure and content of your speech, to that situation. We shall leave a discussion of methods, however, until Chapters 21 and 22, when we shall have a better understanding of speech construction and the materials used in it.

AUDIENCE REACTIONS DURING THE SPEECH

No prior analysis of an audience is proof against mistaken judgment. Moreover, the audience's attitude may change even while you are speaking. Hence, it is highly important to keep a close watch on the reactions of the audience when your subject is announced and throughout your entire speech. The way your hearers sit in their seats, the expressions on their faces, their audible reactions, such as laughter, applause, sharp breathing, shifting about, whispering—all these are vivid symptoms of their attitude toward you, your subject, or your purpose. If you are wise, you will develop a keen sensitivity to these signs and adapt your remarks to them as you go on. This chapter is attempting to help you develop such sensitivity and adaptability.

"I am convinced by my own experience, and by that of others," said Henry Ford, "that if there is any secret of success, it lies in the ability to get the other person's point of view and to see things from his angle as well as your own." [1] A systematic method for finding out the other fellow's point of view has been presented. Your task is to apply this method in the specific situations that arise. Examine carefully the sample analysis outline which follows and notice how the speaker used the facts at his disposal to draw a clear picture of the audience which would confront him.

---

[1] From *Developing Executive Ability* by Enoch Burton Gowin (Ronald Press Company, New York, 1919), p. 10.

Sample Analysis Outline

I. Subject: Representation on the Student Senate.

II. Title: "Neglected Men—And Women!"

III. General End: To actuate.

IV. Specific Purpose: To get the members of the Student Senate to approve a constitutional amendment increasing the number of Senators from the Independent Student Association.

V. Specific Audience: Student Senate, Purdue University.

VI. Specific Occasion: Regular biweekly meeting of the Senate, March 22, 1961, 7:30 P.M., Room 212, Memorial Center. Time: 15 minutes. The regular order of business will precede the speech.

VII. Audience Diagnosis:

A. Size: About thirty persons.

B. Sex and Age: Men and women, 19–23 years old.

C. Occupation: College students but a wide variety of interests and educational objectives are represented.

D. Knowledge of the subject:
1. A general knowledge of the provisions of the Senate constitution and the present system of student representation.
2. A limited knowledge of the dissatisfaction among some independent students toward the present system of representation.
3. A few have specific knowledge of the problem from conversations with the speaker and other students.

E. Primary Interest: Their own educational objectives and problems, including campus organizations and activities.

F. Fixed Attitudes:
1. Political: Believe in the principle of equal representation for all.
2. Professional: Strong desire for success in their chosen professions; believe that participation in civic affairs will contribute to that success and will bring personal prestige.
3. Economic: Most of them are economically dependent upon parents or some other outside source of income and do not classify groups or organizations on this basis.
4. Religious: Attitudes unimportant in consideration of this subject.

G. Attitude toward subject: Interested because of their concern about all issues presented to the Senate.

H. Attitude toward speaker: Personally friendly—a fellow member of the Senate.

I. Attitude toward purpose: Most will be interested in the situation but hostile to the proposed change. They believe existing methods are satisfactory and may fear the loss of some influence or prestige.

VIII. Proposed adaptation to the audience:
   A. Introduce the subject by referring to the Senate's responsibility to treat all student groups fairly.
   B. Use visual aids to show inequities of the present apportionment of representatives.
   C. Primary appeal: To their pride in fulfilling their civic responsibility by giving equal representation to all students.

PROBLEMS

1. Be ready to discuss the following questions in class: How does the nature of the occasion influence the speaker's preparation? How does the predominant audience attitude influence the speaker's preparation? What kinds of audiences are the most difficult to speak before? Will planning eliminate the need for adaptation during the speech? Why?

2. Select the subject and specific purpose for your next speech in class. Using the sample analysis outline above as a model, make a similar analysis of your own speech class.

3. Given the facts stated in the audience analysis you prepared for Problem 2, what would be the difference in attitude toward speaker, subject, and purpose in the following situations:

SPEAKER	SUBJECT	PURPOSE
A. The instructor.	Preparation of class work.	To get students to spend more time in preparing speeches.
B. A visiting student from England.	Life at Oxford.	To secure appreciation of the difference between English and American customs.
C. A senior.	Athletic rally.	To urge attendance at a rally to be held that evening.

4. Review the five subjects you listed for Problem 3 in Chapter 8. For what other occasions and audiences would each topic be suitable?

5. Review several speeches that you have recently read or heard. Did the speakers attempt to adapt their remarks to the audience and the occasion? If so, what methods did they use?

Our chief task, really, is to arouse the more important but slumbering wants into action.

Harry Allen Overstreet

CHAPTER 10 / *Selecting the Basic Appeal*

[handwritten annotations: If we are to influ... their if primary mot... appeal to universal motives of audience. to influence the aud...]

The most carefully built speech is likely to fall flat unless it contains an appeal to the people who hear it. Before going further, then, we will consider briefly the universal motives which control human behavior. If the speech is to influence the audience, the main points of that speech must appeal to these motives, and nothing must be said that will contain a counterappeal.

A comic strip which used to appear in many newspapers described the activities of "Percy, the Mechanical Man." Percy was an automaton made of boiler plate, gas pipe, nuts, bolts, and clockwork. On his back were several rows of push buttons, similar to those on a cash register; these push buttons controlled his movements. When Percy's master wanted his garden spaded, he pressed the "digging" button, and Percy went to work; whenever there were errands to be run, or floors to be painted, or even burglars to be thrown out, pressing the right button immediately set Percy at the task.

In many ways we human beings are like Percy. We are not, of course, automatic machines operated by push buttons, but nearly everything we do or think or feel is based upon some fundamental motive or urge or drive within us that has been set in motion by some event or condition in our immediate experience. Someone calls me a liar, and I order him out of my room; he pressed the fighting button, and I became angry. Someone shows me that the only way I can get a job is to join the union; so I pay my union dues and join. I am told that a membership in a fraternity will insure my social prestige on the campus and help me get into activities, and I become pledged. My bed is so warm and the room so cold that I decide to stay in bed and miss my eight o'clock class; but recalling that I must pass that quiz at nine o'clock or flunk the course, I brave the cold and shiver into my clothes at eight-thirty. In each of these instances some latent force within me has been stirred to action: some button has been pressed.

Psychologists have called these powerful forces by different names depending upon the point of view of the particular psychologist. They have been called instincts, emotions, prepotent reflexes, purposive or wish-fulfilling drives, habitual action tendencies, and many other names. Many have been the arguments about the number of existing basic drives and the degree to which they are inborn or acquired through experience and habit. With the technical details of these arguments we are not concerned here. It is more important for us to realize: (*a*) that in all human beings there are certain universal action tendencies—the organism has within it the capacity and the tendency to move in different directions; and (*b*) that these tendencies are set in motion and modified in their direction by pressure put on the individual by his environment.[1]

---

[1] It will be noted here and elsewhere in the book that the psychological viewpoint of the author is frankly eclectic. He is familiar with the theories of present-day psychologists as well as the traditional psychology of the nineteenth century. He feels that while no one theory forms a complete basis for understanding the psychology of speech, all of them contribute illuminating suggestions. The fact that some of these theories are mutually irreconcilable weighs far less in the author's opinion than the fact that they have a practical value in the speaker's problems of analysis and speech construction. Thus, in the present instance, the author's discussion will be seen to combine the concept of *purposive* reaction originally advanced by McDougall with the idea of *tensions caused by unclosed patterns* advanced by Gestalt psychology.

To translate this in terms of the public speaker, we may say that the normal condition of the people in an audience is one of physical relaxation, mental inertia, and emotional equilibrium unless something has already happened to stir these people into motion or unless the speaker does so through the appeal which he makes. If, then, you are to accomplish the purpose of your speech, you must either overcome the inertia of the audience or counteract an existing tendency in order to move them in the direction of your purpose. You must puncture a hole in their apathy or opposition which will make them feel unsatisfied until they have reacted as you wish. But before you can do this, you must understand what these basic urges or universal action tendencies are, and you must know how to arouse them.

For the purpose of simplicity we shall call the basic forces that motivate human conduct and belief *primary motives;* and, because these primary motives are so often combined in complex patterns and concealed from external observation, we shall use the term *motive appeals* for the appeals to all the specific sentiments, emotions, and desires by which the speaker may set the primary motives into action.

THE PRIMARY MOTIVES

As has been noted, there have been many attempts to list the basic motives that underlie human behavior, and no two attempts have agreed. However, it is probably safe to say that all our behavior—our acts, our beliefs, our emotions—is motivated by one or a combination of these four primary motives:

1. Self-preservation and the desire for physical well-being.
2. Freedom from external restraint.
3. Preservation and increase of self-esteem (ego expansion).
4. Preservation of the human race.

Thus, we build a fire to keep from freezing or even from feeling cold (1); we abhor imprisonment and dislike laws which infringe upon what we call our personal liberty (2); we wear fine clothes, try to excel others in our accomplishments, enjoy praise, and dislike appearing in unfavorable circumstances (3); we marry, have children, organize governments, and impose legal penalties for antisocial conduct (4). The only limit in making an enumeration such as this is, of course, the infinite variety of human conduct itself.

These four basic motives vary in their power with different individuals. One man may care more for his comfort than his freedom; another, more for his family than himself. The influence which these motives have upon us is modified by experience, and there are certain periods in our lives when one or another motive matures and becomes most powerful. Furthermore, the immediate situation confronting us may call one of them into play more than any of the others. Regardless of these variations, however, all four of these forces are powerful factors in the life of every human being.

But the operation of these motives is not so simple. Unlike Percy, human beings do not wear their buttons in full view on their backs. The complexity of human life prevents the simple and direct fulfillment of these desires. Experience produces a large variety of composite desires, combinations of the four primary motives as they relate to the concrete objects of our environment. It is to these more specific and familiar patterns that the speaker must make his motive appeals.

TYPES OF MOTIVE APPEAL

A motive appeal was defined earlier in this chapter as an appeal to some sentiment, emotion, or desire by which the speaker might set the primary motives into action. There are, of course, an infinite number of these specific human wants, and any list of them must of necessity be incomplete and overlapping to some extent. Although the list on page 172 has both of these faults, it will be found quite practical. In it you will find the specific desires and sentiments to which appeals are almost universally effective. It will be worth your while to learn this list, to get a thorough understanding of the meaning of each item as discussed on pages 172–180, and to begin basing your analysis of people and the main points of your speeches upon them. You will note that some of these motive appeals work at cross purposes. An appeal to adventure, for example, may be offset by an appeal to fear. The discussion of methods of using motive appeals on pages 180–182 explains how to meet such problems.

1. Acquisition and Saving.
2. Adventure.
3. Companionship.
4. Creating.
   A. Organizing.
   B. Building.
5. Curiosity.
6. Destruction.
7. Fear.
8. Fighting.
   A. Anger.
   B. Competition.
9. Imitation.
10. Independence.
11. Loyalty.
    A. To friends.
    B. To family (parental or filial love).
    C. To social groups (school spirit, civic pride).
    D. To nation (patriotism).
12. Personal Enjoyment.
    A. Of comfort and luxury.
    B. Of beauty and order.
    C. Of pleasant sensations (tastes, smells, etc.).
    D. Of recreation.
    E. Of relief from restraint (sprees, etc.).
13. Power and Authority.
14. Pride.
    A. Reputation.
    B. Self-respect.
15. Reverence or Worship.
    A. Of leaders (hero worship).
    B. Of traditions or institutions.
    C. Of the Deity.
16. Revulsion.
17. Sexual Attraction.
18. Sympathy.

Acquisition and saving This motive is most generally used in connection with money and property. We all like to get money, to keep it, and to spend as little of it as we can to get other things we want. Bargain basements are filled with people trying to acquire as much as possible at the lowest price. But this motive applies to other things besides money. Many hobbies, such as stamp collecting, the keeping of dance programs or of photo albums, and the gathering of art treasures or rare books, are forms of this tendency. Nevertheless, the most common appeal here is, "You will make money," or "You will save money."

Adventure Most people like the thrill of mild danger. It is high adventure to go to the South Pole, or to climb the Alps, or to fly an airplane for the first time. Youngsters rarely climb the safest tree; roller coasters coin money on the thrills they give; some motorists drive as fast as possible even when they don't have to "get there." When acquisition and adventure are combined—as they are in most forms of gambling, from slot machines to stock speculation—the chance to win exerts a powerful force. Given the assurance that there is a fair chance of safety and that some worth-while objective is in view, most of us like the thrill of a gamble. Note that the healthy vigor of youth, its limited experience, and its lack of heavy responsibilities make it more subject to the motive of adventure than maturity or old age.

Companionship

A few people are hermits, but most of us like company. We cross the street to walk with a friend rather than be alone. We go to parties, join clubs, prefer to live in dormitories or fraternity houses—these and many other things just to avoid loneliness. Even in our beliefs and opinions we tend to go along with the crowd. The most humdrum work becomes more bearable if others are doing it with us.

Creating

We like to be able to say, "I made this myself." The urge to create shows itself in many ways: inventions, books, buildings, business organizations, empires. In addition to the creative *arts* (painting, music, writing, etc.), this tendency takes two more general forms: *building* with physical objects, such as bricks, steel, wood; and *organizing* human beings into working units—political parties, business firms, athletic teams, etc. Indeed, this desire is behind many campus activities.

Curiosity

Children still tear open alarm clocks to find out where the tick is, and adults still crowd the sidewalks to watch a celebrity pass by. Nor is curiosity mere "nosiness," as is so often implied; it forms the motivation of the experimental scientist, the explorer (together with adventure, of course), and every serious-minded student. Without curiosity, life would be a dull and static thing.

Destruction

There seems to be in most of us a frequent impulse to tear down, to break, to cut to pieces, to destroy. Perhaps this impulse arises from the desire to show our superiority over the things we destroy and thus to expand our ego, or it may arise from the desire to break from restraint. In any event, we all are destroyers at times. Build a block house for a baby, and he knocks it down. Let someone present a theory or an argument, and we enjoy tearing it to pieces. There is always a crowd at a fire, and one of the reasons is that something is burning down. Nor is this tendency entirely antisocial; after all, the old must be destroyed before the new can take its place. The radical agitator who shouts "Down with everything" may be disliked by many of us, but he sometimes performs a valuable service.

Fear

Danger has both its positive and its negative effects. It may prevent us from doing things that bring peril, and it may make us act to protect ourselves against that peril. If the other man is bigger than I, I shall hesitate to attack him, but I may go home and put a lock on the door to keep him out. But physical injury is not the only thing we fear. We are afraid of losing our jobs, our property, our friends. Especially do we fear the unknown, the dangerous power of what is hidden. This is one reason for stage fright. As practice makes us familiar with the situation of confronting an audience, this feeling dies.

Fighting

Human beings seem to take a distinct pleasure and interest in conflict. At least all of us have the tendency to fight. In its natural form, fighting is accompanied by *anger* aroused by some opposing force or person. Thus, we become angry at persons who insult us (attack our ego) or destroy our property or interfere with our efforts. The form which our fighting back may take varies all the way from physical attack to subtle gossip or organized financial opposition. Society frowns on assault and battery; so we use more civilized and legal methods of attack such as social ostracism and court action. But show any man that he is being cheated, insulted, or attacked, and he will become angry and fight in some way or other.

But there is another form which this fighting tendency takes in modern society—*competition*. We enjoy matching wit or muscle with antagonists, even though we are not angry with them, for the sheer pleasure of the struggle or the demonstration of greater skill. Most athletic games are based on this tendency; many people argue just for this reason; business competition, card games, and even scholastic rivalry all have the element of competition behind them. The prevalent use of the phrase "We *beat* them" to indicate the winning of such competitive engagements suggests the fighting nature of the effort.

Imitation

People tend to imitate others both consciously and unconsciously. When "cat's pajamas," "twenty-three skidoo," and "I love my wife but oh, you kid" were popular expressions, every college student used them. But slang is not the only thing we imitate. We copy the beliefs, the attitudes, the actions, the gestures and pronunciations of others, especially of those we admire or respect. Tell someone how a famous person does a thing or how he attained his success, and your hearer is likely to imitate that person.

Independence

In spite of the tendency to imitate, we do not like to lose our independence: we do not like to be *forced* to imitate. A woman's dress must be in style, but at the same time it must not be exactly like any other dress—it must be individual. We do not like to be bossed around, or to have to attend class, or to be prohibited from doing things we like. If you can make your hearer feel he is doing a thing from his own choice, he will be much more likely to do it than if you tell him he must do it. Workmen have quit their jobs; members have resigned from clubs; nations have engaged in revolutions—to maintain the feeling of independent action.

Loyalty

The sentiment of loyalty, which is based upon the individual's tendency to identify himself with other persons or groups, is sometimes a very strong motive. The strength of this appeal will vary, of course, with the degree to which the individual has become so identified. Hence, a man's loyalty to his family is usually stronger than his loyalty to his college. A few of the more important types of loyalties are:

Loyalty to friends. We will do more for persons to whom we are affectionately attached than for chance acquaintances or strangers. People resent slurs upon their friends and are more likely to believe in their friends' opinions than in those of strangers.

Loyalty to family. Sometimes family loyalty is referred to as *parental or filial love.* Brothers may fight with one another, but let some outsider attack one of them, and their differences are forgotten in a common loyalty to each other. Men buy life insurance to protect their wives and children; mothers give largely of their time and strength for the good of their children; the pleasure of a visit from mother or father is a very real one.

Loyalty to social groups. Such terms as *school spirit, civic pride,* and *club morale* indicate the types of loyalty included here. Let someone challenge the status of a fraternity, and all its members are up in arms; let some group begin an undertaking, and its loyal members will almost always give that undertaking their full support.

Loyalty to nation: patriotism. A very definite patriotic loyalty is instilled in all of us throughout our lives. Schools, books, newspapers, moving pictures, and civic celebrations constantly maintain the stimulus for this loyalty. We depend upon our government for our safety, and we support it when our support is demanded. In prosperous and peaceful times our loyalty to political parties or sectional interests may be stronger than this larger loyalty, but let danger, economic or military, threaten and patriotic sentiment reasserts itself.

One word of warning should be given. Appeals to loyalty are so easily made that they are often overdone. After too much repetition they lose their force and become nothing but rubber-stamped expressions. Especially avoid such trite and soporific phrases as "the constitushun uv our grea-a-a-t Republic!" When used sparingly and sincerely, the appeal to loyalties is powerful; but it must not become monotonous or shallow.

Personal enjoyment Man's pleasures are many and varied, and he will usually act to prevent their being curtailed or to increase the facilities for enjoying them. A few types of pleasures universally enjoyed are:

Enjoyment of comfort and luxury. Most people prefer to sit on overstuffed furniture. If one can afford it, he gets a reservation in a sleeping car rather than sit up all night in a coach; he takes a cab instead of a crowded bus. What pleasure there is in stopping at a luxuriously appointed hotel with impeccable dining-room service! One reason why people work so hard to get money is to enjoy the comfort and luxury it will buy for them.

Enjoyment of beauty and order. Most of us like to have things clean and neat, even if we may not want to expend the effort to keep them so. There is an esthetic pleasure in the beauty of autumn foliage in the northern woods, in the cadence of the surf, or the product of the skilled artist that gives an exaltation otherwise unknown. But even a neat outline, an orderly boiler room, or a well-pressed suit contributes to one's esthetic pleasure. Many a customer has bought an automobile more because of its luxurious appointments and the beauty of its body lines than essentially because of its economy or mechanical excellence.

Enjoyment of pleasant sensations. Sights, sounds, smells, tastes, feelings that gratify the sensory organs—the eyes, the ears, the nose, the palate, and the like—give special pleasure to most people. Obviously, the pleasures listed in the last two paragraphs are closely associated with this type since they are also sensory in nature. But sensory pleasure exists even without beauty or luxury; it is more direct in its appeal. Regardless of the comfort, luxury, beauty, or orderliness of it, the *taste* of roast turkey on Thanksgiving gives pleasure. The smell and taste of a pipe filled with rare tobacco or of a bowl of steaming tomato soup are further examples.

Enjoyment of recreation. Who does not like to play? The crowded golf courses, the steady stream of tourists to vacation spots, the popularity of certain television programs, and the enormous sale of paperback fiction give an overwhelming answer. Everyone likes to break away from his regular work and engage in interesting activities which have no serious purpose. Show your audience the *fun* they will have in doing a certain thing, and the impulse to do it will grow strong.

Enjoyment of the relief from restraint. Have you ever listened to the laughter and shouts of children when they are let out from school in the afternoon? Similarly, college students appreciate a holiday because it is a relief from the restraint of regular attendance on other days. Note also the joyous attitude of the person who has just been allowed to break from a rigid diet. This tendency to break away after confinement is naturally prevalent everywhere.

Power and authority

Most of us like to exert our influence over others. Men have given up lucrative positions to become President of the United States at a much smaller salary. Why? Among other reasons, they have done so because their power over others is increased and the principles they believed right can be more easily established. Very few persons will refuse the election or appointment to office if that office gives them some authority. Show your audience what additional power your proposal will give to them or to the group or nation to which they belong. To many men, self-advancement means not only an increased income but also an increase in power and authority. Together these two appeals are almost irresistible.

Pride

Perhaps the strongest single appeal that can be made is to pride, especially when you are dealing with young people. A varsity letter has little intrinsic value, but an unbelievable amount of work will be done to earn one. Election to an honorary society has more importance to the average student than a cash award. But the influence of pride is not limited to the age of adolescence; from childhood to old age we are extremely careful of our egos.

It should be noted that pride takes two directions: *reputation* and *self-respect*. Of these two the desire for self-respect is the more fundamental, but in practical situations the desire for a good reputation has a more tangible appeal. Reputation is the estimate others have of you, while self-respect is the opinion you wish to have of yourself. For most of us, it is difficult to have one without the other. To influence an audience, then, show them what effect your idea will have upon their reputation, but be careful not to suggest something incompatible with their self-respect. In particular beware of offering the praise of some person whom your listeners regard so unfavorably that to accept his praise would be to lower their self-respect. Nor can the appeal to pride be too obvious: oily compliments are seldom liked.

Reverence or worship There are times when all of us are aware of a sense of our own inferiority in relation to a superior person or thing. This sentiment shows itself in a feeling of humility and a willingness to subordinate ourselves. It takes three common forms: *hero worship,* or the deep admiration of other persons; *reverence for traditions and institutions;* and *worship of the Deity,* whether it be conceived as religious or as spiritually philosophical. The first of these, hero worship, is more common in children, but it sometimes exists in adults, especially in their admiration of business, political, or social leaders whose personal qualities have made a strong impression on them. Toward certain traditions and institutions we have a strong feeling of reverence: we sit quietly and with bared heads at a funeral; the national anthem brings us to our feet; we consider the principle of democratic government a sacred thing. The feeling of worship for the Deity has come down to us through the ages. It shows itself formally in religious exercises; but even the man who rejects formal religion is awe-struck when he gazes at the immensity of the heavens or feels the full fury of a storm. He may call himself Christian, Jew, Buddhist, Mohammedan, or atheist—but his feeling of reverence is nonetheless real. The wise speaker respects the heroes, traditions, and religious attitudes of his audience and avoids the antagonism which opposition to them may bring. At times an appeal to these sentiments may add an enormous force to the arguments which he may use.

Revulsion Just as a fragrant garden of flowers attracts people, so a dump heap repels them. Just as there is enjoyment in pleasant sensory experiences, so unpleasant ones are revolting. By showing the unpleasant conditions in the city slums, you may create sentiment to clean them up; if you can get people disgusted with graft and corruption in public office, they will vote against those who allow it; by picturing the distasteful results of a proposal, you can turn people against it. While doing these things, however, you must beware of making your description so gruesome that your speech itself becomes revolting. Supreme tact is often needed to make a description of revolting conditions vivid enough without offending the audience's good taste.

Sexual attraction — Men strive for the attentions of women, and women seek to attract men. The importance of this force in human life needs no emphasis here. Whenever a proposal will make us more attractive in the eyes of the opposite sex or will remove an obstacle to that attraction, that proposal gains our support. The taboos society has placed upon sexual matters require that the speaker use extreme care in referring to them. Vulgar stories in particular are revolting to most audiences. Nevertheless, though this appeal is rarely made by itself, using it serves to strengthen other appeals the speaker may employ.

Sympathy — Just as we are likely to identify ourselves with the groups to which we belong or aspire to belong, so we are apt to see ourselves in the plight of those who are unfortunate. This feeling of compassion for the unfortunate, which we call sympathy, makes us want to help them. We pause to help a blind man or to question a crying child. We give money to feed people whose homes have been ravaged by flood, earthquake, or fire. As a speaker, you may influence your audience by arousing in them the sentiment of pity. To do so, however, remember that you must make it easy for them to identify themselves with the unfortunate ones, to put themselves in the others' shoes. You cannot accomplish this with statistics and abstractions; you must describe individuals, and describe them vividly.

USING MOTIVE APPEALS

The sentiments or desires that have been described are some of those to which motive appeals may be made. Remember, though, that these appeals are not always made singly but are often combined. In fact, you have probably noticed that in many of the examples given above some other appeal was present in addition to the one being illustrated. For example, most students attend college in order to improve their chances of self-advancement. But what is involved in this desire for self-advancement? A desire for greater income, the power of higher position, and the pride of a higher station in life—all these, acquisition, power, pride, are combined into the one pattern called "getting ahead." Or let us take another common experience; suppose you were going to buy a suit or a dress. What would influence your decision? One thing would be its price—*saving;* another would be its comfort and appearance—the *pleasure* to be derived from beauty or luxury; another consideration would be its style—*imitation*—or its individuality of appearance—*independence;* and finally, a combination of these items would make an appeal to *pride:* Would other people think the clothes in good taste; would they envy your selection? Some of these desires might be stronger than others, and some might conflict with each other, but all of them would affect your choice, and you would buy whichever suit or dress made the strongest appeal to these desires.

Yet, while using a variety of appeals is valuable in a speech, using too many can dissipate its effect. Usually it is best to select two or three motives which you think will have the strongest appeal to your audience and to concentrate on these few motives, allowing other appeals to be incidental. Be sure that you do not use conflicting appeals—for instance, urging your audience to do something because of the *adventure* involved while describing it so vividly that they *fear* the act or its consequences. To avoid this, select as the main points of your speech arguments that contain basic appeals and examine them for clarity and consistency.

For example, a student who was urging his classmates to participate in interclass athletic contests chose the following as the main points of his speech:

1. Concentrated study without exercise will make your mind stale and ruin your grades (*fear*).

2. By playing with others you will make new friends (*companionship*).

3. Interclass competition may lead to a place for you on the varsity teams (*power* and *pride*).

4. You will have a great deal of fun playing (*enjoyment of recreation*).

In the complete development of his speech, this student made incidental appeals to imitation through examples of those who had previously engaged in interclass sports; he stimulated the desire for competition; he suggested that participation would indicate loyalty to the class; but the principal appeal was made to those few motives which were incorporated in his main points.

In most cases you cannot express your appeal to motives directly or too obviously. To do so would make the technic too prominent and would develop resistance in the audience. You would not say, "I want you to *imitate* Jones, the successful banker," nor would you say, "If you give to this cause, we will print your name so that your *reputation* as a generous man will be known to everybody." Instead, you must make the appeal effective through the suggestion of these things carried in the descriptions and illustrations you use. Furthermore, we are ashamed to acknowledge publicly some motive appeals which are privately powerful, such as the appeal to greed, fear, imitation, or pride. Therefore, when these appeals are used in a public speech, they must be carefully disguised and supplemented by other appeals which we can publicly admit as the cause of our action.

APPEALING TO FIXED ATTITUDES AND OPINIONS

The choice and phrasing of motive appeals may be further influenced by the existence of crystallized and fairly specific attitudes among the listeners. Either as the result of personal experience or because of repeated assertions by parents, teachers, respected friends, and accepted authorities, people tend to develop pretty definite opinions about many things in their environment. They are "for" or "against" labor unions, military preparedness, professional athletics, fraternities; they consider policemen, politicians, nurses, flyers, lawyers, and Frenchmen as good or bad, unreliable or trustworthy, ignorant or intelligent; they like or dislike popular music, flashy clothes, mathematics, traveling on buses. Crystallized attitudes and opinions of this sort are usually based on a combination of motives, but in the process of fixation the underlying motivation becomes submerged, and the specific attitude or opinion becomes the dominating influence. With respect to any particular subject, therefore, you must consider not only the primary motives of your audience and the more universal types of motive appeal but also the specific attitudes and opinions into which these motives have developed. By associating your ideas and proposals with the positive attitudes of your audience and by avoiding negative associations, you can make your appeal more direct and powerful.

PROBLEMS

1. Be ready to discuss the following questions in class: How do primary motives and motive appeals differ? What motive appeals might be most effective for an audience predominantly of young persons? Of older persons? Of men? Of women? What motive appeals might be naturally and effectively combined? What combination of appeals might produce a negative response?

2. Clip ten advertisements from some current popular magazine and for each one list the motive appeals used in it. Select the strongest motive appeal in each advertisement and explain how it was made.

3. Assuming your speech class to be the audience, list the motive appeals which you think would most effectively support each of the following beliefs. Which motive appeals would most effectively serve to oppose these beliefs?
Compulsory class attendance should be abolished.
Motion pictures should be censored to protect public morals.
The United States should unilaterally disarm her military forces.

4. Support your view on any one of the propositions above by preparing a short speech in which you concentrate upon one of the motive appeals you listed. Employ as many different methods as possible to make that appeal strong.

5. Identify the motive appeals used by each speaker in the next group of class speeches. In each case, which one seemed to be the most effective? Were any conflicting appeals used in the same speech?

Every man is born with the faculty of reason and the faculty of speech, but why should he be able to speak before he has anything to say?

Benjamin Whichcote

CHAPTER 11 / *Where to Go for Speech Material*

F or most speeches it will be necessary to find out more about the subject than you already know, and in every case it will be helpful to classify the information you already have. You must investigate the facts before framing your arguments or outlining your explanation, and you will continue to search for additional material as you fill in the details of your speech. The methods of recording and classifying data vary so much that no one method can be exclusively recommended. It is the purpose of this chapter, however, to suggest the variety of sources where speech material can be found, and to explain at least one practicable method of handling the material gathered. Begin by following the suggestions offered below and then modify your method of research to suit your own experience.

Whatever the subject of your speech may be, you must start with what you already know about it. A good way to begin is to jot down on a piece of paper what things you know about your subject and what you have to find out. (You will discover as your study continues that both of these lists will grow: the more you learn, the more you will find there is to learn.) Of particular importance as speech material are the facts and experiences which you acquire first-hand.

Personal experience — Personal experiences are often quite vivid and can be presented realistically to the audience. Such information may come from past experience or from observations planned especially to secure it. First of all try to remember as many personal experiences or observations connected with your subject as you can. Then, if possible, add to your experience by further observations of the conditions you wish to discuss in your speech. Even if your own direct experience cannot appropriately be cited, it will give you increased conviction and depth of insight which will help you talk straight from the shoulder.

Interviews — Few of us realize the vast amount of information that can be gathered merely by asking questions. If you are discussing some subject dealing with athletics, who is better qualified to inform you than a member of your college athletic department? Nearly all faculty members will be willing to discuss with you questions pertaining to their fields of special interest. Whether in school or in later life, you can usually locate experts on some phase of your subject in your own community. Of course, you must avoid being bothersome or impertinent; but sensible questions asked tactfully will give you much that you need.

To save the time of your expert and to insure your getting the desired information, prepare for the interview by writing down the questions you particularly want answered. Be sure to explain your purpose at the beginning of the interview—or when you make your appointment. During the interview, keep in mind that your object is to obtain the expert's facts and opinions on the subject, not to impart your own. If your opinion is asked, give it, of course, but state it briefly and tactfully. Be very sure that you understand the expert's answer; if you are not sure, rephrase his statement or ask him to clarify it. As you listen, make careful mental notes of his points, and record them as soon as you can after the interview. Detailed facts that you think you may want to quote later will need to be written down during the interview. And don't forget to obtain the expert's permission to quote him.

Even if an interview provides you with no quotable facts, it will have given you a broader outlook on the question and may suggest other sources of information. But do not always limit your interviews to experts; sometimes valuable points of view may be secured from the man on the street, from your fellow students, or from neighbors and friends. The broader your background, the better your speech is likely to be.

Letters and questionnaires   Additional information may often be obtained by writing to experts whom it is impossible to see in person. Be sure when you write that you make clear why you want the information and what exact information you want. When there is a difference of opinion on some point and you want to get a cross section of these opinions, send a questionnaire to a number of people and compare their answers. This method is valuable but has been somewhat overdone, so that many people who would answer a personal letter will throw a form questionnaire, particularly a long one, into the wastebasket. Make your questions as easy to answer as possible; and make the list of questions brief. Always enclose a stamped, self-addressed envelope for the reply. If you can find out the man's name and title and address him personally instead of mailing your questions, for example, to "The Head of the Economics Department, X—— University," you will be more likely to receive an answer.

Printed material   The most abundant source of speech material is printed matter—newspapers, magazines, pamphlets, and books. The principal types of printed sources are discussed in the following pages:

Newspapers. A great deal of information about events of current interest will be found in daily papers. The illustrations and unusual instances which fill the papers are especially valuable in holding your audience's attention. You must be careful not to accept everything printed in the newspaper as the gospel truth, however, for the very haste with which news is printed sometimes makes complete accuracy impossible. Your school or city library probably keeps on file copies of one or two papers of the most reliable sort, such as the *New York Times,* the *Christian Science Monitor,* and others. Important presidential speeches and foreign news may be found in these papers. If your library has the *New York Times,* it probably has the published index to that paper, and by using it you can locate accounts of men and events for the past fifty years.

Magazines. Generally, magazines report facts more accurately than do the newspapers because they are edited more carefully. Magazines, however, are usually journals of opinion, and opinions are subject to prejudice. There are many different types of magazines: those containing articles of general interest, such as *The Saturday Evening Post* and *McCall's;* those summarizing weekly events, such as *Time, Newsweek,* and *U. S. News and World Report.* (*The New Yorker* treats "goings on" in a critical vein.) *The Atlantic* and *Harper's* are monthly publications which cover a wide range of subjects. Such magazines as *The Nation, Vital Speeches of the Day, Fortune, The Reporter,* and *New Republic* contain comment on current political, social, and economic questions; discussions of popular scientific interest appear in *Popular Science Monthly, Scientific American,* and *Popular Mechanics Magazine.* There are also many magazines of specialized interest—for example, *Theatre Arts, Field and Stream, The Saturday Review, Better Homes and Gardens, Today's Health, National Geographic Magazine,* and *American Heritage.*

This list is, of course, decidedly incomplete. Its purpose is merely to illustrate the wide range of material to be found in periodicals. When you are looking for a specific sort of information it is usually a waste of time to search haphazardly through a large number of magazines. Learn to use the *Readers' Guide,* which is a classified index of practically all magazine articles. Look in this index under various topical headings that are related to your subject. Similar indexes are also available for technical journals and publications.

Professional and trade journals. Nearly every profession, industry, trade, or field of academic interest is represented by one or more specialized journals. Such publications are: *The Annals of the American Academy of Political and Social Science, American Political Science Review, Quarterly Journal of Speech, Journal of the American Medical Association, Journal of Applied Psychology, AFL-CIO American Federationist, Trade Unionist, Coal Age,* and others. These journals contain a great deal of specialized information in their respective fields.

Yearbooks and encyclopedias. The *Statistical Abstract of the United States* is the most reliable source of comprehensive data on a wide variety of subjects ranging from weather and birth rates to coal production. It is published by the federal government and is available in most libraries. Similar volumes are the *Information Please Almanac* and the *World Almanac and Book of Facts,* published by McGraw-Hill and the New York World-Telegram respectively. Encyclopedias, which attempt to reduce the entire field of human knowledge into a score of volumes, are valuable chiefly for condensed information. Refer to them for quick location of important scientific, geographical, literary, or historical facts.

Special documents and reports. Various governmental agencies, both state and national, and many independent organizations publish reports on special subjects, for example: the reports of Congressional committees, or of the United States Department of Labor or of Commerce; the reports of the experimental branches of state universities on agricultural problems and engineering and scientific experimentation; the reports on business conditions published by such firms as the Babson Institute and the Standard Statistics Company; and the reports of such endowed organizations as the Carnegie, Rockefeller, and Ford Foundations.

Books on special subjects. There are few subjects suitable for a speech upon which someone has not written a book. If you don't know how to find these books in the card catalog of the library, ask the librarian to show you.

General literature. A wide reading of general literature will provide you with a wealth of illustrations and literary allusions which frequently can be used to illuminate your speech. Quick sources of apt quotations are such books as Bartlett's *Familiar Quotations*, H. L. Mencken's *A New Dictionary of Quotations on Historical Principles from Ancient and Modern Sources,* Arthur Richmond's *Modern Quotations for Ready Reference,* George Seldes' *The Great Quotations,* and Burton Stevenson's *The Home Book of Quotations.*

Biography. The detailed accounts of famous people's lives often furnish material for the illustration and amplification of many ideas. *Who's Who in America, Current Biography,* and similar volumes, which contain brief biographical sketches of contemporary persons, are useful in locating facts about famous people and in finding the qualifications of authorities whose testimony you wish to quote.

Radio and television broadcasts — Lectures, debates, and often the addresses of noted persons are broadcast over radio and television. Many of these talks are mimeographed by the stations or by the organizations that sponsor the broadcast, and copies of them may be secured by writing for them. If no manuscript is available and you are taking notes as you hear the broadcast, listen particularly carefully in order to get an exact record of the speaker's words and meaning. Just as you must quote items from other sources accurately and honestly, so you are obligated to respect the remarks someone has made on a radio or television broadcast and to give him credit.

Obviously, you will not have to investigate all the sources listed above for every speech. Your personal experience will often provide you with adequate knowledge, or you will need to locate only one or two additional facts. Usually, however, a search among several of the sources listed above will provide you with material for a more interesting speech. Even though laborious at first, a careful study of these sources will be doubly valuable since you will be learning how to skim rapidly through a mass of material and pick out the important parts. This skill is valuable not only in public speaking but in every type of work where research is required. The time you take to gather material will be reduced as you become more expert in your method of investigation; watch for ways to eliminate waste motion in your pursuit of material.

Have you ever begun to tell a good story you once heard and found that it had slipped your mind entirely? Or have you ever tried in vain to recall an important illustration? Since it is impossible to remember all the data you read, some means of recording these facts is imperative. Many people use notebooks, but they are not so efficient as cards. Cards of various sizes may be secured (3 x 5, or 4 x 6 are recommended) and a few kept in your pocket or briefcase for use whenever you come across material you want to record. These cards may be kept permanently in a classified file. Then when you are ready to organize your speech, they will be easy to sort and rearrange. Furthermore, figures or quotations which you may want to read to your audience will thus be in a handy form to use when giving your speech. The samples opposite show how such cards may be filled out. Note the following characteristics of these record cards which should always be observed:

Use a heading, in the upper left-hand corner, which accurately labels the material recorded on the card. This will simplify the process of sorting and selection when you begin to organize a specific speech.

Note, in the upper right-hand corner, the classification of the material with relation to the subject of your speech. If such classification is not possible early in your research, leave space to write it in later.

Put only one fact, or a few closely related facts, on one card. If you put too many facts or unrelated facts on one card, you will lose the simplicity of classifying and sorting which the card system affords.

Indicate by proper marks whether the quotation is verbatim. In the second sample card, the first note is a direct quotation. Use exact quotations when they are sufficiently brief; condense and paraphrase longer passages, but be sure to interpret fairly.

Note the exact source of the information at the bottom of the card. This point cannot be stressed too strongly. To forget where the information came from is easy, and frequently you will want to go back to that source for further data. Moreover, you may need to defend the reliability of your information. You *must* know the source.

British, Allied, and Neutral Shipping Losses   (classification)
January - June 1945   War at Sea

Month — No. of Ships:	British	Allied	Neutral	Total*
January	9	9	—	18
February	13	12	1	26
March	13	13	1	27
April	11	11	—	22
May	1	3	—	4
June	—	2	—	2

(*Total of 99 ships represents 429,742 gross tons)

Winston S. Churchill, The Second World War: Triumph and Tragedy, Vol. VI (Houghton Mifflin, 1953), p. 724.

Water Supply   (classification)
and Demand   The Problem

"There are three major groups of problems of matching water demand and supply in the United States: (1) those of timing discontinuities when fluctuations in the availability of water supply do not correspond to those in demand for water and water-derived services; (2) those of quality, where the natural supply does not meet quality requirements of one or more important uses; and (3) those of quantity, where there is a consistent inequality between demand and available supply in a region or locality."

Edward A. Ackerman and George O. G. Löf, Technology in American Water Development (The Johns Hopkins Press, 1959), p. 79.

When you first begin to gather material, a simple topical method of classification is satisfactory. Group the cards together according to the apparent similarity of the headings in the upper left corner. But as the number of cards increases, you will need a more systematic method. A few possible methods are the following:

Chronological. You may classify your material on the basis of the time to which it refers—by years, by months, or by its relation, before or after, to some fixed event.

Causal. This method divides material relating to causes into certain classes, and that relating to results into others.

Problem-solution. Here the facts about a problem are grouped apart from the descriptions of the various solutions and the evidence which shows them to be good or bad. (The second sample card uses this method.)

Location. When this method is used, the material is divided according to the localities, countries, states, or other space units to which it refers.

Divide the material into a few large classifications according to one of these methods, and then as the material in any one class gets unwieldy, subdivide that class.

The value of classifying your material as you gather it is twofold. In the first place, you can see at a glance what type of material you lack and in this way plan your further investigation. Secondly, the actual process of organizing material into a speech is made much simpler. Furthermore, if you continue this method of preserving the material you gather over a period of time, you will find a steadily growing mass of information at your disposal.

This process of gathering, recording, and classifying material for your speech is no small part of the task of preparation, and you will do well to begin early enough so that you will have plenty of time to digest the information, organize it, and practice presenting it in its finished form.

PROBLEMS

1. Be ready to discuss the following questions in class: When searching for speech material, what is the first source to consider? What technics

are useful in interviews? What kinds of printed material are available to the speaker? Why should speech material be recorded and classified?

2. Visit the library and list the following:
   A. Five yearbooks or compilations of statistical data.
   B. Three technical magazines.
   C. The different headings under which articles dealing with some subject are listed in the *Readers' Guide.*
   D. A special index that includes publications in your vocational field.

3. Locate the answers to the following in the library:
   A. How many miles of interstate highways have been completed to date?
   B. Where did Adlai Stevenson attend college?
   C. How did the U.S. Senators from your state vote on foreign aid legislation last year?
   D. What were the weather conditions last Christmas in Bangor, Maine, and San Diego, California?
   E. How does your state government help finance local public schools?

4. Select the subject for one of your future class speeches, and:
   A. Outline all the pertinent information you already have on it.
   B. Indicate the possible first-hand observations you can make in regard to it.
   C. List persons whom you can interview on the subject, and decide what questions you will ask each one.
   D. Devise a sample questionnaire which you might employ and indicate to whom it might be sent.
   E. Prepare a bibliography of printed material on the subject, including (1) references from the periodical index, and (2) references from the card catalog of books in the library.

5. Record your material (of Problem 4) on cards; bring five of these cards, properly filled out, to class for criticism. Outline a method for classifying your material on this subject.

6. On slips of paper write three questions beginning "Where would you go to find out about——?" Put these questions in a hat with those submitted by your classmates and take turns drawing them out for discussion.

That which is asserted without proof may also be denied without proof.

Legal Maxim

CHAPTER 12 / *Supporting Main Points*

H uman beings, especially when they compose an audience, are not inclined to accept abstract ideas, bare and unadorned. Nor will they easily believe a proposition or act upon a proposal without proof or stimulation. A contractor proposed to me that I buy a lot and build a house. I was only mildly interested and would have dismissed the matter entirely but for my personal friendship for him. But he did not let the matter drop. He told me the details about the house he was building for one of my colleagues; he produced rough plans and drawings for a house to fit my needs; he figured out the cost and the methods of financing; he showed me an attractive lot upon which the house could be built. Today I am living in the house the contractor talked to me about. He made an abstract idea real to me by various methods of development and proof.

In giving a speech, you must, of course, have clearly in mind the points you wish to clarify or prove to your audience, and you must state them briefly and simply; but if you leave them undeveloped, your audience may miss their meaning or doubt their truth. The two questions listeners most often ask themselves about statements are "What does he *mean* by that?" and "What *proof* is there that he is right?" To answer these questions and drive home your points in a clear and compelling manner, you will need to understand and use the various forms of supporting material.

We may define these forms of support as the types of speech material which are used to amplify, clarify, or prove a statement in order to make it more illuminating or convincing to an audience. Without such supporting material, the thoughts in a speech may be as well organized as the bones in a skeleton, but they will be equally bare and unappealing. The forms of support are the flesh and blood which bring your speech to life. The thought-skeleton of your speech must be there to give it unity and coherence, but it is the meat which you put upon that skeleton that gives it body and warmth and reality for your audience. You must round out your points with examples that will make them clear and vivid—with verbal material that is concrete and specific —and when appropriate, with visible support, such as charts, diagrams, and models.

THE FORMS OF VERBAL SUPPORTING MATERIAL

In general, there are seven forms of verbal support which may be used to develop the ideas in a speech:
1. Explanation.
2. Analogy or Comparison.
3. Illustration (detailed example).
    A. Hypothetical illustration.
    B. Factual illustration.
4. Specific Instances (undeveloped examples).
5. Statistics.
6. Testimony.
7. Restatement.

Many times two or more of these are combined, as when figures are used to detail an illustration, or a comparison is made between two sets of statistics, or the testimony of an expert is given to add weight to a restatement. As you consider the following explanations of these seven types of material, notice that the first three (explanation, comparison, and illustration) are primarily useful in making an idea clear and vivid, while the next three (instances, statistics, and testimony) have the function of establishing and verifying its truth or importance. Restatement, of course, serves for emphasis.

Explanation

A complete explanation often involves the use of several of the other forms of support. In fact, an entire chapter (Chapter 20) will be devoted to speeches in which the whole purpose may be to explain. As used here, however, the term refers to a simple explanation and not to any such detailed development. It is a simple, concise exposition, setting forth the relation between a whole and its parts or making clear an obscure term. Notice how the late Justice Brandeis made clear what is meant by a "profession":

The peculiar character of a profession as distinguished from other occupations, I take to be these: *First.* A profession is an occupation for which the necessary preliminary training is intellectual in character, involving knowledge and to some extent learning, as distinguished from mere skill. *Second.* It is an occupation which is pursued largely for others and not merely for one's self. *Third.* It is an occupation in which the amount of financial return is not the accepted measure of success.[1]

Another example is Bernard Baruch's explanation of the unregulated operation of the law of supply and demand:

To begin with, just how does supply and demand really work? Any number of you students here may be itching to rattle off an answer to that question. Your reply probably would run like this:

When demand rises, prices go up. This stimulates production. With good profits being earned, new producers enter into competition, adding to the supply. Substitutes come onto the market. As prices rise, consumers also buy less. In time, as demand lessens and supply increases, a balance is struck and prices start coming down. With this fall in prices, the processes of adjustment reverse themselves. The newest or highest cost producers are forced out of production or they lower their

---

[1] From "Business—a Profession." Printed in *Modern Speeches* (F. S. Crofts, N.Y., 1926), edited by Homer D. Lindgren, p. 106.

output. As prices fall, substitutes disappear from the market. Lower prices also stimulate demand. People go out to buy that automobile or house or new clothes which they put off buying when prices were high. Again, in time, as demand expands and supply shrinks, a new balance is found and prices start up again.[2]

In neither speech from which the preceding examples were taken did the speakers content themselves with explanation alone. In each case the idea was amplified by the use of one or more of the other forms of support. Be careful, too, not to make an explanation too long and abstract. Many an audience has been put to sleep by a long-winded explanation full of abstract details.

Analogy or comparison   In an analogy or comparison similarities are pointed out between that which is already known, or believed, and that which is not. Analogies may be either literal or figurative. Thomas Edison is reported to have used the following figurative analogy to explain the operation of electricity in a telegraph: it is, he said, "like a Dachshund long enough to reach from Edinburgh to London; when you pull his tail in Edinburgh, he barks in London." [3] Tyler Dennett, former President of Williams College, quoted a Massachusetts statesman as having once described the difference between a democracy and a dictatorship as follows:

It is the difference between a raft and a yacht. On the yacht you are safe if you have a good captain as dictator. On the raft your feet are wet all the time, but you never sink.[4]

Mr. Justice Robert H. Jackson, addressing an audience of college deans, used the following comparison:

In the north country the final test of a man is whether he can safely guide a canoe through "white water," as they call the swirling and rushing rapids. The world has an overabundance of those who paddle pretty well in still water. The world cries for men who can navigate "white water." [5]

[2] From "Making Economic Weather." Printed in *Vital Speeches of the Day*, Vol. XX, June 1, 1954, p. 493.

[3] From *Thomas Alva Edison* by Francis Rolt-Wheeler (Macmillan, N.Y.), pp. 90–91.

[4] From "Democracy as a Factor in Education." Printed in *Vital Speeches of the Day*, Vol. III, May 15, 1937, p. 461. Reprinted by special permission.

[5] *Ibid.*, Vol. IV, December 15, 1937, p. 150.

Note the analogy used by Albert Wass de Czege, a Hungarian writer, in urging an American audience to preserve their freedom by accepting their responsibilities:

If you want to live in your own home, you have to take care of the roof, paint the walls, watch for termites, and repair whatever needs to be repaired. If you are too lazy to do all that, you can live in an apartment, and in this case someone else will do all these things for you. However, the one who owns the building in which you decide to live, will have the right to tell you what kind of pets you can have, how many children, and what colors you can use to paint your rooms.

The same is true about your country. You can keep it a private home that suits your needs, your own way of life. Or you can concentrate it into a huge apartment house in which the government will tell you how to live, as is done in the communist dominated countries. It is entirely up to you.[6]

Abraham Lincoln used a similar technic in an oft-quoted analogy directed against those who were criticizing his conduct of the Civil War. The newspapers had been full of the exploits of Blondin, a famous tightrope walker. Lincoln used this fact to emphasize the precarious position of the government:

Gentlemen, I want you to suppose a case for a moment. Suppose that all the property you were worth was in gold, and you had put it in the hands of Blondin, the famous rope-walker, to carry across the Niagara Falls on a tight rope. Would you shake the rope while he was passing over it, or keep shouting to him, "Blondin, stoop a little more! Go a little faster!" No, I am sure you would not. You would hold your breath as well as your tongue, and keep your hands off until he was safely over. Now the government is in the same situation. It is carrying an immense weight across a stormy ocean. Untold treasures are in its hands. It is doing the best it can. Don't badger it! Just keep still, and it will get you safely over.

As can be observed from these examples, the principal function of the comparison or the analogy is to make an idea clear and vivid. For this purpose it is an excellent tool and deserves to be widely used. Sometimes, however, it is used as a method of proof. For example, in a typical literal analogy the successful operation of a municipal electric-light plant in one city is used to prove its advisability in another city of a similar size. Note how this type of comparison is used in this excerpt:

---

[6] From "The Golden Key to America." *Ibid.*, Vol. XXVI, February 15, 1960, p. 267.

I say to you that if safety can be taught in grade schools, *and it can,* driver education can be just as effective in the high schools. The safety movement has done well in the elementary grades. In the face of an upward trend in adult traffic deaths since 1930, there has been just as steady a downward trend for children. The younger children have learned to walk in traffic better than their older brothers and sisters are learning to drive. Our studies show us that 29,000 pedestrians are now living who might have been killed in traffic had the trend of child accidents followed the adult trend. So there is your evidence—*safety can be taught.*[7]

As proof, the comparison is relatively weak since so many conditions may vary between the two items. At best it indicates only a high degree of probability. If proof is required, it is best to follow a comparison or analogy with other forms of support.

Illustration   An illustration is a detailed example of the idea or statement to be supported. It is the narration of an incident to bring out the point you are trying to make. Sometimes an illustration relates the results obtained from adopting a proposal the speaker advocates; sometimes it describes in detail an individual example of the general conditions the speaker wishes to emphasize. Note its two principal characteristics: the illustration is narrative in form—it tells the story; and the details of the story are vividly described.

There are two principal types of illustration: the hypothetical and the factual. The former tells a story which *could have* happened or *probably will* happen; the latter tells what *actually has* happened.

The *hypothetical illustration* is an imaginary narrative. It must, however, be consistent with the known facts. It must be reasonable. The following is an example of such an illustration:

Let's put ourselves in the other fellow's place. If you got no satisfaction out of your job as employer, if you had no pride in the sense of accomplishment, if you didn't feel yourself a vital part of a dynamic organization, all the pay you would get would be money. Take away all those things that make up your compensation, and every one of you would demand that your pay be doubled, because money would be all that was left.

---

[7] From "The Insurance Side of Highway Safety," a speech by Jesse W. Randall. *Ibid.,* Vol. XIV, June 15, 1948, pp. 515–516.

Out in your shop a man comes to work at 7 A.M. He doesn't know too much about his job and almost nothing about his company or how his work fits into it. He works 8 hours and goes home—with what? His pay and nothing more. Nobody (except the union steward!) took much if any notice of him. Nobody complimented him if he did do well because nobody except a foreman *knows* whether or not he did well, and he realized *that* fact. Nobody ever flattered him by asking his opinion about something. In millions of cases nobody ever told him the importance of his work.

At night he goes home to his family and neighbors—unimportant with nothing to boast about or even talk about. And the union calls a meeting to discuss a grievance—that workman can get up on his feet and sound off while people listen, he can be an officer with a title, he can boast to his family and friends how he "gave those big shots of the company what-for!" A strike vote is exciting!—Being a picket is important!— He gets looked at and talked about; he wears a badge!

Again let's be honest. If you and I were in that worker's situation, wouldn't we do pretty much what he's doing? [8]

The hypothetical illustration is used principally to make an abstract explanation more vivid and concrete. It is particularly useful in explaining a complicated plan. Instead of merely outlining the details, you take some hypothetical person, yourself, or a member of the audience, and put him through the process of actually operating the plan. Note in the above example how the speaker leads his listeners to put themselves in the workman's place.

For clarity the hypothetical illustration is good because the speaker may tell his story as he wants; for proof, however, it is of doubtful value.

The *factual illustration* [9] is a narrative describing in detail a specific event as it actually occurred. It is one of the most telling forms of support that a speaker can use. Since it is described in detail, the incident is made clear and vivid; since it refers to an actual happening, the illustration carries conviction. Note the effect of the following:

Today, man-made law is in conflict with natural law. . . . I met Ed Davis, our guide, on vacation after I had studied engineering at Columbia University. Impressed with scientific methods, I tried to sub-

---

[8] From "Effective Leadership for Better Employee Relations," a speech by Charles J. Stilwell. *Ibid.*, December 15, 1947, p. 157.

[9] In the author's opinion, the term *factual illustration* affords a more accurate description of this form of support than the term *specific illustration* so often used in textbooks of speech.

stitute them for the art of angling. They caught me no fish. Finally, Ed dug down in his tackle box and produced a small yellow, low-wing wooden monoplane with a metal propeller that would spin. He had hung a triple hook where the tail-skid belonged and had soldered a swivel to the prop shaft. Now, as he snapped this to my wire leader, he grinned and remarked, "Try this. It's about time to give 'em something comical!" With that he tossed the contraption over the side.

As I trolled it astern the propeller chugged like the churning screw of an empty tramp steamer riding high in ballast. And, believe it or not, a huge muskellunge, one that must have previously ignored many lures scientifically designed to imitate live bait, rose up and hit that yellow monoplane. When, after a long battle, the fish lay stretched out in the bottom of our canoe, I expressed my amazement to Ed. Pausing to choose his words, Ed vouchsafed another truth germane to our subject. "It ain't how a bait looks to you and me that counts," he said. "It's how it looks to the fish." [10]

In his speech "The Pleasures of Learning," Gilbert Highet uses an illustration to clarify and emphasize his point:

The people for whom classical study has been a success are those who continue, with deepening understanding and appreciation, to read the classics long after they have left school and college. There is one particularly famous example. William Shakespeare was never a linguist; but he had a good schooling at his local high school, where he learnt some Latin and a few smatterings of Greek. Afterwards, when he was an actor and a busy playwright, he still retained his love for and his understanding of the great classics, and discussed them with really learned friends such as Ben Jonson. When he was about 35, he began to read with attention a translation of Plutarch's *Lives of the Greek and Roman Heroes* which had come out not long before. . . . The result was, not only that he found a new mass of material for his plays (the tragedies on Roman history date from this time), but that he achieved a new depth in his creative thinking. The tragedies before 1599 are all either pathetic, like *Romeo and Juliet,* or diabolical, like *Richard III:* it is with *Julius Caesar* that Shakespeare first realized the full meaning of noble failure, the fall of greatness, the doom of the good.[11]

There are three considerations you should keep in mind when choosing a factual illustration to support an idea. First, is it clearly related to the point? If you have to labor to show its connection with your idea, the illustration is of little use. It should be clear within itself. Its point should be obvious. Second, is it a

---

[10] From "The New Role of the Engineer," an address by Eugene E. Wilson. Printed in *Vital Speeches of the Day,* Vol. XIII, November 1, 1946, p. 61.
[11] *Ibid.,* Vol. XXVI, September 15, 1960, p. 729.

fair example? An audience is quick to notice unusual circumstances in an illustration, and if you seem to have picked only the exceptional case, your example will not be very convincing. Third, is it vivid and impressive in detail? The primary value of an illustration is the sense of reality which it creates. If this quality is absent, the advantage of using an illustration is lost. Be sure that your illustrations are pointed, fair, and vivid.

Specific instances Specific instances are condensed forms of factual illustrations. They are undetailed examples. Time may not allow you to relate many detailed illustrations, but you may need to give several brief examples to clarify or support a point adequately. In order to show the widespread nature of a situation or the frequency of an occurrence, you will often need to mention a number of instances, each showing your point to be true. Remember that specific instances are not imaginary happenings. In supporting the point that North Americans are ignorant of Latin America, Charles W. Arnade presented an illustration and then followed it with these specific instances:

> Such cases of geographical illiteracy occur continually. An important Florida businessman trading with Latin America admitted the other day that he had been unaware that Buenos Aires was south of the equator. A Western Union telegraph clerk believed that Bolivia was in Australia and when told it was part of South America was surprised that Australia was not part of Latin America. Very few persons know the difference between Uruguay, one of South America's most progressive nations, and Paraguay which is the most backward nation. Even many experienced editors misspell the name of Colombia by calling it 'Columbia.' Every Latin American visitor to the United States is angered by this geographical ignorance which reaches into high executive positions in business and government.[12]

To clarify what he meant by contemporary reading material, a speaker offered these instances:

> But, by our contemporaries I do not mean merely the authors stacked by the lending library. We should sample modern Japanese verse (the Haikku is currently getting a great play) . . . we should read at least one novel by an author in emancipated India to feel how the world seems

---

[12] From "A Realistic Picture." *Ibid.*, Vol. XXVI, July 1, 1960, p. 575.

from his vantage point. We ought to read the *Manchester Guardian* now and then as well as *Time*. . . . (Incidentally, the *Guardian's* reports on U.S. politics have a fine, cool, sanity about them that I recommend to one and all.) And every now and then I like to look into a quarterly called *Diogenes,* which translates into English the best work of leading scholars from the non-English speaking countries. And *The American Scholar* is another quarterly that deserves an hour or two every three months.[13]

The use of specific instances adds strength and comprehensiveness to an idea. They provide good proof if several of them follow a detailed example which makes the idea clear.

Statistics

Not all figures are statistics; some are merely numbers. Statistics are figures used to show the proportion of instances of a certain kind, to show how many or few or great or small they are. Statistics are useful in covering a great deal of territory in a short time. When judiciously used, they are impressive and convincing. For example:

Between 1960 and 1970 the labor force is expected to increase from about 73½ million workers to 87 million.

This net increase of about 13½ millions, however, is based on a gross entry of 29 million new workers, 26 million of whom will never have worked before since we must counterbalance the expected exit of almost 16 million from our work force due to death, retirement, and other causes.

That is a colossal jump in numbers of people, but we get a real surprise when we see what kinds of people are going to be making up the huge labor force.

Just about one out of every two of them will be young people under 25 years of age.

Another two out of five will be over 45 years of age.

Only 13% will be between 25 and 34, and, most significantly, there will be an actual decline in the number of working people in the labor force in the prime age bracket of 35 to 44.

The low birth rate of the 1930's has given a unique configuration to our population and its distribution through the labor force. It is an hour glass figure, with the wide areas of increase at the bottom and the top, and an actual constriction in the center.[14]

---

[13] From " 'Read—and Grow Up'," a speech by Nicholas Samstag. *Ibid.,* Vol. XXVI, March 1, 1960, p. 306.

[14] From "The Nation's Manpower Picture in the 1960s," a speech by James T. O'Connell. *Ibid.,* Vol. XXVI, April 15, 1960, p. 399.

Or observe how a speaker used statistics to prove his views about the effects of foreign trade on labor in the United States:

The United States Department of Labor has estimated that the jobs of 4½ million workers—or approximately 7 per cent of our labor force —depend on foreign trade. This means that more workers owe their jobs to foreign trade than are employed in such major industries as mining, contract construction, transportation, public utilities or finance. Stated another way, foreign trade provides more jobs than the iron, steel, machinery, and automobile industries combined.

On the production—and thus the profit—side, we find that we export 19 per cent of our total production of trucks, 30 per cent of our track-laying tractors, 11 per cent of our machine tools, 26 per cent of our construction and mining equipment, 14 per cent of our coal, and between 25 and 40 per cent of our cotton, wheat, rice, fats, oils, and tobacco.[15]

Notice in this example that the speaker was not satisfied merely to give figures but that he compared them to one another and related them to our experiences. Numbers by themselves are abstract; they must be made vivid and graphic by comparison with those things which are familiar to us. Note in the following example how another speaker made understandable the small size of an electron. He had first given it as a decimal fraction which was too small for his audience to conceive. Then he said:

If an electron were increased in size till it became as large as an apple, and a human being grew larger in the same proportion, that person could hold the entire solar system in the palm of his hand and would have to use a magnifying glass in order to see it.

Statistics are powerful proof when they are effectively and honestly used, but you must be sure that they are made understandable to your audience. For this reason it is well to use approximate numbers when you are presenting large figures. Say "nearly four million" rather than "3,984,256." If precision is important, write the figures on a blackboard or chart or hand out a mimeographed sheet. Moreover, note that the term *figures* is much easier to pronounce than *statistics;* and although the two terms are not exactly synonymous, most audiences will understand what you mean if you say, "Figures compiled by the Department of Commerce show that. . . ."

---

[15] From "Foreign Trade Competition," a speech by A. J. Hayes. *Ibid.*, Vol. XXVI, July 15, 1960, p. 595.

Frequently an audience which will not take your word alone will be convinced or impressed by the statement of someone else. Another person's statement used to support the ideas of the speaker is called testimony. The following is an example:

In an inspired article "American Education's Greatest Need" in the *Saturday Review* two weeks ago, Yale University President A. Whitney Griswold stressed that he saw the greatest need of the education system not in more money but in a sense of purpose, in higher intellectual aims.

Dr. Clarence Faust, president of the Fund for the Advancement of Education, said over two years ago: "Our school system does need more buildings, more money for operating expenses, teachers' salaries, and more and better prepared teachers. But it needs even more to find ways of making better and more effective use of its resources for the major purposes of education." [16]

Frequently, testimony is used, not in isolated bits as it is above, but in combined and cumulative form. Observe the "piling up" in the example below:

There is a moral law which is inherent in human nature and which is therefore immutable and to which all man-made laws to be valid must conform. By virtue of this law man possesses certain rights which are inherent and inalienable and therefore superior to the authority of the state. . . .

This doctrine has had a long and illustrious history. The basic concept is found in the writings of ancient times, and in one way or another it has been recognized ever since by philosophers and poets, statesmen and lawyers, kings and saints. . . .

From mediaeval sources it came to England, where it characterized the writings of such men as Hooker and Sydney and of the jurists Bracton and Fortescue, Coke and Blackstone and Pollock.

Finally it came to America, where it permeated the writings of the Founding Fathers—of Wilson and Hamilton, of Adams, Dickinson and Otis, while from the pen of Jefferson it received classic, and let us hope immortal, expression in the famous preamble to the Declaration that all men are created equal and that they are endowed by their Creator with certain inalienable rights and that the purpose of government is to secure these rights. Akin to this great expression in the Declaration is the equally beautiful and powerful statement of Hamilton: "The sacred rights of mankind are not to be rummaged for among old records

---

[16] From "Money Alone Won't Cure Schools Ills," a speech by Roger A. Freeman. *Ibid.*, Vol. XXV, May 15, 1959, p. 454.

or musty parchments. They are written, as with a sunbeam, in the whole volume of human nature, by the hand of Divinity itself, and can never be erased or obscured by mortal power." It was this great concept which was given body and visibility by incorporation into our Bill of Rights, especially in the due process clause whereby the life, liberty and property of every least man in the land was brought within its protecting arms.

And now after a century and a half of our national life, it still lives in the expressions of those who see in this principle the bulwark of our liberty and the source of our nation's strength. Among these expressions is that of Chief Judge Irving Lehman of the New York Court of Appeals: "Statesman, prelate and judge, Protestant, Catholic and Jew, are united in the conviction that the inalienable rights of the individual, formulated and assured by our law, rest upon a foundation eternal and immutable because it is divine. There lies America's unity." And in this very year, Mr. Justice Douglas, to the credit of himself and of the great Court of which he is a member, said in a recent case: "The victory for freedom of thought recorded in our Bill of Rights recognized that in the domain of conscience there is a moral power higher than the State."

This, gentlemen, is our birthright.[17]

Your decision to use a particular person's testimony must be governed by a measurement of his reliability and of his reputation with the audience. Ask yourself these questions about him:

1. Do his training and experience qualify him to speak with authority on this subject? Is he an expert in this field?
2. Is his statement based on first-hand knowledge?
3. Is his opinion influenced by personal interest? That is, is he prejudiced?
4. How will the audience regard his testimony? Is he known to them? Do they respect his opinions?

If you had diphtheria, you would not ask a streetcar motorman to prescribe treatment; nor would you ask someone who had never been out of a small town to describe accurately the amount of traffic on Fifth Avenue in New York. It is doubtful how much weight you would give the testimony of a salesman on the quality of the goods he gets a commission for selling. These same measurements must be applied to authorities whom you quote. Be particularly careful about using big names merely because they are well known. A movie star may be famous, but her opinion of a brand of soap flakes is of less value than that of a laundress. When you

---

[17] Abridged from "The Higher Law," a speech by Harold R. McKinnon. *Ibid.*, December 1, 1946, pp. 101–106.

do use an obscure person as an authority, however, be sure to tell your audience *why* he is a good authority—point out his qualifications in relation to the first three questions listed above.

Restatement

This last form of support gains its strength from the power of repetition. Advertisers realize this power and spend thousands of dollars to say the same thing over and over in magazines, on billboards, and on television. The biggest danger lies in the monotony of mere repetition. Restatement, however, is not mere repetition; restatement consists of *saying the same thing*, but saying it *in a different way*. In the example of a factual illustration given earlier in this chapter, the speaker began his speech by saying, "man-made law is in conflict with natural law," and closed by quoting the guide as saying, "It ain't how the bait looks to you and me that counts. It's how it looks to the fish." The same idea is stated, but with different wording. Observe the restatement at the end of Lincoln's analogy: "Now the government is in the same situation. It is carrying an immense weight across a stormy ocean. Untold treasures are in its hands. It is doing the best it can. Don't badger it! Just keep still, and it will get you safely over." By restating an idea in more familiar terms or in more vivid language, you can frequently increase its power.

These, then, are the seven forms of verbal support. Let your speech be full of them. Avoid abstract, unsupported statements. Do not depend on your own assertions of opinion. Amplify and develop them by using explanation, comparison, illustration, instance, statistics, testimony, and restatement.

THE USE OF VISIBLE SUPPORTING MATERIAL

So far we have discussed only the *audible* materials used to explain or prove a point—what you can *say* about it. Equally important, sometimes even more so, are the *visible* materials you can use to *show* what you mean. These materials, which include maps, diagrams, charts, pictures, small working models, and even demonstrations with full-scale equipment, may make your presentation of any of the forms of supports clearer and more effective.

VISIBLE MATERIAL CAN SHOW WHAT YOU MEAN

The saying "One picture is worth a thousand words" holds true for public speakers. Visual aids present information, and the best ones present it with greater clarity than words alone can. To be effective, however, they must be clearly related to the point being discussed, and they must be large enough and placed before the audience so that each person can easily see and understand them. Each of the visual aids used in the speaking situations shown on these three pages has an interest value in itself and contributes to an understanding of the speaker's point.

In testifying before a Senate subcommittee, Walter Reuther (above) uses a bar graph comparing the profits of the auto industry "big three" with those of all manufacturing corporations. The speaker (below) illustrates a televised talk on art with a reproduction of the Mona Lisa.

The teachers pictured on this page know the value of visual aids in making a point clear to their students. Note the variety of visual aids—movies showing a diagram of the ear, a chart and a large-scale model of the crystal structure of a rock, and a human skeleton.

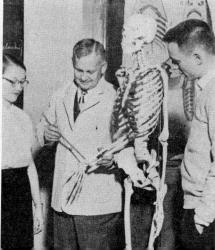

In the United Nations Security Council, Henry Cabot Lodge (top left) uses a map to show how a U.S. reconnaissance plane was forced off its course and downed in international waters. This blackboard diagram of the larynx (top right) is easy to see and understand because it is drawn in a simplified form with heavy lines. A small-scale model (bottom left) makes the Globe Theatre come alive for these students. An officer at West Point (bottom right) stands to one side of a projected line graph and uses a pointer to indicate a pertinent detail.

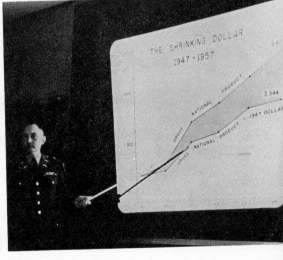

For instance, if you were explaining how to use a complicated camera, your instructions would be much clearer if you took an actual camera, showed your listeners the parts that require adjustment, and demonstrated how to use the camera in typical shots. Sometimes equipment for demonstration is not available or is too big to bring into the room where the speech is to be made. Small-scale models are then very useful. Model airplanes, for example, are widely used to teach aerodynamics. Similarly, in explaining a flood-control project, you will find a large map of the area very helpful. The operation of a gun or machine and the assembly of its various parts can be made more clear by large diagrams showing the important pieces. Statistical data can often be made clear by column graphs and "pies"—circles cut into segments to show proportions. Pictures, including slides and movies, are also extremely useful.

The following list describes in more detail the kinds of visual aids available to the speaker:

The object itself (for example, a camera). The speaker may also supplement the object with diagrams showing its internal parts.

Models, either small-scale models of large objects (model airplane) or large-scale models of small objects, are useful when it is impossible to show the original. A working model has the added advantage of showing both the basic design and the operation.

Slides involve projection equipment and the darkened room obscures the speaker, but they are often effective.

Movies require more equipment than slides but have the advantage of showing action.

Maps should contain only the details vital to the point being made.

Blackboard drawings should be completed before the audience assembles. Be sure that the chalk marks are heavy enough to be seen by the entire audience.

Graphs: Bar graphs show the relationship of two sets of statistics. *Line* graphs show two or more variable facts. *Pie* graphs show percentages by a circle divided proportionately. *Pictorial* graphs show relative amounts by size or number of symbols.

Diagrams: Cut away diagrams of the mechanics of an object show its external aspects as well as its operation. *Simple* diagrams of an object or process may allow a three dimensional view of the subject. *Organization* charts diagram the structure and relationships of an organization.

In using visual aids, be sure that you:

1. Choose visual aids that are relevant. Their importance is in making your point more graphic for the audience; irrelevant material will distract attention from your point.

2. Prepare the displays before giving the speech. Check to see that you have the needed equipment, that blackboard diagrams have been made, and that the material is arranged so that it will be simple to operate. Practice using the visual aids.

3. Keep charts, graphs, diagrams, etc., simple and clear. Use ink in heavy broad lines and possibly in color to emphasize an important fact. Make the displays large enough so that the entire audience can see them easily. Omit unnecessary details. A series of simple charts is better than a single complicated one.

4. Place the material where it can be seen easily. Stand well to the side of the material and use a pointer to indicate specific aspects of the display. When using a model or the object itself, hold it so that your hands do not obscure it.

5. Use the visual aids at the proper psychological point in the speech. If the timing is off, the chain of thought will be broken, and the visual aids will serve only to break the continuity of the speech instead of clarify a point.

6. Have the display visible only when it is in use. Keep it covered until you are ready for it and put it out of sight when you have finished with it. If it can be seen when not in use, it will serve only to distract the audience from the rest of your remarks.

Visible materials may help prove a point by making your facts more vivid. Especially in explanatory talks, try to *show* your listeners what you mean in addition to *telling* them.

THE ONE-POINT SPEECH

Many occasions arise in which the speaker only wants to make clear a single idea or prove one simple point. Such occasions often come in class discussions, in short reports, in simple instructions, in arguments, and at committee meetings or business conferences. In these situations you do not need a complex structure to make your talk effective. In fact, the beginning speaker shows wisdom if he limits himself to single points well supported and leaves the more complex discussions until later. Thus he will avoid hollow abstractions covering a wide range but proving or clarifying nothing; and he will find, when he attempts more complex subjects, that the units of his talks are single points, strategically arranged.

The first thing to do, of course, is to decide definitely on the point you want to explain or prove. Condense your ideas to a single sentence to be *sure* you have only one point. State it simply: for example, "A good truck driver must keep relaxed." Having stated your point, stick to it; don't wander off on another topic. Now assemble the supporting material best suited to your purpose and round out the development of your point in the manner best adapted to that purpose. Keep clearly in mind whether you are trying only to clarify and explain your point or whether you are trying to prove it.

The use of supporting material to explain

How, then, does one assemble supporting material in a short talk explaining a single point? Briefly, you first state the point simply; then you bring in the supporting material—especially explanation, comparison, illustration, and visual material; and finally you restate the point explained. This arrangement can be outlined as follows:

1. State your point in a simple sentence.
2. Make it clear—
   A. by explanation, comparison, and illustration.
   B. by using maps, diagrams, pictures, or models.
3. Restate the point you have explained.

Under (2) above, sometimes the audible and visual materials are presented separately and sometimes together. That is, sometimes you will tell your listeners and then show them; sometimes you will show them while you are telling them. The following outline for a short talk illustrates how supporting material may be assembled to explain a point.

WHAT IS DEMOCRACY?

| *Statement* | I. The essence of democracy is the control of the government by those governed. |
| *Explanation* | A. This means the people have authority to: |

1. Make the laws under which they live.
2. Select public officials to administer these laws.

Hypothetical illustration   B. Suppose a group of students were to plan a party in the democratic way.
1. They would get together to discuss it.
2. They would decide where and when the party would be held.
3. They would agree how much each student should contribute to the cost.
4. In case of disagreement, they would reach a compromise or abide by the vote of the majority.
5. One of them would be selected to collect the money and pay the bills.
6. They might select another person or a small committee to arrange for the entertainment, etc.
7. Each student would have some part in deciding how the party would be run.

Comparison with B   C. If, however, one student took it upon himself to decide all these questions—even to dictating the program of entertainment and how much each one should pay for it—the party would not be *democratic*, regardless of how efficiently it might be run.

Comparison of specific instances   D. Compare these actual cases:
1. In New England, local government is based on town meetings.
   a. All qualified residents are allowed to speak and vote directly on current problems.
   b. Public officials are selected by vote of the citizens.
2. Indiana cities are governed by representatives of the people.
   a. City ordinances are made by the city council, whose members are elected by the voters.
   b. Administrative officials are elected.
3. In Norway and Denmark, under German occupation during World War II, city government was controlled by *gauleiters* or similar officials.
   a. These men were chosen by the Nazi leaders, not by the people they governed.

b. They enforced Nazi laws and issued orders over which the people of Norway and Denmark were permitted no control.

E. This diagram will show why the first two examples just cited are democratic while the third was not. (Arrows show the direction of governmental control.)

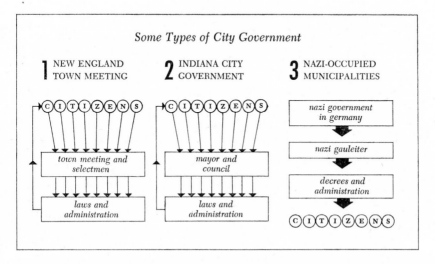

Some Types of City Government

1 NEW ENGLAND TOWN MEETING   **2** INDIANA CITY GOVERNMENT   **3** NAZI-OCCUPIED MUNICIPALITIES

Restatement   II. Democracy, as Lincoln said of the United States, is government "by the people."

The use of supporting material as proof

There are two common methods of assembling the forms of support to establish the proof for a statement —the didactic method and the method of implication.

In using the *didactic method*, you state your conclusion first, then present the proof, and finally restate your conclusion. As the old parson explained, "I tell 'em what I'm going to tell 'em; I tell 'em; then I tell 'em what I told 'em." This is perhaps the clearest and most obvious method of assembling your proof. It can be outlined as follows:

1. State your point.
2. Make it clear by explanation, comparison, or illustration.
3. Support it by additional factual illustrations, specific instances, statistics, or testimony.
4. Restate your point as the conclusion.

In using the *method of implication,* you present the facts first and then state the conclusion which is based on those facts. In other words, you state the conclusion at the end, *after* the evidence to support it has been presented. This method, sometimes called the "natural" method of argument, coincides more nearly with the method by which we reach conclusions ourselves, uninfluenced by another person. For this reason, the method of implication, though not quite so clear or so easy to use as the didactic method, is sometimes more persuasive with the audience. It avoids making them feel that you are pushing something down their throats. It is, in fact, almost the only method to use with an audience that is hostile to the point you wish to present. An outline of this method follows:

1. Present an analogy or illustration which *implies* the point you wish to make.
2. Present additional illustrations, instances, figures, and testimony which point inevitably to this conclusion without stating it.
3. Show how these facts lead unavoidably to this conclusion; use explanation if necessary.
4. Definitely state your point as a conclusion.

Notice that regardless of which of these two methods is used, the first three forms of support (explanation, comparison, and illustration) are primarily useful in making an idea clear and vivid, while the next three (instances, statistics, and testimony) have the function of establishing and verifying its truth or importance. Restatement, of course, serves to emphasize and to assist the memory. Study the sample speech outline below. (Note that the didactic method is used. By omitting the general statement, this outline would illustrate the method of implication.)

INSTRUCTION BY TELEVISION

General
statement
I. Classroom instruction by television is effective.

Hypothetical
illustration
A. Suppose you were to have this experience in your English literature class:
1. When you enter the room, there is a television set rather than an instructor in front of the class.

2. On TV, however, you see the department's best teacher for the course you are taking.
3. In other rooms other classes are watching the same telecast.
    a. The students in each class can see and hear the lecturer and the teaching materials being used.
    b. The students in each class can obtain individual assistance when necessary.
4. You will learn as much about English literature as you would in a conventional class.
    a. Tests on appreciation of literature show this.
    b. Tests on comprehension of literature demonstrate the same result.

Factual illustration

B. Television was used successfully in the Hagerstown, Maryland, public schools.
1. Mathematics classes at nearly every grade level participated.
2. Teachers, student ability, and other variables were controlled so that television was the only major difference in method.
    a. About half of the classes received instruction by television.
    b. The other half received regular instruction.
3. The students who received television instruction scored as high or higher on tests than those who had regular instruction.

Specific instances

C. This experience has been repeated in a number of cases:
1. Miami University of Ohio reported that students in TV sections and those in regular classes did equally well in subject matter learning.
2. The city of Chicago found similar results for high school physics and algebra.
3. In Cincinnati, high school chemistry classes taught by TV were ahead of other classes.

Statistics

D. A special committee headed by Arthur E. Traxler of the Educational Records Bureau and supported by the Fund for the Advancement of Education reported figures that clearly show the effectiveness of television instruction.

    1. Experiments involving almost 27,000 students were conducted in several cities.

    2. Of 110 comparisons made in this study, 68 or over 60% showed the groups instructed by television to have achieved higher scores than the other groups.

Testimony   E. On the basis of studies such as these, experts have expressed their views.

    1. Leslie P. Greenhill, associate director of the Division of Academic Research and Services for Pennsylvania State University, stated in the *National Education Association Journal:*

> "Results of TV research show that when the same teacher teaches in each situation, televised instruction is equivalent in effectiveness to face-to-face instruction."

Analogy   F. Just as training films have assisted in teaching millions of men and women in the armed forces, so television can be useful in the classrooms of our schools.

Restatement   II. Subjects can be effectively taught by television.

Many one-point speeches will not require so many different forms of support as were used in this sample outline. Most one-point speeches are briefer. This sample was given to show how a number of different types of support might be combined.

The use of supporting material to entertain

At times your audience may require entertainment along with your more serious explanation or proof, and occasionally your sole purpose may be to entertain. The development of a speech solely for entertainment is discussed fully in a later chapter and need not be considered here except to note that supporting material for such a speech is assembled around a central theme in much the same way as it is when your purpose is more serious. Even when your purpose is a serious one, however, you may need to include material with a lighter tone. When this is true, the illustrations, comparisons, instances, and even figures and quotations will be chosen for their entertaining value as well as for their clarity or substance. Humorous anecdotes, tales of odd experiences, curious facts about important people and events, exaggerated descriptions—all these serve to illuminate the point you are making in an entertaining way. Be careful, however, that entertainment does not run away with your speech. See that your tales are to the point and that your humor does not divert attention from your explanation or proof unless entertainment is your only object in speaking.

In this chapter we have discussed the types of supporting material both verbal and visible, and we have seen how the material may be assembled to clarify and prove the points a speaker wishes to make. Begin practicing the use of these forms of support by making several one-point speeches. Study carefully the sample outlines for such speeches printed earlier in this chapter. Phrase the main point of your talk in a simple, straightforward manner; choose supporting material that is clear and substantial and entertaining; arrange your material so that it develops and emphasizes your main point.

SAMPLE SPEECH

Note how all these things were done by James Robertson to develop his central theme in the one-point speech printed below. When you have learned to do this with one main point, you will be ready to prepare speeches that are more complex, where several main points are put together in an integrated pattern.

ONE IDEA [18]

> *The following speech was delivered to the Kiwanis Club of Birmingham, Michigan, by James Robertson.*

If I had a choice given me of one idea or all the atomic bombs in existence, I'd unhesitatingly choose the one idea. You would too. If you don't think so, then let's look closely at some simple ideas.

---

[18] From *Vital Speeches of the Day*, Vol. XIV, June 15, 1948, pp. 527–529. Abridged here to conserve space.

For instance, Henry Ford just had one idea. His idea was to produce a car cheap enough so that the man in the street, the common man, could afford to buy it. If you look in the files of almost any newspaper for September 1922 you will find advertised there a Ford chassis and motor delivered complete for $290 and a five passenger touring car complete and ready to go for $450.

We Americans paid Henry Ford more than a billion dollars for his one idea. And we got our money's worth.

Ford's one idea transformed the United States. Ford had no notion that it would do all this. Nevertheless Ford's one idea brought highways of concrete across this great land east and west and north and south. It brought Fifth Avenue styles to the smallest hamlet and broadened our whole mental outlook. It added a huge set of new businesses and vocations.

Of course, it also got us to abandon the horse and buggy and many other activities of the gay nineties. Ford was 40 years old when he started the Ford Motor Co. in 1903.

"A conception of what ought to be," was Henry Ford's idea and it gave us a whole new scheme of things.

Abraham Lincoln is an example of one idea. Honored and revered above any other American, Lincoln is an example of the power of one idea. Stripped of all secondary and lesser qualifications Lincoln stands, simple proof that here in America a boy can be born in a lowly log cabin and rise above poverty and hardship to the position of highest honor, the presidency of the United States. No other idea expresses the freedom that is ours in America better. No other idea stimulates the imagination more truly than the Abe Lincoln example.

"Every idea that enters the mind tends to express itself in suitable action," says William James. And the Encyclopaedia Britannica says, "Man has only had 102 BIG IDEAS since the beginning of time." All other ideas men may have had fit into these categories and are subordinate to them. . . .

And that's just it. You run your whole life on one or two ideas. Here's an example:

Everyone is familiar with the boy who won't wash behind his ears. Nor will he comb his hair. He stands in a slouchy manner, has a hang-dog look, isn't interested in clothes and permits buttons to dangle. Altogether, with his chin whiskers and carelessness, he is a decidely unprepossessing creature. Then suddenly a miracle takes place. It happens in every block in the city. There's one on your street right now. All over America it takes place. Almost over night there comes a magical transformation. All because of one idea: BOY MEETS GIRL. When Boy meets Girl this one idea takes hold of him and shakes him to the tip of his toes. It ransacks every nook and cranny of his being. It twists him inside out and explores every possibility he will eventually achieve. This one idea remakes him into the grandest creature that walks the earth.

Just analyze it for a moment. Why does it take such hold of a being? Why does it reach into the innermost recesses of his soul and bring out all that is good and true and beautiful?

Here's why. It's because he has so much at stake. By that simple device he seals his doom for half his waking hours from that day until the day he dies. The one idea—BOY MEETS GIRL—runs him half a lifetime.

This is no time for fuzzy thinking. One or two ideas clearly understood will fill America with purpose once more. We need to drain off the obnoxious ideas and deftly insert the clear ideas. It's time for high-mindedness.

Let's go back a little way. This planet has existed for two billion years but man has lived for merely a small fraction of that time, namely one million years. So the world got along without man for 1,999,000,000 years. Strangely enough man has not always been the supreme creature of this world. The dinosaurs ruled the earth for 140 million years before becoming extinct 60 million years ago. Man has a long way to go to equal them in point of time. And yet a million years in itself is no small achievement.

Now, of that million years that man has lived, only the past 7,000 years has had real significance. It has been so short a time that we have been able to read and write. Man's first truly great achievement was in being able to record his activities and transfer ideas from one mind to another—store ideas in libraries for future generations. That's when civilization began.

So man's achievement in recording his history gave us our biggest boost, pushed us ahead faster than all other devices up to that time. Man's ability to record his history was one idea. And it took a million years of muddy or fuzzy thinking before he managed to get a clear idea —one idea.

The next tremendous achievement was as recently as 2,000 years ago, a mere fraction of time compared to the million years man has been on this planet. The discovery of the divine in human life was the one idea that pierced man's consciousness at that time. That life holds ultimate lasting meaning for everyone who lives is the one idea we caught up and adopted. The integrity of the individual. The dignity of the individual. The worthwhileness of man—every man, everywhere.

And only as recently as 172 years ago was there a nation built on this one idea. Some call it freedom. Some call it private enterprise. Some call it individual initiative. In truth it is simply one idea: that every life has ultimate lasting meaning; the integrity of the individual; the dignity of every life, everywhere.

What we need in America today is a modern P. T. Barnum to sell us on the American idea. We need genuine shouting enthusiasm about this land of ours—not just a complacent acceptance. The whole world is looking to us and we need a clear idea—yes, crystal clear—idea of what America means.

PROBLEMS

1. Be ready to discuss the following questions in class: Why should the speaker support the main points of his speech? What are the forms of verbal supporting material? What is the chief purpose of each type of support? When can visual aids help the speaker? How should the speaker select and use visual aids? How can supporting material be arranged to explain a point? To prove a point? For entertainment?

2. Select speeches in *Vital Speeches of the Day* or in some good anthology of speeches and find several samples of each of the forms of support.

3. Listen to a recorded speech. (Your instructor may wish to play a portion of a speech in class.) Identify the forms of support used as you listen to the speech. (Notice whether your purpose helps you listen more carefully than you usually do.)

4. Use at least four of the forms of support to present your views for or against one of the points listed below or on a point suggested by one of these. Analyze the audience's attitude toward your purpose to determine whether you should use the didactic method or the method of implication.

> Classroom instruction by television is economical.
> Labor unions are democratic.
> Driver license regulations need revision.
> Voting rights for eighteen-year-olds would increase national interest in politics.
> Fluoridation of water is safe.
> Advanced ROTC develops good officers for the army.

5. For which of the above points might you effectively use visible supporting materials? What kinds of aids would be appropriate?

6. Prepare a short speech answering an argument made previously by some other member of the class. Do two things:
   A. Point out any weakness, insufficiency, or lack of reliability in the support offered by the other speaker for his point.
   B. Present your own supporting material—show that it is strong, sufficient, reliable.

7. Make a similar speech answering an argument found in a magazine article or a speech heard outside of class.

Condense some daily experience into a glowing symbol,
and an audience is electrified.

Ralph Waldo Emerson

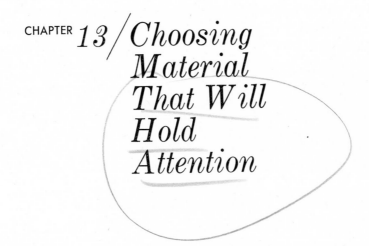

CHAPTER *13 / Choosing Material That Will Hold Attention*

The preceding chapter discussed the seven types of material which may be used to support the main points of a speech. This chapter is concerned with the question of choosing from the available material those things which will hold the attention of the audience.

Attention is a great deal like electricity: we don't know exactly what it is, but we do know what it does and what conditions bring it about. A baseball fan is sitting in the bleachers. The count is three and two. The pitcher wraps his fingers round the ball, winds up, and sends a hot one sizzling over the plate. The umpire bawls out, "Strike three; yer out!" Only then does the spectator lean back, take a long breath, and notice what has been going on about him: the man behind him who has been thumping him on the back, the sack of peanuts he dropped, the threatening clouds that have suddenly come up, the hornet buzzing round his ankles. What has happened? We say his attention was focused on the game. Those things to which he was paying attention controlled his entire thought and action, forcing everything else into the background.

THE NATURE OF ATTENTION

Dr. Floyd Ruch suggests that, psychologically, attention can be looked upon as having three interrelated aspects: (1) an adjustment of the body and its sense organs, (2) clearness and vividness in consciousness, and (3) a set toward action.[1] Thus, during attention, posture is adjusted and the sense organs are "aimed at" the stimulus in order to receive impressions from it more readily. Just as the robin cocks its head to listen for the worm underneath the sod, so people lean forward and turn their eyes and ears toward the object which captures their attention. You have only to call your friend by name, and he will turn toward you in order to attend to your remarks. By gaining the attention of your audience, then, you increase their capacity to hear what you say since they will have adjusted themselves physically to listen.

Of greater importance to the speaker, however, is the second characteristic of attention—the fact that when we pay attention to a stimulus it becomes more clear and vivid in our consciousness while other equally strong stimuli seem to get weaker or to fade out altogether. This explains why the spectator at the ball game was unconscious of so many things going on about him as long as his attention was focused on the game. Every moment of our lives innumerable stimuli are impinging on our senses. We can hear the wind whistling, the birds calling, or the trucks rumbling; the temperature is warm or cold; a hundred different sights are before our eyes. Why don't we notice them all? It is because of the selective nature of attention. Thus some stimuli become strengthened and our reaction to them increases, while other stimuli recede and become less influential. If you as a speaker can catch and hold the attention of your audience, the ideas you express will make a more

[1] From *Psychology and Life*, 5th ed., by Floyd L. Ruch (Scott, Foresman and Company, Chicago, 1958), p. 267.

clear and vivid impression on them while distracting sights and sounds or conflicting ideas will tend to fade into the background.

Finally, the condition of a set toward action which accompanies attention is important. We have a tendency, while attending to a series of stimuli, to "get set" to do something about them. Thus the driver of an automobile who pays attention to highway signs is *ready* to steer his car around the curve or to stop at the intersection. Similarly, assuming that what you say makes sense and contains the proper motivation, the closer your audience pays attention to you, the more likely they will be to act as you suggest. As they listen, they will tend to "get set" to think or act as you propose and will be more apt to do so without wavering or hesitation. It has been said that *what holds attention, controls action;* and while this is perhaps an overstatement, there is no doubt that speakers who do not secure the audience's attention rarely get the action they desire. Certainly the most influential speakers have been those who have gripped the attention of their audiences.

We must not assume, however, that paying attention is entirely a spontaneous and involuntary reaction of the audience governed solely by what the speaker says. Many times we force ourselves to concentrate on something which in itself does not attract our attention. Thus a student may compel himself to focus his attention on a textbook assignment in spite of the distractions around him or to listen attentively to a dull lecture in a subject he is required to pass. Necessity or strong motivation often leads us to exert this type of conscious effort in order to focus our minds on stimuli which are not attention-provoking in themselves.

Psychologists refer to attention which results from such conscious effort as *voluntary* or *forced* attention as distinguished from the *involuntary* or *effortless* attention paid to things which are striking or interesting in themselves. Audiences sometimes force themselves to listen to a speaker out of mere politeness or respect for his prestige or position. More often, however, such voluntary attention results from the audience's feeling that the subject is very important to them. Early in your speech, therefore, make clear to your audience the importance of your subject so that they will exert voluntary effort to concentrate.

The very fact that voluntary attention requires conscious effort on the listener's part makes it tiring to him. As the psychologists say, "it is accompanied by a mass of strain sensations" resulting in a feeling of fatigue and, ultimately, boredom. Unless you want to tire your audience or to risk having their interest wane as you go on, you cannot depend on their voluntary attention alone. Desirable as it is to give your listener a reason at the start for paying attention, it is still your task to retain that attention and to make it as effortless and involuntary as possible. By using material containing the factors of attention discussed below, you can make it easier for your audience to listen to you and to focus attention on what you have to say. Thus, voluntary attention on their part will become involuntary, effortless, and sustained, and your ideas will be left sharply impressed upon your listeners' minds, unblurred by dullness or fatigue.

THE FACTORS OF ATTENTION

How, then, can we capture and hold the attention of an audience? Chapters 3 and 5 described ways in which a speaker could use his platform manner and his voice as methods of getting and holding attention; the reputation of the speaker and his prestige will also help determine the degree of attention accorded him. But here we are concerned with the content of the speech itself. What type of things can a speaker say that will command the attention of his audience? The *factors of attention*—those qualities of subject matter which capture the spontaneous attention of an audience—are:

1. Activity or Movement.
2. Reality.
3. Proximity.
4. Familiarity.
5. Novelty.
6. Suspense.
7. Conflict.
8. Humor.
9. The Vital.

These qualities, of course, overlap and frequently combine in a single appeal, but for convenience let us consider them separately.

Activity

If you were standing on the sidewalk and two cars of the same make and style were in your view, one parked by the curb and the other speeding down the street at sixty miles an hour, which one would you look at? The moving one, of course. Your speech likewise must move. Stories in which something happens have this quality. The more active are the things you talk about, the more intently will people listen. Instead of describing the structure of a machine, show how it works —get the wheels turning.

Your speech as a whole should also move. Nothing is so boring as a talk that seems to get nowhere. Make the movement of your speech clear to your audience by indicating when you are done with one point and are ready to move on to the next; and don't spend too much time on one point.

Reality

The earliest words a child learns are the names of objects and of tangible acts related to them. This interest in reality persists throughout life. The abstract proposition $2 + 2 = 4$ may be true, but it holds little interest. Instead of talking abstract theory, talk in terms of people, events, places, tangible circumstances. Use pictures, diagrams, and charts; tell what happened to Dr. Smith; use all the forms of support possible; make your descriptions vivid. And remember particularly that individual cases are more real than general classifications. Instead of saying, "A certain friend of mine," call him by name. Instead of "house," say *what* house or *what kind* of house.

Proximity

A direct reference to someone in the audience, to some object near at hand, to some incident which has just occurred, or to the immediate occasion at which the speech is being made will usually get attention. A reference to some remark of the preceding speaker or of the chairman has the same effect. The next time an audience starts dozing while you are speaking, try this: use a hypothetical illustration in which you name some person in the audience as the supposed chief character. Not only that man but everyone else as well will wake up.

Some things which are not near at
Familiarity　　　　　hand are still familiar to us because
of the frequency with which we
meet them in our daily lives. Thus, knives and forks, rain, automobiles, shaving, classes, and a host of other common objects and
events are closely built into our experiences. Because of their very
intimate connection with ourselves, familiar things catch our attention. We say, "Ah, that is an old friend." But, as with old
friends, we become bored if we see too much of them and nothing
else. The familiar holds attention only when it is brought up in
connection with something unfamiliar or when some unknown
aspect of it is pointed out. Thus, stories about Lincoln and Washington are interesting because we feel familiar with their characters; but we don't like to hear the same old rail-splitter or
cherry tree stories about them unless the stories are given a new
twist.

An old newspaper proverb has it
Novelty　　　　　that when a dog bites a man, it's
an accident; when a man bites a dog,
it's news. We pay immediate attention to that which is new or
unusual. Airplanes fly daily the hundreds of miles from New York
to San Francisco, but there is nothing in the papers about them
unless they crash. Even missile launching has begun to lose its
novelty, but human exploration of space still is news.

Be careful, however, not to discuss things so novel that they are
entirely unfamiliar. Remember that your audience must know
what you are talking about, or their attention will be lost. The
proper combination of the new and the old, of the novel and the
familiar, brings the best results.

There are two special types of novelty, that produced by *size* and
that brought out by *contrast*.

Size. Objects that are extremely large or extremely small attract
our attention. People are often startled into attention by large
figures, especially if they are much larger than commonly supposed or than numbers with which they are familiar. In an address
given at the University of Virginia, Henry W. Grady remarked, "A home that cost three million dollars and a breakfast
that cost five thousand are disquieting facts." Notice that mere

size alone will not always attract attention, but *unusual* size will. Reference to a truck costing five thousand dollars or a bridge worth three million would hardly have been striking. The New Yorker pays no attention to the great height of the skyscrapers, but the newcomer may get a cramp in his neck gazing up at the Empire State Building.

Contrast. At a formal dance, tuxedo suits pass unnoticed; but let a student come to class dressed in one the next morning and he becomes the center of amused attention. He would have been equally conspicuous had he gone to the dance in sport clothes. Of course, impropriety of this sort is not advised for the speaker; but contrast is not necessarily of this sort. How much more compelling the facts mentioned by Grady become when he throws them in contrast with others: "Our great wealth has brought us profit and splendor, but the status itself is a menace. A home that cost three million dollars and a breakfast that cost five thousand are disquieting facts to the millions who live in a hut and dine on a crust. The fact that a man . . . has an income of twenty million dollars falls strangely on the ears of those who hear it as they sit empty-handed with children crying for bread." [2]

Suspense   A large part of people's interest in a mystery story arises from their uncertainty as to its solution. If the reader were told at once who had killed the murdered man and how and when the deed was done, the rest of the book would never be read. An effective advertisement began in this way: "The L. J. Smithson Co. had been writing its balance in the red for two years, but last year it paid a dividend of twelve per cent." This statement was accompanied with a picture of a dividend check. Immediately you wonder, "How did they do it?" and you read on to find out. Few people go to see what they know will be a one-sided football game; the result is nearly certain. But the suspense of an evenly matched game draws a crowd. Hold the attention of your audience by pointing out results the cause of which must be explained (like the dividend mentioned above) or by calling attention to a force the effect of which is uncertain. Keep up the suspense in the

---

[2] From an address before the Literary Societies of the University of Virginia by Henry W. Grady, June 25, 1889.

stories you use to illustrate your points. Mention some valuable information that you expect to divulge later on in your speech but that first requires an understanding of the immediate point. Make full use of the factor of suspense, but remember two things: (*a*) Don't be so vague that the listeners lose all hope of solving the riddle; give them a large enough taste to make them want to hear more. (*b*) Make sure the situation is important enough to the audience that the suspense matters; attention is seldom drawn by uncertainties which are too trivial.

Conflict The opposition of forces compels attention. In a sense conflict is a form of activity, but it is more than that —it is a clash between opposing actions. In another sense it suggests uncertainty; but even when there is little doubt of the outcome, the very conflict draws some attention. Dog fights, election contests, the struggle of man with the adverse elements of nature and disease—all these have the attraction of conflict, and people are interested when you describe them. Controversial issues are of more interest than those agreed on. Disagreeing with your listeners will bring more attention than agreeing with them, though it is sometimes dangerous. A vigorous attack upon some enemy force, be it crime, graft, or a personal opponent, will draw more attention than a quiet analysis, though it is not always so effective. Describe a fight, show vividly the opposition between two forces, or make a verbal attack yourself, and people will listen to you. Be cautious, however, of sham battles: if you set up straw men and knock them down, the reality of your speech will be destroyed.

Humor Laughter indicates enjoyment, and people pay attention to that which they enjoy. Few things will hold the attention of an audience as well as a judicious use of humor. It serves as relaxation from the tension which other factors of attention often create and thus prevents fatigue while still retaining control over the thoughts of the listener. Funny anecdotes and humorous allusions serve to brighten many speeches. For the present let us be content with two requirements for its effective use: *Relevancy.* Beware of getting off the point being discussed.

Good taste. Avoid humor at occasions where it would be out of place, and avoid particular types of humor which would offend the specific audience before you.

The vital People always pay attention to those things which affect their life or health, their reputation, their property, or their employment. If you can show a man that what you say concerns him or his family, he will consider your discussion vital and will listen intently. In a larger sense, the satisfaction of any of the desires based on the primary motives discussed in Chapter 10 is a vital concern. Even the danger to someone else's life attracts attention because of our tendency to identify ourselves with others. If the other eight factors of attention are important in speech, this one is indispensable. Make your comments concern vital problems of your audience.

These nine factors of attention should be your constant guide in selecting material to develop your speech. Given adequate support in the manner described in the preceding chapter, your speech will be effective in proportion as it contains these factors.

SAMPLE SPEECH

The application of these factors of attention can best be illustrated by examining the text of an effective speech. Note the factors of attention contained in the following passage from a speech by Robert J. Havighurst.

THE AMERICAN FAMILY [3]

> *This excerpt is from a speech delivered by Robert J. Havighurst at the twenty-fifth annual Conference of the National Congress of Parents and Teachers held at Cleveland, Ohio, May 24–26, 1948.*

T he bare words, "we live in a changing society," hardly do justice to the process which has almost turned our society upside down and inside out within the lifetime of the older of us.

---

[3] From *Vital Speeches of the Day*, Vol. XIV, July 1, 1948, p. 565 ff.

Consider what has happened to the home, the stage on which the drama of family life is played. What was the home like, fifty years ago? There was the parlor, always cold and clean and quiet, with an organ which was pumped with the feet, a hard horsehair sofa, and a photographic album. The sitting room was more cheerful, with its base-burner standing in the middle of the room on a metal sheet to protect the carpet, the coals glowing red-hot through the isinglass windows of the stove, the stove pipe going straight up through the ceiling to lend a little warmth to the bedroom above; the coal scuttle beside the stove, half full of coal, and garnished with nutshells and apple cores. On the library table a big kerosene lamp shedding a yellow glow, and the latest copies of *Harper's Bazaar* and the *Youth's Companion*. Beside the table a big rocking chair, in which mother rocked the baby to sleep, singing lullabies. And I almost forgot to mention the brick sewn up in a piece of carpet, and used as a doorstop.

In the kitchen there was the range, with a fire burning briskly, and the oven door open to warm the room on a cold morning, while oatmeal cooked in the double boiler and eggs and bacon sizzled in the frying pan. At the sink was the cistern pump for rain water, and beside it stood the pail of drinking water, with a long-handled dipper. Down in the cellar was the vegetable room with a bin of potatoes and a sack of turnips and a barrel of apples.

Let us not omit from this picture the icy-cold bedroom, with the wash-water frozen in the washbowl on the washstand on winter mornings; the Saturday-night bath ritual in the washtub in the kitchen; the souring milk and the running butter during hot summer days, and the dread of typhoid fever always threatening to break into epidemic proportions.

Would we trade the old home for the modern one, with thermostatically-controlled heat coming through radiators at the turn of a valve, light at the turn of a button, clean white kitchen equipment, electric refrigeration, and electrical cleaning equipment which makes unnecessary "beating the rugs" until one gets blisters on the hands and knees?

Whether we approve of modern gadgets completely or not, we will take most of them and enjoy them. They are results of man's unquenchable thirst for knowledge, which produces a technology that changes the conditions of life and sets in motion great social forces which change the social landscape as irresistibly as the glacier, creeping down from the north in the ancient days, changed the physical landscape. . . .

Is the destiny of the family outside of man's control, like the coming of an ice age? We know that some time, a few thousand or a few million years hence, the earth's axis may tip, or some other cosmic process may occur which will bring another ice age on this continent. The winters will gradually grow longer. The sun will seem to lose its heat and will shine wanly from the south during the short winter days, unable to melt the snow and ice that lock the land and water in rigid embrace. Slowly but relentlessly an ice sheet will form in Canada and move south, a few feet or a few inches in a year. This glacier will surmount and grind into debris the cities and farms and all the handiwork of men. As the glacier reaches the Great Lakes, the cities of Buffalo and Cleveland and Toledo and Detroit and Chicago will become uninhabitable. Industry and business will move south, and so will most of the people, leaving only a few hardy souls to turn Eskimo and hack out a living from the frozen wilderness at the edge of the advancing ice.

This physical event, when and if it comes, will be irresistible. Even atomic energy will not avail against it. It lies outside of man's control.

But the forces of social change are not like the blind forces of physical change. Social change is man-made, and can be man-controlled. Men can foresee consequences and can modify their institutions so as to preserve old values and gain new ones.

The problem, then, of the family is the problem of controlling social forces and modifying institutional forms so as to achieve values which the family has given in the past or may give in the future.

The great difficulty of this problem can be estimated from a look at the recent vicissitudes of the American family since World War I.

First, immediately after World War I, there were the mad and riotous 1920's. This was the age of the flapper, when divorce rates first commenced their alarming rise; when the movie and the automobile drew people out of their homes, and the front porch lost its function in the American home.

Then came the gloomy thirties, when the economic base of the family crumbled. People could not afford to marry. People could not afford to have children. The birth rate dropped to its lowest point in America's history in 1933. Families were held together, like the old Fords, with baling wire provided by the W.P.A.

Just when it seemed that we might climb out of the Great Depression, there came the anxious forties, when young men and women married and then the men went off to war. When children were born to hundreds of thousands of women without the supporting presence of a father. When young mothers had to move in with their parents, and families of war industry workers lived in trailers.

And finally comes the frustrating and pressing present—a postwar period of confusion of purposes and of doubt as to our ability to re-create a stable and peaceful society on a world scale. This is an age in which we see clearly our social weakness, but seem impotent to do anything about it. We can describe our social ills with a wealth of statistics. It is an age of great understanding and little will power.

PROBLEMS

1. Be ready to discuss the following questions in class: What is the nature of attention? How is the concept of attention important to the

speaker? How can the factors of attention be employed in the content of a speech?

2. From your own experience, make a list of instances when you "paid attention" to something. For each instance on your list, determine whether that attention was voluntary or involuntary. Then try to recall the manner and degree with which you made physical adjustments, whether you received a clearer impression of what your attention was focused on than of background impressions, and whether you "got set" to respond.

3. Find samples of each of the factors of attention that are used in the speech printed above and in the speeches at the ends of the chapters in Parts IV and V.

4. List three or four subjects which have little interest for your classmates. What factors of attention could you use to catch and maintain their attention in these subjects? How could you develop your speech using these factors?

5. Rework the speech prepared for Problem 4 in the last chapter, introducing more attention factors into it. Make the speech more vivid and striking.

6. Prepare a three-minute speech advertising the next activity of a campus organization to which you belong. Include several of the factors of attention.

Everything that can be thought at all can be thought clearly. Everything that can be said can be said clearly.

Ludwig Wittgenstein

CHAPTER 14 / *Arranging and Outlining Points of a Speech*

We have considered the analytical aspects of speech preparation and have discussed the material of which speeches are built. Moreover, we have seen in Chapter 12 how this material may be arranged to explain or to support a single point or idea. Most speeches, however, contain more than one point. In this chapter, therefore, we shall discuss a number of ways to arrange the main points in a speech together with their subordinate points and supporting material and then consider how these points may be written down in outline form. In the next chapter we shall consider the means of completing the speech by adding appropriate beginnings and endings.

SELECTING AND ARRANGING MAIN POINTS

When you get up to speak, nothing will help you remember what you have planned to say quite so much as having the points in your speech arranged in a systematic sequence so that one point leads naturally into the next. Moreover, your audience will follow your thoughts more easily and grasp them more firmly if the pattern of your speech is clear. As H. A. Overstreet once said, to hold the interest of your audience you must *"let your speech march!"* [1] Your listeners should not get the impression that you are wandering aimlessly from point to point; you must make it evident to them that your ideas are closely related to one another and are marching forward to completeness in a unified and orderly manner. There are several ways of selecting and arranging the points in your speech to accomplish this result.

Time sequence   Begin at a certain period or date and move forward or backward from that. (Be careful not to reverse the order once you have started.) For example, weather conditions may be discussed by considering the conditions which exist in the spring, summer, fall, and winter, respectively; methods for refining petroleum, by tracing the development of the refining process from the earliest attempts down to the present; for the manufacture of an automobile, by following the assembly-line process from beginning to end. A time sequence may be appropriate to your subject no matter what your purpose in the speech may be. As in each of the instances above, however, it is often the most effective means of determining and arranging the main points in a speech to inform. Here is an example of this method:

THE EARLY HISTORY OF TEXAS

  I. Until 1822, Texas was under Spanish colonial rule.
 II. From then till 1835, Texas remained a part of the Mexican Republic.
III. For the next ten years, Texas was an independent nation.
IV. In 1845, Texas became one of the United States.

Space sequence   Arrange your material from east to west, from the bottom up, from right to left. Thus, the density of population may be discussed according to geographical areas; the plans of a building may be considered floor by floor; or the

---

[1] See *Influencing Human Behavior* by H. A. Overstreet (W. W. Norton & Company, N. Y., 1925), pp. 82–83.

layout for a city park may be explained by proceeding from one end to the other. The aspects of a problem or a solution are often arranged according to a space sequence. The following example shows a problem analyzed according to this method:

OUR DECLINING SALES

  I. New England sales have dropped 15 percent during the past year.
 II. The Gulf States have had the same decline in sales.
III. In the Great Lakes area sales have fallen off 20 percent.

Cause-effect sequence

While a cause-effect sequence may be used in a speech to inform (as in explaining the relationships involved in some past or present event), this sequence is more commonly used in speeches to persuade. When you discuss certain forces and then try to convince your audience that these forces have produced or will produce certain results, or when you describe conditions or events and then attempt to prove that certain forces created them, you are dealing with causal relationships. Thus you might first discuss a community's zoning ordinances and second try to prove that present conditions (good or bad) are the effects of those regulations; the number of individuals who commit crimes after they have served prison sentences can be reported and then attributed to certain major causes—ineffective methods of rehabilitation, public misunderstanding, or others. The arrangement of an argument of this sort (on which there is agreement as to the conditions or effects but seldom as to their causes) may be arranged as follows:

THE RISING COST OF LIVING

  I. Each year the cost of living increases. (A, B, C, etc.: cite examples and statistics.)
 II. The causes of the increase are: (A, B, C, etc.: list and explain causes.)

Problem-solution sequence

Many times, your material can best be presented by dividing it into two major sections: the description of a problem (or related problems) and the presentation of a solution (or solutions) to it. Thus you might describe the problems involved in building the Mackinac bridge connecting the Upper and Lower Peninsulas of Michigan, and then explain how the problems were solved. Usually, however, this type of arrangement will be applied to problems facing the immediate audience for which you wish to present a solution. For example, you might discuss the problem of declining interest in a campus activity and then try to convince the members of your audience that they should adopt one or more ways of solving this problem. It is also possible to apply this method to discussions of future contingencies: for example, one could outline the problems to be faced by the American school system after twenty more years of increasing population and then present suggested solutions to these problems. When this type of sequence is used with a multiple problem or solution, each of the two main divisions of your discussion must itself be arranged in an orderly way, and you may use one of the other sequences for this purpose. Here is an example of how one speaker employed the problem-solution sequence:

CONTROLLING CRIME

I. Our criminal problem is becoming serious.
   A. Serious offenses are more common.
   B. Juvenile crimes have become alarming.
II. We must meet this problem in three ways:
   A. We must begin a crime-prevention program.
   B. Our police force must be strengthened to insure arrests.
   C. Our court procedure must be freed from politics.

Special topical sequence   Certain types of information are customarily presented in divisions with which the audience is familiar. For example, financial reports are divided traditionally into assets and liabilities, or into income and expenditure. Some organizations are often discussed by departments; a talk on the organization of the United States government, for instance, would naturally be divided into three sections: the legislative, the executive, and the judicial branches. Whenever a partition is already established in the information or argument you are about to present, the best method usually is to follow that partition. Moreover, your points may sometimes consist of a series of qualities or functions of the thing you are discussing; or you may wish to present a series of parallel "reasons why" or "basic objections." When such a series cannot be arranged easily in a time or space sequence, a special topical sequence should be used. Thus, you might have a series of points like this:

DEMOCRATIC GOVERNMENT IS BEST
  I. It guarantees legitimate freedom to the individual.
 II. It reflects the will of the majority.
III. It deepens the citizen's feeling of responsibility.

Similarly, your points may be arranged to answer a series of questions known to be uppermost in the minds of the audience. It would be foolish to diffuse the answers to these questions by adopting a different partition of the subject.

The fact that one of the above methods has been chosen for the main topics does not prevent the use of another method for the subordinate points. On no condition, however, shift from one method to another in the order of the main points themselves. The following outline will illustrate the proper way to combine two or more methods:

MAJOR INDIAN TRIBES OF THE WEST
  I. Southwest.
      A. Apache.
          1. Early history.
          2. Contacts with explorers and settlers.
          3. Present conditions.
      B. Navaho.
          1. . . . etc.
      C. Pueblo.
 II. Pacific coast.
      A. . . . etc.
III. Northwest.

Notice that in this outline the space sequence is used in the main points, the special topical sequence is used in the subpoints, A, B, and C, and the time sequence is used in the sub-subpoints, 1, 2, and 3.

The main points in your speech should be expressed clearly and emphatically. While your illustrations, arguments, and facts will constitute the bulk of your speech, the statement of your main points ties these details together and points up their meaning. Good speakers take particular pains to phrase these main points in such a way that the meaning will be clear, persuasive, and easily remembered by their listeners. To achieve this result, you should keep in mind four characteristics of good phrasing: conciseness, vividness, motivation, and parallelism.

Conciseness   State your points as briefly as you can without sacrificing their meaning. Use the fewest words possible. Boil it down. A simple declarative sentence is better than a complex one. Avoid using a clumsy modifying phrase or distracting subordinate clause. State the essence of your idea in a short sentence which can be modified or elaborated as you present the supporting material, or phrase your point as a simple question to which your detailed facts will provide the answer. Thus "Our state taxes are too high" is better than "Taxes in this state, with one or two exceptions, are higher than the present economic conditions justify." The latter statement may present your idea more completely than the first, but it contains nothing that your supporting material should not make clear anyhow, while its greater complexity makes it less crisp and emphatic.

Vividness   Wherever possible, use words and phrases that are colorful and provoke attention. If the wording of your main points is dull and lifeless, you cannot expect them to stand out and be remembered. Since they *are* the main points, they should be phrased so that they *sound* that way. They should be the punch lines of your speech. Notice how much more vivid it is to say, "We must turn these rascals out!" than to say, "We must remove these incompetent and dishonest men from office." Remember, of course, that vivid phrasing can be overdone. The sober presentation of a technical report at a scientific meeting does not require the colorful language needed at a political rally; on the other hand, neither does it justify the trite and sterile jargon too often employed. Keeping in mind the nature of your subject and the occasion, avoid equally a superficial and exaggerated vividness that seems to be straining for effect and a lifeless, ordinary wording that lacks strength or color.

Motivation   Whenever possible, word your main points so that they appeal to the interests and desires of your audience. Review the factors of attention listed in Chapter 13 and the motive appeals discussed in Chapter 10. Try to phrase your main points so that they incorporate these elements. Instead of stating, "Chemical research has helped improve medical treatment," say, "Modern chemistry helps the doctor make you well." Rather than asserting, "Travel by air is fast," why not say "Travel by air saves time." Remember that you will not be speaking merely about something, but *to* somebody; your main points should appeal to each person in the audience.

Parallelism   Try to use the same sentence structure and similar phrasing for each of your main points. Since these points represent coordinate major units of your speech, word them so they sound that way. Avoid unnecessary shifts from active to passive voice or from question to assertion. Where possible, use prepositions, connectives, and auxiliary verbs which permit a similar balance, rhythm, and direction of thought. Instead of wording a series of main points thus:

I. The amount of your income tax depends on the amount you earn.
II. Property tax is assessed on the value of what you own.
III. You pay sales taxes in proportion to the amount you buy.

Phrase them like this:

I. The amount you earn decides your income tax.
II. The amount you own controls your property tax.
III. The amount you buy determines your sales tax.

Note that part of each statement in the series above was repeated, while the rest of the statement changed from point to point.

Such repetition of key words is often used to intensify the parallelism. Similarly, in discussing the industrial value of aluminum, you might say:

    I. Aluminum is strong.
   II. Aluminum is light.
 III. Aluminum is cheap.

Parallelism of phrasing, together with conciseness, vividness, and motivation, will help make your main points stand out.

ARRANGING SUBPOINTS AND
SUPPORTING MATERIAL

After you have put the main points of your speech in a sequence, you must then decide how to arrange the subpoints and supporting material so that the internal structure of your speech has orderliness and substance.

Subordinating the subpoints   A string-of-beads discussion, in which everything seems to have equal weight—tied together usually by "and-uh," "and next," "and then," "and so"—lacks vigor and soon gets tiring. If you emphasize everything, nothing will seem prominent. Regardless of how well you have chosen, arranged, and worded your main points, they will not stand out unless your subpoints are properly subordinated to them. Therefore, avoid listing subpoints as if they were main points, and avoid listing under a main point items that have no direct subordinate relation to that point. Here are a few types of items that are commonly subordinate:

Parts of a whole. Frequently the main point concerns an object or a process which consists of a series of component parts; the subpoints then take up each of the parts. Or sometimes the main point expresses a summation of items; the subpoints then list the facts which add up to that summation. Thus the grip, shaft, and head may be the parts of a golf club; or the number of churches in England, Scotland, Ireland, and Wales may be cited as subtotals of the sum total of churches in the entire British Isles.

Lists of qualities or functions. When the main point deals with the nature of something, the subpoints often list the qualities which constitute that nature. If the main point suggests the purpose of some mechanism, organization, or procedure, the subpoints may list the specific functions it performs. Thus timbre, pitch, and loudness may be the qualities under which the nature of sound is discussed; the purpose of a police department may be made clear by discussing its various duties or functions.

Series of causes or results. If the cause-effect sequence is used for your main points, you will often find that neither cause nor effect is single. The series of causes and results will then constitute the series of subpoints. Even when another type of sequence is used for main points, a list of causes or results often forms the subitems of a major point. In this way, the causes of a crop failure might be listed as drought, frost, and blight; or the results of proper diet could be given as greater comfort, better health, and longer life.

Items of logical proof. In an argumentative speech the subpoints should always provide logical proof of the main point they support. Often they consist of a series of reasons or of the coordinate steps in a single process of reasoning. When this is done, you should always be able to connect the main point and subpoints with the word "because" (main point is true, *because* subpoints are true), and, in reverse, you should be able to use the word "therefore" (subpoints are true, *therefore* main point is true). An example of this type of subordination is this: Strikes are wasteful, because (*a*) workers lose their wages, (*b*) employers lose their profits, and (*c*) consumers lose the products they might have had.

Illustrative examples. Many times the main point consists of a generalized statement for which the subpoints provide a series of specific illustrative examples. This method is used both for exposition and for argument, the examples constituting clarification and proof respectively. The general statement that fluoride helps reduce tooth decay, for example, might have as its subpoints a series of examples citing the experience of those cities which have added fluoride to their drinking water.

These are by no means all the types of subordinate items, but these common types should serve to illustrate the general principle of subordination. Remember also that the same principle applies to further subordination under subpoints. In longer and more detailed speeches you may have sub-subpoints and even sub-sub-subpoints. Don't become too intricate and involved in this process, but however far you go, keep your subordination logical.

Arranging coordinate subpoints　　　Preferably there should be two or more subpoints under every main point in your speech. While these are subordinate to the main point, they should be coordinate with each other. In what sequence, then, should they be arranged? The answer is simple: list them according to one of the types of arrangement given at the beginning of this chapter. Choose whichever sequence—time, space, causal, etc.—seems most appropriate. You may want to use one sequence for the items under one main point and a different sequence for those under another, but do not shift from one to another in the same coordinate series. Above all, be sure you do employ some systematic order; don't crowd items in haphazardly just because they are subordinate points.

Supporting subpoints　　　The importance of supporting material was emphasized in Chapter 12. The general rule is: never make a statement in a speech without presenting at least one of the forms of support to clarify, illustrate, or prove it. Too often, speakers think that if they have set down subpoints under every main point they have done enough. The fact is, however, that you can subdivide points all day without doing any more than add detail to the *structure* of your speech. The *substance* of it lies in the figures, illustrations, facts, and testimony introduced. The manner in which such material is used to support a point was fully discussed in connection with the one-point speech (p. 212 ff.) and need not be repeated here. While you may not need as much support for every subpoint in your talk as was suggested for a one-point speech, remember that the more you have, the stronger that point will be.

We have now considered the principles and some of the methods for logical and coherent arrangement of the ideas in a speech. Even with a thorough grasp of these principles and methods, however, few persons can sit down with a mass of material and work out the details of a speech in their minds. Some orderly method must usually be followed for setting these ideas and facts down on paper so that the relationship between them can be kept clear and any weak points can be discovered and corrected. The method used by most speakers is to construct an outline. This method is particularly effective because it throws into bold relief the structure as well as the content of the speech. Noting first the requirements of good outline form, we shall then see how to go about preparing an outline which sets forth in orderly fashion the main points, the subpoints, and the supporting material of a speech.

REQUIREMENTS OF GOOD OUTLINE FORM

The amount of detail and the type of arrangement used in an outline will depend on your subject, your analysis of the situation, and your previous experience in speech composition. But regardless of these factors, any good outline should meet certain basic requirements:

1. *Each unit in the outline should contain only one item or statement.* This is essential to the very nature of outlining. If two or three items or statements are run together under one symbol, the structural relationship does not stand out clearly. Notice the differences in the following examples:

Wrong
I. Our city should conduct a campaign against the thousands of flies that infest the city every year, breeding everywhere and buzzing at every kitchen door, because they spread disease by carrying germs and contaminating food, and because they can be eliminated easily by killing them with insecticides and preventing their breeding by cleaning up refuse.

Right
I. Our city should conduct a campaign against flies.
   A. Thousands of flies infest the city every year.
      1. They breed everywhere.
      2. They buzz at every kitchen door.
   B. Flies spread disease.
      1. They carry germs.
      2. They contaminate food.
   C. Flies can be eliminated easily.
      1. Widespread use of insecticides kills them.
      2. Cleaning up refuse prevents their breeding.

2. *The items in the outline should be logically subordinated.* Those statements or facts that are listed as subpoints under a larger heading should really be subordinate in meaning and not of equal or greater importance. Moreover, nothing should be included as a subpoint unless it has some direct connection with the main point under which it appears. Each subordinate point should directly and logically support or amplify the superior point under which it stands.

Wrong

I. Radio is a direct benefit to humanity.
    A. It has saved many lives at sea.
II. It makes easier the spreading of news.
III. Present broadcasting methods are not as good as they might be.
    A. There are too many stations cluttering the air.
        1. Programs are becoming worse.
        2. There are too many disk jockey programs and high-pressure sales talks.
    B. This is true even though a great many criminals have been tracked down by means of radio.

Right

I. Radio is a direct benefit to humanity.
    A. It has saved many lives at sea.
    B. It makes easier the spreading of news.
    C. It has aided in tracking down a great many criminals.
II. Present broadcasting methods are not as good as they might be.
    A. There are too many stations cluttering the air.
    B. Programs are becoming worse.
        1. There are too many disk jockey programs.
        2. There are too many high-pressure sales talks.

3. *The logical relation of the items in an outline should be shown by proper indentation.* The greater the logical importance of a statement, the nearer to the left-hand margin should it be started. If a statement runs over one line, the second line should be indented the same as the beginning of the statement.

Wrong

I. Shortening the college course to three years is not necessary.
    A. Provision is already made for students who are unable to spend four years in college.
    B. Other parts of one's educational career can be cut short with less loss than would result from this proposal.
        1. The preparatory-school course could be shortened.
        2. The course in professional school could be shortened.

Wrong

I. Shortening the college course to three years is not necessary.
A. Provision is already made for students who are unable to spend four years in college.
B. Other parts of one's educational career can be cut short with less loss than would result from this proposal.
1. The preparatory-school course could be shortened.
2. The course in professional school could be shortened.

Right

I. Shortening the college course to three years is not necessary.
  A. Provision is already made for students who are unable to spend four years in college.
  B. Other parts of one's educational career can be cut short with less loss than would result from this proposal.
    1. The preparatory-school course could be shortened.
    2. The course in professional school could be shortened.

4. *Some consistent set of symbols should be used.* One such set is exemplified in the outlines printed in this chapter. But whether you use this set or some other, be consistent—do not change systems in the middle of the outline. Items of the same logical importance should have the same type of symbol, and those which differ in their logical importance should *not* have the same type of symbol. Thus:

Wrong

I. There is a need for better traffic regulation.
  II. Figures show the extent of traffic-law violations:
    A. 300,000 motorists were arrested in New York last year.
    2. One million dollars was paid in fines last year by New York motorists.
      I. This is more than the total paid in all England, Scotland, and Wales.
      a. This amount would buy about 500 new automobiles.

Right

I. There is a need for better traffic regulation.
  A. Figures show the extent of traffic-law violations:
    1. 300,000 motorists were arrested in New York last year.
    2. One million dollars was paid in fines last year by New York motorists.
      a. This is more than the total paid in all England, Scotland, and Wales.
      b. This amount would buy about 500 new automobiles.

In addition to these four requirements which apply to all types of outlines, there is one more that applies to the final draft of a complete and finished outline. *All the main points and all the subpoints should be written down as complete sentences.* Only by writing complete sentences can you be sure that the meaning of each point and its relation to the other points in the outline are completely clear.

HOW TO PREPARE AN OUTLINE

We turn now to the actual process of getting an outline down on paper. Our objective is to develop in outline form a logical and usable framework for the ideas we intend to present in the speech itself. Our outline should obey the principles of orderly arrangement and logical completeness discussed earlier in this chapter, and its form should fill the requirements just listed. Obviously, one does not arrive at this result in one sudden step: he does not stare thoughtfully into space for a period of time and then begin writing down an outline in a finished and final form. An outline, like the speech it represents, grows, develops, and becomes more definite in a series of orderly stages. While the details of this process may vary from person to person just as study habits differ, the basic procedure is the same. Your work will move along more easily and systematically if you follow this basic procedure:

I. Select and limit the subject of your speech:
   A. Phrase your general topic.
   B. Consider your purpose and the limiting factors of time, audience, and occasion.
   C. Restate your topic to fit these limits.
II. Develop a rough draft of your outline:
   A. List the main points you expect to cover.
   B. Rearrange these main points in some systematic sequence.
   C. Insert and arrange the subpoints under each main point.
   D. Note roughly the supporting material to be used under each point.
   E. Check your rough draft: see whether it covers your subject and fits your purpose. (If not, revise it or start over with a different sequence of main points.)

III. Recast the outline into final form:
   A. Rephrase the main points to make them concise, vivid, parallel, and motivated.
   B. Write out the subpoints as complete sentences.
      1. Check them for proper coordination.
      2. Check them for subordination to the main point.
   C. Fill in the supporting material in detail.
      1. Check support for pertinence.
      2. Check support for adequacy.
   D. Recheck the entire outline for:
      1. Good outline form.
      2. Coverage of subject.
      3. Accomplishment of purpose.

Now let us see how this process might be applied to develop a finished outline.

Selecting and limiting the subject Suppose that because of your work with an urban renewal project you have been asked to speak on urban renewal to an audience of business and professional men at a luncheon club in a small city. Your general topic, of course, would be:

URBAN RENEWAL

But before attempting to develop your outline, you know you need to limit this topic somewhat to keep your talk within the thirty minutes allotted you. A review of Chapters 8 and 9 reminds you to limit and organize your subject according to the probable interests and information of your audience. As business and professional men and also as city dwellers, your audience will be interested in the general topic, you decide, but not necessarily informed about how urban renewal developed nor fully aware of its vital importance to each of them. Thus it seems a good idea to begin with an account of its development and then to point up its vital importance to all citizens. Since you have only thirty minutes in which to deliver this speech, you must select the remaining content carefully. In order to prove to your audience that urban renewal is not all theory, you plan to describe in detail a specific example of the urban renewal program with which you are familiar. Knowing the interest of your audience in money matters, you decide to include a discussion of urban renewal finance. Accordingly, you have now limited your topic to:

URBAN RENEWAL

(A discussion of the development and importance of urban renewal, a specific example of an urban renewal program and financing of urban renewal.)

Only your general topic will be announced to your audience, of course, as the title of your speech; but the entire statement included within parentheses will appear on your outline to indicate the limits you have set for yourself.

Developing the rough draft

In deciding on the limits of your subject, you will already have selected in broad terms the main topics to be covered in your speech. Now set these down in rough form to see how they may be modified and arranged. At this stage your list may be:

1. Development and importance of Urban Renewal.
2. Specific Example of Urban Renewal.
3. Financing of Urban Renewal.

This list covers what you want to say, but the sequence is a little doubtful and the first point should be divided. A time sequence could be used for the whole speech, discussing the gradual development of the concept of urban renewal with the associated methods of management and finance, but this would result in too much repetition and might subordinate the ideas you want to emphasize. After considering several other types of arrangement, you might finally decide on a special topical sequence based on the questions you know will be of interest to your audience, namely:

1. How did urban renewal develop?
2. How is it financed?
3. Why is it important to the citizen?
4. What is a specific example of an urban renewal program?

Your next step will be to phrase these points as answers to the above questions and put them in outline form, inserting subpoints under each of them. In this way you can test the sequence you have tentatively chosen; you can see whether it hangs together when the details are added. After inserting and arranging your subpoints, you will make rough notations under each to indicate what supporting material can be used to illustrate and amplify them. When you have done this, your rough draft will look something like the sample on pages 252 and 253.

Now examine your rough draft carefully. See whether it covers all the points you want to include. Note whether you have thrown it out of balance by expanding unimportant points too greatly or by skimping on the more important items. Ask yourself whether it is likely to accomplish its purpose with the audience for which it is designed. Check your supporting material thoroughly to see that you have enough examples, facts, and quotable references throughout; if you do not, seek out the additional material you need. When you are satisfied with your rough outline, you are ready to recast it into final form.

Putting the outline into final form
This phase of your preparation consists mainly of improving your phraseology and of filling in details. Write out your points as sentences which state your meaning exactly, and see that your outline form meets the requirements listed on pages 245 to 248. As you do so, you may discover errors in logical sequence or weakness of support in some places. These should be corrected as you go along.

Your work will be speeded if you follow the order suggested on pages 248 and 249. First, rephrase your main points so they make your meaning clear and vivid. Then taking each main point in turn, restate the subpoints under it, checking coordination and subordination carefully. As you do this, fill in the supporting material in more complete detail, testing it for pertinence and adequacy. When you have done this in detail for each part of the outline, go back and review the outline as a whole: check its form, its coverage of the subject, its adaptation to your purpose. Perhaps by this time your revision will look like the sample on pages 254 to 257.

Urban Renewal
(A discussion of the development, finance, and importance
of urban renewal, and a specific example of an urban
renewal program.)

I. Federal government supported urban renewal
    A. Housing Act of 1949
        1. Federal aid for clearance of slum areas
        2. Concentrated on elimination of substandard
           housing
    B. Housing Act of 1954
        1. Federal aid for clearance of slum areas
        2. Stressed restoration through voluntary repair
           and rehabilitation
    C. Housing Act of 1959
        1. Endorsed long-range community renewal programs
        2. Enabled more effective use of federal and
           local funds
        3. Aid urban renewal program on national
           basis

II. Urban renewal financed by federal government and
    by the community
    A. Federal assistance available for specific
        projects
        1. Elimination of residential slums
        2. Redevelopment of nonresidential blighted
           areas for residential uses
        3. Redevelopment of open areas impairing
           growth of community
        4. Acquisition of open land for residential uses
        5. Acquisition of land for industrial
           redevelopment
    B. Various forms of federal assistance available
        1. Advance loans for surveys and plans
        2. Temporary loans to pay gross project costs
        3. Loans for leasing land in accordance
           with redevelopment plan
        4. Capital grants of 2/3 net cost
        5. Grants for relocation of families and businesses

C. Community may use several methods to finance cost
   1. Appropriations
   2. Bond issues
   3. Funds from state, county, or private organizations

III. Urban renewal is important to every citizen
   A. Areas in need of urban renewal are costly
      1. Provide only 6% of city's tax revenues
      2. Account for 45% of city's municipal service costs
   B. Areas in need of urban renewal are dangerous
      1. Unsanitary conditions prevalent
         a. 50% of city's disease
         b. 60% of tuberculosis victims
      2. Delinquency and crime rate high
         a. 55% of the juvenile delinquency
         b. 45% of the major crimes
         c. 50% of the arrests

IV. Chicago established Chicago Land Clearance Commission to direct portion of its urban renewal program
   A. Designates projects with approval of City Council and State Housing Board, concentrating on specific areas
      1. Areas detrimental to public welfare
      2. Areas with clouded titles, diversity of ownership, and tax delinquencies
   B. Current program has 26 projects
      1. 11 residential projects will provide 11,000 new dwelling units
      2. 8 projects will provide land for community parks and expansion of hospitals and schools
      3. 3 projects will be redeveloped as shopping centers
      4. 4 projects will provide industrial and commercial buildings

URBAN RENEWAL
(A discussion of the development, finance, and importance of urban renewal and a specific example of
an urban renewal program.)
  I. Urban renewal has been speeded up through fed-
    eral legislation.
    A. The Housing Act of 1949 was an important step
      in promoting urban renewal.
      1. It was the first attempt to join private
        enterprise and local government to clear
        the slums.
      2. It offered federal aid to the cities for
        slum clearance.
      3. It concentrated primarily on the elimi-
        nation of substandard housing.
    B. The Housing Act of 1954 had several im-
      portant new aspects.
      1. It asked private enterprise to assume a
        greater part of the job of blight removal
        and prevention.
      2. It continued to offer federal aid for
        slum clearance.
      3. It stressed restoration through voluntary
        repair and rehabilitation.
        a. Rehabilitation was less costly than
          land acquisition and building demoli-
          tion.
          1) As Fred Smith, Vice President of the
            Prudential Insurance Company, said
            recently, "New structures should go
            up only when older ones cannot suc-
            cessfully be rehabilitated."
        b. Task was too expensive to be accom-
          plished solely through slum clearance.
    C. The Housing Act of 1959 emphasized the con-
      cept of urban renewal.
      1. It endorsed long-range programs involving
        urban renewal needs of the whole com-
        munity.
      2. It enabled more effective use of federal
        and local funds by permitting the best
        scheduling of urban projects in the com-
        munity.
      3. Its method may help furnish information
        concerning urban renewal needs on a na-
        tional basis.

II. Urban renewal projects are sponsored cooperatively by the federal government and by the community.
   A. The federal government provides assistance for specific projects.
      1. It supports elimination of residential slum or blighted areas.
      2. It promotes redevelopment of nonresidential blighted areas for residential uses.
      3. It encourages redevelopment of open areas which impair the sound growth of the community.
      4. It offers assistance for the acquisition of open land for residential uses essential for sound community growth.
      5. It aids the acquisition of land for industrial redevelopment within the limits of fund and law.
   B. The federal government provides financial assistance of various kinds.
      1. It provides advance loans for surveys and plans.
      2. It provides temporary loans to pay gross project costs.
      3. It provides loans for leasing of land.
      4. It provides capital grants not exceeding two thirds of the net project cost.
      5. It provides grants for relocation repayments to displaced families and businesses.
   C. The community may finance its share of the cost variously.
      1. It may make direct appropriations from the annual budget.
      2. It may issue general obligation bonds on the faith and credit of the community.
      3. It may issue funds from state, county, or public bodies or from any private organization.
III. Urban renewal is of vital importance to every citizen.
   A. Slums are expensive.[2]

_____
   [2] Data selected from "ABC's of Urban Renewal," Urban Renewal Division of Sears Roebuck and Co., Chicago, Illinois, page 7.

1. Slum and substandard areas comprising 20 percent of a city's residential area provide only 6 percent of the city's total real estate tax revenues.
2. Slum and substandard areas are responsible for 45 percent of the city's municipal service costs—police, fire, health, welfare.

B. Slums are dangerous.
   1. Unsanitary conditions are prevalent.
      a. Fifty percent of the city's disease occurs in slum areas.
      b. Sixty percent of the tuberculosis victims live in slum areas.
   2. Crime rates are high.
      a. Fifty-five percent of the city's juvenile delinquency occurs in slum areas.
      b. Forty-five percent of the city's major crimes occurs in slum areas.
      c. Fifty percent of the city's arrests are made in slum areas.

C. Slums are cruel.
   1. Children's lives may be stunted or warped.
   2. Elderly people may finish out their lives in misery.
   3. Adults of all ages may be trapped and hopeless.

IV. Chicago's urban renewal work includes a huge redevelopment program.
   A. The program is directed by the Chicago Land Clearance Commission.
      1. The Commission was established on September 26, 1947.
      2. It works with the City Council and the State Housing Board to decide on projects.
   B. The program concentrates on specific areas.
      1. Built-up areas detrimental to the public welfare are considered for urban renewal.
      2. Vacant land with clouded titles, diversity of ownership, and tax delinquencies is usually in need of urban renewal.
   C. The current program[3] has twenty-six projects underway.

_____

[3] Facts and figures cited here were current in October 1961.

1. Eleven residential projects containing 514 acres will provide 11,000 new dwelling units.
2. Eight projects containing 230 acres will provide land for community parks and the expansion of hospitals and schools.
3. Three projects containing 12 acres will be redeveloped as shopping centers to serve adjacent neighborhoods.
4. Four projects containing 163 acres will provide industrial and commercial buildings with off-street parking and loading facilities.

A final word of advice is here in order. Arranging and outlining the substance of a speech cannot be casually tossed off in a few odd moments. Time and effort are required to do it well. Allow yourself the time and exert the effort; the resulting clarity and force with which you speak will more than compensate you. Remember, too, that there is a certain knack to outlining which develops with experience. If you have not done much of it before, outlining a speech will take you more time. As you do more of it, your skill will increase and with it the speed at which you work. Begin now by carefully outlining every speech you make in class.

PROBLEMS

1. Be ready to discuss the following questions in class: Why is careful organization important to the speaker? To the audience? What are the characteristics of good phrasing for main points, and why is good phrasing important? How should subpoints and supporting material be arranged? What are the requirements of good outline form? What main steps should be followed in preparing an outline?

2. Decide on suitable arrangements for four of the following topics or for four topics of your own choice and write down three or more main points for each. Try to use a different type of arrangement for each topic.

Foreign Neighborhoods in ———— City
Family Disagreements
Administration of My Home Town
Careers for Speech (History, Mathematics, etc.) Majors
Facilities of the College Library
Methods of Preparing for a Final Examination

My Preparation for College
My Changing Reading Interests
Factors in the Location of ———— City

3. Reword the main points for one or more of the topics chosen for Problem 2 so that they exemplify the characteristics of good phrasing.

4. As you listen to the next group of speeches in class, determine the main points and the type of arrangement employed in each speech. In class discuss whether the organization was suitable and clear.

5. After listening to some good speaker, make a rough outline of the substance of his speech. Revise the rough draft critically as if you were expecting to develop a speech on the topic.

6. Study the final outline for Urban Renewal, pages 254 to 257. What changes, if any, do you think might be made? Try outlining the speech in a different way. Can you improve the outline? What difficulties did you encounter?

7. For your next class speech, develop an outline following the procedure recommended on pages 248 ff. Arrange with a classmate to criticize each other's outlines with reference to the requirements of good organization and good outline form.

Beginning and end shake hands with each other.
German Proverb

15 / *Beginning*
and
Ending
a Speech

[handwritten: get Attention right off bat.]

E very speech, whether long or short, must have a beginning and
an end. Too often, speakers devote all their time to preparing
the main substance of the speech and fail to plan how to start it
off and how to close it neatly. Of course, the development of your
main points deserves the major share of your preparation time
and must be worked out before you can sensibly plan how to lead
into them or how to pin them down at the end. But it is folly to
leave the start and finish to the inspiration of the moment. Frequently the inspiration fails to come, and a dull or hesitant beginning and a weak, indefinite ending may result. The impact of
your speech will be greater if you plan in advance how to direct
your listener's attention to your subject at the start and how to
bring your ideas together in a firm and vigorous close. First, we
will discuss the characteristics of good beginnings and the various ways they can be achieved; then, we will discuss effective endings and how they may best be planned. Finally, we will see how

to integrate the beginning and ending with the main content of the speech.

BEGINNING THE SPEECH

The audience's attention must be maintained throughout your speech, but at the beginning, _gaining_ their attention is your main task. Obviously, the first part of your speech should be built with materials containing one or more of the factors of attention discussed in Chapter 13. Nowhere is the need for novelty, reality, activity, humor, etc., greater. But mere attention is not enough; you must gain the goodwill and respect of the audience. In many situations your reputation or the chairman's introduction may have created a favorable attitude toward you even before you begin to speak. When this is true, all you must watch is to avoid making tactless remarks and to be sure you start off in a modest but confident manner. When you are confronted by hostility, distrust, or skepticism, however, you must take steps to overcome that handicap at the very beginning of your speech. This can be done by establishing common ground with your audience in the manner described in Chapter 9 (see p. 161). Finally, you must remember that gaining attention and establishing goodwill are useless unless you lead the minds of your listeners naturally into the subject of your speech. The beginning of your speech must point ahead to that which is to follow. In short, a good beginning should gain attention, gain goodwill and respect, and lead into the subject.

If the factors of attention are adequately applied, there are several methods of attaining these results:
1. Reference to the Subject or Problem.
2. Reference to the Occasion.
3. Personal Greeting.
4. Rhetorical Question.
5. Startling Statement.
    A. Of fact.
    B. Of opinion.
6. Quotation.
7. Humorous Anecdote.
8. Illustration.

Reference to the subject or problem When you are sure that your audience already has a vital interest in the problem or subject you are to discuss, it is often enough merely to state it and then plunge directly into your first main point. The very speed and directness of this approach suggest movement and alertness. For example, a speaker began a talk to college seniors with, "I'm going to talk to you about jobs: how to get them, and how to keep them." Such an appeal is both brief and forthright. Here is how Erwin D. Canham, editor of the *Christian Science Monitor,* began a speech:

This morning, I would like to talk to you for a little while about the value of self-criticism. Or, you could call it self-appraisal—self-analysis —or—the proposition of letting your conscience back you into a corner— and trying to defend yourself against the questions which your own conscience might ask.[1]

Another example is the beginning used by Edith Kermit Roosevelt for a speech about "American Education and the Child":

I'd like today to say a few words about education to you. This is a vast subject which certainly cannot be discussed in the time allotted. It would be presumptuous of me to even attempt to solve the many complex questions raised by the great debate on education now underway. So I'd like to narrow our consideration of educational problems to a brief examination of the philosophy which produced our present-day educational system and also to consider some of the newer ideas and the research which we hope will improve this system.[2]

Do not make the mistake, however, of beginning all speeches this way. To a hostile audience, such a beginning would be a slap in the face; and to an apathetic one, it would not have enough novelty. Only when your subject is of vital interest to the audience should you use this method alone—though a statement of subject is often used to point up some more striking methods.

Reference to the occasion Speeches which are made for a special occasion are often best begun by a reference to that occasion. For example, Dr. Ralph Eubanks began a commencement address entitled "Know Thy Worth" in the following way:

---

[1] From "The Value of Self-Criticism for Business and Labor." *Vital Speeches of the Day,* Vol. XXVI, December 15, 1959, p. 147.
[2] *Ibid.,* Vol. XXVI, March 15, 1960, p. 334.

I'm genuinely pleased to share with you these important moments in your lives. I'm pleased, first of all, because this ceremony of commencement represents a celebration of one of the most cherished cultural values of the human race—enlightenment. I'm pleased, secondly, because this ceremony represents for us all an occasion for sober reflection on the deeper meanings of life. And it is to this purpose that I wish to invite your attention for a few moments this morning.[3]

This method is particularly useful at anniversaries, dedication ceremonies, conventions, and other such special events, where the occasion is the central motif for the whole program.

Personal greeting or reference

At times, a personal word from the speaker serves as an excellent starting point. This is particularly true when the speaker occupies a position of prestige. Leroy Collins, former governor of Florida, began his speech to a Princeton University conference with this personal reference:

Meeting with you here tonight is a doubly pleasant experience for me. First of all, it is wonderful to be back again in Princeton. My family and I spent one of the most delightful periods of our lives while I studied here for four months as a Navy lieutenant during the war. We came to regard this beautiful town with a deep affection. Our children attended school in Princeton and here saw their first snow.

In fact, we had a beautiful white Christmas that year. Palmer Square, and its carolers in the moonlight, validated completely the Dickens picture of Christmas, which before had called for quite an exercise of the imagination by people accustomed, as we all were from birth, to Florida's hot suns and white sands.

I welcome this opportunity, also, to talk with such a distinguished group on one of my favorite subjects, the American Southland. My interest is not exclusively that of a native who loves his homeland; I think I would have become fascinated by the story of what is happening in the South regardless of where my home had been.[4]

Mr. William A. Irwin, then Associate Educational Director of the American Institute of Banking, used a personal reference in introducing his address, "The American Way," given before the Pittsburgh Advertising Club:

When I first came to America some eighteen years or so ago there was a good deal of talk, as there is today, about un-American activities. At

---

[3] Delivered at Commencement, University High School, Fayetteville, Arkansas, June 1, 1961. *Ibid.*, XXVII, July 15, 1961, pp. 604–606.
[4] From "Industrialization of the South." *Ibid.*, Vol. XXVI, July 1, 1960, p. 564.

that time a committee was active, investigating so-called subversive movements and the newspapers were filled with stories about various groups and about the things they were doing to undermine American life. Wherever a man went to attend an American Legion meeting, a Rotary Club, or any similar group, it was not uncommon to hear some reference made to Americanism or to the American Way.

I used to ask myself this question: What is this American Way? And I did it for this reason—my old Scotch-Irish father and mother had taught me, as a boy in a Scottish coal mining town, that if I should ever live in any other country I should try to discover what its people fundamentally believed.—Because, they said, unless you understand what people fundamentally believe, you cannot understand them.

So, for the past eighteen years I have been trying to tell myself just exactly what an American means when he speaks about this American Way. I think I have discovered the answer.[5]

As long as such a beginning is modest and sincere, it may establish goodwill as well as gain the attention of the audience. Beware, however, of apologizing. Avoid saying, "I don't know why the chairman picked me out to talk on this subject when others could do it so much better," or "The man who was to speak to you couldn't come, and so at the last minute I agreed to speak, but I haven't had much time to get ready." Such apologetic beginnings defeat their own purpose by suggesting that your speech isn't worthy of attention. Be cordial, sincere, and modest, but don't apologize.

Rhetorical question   Often a speech may be opened by asking a question which the audience will be impelled to answer in their own minds, thus causing them to start thinking about the subject of the speech. A student began his discussion of the fire hazards of the building in which his class was being held by asking, "What would you do if a fire should break out downstairs while I am talking and the stairway should collapse before you could get out?" Questions of this kind are especially effective if they impinge upon some vital concern of the audience or if they set forth some unusual or puzzling problem. Note how Robert M. Hutchins, former chancellor of the University of Chicago, used this method to open a discussion of the problems facing education in this atomic age:

[5] *Ibid.*, Vol. VI, April 6, 1940, p. 362.

The great problems before us are, first, can we survive, and second, what kind of life are we going to lead if we do.[6]

Another effective method, called the

Startling statement   "shock technic" by H. A. Over-
street,[7] consists of jarring the audience into attention either by a statement of some startling fact or by an unexpected phrasing of your opinion. General Thomas S. Power began a speech before the Economic Club of New York in this way:

> The American people today are faced with the most difficult and far-reaching decisions in the history of this nation. Through their elected representatives they must decide what course to follow in their quest for peace and what tools to furnish to insure the successful pursuit of that course.[8]

Note the striking statements used by H. S. Aurand, Jr., in opening his speech on "The Balance of Terror":

> The pace of scientific discovery and technological development is so rapid today that even the most thoughtful and best-informed members of our society do not have the opportunity to digest the meaning and significance of technological developments before new and more complex ones occur. This situation is dangerous because it affects the timeliness and quality of decisions concerning weapon developments and foreign policy. In particular the multi-national possession of nuclear weapons gives rise to difficult and complex problems which appear to me only vaguely understood as yet in the public press.[9]

More briefly, Alfred E. Smith began a speech before the New York League of Women Voters by saying, "I have repeatedly said that the State of New York to a certain extent is the victim of its own growth."[10] Whether startling statements are used as the sole method of beginning a speech or are combined with other methods, unusual phrasing serves an important part in catching the audience's attention.

---

[6] From *Representative American Speeches: 1945–1946* (The H. W. Wilson Company, N. Y., 1946) edited by A. C. Baird, p. 262.
[7] From *Influencing Human Behavior* by H. A. Overstreet (W. W. Norton & Company, N.Y., 1925) p. 120 ff.
[8] From "Military Problems and Prospects of Deterrence." *Vital Speeches of the Day*, Vol. XXVI, February 15, 1960, p. 285.
[9] *Ibid.*, Vol. XXVI, July 1, 1960, p. 549.
[10] From *Modern Speeches* (Crofts, N.Y., 1930) edited by Homer D. Lindgren, p. 490.

	Frequently a speaker gains atten-
Quotation	tion at the beginning of his speech
	by using a quotation which aptly

states his viewpoint. Sometimes, a well-known phrase is quoted
which is then applied in an unusual way. Ernest F. Hollings
used this method in a commencement address before the Medical
College of South Carolina:

> Hippocrates, the greatest of Greek physicians, warned, "Strong mala-
> dies require strong medicine." This forebear of today's medical profes-
> sion also wrote, "in order to cure the human body it is necessary to have
> knowledge of the whole of things." With the prophetic greatness of the
> ancient Greeks, Hippocrates' words have special meaning today.
>
> The transcending malady of our time is the plague of compromise.
> Insidiously, it eats away at American principle and the free enterprise
> system in America. The strong medicine we need is vigorous action to
> reverse this deterioration. The medical profession must play a major
> role in treating this malady. It will require that you be broad enough in
> scope, and incisive enough in insight to help diagnose and treat the ills
> of compromise and equivocation. You must "have a knowledge of the
> whole of things." [11]

Here is how H. Bruce Palmer began an address before the Los
Angeles Town Hall:

> America's Number One problem is what I would discuss with you
> today—the problem that Bernard Baruch, that pre-eminent financial
> advisor to American Presidents of both political parties, calls "the most
> important economic fact of our time—the single greatest peril to our
> economic health." This problem is the primary cause of our mountainous
> national debt. It is the reason for our high tax rates and record expendi-
> tures in what is called a time of peace. It is the force which has put our
> price structure on stilts and eroded the purchasing power of the dollar.
> I am talking about inflation.[12]

The use of a quotation to begin a speech depends for its effectiveness on one of two things: it must either be unusual or be applied in an unusual way, or it must have come from some person
who enjoys the esteem of the audience. In either case, beware of a
quotation which is too long.

---

[11] From "The Equivocal Man." *Vital Speeches of the Day*, Vol. XXVI,
August 15, 1960, p. 662.
[12] From "Inflation Control." *Ibid.*, Vol. XXVI, April 15, 1960, p. 386.

| | A funny story or experience often |
| *Humorous anecdote* | gets a speech off to a good start. If |

you use this method, however, be sure that the anecdote is really funny. If it falls flat, you will have started off on the wrong foot. Moreover, to be effective, the anecdote must be in good taste and to the point. Nothing is worse than telling a joke which has nothing to do with the subject. The audience will listen to the joke, but their attention will not be directed by it to the speech proper. Note how Dr. George Hedley extracted from the anecdote below the two main ideas toward which he was leading in his talk, "Religion: What It Isn't, and Is."

Mr. Chairman and fellow-students: Since our subject tonight is that of the nature of religion, I think I shan't be too far afield if I begin with an ecclesiastical story. It is one which was told me by an Episcopal clergyman in Massachusetts; and so of its truth I can hold no possible doubt.

It appears that this friend of mine was one of a party of tourists who were being shown around one of the old English cathedrals. Their guide was the verger: one of those grand old men who apparently had been born just about the time that building's foundations were laid, and who had been growing up with it ever since. Proudly the old gentleman led the visitors through the structure. He dated its every wall and transept and bay and spire, and well nigh every pane of glass in the great windows. He recited the heroic deeds of the knights of old, whose effigies lay graven in stone upon their tombs. He pointed to the battle-flags hanging dusty and tattered from the arches, and spoke of the wars of long ago.

At last he brought the party up to the chancel railing. Now this was one of those very old-fashioned railings, with every here and there a large, round wooden knob. Before one of these knobs the verger paused, and portentously cleared his throat. "Now ladies and gentlemen," he said, "I want you to notice this here post. This here post, ladies and gentlemen, already has been confirmed by two near-sighted bishops."

Of course that story could be used to point to any number of different morals. Basically, however, I think it suggests that the good bishops had failed to discriminate between living values and dead lumber; and so that they had wasted a lot of divine unction on wholly unresponsive wood. It is clear, too, that their failure to discriminate arose from their near-sightedness. And it may be that we who are not bishops, and who to-night are concerned with religion itself rather than with its adjunct of ecclesiasticism, need ourselves to be sure that our discrimination is precise and our vision clear.[13]

---

[13] *Ibid.*, Vol. XIV, December 15, 1947, p. 148.

Real-life incidents, stories taken from literature, and hypothetical illustrations may be used to start a speech. The attention of the audience is caught by the story and directed toward the main discussion by the point of the illustration. Be sure that the story has interest in itself and that it is connected to the main idea. The chances that an illustration or story will gain attention are twice as good as those of any of the other methods listed above. Notice how Roberta West gained attention and directed it to the theme of her speech, "Identifying and Training the Gifted":

In 1948, the year of Partition, an Arab refugee family of seven took up "existence" in a crude one-room stone hut in Old Jerusalem. A few years later the eldest son, sponsored by an American pastor, came to the United States, entered college, and, in spite of language and cultural differences, received his A. B. degree cum laude. Possessed of outstanding ability in Christian leadership, he is now studying in a theological seminary. In the meantime his next younger brother had come to America under the same sponsorship, and last year graduated from college, in chemistry, at the age of 20, also cum laude! Last fall another brother entered high school in America, as a senior, at the age of 15!

The superior abilities and scholastic achievements of these three boys from a refugee hut in Jordan lead one to wonder: How many others of the present 963,958 Arab refugees are also of this mental caliber? How may they be found and helped? Also, how many gifted are there in other groups in other lands, including our own? Immediately we are faced with the need for universality in this quest for giftedness.[14]

These eight methods are the principal ways of beginning a speech. Sometimes one method alone is used. More often two or more are combined. Notice that some of the examples cited earlier demonstrate the effective combination of methods. Lester Thonssen combines an illustration with a personal reference and a reference to the occasion in the opening of his commencement address at Huron College, South Dakota:

In his essay on "The Anthropology of Manners," Edward T. Hall, Jr., tells of a tribesman who came to a prearranged spot in Kabul, the capital of Afghanistan, to meet his brother. But he couldn't find him. So he left, giving instructions to the local merchants where he might be reached if his brother showed up. Exactly a year later, the tribesman

---

[14] *Ibid.*, Vol. XXVI, April 1, 1960, p. 379.

returned to the same place in Kabul, and sure enough, there was his brother. It seems that the brothers had agreed to meet in Kabul on a certain day of a certain month at a particular place, but they had failed to specify the year.

My plans have been like those of the tribesman. Often I've agreed to meet friends on a return to the campus at commencement time, but the year was never definitely set. Now thirty-two years after graduation— a disturbingly grim statistic—I'm honored and privileged to keep an appointment on this important occasion in the life of a fine institution.[15]

Whatever method or methods you use to begin a speech, remember that gaining attention is your main task and that you must lead the minds of your listeners naturally into the subject of your speech. Remember, too, that you must gain the goodwill and maintain the respect of your audience and that this will sometimes require special effort on your part to establish common ground.

ENDING THE SPEECH

The principal function of any method used to end a speech is to focus the thought and feeling of the audience on the central theme developed in the speech. If you present a one-point speech, that point must be restated at the end in a manner which will make your meaning clear and forceful.[16] If your speech is more complex, you must bring its most important points together in a condensed and unified form or else suggest the action or belief to which these points lead. In addition to bringing the substance of the speech into final focus, a good ending should leave the audience in the proper mood. If you expect your listeners to express vigorous enthusiasm, you must stimulate that feeling in the way you close your speech. If you want them to reflect thoughtfully on what you have just said, the end of your speech should encourage a calm, judicious attitude. Decide whether the response you seek requires a mood of serious determination or good-humored levity, of warm sympathy or cold anger, of thoughtful consideration or vigorous immediate action; then plan to end your speech in such a way as to create that mood. Finally, remember that the end of a speech should convey a sense of completeness and finality. Nothing annoys an audience so much as to think the speaker has finished only

---

[15] From *Representative American Speeches: 1958–1959*, pp. 132–133.
[16] See previous discussion of the one-point speech on pages 212–218.

to have him go on again. Avoid false endings. Tie the threads together so that the pattern of your speech is brought to completion, deliver your final sentence with finality—and then stop. If you bring the central theme into sharp focus, create the proper mood, and close with decisiveness, you will be more likely to achieve the purpose of your speech.

Some of the methods most frequently used by speakers to end their speeches are:
1. Challenge or Appeal.
2. Summary.
3. Quotation.
4. Illustration.
5. Inducement.
6. Personal Intention.

Challenge or appeal
This method is a definite and more or less emphatic appeal to take a specific course of action or to feel or believe in some particular way. Such an appeal should be short and compelling and should contain within it a suggestion of the principal reason presented in the speech for doing as you propose. Note how this is done:

Gentlemen: The City Engineer has placed in the hands of each of you the detailed plans for improving the purity of our water supply; he has shown that the safety of our children and the health of our entire city demand the approval of these plans; the decision can no longer be delayed. I ask you to appropriate the necessary funds.

A similar method was used by Charles G. Mortimer to end his speech before a meeting of the New York State Bankers Association:

I earnestly urge that you begin to look upon every contact with your customers, as well as your daily dealings with your employees, as opportunities to do valuable missionary work for a saner, sounder—yes, and sterner—appreciation of what it is going to call for, in work, in self-discipline, and in devotion to high principles in our national life, on the part of each and every one of us, to carry our country safely through the soul-searching sixties.[17]

---

[17] From "All Set for the Sixties?" *Vital Speeches of the Day*, Vol. XXVI, March 1, 1960, p. 320.

In a somewhat longer ending, M. Shoaib of Pakistan appealed for continued economic support from the United States:

> We are grateful for all the assistance we have hitherto received from our friends abroad, particularly from this great country, in the gigantic task of raising the living standards of our people. You have accorded us a generous measure of support in the past. Now we are asking you, in co-operation with other countries of the West, to assist us on an even more generous scale. We do not want simply to keep our heads above water. We are pleading for that decisive boost which will enable us to gain dry land and to stand in time on our own feet. We consider that the task that we are engaged in is of great concern, not only to us, but also to nations like yours which value human dignity and freedom. But our joint cause will triumph only if we can reconcile freedom and economic progress, only if through our common effort we can satisfy the aspirations of all our peoples for a better life, free from the cares and worries of grinding poverty. We ourselves are doing our best. We hope we merit your confidence and support.[18]

Summary

The summary is a short recapitulation of the main points in your speech together with whatever important conclusion you have drawn from them. In a speech to inform, the summary ending is nearly always useful. It brings together the important points of information you have presented and impresses them upon the memory of your audience. For example, note how Dr. Arthur H. Compton used this method to close his address on "The Social Implications of Atomic Energy" before the American Physical Society:

> In summary, therefore, I would note that by far the most significant direct social effect of the release of atomic energy is to unite the world in an effort to eliminate war. We have reason to hope that this effort may be successful.
>
> The anticipated peacetime consequences of atomic energy are significant, but far from revolutionary within the visible future. Atomic power used in large units is a promising development. The scientific use of radioactive tracers may well open to us new levels of understanding of chemicals and biological processes.
>
> Most significant of the social implications of atomic energy may be perhaps the indirect effects of the program in accelerating the social trends toward increased education and training, toward a more complex

---

[18] From "Economic Trends in Pakistan." *Ibid.*, Vol. XXVI, May 1, 1960, p. 433.

and hence more cooperative society, and toward finding common objectives for which people will willingly devote their efforts. These are constructive trends which add to the richness of human life.[19]

The summary ending is equally useful when your purpose is to influence belief or action. Then the recapitulation of main points is followed by a definite suggestion of what belief or what course of action the audience is to adopt. Here is an example of such a summary used by Margaret Armstrong of Middlebury College in a debate on the control of atomic energy patents. Note how the tone and purpose of this summary differ from the one above even though the general subject is the same:

For three basic reasons patents on atomic energy should be the property of the Federal Government: first, to give our government a free hand in any atomic energy agreements with other nations or the UNO; second, to insure to the people of this country full utilization of all benefits from peacetime development of atomic energy; and third, to prevent private cartels and other arrangements with nationals of foreign countries, which did much to keep us unprepared for war before and at the start of this war.

For these reasons, I believe that the Federal Government should continue to own all patents on atomic energy. International government is not capable of taking over ownership of these patents. It is not able to prevent cartels, and until some unforseeable future, some Utopian ideal, all patents on atomic energy within the United States should remain the property of the Federal Government, to insure international cooperation.[20]

Sometimes a speaker urges his audience to accept not one but a series of related beliefs or urges support for a series of related actions. The summary then contains a restatement of this series of beliefs or proposals. Such a summary was used by J. Edgar Hoover in a speech on "Citizenship":

Here are seven basic points which should be part of our everyday lives: We must:
1. Be alert and learn the true nature and tactics of the communist and criminal enemy.
2. Make civic programs for social improvement our business.
3. Exercise our right to vote; elect representatives of integrity.

---

[19] From *Representative American Speeches: 1945–1946*, p. 119.
[20] From the *University Debaters' Annual* (The H. W. Wilson Company, N.Y., 1946), edited by E. M. Phelps, p. 141.

4. Respect human dignity—individual rights cannot co-exist with crime and communism.
5. Be informed—know the history, traditions, and heritage of our country.
6. Combat public apathy—indifference can be fatal when national survival is at stake.
7. Attack bigotry and prejudice wherever they appear; justice for all is the bulwark of democracy.

These points—in all their simplicity—mean America—the land we love and cherish. This is the America we must all work to protect against those enemies who seek to destroy her historic freedoms. This is the America which merits our entire devotion and support. This is the America which is the hope of free men everywhere.[21]

Quotation

If you use a quotation in ending your speech, it should bear directly on your central idea and suggest the attitude or action you want taken. Senator George D. Aiken of Vermont closed an address on "Foreign Policy for the 1960's" in this way:

To sum up, my prescription for our foreign policy in the 1960's is to concentrate on doing what is feasible and to stop worrying about doing what is impossible.

And in this connection, the advice which comes to us over the ages from that wise old Greek—Demosthenes—is still sound:

"As a general marches at the head of his troops, so ought with politicians, if I dare use the expression, to march at the head of affairs; insomuch that they ought not to wait the *event,* to know what measure to take; but the measures which they have taken, ought to produce the *event.*" [22]

Another example of this method is seen in a speech by Senator J. W. Fulbright:

Our task as champions of human liberty is to draw closer together in all fields of international activity and at the same time to preserve the essentials of human freedom. Recently a distinguished Spaniard, Senor de Madariaga, put it quite well when he wrote:

"The trouble today is that the Communist world understands unity but not liberty, while the free world understands liberty but not unity. Eventual victory may be won by the first of the two sides to achieve the synthesis of both liberty and unity."

---

[21] From *Vital Speeches of the Day*, Vol. XXV, August 15, 1959, p. 658.
[22] *Ibid.,* Vol. XXVI, July 15, 1960, p. 587.

To achieve the unity of the free peoples while preserving their liberty is a worthy purpose for our great nation. To make progress toward this objective would cure our frustrations and would be an inspiration to people in all parts of this world.[23]

Illustration

You may close with a telling incident or story which contains the kernel of your idea or suggests the action you wish the audience to accept.

As I was walking toward the library the other evening, I saw a car coming down Sheridan Road at what I considered too fast a speed for so slippery a night. I turned to watch it as it went past, and it began to skid. All the way around it went, and then, hitting a dry spot in the pavement, tipped over. But it didn't stop. It went all the way over and back onto its wheels again! And then—more slowly—it drove on down the street.

And I said to myself as I turned away, "Thank heaven for the strength of modern automobile bodies." And I say to you now, "Thank heaven for the foresight of the automotive engineers who design those bodies and in whose honor we have met tonight."

To close a longer address, a somewhat longer illustration may be appropriate, especially if it is vividly and dramatically told. The following illustration was used some years ago by Lewis H. Brown at the close of a commencement address to emphasize the individual responsibility of each graduate:

"But," you may say, "how can I, one little person, affect the destiny of more than 130,000,000 Americans?" Let me give you my answer by telling you of an incident that took place out in Los Angeles about a year ago. In an effort to bring home the vital importance of individual effort in winning the greatest war in history, the United States Army staged a gigantic war show in the Olympic Stadium. More than 120,000 workers, from shipyards and airplane factories, filled the great stadium.

But the culmination of this evening came when a wounded Marine sergeant stood up to speak. He said he supposed that it was a little difficult for each person who made some small airplane part or a spring for a machine gun to understand how their small effort was important in such a nation-wide and gigantic undertaking.

Then he said he'd show them. He asked that all the lights be put out. When the huge stadium was in total darkness, he struck a match and

---

[23] From "The Synthesis of Both Liberty and Unity." *Ibid.*, Vol. XXVI, October 1, 1960, p. 742.

held up the tiny flame, which was hardly visible from the opposite end of the great arena.

"This single match doesn't give much light," he said, "compared to one of those powerful searchlights. But now when I give the signal, I'm going to ask every person here to strike a match. And if any of you haven't a match, borrow one from your neighbor."

There was a moment of rustling around in this darkened stadium. Then the wounded sergeant gave the signal. From all over the place tiny flames appeared and everyone held a lighted match aloft.

Suddenly the stadium was suffused with a stronger illumination, a clearer light, than the searchlights had produced. In it were to be seen plainly the uplifted faces of one hundred and twenty thousand people, each one of whom was inspired as he realized his tiny flame was contributing to a mutual effort that resulted in an almost supernatural brilliance.[24]

Inducement   Inducement is achieved at the end of a speech by the quick cumulation of a few additional reasons for taking the action proposed. This method should not be drawn out or allowed to become too much of a "bargain sale." It is more useful in speeches for sales purposes than for other purposes. For example:

We are quite anxious to increase the number of these small airplanes in actual use. The more businessmen there are who actually own and fly them, the more their friends and associates will see how convenient and practical they are. Therefore, we are authorizing you dealers to extend at our expense in your usual service guarantee an extra hundred flying hours on the first three planes you sell; and in addition, we will give you an extra five percent reduction in the cost price of each plane sold this month.

Even in talks of a more general character, however, this method is sometimes used to show some additional benefit accruing to the audience if they take the proposed action. Note the suggestion of such benefits contained in the last sentences of the speech by Senator Hubert H. Humphrey urging American aid for the improvement of the facilities of higher education in foreign countries:

I ask you for your consideration of this proposal. If you will give it your thoughtful criticism and your intelligent support, we may be able

---

[24] From *Representative American Speeches: 1946–47*, p. 143.

to help our country take another long step toward a more balanced and vital foreign policy and eventually a stable, just and serene peace.[25]

Personal intention

A statement of your own intention to take the course of action recommended is particularly valuable when your own prestige with the audience is high. The most famous example of this method of closing a speech is that used by Patrick Henry: "As for me, give me liberty or give me death!" A more formal close of this type was used by New York's Governor Nelson A. Rockefeller in his inaugural address:

> Let us unite in common cause—with hope and faith and love, with vision and courage. Together we can thus work toward the goal of freedom of opportunity for men everywhere in a world of peace.
> I shall need your help and your trust.
> I ask that help—and I pledge myself consistently to serve that trust.[26]

Winston Churchill closed his great speech to the British Parliament on June 4, 1940 (when the German panzer armies which had swept across Holland, France, and Belgium, pushing the English armies into the sea at Dunkirk, were expected to cross the English Channel to invade Britain at any time) with this ringing statement of determination:

> Even though large tracts of Europe and many old and famous States have fallen or may fall into the grip of the Gestapo and all the odious apparatus of Nazi rule, we shall not flag or fail. We shall go on to the end; we shall fight in France; we shall fight on the seas and oceans; we shall fight with growing confidence and growing strength in the air; we shall defend our Island, whatever the cost may be; we shall fight on the beaches; we shall fight on the landing grounds; we shall fight in the fields and in the streets; we shall fight in the hills. We shall never surrender, and even if, which I do not for a moment believe, this Island or a large part of it were subjugated and starving, then our Empire beyond the seas, armed and guarded by the British Fleet, would carry on the struggle, until, in God's good time, the New World, with all its power and might, steps forth to the rescue and the liberation of the old.[27]

These, then, are six methods of ending a speech. Remember that, whichever you use, care should be taken to focus the thought

---

[25] From "College Teaching in Today's World." *Vital Speeches of the Day*, Vol. XXV, April 15, 1959, p. 413.

[26] From *Representative American Speeches: 1958–1959*, p. 115.

[27] From *Blood, Sweat, and Tears* by Winston S. Churchill (G. P. Putnam's Sons, N.Y., 1941), p. 297.

and feeling of your audience on the central theme developed in your speech, to leave the audience in the proper mood, and to convey a sense of completeness and finality.

FITTING THE BEGINNING AND END
TO THE MAIN STRUCTURE

At the start of this chapter, the importance of fitting the beginning and ending to the principal substance of a speech was mentioned. Generally you will want to develop the main points of your speech in considerable detail before working out a method of starting and finishing it; otherwise the beginning and the end may stand out as separate and disconnected pieces. Try, instead, to fit them smoothly to the principal content of your speech so that the whole is closely knit. This unity can be achieved with the above methods regardless of the type or purpose of your speech.

In a one-point speech For a one-point speech, you may start, for example, with a simple reference to your subject (the main point you plan to make), and after citing the supporting material in detail, you may close with a challenge or appeal (essentially, a restatement of your principal point). In a somewhat longer one-point speech, or in one before an audience whose attitude precludes an opening quite so forthright, you may need to use one of the other methods. You might begin, for instance, with an illustration, a quotation, or even a personal statement, leading more tactfully to the statement of your point. Likewise, the close may be developed with a quotation, illustration, or statement of your personal intention. The basic structure of the one-point speech will still remain unchanged, but your method of leading up to it and of pressing your point home at the end will have been adapted to your audience and your purpose.

In speeches having a more complex structure For a more completely organized speech, you will need one or more of the methods described above. Regardless of whether the main points are arranged in a time sequence or in a space sequence or in any of the other methods suggested in Chapter 14, you will need to lead your audience into that sequence and tie it together for them at the end. The basic structure and substance of your speech may be prepared as indicated in that chapter, but you must add a section to the start and finish of it. These sections may be marked off separately on your outline and labeled *Opening* and *Close,* or *Beginning* and *Ending,* or *Introduction* and *Conclusion,* depending on the terminology which is familiar to you. The structure of your outline should then appear somewhat like this sample of the outline prepared in Chapter 14, now completed with a beginning and an ending:

URBAN RENEWAL

(A discussion of the development, finance, and importance of urban renewal and a specific example of an urban renewal program.)

Introduction

I. Do you know how big the slum problem has become?
   A. Seventy percent of our population lives in urban areas.
   B. Thirty-three percent of our urban population lives in slum areas.
   C. Twenty percent of the city is comprised of slum areas.
II. Do you know that attempts to solve the slum problem are costing you and your fellow citizens millions of dollars?
III. Do you know that the proposed solutions— comprehensively referred to as urban renewal —may prevent your own community from becoming a slum?

Body

I. See pp. 254–257 for the main substance of the outline.)
II.
III.
IV.

Conclusion

I. Remember that urban renewal is of concern to the nation as well as to the community involved.
   A. It has been stimulated by federal legislation.

B. It is supported partly by various forms of federal aid and partly by the community.
C. Its success is vital to all citizens, not merely those living in slums.
D. Projects like Chicago's are dramatic evidence of what can be done.

In the next two chapters we shall modify this basic plan somewhat as we study how to adapt the structure of a speech to the psychology of the audience. As we do so, we shall use a better set of terms to mark off the sections of a speech, terms which reflect their psychological functions. But we shall see that the methods of beginning and ending a speech just described remain unchanged and that the logical structure of a speech may easily be adapted to the normal patterns of human thought and action.

PROBLEMS

1. Be ready to discuss the following questions in class: What are the chief purposes of the beginning of a speech? Of the ending? How does the audience's attitude affect the choice of method for beginning a speech? What are the methods most frequently used to end a speech?

2. Analyze the beginnings and endings of the speeches in a recent issue of *Vital Speeches of the Day* or in the latest volume of *Representative American Speeches*. What methods do you find used most frequently? In each case, note what methods were used to accomplish the purposes of the beginning and the ending and how successful they were.

3. After listening to one of the following types of speech, prepare to report in class your analysis of the beginning and ending used:
    A. A classroom lecture.
    B. An address at a student convocation.
    C. A talk given at a meeting of a local young people's society.
    D. The remarks made by one of the speakers at a meeting of your fraternity, sorority, or dormitory council.

4. As a result of your analysis in 2 and 3 above, what common faults can you list for the beginnings and endings of these speeches? Do they seem typical of other speeches you have heard or read?

5. Using one of the topics for which you outlined the main points in Chapter 14 (Problem 2, p. 257), prepare three alternative methods of beginning and of ending which would be suitable for use with your class as the audience.

6. Assuming that you are to speak before some other audience on the same topic used for Problem 5, work out a new beginning and ending suited specifically to that audience and occasion.

7. Prepare a short speech urging a point of view toward which your audience is likely to be apathetic or hostile. Work out a beginning for this speech designed to arouse interest in the subject and to secure the audience's good will and respect.

8. Select a topic likely to arouse heated controversy among members of your class. Work out three different endings for speeches on this topic as follows:

    A. One that would leave them in a thoughtful mood.

    B. One that would arouse them to enthusiasm and excitement.

    C. One that would encourage in them a quiet determination to take some definite course of action.

All speech, written or spoken, is a dead language, until it finds a willing and prepared hearer.

Robert Louis Stevenson

CHAPTER 16/*Adapting Speech Organization to the Audience:*

The Motivated Sequence

The earlier chapters of this section gave special emphasis to the importance of analyzing the audience, of determining clearly the speaker's purpose, and of remaining constantly aware of the probable attitude of the audience toward it. Then in later chapters we saw how supporting material could be used to develop and substantiate a single point, how these points could be arranged in various types of logical and coherent sequence, and how beginnings and endings could be constructed to complete the speech. We are now ready to consider how the logical sequence of points within a speech can be adapted to the audience so that the proper response may be secured. We shall see how to modify the traditional organization of a speech so that its points will combine, both logically and psychologically, to achieve its purpose with the audience.

First of all, we must remember that a speaker cannot cram things down people's throats. He must lead the thoughts of his audience naturally. The structure of a speech, then, must not be planned with no thought of the audience and then brought out and displayed before them. Rather, the speech must be built with the specific audience always in mind, and the structure of the speech must conform to the thinking process of the listener. To do otherwise is as foolish as trying to make a man fit a suit.

THE LISTENER'S MENTAL PROCESS AND THE MOTIVATED SEQUENCE

At first thought, the listener's mental process would seem to vary depending on the type of reaction asked of him; entertainment would seem to call for a different mental process from that required in learning or coming to a decision. But this difference, so far as the reaction to a public speech is concerned, is not so much a difference in the type of mental process involved as in the completeness of that process. Thus, when the only reaction required of the listener is that he be entertained, the only mental reaction necessary is that he give his complete attention, free from conflicting worry and distraction. Attention is still necessary when the object is to inform him, but now his mind must proceed further—he must become conscious of a need or desire to be informed, and then he must absorb and understand the information presented. Now let us suppose that he is confronted with making a decision to act. He still must first direct his attention to the subject, become conscious of a need, and understand the proposal; but he must go even further in his mental process—he must be convinced of the soundness and desirability of the proposal, and he must be stimulated to act upon it. Normally, therefore, the mental process of the listener as applied to the various general ends of speech is not different in kind, but cumulative—the completeness of it depending on the completeness of the reaction required.

Moreover, this normal process of human thinking is sufficiently uniform that, in spite of variations in individuals, we can outline a form of speech structure that will conform to it rather closely on nearly all occasions. This form of speech structure we shall call *the motivated sequence: the sequence of ideas which, by following the normal process of human thinking, motivates the audience to respond to the speaker's purpose.* This sequence will serve as the backbone for all types of speeches, needing only to be modified by omitting or lengthening certain parts according to the particular situation.

Let us first consider the motivated sequence in its most complete form, that used when the object is to secure action. Although not a speech, the following advertisement will briefly illustrate the sequence:

The South Sea Bubble had burst. All England clamored for the punishment of its directors. Parliament re-echoed with angry recriminations. "Sew them in sacks and throw them in the Thames!" cried one indignant peer.

Yet only a short time before, hopes had run high. The fabulous wealth of South America was to make everybody rich. Shares in the South Sea Company had skyrocketed from £100 to £1000. Landlords sold their estates. Clergymen and widows brought their savings to invest in it.

And now these towering castles in the air had crashed. The King's most important ministers were involved in the scandal. There were suicides, sudden deaths, prison sentences, ruin on every side. But the money was gone forever.

*　　*　　*

Today, or two hundred years ago—speculative frenzy meets one inevitable end. But though "bubbles" burst and fancy prices fall, solid values still endure.

These values rest on *facts*—not guesses. The investor who makes *facts* his guiding principle in the selection of securities has nothing to fear. Prices at times may be temporarily depressed, but in the long run they will adjust themselves. The chief problem is to get those essential facts that will make possible a true estimate of *value*—current and prospective.

*　　*　　*

Here is where Standard Statistics Company can be of invaluable assistance to you. The largest statistical and analytical organization in the world today, "Standard" spends millions of dollars every year for the sole purpose of collecting, analyzing, and distributing accurate, unbiased, pertinent, up-to-the-minute *facts*—facts that will make business ventures and investing in securities less hazardous and more profitable for you.

Its staff of nearly one thousand people numbers highly-trained specialists in analyzing security values and financial conditions, as well as field investigators located at strategic points through the country to study industrial and other properties at first hand.

Regularly, the many varied Standard Services go out to an impressive list of clients, including the largest banks and financial houses in North America and Europe, as well as to thousands of individual investors both large and small.

* * *

Whether you have a few thousands, or millions, to invest—whether you are interested in stocks or bonds—whether you want to keep posted on the largest corporation reports and dividend declarations or desire sound, authoritative data on commodity price movements, business trends, or general industrial conditions—whatever *your* particular problem may be, there is a Standard Service to meet your individual need. *You may have the facts on your desk when you need them.*

* * *

We will gladly give you further information. Simply write us. Address *Standard Statistics Company, Inc., Dept. P-50, 200 Varick St., New York City.*[1]

Notice that five distinct steps were taken in this advertisement: (1) your *attention* was caught; (2) you were made to feel a definite *need;* (3) you were shown a way to *satisfy* this need; (4) you were made to *visualize* the application of this proposal to you personally; and (5) a definite suggestion was made as to how you should *act.* Thus the five steps in the motivated sequence are named:

1. Attention.
2. Need.
3. Satisfaction.
4. Visualization.
5. Action.

We might outline these five steps in the advertisement as follows:

1. Attention	The South Sea Bubble caused a violent financial panic because guesswork was substituted for knowledge.
2. Need	Today, you as an investor need to know the facts in order to make safe investments.
3. Satisfaction	The Standard Statistics Company is specially equipped to secure and analyze these facts for all types of investors.
4. Visualization	Your particular problems will be more effectively solved by the facts we can place on your desk.
5. Action	Write us.

---

[1] From the *Saturday Evening Post,* May 10, 1930.

Observe that the general end of the advertisement was *to actuate*. One might use the same outline for a speech with a similar purpose, because people react in much the same way to a persuasive speech as to an advertisement and must be guided through these same steps. Attention must be diverted from other things and converged on what the speaker has to say; the audience must be made to realize that a need exists; a method of satisfying this need must be presented and shown to be effective; the audience must be made to visualize the desirable conditions which the solution will create; and they must be given directions on how to act or what to believe.

Notice how these five steps were used by David Sarnoff in his appeal for popular support of the Metropolitan Opera:

(1) This in the ninth consecutive year in which the National Broadcasting Company, through the miracle of radio, has been privileged to bring the Metropolitan Opera into the homes of America. On Christmas Day in 1931, the nation-wide radio audience heard the first of these programs, a performance of "Hansel and Gretel," direct from the stage of this historic opera house. Since then, every single week of the New York season of the Metropolitan, for nine years, one of the great operas —performed by great artists—has been broadcast to you.

The American system of broadcasting has made it possible for radio listeners everywhere to hear the world's finest opera week after week, without having to pay a cent for the privilege.

But over this same period of nine years, the National Broadcasting Company has paid directly to the Metropolitan Opera Association one million dollars for the privilege of bringing grand opera to its radio audience. This has been an important and necessary source of income to the Metropolitan. The National Broadcasting Company will continue to pay the Metropolitan Opera for the opportunity to broadcast these programs to you.

(2) Today the Metropolitan faces a critical financial situation, if grand opera of the first rank is to continue in America. As a member of the Board of Directors of the Metropolitan Opera Association, I have been asked to explain this situation to the radio audience. As a radio man, who knows from experience how widespread in America is the appreciation of grand opera, I have taken upon myself an even greater responsibility. I have told the management and the artists of the Metropolitan that I have full faith in the willingness of the opera's national radio audience to help them.

You who constitute this vast audience may not realize what an important part you play in the operation of the Metropolitan today. While you cannot see the other millions who are gathered around their radios,

A SPEECH STRUCTURE TO MOTIVATE AUDIENCE RESPONSE

In daily conversation most of us speak to get a certain response from our hearer. We may shout "Hey!" simply to get a friend's attention, we may tell him that he needs a haircut, or we may ask him to help us with our work. In each case we had an objective in mind, one that we tried to reach by speaking.

The public speaker also seeks a definite response when he faces an audience. Because public speaking situations are generally more complex and formal than private conversations, however, he must organize and construct his speech beforehand so that it will have the best chance of achieving his purpose. The motivated sequence is a method to help him do this successfully.

The five steps below make up the complete motivated sequence. This basic plan is applicable to almost all types of public speech and can be modified to fit the general end of a particular talk.

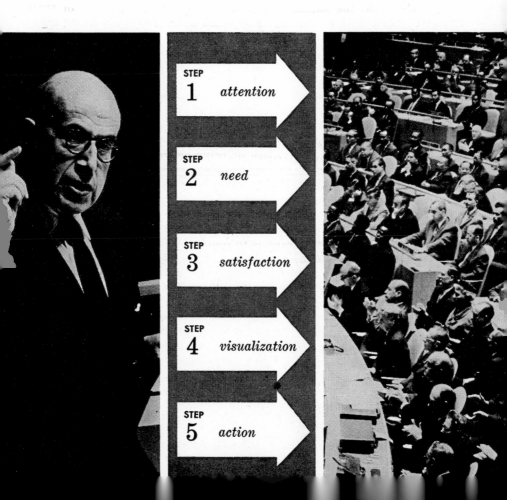

STEP **1** *attention*

STEP **2** *need*

STEP **3** *satisfaction*

STEP **4** *visualization*

STEP **5** *action*

all of you, together, form the greatest opera audience in the history of the world. It is estimated that this afternoon in the United States alone, more than 10,000,000 people are listening to this inspiring performance of "Lohengrin." This famous old building on Broadway has ceased to be a local opera house. It is now the nation's opera—the People's Opera—your opera.

Many of you may not know that this historic house is not owned or controlled by the company which produces the opera—that is, the Metropolitan Opera Association. The time has now come when the future of the opera, and its ability to advance as a national institution, demands permanent ownership of a house, supported by the general public, and serving broad public interests.

The Metropolitan Opera Association has an option on the opera house, which in its terms requires $500,000 in cash. It faces the problem of taking up this option by May 31, 1940, and maintaining opera in the present house, or of working out other plans which will insure the continuance of opera in some other appropriate location. An additional $500,000 is needed to carry out plans for essential improvements, and for the advancement of the Metropolitan Opera as a national music center.

(3) The Metropolitan Opera Association therefore has undertaken a campaign to seek $1,000,000 from public-spirited citizens, including radio listeners, in gifts both large and small. The Directors of the Metropolitan have made a public announcement of the need and purposes of this campaign, and the details have been published in newspapers throughout the country.

I have been asked to serve as Chairman of the Radio Division of this campaign, and I am happy to announce that Mrs. August Belmont and Miss Lucrezia Bori have consented to serve with me as Vice-Chairmen. Their deep interest and great service to the Metropolitan over a period of many years is well-known throughout the United States.

I believe that there are many radio listeners who will be willing and happy to contribute a small sum to help insure the continuance of the Metropolitan Opera. I therefore earnestly appeal to all of you who can afford to do so, to send one dollar directly to the Metropolitan Opera Association, as your contribution toward helping preserve in America the world's finest opera.

(4) Please ask yourself this question: "If I knew that I could not hear another Metropolitan Opera on the radio unless I gave one dollar, would I give it?"

I am sure your answer will be "yes," because I feel certain that you want Metropolitan Opera to go on. Surely you want to see continued an American institution which has won a reputation all over the world; an unchallenged reputation for its interpretation of the great beauty that lies in the operas of the world's great masters.

(5) The Metropolitan Opera asks you who are its friends to express that friendship now in a practical way. We ask for one dollar from each

listener who can afford to give it. Naturally, larger gifts will be most welcome.

I particularly ask the organized listening groups in schools and clubs and homes throughout the country to help make this campaign a success, and thereby to insure the continuance of the Metropolitan Opera.[2]

Observe that Mr. Sarnoff (1) called attention to his subject by reference to a few striking facts, (2) pointed out the pressing need for funds to maintain the Metropolitan Opera program, (3) explained how popular subscription could provide these funds, (4) briefly visualized the personal pleasure of helping maintain the opera, and (5) appealed for direct action in the form of contributions from his listeners.

If this sequence is kept in mind, organizing a speech becomes comparatively simple. In its complete form, as used for persuasive speeches (those to stimulate, convince, or actuate), the motivated sequence consists of five steps.

THE MOTIVATED SEQUENCE APPLIED TO PERSUASIVE SPEECHES
(General ends: to stimulate, to convince, to actuate.)

STEP	FUNCTION	AUDIENCE RESPONSE
1. Attention Step.	Getting attention.	"I want to listen."
2. Need Step.	Showing the need: describing the problem.	"Something needs to be done (decided, or felt)."
3. Satisfaction Step.	Satisfying the need: presenting the solution.	"This is what to do (believe, or feel) to satisfy the need."
4. Visualization Step.	Visualizing the results.	"I can see myself enjoying the satisfaction of doing (believing, or feeling) this."
5. Action Step.	Requesting action or approval.	"I will do (believe, or feel) this."

[2] From *NBC Presents*, February 1940, Vol. II, No. 5. This speech was delivered from the Metropolitan Opera House on January 27, 1940, during a matinée broadcast of *Lohengrin*. Needless to say, the campaign was successful.

Note how this sequence is followed below in the abbreviated student outline for a persuasive speech on fire prevention:

FIRE PREVENTION AT HOME

Attention step   I. If you like parlor tricks, try this:
  - A. Place a blotter soaked in turpentine in a jar of oxygen.
  - B. The blotter will burst into flames.

    II. If you have no oxygen jar around the house, try this:
  - A. Place a well-oiled mop in a storage closet.
  - B. In a few days the mop will burst into flames.

Need step   I. Few homes are free from dangerous fire hazards.
  - A. Attics with piles of damp clothing and paper are combustible.
  - B. Storage closets, containing cleaning mops and brushes, are dangerous.
  - C. Basements are often filled with dangerous piles of trash.
  - D. Garages attached to houses are a danger spot.

Satisfaction step   I. To protect your home from fire involves three things:
  - A. A thorough cleaning out of all combustible materials.
  - B. Careful storage of such hazards as oil mops, paint brushes, etc.
    1. Clean them before storage.
    2. Store them in fireproof containers.
  - C. A regular check to see that inflammable trash does not accumulate.

    II. Clean-up programs show practical results.
  - A. Clean-up campaigns in Evansville kept insurance rates in a "Class 1" bracket.
  - B. A clean-up campaign in Fort Wayne helped reduce the number of fires.

Visualization step   I. You will enjoy the results of such a program.
  - A. You will have neat and attractive surroundings.
  - B. You will be safe from fire.

Action step   I. Begin your own clean-up campaign now.

Remember that these steps are not of equal length in every speech, nor are they always the same. Each situation will demand variations. At times, for example, one or more of the steps may be left out entirely because the attitude of the audience does not require them. For instance, if the audience already realizes that a need exists—that something must be done—there is no necessity for expanding this point; merely remind the audience of the nature of the problem and show how your proposal will satisfy the need.

Moreover, the general end of your speech will substantially modify your use of the motivated sequence. Indeed, only when the general end is *to stimulate, to convince,* or *to actuate,* are all five steps employed. When the end is *to inform* or *to entertain,* the steps are followed only as far as is necessary in order to obtain the desired response. Hence, the speech to inform employs only the first three steps, thus:

THE MOTIVATED SEQUENCE APPLIED TO INFORMATIVE SPEECHES

STEP	FUNCTION	AUDIENCE RESPONSE
1. Attention Step.	Getting attention.	"I want to listen."
2. Need Step.	Demonstrating the need to know.	"I need information on this subject."
3. Satisfaction Step.	Presenting the information itself.	"The information being presented helps me understand the subject more satisfactorily."

A student organized his speech on how to rescue drowning persons like this:

"ROW—THROW—GO"

Attention step   I. Holiday deaths by drowning are second only to auto accidents.

Need step   I. Every person should know what to do when a call for help is heard.
   A. This information may help you save a friend.

B. This information may help you save a member of your family.

Satisfaction step I. Remember three important words when someone is drowning: row, throw, go.
    A. Row: Look for a boat.
      1. You can well afford to take a little time to look for a means of rowing to the rescue.
        a. Look for a boat.
        b. Look for a canoe.
        c. Look for a raft.
      2. Rowing to the rescue is always the wisest way.
    B. Throw: Look for a life buoy.
      1. See if you can locate something buoyant to throw the person in distress.
        a. Look for a life buoy.
        b. Look for an inflated inner tube.
        c. Look for a board.
        d. Look for a child's floating toy.
      2. You can throw an object faster than you can swim.
    C. Go: As a last resort, swim out to the drowning person.
      1. Approach the victim from the rear.
      2. If you are grabbed, go under water.
      3. Clutch the person's hair.
      4. Swim for shore.
 II. Remember when you hear the call for help:
    A. Look first for something in which to row.
    B. Look for something buoyant to throw the victim.
    C. Swim out only as a last resort.

And finally, the speech to entertain consists entirely of an expanded attention step. The other four steps are omitted.

THE MOTIVATED SEQUENCE APPLIED TO ENTERTAINING SPEECHES

STEP	FUNCTION	AUDIENCE RESPONSE
1. Attention Step.	Getting attention and retaining interest through entertainment.	"I want to listen, and I'll continue listening because I'm enjoying myself."

The brief outline below illustrates how one student developed an entertaining speech in this way:

A TOAST TO THE APPLE

Attention step I. The apple should be our national fruit.
  A. Adam and Eve started our life of joy and confusion because of an apple.
  B. Apples saved the lives of our favorite childhood characters.
    1. The third little pig in the *Three Little Pigs* was saved from the wolf by an apple.
    2. Alex in the *Bear Story* was saved from starvation by eating the apples growing on the sycamore tree.
  C. Apples are the symbol of our early education.
    1. "A was an apple pie; B bit it; C cut it."
  D. Apples enter into our courtship songs.
    1. We sing to our sweetheart, "I'll Be with You in Apple Blossom Time."
    2. We then serenade her with "In the Shade of the Old Apple Tree."
    3. We warn her, "Don't Sit Under the Apple Tree with Anyone Else But Me."
  E. Our own health may depend upon an apple.
    1. As the proverb says, "An apple a day keeps the doctor away."
  F. Johnny Appleseed is rightfully a national hero.
 II. So here's to the apple—our national fruit!

From what has been said thus far, it is apparent that the divisions of a speech are functional in nature: that is, each part or step has a particular duty to perform in directing the mental process of the listener. The ideas and supporting material included in each step, therefore, must be such as to achieve the purpose of that step. While the general function of each step remains the same, it must be modified to suit the general end of the speech. The chart on the following page will give you a general idea of the way in which the motivated sequence is adapted to each of the general ends. Study the chart very carefully before going further. You will then be ready to consider how each step in the motivated sequence may be developed.

ADAPTATION OF THE MOTIVATED SEQUENCE TO THE GENERAL ENDS

Type of Speech	PERSUASIVE			INSTRUCTIVE	RECREATIVE	
General End	1. TO STIMULATE	2. TO CONVINCE	3. TO ACTUATE	4. TO INFORM	5. TO ENTERTAIN	
Reaction Sought	*Inspiration* (Emotional Arousal)	*Belief* (Intellectual)	*Specific Action* (Observable)	*Understanding* (Clarity)	*Interest and Diversion* (Enjoyment)	
					(A)	(B)
Attention step	Draw attention to the need.	Draw attention to the need.	Draw attention to the need.	Draw attention to the subject.	Draw attention to an absurd problem and entertain by an exaggerated treatment of it, thus burlesquing the entire motivated sequence as used in a serious persuasive speech; present the discussion in mock seriousness, with marked and obvious exaggeration.	Draw attention to an interesting idea. Keep interest in it alive by a series of illustrations, anecdotes, and a humorous treatment: relate these to things in which the audience is already interested. Organize as a one-point speech. Stop while interest is still high. Omit last four steps of the motivated sequence.
Need step	Increase the feeling that the need is vital; create emotional dissatisfaction with present situation through the use of striking facts and illustrations.	Present logical evidence to prove the existence of a situation which requires that something be decided and upon which the audience must take a position.	Combine methods outlined in the two preceding columns (1 and 2) to show the need for action.	Show why the listeners need a knowledge of the subject; point out what problems this information will help them meet.		
Satisfaction step	Briefly state the heightened emotional attitude (enthusiasm, reverence, etc.) required of the audience.	Get the audience to believe that your position on this question is the right one to take, by using logic and evidence as proof.	Propose the specific action required to meet this problem; get the audience to believe in it by presenting logical evidence (as in column 2).	Present information to give them a satisfactory knowledge of the subject as an aid in the solution of these problems; begin and end this presentation with a summary of the main points presented. (Normal End of the Speech.)		
Visualization step	By means of vivid description, picture the results which such an attitude will bring, especially the emotional satisfaction to be gained by the audience.	Briefly stimulate favorable emotion by projecting this belief into imaginary operation.	Picture the results which such action or the failure to take it will bring; use vivid description (as in column 1).	Sometimes: briefly suggest pleasure to be gained from this knowledge.		
Action step	Request the audience to actually assume this attitude, or express the assumption that they already have.	Arouse determination to retain this belief (as a guide to future action if need should arise).	Urge the audience to take definite action.	Sometimes: urge further study of the subject.		

Your first step in the motivated sequence is to *gain attention,* but merely securing attention is not enough; you must gain favorable attention and direct it toward the main ideas in your speech. Since the methods for doing this were thoroughly explained in the preceding chapter, we will merely repeat the list here for emphasis:

1. Reference to the Subject.	5. Startling Statement.
2. Reference to the Occasion.	6. Quotation.
3. Personal Greeting.	7. Humorous Anecdote.
4. Rhetorical Question.	8. Illustration.

Review these eight methods of beginning a speech and examine the samples of them printed on pages 260 to 268. Remember that while frequently only one method is used to develop this step in your speech, quite often two or more are combined. Almost always a reference to the subject is inserted to point up whatever other methods are employed. With the exception of the speech for entertainment, however, the gaining of attention is only a means to an end, not an end in itself. Be sure that your attention step leads naturally into the next step of your speech.

The kind of need step you develop will vary with the purpose of your speech and, as we shall see in later chapters, with the audience's attitude toward that purpose. Even for speeches in which the general purpose is persuasion, the development of the need step will depend upon the specific purpose of the speech. For instance, one common purpose of persuasion is to urge a change. In this case the need step attempts to create dissatisfaction with existing conditions in order to convince the audience that something must be done. A definite problem must be shown to exist. The campaign strategy of the political party out of power is a good example of this; it is the process of condemnation, of pointing out flaws and failures. Other kinds of need steps for persuasive speeches will be explained and illustrated in Chapter 22. Speeches to inform require a need step in which the audience must be made to feel the limited scope of their own knowledge on the subject to be discussed and to realize how important information on that subject is to them.

Not only must the ideas and points of view expressed in the need step vary according to the purpose of the speech, but the structural development of the need step must be suited to the nature of the material to be presented. Suggestions for the structure of the need step are made in the following chapters on the various types of general ends. One pattern of development should be presented at this time, however, because of its general usefulness. This technique of development is fourfold: (1) *Statement:* a definite, concise statement of the nature of the problem. (2) *Illustration:* one or more detailed examples illustrating it. (3) *Ramification:* an enumeration of additional examples, statistical data, testimony, and other forms of support to whatever extent necessary. This additional support shows that the need is an important one, that you are not enlarging on a few isolated cases. (4) *Pointing:* showing the direct relation of the need to the people you are addressing. Make them see that the problems discussed affect them personally; otherwise they will say to themselves, "That is too bad, but what has it got to do with me?"

Let us put this method of development in outline form so that we may clearly see its essential structure:

1. *Statement.* State the need. (The specific problem or the importance of the information to the audience.)
2. *Illustration.* Tell one or more incidents to illustrate the need.
3. *Ramification.* Employ as many forms of support as are required to make the need convincing and impressive.
4. *Pointing.* Show the importance of the need to your audience.

You will notice how similar this development is to the structure of the one-point speech described on pages 212 to 219. Many need steps, if taken by themselves, are one-point speeches: they point out one thing—need. Combined with similar units in each of the other steps, this point becomes a part of the larger unit, the complete structure. When appropriate, therefore, develop your need step just as you would a one-point speech. Use the didactic method or the method of implication, depending upon the attitude of the audience toward your purpose.

Some needs are, of course, complex and consist of more than one main aspect. In this case, you can develop each main aspect separately and then draw the various aspects together and show their interrelation. The result will be like a series of one-point speeches related to one another and tied together at the end.

Although it is usually desirable, you will not always have to use all four items when you develop the need step in this way. The statement and the pointing should always be made, but the amount of illustration and ramification will depend upon the amount of detail required to impress any particular need on the audience. But regardless of whether you use the complete fourfold development, only part of it, or some other structure, you will often find this step to be the most important one in your speech because it relates your subject to the needs of your audience.

THE SATISFACTION STEP

We have said that the purpose of the satisfaction step is to get the audience to agree that the belief or action you propose is the correct one or to get them to understand the subject you have chosen to explain. The structure of this step differs somewhat, however, depending on whether the purpose of the speech is persuasion or instruction. Accordingly, the types of development for the satisfaction step are discussed separately.

In persuasive speeches When the purpose of the speech is to stimulate, convince, or actuate, five items may be involved in the development of the satisfaction step: (1) *Statement:* briefly state the attitude, belief, or action you wish the audience to adopt. (2) *Explanation:* make sure your proposal is understood. Often diagrams or charts are useful here. (3) *Theoretical demonstration:* show how the solution logically and adequately meets the need pointed out in the need step. (4) *Practical experience:* give actual examples showing that this proposal has worked effectively or that this belief has been proved correct—use facts, figures, and the testimony of experts to demonstrate this conclusion. (5) *Meeting objections:* forestall opposition by showing how your proposal overcomes any objections which might be raised.

As was the case in the need step, not all of these items are used every time. Nor must the order always be the same as that listed above. Indeed, meeting objections can be better done if scattered throughout the solution step wherever the individual objections are most likely to arise. The first four items, however, form a convenient and effective sequence for developing the satisfaction step in a persuasive speech:

1. Briefly state the attitude, belief, or action you propose.
2. Explain it clearly.
3. Show logically how it will meet the need.[3]
4. Cite examples from practical experience to show its soundness. Supplement these examples with facts, figures, and the testimony of experts.[3]

If the satisfaction step is carefully developed in this way, it should cause your audience to feel, "This is the best attitude, belief, or action." Of course, in this step, as in the need step, other items and arrangements may be necessary; several other important methods will be presented in Chapter 22.

In speeches to inform When the purpose of your speech is to give the audience a clear understanding of some subject, the satisfaction step will constitute the bulk of your speech. It will include the information that the need step pointed out was necessary. Briefly, the development of this step usually involves: (1) *initial summary*, (2) *detailed information*, and (3) *final summary*.

The *initial summary* gives a brief preview of the information you expect to present, usually an enumeration of the main points around which you expect to group your facts. In this way you make the direction of your discussion clear in advance. Obviously, the main points listed in this initial summary should parallel the order in which you intend to discuss them, or you will give your audience a false lead. When it is properly used, the initial summary acts as an excellent guidepost.

Next, the *detailed information* is presented; the main points mentioned above are considered in turn, and the detailed facts and explanations relating to them are grouped around these points in an orderly fashion. Some consistent order of discussion, such as the time sequence, space sequence, etc., ought to be used. (See pp.

---

[3] When the end is to stimulate only, items 3 and 4 are omitted.

235–239 in Chapter 14.) You must be sure at all times that your speech moves along in a definite direction; do not let your audience get lost.

The *final summary* recapitulates the main points discussed, with the inclusion of whatever important conclusions you have made clear in relation to them. The final summary is similar to the initial summary in structure, but it is usually not quite so brief.

Thus the development of the satisfaction step as used in the informative speech can be outlined as follows:

1. *Initial Summary.* Briefly state in advance the main points you intend to cover.
2. *Detailed Information.* Discuss the facts and explanations pertaining to each of these main points in order.
3. *Final Summary.* Restate the main points presented, together with any important conclusions you have made.

If presented as outlined above, your information will tend to be clear and coherent.

Parallel development of need and satisfaction steps Frequently, the need you want to present has two or more important aspects. To give these aspects special emphasis and to make your discussion clearer, you can develop the need and satisfaction steps in a parallel order. First present one aspect of the need and show how your proposal or information satisfies it; then present the second aspect and its solution; then the third, and so on. This method weakens the cumulative effect of the motivated sequence, but the additional clarity often makes up for the loss.

The two skeleton outlines below compare the normal order and the parallel order.

NORMAL ORDER

Attention I. The test flights I saw were exciting events.
   A. Description of test flights and accidents.

Need I. The faults of new airplane body design often are:
   A. Parts in the wing structures may be too heavy.

B. The strength of the structures has not been accurately determined in relation to the strain they must stand.

II. There may also be faults in the design of new airplane engines.

Satisfaction   I. Test flights throw light on how the new body design may be improved.

A. The extra strain of these flights tests the strength of body structures.

II. The testing of new engine designs helps improve engine performance.

A. Engine reliability is given strenuous tests in these flights.

Visualization   I. There is hope for great development in airplane engine and body design in the near future.

Action   I. Increased expenditures for test flying are thoroughly justified.

PARALLEL ORDER

Attention   I. The test flights I saw were exciting events.

A. Description of test flights and accidents.

Need and satisfaction (First aspect)   I. Airplane body design.

A. The faults of new airplane body design often are:
    1. Parts in the wing structures may be too heavy.
    2. The strength of the structures has not been accurately determined in relation to the strain they must stand.

B. Test flights throw light on how the new body design may be improved.
    1. The extra strain of these flights tests the strength of body structures.

(Second aspect)   II. Airplane engine design.

A. There may also be faults in the design of new airplane engines.

B. The testing of new engine designs helps improve engine performance.
    1. Engine reliability is given strenuous tests in these flights.

Visualization   I. There is hope for great development in airplane engine and body design in the near future.

Action   I. Increased expenditures for test flying are thoroughly justified.

Whether you use the normal order or the parallel order, you will always need to develop support for your statements by the methods already discussed.

THE VISUALIZATION STEP

The visualization step is ordinarily used only in persuasive speeches. Speeches to inform or to entertain achieve their purpose before they go this far in the motivated sequence. (See chart on p. 292.) Hence, this discussion relates only to speeches whose end is to stimulate, to convince, or to actuate.

The function of this step is to intensify desire—to make the audience really want to see the belief accepted by everyone or to see the proposal adopted and carried out. The visualization step should project the audience into the future so that they are emotionally impressed with an image of future conditions. Indeed, this step might just as correctly be called the "projection" step, for its effectiveness is determined by the vividness of the picture conveyed. This result may be obtained in one of three ways: by projecting a picture of the future that is *positive,* or one that is *negative,* or one that *contrasts the two.*

The positive method   When using the positive method, you describe conditions as they will be in the future if the solution you propose is carried out. Do not be abstract about this. Select some situation which you are quite sure will arise in the future, and picture your audience in that situation actually enjoying the safety, pleasure, pride, etc., which your proposal will have produced. Repeat your satisfaction step in terms of the audience's future.

The negative method   When using the negative method, you describe conditions as they will be in the future if the solution you propose is *not* carried out. You develop this method exactly as you would the positive method, except that you must picture your audience feeling the bad effects of the danger or the unpleasantness which the failure to effect your solution will have produced. Go back to the need step of your speech and select the most strikingly undesirable things and put these into the picture of future conditions.

The method of contrast   The method of contrast combines the two preceding methods. The negative method is used first, showing the bad effects of failure to adopt your proposal; then the positive method follows, showing the good results of adopting it. Thus, the undesirable situation is followed by the desirable one in immediate contrast.

Whichever of these methods you use, the important thing to remember is that the visualization step must stand the test of reality. The conditions you picture must at least be probable. You must make the audience virtually put themselves in the picture. Use vivid imagery: make the audience see, hear, feel, taste, and smell. The more vividly real you make the projected situation seem, the stronger will be the reaction of the audience.

The following is an example of the visualization step using the method of contrast between positive and negative projection. It was developed by a student in a speech urging the use of fireproof materials in home construction.

But suppose you do build your home of the usual kindling wood: joists, rafters, and shingles. Some dark night you may awake from your pleasant sleep with the smell of acrid smoke in your nostrils, and in your ears the threatening crackle of burning timbers. You will jump out onto the cold floor and rush to wake up the household. Gathering your children in your arms you will hurry down the stairs—if they are not already in flames—and out of doors. There you will watch the firemen chop holes in your roof, pour gallons of water over your plaster, your furniture, your piano. You will shiver with cold in spite of the blazing spectacle and the plastic minds of your children will be indelibly impressed with fright. No fire insurance can repay your family for this horror, even though it may pay a small part of the financial loss.

How much better to use safe materials! Then throughout the long winter nights you can dig down under the warmth of your bedclothes to sleep peacefully in the assurance that your house cannot burn, and that any fire which catches in your furnishings can be confined to a small space and put out. No more the fear of flying sparks. Gone the danger to your wife and children. Sleep—quiet, restful, and secure in the knowl-edge that the "burning horror" has been banished from your home.[4]

THE ACTION STEP

The action step, like the visualization step, occurs only in per-suasive speeches. Its function is to translate the desire created in the visualization step into a definitely fixed attitude or belief or into overt action. There are many methods for developing this last step in the motivated sequence, but the six most frequently used were fully described and illustrated in Chapter 15 as "methods of ending a speech":

1. Challenge or Appeal.
2. Summary.
3. Quotation.
4. Illustration.
5. Inducement.
6. Personal Intention.

These same methods applied to persuasive speeches constitute the action step. Thus a review of pages 268 to 276, where these six types of ending were described, will indicate how this last step in the motivated sequence can be developed to secure the final reac-tion you want from your audience.

The greatest care must be taken, however, not to make the ac-tion step too long. Someone has given the following three rules of public speaking: "Stand up; speak up; shut up!" It is well here to emphasize the final admonition. Clinch your points; finish your speech briskly; and sit down.

The motivated sequence, then, consists of five steps which cor-respond to the natural process of people's minds. Speeches con-structed on this basis are not sure of success, but they are more likely to be successful than those put together without considering their psychological effect upon the listener. The discussion in this chapter has concerned itself chiefly with the basic development of the motivated sequence. There has been no attempt here to enter into a detailed discussion of the modifications required to adapt it to different types of occasion and differing audience attitudes. Consideration of such details has been deferred to later chapters dealing with specific types of speeches. For the purpose of sum-marizing the general direction of these modifications, a chart

---

[4] From a student speech by James Fulton.

has been prepared and placed in the Appendix to which you may refer if any immediate problems of adaptation arise. In general, you will find that your skill in speech organization will develop more easily if you master the basic methods outlined in this chapter first and leave the details of modification until later.

PROBLEMS

1. Be ready to discuss the following questions in class: How does the motivated sequence follow the normal process of human thinking? How is the motivated sequence applied to persuasive speeches? To informative speeches? To entertaining speeches? Describe the fourfold need step. In persuasive speeches, what five items may be involved in the development of the satisfaction step? In developing the satisfaction step for a speech to inform, what three items are usually included? When is a parallel development of need and satisfaction steps desirable? What three different methods are used in developing the visualization step? To what in the traditional outline do the attention and action steps correspond?

2. Read a persuasive speech and identify the five steps of the motivated sequence. Write a brief statement of what is included in each step.

3. Go to hear some speaker and make a similar analysis (see Problem 2) of his speech.

4. Supposing your speech class to be the audience, determine a specific purpose requiring an active response from them, and prepare a speech, containing only five sentences, to secure that response—one sentence for each step in the motivated sequence.

5. Expand the five-sentence speech prepared for Problem 4 into a five-minute speech. What portion of the total time have you given to each step of the motivated sequence?

6. Prepare a short talk instructing the class how to perform some important task or operation. Develop the talk as suggested in this chapter, using the first three steps in the motivated sequence.

7. Prepare a short speech urging the members of the class to buy some article, a sample of which you can bring to class for demonstration.

8. Work up a speech urging support for some much needed reform in college life or administration, in local civic affairs, or in nation-wide social justice. Prepare three different visualization steps: one using the positive method, one the negative method, and the third the method of contrast. Which method seems the most effective for the subject you have selected?

In securing coherence, much is gained by making a clear plan, with main heads showing clearly their relation to each other and to the theme, and with each subhead clear in its relation to its main head.

James A. Winans

CHAPTER 17 / *Outlining a Speech Using the Motivated Sequence*

We now come to the method of writing down in outline form the complete pattern of a motivated speech—that is, one that employs the motivated sequence to gain the audience response desired. We have seen, in Chapter 14, how to arrange and outline the main substance of a speech in logical and coherent form. In Chapter 15, we examined the methods of constructing a beginning and ending for a speech and saw how they were fitted to the main structure of the speech in the traditional outline. In Chapter 16, we developed a pattern for arranging the psychological structure of a speech to fit the thinking and reaction process of our listeners. We need only combine the procedures explained in Chapters 14 and 15 with those explained in Chapter 16, then, to develop the outline for a speech that is both logical in structure and psychologically effective.

There are two principal types of outlines, each of which fulfills a different purpose in the preparation of a speech—the *full-content* outline and the *key-word* outline. The former serves to make the process of building the speech both systematic and thorough; the latter serves as an aid to memory in the early stages of oral practice. In addition, constructing an outline of the *technical plot* is often a good way to test thoroughly whether the speech is soundly structured and adequately developed. As an inexperienced speaker, you should work out all three types of outline.

THE FULL-CONTENT OUTLINE

As its name implies, the full-content outline contains the complete, detailed factual content of the speech in outline form. The various steps in the motivated sequence are set off in sections. In each of these sections, the main points are stated, and under them, properly indented and marked with proper symbols, is put all the material used to amplify and support them. Each main point and all of the minor ones are written down in complete sentences so that their full meaning and their relation to other points are made completely clear. After each piece of evidence or supporting material, the source from which it was obtained is indicated, or these sources are combined in a bibliography at the end of the outline. Thus, when the outline has been completed, not only the speaker but any other person could get a clear, comprehensive picture of the speech as a whole and in its detail by reading the outline. The only thing lacking would be the specific wording to be used in presenting the speech and the visible and audible effect of the speaker's delivery. The purpose of this type of outline is obvious. By bringing together all the material you have gathered and arranging it in the most effective manner, you insure thoroughness in the preparation of your speech.

A full-content outline requires careful preparation. It cannot be written offhand even by one who has had a great deal of experience; the beginner will be wise to allow plenty of time for developing one. The time required can be reduced, however, by going at the task systematically.

1. Begin by setting down the subject of your speech, the general end, the specific purpose, and the probable audience attitude to-

ward the purpose. If you have made an analysis of the audience and occasion as suggested in Chapter 9, you will already have done this.

2. Next, block out a skeleton plan of your outline. This plan will be a sort of blueprint to be filled in later; it will not contain the actual material of the speech but will merely indicate the structure of it. The nature of this skeleton plan will depend upon the general end. If your object is to entertain, the plan will normally contain only the attention step and will follow the method of the one-point speech (see pp. 212–219). Thus your skeleton plan will look something like the following:

Subject: _____
General End: To Entertain
Specific Purpose: _____
Probable Audience Attitude: _____

Attention step

   I. (Statement of the central
      entertaining idea) _____
      A. (Illustration) _____
         1. (Detail) _____
         2. (Detail) _____
         3, 4, etc. _____
      B. (More support) _____
      C. (More support) _____
      D, E, etc. _____
  II. (Restatement of central
      entertaining idea) _____

If your object is to inform, your skeleton plan will contain attention, need, and satisfaction steps. In each step there will be one or more main points each of which will require amplification and support very much as if it were a one-point speech itself. Your skeleton plan will therefore be somewhat like this:

Subject: _____
General End: To Inform
Specific Purpose: _____
Probable Audience Attitude: _____

Attention step

   I. (Opening statement) _____
      A. (Support) _____
         1, 2, etc. (Details) _____
      B. (Support) _____
  II. (Statement or restatement) _____

Need step I. (Statement of need for information) _____
     A. (Main supporting statement) _____
        1, 2, etc. (Support) _____
     B. (Main supporting statement) _____
     C, D, etc. _____
   II. (Pointing statement
       relating to audience) _____
       A, B, etc. (Support) _____
  III. (Summary statement)

Satisfaction step I. (Statement of subject, including
       preliminary summary) _____
     A. (Statement of first main
        division of subject) _____
        1. (Support) _____
           a. (Detail) _____
           b. (Detail) _____
        2. (Support) _____
     B, C, etc. (Statements of other main
        divisions of subject) _____
   II. (Summary statement) _____
       A, B, C. (Recapitulation
          of main points) _____

When your talk is intended to convince, to stimulate, or to actuate, all five steps in the motivated sequence will be contained in your skeleton plan:

Subject: _____
General End: To Convince (stimulate, actuate)
Specific Purpose: _____
Probable Audience Attitude: _____

Attention step   (Same form as for speech to inform; see p. 305.)

Need step I. (Statement of need: the problem) _____
       (The form used here will depend upon the spe-
       cific purpose of the speech and the nature of
       the material. One common development in-
       cludes supporting detail, pointing, and sum-
       mary: same form as for speech to inform;
       see above.)

Satisfaction step I. (Statement of idea or plan proposed) _____
     A. (Explanation) _____
        1, 2, etc. (Details) _____
     B. (Main supporting statement) _____

                    1. (Support) _____
                       a, b, etc. (Details) _____
                       2, 3, etc. (Support) _____
                    C, D, etc. (Main supporting
                       statements) _____
                II. (Summary statement) _____

Visualization step   I. (Statement of negative projection) _____
                   A, B, etc. (Support or details) _____
                   II. (Statement of positive projection) _____

   Action step   I. (Statement of action requested) _____
                   A, B, etc. (Support or
                      recapitulation) _____
                   II. (Restatement or appeal) _____

Do not consider the preceding examples as rigid models; they
are included merely to illustrate the general structure of the skeleton plan. The number of main points and the details of support will
vary from speech to speech and cannot be determined in advance
anyway. For a particular speech, merely lay out the general structure in the appropriate type of skeleton plan.

3. The next step is to set down the main points of your speech.
Fill in the main points on your skeleton plan with statements of
the main ideas you expect to present. See that these statements
help perform the functions required of the part of the speech
in which they are used; that is, in the attention step see that they
are designed to secure attention; in the need step, to emphasize
the need, and so on. Apply the principles of arrangement—of
proper sequence, coordination, subordination, etc.—studied in
Chapter 14. At this stage an outline for a speech to persuade
might look like this:

Title   OUR PLENTY IS NOT SO PLENTIFUL

Attention   I. 125,000 160-acre farms become silt.
step   II. Importance to your future.

Need   I. Principles vital to conservation.
step   A. Economy.
                      B. Foresightedness.
                      C. Preserving balance of nature.
                  II. Past disregard of these principles.

```
                     A. Waste.
                     B. Lack of foresight.
                     C. Balance of nature ignored.
              III. Summary.

Satisfaction     I. Establish threefold program.
step                 A. Planned valley programs.
                     B. Modern conservation methods.
                     C. Scientific research.
               II. Program follows vital principles.
                     A. Economy.
                     B. Foresightedness.
                     C. Regard for balance of nature.
              III. Past success of these measures.

Visualization    I. If plunder continues—
step                 A. Destitution.
                     B. Weakening national defenses.
               II. Plan will prevent catastrophe.

Action           I. Delay no longer.
step            II. People must realize the problem.
              III. You tell others about the danger.
```

4. Finally, fill in this rough draft with detailed support, and re-vise, reword, and rearrange the statements so that the result is logical and persuasive. Each item should be phrased as a complete sentence so that its logical relation to superior and subordinate points can be tested. You may find that you lack support for some statements; you may have to omit these or secure additional proof. Thus your outline will both change and grow until it has reached its final form. Then it will perhaps look like the full-content outline below. Notice the sense of thorough treatment obtained.[1] Even though there are a number of defensible plans different from the one the speaker uses here, you cannot read through the outline without being at least partially convinced by it. Any good full-content outline for a persuasive speech should have this effect on the reader.

---

[1] Students who have studied elsewhere the making of briefs, or logical outlines, in contrast to rhetorical outlines for persuasive speeches, will observe that the full-content outline based on the motivated sequence is really a combination of the two.

OUR PLENTY IS NOT SO PLENTIFUL

Attention
step

    I. We may think that the ground under our feet is solid enough, but each year 125,000 160-acre farms float down our rivers as silt.

   II. Did you know that many of our natural resources are in danger of total depletion?

      A. At present consumption rates, petroleum reserves may not last over twenty years.

      B. The number of trees cut for commercial use exceeds the new growth by 50 percent.

  III. You can be directly affected by this danger.

      A. Shortages of wood, coal, and oil will mean less fuel for your homes.

      B. Erosion and sedimentation will mean a scarcity of food and water.

      C. Depletion of resources could endanger our defense in wartime.

   IV. You need to know how a national catastrophe can be prevented.

Need
step

    I. Three principles are vital to any conservation program.

      A. We must make the most of what we have.

      B. We must renew what resources we can.

      C. We must preserve the balance of nature.

   II. In the past these "musts" have been ignored.

      A. Irreplaceable metals and oils were wasted.

         1. Petroleum and petroleum products were mercilessly exploited.

            a. Van Hise estimates that for every barrel used, five are left unrecoverable in the ground.

  b. According to the National
   Resources Board, the heat
   value of the gas wasted at
   Kettleman Hills in 1930 was
   equal to a year's energy
   output at Hoover Dam.
 2. Copper mines were abandoned
  before the ore was exhausted.
  a. It is now too expensive to
   reopen the water-filled
   shafts.
  b. We are being forced to im-
   port more and more copper.
 3. Stuart Chase says that the
  avoidable waste in mining coal
  in the United States is 35 percent, compared to 5 to 10 percent in Europe.
B. No provision was made for renewing resources.
 1. Early settlers looked upon
  America as infinitely wealthy.
  a. When cotton fields became
   sterile, farmers simply
   moved to new land.
  b. Up to now, lumber companies
   have assumed a never-ending
   supply of high-grade timber.
 2. This lack of foresight has
  started a vicious chain of
  spoilage.
  a. With the forests went the
   protective soil covering of
   decayed leaves and pine
   needles.
  b. Rain and melted snow rushed
   down the hillsides instead
   of being gradually absorbed
   by this cover.
  c. Precious topsoil was carried
   away by the surging waters.
   i. The torrents eroded gul-
    lies in the farmlands.
   ii. The silt thus formed
    polluted the water
    supply.

C. The interrelation of natural resources was ignored.
 1. What happened in Decatur, Illinois, is a glaring example.
  a. In 1922 this city built a two million dollar dam across the Sangamon River.
  b. By 1946, silt had deprived the reservoir of 26 percent of its capacity.
  c. The city had not taken heed of the shift to intertilled crops in the watershed area.
   i. Corn and soybeans had replaced hay, grass, and grain.
   ii. Lack of close-growing crops had increased erosion.
  d. Decatur must soon invest more money to re-establish its water supply.
 2. Taxpayers of Baltimore are paying for the poor farming methods in the upper river valleys.
  a. Sediment from the farms clogs the harbor.
  b. In a century, the city has paid 17 million dollars to dredge 111 million cubic yards of sediment.
III. Past disregard of the principles vital to conservation makes it imperative that we observe them now.

Satisfaction step I. A threefold program is the only way to meet the urgent need.
 A. Planned programs for whole river valleys should be established.
 B. Reforestation and proper soil practices should be instituted.
 C. Expert scientific advice should be provided.
II. Such a program satisfies the three "musts" for effective conservation.

A. By establishing valley programs, we can restore and maintain the balance of nature.
   1. Forests can be restored in watershed areas to prevent floods and erosion.
   2. Below the watershed area, dams can be constructed.
      a. They will prevent floods in the lower valley.
      b. They will maintain water supply.
      c. They will furnish electric power.
   3. Below the dam, land can be reclaimed for cultivation.
      a. Arid land can be made productive by irrigation.
      b. Fertility can be maintained by growing the proper crops.
B. By applying modern methods of forestry and farming, we can produce more and still replenish the land.
   1. According to the NEA report, 70 million acres can be cleared, drained, or irrigated to make suitable farmland.
   2. The quality of the soil can be improved.
      a. Crop rotation can prevent excessive erosion and restore nitrates.
      b. Proper fertilization can increase productivity.
   3. Reforestation can supply the necessary lumber and soil protection.
C. By providing for scientific research, we can get the most from irreplaceable mineral resources.
   1. The most efficient methods of extraction and refining can be worked out.
   2. The possibility of new mines and oil fields can be explored.

3. Synthetics can be developed for the time when we do run out of natural resources.
III. Results already obtained guarantee the success of such a program.
    A. Harnessing the Colorado River has resulted in benefits for the whole valley.
        1. Hoover Dam has conquered the floods which threatened the Imperial and Yuma valleys.
        2. Farmers in these valleys can now irrigate their lands.
        3. Navigation above and below the dam has been extended and improved.
        4. According to the Department of the Interior, the dam has produced 130 million kilowatt-hours of energy.
            a. It will return the entire cost in fifty years.
            b. It has returned over $290,000 to the United States Treasury each month.
    B. Startling results have been achieved from farming with modern conservation methods.
        1. In a study reported by the NEA, the average annual increase for the four million acres where conservation was practiced was 36 percent.
        2. Farmers grew 1,300,000 more bushels of corn on 32,000 fewer acres.
        3. Their average income was $4.90 per acre higher than that of other farmers.
    C. C. E. Behre of the Forest Service says that saw-timber growth is now about 3 billion board feet greater than the 1938 estimate.
    D. So far scientists have been responsible for important advances in conservation.

1. The Bureau of Mines developed a
   way to make potassium, formerly
   imported from Germany, out of
   potash rock.
2. Between 1931 and 1936, newly
   discovered oil fields averaged
   580 million barrels a year.

Visualization
step

I. If we don't stop destructive prac-
   tices now, the damage will be irrepa-
   rable.
   A. We will find ourselves without
      coal and copper, loam and white
      pine.
      1. Industry will decline for lack
         of raw material. (Description
         of ghost town)
      2. When the soil can no longer
         feed our growing population,
         famine will strike. (Descrip-
         tion of famine in China)
   B. Our lack of economy will lower our
      resistance to possible enemy in-
      vaders.
II. By valley projects, by renewing the
    soil and forests, and by further
    scientific research, we can prevent a
    national catastrophe.

Action
step

I. A unified conservation program can be
   delayed no longer.
   A. We don't want continued water
      shortages, dust storms, and
      floods.
   B. We don't want our children to be
      the victims of our own wasteful
      practices.
II. Action will come only when enough
    people are made aware of the problem.
III. You must help others understand the
     dangers we face.

Of course, outlines for speeches to entertain or to inform will
differ from the one above since they will not contain all five steps
in the motivated sequence. In all other details of form and con-

tent, however, they will be just as complete. We saw, in Chapter 14, how the principal substance of an informative speech on urban renewal was outlined and, in Chapter 15, how an introduction and a conclusion were added to complete this traditional outline; now let us see how a speech on this subject might be outlined using the motivated sequence:

URBAN RENEWAL

Attention step

I. Do you know how big the slum problem has become?
   A. Seventy percent of our population lives in urban areas.
   B. Thirty-three percent of city-dwellers live in slum areas.
   C. Twenty percent of the city is comprised of slum areas.
II. Do you know that attempts to solve the slum problem are costing you and your fellow citizens millions of dollars?
III. Do you know that the proposed solutions—comprehensively referred to as urban renewal—may prevent your own community from becoming a slum?

Need step

I. Information about urban renewal is important to everyone.
   A. Slums are expensive.
      1. Slum and substandard areas provide only 6 percent of the city's total real estate tax revenues.
      2. Slum and substandard areas require 45 percent of the city's municipal service costs—police, fire, health, welfare.
   B. Slums are dangerous.
      1. Unsanitary conditions are prevalent.
         a. Fifty percent of the city's disease occurs in slum areas.

    b. Sixty percent of the tuber-
    culosis victims live in slum
    areas.
   2. Delinquency and crime rates
   are high.
    a. Fifty-five percent of the
    city's juvenile delinquency
    occurs in slum areas.
    b. Forty-five percent of the
    city's major crimes occur
    in slum areas.
    c. Fifty percent of the city's
    arrests are made in slum
    areas.
  C. Slums are cruel.
   1. Children's lives may be stunted
   or warped.
   2. Elderly people may finish out
   their lives in misery.
   3. Adults of all ages may be
   trapped and hopeless.
 II. Urban renewal is aimed not only at
 destroying slums but at preventing
 their development.
 III. Information about urban renewal is
 important to you.
  A. As city business and professional
  men, your livelihood may be
  affected by the prevalence of
  slums.
  B. As city or suburban homeowners,
  your community is never entirely
  free from the encroachment of
  slums.
  C. As heads of households, your life
  and the lives of your wife and
  children may be endangered by the
  presence of slums and blighted
  areas.

Satisfaction I. This discussion will provide informa-
step tion about the development of urban
(Preliminary renewal, its financing, and one
summary) example of its work.
  A. Urban renewal has been speeded up
  through federal legislation.

    1. (Details)[2]
   B. Urban renewal projects are spon-
    sored cooperatively by the federal
    government and the community.
    1. (Details)
   C. Chicago's urban renewal work in-
    cludes a huge redevelopment
    program.
    1. (Details)

(Final
summary)

 II. Remember that urban renewal is of
   concern to the nation as well as to
   the community involved.
   A. It has been stimulated by federal
    legislation.
   B. It is supported partly by various
    forms of federal aid and partly
    by the community.
   C. Projects like Chicago's are dra-
    matic evidence of what can be
    done.

BIBLIOGRAPHY

"ABC's of Urban Renewal," Urban Renewal
 Division of Sears, Roebuck and Co.,
 Chicago, Ill.
Miles L. Colean, Renewing Our Cities,
 The Twentieth Century Fund, N.Y., 1953.
"An Explanation of Urban Renewal," The
 Milwaukee Journal, July 8, 1958.
Fact sheet, Chicago Land Clearance Com-
 mission, 320 N. Clark, Chicago, Ill.
Joseph A. Gerak, "Are Urban Renewal Pro-
 grams for Large Cities Only?" Traffic
 Quarterly, Oct. 1959, Eno Foundation at
 Saugatuck, Conn.
Edward J. Logue, "Urban Ruin—Or Urban
 Renewal?" Development Administrator of
 New Haven, New York Times Magazine,
 Nov. 9, 1958.

---

[2] Details of information are omitted here and below; for complete details
see pages 254 to 257.

"A Memorandum on Urban Renewal," Citizens Research Council of Michigan, Memorandum No. 193, Aug. 1958, 810 Farewell Building, Detroit 26, Mich.

"1959 Combined Annual Report," Chicago Plan Commission and Department of City Planning, Public Information Section, Chicago, Ill.

"Urban Renewal, Part I," Law and Contemporary Problems, School of Law, Duke University, Vol. 25, No. 4, Autumn 1960, Durham, N.C.

"Urban Renewal Outline," City Planning Associates, Inc., 708 S. Main, Mishawaka, Ind.

THE KEY-WORD OUTLINE

After you have constructed your speech and written out a full-content outline for it, you are ready to begin your oral practice. The key-word outline is an excellent aid to memory in such practice. This outline has the same indentation and symbols as the full-content outline, but it boils down the statements of the full-content outline to key-words that can be more easily remembered. Although this condensed outline is valuable in helping you memorize the sequence of ideas while you practice your speech, it should *not* be used as a prop or crutch while you present your speech to an audience. Some speakers do use such an outline during the speech, but the result is often disastrous to the effectiveness of the presentation. If you cannot remember the sequence of ideas in your speech, you have not prepared it thoroughly, or you have not practiced it aloud enough. Of course, to insure accuracy, you may read specific quotations or figures from note cards.

The following is a sample key-word outline based on the full-content outline beginning on page 309.

Title	OUR PLENTY IS NOT SO PLENTIFUL
Attention step	I. 125,000 160-acre farms become silt. II. Know danger to natural resources?

          A. Petroleum gone in 20 years.
          B. Timber cut 50% more than growth.
    III. Shortages of fuel, food, water may
          affect you directly.
     IV. Know how to prevent catastrophe.

Need   I. Three principles of conservation:
step   economy, renewal, preserving balance.
     II. Past disregard.
          A. Minerals wasted.
              1. Petroleum exploited.
                 a. Van Hise.
                 b. National Resources Board.
              2. Copper mines abandoned.
                 a. Water-filled shafts.
                 b. Forced to import.
              3. Chase on avoidable coal waste.
          B. No provision for renewing.
              1. Early settlers.
                 a. Cotton fields.
                 b. Lumber companies.
              2. Chain of spoilage.
          C. Interrelation ignored.
              1. Example of Decatur.
                 a. 2 million dollar dam.
                 b. Capacity lowered 26%.
                 c. Shift to intertilled crops.
                 d. Must invest more money.
              2. Baltimore.
                 a. Harbor clogged.
                 b. Figures on dredging.
    III. Must observe principles now.

Satisfaction   I. Threefold program.
step   A. Valley programs.
                 B. Reforestation, soil practices.
                 C. Scientific advice.
     II. Program satisfies "musts."
          A. Valley programs restore balance.
              1. Forests prevent floods and
                 erosion.
              2. Constructing dams: floods,
                 water, power.
              3. Reclaim land.
                 a. Irrigation.
                 b. Suitable crops.

                                    Key-word outline   **319**

B. Modern forestry and farming.
  1. 70 million acres reclaimable--NEA.
  2. Improving soil.
  3. Reforestation.
C. Scientific research.
  1. Efficient extraction and refining.
  2. New mines, oil fields.
  3. Synthetics.
III. Previous results insure success.
A. Colorado valley benefits.
  1. Hoover Dam prevents floods.
  2. Water for irrigation.
  3. Navigation extended.
  4. 130 million kw.-hrs. of energy.
B. Results of modern farming--NEA.
C. Saw timber growth--Behre.
D. Scientific advances: potassium, oil.

Visualization step

I. No change--irreparable damage.
A. Industrial decline, ghost towns, and famine.
B. Possible invasion.
II. Threefold program: no national catastrophe.

Action step

I. No delay.
II. People must be aware of the problem.
III. Help others understand the dangers.

THE OUTLINE OF THE TECHNICAL PLOT

Sometimes you may wish to examine your full-content outline minutely to discover if there are any weaknesses not readily apparent. For this analysis you should make an outline of the technical plot of your speech. Lay your completed full-content outline beside a sheet of paper which is blank. On this second sheet, set down line for line and symbol for symbol a statement of the technical devices which you have employed. Where you have used statistics in the content outline, set down the word *statistics* in the outline of technical plot, together with a brief statement of their functions. In this manner indicate all the various forms of support, attention factors, forms of imagery, motive appeals, methods of development, etc.

The outline of the technical plot is a testing device. It can help you determine whether your speech is organically sound; whether there is adequate supporting material; whether you have used too much of the same kind of material; whether the various appeals are well adapted to the audience and occasion. Many speeches, of course, do not need to be tested so thoroughly, and experienced speakers can make this analysis without writing down an outline of this type. For the beginner, however, there is no more effective method of testing the actual structure and technic of his proposed speech. The following sample [3] is an outline of the technic employed in the full-content outline printed earlier in the chapter (p. 309 ff.).

Attention step

I. Startling statement of fact.
II. Rhetorical question, appeal to fear.
    A, B. Specific instances, novelty of size.
III. Statement relating subject to audience.
    A, B, C. Detailed application to audience; vital attention factor.
IV. Summary restatement relating the subject to the audience.

Need step:
developed
to show a need
for a change

I. General statement of standards by which situation is to be judged.
    A, B, C. Statements enumerating these standards, based on motive appeals of saving, preservation of the race, organizing, fear.
II. General statement of the need.
    A. Statement relating need to the first standard; appeal to saving.
        1. Statement of fact for support.
           a, b. Testimony and statistics referring to specific instances.
        2. Specific instance.
           a, b. Description of effects.
        3. Testimony referring to a specific instance, statistics.

---

[3] By no means are all available terms for structural outlines used in this sample. Additional terms from the text or from the student's own coinage may be useful.

B. Statement relating need to second standard; appeal to preservation of the race, organizing.
  1. Statement of fact by way of explanation (historical reference).
    a, b. Examples.
  2. Factual illustration.
    a, b, c. Cause and effect sequence to develop illustration.
    i, ii. Further effects for ramification.
C. Statement relating need to third standard; appeal to organizing, fear.
  1. Factual illustration used as support.
    a, b. Statistics.
    c. Statement of fact.
      i. Specific instance as explanation.
      ii. Effect.
    d. Conclusion based on preceding statements.
  2. Another factual illustration used as support.
    a. Statement of fact.
    b. Statistics as support.

III. Summary: restatement of the general need.

Satisfaction step: developed to secure belief in plan proposed

I. General statement of the plan proposed.
A. Statement explaining first part of the plan.
B. Statement explaining second part of the plan.
C. Statement explaining third part of the plan.

II. General statement that plan meets need in terms of standards set up.
A. Statement that first part of plan meets third standard; appeal to saving, organizing.
  1, 2, 3. Enumeration of results of projected plan.
  2a, 2b, 2c. Further effects.
  3a, 3b. Explanation.
B. Statement that second part of plan meets second standard; appeal to saving, preservation of the race.
  1. Statistics, testimony.
  2. Statement of fact as support.
    a, b. Specific methods as explanation.

3. Explanation of the way plan meets standard.
   C. Third part of plan meets first standard; appeal to saving.
     1, 2, 3. Enumeration of projected results.
III. Statement indicating successful operation of plan; appeal to imitation.
   A. Specific instance of successful operation of first part of plan.
     1, 2, 3. Statements of fact for ramification.
     4. Statistics, testimony.
       a, b. Further statistics for additional proof.
   B. Instance of successful operation of second part of plan.
     1, 2, 3. Statistics and testimony referring to a specific instance of operation.
   C. Testimony and statistics indicating success of second part of plan.
   D. Statement indicating success of third part of plan.
     1, 2. Statistics referring to specific instances.

Visualization step: developed by the method of contrast; combining negative and positive projection of future conditions

I. Projection of future conditions with present defects unremedied.
   A. Specific instance of consequences; appeal to saving.
     1, 2. Detailed descriptions appealing to fear and revulsion using visual, auditory, and olfactory imagery.
   B. Another specific consequence; appeal to patriotism.
II. Projection of future conditions with proposal adopted; appeal to pride, patriotism.

Action step

I. Statement emphasizing urgency of need.
   A. Specific restatement of present need.
   B. Statement underlining future need; appeal to sympathy. (Parallel structure of A and B for emphasis)
II. Statement of condition for action to meet the need.
III. Personal appeal for audience action.

Of course, not all speeches require as detailed or complete a development as the one outlined above. The number of subpoints and the quantity of proof will vary greatly with the subject and purpose of the speech. Regardless of this fact, however, each part of your speech should be clear and accurate.

You have probably noticed that the traditional divisions of material—introduction, body, and conclusion—have not appeared in the outlines in this chapter. The relation between these traditional divisions and the five steps of the motivated sequence is shown on the chart at the close of this chapter (p. 328). Study this chart and you will see that while taking care to include each of the traditional divisions, you can still follow the motivated sequence. It is much easier to keep this process in mind, however, by labeling the steps of the motivated sequence clearly on the outline and developing each step with its function clearly in mind. You will find, therefore, that for outlining, the method in this chapter is superior to the traditional method.

Of course, the only way to develop skill in outlining is to examine critically the outlines prepared by someone else and to prepare outlines of your own. Several problems are suggested at the end of the chapter to provide this sort of practice. Further outlines are presented here for your study and criticism. Examine them carefully, noting both their good and bad points. Apply to them the tests for a good outline explained above and in Chapter 14, and determine whether their structure and content are both clear and psychologically adequate. The first is an outline of a speech prepared by Charles C. Higgins at Purdue University explaining gas-turbine engines to a group of engineering students.

Outline	Technical Plot
I. Power is the master of time and distance.	*Attention step:*
A. Today, distance is measured in time units.	*Arouse interest*
1. Last Sunday morning, I rode downtown on a bus in 18 minutes.	*by striking comparison.*
2. Later that same day, a P-80 from the Air Show flew the same distance in 8 seconds.	
B. But speed depends on driving power.	*Direct attention*
1. Why can the P-80 go so fast?	*toward the*
2. Because of its powerful gas-turbine engine.	*subject.*
II. You engineering students should learn all you can about gas turbines.	*Need step:*

A. As future engineers, you may need to apply gas-turbine power to the units you design.
B. Your personal car or plane may be powered by a gas turbine in the future.

III. Consider the main parts of the gas turbine from front to rear: the compressor, the combustion chamber, and the turbine rotor.
  A. The compressor squeezes the air into the combustion chamber.
    1. The compressor may have one of two possible arrangements.
      a. The centrifugal compressor has a single rotor with blades shaped to take the air in at the center of the rotor and fling it outward into a collector ring connected to the combustion chamber.
      b. The axial compressor uses a number of rotors (usually 7 to 11) composed of many windmill-like blades which decrease in size toward the combustion chamber.
        i. The air is thus compressed by the large number of blades and the decreasing size of the rotors and blades.
  B. The combustion chamber mixes and burns fuel with the compressed air.
    1. Combustion chambers may be arranged in one of two ways.
      a. The centrifugal compressor usually requires a number of small radially arranged chambers which are connected to the collector ring.
      b. The axial compressor feeds the air into a single large combustion chamber which is the type used when streamlining and weight are most important.
    2. Fuel is mixed with the air at the front opening of the combustion chamber.
    3. The rear exit of the combustion chamber varies according to the combustion chamber used.

Pointing—the importance of the subject to this audience.

Satisfaction step: Initial summary.

Detailed information in space sequence.

Details on first main topic: Use drawings to show difference between two types.

Second main topic developed by detailed explanation: Two types shown by diagrams and pictures.

a. The small radially arranged chambers have individual exits leading to the turbine rotor.
b. The large combustion chamber of the axial turbine has only one outlet leading to the turbine rotor.

C. The turbine rotor absorbs energy from the hot, expanding gases that come from the combustion chamber.   *Third main topic explained in detail:*
  1. The turbine may have one of two forms.   *Show two types with drawings.*
    a. The turbine rotor is only large enough to drive the compressor if jet propulsion is to be used.
      i. The energy absorbed by the rotor must be small in this case to leave as much for the jet as possible.
    b. The turbine rotor is a very large multistage affair if the power is to be used in driving machines by means of a shaft.
      i. The rotor must be large enough to remove all of the energy possible from the expanding gases.

IV. Remember these things about the gas turbine: *Final summary:*
  A. The compressor, combustion chamber, and turbine rotor are placed one behind the other in that order.
    1. The compressor packs the air in.   *Restatement of*
    2. The combustion chamber expands the air.   *three main topics.*
    3. The turbine rotor absorbs the energy of the expanded air or passes it to the jet.
  B. Each component may have one of two internal arrangements.   *Reiterate two alternate types.*
  C. All three components in assembled form produce the tremendous power of the gas-turbine engine.   *Concluding statement.*

The following is the outline of a speech prepared by Herschel Womble of the University of Denver for a presumed audience composed of the directors of a museum. The purpose of the speech was to raise money for an anthropological expedition.

Outline	*Technical Plot*
I. Parts of South America have never been explored anthropologically.	*Attention step: Direct attention*

A. The Highlands of Eastern Brazil is the largest blank spot on the map.
   1. Inaccessible.
   2. Hostile natives.
B. Has never been covered by an anthropologist.

to basic elements of problem: Define. Narrow the question. Use historical data.

II. The problem is how to get to the area.
   A. Highland rivers are hard to navigate by boat.
   B. There are no roads.
   C. Native packers offer labor problems.

Need step: Show causes of problem. Make certain audience is aware of problem. Show why it exists.

III. An air expedition is the only practicable way to explore this territory.
   A. Amphibian planes can find landing places in various parts of territory.
   B. The party could protect themselves.
      1. They could carry machine guns and automatic rifles.
      2. They could easily fly away if the going was too hot.
      3. They would not be in the hands of native crews or porters.
   C. A great deal of territory could be covered in a short time and at less expense than with other methods.
      1. Preliminary exploration could be finished in six months.
      2. The cost would be ten thousand dollars.
   D. Other air explorations have succeeded.
      1. The Southwest has been mapped in this way.
      2. Lindbergh's flights over Yucatan furnish added examples of the effectiveness of this method.

Satisfaction step: Show that this plan is the best solution: Explain the plan. Demonstrate that it removes causes of the problem.

Examples of operation.

IV. This expedition will bring scientific light to what is now darkness.
   A. Native life can be studied.
      1. Their language.
      2. Their customs.
   B. Archeological finds are likely.

Visualization step: Make results more vivid.

THE RELATIONSHIP BETWEEN THE STEPS OF THE MOTIVATED SEQUENCE AND THE TRADITIONAL DIVISIONS OF A SPEECH

GENERAL ENDS	INTRODUCTION	BODY OR DISCUSSION	CONCLUSION
To *entertain*	*Attention Step* Illustration or statement of the idea or subject.	*Attention Step* (continued) Further illustration or ramification of it.	*Attention Step* (concluded) Final illustration, quotation, or restatement of it.
To *inform*	*Attention Step* Provoke curiosity in subject. *Need Step* Show its relation to the listeners: why they need to know.	*Satisfaction Step* 1. Initial summary, outlining points to be covered to satisfy this need. 2. Detailed discussion of points in order.	*Satisfaction Step* (concluded) 3. Final summary: a recapitulation of the main points and of important conclusions.
To *stimulate*	*Attention Step* Stimulate attention and direct it to—	*Need Step* Present the conditions, objects, subject, which demand an emotional reaction from audience. *Satisfaction Step* Briefly state attitude desired.	*Visualization Step* Bring about climax of emotional stimulus by picturing desired attitude. *Action Step* Restate the attitude desired or challenge to audience.
To *convince*	*Attention Step* Direct attention to basic elements of the proposition.	*Need Step* Demonstrate that a need for decision exists and lay down criteria for judgment. *Satisfaction Step* State the proposition and evidence to induce belief in it and its benefits.	*Visualization Step* Briefly make its desirability vivid through imagery. *Action Step* Restate the proposition and recapitulate the reasons for belief.
To *actuate*	*Attention Step* Direct attention to—	*Need Step* Present conditions showing a need for action. *Satisfaction Step* State proposed action and prove its workability and benefits.	*Visualization Step* Picture future conditions as a result of the action taken. *Action Step* Appeal for or demand the specified action.

Note: Not everything listed above is always included. The chart is used merely to show the relationship between the two methods of organization.

1. No doubt some artifacts will be found for the museum shelves.

Project them into future.

2. Possibly we will find something the equal of the Chichen Itzá or Cuzco.

C. The expedition will bring prestige to this museum.

V. Finance this expedition.

Action step:

A. Give all you can from your treasury.

Request definite action:

B. Approach all those you are connected with and ask them to make up the difference necessary to put this expedition in the field.

Specific means by which individuals can help.

PROBLEMS

1. Be ready to discuss the following questions in class: What is a full-content outline? A key-word outline? An outline of the technical plot of the speech? What is the purpose of each of these outlines?

2. Review the material in Chapter 14 on the preparation of an outline. With reference to those requirements and the material in this chapter, revise the outline you prepared for your last class speech.

3. For your next class speech, construct each of the three types of out-line: full-content, key-word, and technical plot. What changes in the arrangement and in the wording of the main points did you find necessary or desirable as you prepared these outlines?

4. Listen to a recording of a speech or go hear some speaker and make a key-word outline as the speech is being presented. Compare your outline with those of your classmates who heard the speech.

Think like a wise man but communicate in the language of the people.

William Butler Yeats

CHAPTER 18/*Wording the Speech*

An outline sets forth the structure of a speech and the material to be used in supporting that structure, but it does not provide a finished speech. The problem of phrasing a speech in vivid and compelling language, of making transitions from one point to another clearly and smoothly, of transforming the outline into a complete, well-worded speech still confronts you. We are not concerned here with your method of composing a speech—whether you write it out and memorize it or work it out orally through continued practice (see Chapter 7, pp. 139–140); but we are concerned with the wording itself. This chapter, therefore, will consider some of the principles that underlie the effective use of words and will offer specific guidance for their selection.

ACCURACY OF MEANING

Precise meaning can be expressed only if words are carefully chosen. The man who told the hardware clerk that he had "broken the hickey on my hootenanny and needed a thing'ma-jig to fix it," expressed his meaning vaguely; but his vagueness was only a little greater than that of the orator who proclaimed, "We must follow along the path of true Americanism." The sentiment is to be admired, but just what did the orator mean by his statement? Remember that words are only the symbols of meaning and that your listener may attach a different meaning to the symbol from what you intended. *Democracy* means something different to a citizen of the United States from what it means to a citizen of Soviet Russia. An *expensive* meal to a college student may seem quite moderate in price to a wealthy man. A mode of travel that was *fast* in 1860 seems slow a century later; likewise the *United States* today is not the same as it was in the days of George Washington —in area, in population, in industry, or even in much of its governmental structure. Nor are all members of a general class alike: Frenchman A differs from Frenchmen B and C; thus one must be careful in his use of class terms. Depending upon the type of *liberals* your listeners have known, they will variously interpret what you mean by calling a statesman liberal. Students of general semantics [1] continually warn us that words are not things or qualities or operations in themselves but only symbols for them; our gravest errors of thinking and of communication arise from treating words as if they were the things to which they refer, universal and timeless in meaning.

If you think your audience may misinterpret what you say, define your words in more concrete terms. Notice, for example, how Elliott V. Bell in the following passages made clear what he meant by *structural unemployment* and *fiscal policy:*

"Structural unemployment" is just another name for what we used to call technological unemployment except that it has a broader meaning. It means not merely the unemployment that results when, for example, a textile plant is fitted out with labor-saving machinery and handworkers are displaced by automation. It also means what happens when the old textile plant in New England is abandoned and the new automated plant is erected in North Carolina. It means what happens when

---

[1] For a more extended treatment of this subject, read *Language Habits in Human Affairs* by Irving J. Lee (Harper & Brothers, N.Y., 1941), *People in Quandaries* by Wendell Johnson (Harper & Brothers, N.Y., 1946), *Putting Words in Their Places* by Doris B. Garey (Scott, Foresman, Chicago, 1957), and *Words and Things* by Roger Brown (The Free Press, Glencoe, Ill., 1958).

homes and factories switch from coal to oil. Coal miners in West Virginia or Pennsylvania lose their jobs. Even if there are unfilled jobs elsewhere, the miners may not be able or willing to move away and learn new skills. . . .

"Fiscal policy" is a term that is often used and seldom defined. By it I mean all of the taxing, spending and borrowing operations that the Government conducts—all of the ways in which the Federal Establishment puts money into the national economy or takes money out of it.[2]

A speaker concerned about the interpretation his audience will give his remarks will choose words which express the exact shade of meaning he intends to convey. Although dictionary definitions are incomplete guides to the meaning which any particular listener will attach to the words you use, they do represent the commonly accepted meanings stated as precisely as possible. The careful speaker uses his dictionary constantly to verify or correct his choice of words. He will note and observe in his speech the distinctions dictionaries make among related words, such as *languor, lassitude, lethargy, stupor,* and *torpor.* He may use a book of synonyms (such as Roget's *Thesaurus*) in an attempt to select words which exactly express his meaning. For example, among the synonyms for the verb *shine* are: *glow, glitter, glisten, gleam, flare, blaze, glare, shimmer, glimmer, flicker, sparkle, flash, beam.* The English language is very rich in subtle variations of meaning. To increase the precision of your expression, make use of this variety in your choice of words.

IMAGERY

We receive our impressions of the world around us through our senses. By means of the stimuli that impress themselves upon our eyes, our noses, our ears, and other sense organs, we learn about the world around us and respond to the situations we observe. The desire to live is always present, but only when we experience something like the sharp crackle of lightning as it strikes a nearby tree do we tremble with fear and look for some protection. In order to get a reaction from your audience, you must in some way stimulate them through one of their senses. But you cannot punch their noses, scatter-exotic perfume for them to smell, or give them

---

[2] "Economic Outlook," *Vital Speeches of the Day,* Vol. XXVII, June 1, 1961, pp. 499, 500.

delicious samples of the meal you are describing. The only senses through which you can reach them directly are the visual and auditory senses: they can see you, your movements, and your facial expressions, and they can hear what you say.

Nevertheless, you can indirectly stimulate all types of sensation through imagery—through the use of words that have the power of producing imagined sensations in the one who hears them. When I say "book," the only direct sensation you get is the sound of my voice; but the word has become a symbol for the sight of a certain object, or for the sight of printed pages, or the feeling of that object in your hand. The symbol "book" creates an image in your mind based upon past sensations that have become associated with it. Through the effective use of image-producing words, therefore, you can indirectly stimulate many different types of sensations in your audience.

Reproduced and produced images
There are two types of images: one based on the memory of a past experience in its entirety; the other a new image produced by putting together in a new pattern details which have been experienced. Thus, if I describe the football game which you attended yesterday, I am able to reproduce an image of the experience you had; if, however, I describe a cricket match —a sport which you have never seen—by putting together details of clothing, action, and sound which you have experienced in another circumstance, I produce a new image in your mind.

The principle of reference to experience
Word symbols are effective in direct proportion to the strength of the experiences with which they are associated. Some words create stronger images than others; for example, *wrench* is more vivid than *pull* simply because stronger sensations have been associated with it. For the man who has never seen a *dirigible*, the word creates at best an indistinct picture; you must use language with which he is familiar or make comparisons to experiences which are common to him. Notice, for example, how much more vivid the image becomes when you say that the dirigible is like a "huge football, painted silver, moving through the air."

The principle of detail

Remember, too, that while you can speak only one word symbol at a time, direct sensation is experienced in multiple form. A large number of detailed sensations are received at once. If you are to create a vivid image, you must take time to describe the details of the object or event. Except in rare instances, the details of sight, sound, color, movement, and the like must be included to make the image complete.

A more complete discussion of various types of imagery will be presented in Chapter 21, pages 393 to 397. For the present, concentrate on using phraseology that describes concrete detail and is related closely to the experiences of your audience. Note how Robert J. Havighurst applied both these principles in the short passage from his speech on "The American Family," printed on pages 231 to 233, and how Henry W. Grady applied them in the following passage from his famous address on "The New South":

> Let me picture to you the footsore Confederate soldier, as, buttoning up in his faded gray jacket the parole, which was to bear testimony to his children of his fidelity and faith, he turned his face southward from Appomattox in April, 1865. Think of him as, ragged, half-starved, heavy-hearted, enfeebled by wounds and exhaustion—having fought to exhaustion—he surrenders his gun, wrings the hands of his comrades in silence, and, lifting his tear-stained and pallid face for the last time to the graves that dot the old Virginia hills, pulls his gray cap over his brows and begins the slow and painful journey.[3]

SIMPLICITY OF LANGUAGE

What has been said about imagery must not be taken to imply that the wording of a speech should be flowery and ornate. Straightforward simplicity both of words and sentences is always more effective than a flamboyant style. Use words that you know your audience will understand; use sentences such as you would in conversation with a friend; use phrasing that is vivid and direct. On being admitted to the French Academy in 1753, the Compte de Buffon made an observation as true today as it was then: "Nothing is more opposed to the beauty of naturalness than the pains people take to express ordinary, everyday matters with

---

[3] From an address at the New England Society Dinner in New York by Henry W. Grady, December 22, 1886.

an air of singularity or pretense; . . . accordingly they juggle with diction, and fancy that they have refined the language, when they really have corrupted it by warping the accepted forms. . . ." [4]

You should particularly avoid words that are long, abstract, and technical. Herbert Spencer illustrates this point in his *Essay on Style* by comparing two sentences:

(1) "In proportion as the manners, customs, and amusements of a nation are cruel and barbarous, the regulations of their penal code will be severe."—How much better to have said—

(2) "In proportion as men delight in battles, bullfights, and combat of gladiators, will they punish by hanging, burning, and the rack."

Billy Sunday, though by no means an authority on style, has given us another example of the same point:

If a man were to take a piece of meat and smell it and look disgusted, and his little boy were to say, "What's the matter with it, pop?" and he were to say, "It is undergoing a process of decomposition in the formation of new chemical compounds," the boy would be all in. But if the father were to say, "It's rotten," then the boy would understand and hold his nose. "Rotten" is a good Anglo-Saxon word and you do not have to go to the dictionary to find out what it means. [5]

Use short words; use simple words; use words that are specific; use words whose meaning is obvious at once.

LOADED WORDS

Simplicity of language does not mean dullness or lack of color. On the contrary, a proper choice of simple words will add vividness to your speech. Many words contain within themselves not only their dictionary meaning but, in addition, an aura of implied meaning. Such words are "loaded"; they have a strong effect on the reaction of an audience. Observe your own reaction to the following words: *man, fellow, guy, person, savage, cheapskate, piker, chiseler, sportsman, father, dad, baron, miser, dictator.* Although each of these words denotes a human being, what different types of human beings they suggest.

---

[4] From *Discours sur le Style.*
[5] Quoted in *Essentials of Speech* by J. R. Pelsma (Crowell, N. Y., 1924), p. 193.

Because of their influence on audience reaction, loaded words must be used with caution. Be sure you can answer these two questions affirmatively: Does the audience understand the meaning I intend to convey? Do I have sound facts and reasoning to support my position so that the words are not mere labels? Select words which will add vividness to your speaking, but take care to apply them accurately.

Meaning derived from associations Many words become loaded as a result of experiences with which they have become associated. Thus, after the repeal of national prohibition, places where liquor was sold came to be called *taverns* in order to avoid unpleasant associations with the old saloon. The word *politician* suggests to many people a scheming, dishonest man, making promises which he does not expect to keep and uttering pious platitudes while he secretly accepts illegal pay from "special interests"; this picture has been repeatedly painted of him by cartoonists and novelists and by opposing politicians. Yet the intrinsic meaning of the word denotes only one who is occupied in the management of public affairs or who works in the interest of a political party.

Since different people have different experiences, the connotation of words varies a great deal, and you must be tactful in adapting words to the audience. Shoe clerks, for example, tell a woman, "Madam, this foot is slightly smaller than the other," instead of "That foot is bigger than this one." Observe in the following example how Dr. Ernest F. Tittle uses words loaded with associations in his description of words themselves.

There are colorful words that are as beautiful as red roses; and there are drab words that are as unlovely as an anaemic-looking woman. There are concrete words that keep people awake; and there are abstract words that put them to sleep. There are strong words that can punch like a prize-fighter; and weak words that are as insipid as a "mama's boy." There are warm, sympathetic words that grip men's hearts; and cold, detached words that leave an audience unmoved. There are warm, sympathetic words that lift every listener, at least for a moment, to the sunlit heights of God; and base words that leave an audience in the atmosphere of the cabaret.[6]

---

[6] From a commencement address before the Northwestern University School of Speech, June 1924. Reprinted in full on pages 401–409.

Meaning derived from the sound of the word   Some words gain a particular value from the very sounds they contain. Such words as *hiss, crash, rattle, slink, creep, bound, roar,* and the like suggest by their sound their exact meaning. The poems of Edgar Allan Poe and of Vachel Lindsay abound in words of this kind—*clanging, tinkle, mumbo-jumbo,* etc. As H. A. Overstreet has said, "There are words that chuckle; words that laugh right out; words that weep; words that droop and falter." [7] A proper appreciation of the sound value of words will help make your speaking vivid.

TRITENESS

Words which are effective in themselves are often made ineffective by too continued use. A once powerful phrase is stripped of its significance by repetition and serves only to display a lack of originality in the person who uses it. Thus, when one says that he "sat down to a sumptuous repast placed on a table loaded with delectable delicacies," he is not only violating the rule of simplicity but is using worn-out phrases as well. The words *gorgeous, fabulous, terrific,* and others have been so overworked that they are no longer as effective as they once were. Figures of speech especially are likely to become trite; avoid such expressions as "slept like a log," "dead as a doornail," and "pretty as a picture." On the other hand, beware also of grotesque combinations and mixed metaphors. The speaker who spoke of a dump heap as a "picturesque eyesore" was original, but ludicrous, as was the man who remarked that "The years roll on, drop by drop." Note in contrast the forcefulness of Justice Learned Hand's statement:

Liberty lives in the hearts of men and women. When it dies there, no constitution, nor court, nor law can save it." [8]

Note also the strength of Yale president A. Whitney Griswold's comparison of the free mind and the unfree mind:

---

[7] From *Influencing Human Behavior* by H. A. Overstreet (W. W. Norton & Company, N. Y., 1925).
[8] Quoted in a speech "The Bold Go Toward Their Time," by William C. Lang, printed in *Vital Speeches of the Day*, Vol. XXVII, March 15, 1961, pp. 333, 334.

The mind that is unfree, the mind that is possessed, the mind that is indoctrinated or forced does not learn. It copies. Discovery is the true essence of learning. The free mind travels while the unfree simply looks at the maps. The unfree mind locks the doors, bars the shutters, and stays at home.[9]

SLANG

Slang words and phrases are on occasion both acceptable and effective. They sometimes represent a transitional stage between new and accepted usage. When a slang phrase is inherently precise or vivid, it may become standard usage; but too often slang is only temporary and weak. It is never wise to use slang on dignified occasions and only rarely on others. College slang tends to become trite and to substitute one word for a variety of more specific and effective ones. Thus, a young woman is "terrific" but so is a football game, a chocolate soda, a dance, a class lecture, and a pair of shoes. To use slang for a particular effect is no sin, but to use it merely to avoid the search for more precise words is slipshod and inexcusable.

CONNECTIVE PHRASES

Wording a speech involves more than mere vividness and precision. Unlike written composition, speeches cannot be divided into units by paragraph indentation and by underlined headings. The relation between the points of a speech must be made clear by the wording itself.

Preliminary and final summaries, such as those already described in Chapter 16 and more fully explained in Chapter 20, are useful in mapping out for the audience the road you intend to follow and in reviewing it when you are through. But you must continually set up signposts as you go along to assist your audience in following you. For this purpose, you will find a variety of connective phrases useful. The following list contains a few of the more common ones:

Not only . . . but also . . .
In the first place . . . The second point is . . .

---

[9] *Ibid.*

In addition to . . . notice that . . .
More important than all these is . . .
In contrast to . . .
Similar to this . . . is . . .
Now look at it from a different angle . . .
This last point raises a question . . .
You must keep these three things in mind in order to understand the
    importance of the fourth . . .
What was the result of this . . . ? Just this: . . .

Clarity often depends upon the effectiveness of the speaker's connective phrases. Expand your list of such phrases until you can make easy, smooth transitions instead of awkward, jerky ones.

BUILDING A VOCABULARY

The larger your working vocabulary, the easier will wording your speech be. Wide reading, close observation of the language used by cultured people, even the systematic attempt to "use a new word every day"—all these are methods of building a vocabulary. More important, however, is the process of putting into active use the vocabulary you already possess. Most people know the meaning of ten times as many words as they actually use. Work to transfer the words in your recognition vocabulary to your active vocabulary. Great speakers are often noted not for the large words they use but for the skill with which they combine the simple words of the average man's vocabulary to state even complicated ideas vividly and precisely.

PROBLEMS

1. Be ready to discuss the following questions in class: What cautions should you take to be sure you are using words accurately? Is there anything contradictory in the suggestion that you should use image-producing words and also simple, direct words? What are the values and dangers of loaded words? Are trite words and slang the same? How do connective phrases add clarity and unity to a speech?

2. Prepare to present orally brief descriptions containing vivid imagery of one or two simple things such as:

Sailboats on a lake.   A cold roast beef sandwich.
A faulty loud-speaker.   Kitchen on Sunday noon.
Frogs in the biology laboratory. Traffic at a busy intersection.

3. Find as many samples of imagery as you can in the speeches by Mr. Havighurst (pp. 231–233) and Dr. Tittle (p. 336).

4. Prepare to describe orally some personal experience or some event you have witnessed. Employ imagery vivid enough to make your audience relive the experience with you.

5. Compile a list of synonyms for the following words: *good, active, brutal, plan, group, school, game, house, walk, speak, quickly, smile.* Expand this list to include synonyms of other common words. Note the different shades of meaning carried by the various synonyms.

6. For each of the words listed below, set down two or more *different* meanings which the word is frequently used to convey. Add to this list other such multiple-meaning words.

average	good	popular
fair	normal	right

7. Make a list of loaded words, putting in one group those words and phrases to which members of your class would react favorably, and in another group those to which they would attach a feeling of dislike.

8. Pick out twenty loaded words used in the speech by Dr. Tittle, page 336, and indicate whether they are favorably or unfavorably loaded.

9. Read a recent issue of *Vital Speeches of the Day* to find passages (*a*) illustrating particularly good choice of words (simple, direct, exact, and vivid words); (*b*) illustrating particularly helpful use of connective phrases.

10. In the library find a speech by Edmund Burke, one by Daniel Webster, and one by Abraham Lincoln. Compare the wording in these three speeches on the basis of (*a*) simplicity, (*b*) vivid imagery, and (*c*) use of loaded words.

11. Expand the list of connective phrases listed on pages 338 to 339 until you have twenty or more; make a short speech in which you use as many of them as possible.

12. In practicing for your next class speech, pay particular attention to your choice of words. Check your words for accuracy, vividness, simplicity, concreteness, and appropriateness.

part four

Basic Types of Speech

The speech to entertain • The speech to inform • The speech to stimulate

(or to actuate through emotional stimulation) • The speech to convince

(or to actuate through conviction) • Answering questions and objections

The essence of language is that it utilizes those elements in experience most easily abstracted for conscious entertainment, and most easily reproduced in experience.

Alfred North Whitehead

CHAPTER 19/*The Speech to Entertain*

Many public speakers have never given much attention to the technics of the speech to entertain, and consequently, when they attempt one, they succeed only in boring their audiences. On the surface, developing and presenting a good speech to entertain would seem easy, but this is far from the fact; a lot of practical experience is necessary to succeed in this kind of speaking.

A common misconception is that the speech to entertain must be funny. Of course humorous speeches are popular with audiences, but speeches about travel experiences or about unusual people or events, for example, may be even more entertaining. Indeed, nearly anything which would provide interesting conversational material for the audience you are addressing may be appropriate material for a speech to entertain. The purpose of such a speech, however, is not to impart a basic understanding of the subject but to provide an interesting diversion. Careful explanation is omitted in favor of lively description, novelty, and humor.

Moreover, entertainment, whether provided through humor or through novelty, is often necessary in a speech with a more serious purpose. For example, audiences that have been fatigued by a long program preceding a speech may require an abundance of entertainment along with the more serious discussion. Remember, therefore, that the suggestions presented here can be applied to all kinds of speeches, not just the speech to entertain.

TYPICAL SITUATIONS REQUIRING SPEECHES OF ENTERTAINMENT

Speeches of entertainment are given on many and varied occasions, including: (1) *Parties*. Social occasions sometimes offer the opportunity for an entertaining speech. When a gathering is large, a special program including speeches to entertain is frequently arranged. (2) *Club meetings*. Organized groups—religious, social, and political—often arrange sessions that are frankly for the purpose of entertainment and include speeches. (3) *Dinners*. The after-dinner speech is undoubtedly the most common type of entertaining speech. Certainly it is the best known, the most abhorred when poorly done, and the most enjoyed when cleverly done.

THE PURPOSE: TO ENTERTAIN THE AUDIENCE

When your object in speaking is entertainment, everything else must be subordinated to that purpose. Of course, a serious thought may be injected occasionally for mild contrast. No matter how much people like froth, they do not like froth alone. Underlying your humor, there should be something a little more substantial— some sentiment of loyalty or appreciation for the group addressed or of the subject discussed. Sentiments of this sort, however, must never be allowed to dominate the purpose of the speech; they must be used only as foils for the entertainment.

SOME CHARACTERISTICS OF DELIVERY AND CONTENT

Remember that you want your audience to have a good time and that you cannot encourage enjoyment in others unless your manner suggests you are having a good time yourself. Be genial and good-natured—this is of extreme importance—but beware of appearing as though you were forcing yourself. Do not put on the sickly grin of the boy who was bound he would laugh harder the more he was thrashed. On the other hand, stay clear of the scowling determination of the overzealous reformer. As Mr. Dooley, a character created by Finley Peter Dunne, put it, "Let your spakin' be light and airy." Be quick and alert, lively and animated; above all, don't let your speech drag. Over three centuries ago, Milton expressed the proper mood in these lines:

> . . . bring with thee
> Jest, and youthful Jollity,
> Quips, and cranks, and wanton wiles,
> Nods, and becks, and wreathéd smiles . . .
> Sport that wrinkled Care derides,
> And Laughter holding both his sides,
> Come, and trip it as ye go,
> On the light fantastic toe. . . .

What you say ought to reflect the same mood as your delivery. Lightness, good humor, novelty, fun—these are the elements of which the entertaining speech is built.

Be optimistic. This is not the place to unload your troubles, or to be argumentative, or to paint a dark picture of the future—unless you are obviously doing it in fun. Be gay and let the troubles of tomorrow take care of themselves.

Avoid a complicated arrangement of ideas. Don't make your audience strain to understand you. Develop the speech around one or two simple ideas that can be easily grasped. Be very sure, however, that these few points have in them something novel or original.

Liberally sprinkle stories and illustrations through your speech. Do not rely on "canned" jokes. Humorous anecdotes and tales of your own or of someone else's experiences, however, will serve to illuminate the point you are making and should be used generously. Unless you are clever at turning phrases, avoid too much intervening discussion between your illustrations and descriptions; let one story lead naturally into another, each serving to bring out the theme around which your speech is built. See that your tales are to the point; never drag one in by the heels.

Include humor in your speech whenever it is appropriate. Humor, you must remember, ranges all the way from the inward chuckle to the loud guffaw. You do not have to make your listeners roar, but at least loosen them up to the point of smiling. There are a number of ways to do this, but fundamental to all of them is a spirit of fun on the part of the speaker and an ability to see and portray the incongruity of situations. It is the out-of-order things which cause us to laugh. A big man on a big horse is not funny; but the same man astraddle a donkey so small that the stirrups almost reach the ground will cause the most matter-of-fact person to smile. But, you may ask, how can a speaker put all this into practice? A brief enumeration of some forms of humor follows.

Exaggeration

You can often add humor to your speech and at the same time make your point obvious by a skillful use of exaggeration or overstatement. For example, "This traffic problem is becoming serious—the pedestrian has the right of way only after the ambulance picks him up" (*Arkansas Gazette*). The Reverend Sidney Smith is reported to have replied to one of his parishioners who complained of the heat, "Yes, it is very hot. Let us both take off our flesh and sit in the garden in our bones!" Exaggeration of course, is the basis of humor in many "tall tales." Louis Untermeyer tells one about the rancher in the Texas Panhandle who went to town to borrow money on his ranch during one of those big—and what isn't big to a Texan?—dust storms. "Before I can let you have anything," said the banker, shouting above the high wind, "I'll have to go out and take a look at your place." " 'Twon't be necessary," said the rancher. "Here comes the place now."

Puns

Using words which have a double meaning or which sound like other words with a different meaning often provokes laughter. For example, a financial writer once said that the stock market slump "has had a sobering effect on Wall Street; money, however, is still very tight" (*London Opinion*).

The Saturday Review printed these two stories: (1) The receiver of a corporation about to go into bankruptcy glared across the director's table at the outgoing president and said: "This is no concern of yours!" (2) An industrialist was complaining that court decisions were constantly hemming in business: "Corporations are losing their strength today—gradually, by decrees!" [1] *Puns, Puns, Puns* is responsible for this example: "The Chairman of the Management Board replied in a few appropriated words." [2] A classic example is the very particular matron who looked down her nose at the butcher and said, "I'll have two dozen chops, and see that you make them lean." "Yes, ma'am," replied the clerk meekly, "to the right or left?" Finally, there is the answer Johnny gave when the teacher asked why Lapland was so thinly populated: "Because there are so few Lapps to the mile."

Poking fun at authority or dignity

People like to see someone take a dig at those who are on top and, even more, at those who falsely think they are. There is the famous quip made by a member of the House of Commons when an extremely dignified and serious-looking cabinet member walked by: "There, but for the grace of God, goes God." In his speech on "The American Tax System," Roger A. Freeman remarked, "Most of us have participated in, attended, or read the transcripts of legislative tax hearings. We have sympathized with some groups, but occasionally felt like Mr. J. P. Morgan, who one day, when he was besieged by a mendicant, rang for his butler and ordered him: 'Jim, throw him out; he is breaking my heart.'" [3] Thomas A. Edison is reported by Louis Sobol to have begun a speech, after the toastmaster had given him a complimentary but very long introduction dwelling on his invention of the talking machine, by saying, "I thank the gentleman for his kind remarks but I must insist upon a correction. God invented the talking machine. I only invented the first one that can be shut off." Bennett Cerf tells about the inspecting colonel who stopped two soldiers staggering under the weight of a steaming kettle they

---

[1] August 23, 1958, p. 6.
[2] Helen Hoke (Franklin Watts, Inc., N. Y., 1958), p. 91.
[3] *Vital Speeches of the Day*, August 15, 1961.

were hauling from the mess truck. "Get me a ladle," he commanded. One of the soldiers rushed for it. The colonel dipped it into the kettle, swallowed a mouthful, gulped, and roared, "Do you call that soup?" "No, sir," came the meek reply, "that's the water we've been washing mess kits in."

Irony

Say something in such a way that the opposite meaning is obviously implied. While James A. Whistler, the famous American painter, was being honored at a reception, a gushing woman bustled up to him and announced, "Oh, Mr. Whistler, I was out your way this afternoon and I walked right by your house!" To which Whistler replied, "Thank you so much, madam." Ambrose Bierce, in his *Devil's Dictionary*, defined an *egotist* as "a person of low taste, more interested in himself than me" and remarked that to be *positive* meant "to be mistaken at the top of one's voice."

Burlesque

The fundamental characteristic of burlesque consists of treating absurd things seriously or serious things absurdly. In this vein, the Duke of Manchester is reported to have said, "I believe that the energy expended by a society woman in one year is enough to lift Buckingham Palace $9\frac{1}{4}$ inches off the ground and hold it there 43 seconds." Louis Untermeyer tells of the Reno lawyer who said, "Some people object to divorce, but a large number of divorces proves that America is the land of the free." "Perhaps," replied the lawyer from New York, "but the steady persistence of marriage shows that it's also the home of the brave." A parody or take-off on something which is usually treated with seriousness often provides humor. A sense of incongruity can be developed by describing absurdities in the dignified language usually reserved for serious subjects or by treating minor problems as if they were complicated and important. Edward C. Elliott, former President of Purdue University, in mock seriousness advised the new President of Wabash College at his inaugural dinner that the three essentials for success in his new office were "a sound stomach . . . to eat all the food placed before you in public, a good thick skin . . . for resisting your foes and particularly your friends, and an operation to remove your conscience, which for a president is a discouraging handicap."

Unexpected turns

Lead your audience to believe that you are going to say the normal thing; then say the opposite. Frederick Landis used this method while poking good-humored fun at Will H. Hays during a program at which they both spoke: "I knew that he had been successful in politics for twenty years—and never had been caught at it." That the unexpected twist adds life to any type of humor is exemplified in many of the samples above. Often it is the principal ingredient of humorous anecdotes. Louis Sobol tells of a distinguished scientist who was observing the heavens through the huge telescope in an observatory. Suddenly he announced, "It's going to rain." "What makes you think so?" asked his friend. "Because," said the astronomer, still peering through the telescope, "my corns hurt." The story is told of a woman who went to a psychiatrist confessing that her friends thought she was crazy. The psychiatrist asked for her symptoms. She said, "I like pancakes, that's all." "Well," replied the doctor, "that isn't a sign of insanity. I like pancakes myself." The old girl jumped from her chair, clapped her hands with delight in finding a kindred spirit, and exclaimed, "Really, doctor, I'm so glad. You must come visit me some day. I have two trunks full of pancakes in the attic!" During one of his campaign speeches, Theodore Roosevelt is said to have been continually interrupted by a heckler who kept shouting, "I am a Democrat." Finally, Roosevelt inquired gently, "May I inquire why the gentleman is a Democrat?" "My grandfather was a Democrat," replied the heckler, "my father was a Democrat, and I am a Democrat." "And suppose," asked Roosevelt, "that your grandfather had been a jackass, and your father had been a jackass, what would you be?" To the delight of the audience, the heckler shouted back, "A Republican!"

Peculiar traits of people

Tell about some person's idiosyncrasies, or illustrate peculiarities which are characteristic of certain classes of people. The musical show "Of Thee I Sing" obtained much of its humor by painting in bold relief the peculiar traits of certain types of politicians. During a supposed meeting of the Senate, for example, one "Senator" described a bridge hand as follows, "North had four aces; east held four kings; west, four queens; and south held four knaves." At this point the "Senator from Virginia" interrupted with, "Mr. President, I object. The South would never consent to a hand like that." Then there were the three somewhat deaf gentlemen aboard a train from London, one of whom inquired, "What station is this?" "Wembly," answered the guard. "Heavens," remarked the second gentleman, "I thought it was Thursday." "So am I," exclaimed the third. "Let's all have a drink." And, of course, McTavish was the typical legendary Scotsman who bought only one spur; he figured that if one side of the horse went, the other was sure to follow. Another story concerns the two good friends, Father Kelly and Rabbi Levi, who sat opposite each other at a banquet where roast ham was served. Serving himself liberally, the good Father turned to his friend and said, "Rabbi Levi, when are you going to become liberal enough to eat ham?" To which the rabbi gently retorted, "At your wedding, Father Kelly." Then, of course, Uncle Ezra coming to town for the first time in twenty years saw a sign in the store window reading, "Ladies Ready to Wear Clothes." "Gosh," he remarked, "it's about time." In Hollywood, meanwhile, an absent-minded clerk waited on a movie star in a specialty shop. "I'd like a pair of shorts to wear around my gymnasium," she said. "Excellent," said the bemused clerk reaching for the tape, "don't you think we better measure it for size?"

These are only a few of the many ways in which the absurdities of life can be presented humorously.[4] Your ability to use humor depends in large measure upon your ability to see the contrasts, the incongruities of events around you. Watch the funny things that happen. Often the unusual little mishaps of word or action which occur before you speak will furnish you with spontaneous

---

[4] Among collections of anecdotes and humor to which you may refer are Louis Untermeyer's *A Treasury of Laughter* (Simon and Schuster, N. Y., 1946) ; Bennett Cerf's four collections, *Anything for a Laugh* (Bantam Books, N. Y., 1946), *Shake Well Before Using* (Simon and Schuster, N. Y., 1948), *Encyclopedia of Modern American Humor* (Doubleday, N. Y., 1954), and *The Life of the Party* (Hanover House, Garden City, N. Y., 1956) ; and Benjamin Botken's *A Treasury of American Anecdotes* (Random House, N. Y., 1957). Several examples in this chapter are adapted from items in these volumes.

bits of humor. Moreover, don't take your speech too seriously. If you throw off all care and proceed to enjoy yourself, you will find that your own carefree attitude will help produce a spirit of good humor in your audience.

ORGANIZATION

The organization of a speech to entertain is controlled by the fact that the listeners need to be led through only the first step of the motivated sequence—the attention step. They need not be made aware of any pressing problem or given clear explanation and argument. It is only necessary to secure their attention and maintain their interest in an enjoyable manner. To do this, the speaker might use the technic of the one-point speech, or he might burlesque the entire motivated sequence.

Using the technic of the one-point speech

When you use this first method, your speech will be a series of illustrations, anecdotes, and humorous contrasts following one another in rapid order. Each item should refer in some way to one central idea. The following is a simple formula for this type of organization:
1. Tell a story or give an illustration.
2. Point out the essential idea or point of view expressed by it, around which you intend to unify the details of your speech.
3. Follow with a series of additional stories and illustrations, each of which amplifies or illuminates this central point. Arrange these items so as to maintain a balance of interest or humor. Avoid grouping all the funniest material in one spot, and particularly beware of a letdown at the end. Save an especially striking or humorous anecdote for the last.
4. Close with an unusual restatement of the central point which you have illuminated. At this point bring in whatever serious sentiment may underlie your fun.

By developing your speech in this way, you will not only entertain your audience but will also help them remember your talk. A skeleton plan for this method of organizing an entertaining speech was presented on page 305. (See also the sample outline on p. 291 in Chapter 16.) This method is followed in "The Babies" by Mark

Twain, and in "A Toast to Sir Thomas Lipton" by George Ade (listed in the *Speeches for Collateral Study*, pp. 355–356).

Burlesquing the entire motivated sequence

When you use this second method, your speech will contain only the attention step insofar as the psychological reaction of your audience is concerned; but the structure of the speech will contain all five steps, each one an absurd burlesque of that used in serious persuasion.

Attention step. Begin your speech in one of four ways: refer to the occasion, allude to some recent humorous incident, poke fun at the chairman or someone else (don't be mean; make it obvious that you are not serious), tell a story or anecdote. Then in some way relate the beginning of your speech to the:

Need and satisfaction steps. Either present a serious problem (such as the difficulties of making income meet expenditures), exaggerate the seriousness of it beyond all proportions, and then offer an absurd solution or show how the actual solution is absurd; or present an absurd problem (such as the harm caused by eating with one's knife), detail a number of fictitious stories illustrating it, then launch into an equally preposterous method of solving this problem. Incorporate a series of humorous anecdotes to amplify the incongruity.

Visualization step. Heighten the absurdity already developed by adding a more exaggerated picture of conditions.

Action step. Close your speech swiftly by burlesquing an exorbitant demand for action, or by telling a story to illustrate the irony of your argument, or by summarizing the "vital" points of your argument. Make this final thrust short and funny.

A good example of the speech that burlesques the motivated sequence is Will Rogers' "Settling the Corset Problem of This Country," which is listed on page 356.

Two final cautions. First, don't talk too long. Nothing spoils humor so much as dragging it out. Bring your speech to a point; illuminate that point brilliantly for a moment; then sit down. Unless you are the only speaker, five or ten minutes ought to be your limit. Second, be sure that your humor is in good taste. If it leaves a sting or a feeling of shame you will not create good feeling.

At a testimonial dinner for George Jessel, several humorous tributes were paid to the guest of honor. In his response, Mr. Jessel picked up and further developed some of the themes of the preceding speakers. For each of these speeches printed in his book *This Way, Miss,* Mr. Jessel provided a brief "clinical note." In the following pages are printed (1) a clinical note by Mr. Jessel for Jack Benny's speech, (2) excerpts from speeches by Jack Benny, Eddie Cantor, and Samuel Goldwyn, and (3) Mr. Jessel's speech, pages 353 to 355.

TESTIMONIAL DINNER FOR GEORGE JESSEL [5]

Clinical note by George Jessel: Jack Benny has more ease when speaking at a dinner than any of his contemporaries. First, he is always well prepared and has tried out most of his gags for his staff and his smart wife. His method is that he is never punching too hard, so that should some of his lines fall without laughter, you never hear the thud. Added to this, he has a gentleness that no matter what he says, it never offends anyone. Also, you can tell by what he says that he likes everybody. I never heard him say an unkind word in private or before the public. . . .

Jack Benny: Brother Friars, ladies and gentlemen: Unaccustomed as I am to speaking ahead of our guest of honor—I am going to tell you, which you may or not believe, but Jessel did everything in his power to take this job away from me tonight. He wanted to be the guest of honor *and* the Toastmaster—but fortunately, ladies and gentlemen, I happen to be an officer of the Friars' Club, and I put a stop to it. I am the Proctor of the Friars. I was elected Proctor about three months ago. The Proctor of the Friars is equivalent to a photographer on the *Reader's Digest.*— Just the same, ladies and gentlemen, I am highly flattered that I was asked by our club to be Toastmaster for a dinner given to the greatest Toastmaster in America.—I mean, it gives me a feeling, even though it may be temporary, that at least I am next best—and being next best to Jessel, whether it is toastmaster, producer, entertainer, or any of his other accomplishments, is quite an achievement. . . . Being Toastmaster means that I'll have to jump up here every few minutes—I'll have to be up here all night, so I am not going to take up any more of your time at this moment. If you look up at the dais, you will see what a grand

---

[5] From *This Way, Miss* by George Jessel. Copyright 1955 by George Jessel. Abridged and reprinted by permission of Holt, Rinehart and Winston, Inc.

array of speakers we have—the finest dais that I've ever seen. I know that if these gentlemen were paid, it would cost one hundred or two hundred thousand dollars for their performances. Even I have cut my regular fee in half. . . .

Eddie Cantor: . . . Jack has told you that he is the greatest Toast-master ever. He is a great comedian, and a producer—but did you ever catch him at a funeral? He is wonderful—most wonderful. These things are nothing for Jessel—he loves to go to a funeral. And all through the years he makes notes on all his friends, because he is a busy man—he wants to be ready. And many times he has called me on the phone. I said, "Hello," and he hung up. He is just checking on my health.—

Samuel Goldwyn: Governor, Your Honor the Mayor, ladies and gentlemen, and Brother Friars: Before, a little while ago, I had a couple of gags and I tried them out on Bob Hope, and he said, "You are supposed to be a producer, not be funny, and don't try it." So, I am not going to try it and be funny. . . . I wanted to sit at this distinguished table for two specific reasons, first to pay my tribute to the show business ambassador of the world. And second, you don't know what a novelty it is for me to sit and listen to Hope, Cantor, and [Danny] Kaye speak dialogue that I don't have to pay for.

It is a great satisfaction to me to be able to pay tribute to a man who has been a credit to the show business for so long—and believe me, Georgie has been in business a long, long time. As a matter of fact, he has been in it so long that there are some people that say that Jessel was the actor that shot Lincoln, but I know that couldn't be true. If Lincoln had ever heard Jessel sing, he'd have shot him first. But even if you have any doubts about that Lincoln business, it is a fact that Georgie was tied in closely with another president. As a matter of fact, he was the advance man for Woodrow Wilson. I mean the picture. He made so many speeches for Wilson and Darryl Zanuck, you would have thought that Darryl was running for vice-president.

George Jessel: This has been a most trying evening for me, listening to many gentlemen highly successful in their own vocations, attempting to be after-dinner speakers. Considering this great fund of inexperience, they have done remarkably well, and I compliment them, as I would compliment a sixty-year-old baseball umpire who had crocheted a fine lace tablecloth. Most men who are recipients of testimonial dinners such as this are immediately overcome with emotion when called to their feet, and they generally begin a hesitant address by saying, "Oh, my friends, I have no words for this . . ." I have more words than in *Gone with the Wind*. And as to the phrases and the many shafts that have been wafted at me by some of the speakers, it would be nice if I were overcome by the close proximity of these celebrated people. Unfortunately I am not. I don't think that posterity will be as generous as you have been with your laughter and applause to most of the speakers. Look through your mind's eye and see what might be written of most of them in the future—a short word-portrait of their careers: Mr. Cantor, favorite radio star of the Crystal Set day—Mr. George Burns, whose lifeline of existence is depending on what Gracie will say when he says, "—and then what happened to your brother??" Mr. Danny Kaye, current favorite of a shattered and bankrupt Great Britain—Mr. Bob Hope, the most popular comedian of an era when America was in its most bewildered state— Mr. Pat O'Brien, a Vine Street Parnell—Mr. Jolson, with a great success shielded from the public eye by a handsome boy in his twenties and a thousand fat Victor records. And the Toastmaster! I am not particularly gratified when complimented by so many insinuations that it is about time that honor was paid to me.

I am glad the young lady with whom I have a date later in the evening is here to hear these nice things about me; but there's much more I'd like her to hear about me. As a child I made up many sayings which are known the world over: "A friend in need is a friend indeed" is one of them. Another: "Money you make like that will never do you any good." "Rockefeller can only wear one suit at a time," was one of my phrases,—and I should have been happy if the preceding speakers had mentioned the help I had been to men throughout the years. I wish I could say this in the second or third person.

I recall working along the waterfront in Albany many years ago, and seeing a young man having trouble starting his boat. I helped him. He never forgot it. That man was Robert Fulton, ladies and gentlemen.

The world does not know this, nor did you hear it from the mouth of the speakers—of how I was called up to Washington by a great man at a time when our country was in great hazard. When he said to me, "Georgie, I don't know what to do about this general I have. He drinks, he smokes, and with his beard people think he looks Jewish; I am being terribly criticized . . ." And I said, "Abe, keep Grant, and let McClellan go . . ." A publisher who lives in San Simeon sent for me some months ago and said to me, "Georgie, I have a man who I feel is right for the presidency, and I want you to help him in public utterance." So, while most of you think I was appearing at the Carnival—a saloon in New York—I was in Loew's Tokyo, ladies and gentlemen. And I helped this man. I said to him, "MacArthur, your speeches are too flowery—you sound as if you have a Godhead complex. The public don't want that. Remember you are just a man, Doug—you aren't Zanuck." Not only have I helped my fellow men, but I have helped dumb animals as well. Some years ago I met a horse as a two-year-old and nobody wanted to bet on him . . . a thin, skinny horse, Rosenberg was his name. I made him change his name to Rosemont, and he won at the Santa Anita Handicap.

But all this is yesterday's roses. . . . More than anyone . . . I know how much bunkum there is in testimonial dinners. I have had, through my years in public life, to tell more lies about guests-of-honor than any one of my contemporaries. I have screamed their virtues from the speaker's table, hiding their vices in my own conscience. But I've found this to be true—I have never known anyone who was the recipient of a testimonial dinner who did not have something that was pretty good—some slight decent quality. No one ever gave a dinner for Lefty Louie or Sittin' Bull—and so, after forty years in show business, I am inclined to look at things philosophically. I don't know whether or not life begins at forty. If it does, it begins from the neck up. For the manuscript of life is a tragi-farce, there is very little mystery in it. And we know very soon the finish and we reach for our hats and our hearts. At this moment the scene is light and gay, and for me completely is the manuscript sweetly scented. As the curtain rises, I find myself at this moment basking on the right side of the stage. I am not a rich man, but at this milestone in a minstrel's career I find myself blessed with good health and a little daughter who gives every sign of being a comfort to me in the twilight years. And I am further blessed having so many acquaintances and friends, not only here but throughout all America—but particularly these who have come tonight to break bread in this intimate scene with me. And as for myself and the manuscript, I find the part that I play is a good part, for I play a man with many faults, who makes many mistakes and many, many speeches. It is natural that a man pause at this stage of his life and think of those of close kinship that we want with us only at moments of compliment. And as I say that, because by force of being middle-aged and sentimental, my eyes fill up—and this is a cue to end my speech—and I take it—and like so, I salute the distinguished gentlemen who have said words in praise—and like so, I throw a kiss to you assembled—and like so, I sit down.

SPEECHES FOR COLLATERAL STUDY[6]

1. George Ade, "A Toast to Sir Thomas Lipton,"—Wilbur D. Nesbit, *After Dinner Speeches* (Reilly and Lee Co., Chicago, 1927), p. 180 ff.
2. Robert Benchley, "The Treasurer's Report"—*Benchley Beside Himself,* 3rd ed. (Harper and Bros., N. Y., 1943) p. 193 ff.
3. Edward C. Elliott, "The Qualifications of a College President"—W. N. Brigance, *Classified Speech Models* (Crofts, N. Y., 1928) p. 305 ff.
4. Strickland W. Gillilan, Address at National Rivers and Harbors

---

[6] The speeches for collateral study in the short lists here and in following chapters are selected principally from books of collected speeches because they contain a variety of speech types and because they are found in nearly every college library. Many other excellent examples of these speech types may, of course, be found elsewhere. Some of the speeches listed overlap into other classifications besides the one under which they are named; their subsidiary function, as well as the primary one, should be observed in reading them.

Congress—Sandford and Yeager, *Business Speeches by Business Men* (McGraw-Hill, N. Y., 1930) p. 715 ff.

5. Frederick Landis, "Our Guest of Honor"—Brigance, *Classified Speech Models*, p. 302 ff.

6. Will Rogers, "Settling the Corset Problem of This Country"—Nesbit, *After Dinner Speeches,* p. 197 ff.

7. Cornelia Otis Skinner, "A Toast from the Ladies of America"—Charles Hurd, *A Treasury of Great American Speeches* (Hawthorn Books, Inc., N. Y., 1959) p. 311 ff.

8. Mark Twain (Samuel L. Clemens), "The Babies"—Nesbit, *After Dinner Speeches,* p. 108 ff.

9. See also *Intercollegiate After Dinner Speaking,* edited by L. S. Judson and F. W. Lambertson (Noble and Noble, N. Y., 1937).

PROBLEMS

1. Be ready to discuss the following questions in class: What occasions are appropriate for speeches to entertain? What qualities will make the delivery and content of the speech appropriate to the occasion? In what ways can humor be used in the speech to entertain? How may this type of speech be organized?

2. Identify the forms of humor used in the speeches on pages 352–355.

3. Identify the forms of humor used in some television or radio program. If any of it falls flat, try to ascertain the reason.

4. Go to hear some popular lecture. Determine whether the purpose of the speech was primarily to entertain by presenting novel bits of information or whether it was a real attempt to inform.

5. Prepare a speech of entertainment on one of the following topics or on a subject of your own choice.
> Men deserve equal rights.
> You can't take it with you.
> How to swallow a pill.
> What this country really needs————.
> Gentlemen prefer blondes—and brunettes and redheads.
> There's many a slip 'twixt the cup and the lip.
> Professors I have known.
> Campus traditions in the year 2000.
> My solo flight in an automobile.

6. For which of the above topics would you recommend the one-point method of organization? The burlesque of the motivated sequence?

7. What factors would you consider before presenting this or any other speech to entertain as an after-dinner speech?

The improvement of the understanding is for two ends;
first, for our own increase of knowledge; secondly, to en-
able us to deliver and make out that knowledge to others.

John Locke

20/The Speech
to
Inform

O ne of the primary functions of speech is to provide man with
a means of transferring knowledge. Through speech, one
man is able to give others the benefit of his own experience. This
chapter will discuss this important function of speech—the presentation of information in an understandable fashion.

TYPES OF INFORMATIVE SPEECHES

To enumerate all the situations in which informative speeches
are necessary is impossible. Three types of informative speech,
however, occur most frequently: (1) *Reports*—scientific reports,
committee reports, executive reports, and the like. Experts are often engaged to make special investigations and to report their

findings. Teachers, fraternal representatives, and businessmen are sent to conventions and later asked to tell about their experiences and the information they have obtained. Such reports are often submitted in written form as well as given orally. (2) *Instructions.* Supervisors have to inform their subordinates how their work should be done, particularly when the task is different from what they have previously done or is of a special nature. For convenience, instructions are often given to the entire group of workers rather than to individuals. Experience has shown that written instructions may be misunderstood unless first explained orally. (3) *Lectures.* Men are often called upon to tell of their experiences and knowledge to groups other than those with which they are directly associated. Four or five such talks are given every week at the luncheon clubs of nearly every American city. The teacher must explain his subject to the class he is instructing. Club meetings, conventions, extension classes—at all these and others, speeches of information are presented, offering people the opportunity of learning about other men's affairs. At all such occasions, it behooves a speaker to present his facts in an interesting and understandable fashion.

THE PURPOSE: TO SECURE UNDERSTANDING

The main purpose of the speech to inform is to secure a clear understanding of the ideas presented. Do not mistake the informative speech as an opportunity to show off how much you know. You should not try to see how much you can get off your chest in a given length of time, but rather you should try to help others get a firm grasp of the facts or ideas you have to present. This does not mean that such speeches should be dull and dry. People absorb information more easily when it interests them. Hence, a secondary purpose of such a speech is to make your information interesting to your audience. But although this secondary purpose is important, it must never become your primary object. Too often the speaker rambles from one interesting point to another without connecting them in any clear fashion. Such procedure may be permissible when your purpose is to entertain, but not when your main object is to inform. Remember that your principal duty is to make the conclusions of your report clear, to have your instructions understood, or to insure a proper grasp of the content of your lecture.

THE MANNER OF SPEAKING

The manner in which you deliver an informative speech will depend almost entirely upon your subject and your audience. In general, talk slowly enough to be understood and rapidly enough to hold interest. Too rapid a rate of speech will confuse your listeners; too slow a rate will put them to sleep. The more difficult the information, the more slowly you should proceed; but on the first sign of inattention speed up a little.

CHARACTERISTICS OF CONTENT

Clear organization is the first essential. To be sure your speech is organized clearly, remember the following requirements: (*a*) Do not have too many main points. If possible, reduce your ideas to three or four principal topics, and then group the remaining facts under these main headings. (*b*) Make the logical relation between your main points clear. Keep moving in the same direction; don't jump back and forth from one point to another. (*c*) Make your transitions clear. As you move from one main topic to another, let your audience know about it. In a discussion of sports, for example, if you start to talk about baseball, say so definitely, or your hearers may think that you are still talking about football. If necessary, enumerate your points, "First, second, third, etc."

Use concrete data—don't be abstract. This is the second essential. Your speech must not only have a clear structure but must also be meaty. However, there are ways and ways of presenting facts; they may be made dull or interesting, vague or clear. Two things need to be kept in mind: (*a*) In your concern for accuracy of detail, do not sacrifice clarity. Nearly every rule has exceptions, but do not endanger the understanding of a rule by too detailed a discussion of the exceptions. Present statistics in round numbers in order that the smaller digits may not prevent a comprehension of the larger one. Say "a little over two million" rather than "2,001,397." If extreme accuracy of detail is essential (as in a financial report), accompany your speech with a written report;

but do not clutter your speech with detailed figures. (*b*) Use charts, graphs, and printed material whenever appropriate and helpful. Your audience will often understand a point better if they can see it as well as hear it. A diagram of a machine will make its operation easier to explain; columns and pied circles make proportions clearer; written tabulations of assets and liabilities make their explanation simpler. Diagrams or charts of this sort should be put on a blackboard or hung on a standard where they can be seen easily, or they may be projected on a screen or put on paper and distributed. (Review the discussion of visual aids, p. 207 ff.)

Avoid dullness by the occasional use of figures of speech and humor. There is a limit to any person's capacity for absorbing facts. Recognizing this, the wise speaker uses vivid phrasing and includes occasional bits of humor.

Connect the unknown with the known. People learn new things by associating them with what they already know. If you are talking to a group of physicians, for example, compare the facts you are presenting to the things with which they are familiar because of their profession. An educator talking to a group of manufacturers on the problems of higher education presented his information in terms of *raw material, casting, machining, polishing,* and *assembling.*

ORGANIZATION

First of all, remember that you must not develop your points too rapidly. You must lead the thoughts of your listeners rather than force them. Ordinarily you should not plunge right into the middle of your subject but should prepare the listeners' minds for what you have to say. To do this, you must gain their *attention* and demonstrate to them their *need* to know about your subject.

Attention step   Of course, when you are sure that the subject of your speech is of considerable interest to the audience, you can frequently save time by going immediately into it. You can attract attention simply by reference to your theme. However, when your listeners are not vitally concerned with the subject or are not aware of its importance to them personally, use a startling statement or an unusual illustration at the very beginning of your speech in order to focus their attention.

Need step

Although it should be short, the need step is exceedingly important. Many a speaker has failed because he assumed that his audience would be eagerly waiting to seize the pearls of knowledge as they fell from his lips. Unfortunately, this is not often the case. You must show your audience that the information you are to present will be valuable to them—that it is something they need. Suggest how your information will help them get ahead, or save money, or do their work more easily, and they will listen to you.

The development of the need step is largely determined by the degree of interest the audience has in your subject. When interest is high, a brief reference to the value or utility of the information you will present is all that is necessary; when the audience is apathetic, however, the fourfold development as outlined in Chapter 16 (pp. 293–294) may be called for. Remember these steps: a statement of the importance of the information to the audience; an illustration to clarify that statement; proof of its importance by means of examples, testimony, and statistics; and pointing, that is, relating the problem to the audience. The emphasis on the second and third steps in this sequence will vary with the nature of the information you are going to present. In every case when there is doubt about the audience's interest, however, you should at least state the importance of the information and show how the information relates to the audience.

There are times, of course, when the information you are going to present is not of the practical workaday variety. You must then build your need step on the basis of curiosity. Everyone has a latent desire to understand curious or unusual things; you must awaken this desire with respect to your subject. Set up a situation containing some mysterious elements and suggest that you are about to make the mystery clear. For example, a noted chemist began his speech by telling about an unusual murder case. He made his audience wonder who the guilty man was and then proceeded to tell them the principles of chemistry by which the guilty man was found.

Satisfaction step:
the information itself

Having captured the attention of your audience and convinced them of their need or desire for your information, you are now ready to present the information itself. The satisfaction step will be the longest part of the speech to inform—from three fourths to nine tenths of it. In this step you must exercise the greatest care to make your organization clear. You will recall that methods of selecting and arranging the main points of a speech were described in Chapter 14. A thorough review of the explanations and illustrations on pages 235 to 239 will help you plan your organization. Briefly stated, the time sequence arranges points in the order in which they occur; the space sequence uses location or position as the basis for arrangement; the cause-effect sequence presents conditions and then the forces that created them or discusses some forces and then the resulting conditions; the problem-solution sequence describes a difficulty and the method or methods used to correct it; and the special topical sequence utilizes the familiar or special divisions by which the information is already cataloged. Decide early in your preparation what type of arrangement will make the information you present most easily grasped by your audience and then organize your information in that way.

In order to unify the presentation of this information, however, you will want to begin and end it with a summary. As pointed out on page 296 ff., the satisfaction step of a speech to inform usually includes an *initial summary,* the *detailed information,* and the *final summary.*

The *initial summary* usually consists of a brief enumeration of the main points you expect to cover, thus showing your audience the skeleton of your discussion around which you expect to group your facts. In this way you make clear the direction of your discussion and help your audience get a clear picture of it in advance. For example, if you were going to explain the organization of athletic activities on your campus, you might begin your satisfaction step:

> In order to make clear the organization of athletic activities on our campus, I shall discuss first, the management of our intercollegiate sports; second, our intramural system; and last, the class work in physical education.

Robert Havighurst began a discussion of the functions of the American family with an initial summary like this:

To see what the needs of the American family are in this situation, it would be well to make a distinction between the essential functions of the family and its accidental functions. The essential functions are the things the family does for human life and happiness which no other institution can do nearly as well. The accidental functions are things the family has done or is doing which are useful, but can be done as well or better by other social institutions.[1]

Of course, the order in which you list the main points in your initial summary should follow the same sequence you intend to use in your detailed discussion; otherwise you will confuse your listeners by setting your initial guidepost in the wrong direction. Properly used, the initial summary will help your audience follow your discussion more easily and will aid them to see the relation of each point to the whole.

Detailed information is presented next, covering in order the main points enumerated in your initial summary. The explanations, detailed facts, comparisons, and other information are grouped around each main point in a systematic fashion, often amplified and illustrated by maps, pictures, tables, demonstrations, or other visible aids to understanding. As you move from one main point to the next, be sure you make it clear that you are doing so. Use connective sentences or phrases freely to emphasize the shifts (see p. 338). At all times be sure that your audience knows where you are and in what direction your discussion is moving. Follow a consistent plan of arrangement as you move along, and amplify your points with plenty of support, both verbal (p. 195) and visible (p. 207).

A few suggestions are in order here about the detailed content of some common types of informative speech. The presentation of a *research report*, for instance—whether historical, scientific, or literary—usually contains the following items: first, a clear statement of the hypothesis to be tested or the problem investigated; second, a brief review of previous research upon this subject; third, an explanation of materials used, the apparatus employed, or the literary or historical sources investigated; fourth, an ex-

---

[1] From *Vital Speeches of the Day*, Vol. XIV, July 1, 1948, p. 566.

planation of the procedure followed in the study; and finally, a discussion of the facts or results obtained. *Other types of reports,* such as those resulting from committee discussion, financial operations, travel, or direct observation, vary a great deal but nearly always include: first, a statement of the nature or scope of the report; second, the source of the material—discussion, observation, written records, etc.; and third, a discussion of the salient points.

When the speech is for the purpose of *giving instructions,* it usually contains: first, an overall statement of the nature and purpose of the operation to be performed; and second, an explanation of each step in that operation in the order it is to be taken. The discussion of each step usually covers the reason for it, the materials or tools or special information required, and the precautions to be taken. Frequently in giving such talks, the speaker interrupts after explaining each step in the process to ask questions of his listeners to test their understanding as he goes along.

The detailed development of an *informative lecture* varies so much with the subject that no single list of items would suffice to describe it. In the main, its substance is organized in the manner natural to the subject matter, as explained in Chapter 14.

Regardless of what the subject or specific purpose of an informative speech may be, remember that its main objective is to secure clear and thorough understanding on the part of your audience. The detailed information must therefore be clearly organized and fully amplified with concrete and specific material.

The *final summary* ties together the information you have presented in order to leave your audience with a unified picture. It consists of a restatement of your main points, together with any important conclusions or implications which have grown out of your discussion. It is similar to the initial summary but is usually not so brief. Notice the difference between the following final summary and the initial summary (p. 362) for the speech on athletic activities.

From what I have said, you can readily see that the three main divisions of our athletic system are closely related to one another. The intercollegiate sports serve as the stimulus for interest in developing superior skill as well as a source of revenue for financing the rest of the program. Our intramural system extends the facilities for physical recreation to a large part of our student body—three thousand last year. And our physical education classes not only serve in training men to become the coaches of the future, but also act in systematically building up the physical endurance of the student body as a whole and in giving corrective work to those who have physical defects. The work of these three divisions is well organized and complete.

In addition to the initial summary, the detailed information, and the final summary, the satisfaction step of the speech to inform sometimes requires a fourth item—*definitions of important terms*. There is no fixed point at which these should be introduced, but they are most frequently given either just before or just after the initial summary when they relate to the whole body of information to be presented. Note how Mr. Havighurst distinguished between the essential and accidental functions of the family in his initial summary (p. 363). When definitions are related only to one part of the information, they are introduced at that point. Frequently, no definition of terms is needed. Be sure, however, that all technical terms are understood by the audience. Observe how Lee A. DuBridge, President of California Institute of Technology, defined *space* at a Science Youth Day Dinner:

We begin with the question of "what is space?" Are we "flying through space" in an airplane at an altitude of 10,000 or 20,000 feet above the earth's surface? No, for in an airplane one is being supported by the lift of the earth's atmosphere on the wings, and therefore he is clearly not yet in "empty space." For our purposes tonight, let us say that space begins beyond the atmosphere at a distance of about 200 miles above the surface of the earth. From here on out, space is very empty indeed.

Nevertheless, space is still not completely empty. Even out to several thousand miles, there are a certain number of atoms or molecules in each cubic yard which can be thought of as the outer fringes of the earth's atmosphere. As we leave the earth's atmosphere, we still find there are a few atoms or molecules which constitute the outer fringes of the sun's atmosphere. Also, we shall occasionally encounter specks of dust and, once in a great while, even larger particles of matter floating in various orbits and trajectories in space.

One of the interesting aspects of space research, therefore, is to learn more about the contents of so-called "empty space." It will be interesting indeed to sample the extremely rare matter in the far reaches of space to see what it consists of and to find out where it has come from and where it is going. When the density of matter in space amounts to only a few atoms per cubic yard, it is evident that the task of capturing and identifying those few atoms is going to be a very difficult one indeed—a really challenging scientific problem![2]

When you have presented your information and secured an understanding of it, you should have accomplished the general purpose of your speech. Ordinarily the final summary given at the end of the satisfaction step marks the end of the speech. There are times, however, when you may wish to encourage further interest in the subject you have been discussing—in a sense, to actuate as well as inform. In this event, suggest to your audience how valuable this knowledge will be to them. Then close quickly by suggesting that they make a further study of the matter. Give them one or two sources of information or call attention to instruction books they already have.

The following sample outline will illustrate how to organize material in a talk for instruction or information.

TAKING CARE OF YOUR ROADS [3]

This speech was presented before the Lafayette Optimist Club by the late Professor Ben Petty, Director of Indiana Road School for County Highway Superintendents.

Attention
    I. It is a pleasure to be back with old friends.
   II. You have asked me to talk on roads, a subject in which I am extremely interested.

Need
    I. Most businessmen are too busy to investigate the facts about roads.
   II. Yet you use the roads, and *pay* for them.
      A. Indiana spends one hundred million dollars a year this way.
      B. Most of this money comes from license fees and gasoline taxes.
   III. You ought to be sure this money is spent wisely.

Satisfaction
(Initial summary)
    I. To understand road expenditures, it is necessary that you grasp the distinction between two kinds of roads: county roads and state roads.
      A. County roads are important for local and intermediate traffic.

---

[2] From "Adventures in Space." *Ibid.*, Vol. XXVI, May 1, 1960, p. 433.
[3] This outline was originally made by the author while listening to Professor Petty speak and was revised to include 1957 data.

1. There are 76,700 miles of these roads in the state.
2. They are controlled by County Highway Superintendents.
   a. These men are political appointees.
   b. It is important for you to see that the right man gets this position in your county.
      i. He will spend $379,000 in this county this coming year.
      ii. The quality of road maintenance is in his hands.
3. Upkeep cost is $430 per mile—$1.43 each working day.
4. Traffic has increased greatly on these roads in forty years.
   a. There used to be twenty-five horse-drawn vehicles per day.
   b. Now, 1000 high-speed autos, trucks, and buses use them.
5. Formerly, some of these roads were under township control.
   a. The expenditure was large.
   b. The administration by township trustees were often poor.
      i. These men were too busy with other duties.
      ii. They rarely understood the road problem.
6. Management of the roads in this county has been efficient under your present superintendent.
   a. The county unit offers good organization.
   b. The county has better equipment.
B. State roads handle the through traffic.
   1. During the past ten years, traffic on state roads has increased greatly.
      a. Passenger cars have doubled in number.
      b. Trucks have more than doubled.
   2. State roads are under the jurisdiction of the Chairman of the State Highway Commission.
   3. Yet these roads are less important to your local community than the local roads.

a. The function of local roads is to make them feeders for state roads.

b. Most local business comes to town on local roads.

4. The real purpose of paved state roads is to concentrate the heavy traffic and save the more important local roads.

(Final Summary)

II. Remember that *all* your roads are important.

A. You may call county roads secondary.

B. You should call them *primary*.

1. Because of better county roads, you can travel more easily in Indiana than in most other states.

2. Brief illustration from personal experience.

C. Your state roads serve to keep traffic off these primary local roads.

D. Your roads require more of your attention.

SAMPLE SPEECHES

In the following two informative speeches, observe how the technics suggested in this chapter have been employed. The first speech ("Your Story Must Be Told" by Dean F. Berkley, p. 370 ff.) is provided with relatively full comments and analysis; the second ("The Historian's Job" by Gilbert Highet, p. 382 ff.) is provided with only brief comments and indications of its main divisions. Using the technics illustrated in the analysis of the first speech, you may wish to attempt a similar analysis of the second speech.

Preliminary comments on Dr. Berkley's speech

On February 23, 1960, Dr. Dean F. Berkley of the School of Education at Indiana University delivered the following speech at the annual convention of the National Institute of Drycleaning meeting in Chicago. Later published in *Vital Speeches of the Day* [4] under the title "Your Story Must Be Told," Dr. Berkley's address reveals many of the qualities of a good informative talk as described in this chapter.

Adhering strictly to the three steps of the motivated sequence applicable to speeches to inform—attention, need, and satisfaction

---

[4] Vol. XXVI, May 1, 1960, pp. 424–428.

—Dr. Berkley quickly arouses interest at the outset by presenting two familiar examples. He then states and clarifies the central idea of his talk and defines the crucial term *communication*. The need step is given more extended development than is customary in informative speeches and contains an abundance of concrete material. Moreover, it is specifically pointed to the interests and concerns of operators of drycleaning establishments (see paragraph 9). The satisfaction step presents a limited number of ideas in a clear and orderly fashion. Each idea is effectively explained and supported by several stories, examples, illustrations, or analogies. Although the satisfaction step lacks an initial summary, the information presented in the speech is adequately previewed in the attention step (see sentence 4 of paragraph 4). A restatement of the leading ideas offered and a story epitomizing and reinforcing them conclude the satisfaction step. As is usually the case in informative speeches, both the visualization and the action steps are omitted.

Throughout his talk Dr. Berkley not only introduces a great deal of concrete data but frequently uses material of a humorous nature, thus enlivening the subject and giving the speech a verve and sparkle it would otherwise lack. In addition, interest is stimulated and important ideas emphasized by the use of striking phrases or figurative language (see, for example, the expression "penetrate beyond . . . walls" in paragraphs 1–3; the first sentence of paragraph 7; the last three sentences of paragraph 25).

Throughout, Dr. Berkley relates his remarks directly to his hearers. Drycleaners and their shops or equipment are specifically mentioned no less than five or six times, and the "pocketbook motive" is repeatedly stressed. By these references to the drycleaning business, the speaker not only brings his remarks directly home to his hearers but also eases the learning process by relating the new or unknown with the familiar. Learning is further facilitated by the use of an especially memorable story or clear summary to conclude each major point and by the uniformly clear and simple style in which ideas are expressed.

A single major criticism of Dr. Berkley's talk is the absence of badly needed transitions at several places. It should be pointed out in the speaker's defense, however, that some of the transitions present in the oral version were necessarily omitted in condensing the speech for publication.[5] Moreover, at least two examples of effective transitions remain (see paragraphs 11 and 34), and the major divisions of the talk—the attention, need, and satisfaction steps—are clearly set off (see, for example, paragraphs 5 and 11).

Dr. Berkley, a native of South Dakota, received his bachelor's degree from Dakota Wesleyan University and his M.A. and Ed.D. from the University of Denver. For a number of years he was a teacher of speech and coach of debate in various South Dakota high schools, and from 1955 to 1957 he served as assistant to the Superintendent of Schools in Sioux Falls, South Dakota. Since 1957 he has been Director of College and University Placement and Professor of School Administration at Indiana University. He delivers on the average of a hundred speeches a year in all parts of the country.

Asked to comment on his philosophy of effective speaking, Dr. Berkley replied as follows:

It is my belief that in the preparation of a speech there must be (1) adequate analysis of the group, (2) identification of the areas that will have some "take home value" for such a group, (3) organization of the ideas into a discussion of three or four points, and (4) the statement of these points in language that is easily understood and simple enough to remember. I normally surround each point with a catchy phrase and sufficient illustrations, anecdotes, and humor so that the serious thesis of the talk becomes palatable. Effective speaking necessitates a physical delivery that is restrained, yet vigorous in its over-all effect; gestures and vocal variety that are viewed as means of punctuation; and eye contact *cannot* be established if one must constantly refer to notes or manuscript —this implies familiarity with the material and sufficient enthusiasm about the topic to develop the necessary confidence to speak with conviction uninhibited by copiously written notes.[5]

YOUR STORY MUST BE TOLD

> *Dr. Dean F. Berkley's speech was delivered to approximately three hundred persons representing drycleaning establishments in all parts of the United States. The text as here printed has been taken from* Vital Speeches of the Day, *and has been approved by Dr. Berkley.*

---

[5] Letter to the author, November 28, 1960.

*Attention step.
Familiar
examples which
by implication
support the
central idea
of the speech*

I was ready to tuck the children into bed. As I went over to open the window I noticed the next door neighbor was practicing the piano. I could hear his music clearly though I knew his windows were closed. It had never occurred to me that perhaps my own practicing penetrated beyond my walls. The most amazing walls are penetrated. We go back hundreds of years and see a man seated at a bare writing table behind blocks of stone and bars of steel. In order to consume the burden of time and release nervous energy, he jotted down some of his thoughts. John Bunyan would have been the last to have presumed that what he did at that bare writing table would penetrate beyond those walls and result in one of the three or four most influential books in the history of Western Christendom. /1

In Frauenberg there is a drab two-story house. On the second floor is a small workroom, which in the 16th Century was the workroom of a monk named Copernicus. In imagination we can see him peering into the heavens at night and jotting down his observations. Copernicus would have scoffed at the suggestion that what he did in that little room would create one of the major scientific revolutions in the history of mankind. Some time later another man used his astronomical telescope to prove that the earth rotated daily upon its axis. Galileo had no reason to believe that he too had penetrated beyond the span of history by proving the Copernican theory. /2

One of the illusions of life is that we can choose to penetrate beyond our walls or not. There is an axiom as old as the human race which says that irrespective of what we do in our political, social, economic, or physical endeavors we penetrate beyond our walls. Far-fetched? Not for a moment.

*Central idea
clarified and its
truth impressed
upon audience by
direct reference
to drycleaning
business*

You might observe that the manager of a shop might lock himself in the office and he wouldn't penetrate beyond his walls. But you cannot isolate the influence of that man and the lives he touches. Put your drycleaning machine in a soundproofed room behind opaque glass. You can push a button to start it, but you have no way to know whether the machine is operating. Now, an electrician would have a light to indicate whether all was well within. Even in automation there is provision for feedback

—for penetration, if you please. In a small operation the reliance is more on verbal communication for this penetration and we penetrate whether we like it or not. Our only choice is the kind and the quality of penetration. It is not a case of your story being told, but rather that it must be told in terms of degree and quality. /3

Communication defined, first facetiously and then seriously

One of the first questions we must ask ourselves is what is meant by communication? By telling your story? Someone has said that communication is the art of telling people who don't want to listen something they don't want to hear, doing it in such a way that they will do something they didn't want to do before—and leaving them pleased with themselves and with you. In that statement, facetious or not, are the ingredients of communication: listening, persuading, responding, promoting, and telling. Our concern, therefore, is to tell our story by using the elements of communication to convey our intention—always remembering that good intentions are not enough. What a man intends to communicate is not the determinant, but rather the ultimate interpretation. Herein is the first lesson of human relations. Penetrating beyond our walls in terms of communication. /4

Need step. Need for effective communication stated and illustrated by examples, analogies, and humorous stories

We must now pause for a moment and examine the need for more effective communication in telling our story. We must first consider the need before we assess the communication strategy applicable in telling the story. /5

An early biblical account relates the activities of a group of men building a high tower. The Lord decided these men had evil purpose so he "smote them with a confusion of tongues" and project, Tower of Babel, went out of business. Think what a bit more confusion of tongues would do to our airline flight schedules, drycleaning deliveries, repair orders or our choices in a restaurant. Apparently men have always been impressed with the importance of being able to pass the word along—or have they? A classic illustration takes us back to the late 1700's when Captain John Paul Jones found things going against him out on the Atlantic. This prompted a Captain Pearson of the British Navy to pose the question, "Sir, do you give quarter?" Jones retorted with the classic statement, "I have not yet begun to fight." But that isn't the end of the story. Behind Jones, on that bloody deck, lay a wounded Marine who, when he heard that remark, lifted himself up on one elbow and cried out in anguish, "Always somebody don't get the word!" /6

As an educator, I see first-hand some of the caustic, critical and cantankerous questions raised about American education. Many of these questions are raised by people who are well-intentioned but either misinformed or uninformed. As a result, thousands of Americans are raising questions simply because they didn't get the word. A cursory examination will direct one to view many professions—beset with internal and external issues—simply because someone either in the ranks or on the outside didn't get the word. The labor movement today, the greatest of its kind in the history of man, has recently revealed some insidious practices prompting us to wonder whether somebody didn't get the word. American business, having risen to a pinnacle never before evidenced in the history of man, is beset with leaders who are unable to relate articulately the role of private enterprise in a democracy. This, in some quarters, prompts one to ask whether capitalism has gone soft. The cry raised by millions of Americans regarding the in-roads of socialism may well have resulted because somebody didn't get the word. Scientists, engineers, skilled technicians and many of our professional people are trapped in the prisons of their specialized language. This has resulted in misconceptions, open hostility, needless controversies, and even defeat—stemming from a lack of understanding. /7

There are some at this point who might wonder why we should get so concerned about this problem. Many would infer that business is going well and there is no reason for such concern. Typically, these same people also proclaim that anybody can talk. Such a statement is not false—it's just half true. Your little daughter or granddaughter who cuts out paper dolls cannot cut out an appendix. To follow this line of reasoning to its logical conclusion would indicate there are degrees of speaking just as there are degrees of cutting, ranging all the way from elementary chatter to the formal discipline of speech. /8

Those who would mix the charms of sound with nonsense by proclaiming communication as not being important, ignore 23 centuries of history and its obvious lesson that speech-making is inherent in human relations and a free society cannot exist without it. To reduce it to simple terms, we have the choice today to either shoot it out or talk it out. This was so succinctly related by Vice President Nixon upon his return from Russia when he said, "We have the alternative of either talking with the Russians or someday we may be shooting them." What we must make clear is that the ability of men to live together, to coordinate their efforts, to avoid destructive conflicts is determined by and large by their skill in communication. This is true on the international scene; this is true in your state dry-cleaners association; this is true in your shop at home. No matter how much skill you need in your job, no matter how varied your activities, no matter how large or small the organization—in the final analysis the biggest single task you have is one of communication. In the normal course of a day's work you may speak between 40 and 50 thousand words. These cannot be words of indecision, of an inarticulate nature, or of vacillation if we are to sustain effective human relations. Perhaps there is a message in the incident of a mother of ten children in southern Indiana. Her husband divorced her because he didn't like her any more. Her only comment was, "Well, what would have happened if he really loved me!" What would happen to the effect of your story if you really became concerned about those 40 to 50 thousand words each day? /9

Need "pointed" by relating importance of communication directly to drycleaning business

We dare not forget that man's first great human invention was the power to communicate. From this power he designed the mastery of man over nature and, more important, man over himself. The need for more effective communication is perhaps summarized adequately in these lines of Will Carleton:

Need step summarized and concluded

"Boys flying kites haul in their white-winged birds;
But you can't do that way when you're flying words.
'Careful with fire,' is good advice, we know;
'Careful with words,' is ten times doubly so.

Thoughts unexpressed may sometimes fall back dead,
But God Himself can't kill them, when they're said."

/10

Transition from need to satisfaction step

Let us turn our attention to *how* the story must be told. Some of the dimensions of communication, if you please. /11

Satisfaction step. Detailed information starts immediately. Initial summary appears in the attention step. Story and statistics introduce first major point of satisfaction step

Recently I returned home before the neighborhood bridge party at our house had been adjourned. After all had left, I posed this question to my wife, "Who listens?" This is a legitimate question for all of us. There is increasing evidence of both the relationship of listening to communication and our failure to be effective listeners. One of the things that we must do to tell our story is to develop an acuity in listening. It was my opportunity some time ago to assess the listening effectiveness of workers in an industrial installation. We were shocked to find that about 50 per cent of the time of the white-collar workers was spent in listening.

/12

Dr. Ralph Nichols, of the University of Minnesota, has done much research in this area and variously estimates from 40 to 80 per cent of the time of the typical worker is spent listening. I also know, on the basis of research, that in the period of a week you will only recall about 25 per cent of the central ideas of this talk! I also know that as soon as you leave this meeting you will be able to recall only one-half of the central ideas! This implies that we must penetrate beyond our walls through effective communication for it can be translated into a dollar and cent handicap. On the basis of typical adult communication habits, it was found, in a Detroit Study, that we devote 9 per cent of our time to writing, 16 per cent to reading, 30 per cent to talking, and 45 per cent listening. No, it was no coincidence that the University of Minnesota, in advertising evening courses, related the following in sequence: *Effective Listening* and *Preparation for Marriage!* /13

Importance of listening further emphasized by relating it to "pocketbook" motive

Point clinched by humor. Importance of listening directly related to drycleaning business

We typically graduate from school as rather good readers into a world of telephones, television, radio, conferences, and trial by jury. Does this apply to us? Think for a moment of the importance of your seamstresses, spotters, routesalesmen and counter-girls ability to listen. /14

Think for a moment how the story can be told by the girl at the receiving counter who listens effectively—and then translates what she has heard into written or verbal orders easily understood in the back room. The importance of this certainly doesn't minimize the necessity for the manager to listen when an employee has a suggestion, relates a complaint or wants a day off. Just as applicable is the necessity to listen when a salesman comes to call, or we hear the ideas of a competitor, or have research related to us by the National Institute of Drycleaning. /15

A practical suggestion for using listening to help solve disagreements

One of the most interesting communication experiments I have encountered is one suggested by Dr. Carl Rogers. He suggests that when you get into a disagreement with your wife, employees, or friends, just stop the discussion and apply this rule. "Each person can speak up for himself only *after* he has first restated the ideas and feelings of the previous speaker accurately and to the speaker's satisfaction." Can you see what this would do in employer-employee discussions? Think what would happen were this applied to labor-management negotiations! This implies that before you can continue you must *really* see the other point of view. Try it sometime. You will find it extremely difficult, but if you are successful in seeing and feeling the other point of view, your own communication will be modified considerably. /16

A final story to sum up and clinch importance of listening

A little boy once asked how he might become a good conversationalist (what he meant was to be effective in human relations). The wise old sage, who was asked the question, responded, "Listen, my son . . ." and paused then momentarily. "Yes, yes," cried the boy, "Go on." "That is all. Listen, my son," responded the wise man. This then becomes our first method of telling our story. /17

Begins discussion of second major factor in communication —the "face-to-face" approach

There is no substitute for a person-to-person approach. We cannot forget that the "climate" is important—and we create it. The "climate" is created more by the face-to-face approach than in any other way. /18

A recent discussion with an advertising director for a large Ohio firm brought this point home to me rather emphatically. He indicated that there is a concerted effort at present to find out how we can complement advertising via mass media by a more personalized method. It was his contention that unless we make provision for effective communication on a person-to-person basis, the effects of the gimmicks, techniques, slick ads, and advertising psychology would be rendered impotent. When one stops to consider that during the ensuing year you will influence 900 persons (either negatively or positively—and we hope the latter) this becomes a matter of paramount importance. You see, the penetrating beyond our walls we render in terms of those 900 people will be on the basis of a person-to-person contact! */19*

Some of you may have noted the recent innovation on some of our toll roads whereby, if you have the appropriate change, you merely toss it into a receptacle and proceed. Such is the case on one of the routes into Chicago. Frankly, I refuse to use that automatic lane! Why? Because I refuse to submit to such a grim reminder of an increasingly impersonal and mechanical world. You see, I prefer to be able to hear the attendant say "thank you." He creates a "climate" by this personal contact. How well I recall my first day at school. Upon entering that one-room rural school, with fear and trepidation, the teacher in a very gracious and courteous manner merely said, "We've been waiting for you." I began to wonder how she knew I was coming! I am still amazed at the "climate" she created in her person-to-person communication. Frankly, I must admit that the following year when I entered the schoolroom she stood there to meet me. But this time, with hands on her hips and no evidence of a smile, she said, *"We've* been *waiting for you."* You see, I had created a "climate"! */20*

I know a high school principal in one of the largest schools in the country who practices the person-to-person method effectively. He listens well enough to pick up bits of information about various pupils each day. Armed with this information, he "accidentally" meets the appropriate students and asks them how their father feels after his illness, congratulates them on election to an office, pats them on the back for a better term mark, or wonders how the new baby sister is getting along. You would be amazed at the morale in this building, all a result of a man who is convinced the story must be told personally. /21

Face-to-face principle directly applied to dry-cleaning business

A "climate" is in evidence in every shop we enter. In some it is bright and sunny; in others cold and cloudy. This is true simply because we create a "climate" through a person-to-person relationship. This is the most important single reason why I go to a particular drycleaner and, on the basis of a limited survey of my friends, the reason for their choosing a plant. This is the reason one gasoline station gets over a thousand dollars a year business from me. It all happened one rainy afternoon. With one windshield wiper out of commission, I pulled into a station and asked for a new wiper blade. The young fellow on duty said, "I'm sorry we're out, but I'll get one for you in 15 minutes." He created a "climate"—an attitude—an image simply because of what he said and the way he said it. This decision was accentuated all the more because the man in the station across the street, where I had first asked for assistance, responded in terms indicating this was a most inconvenient request on that busy afternoon. /22

Poem summarizing and clinching face-to-face point

This is nothing new or different but it represents a constant challenge in telling our story. Examples and illustrations are numerous, but perhaps the following lines by a little-known poet say it more effectively than can I:

If I possessed a shop or store, I'd drive the grouches off my floor!
I'd never let some gloomy guy offend the folks who come to buy;

I'd never keep a boy or clerk—with mental toothache at his work,
Nor let a man who draws my pay drive customers of mine away.

I'd treat the man who takes my time—and spends a nickel or a dime
With courtesy, and make him feel that I was pleased to close the deal,

Because tomorrow, who can tell? He may want stuff I have to sell,

And in that case, then glad he'll be to spend his dollars all with me.

The reason people pass one door—to patronize another store,
Is not because the busier place—has better silks, or gloves, or lace

Or special prices, but it lies—in pleasant words and smiling eyes;
The only difference, I believe, is in the treatment folks receive! /23

Third major idea of satisfaction step introduced

One of the troubles in running a business is that it is full of human beings! The presses never sulk; the drycleaning machine doesn't get jealous; and the tumbler may run for a whole year without affecting its willingness. Men are not so constituted. As a result, there are problems of preventative maintenance, premature obsolescence, and even complete operational failure! ! These factors, however, are much harder to solve and thus necessitate looking at some of the techniques of telling the story. /24

Specific technics stated and explained

In considering the how of communication, it is imperative to recognize the importance of the psychological climate. This factor is as variable as the atmospheric pressure. Unless our communication takes into account the basic drives for recognition, acceptance, accomplishment, and the need to belong, the reactions to your story will become evident. Creating the proper psychological climate can decrease both the unavoidable social barrier between employer-employee and the business house and its clientele. The average person wants to matter and he glows with pride when you communicate your compliments to him. This factor probably accounts for someone indicating that the five most important words are: I am proud of you; the four most important: What is your opinion?; the three most important: If you please; the two most important: Thank you; and the least important word: I. Of the more than 600,000 words in the English language we use one word 450 times more than any of the others and that word is *I*. Such overuse of this word does not, by and large, bring about an appropriate psychological climate. /25

Another important factor is that communication must be active. This means a two-way process. View your discussions with people as you might a tennis game. Unless they are able to field the ball and return it, there is no two-way activity. Communication experts call this "feedback"—for it is the only way we can arrive at mutual understanding. The fundamental phase of training by one of the Roman speech teachers centuries ago was boxing and fencing. His reasoning is now apparent to us and we too must view communication as a two-way street. /26

The list would not be complete without mentioning some factors in communicating that might help tell your story—other than the mass media. /27

The "grapevine" is operative in every organization and can have a real value in building team spirit if properly cultivated. It can become highly destructive if there is ineffective and impersonal communication on the part of the boss. Often new employees must turn to the more experienced workers to get their information and have ideas and orders interpreted. If communication is restricted then one has only to wonder, speculate, and give vent to rumors. /28

Such factors as social events, time schedules, written employment policies, punctuality, extending greetings to an acquaintance, and taking time for social amenities over the telephone are all important channels that tell your story. /29

A word of warning: danger in the overuse of any one avenue of communication

When we overuse any one avenue it may lose its effectiveness. This is well illustrated in the story of the woman who brought a dress into the cleaners and asked that she have immediate service and the clerk said it would be ready late that afternoon. She wrote on the ticket the word RUSH. Now what does this word mean? It went to the back room and one of the employees said, "When shall I do it, I am all tied up?" The response by another employee went something like this, "Just do the best you can. They always mark everything rush!" /30

You see, this represented a communication failure because the word had lost its meaning. It used to mean to do it first. Apparently the current meaning is, don't put it at the bottom of the pile. The "rush" order lost its meaning because that particular line of communication was overloaded by overuse. We must be aware of alternate lines and channels to use in the event of overloading. /31

The communication channels are important. So important that if they aren't recognized the boss can easily become a prisoner of his own organization. The decisions you make are no better than the information you use to make the decision. Should you want to arrive at decisions regarding expansion of the building, new equipment, re-arranging facilities, or employee needs, it forces us to ask the following questions:

Point summarized and made specific by outlining questions the employer can ask himself

How good is that information?

Is any omitted?

How much is swept under the rug?

Have the elements of fear, jealousy, insecurity, ambition, flattery and incompetence influenced the information which comes to you? /32

Last major idea of the satisfaction step introduced and explained

Finally, mention must be made of telling the story through your leadership in association work and in the home community. As people in positions of responsibility, we must think of the leadership role and the fact that self-expression is the first step in assuming that role. A great deal of time should be devoted to discussing this factor alone. A multitude of avenues are open to tell your story in the community, at state or regional meetings of your associations, and with your civic friends. We cannot deny that others will judge the quality of your shop by the quality of your telling the story—not by direct account, but through association of your leadership capacity to the type of business you operate. /33

Transition to summary of satisfaction step

In summary, what then are the key words or phrases related to this discussion so that you might best tell the story? /34

Final summary of points in detailed information of satisfaction step

We penetrate beyond our walls and control only the matter of degree and quality—recognize the need for effective communication—effective listening—person-to-person—channels of communication—leadership. /35

If you recall nothing else, take these words with you and perhaps your story will be told a bit better. /36

Story epitomizing central idea

The conversation of two receiving clerks in a drycleaning establishment may have a final message for us. At the end of a busy day one commented: "What a day. Sometimes I think I hate people." The response by her co-worker went like this: "Oh, I like people all right, but sometimes I forget that I do." /37

Final appeal to "pocketbook" motive

Sometimes we might not like the effort it takes in telling our story, but we dare not forget its importance. Your survival in business depends on it. /38

THE HISTORIAN'S JOB [6]

The following speech was one in a series of radio talks on literary subjects presented in 1952 by Gilbert Highet, teacher and writer. Note that the speaker combines attention and need steps, relying on arousing the curiosity of his listeners to create a feeling of need for the detailed information. Would a more pointed need step have improved or weakened this speech? Note also the very brief initial summary and the clear arrangement and development of information in the satisfaction step.

Attention and need steps combined

The historian's job is to tell us about the past. If you think about it for a moment, that really is an astonishing notion. We are often informed how remarkable it is that an astronomer is able to describe the constitution and motions of a star on the other side of the universe, or that a physicist can explain the behavior of tiny entities which are too small to see (even through a microscope) and yet too complicated to diagrammatize. But it is almost equally strange that a man writing a book in 1953 should be able to tell us about the actions, the appearance, the very thoughts of scores of people whom he never saw, living and working in a world which has long since disappeared. Some historians have—after laboring long at the task—concluded that it was almost impossible to achieve. There is a fine passage from Froude, describing the end of the Middle Ages:

"The paths trodden by the footsteps of ages were broken up: old things were passing away, and the faith and the life of ten centuries were dissolving like a dream. Chivalry was dying; the abbey and the castle were soon together to crumble into ruins; and all the forms, desires, beliefs, convictions of the old world were passing away, never to return . . . And now it is all gone—like an unsubstantial pageant faded; and between us and the old English there lies a gulf of mystery which the prose of the historian will never adequately bridge. They cannot come to us, and our imagination can but feebly penetrate to them. Only among the aisles of the cathedral, only as we gaze upon their silent figures sleeping on their tombs, some faint conceptions float before us of what these men were when they were alive; and perhaps in the sound of churchbells, that peculiar creation of medieval age, which falls upon the ear like an echo of a vanished world." *

Handsome prose, isn't it? And filled with the right emotions for the historian: nostalgia, imagination, and humility. There is a fine thirteenth-century Spanish tomb in the Cloisters, the tomb of the Count of Urgel, which I often look at with the same feelings of wonder and distance.

Satisfaction step: Initial summary The historian's job is difficult, then, but not impossible. There are at least three different ways of doing it. We can easily be disappointed if we overlook this and expect all historians to follow the same plan.

Detailed information The first type is not, strictly speaking, a professional historian's work at all; but it is history none the less. This is a collection of materials, memories of interesting events set down by an eyewitness. Such a book never tells the whole story, because its author does not care about the whole story and does not know enough to relate it. And it does not usually interpret events by fitting them into a large pattern of social, economic, and political change. But it is nearly always an invaluable collection of facts which all other historians must take into account (or else show good reason for disbelieving) ; it bridges the gulf between the present and the past, by speaking of things really seen and experienced; and it usually has the brisk variety and unexpectedness of life. A famous example of this type is *The Acts of the Apostles,* which was either written by a man who had shared in the experiences described, or else based on his memoirs. There are two other such books, which have long been cordially hated and hopelessly misunderstood. These are the two sets of "Memoirs" by Julius Caesar—sometimes wrongly called his *Commentaries.* They are cool, dry, apparently factual accounts of the war in France in which Caesar trained his private army, and of the civil war in which he attacked and overthrew the constitutional government of his country. I say "apparently factual" because he himself deliberately chose to write them not as history, in the highly developed sense which the Greeks and Romans knew, but as objective notes ostensibly intended for future historians to use and to believe. They are about as honest and well balanced as *Mein Kampf;* but the skill with which they are composed has led some historians to accept them as the plain statement of unadulterated facts.

---

* J. A. Froude, *History of England*, Chapter I.

Still, there are few writers of this kind of history who have much adroitness in disguising reality. Most of them do tell something like the truth as they saw it, although they do not attempt to tell the whole truth. Two of my favorite autobiographies fall into this class. One is the life story of William Cobbett, the tough, bluff Englishman who lived in the United States from 1792 to 1800 and made the country too hot to hold him by issuing torrid anti-revolutionary propaganda; returned to Britain and was soon tossed into prison for denouncing the abuse of discipline in the army; ran a first-rate popular newspaper; sat in Parliament; and loved his country with a warm physical love and deep knowledge. The other is the autobiography of Dr. Benjamin Franklin, filled with his peculiar blend of ingenuity and ingenuousness, which makes it easy to see why President Jefferson called him "the most agreeable man in company that he had ever known."

Two charming collections of such memories, recently published, are well worth reading. One of them is *The Memoirs of a Monticello Slave*— the reminiscences of Isaac, one of Mr. Jefferson's slaves, who dictated to an interviewer all that he remembered, just over a century ago. The other is *The Letters of Private Wheeler,* a regular soldier who served under Wellington and wrote a splendid series of letters home about his adventures. The beauty of such books is that, while we read them, we seem actually to hear the voice of a man who knew Mr. Jefferson, of a soldier who marched up to the terrible walls of Badajoz and fought for three days at Waterloo. The past speaks through them.

The second type of history book is a reconstruction. This is an attempt to re-create the past from a few facts, and usually from inadequate facts. It is hard to do this. To succeed, the historian must carefully combine isolated data so that they support and explain one another; interpret documents which were written with no thought of aiding him; often combine the talents of a lawyer, an art critic, an anthropologist, and a psychoanalyst; and always be prepared to admit that he does not know, and is only inferring. Much of the history of the distant past has to be reconstructed in this manner.

If both the writer and the reader will fairly admit that certain knowledge cannot usually be attained, then such works are delightful and valuable. In his presidential address to the American Historical Association in December 1951, Professor Robert Schuyler praised the historian Maitland for just this virtue. Haziness, he said, was recognized by Maitland for what it was. It was allowed to remain hazy. It was not "given the semblance of clarity by having an unhistorical and false lucidity forced upon it."

There is a fine example of this in *The Oxford History of England.* This majestic series of fourteen volumes is not yet complete, but ten are now out, and they are indispensable works. In Volume 1, the late R. G. Collingwood, that brilliant man who was both a historian and an archaeologist and (unlikely combination!) a philosopher, applies his mind to the legend of King Arthur. Who was Arthur? Who were his knights? Fables? Myths? Retrojections of medieval men into the late Roman empire? Collingwood takes the stories as we have them in the earliest form: King Arthur was recorded, by men who lived not many generations after his death, to have fought the pagan invaders of Roman Britain. He had an odd title, *dux bellorum*, leader in the wars. He fought all over Britain. He had knights in armor. He was finally killed by one of his own men. Not much more is recorded. But out of this Collingwood constructs the admirable inference that Arthur was in fact a gifted Roman-British professional soldier, who led a force organized to meet the recurrent barbarian invasions—namely, a mobile unit of heavy cavalry, with men, and perhaps horses too, armored so that even when outnumbered they could still rout a horde of savages poorly organized and lightly equipped. He was not a territorial ruler, but was apparently employed by the various Christian chiefs of different areas of Britain—hence his adventures far and near. And he was the last hope of the Celtic people of Britain, so that when he was killed (Collingwood suggests that the Mordred story means there was dissension within the ranks of his own small force) they would not believe he was really dead, but spoke of him as still alive, waiting his time to return and champion their cause once again.

This is not all the story, of course. Professor Roger Loomis and other scholars have shown how Arthur and his men also gathered much of their strength and magic from the pre-Christian stories of Celtic gods, and from a religion which, although the Christian missionaries drove it out, still lingered in the recesses of men's minds and in that strange region where poetry is born. And tomorrow a British plowman might quite well turn up a stone, with an inscription on it, which would disprove Collingwood's reconstruction of the basic story of the human Arthur. But if that possibility is acknowledged, as it is in the *Oxford History,* then we can accept the story and, by using it, understand a little more about that grim time when the empire was falling and even Christianity seemed in danger, as it often has seemed to be since then.

There is a third kind of history book, which is not so much a reconstruction as a selection and a compression. Here there are plenty of facts, lots of records, dispatches and deeds, private letters and public announcements, maps, and even photographs. The historian has to choose those which will make the story clear; arrange them so as to bring out the essentials of historical change; and then, with such gifts of style and imagination as he possesses, convert them into something less like a scientific statement than a work of art. The professional scholars distrust this kind of writing; but when it is proved trustworthy they usually acknowledge that it is the crown of their profession. Life is sometimes exciting; and this type of history can convey the excitement. Life contains nobility and beauty; such histories will evoke the beauty and reflect the nobility. Life is frequently very funny: the right historian can make us laugh. For instance, take John Miller's history of the War of

Independence, called *Triumph of Freedom,* and turn to his account of the Battle of Trenton. We knew that Washington crossed the Delaware among floating blocks of ice on a bitter Christmas night, and attacked the Hessian troops on 26 December 1776. But the Hessians had been doing some serious Christmas drinking, and their colonel, Rahl, had to be awakened by his orderly to confront the double perils of Washington's artillery and a terrific hangover. The strategic surprise conducted by Washington was complete. After less than an hour's fighting, the Hessians surrendered; and, Mr. Miller tells us,

"Among the slain was Colonel Rahl. He died as he had lived—brave and drunk."

I can recommend Mr. Miller's book heartily. And just as heartily let me recommend a splendid trilogy by Arthur Bryant, dealing with the Napoleonic era. They are called *Years of Endurance* (1793–1802), *Years of Victory* (1802–1812), and *The Age of Elegance* (1812–1822). They began to appear at just the right moment, when the British were standing alone against Hitler and when the entire continent of Europe appeared to be united under a single master who was forging it into a weapon with which to destroy or enslave Great Britain—just as it had appeared under the Emperor Napoleon. It is one of the highest uses of history, to remind individuals and nations that greatness is always possible; and I believe that Bryant's books had that effect. But apart from their patriotism, they are full of general interest and charm. Battles, as we know, are terribly hard to describe. Stendhal thought no soldier had much chance of understanding what went on in them; and Tolstoy believed that not even the generals knew. But as we read Bryant's descriptions of great battles we know very well that the generals on both sides (and many of the experienced officers) in the Napoleonic wars were fully aware of everything essential that was happening; and yet Bryant manages to give us the enlisted man's point of view, too, and reports how he drank or swore; and he tells us how the young officers joked and capered even in the toughest spots. There is an entire chapter of nearly forty pages on Waterloo, and I cannot read it without wild excitement.

History is more than battles. And so Bryant shows us what England, France, Spain, and Portugal actually looked like: how their people fed, and worked, and amused themselves: he makes them live. To describe London in 1814, he uses an admirable device. He shows us the Czar of Russia (who had come to England for the peace celebration) riding round the city early in the morning, followed by his Cossack attendants with long lances and sheepskin cloaks; and he tells us what the Czar saw. It is like a fine set of Rowlandson drawings, with something grander in it, that Rowlandson never saw:

"the tottering old taverns and warehouses of Scotland Yard, the gardens of Northumberland House, the conical water tower of York Buildings,

Somerset House rising like a Venetian palace from the water, and Paul's dome floating above the houses and spires. And binding Westminster to the city, the city to the world, and man to the ages, the great stream flowed seawards, green and grey. . . ."

Final summary — Well, these are the three types of history: the memories, which give individual experience; the reconstructions, which apply logic to scanty records; and the imaginative descriptions, which, from the endless flow of facts and events spawned in millions by the tireless human race, selects those which are truly important and gives us not only their casual connections, but something of the rich emotion and imagination which accompanied them when they occurred, and without which the past is truly dead. It is a noble task, to keep it alive.

SPEECHES FOR COLLATERAL STUDY

1. Ernest C. Arbuckle, "Tomorrow's Manager"—*Vital Speeches of the Day*, Vol. XXVII, October 15, 1960, p. 24 ff.

2. Louis D. Brandeis, "Business—A Profession"—Homer D. Lindgren, *Modern Speeches* (Crofts, N. Y., 1930) p. 106 ff.

3. A. W. Bruce, "The Locomotive Yard Stick"—William P. Sandford and W. H. Yeager, *Business Speeches by Business Men* (McGraw-Hill, N. Y., 1930) p. 633 ff.

4. Winston Churchill, "The Twentieth Century—Its Promise and Its Realization"—Harold F. Harding, *The Age of Danger* (Random House, N. Y., 1952) p. 3 ff.

5. Carl T. Compton, "The State of Science"—Harding, *The Age of Danger*, p. 249 ff.

6. Anson Getman, "State and Private Rights to Real Property"—James M. O'Neill and F. K. Riley, *Contemporary Speeches* (Century, N. Y., 1930) p. 300 ff.

7. Robert F. Goheen, "The University in the World Today"—*Vital Speeches of the Day*, Vol. XXVII, February 15, 1961, p. 281 ff.

8. Clarence H. Mackay, "The History of Communications"—Lindgren, *Modern Speeches*, p. 260 ff.

9. Dr. Charles H. Mayo, "What Is Being Done in the Field of Medicine to Lengthen the Span of Life?"—Sandford and Yeager, *Business Speeches by Business Men*, p. 501 ff.

10. See also the annual volumes of *Representative American Speeches*, edited by A. Craig Baird or Lester Thonssen (H. W. Wilson Company, N. Y.).

PROBLEMS

1. Be ready to discuss the following questions in class: What are the most common types of informative speeches? In every case, what is the

primary purpose of the speech? What requirements should be followed for the selection and arrangement of speech materials? Which steps of the motivated sequence are used for the speech to inform? How does audience interest affect the content of the speech?

2. Make skeleton outlines of the speeches by Dean F. Berkley and by Gilbert Highet printed at the end of this chapter and compare the methods used to organize the information presented in the satisfaction steps with that used in the outline of Professor Petty's speech on roads.

3. Outline one of the speeches in the list for collateral study and determine the method used to organize its information.

4. Outline a classroom lecture and determine the method used to organize its information.

5. Make a list of as many devices for presenting information visually as you can remember having seen speakers use. Note (*a*) the device, (*b*) whether used separately or simultaneously with oral explanation, (*c*) what type of material was presented visually, (*d*) whether the points were clarified or not, and (*e*) whether attention was distracted from the discussion.

6. Select some principle of physics, chemistry, or biology, and plan some method by which it may be connected with concepts familiar to: (*a*) a farmer, (*b*) an automobile repairman, (*c*) a twelve-year-old child, (*d*) a housewife. Write out a paragraph or prepare a one-minute speech calculated to make this point clear to each of these four in turn.

7. Prepare a speech to inform for presentation to your class. Select and narrow your subject from the topics below or one of your own choice. Introduce visual aids whenever they will assist your presentation of information.

Recent research in pharmacy.
Contemporary American composers.
New developments in audio-visual materials for the classroom.
Foreign language teaching in elementary schools.
What your state taxes buy.
The speeches of Henry Clay.
The organization of the Federal Reserve System.
How to prepare visual aids for a speech.
How to write a constitution.
How to locate special documents in the library.
How to listen.

Enthusiasm is the leaping lightning, not to be measured by the horse-power of the understanding.

Ralph Waldo Emerson

CHAPTER *21* / *The Speech to Stimulate*

(or to Actuate Through Emotional Stimulation)

This chapter will discuss the speech intended to stimulate or inspire—the speech planned to uplift the ideals and ambitions of men. Sometimes such a speech has inspiration as its only purpose. Often, though, the speaker may also wish to stimulate the emotional attitudes of the listeners so that they will be impelled to take some definite action.

TYPICAL SITUATIONS REQUIRING SPEECHES WHICH STIMULATE

Occasions for speeches to stimulate or inspire (or to actuate through emotional stimulation) are frequent. *Memorials, dedications, commencement exercises,* and the like usually require such speeches. At such times it is customary for speakers to recall the traditions and ideals—patriotic, religious, and social—to which people give lip service but which need periodic revivification if they are to be retained as powerful forces in daily life. Moreover, such occasions offer a speaker the opportunity of deepening the reverence and enthusiasm of the audience for the lives and principles of great men.

At *conventions,* the wise program committee sees that an inspirational speech is presented early in the proceedings; the delegates must be made to feel that their presence is important and that the convention is worth while. Indeed, the primary function of many conventions is to inspire the delegates with greater loyalty and zeal for the cause or occupation which the convention represents. Thus keynote addresses, intended to inspire or stimulate, are made quite frequently at conventions. At any meeting or series of meetings the opening speaker should endeavor not only to acquaint his listeners with the purpose of the meeting but also to stimulate their enthusiasm and establish an appropriate mood for the business at hand.

Nearly all *meetings of sales or promotional organizations* require speeches to inspire. Salesmen who are likely to become self-satisfied or disheartened need repeated stimulation, and promotional groups—particularly amateur ones, such as a local committee handling a community drive—need frequent encouragement. Thus a good sales manager or committee chairman should be able not only to criticize when criticism is needed but also to arouse the latent enthusiasm of his subordinates. *Organization banquets or meetings* present similar problems to the leaders. More than mere argument is required to get most people into anything new or persuade them to work for an organization. If you try to start a club, or an improvement association in your local community, or even a baseball team in your club or fraternity, you will always face the problem of stimulation. Usually you will find that everyone approves of the idea but that each person suddenly becomes very busy when he is asked to help. People need to be inspired to do their part. *Campaign rallies* present the same problem. During any campaign—political, sales, membership, or financial—the staff of workers usually needs to be inspired frequently to carry through their work to the end.

This list by no means covers all the situations in which speeches to stimulate and inspire are appropriate. Wherever there is a problem of stirring men, women, and children to greater activity or higher ambition, the technics discussed in this chapter will be useful. Teachers, ministers, parents—all must deal with the problem of stimulating their charges to greater devotion and more vigorous effort.

THE PURPOSE

Obviously the purpose of the speech to stimulate is primarily to arouse enthusiasm or to deepen emotion. But it should not end there. Enthusiasm or deep emotion without direction is like a steam engine running wild. The speaker must endeavor not only to stimulate his listeners but also, whenever possible, to direct them toward a definite course of action. Too many speakers thrill their hearers into great excitement but leave them nothing to do about it. The speaker should not just arouse the audience but should arouse them about something definite and, if possible, give them something to do. Then, if he is to secure the best results, he should also strive to make that enthusiasm or emotion lasting. To inspire men while you are talking to them is one thing; to build the inspiration upon a strong enough foundation for it to last after you have finished speaking is quite another. A sales manager, for example, may inspire a group of salesmen momentarily by painting a picture of the glorious expansion of the business or of the ease with which someone else has made large sales; but unless he builds in the salesman a sincere belief in his goods, a confidence in his own capacity, and an assurance of personal gain from his work, all the talk of loyalty to the company and of glorious expansion will melt away on the first hot summer day. High-pressure methods may stimulate temporarily, but they are seldom as permanently stimulating as those based on good sense and sincerity.

THE MANNER OF SPEAKING

Your presentation of a speech to stimulate should be dynamic. The outward expression of this dynamic quality should, of course, vary with your specific purpose and with the occasion. If you wish to stir your listeners to strong enthusiasm, be enthusiastic yourself. Be vigorous both in mind and body; move around; use your arms and hands to emphasize your ideas. On the other hand, if you wish to instill a deep feeling of reverence or devotion, you must be poised physically and must let your voice suggest the depth of your feeling. At an athletic rally, your speaking may be somewhat unrestrained; at a commencement exercise it may be just as dynamic but more controlled. A sales meeting demands brisk and decisive utterance, while a dedication exercise calls for dignity and polish in speaking. Above all, be well enough prepared that you will not have to hesitate or use notes; you will have difficulty stimulating people if you falter or must constantly refer to a sheet of notes.

CHARACTERISTICS OF CONTENT

Since your listeners probably agree in principle with you already, don't argue with them. Your job is to jar them loose, to stir them up, to move them. To do these things, follow the suggestions listed below.

Use striking phraseology. For example, in the speech at the end of this chapter, notice the effectiveness of such statements as these: "If you cannot gather grapes from thorns, or figs from thistles, neither can you gather golden sentences from an empty mind. The reason why most of us do not say more is just because we have nothing more to say. We cannot speak in public because we do not think in private."

Use a slogan as your keynote whenever possible. Of course slogans are not always appropriate, but if the gist of your speech can be expressed in a slogan, use it and hook it up with each illustration in your speech. To be good, a slogan must have some or all of the following qualities: brevity, rhythm, vividness, alliteration, contrast, active suggestion. Consider the effectiveness of this famous slogan: "Millions for defense, but not one cent for tribute!" or of this advertising slogan: "Progress is our most important product."

Be concrete and specific. Instead of saying, "a certain great aviator," call him by name. Instead of referring to "huge sums of money," say definitely "a hundred million," or "enough money to buy up our whole town." Don't talk abstract principles; your audience agrees with them already. Use vivid examples and stories and incidents to make those principles come alive. Notice the effectiveness of the illustrations in the speech on page 401 ff.

Use contrast. Follow an example of failure with one of success. Contrast humor with seriousness. Stand the "big and little of it" side by side for your audience to see.

Use strong motivation. Be sure that your speech is not all glitter. Build it upon the foundation of a strong appeal to fundamental human desires. Touch the pocketbooks, pride, sympathy, fighting spirit, family affection, desire for self-advancement, or any of the other motives of human action. Be careful, however, not to appeal only to selfish motives. Although people often do act for selfish reasons, they usually don't like to admit that fact. Therefore, couple any selfish motives with loftier ones, such as loyalty or patriotism.

Use vivid imagery. Particularly in a speech to inspire, you should try to stir the imagination of your audience. To do so, you will need vivid description which calls up sharp, compelling images in your listeners' minds. Read again the discussion of imagery on pages 332–334 and note especially the importance of reference to experience and use of detail in creating vivid images. Then consider the types of imagery explained below. You will find their effective use one of the most important requirements for stimulating the emotions of your audience.

THE TYPES OF IMAGERY

Imagery, as used in speaking, falls naturally into seven types—each type related to the sensation which it portrays:

1. Visual—(sight).
2. Auditory—(hearing).
3. Gustatory—(taste).
4. Olfactory—(smell).
5. Tactual—(touch).
   A. Texture and shape.
   B. Pressure.
   C. Heat and cold.

6. Kinesthetic—(muscle strain).
7. Organic—(internal sensations).

Visual imagery

Try to make your audience "see" the objects and situations you are describing. Mention size, shape, color, movement, and the relative position of one object to another. Notice how C. P. Snow uses visual imagery to emphasize his point that we should help people in the poor countries "live as long as we do and eat enough." As he said, "We are sitting like people in a smart and cozy restaurant and we are eating comfortably, looking out of the window into the streets. Down on the pavement are people who are looking up at us, people who by chance have different colored skins from ours, and are rather hungry. Do you wonder that they don't like us all that much? Do you wonder that we sometimes feel ashamed of ourselves, as we look out through that plate glass?" [1]

Auditory imagery

Make the audience hear not only what you say but also the sounds which you are describing. Example: "As we stepped inside the power plant at Niagara, the roar of the mighty cataract was still in our ears, and it was some moments before we could hear any other sound at all. Then we began to hear the steady, high-pitched whine of the dynamos and, as the men below us moved around, the quiet patting of rubber-soled shoes against cement." Note that sounds vary in loudness, pitch, and rhythm, as well as in quality. By calling attention to these details, you can create a vivid auditory image.

Gustatory imagery

Get your audience to imagine the taste of what you are describing. Mention its saltiness, sweetness, sourness, bitterness, or its spicy flavor. Observe how Charles Lamb (in his "Dissertation upon Roast Pig") describes roast pig: "There is no flavor comparable, I will contend, to that of the crisp,

---

[1] From "The Moral Un-Neutrality of Science." *Representative American Speeches: 1960–1961*, ed. Lester Thonssen (H. W. Wilson Co., N.Y., 1961), p. 53.

tawny, well-watched, not over-roasted, *crackling,* as it is well called—the very teeth are invited to their share of the pleasure at this banquet in overcoming the coy, brittle resistance . . . the tender blossoming of fat . . . the lean, not lean, but a kind of animal manna—or, rather, fat and lean so blended and running into each other, that both together make but one ambrosian result . . . too ravishing for mortal taste."

Olfactory imagery

Make your audience smell the odors connected with the situation you describe. Do this not only by mentioning the odor itself but also by describing the object having the odor or by comparing it with some familiar one. Example: "As he opened the door of the old apothecary's shop, he breathed the odor of medicines, musty, perhaps, and pungent from too close confinement in so small a place, but free from the sickening smell of stale candy and cheap perfume."

Tactual imagery

Tactual imagery is based upon the various types of sensation we get from our skin when it is touched. Particularly we notice shape and texture, pressure, and heat or cold.

Texture and shape. Try to get your audience to feel how rough or smooth, dry or wet, or sharp, or slimy, or sticky a thing is. The following example is from H. G. Wells' *The Time Machine:* "While I stood in the dark, a hand touched mine, lank fingers came feeling over my face, . . . I felt the box of matches in my hand being gently disengaged, and other hands behind me plucking at my clothing."

Pressure. "As he pulled himself down foot by foot toward the bottom, he felt the water pressing against him until the enveloping squeeze was all that he could stand."

Heat and cold. This is sometimes called "thermal" imagery. "After the night spent with icy spray whipping over me from the prow of the boat, the warmth of the morning sun and the steaming hot cup of coffee which the steward brought me were welcome indeed."

Kinesthetic imagery Kinesthetic imagery relates to muscle strain and movement. Get your audience to feel themselves active, to feel the pull upon muscle and tendon: "Had it been an ordinary trapdoor, we could have pushed it open with no effort at all. As it was, the three of us braced ourselves firmly, but heave and shove as we might, we could not budge it. Our muscles became great hard knots; the sweat stood on our foreheads; it seemed as though our backs would break with the effort. But not a fraction of an inch would it move." To emphasize his point that the networks had foolishly "been spending their time trying to bat down the arguments" on what to do about broadcasting, LeRoy Collins, former Governor of Florida, made use of kinesthetic imagery as well as other kinds of imagery in the following story:

> Once, down in South America, I went to a bullfight. After the bull was turned into the arena, a series of efforts were made to agitate and weaken him.
> The picadores came on horseback, driving their barbed sticks into the big neck muscles and causing the bull to charge in pain and frustration.
> Then, another group came after him. They were the banderilleros with their torturous barbs. And the bull got more of the same treatment.
> Finally, the matador came with a red cape. The slowly exhausting bull charged with all his remaining strength after the elusive man with the sword. But when all his strength was gone and the huge neck muscle had been weakened from the barbs, the bull's head lowered, and the matador could, with apparent ease, drive the keen steel through the shoulder blades to the heart.
> Broadcasting is getting a lot of barbs in the neck muscle at this point.
> Are we going to exhaust ourselves by thrashing around with defensive movements? [2]

Organic imagery Hunger, dizziness, nausea—these are a few of the feelings organic imagery calls up. There are times when an image is not complete without the inclusion of details relating to the inward feelings. Be careful, however, not to offend your audience by making the picture too revolting. A fine taste is required to measure the detail necessary for vividness without making the image so gruesome that it becomes either disgusting

[2] "Speech to the Directors of the National Association of Broadcasters." *Ibid.*, p. 183.

or laughably grotesque. Observe the use made of organic imagery by H. G. Wells: "That climb seemed interminable to me. With the last twenty or thirty feet of it a deadly nausea came upon me. I had the greatest difficulty in keeping my hold. The last few yards was a frightful struggle against this faintness. Several times my head swam, and I felt all the sensations of falling. At last, however, I got over the well-mouth somehow and staggered out of the ruin into the blinding sunlight."

These, then, are the seven types of imagery. Victor Alvin Ketcham [3] calls them the "Seven Doorways to the Mind" which the speaker must open with his words if he expects his audience to understand him. As Professor Ketcham points out, people differ in the degree to which they are sensitive to one type of imagery or another. The public speaker is wise, therefore, to employ as many different kinds of imagery as possible.

In the example which follows, notice how the different types of imagery have been combined to create a vivid picture:

I was lately taken by a friend, with whom I was staying in the country, to a garden party. . . . The day was hot, and I was uncomfortably dressed. I found myself first in a hot room, where the host and hostess were engaged in what is called receiving. A stream of pale, perspiring people moved slowly through, some of them frankly miserable, some with an air of false geniality, which deceived no one, written upon their faces. "So pleasant to see so many friends!" "What a delightful day you have for your party!" Such ineptitudes were the current coin of the market. I passed on into another room where refreshment, of a nature that I did not want, was sadly accepted. And I passed out into the open air; the garden was disagreeably crowded; there was "a din of doubtful talk," as Rossetti says. The sun beat down dizzily on my streaming brow. I joined group after group, where the conversation was all of the same easy and stimulating character, until I felt sick and faint . . . with the "mazes of heat and sound" in which my life seemed "turning, turning." . . . I got away, dizzy, unstrung, unfit for life, with that terrible sense of fatigue unaccompanied by wholesome tiredness, that comes of standing in hot buzzing places. . . . As I went away, I pondered sadly upon the almost inconceivable nature of the motive which could lead people to behave as I had seen them behaving, and resolutely to label it pleasure.[4]

[3] From "The Seven Doorways to the Mind." *Business Speeches by Business Men* (McGraw-Hill, N. Y., 1930), edited by William P. Sandford and W. H. Yeager.
[4] From "Sociabilities" by Arthur Christopher Benson.

In the speech at the end of this chapter, note how Dr. Tittle also combines imagery of several kinds to heighten the effect of his descriptions.

ORGANIZATION

A speech to stimulate may sometimes be organized as a one-point speech. When your purpose is just to intensify your listeners' feelings about the seriousness of a problem, your speech may consist of only a one-point need step, beginning with a striking statement of that need, to get attention at the start, and developed with striking and vivid examples illustrating that need. If the need is perfectly clear, you may begin your speech with a vivid statement of the attitude or action which you urge, then present a series of descriptions and illustrations to visualize the desirable results to be obtained, and close with a compelling restatement of the recommended attitude or action. Thus your first sentence is the attention, need, and satisfaction steps combined, the bulk of your speech is visualization, and the final statement is your action step. The speech on "One Idea" (pp. 219–221) is essentially a stimulating speech of this type. More often, however, especially at occasions which require a longer speech, the steps in the motivated sequence are fully developed as follows:

Attention step

A keynote speech or the opening speech of a presiding officer is usually begun with a reference to the occasion. In other types of speeches, the attention step may consist of an unusual statement or of a telling illustration. In his attention step, Dr. Tittle employed an unusual combination of quotation, personal reference, and statement of theme (p. 401 ff.).

Need step

In the need step, stress the importance of greater activity or enthusiasm or a deeper feeling of some emotion, such as anger, reverence, etc. This is done by pointing out how the present situation is unsatisfactory in contrast to what has been or to what is possible. Frequently the audience is awakened to a consciousness of present weaknesses merely by a vivid picture of possible strength; thus the contrast between the present and the past or future is implied rather than stated. In the sample speech, for instance, observe how Dr. Tittle, by calling attention to the achievements of great speakers of the past, creates in his student audience a feeling of the importance of speech and a need for further self-development to make similar accomplishments possible. Remember that a feeling of need cannot be created effectively by mere argument or by the mere statement "Be enthusiastic" or "Be angry." Illustration, narrative, startling facts, vividness—these are required. Keep the picture active and moving, and, above all, keep your audience at a high pitch of attention. Sometimes this step is short if the audience is already keenly aware of the problem. More often, particularly when the audience is apathetic, it is longer—from a third to more than half the speech.

Satisfaction step In a speech to stimulate, the satisfaction step is usually short unless it is combined with the visualization step (as in the sample speech). Ordinarily, the satisfaction step proposes one of two things: (*a*) a general frame of mind that the audience is to assume, such as enthusiasm, anger, reverence, devotion, loyalty, renewed activity; or (*b*) a definite plan of action briefly outlined. If the latter method is used, some device, such as alliteration, is helpful to impress the plan on the minds of your listeners. Thus, a speaker making a health talk to middle-aged businessmen suggested that they "sleep more; stuff less; and see a doctor often." When a definite course of action is proposed, state it positively but don't argue; argument sometimes convinces but seldom inspires.

Visualization step Ordinarily the greater part of the speech will come in the visualization step. The development will be of the positive type mentioned in Chapter 16, page 299. Picture conditions as they will be when your plan is put into operation or heighten the desirability of the attitude you are urging the audience to assume. Here you can even afford a bit of mild exaggeration; everyone is with you in principle, and a mild overstatement will seem natural. Again, avoid the abstract—be vivid, concrete; make the picture both lively and realistic. Fill the speech with imagery. Use illustration and narrative profusely.

Parallel development of need, satisfaction, and visualization steps Frequently a parallel development (such as that explained in Chapter 16, pp. 297–299) is effective. If the need has more than one main aspect, each aspect may be followed through the need and satisfaction steps separately and drawn together in the visualization step; or more frequently, the need may be treated as one unit, and then the various aspects are separately followed through the satisfaction and visualization steps. This latter method is used in the sample speech: first the need for great speakers is pointed out; then qualities required for greatness are mentioned (satisfaction) and vividly pictured (visualization) one by one. There are times, though somewhat rare, when all three steps—need, satisfaction, visualization—are thus developed in parallel. When this parallel structure is used you must take care to limit the units to a few basic aspects; too many units will result in a stringy, unstimulating speech.

Action step In a speech to stimulate, no definite action step is included unless the purpose of the speech is to request some specific act. Requests for generalized activity or emotional attitude are usually implied rather than stated. If the visualization step is adequately developed, the implication will be clear. When an action step is included, it is usually developed in one of three ways: by a *rapid summary* of the specific action required, by a *quotation* which vividly suggests the action or emotion urged, or by a *challenge* which requires personal commitment on the part of the audience—a show of hands, signature, or vocal assent. The last method should never be used unless you are sure the audience is sufficiently aroused to react without hesitation or inhibition; if people do commit themselves publicly, they will, of course, feel a certain additional obligation to keep their pledge.

Experience will doubtless suggest many variations to the technics suggested here for the preparation and presentation of speeches to stimulate. Each individual occasion will certainly dictate modification, but the fundamental technic presents a definite and effective groundwork for any speech problem of this nature. The outline for this type of speech usually follows the skeleton plan shown on page 306 f. except that the satisfaction step will always be abbreviated and the action step will sometimes be omitted. A short but telling speech of this type, which shows how content and organization may be combined to stimulate action, is the appeal made by David Sarnoff printed on pages 284 to 286. Note how he used striking phraseology, vivid imagery, and strong motivation in making his appeal.

SAMPLE SPEECH

Read carefully the sample speech which follows, delivered at an occasion where a more deliberate development was possible and a more polished style required. Note especially the wealth of illustration, the parallel development of the satisfaction and visualization steps, and the absence of any definitely stated action step.

LEARNING TO SPEAK [5]

> *This commencement address was delivered to the graduates of the Northwestern University School of Speech in June 1924 by Dr. Ernest Fremont Tittle, then the pastor of the First Methodist Church of Evanston, Illinois, a church which a majority of the audience regularly attended.*

Attention step   One day, without any very definite outline in mind, Robert Burns sat down to write a poem and frankly confessed:

> Which way the subject theme may gang
> Let time and chance determine;
> Perhaps it may turn out a sang—
> Or probably a sermon.

I wish—how I wish tonight—that I might produce a song. But, if I succeed in producing anything, it will probably be a sermon. When Coleridge asked Lamb, "Did you ever hear me preach, Charles?" Lamb replied, "I n-never heard you do anything else." The bearing of

---

[5] Reprinted by special permission.

this famous retort upon the present instance is, I am afraid, only too obvious.

But be it a "sang," or be it a "sermon," the theme which I have chosen for this occasion is Learning to Speak. And I marvel at my own temerity. I can only hope that some of you will consider it pertinent. You need not suggest—I already know—that it is also impertinent!

Need step Everybody ought to learn how to speak. First, because speaking clarifies thought. I am going to suggest farther on that clear thinking is the primary requisite for good speaking; but just now I should like to suggest that honest effort to express thought usually results in clarifying it.

When some one complains, "I know what I want to say but cannot say it," you may not confess your well-founded suspicion that he doesn't quite know what he wants to say; but you may, perhaps, tactfully suggest that if only he will try to say what he knows, he will even better know what he is trying to say.

Once you have got your thought expressed you have a clearer understanding of the thought that you have wanted to express. Everybody, therefore, ought to learn how to speak if for no other reason than for the purpose of clarifying his own thinking.

But is it not also true that "a word fitly spoken is like apples of gold in pictures of silver"? It gives pleasure. Listening to good English, like listening to good music, is one of the most satisfying enjoyments of life. The brilliant conversationalist is a social asset even though it must be said of him, as it was said of W. T. Stead, that "his idea of good conversation is to have another man to listen to him."

And is not the clever after-dinner speaker a public servant? There is, to be sure, a vast difference between post-prandial orators. Once upon a time a mayor of Chicago introduced Chauncey Depew by suggesting that he was like an automatic machine—"You put in a dinner and up comes a speech." When Mr. Depew gained his feet, he suggested that the difference between his after-dinner speaking and the chairman's was that his Honor, the Mayor, "puts in a speech and up comes your dinner." But you will, I think, agree with me that the accomplished after-dinner speaker is a public servant. If he adds but little—and he usually does—to the sum total of the world's knowledge, he adds considerably to the sheer enjoyment of life.

Moreover, the pleasure which may be given by a gifted speaker is by no means the only service which he is able to render. For, as Walter Savage Landor once remarked, "On a winged word hath hung the destiny of nations." The speeches of Demosthenes in Athens, of Cicero in Rome, of Pitt and Burke and Gladstone in England, of Webster and Lincoln and Wilson in America, were not only utterances; they were events. They not only appealed to history. They made history. And this, at least to some extent, has been true of speeches made by far lesser men.

History used to be written as though it were merely a string of great men's biographies. This, as you remember, was the method of Plutarch. It was the method, also, of Carlyle, who once said of England that she boasted twenty-seven millions of people—mostly fools; and of the United States, "They have begotten with a rapidity beyond recorded example eighteen million of the greatest bores ever seen in this world before."

History for Carlyle was simply a succession of great men's biographies. He worshiped the hero and despised the crowd.

But the crowd, as we are beginning to realize, is not to be despised.

Think of the reformers before the Reformation: the unnumbered thousands who prepared the way for Luther; who helped to create the intellectual and moral environment of which Luther availed himself when he nailed his ninety-eight theses to the door of the old church in Wittenberg, and carved for himself a conspicuous place in the memory of mankind. Think of the unpictured, unpraised persons who fanned the fires of conviction which lighted the way for Abraham Lincoln to move into immortality as the emancipator of four million slaves. Think of the unfamous persons in every country in the world today who are forging the demand that war shall be placed in the same category with dueling, piracy, and human slavery.

It has been said that "The frail snowflake has sculptured continents." Is it not equally true that the spoken thought, not only of great men, but of millions of ordinary men, has molded the lives of nations and determined the course of civilization? How important, then, it is that everybody should learn how to speak. The voice of the ordinary man may not carry very far. All the more reason why, as far as it does carry, it should be made as clear and compelling as possible.

Satisfaction and visualization steps in parallel Everybody may learn how to speak. By learning to speak, of course, I mean something different from learning to talk. Not long ago I heard an American Indian suggest that when the White man says to the Red man, "Why don't you talk more?" the Red man would like to reply to the White man, "Why don't you say more?" A vivacious representative of the gentler sex once asked Henry James whether he did not think that American women talk better than English women. "Yes," he replied, "they are more ready and much more brilliant. They rise to every suggestion. But," he added reflectively, and with rare tactfulness, "English women so often know what they are talking about." And has not Christopher Morley sententiously remarked that "The unluckiest insolvent in the world is the man whose expenditure of speech is too great for his income of ideas"?

By learning to speak one wishes to mean something more than learning to vocalize. The latter accomplishment is not beyond the reach of a parrot.

But everybody who is not an idiot may learn not only how to talk but how to speak. Ability to speak like ability to swim, or to drive a golf ball, or to play the piano, may be cultivated. You may never develop into a Wendell Phillips, or a Frances Willard, any more than you may develop into a Sybil Bauer, or a Bobbie Jones, or a Paderewski; but you need not go stuttering and stammering through life. As a biological descendant of Adam and Eve, you have a tongue and some teeth, and a modicum at least of intelligence. As a linguistic descendant of Shakespeare and Milton, you have nine parts of speech and a possible vocabulary of more than three hundred thousand words to choose from. If, therefore, you do not learn how to speak, it is your own fault. It is not because you cannot learn. It is merely because you will not go to the trouble of learning.

What then are some of the essential requirements for learning to speak as over against the mere ability to vocalize in a half-dozen languages? Let me mention, first, the ability to think. The man who has something to say can and will find some way to say it. If any man remains a "mute inglorious Milton," it is not because he cannot say what he thinks; it is rather because he has never thought anything worth saying.

If you cannot gather grapes from thorns, or figs from thistles, neither can you gather golden sentences from an empty mind. The reason why most of us do not say more is just because we have nothing more to say. We cannot speak in public, because we do not think in private.

A somewhat distinguished English preacher, who was naturally fluent, once declared that he could always go on saying something until he had something to say. But a far safer guide for most of us to follow is that deservedly famous stump speaker who advised, "Fill yourself with your subject, then knock out the bung and let nature caper."

Remy de Gourmont has remarked that "Works well thought out are invariably well written." Allowing for the inevitable exceptions, he has, I suspect, stated the rule—a rule which applies not only to effective writing but to effective speaking. Works well thought out are almost invariably well written; and ideas well thought out are almost invariably well spoken. A poor speech may be the result of a number of causes, including, perhaps, milk-fed chicken, vanilla ice cream, and French pastry; but it is even more likely to be the result of sloppy thinking. The ambitious speaker would do well to spend more time in clarifying his thought than in choosing his words.

Yet words, too, are important. There are colorful words that are as beautiful as red roses; and there are drab words that are as unlovely as an anaemic-looking woman. There are concrete words that keep people awake; and abstract words that put them to sleep. There are strong words that can punch like a prize-fighter; and weak words that are as insipid as a "mamma's boy." There are warm sympathetic words that grip men's hearts; and cold detached words that leave an audience unmoved. There are noble words that lift every listener, at least for a moment, to the sunlit heights of God; and base words that leave an audience in the atmosphere of the cabaret. And so, other things being equal, including abstemious eating and clear thinking, the most effective speech will be the speech that contains the greatest number of colorful, concrete, strong, sympathetic, and inspiring words. Provided . . . What?

Very much of the effectiveness of public speaking depends upon the technic employed by the speaker.

An exasperated parishioner, who felt it incumbent upon him to protest against the feebleness of the clerical profession, remarked to the Reverend Sidney Smith, "If I had a son who was an idiot, I would make him a parson." To which the Reverend Sidney Smith replied, "Your father evidently was of a different opinion." Some protest, no doubt, needed to be made; but the gentleman who ventured to make it had not developed the right technic.

There are, as I have discovered, two very different ways of calling someone's attention to the fact that he has taken certain unwarranted liberties with the truth. If you employ the wrong way, the response is very likely to be, "You're another!" But if you employ the right way, the response may be, "Perhaps I have; and I shall endeavor hereafter to confine myself strictly to facts."

I was present some time ago at a meeting at which two speeches were made on the same theme. Both speakers, as it happened, took substantially the same position. But when the first speaker sat down, the audience was distinctly unfriendly; and when the second speaker sat down, the same audience vigorously applauded him. Both had said the same thing; but the first had said it in a way that merely irritated his audience, whereas the second had said it in a way that had convinced his audience. Many a speaker has met with opposition not so much because of what he said as because of the way in which he said it.

There is, of course, the exactly opposite danger that a man may say something that needs to be said, but say it so cautiously that no one will realize that he has said it. He will get it out, but he will not get it over; and if he fails to get it over, he has made an ineffective speech.

Not long ago, in the course of an address, I repeated the deservedly famous story of the merchant who hung out a sign reading, "I am a One Hundred Per Cent American: I hate Jews, Catholics, Negroes, and foreigners"; whereupon his competitor across the street hung out a sign reading, "I am a Two Hundred Per Cent American: I hate everybody." At the close of the meeting, an ardent member of the local Ku Klux Klan came forward and warmly congratulated me! I had gotten it out; but I had not, apparently, gotten it over.

One way to get something out without getting it over is to confine yourself to glittering generalities. Almost any audience will applaud glittering generalities, especially if they are couched in familiar rhetorical phrases.

Some one gets up and affirms, with the air of Christopher Columbus discovering America, that what this country needs is a good old-fashioned revival of religion. Shouts of Amen! from the Methodist corner. Decorous cries of Hear! Hear! from the Presbyterian corner. Smiles of approval from the Congregational corner. Slight intimations of approval from the Episcopalian corner. Even the out and out pagan in the audience feels an impulse to applaud! A good old-fashioned revival of religion sounds harmless enough. To the traditionalist it suggests the theology on which he was brought up. To the dogmatist it suggests the truth —as he sees it. To the emotionalist it suggests a perfectly wonderful opportunity to enjoy the luxury of inexpensive tears. To the pious profiteer and the orthodox exploiter, it suggests a type of religion which raises no embarrassing questions, makes no inconvenient demands, but leaves men undisturbed in the enjoyment of the fruits of other people's labor, and furnishes a divine sanction for the maintenance of the status quo. And so, as a sonorous platitude, almost any audience will endorse the statement that what this country needs is a good old-fashioned revival of religion.

But suppose the speaker feels under some obligation to descend from the pleasant heights of glittering generalities to the arduous lowlands of particular applications. Suppose he feels impelled to suggest that a good old-fashioned revival of religion would involve, as it did in the days of John the Baptist, an urgent, unflinching demand that the rough ways of industry shall be made smooth; and that the crooked ways of politics shall be made straight; and that every mountain and hill of unearned wealth shall be brought low; and that every valley of undeserved poverty shall be filled; and that all flesh shall be given equality of educational and economic opportunity; and that nothing less than this shall be termed the salvation of God. Having made a suggestion of this sort, would not the preacher discover a sudden drop of at least forty degrees in the temperature of the audience?

To be effective, a public speaker must develop a technic which will enable him to get out what needs to be said without needless and fruitless irritation, and at the same time to get it over.

But if much depends upon the technic of speaking, much more depends upon the life of the speaker. You cannot make silken purses out of sow's ears; nor can you get a big speech out of a little speaker. Schools of speech may give you a faultless technic. But what shall it profit a speaker if he acquire a faultless technic but fail to develop his mind and to enrich his soul?

When Senator Hayne had delivered, in the United States Senate, his famous speech defending the right of a sovereign state to withdraw from the Union, there were men of no little discernment who declared with heavy hearts that his argument was unanswerable. But, on the following day, Senator Hayne's unanswerable argument was brilliantly answered by Daniel Webster; and the Senate chamber had witnessed probably the most wonderful burst of pure oratory yet heard on the continent. Afterwards, Webster was asked how long he had been in the preparation of his great Reply. His answer was, "Twenty years." Said he, "When I stood up in the Senate Chamber and began to speak, a strange sensation came to me. All that I had ever thought, or read in literature, in history, in law, in politics, seemed to unroll before me in glowing panorama; and then it was easy, whenever I wanted a thunderbolt, to reach out and take it as it went smoking by."

Great speeches are not born in a day. It may require as long as twenty years to bring them forth. For they come out of the slowly nourished minds of men. They come out of the slowly maturing souls of men. They come very often out of suffering and heartache and loneliness and all but despair. They never come out of shallow minds and sordid secular souls.

How fearfully flat mere declamation falls. "Give me liberty or give me death," cries the school boy; and his declamation may be rhetorically impeccable. Yet somehow it is unconvincing. The words appear; but they are like wax figures in a museum. Only the flaming soul of a Patrick Henry could give them life.

I do not mean to suggest that it is beyond the power of a great actor to give convincing expression to words that another has written or spoken. I do mean to suggest that, in order to do so, the actor himself must, as a man, be great enough actually to experience the sentiment he is expressing.

Carlyle used to insist that "Sincerity is the first characteristic of all men in any way heroic. All the great men I have ever heard of," he declares, "have [sincerity] as the primary material of them."

Can you think of any permanently effective public speaker who was not deeply and even passionately sincere? I except, of course, the mere rhetorician: the popular preachers, the political spell-binders, the matinée idols, and every other kind of vocalizing idol whose feet are of clay. They have, to be sure, their little vogue, their little coterie of worshipers. But if they go up like a rocket, they come down like a stick, leaving no permanent light in the sky. It is not of such, but only of men who, being dead, yet speak, that I am thinking when I ask: Can you recall any single permanently effective public speaker who was not deeply and even passionately sincere?

In preparation for the important speech which he was to deliver on the occasion of his nomination to the United States Senate, Mr. Lincoln read that famous classic to which I have already referred, Webster's "Reply to Hayne." It begins, as you may remember, in this fashion:

"Mr. President: When the mariner has been tossed for many days in thick weather, and on an unknown sea, he naturally avails himself of the first pause in the storm, the earliest glimpse of the sun, to take his latitude, and ascertain how far the elements have driven him from his course. Let us imitate this prudence, and before we float farther on the waves of this debate, refer to the point from which we departed, that we may at least be able to conjecture where we now are."

But the sonorous sentences of the silver-tongued orator of the East were not natural to the plain-speaking lawyer of the West; and when Lincoln sat down to compose his speech, he began:

"Mr. Chairman: If we could first know where we are and whither we are tending, we could better judge what to do, and how to do it."

And, having before him, as I cannot but believe, these two classical examples, Woodrow Wilson began his own last published article in this fashion:

"In these doubtful and anxious days, when all the world is at unrest, and, look which way you will, the road ahead seems darkened by shadows which portend dangers of many kinds, it is only common prudence that we should look about us and attempt to assess the causes of distress and the most likely means of removing them."

In this last introduction one finds neither the ponderous oratory of a Webster—quite natural to him; nor the homespun speech of a Lincoln—equally natural to him; but just that peculiar combination of embroidered Latinity and Anglo-Saxon simplicity which was natural to Woodrow Wilson.

Webster, Lincoln, Wilson—three Americans whose speeches became historical events. And different as they were in many respects, they were alike in this respect that Webster, during his great days, and Lincoln and Wilson during all their days, were passionately sincere.

Whosoever would be permanently effective as a public speaker must be sincere. If a personal confession be allowed, I may say that no man, however brilliant or eloquent, can move me to anything save anger if I have reason to believe that what he is contradicts what he says.

Is it not also true that whosoever would move his audience must lose sight of himself?

An old schoolmate of Joseph Parker once came to him in great distress. Joseph Parker was, at that time, one of the greatest of living preachers. The schoolmate was an undistinguished country curate.

"Parker," he said, "what is the matter with me? I have got a brain that is just as good as yours is; but for some reason, I am not able to get anywhere with it."

"Well," said Joseph Parker, "let me see what you do. Stand at the other end of this room and deliver for me your last Sunday's sermon."

The undistinguished curate did so, and received this criticism: "My old friend, the trouble with you is that you are trying to get something off instead of trying to get something in."

In the year 1858, the eyes of the American people were fixed upon two men. These men were engaged in a series of debates. And they were debating the greatest question of the age. One of them was trying to be eloquent; the other was trying to be honest. One was endeavoring to get something off; the other was endeavoring to get something in. One was seeking to win an election; the other was seeking to win a cause.

When Judge Douglas finished speaking, men shouted themselves hoarse, and exclaimed, "What a wonderful speech!" When Mr. Lincoln sat down, they said to one another, "Old Abe is right."

Douglas won the election. Lincoln said in a letter to a friend: "I am glad I made the late race. It gave me an opportunity to be heard on the greatest question of the age such as I could have gotten in no other way; and now, though I sink out of sight and become forgotten, I think I have made some marks which will tell for the cause of Liberty after I am gone." But, Abraham Lincoln did not sink out of sight or become forgotten. The American people—a determined portion of them—were looking for just such a man. It now appears that God Almighty was looking for just such a man. And when He found him He highly exalted him, and gave him a name that is above every name in American history.

When Douglas died, he moaned, "I have failed." When the spirit of Abraham Lincoln returned to the God who gave it, Edwin M. Stanton remarked, "And now, he belongs to the ages."

How everlastingly true it is even of public speakers; whosoever would save his life shall lose it; but whosoever will lose his life in devotion to a great cause will save it.

(*No stated action step—the general attitude and course of action are implied.*)

SPEECHES FOR COLLATERAL STUDY

1. Virgil L. Baker, "The Art of Public Speaking"—*Vital Speeches of the Day,* Vol. XVII, March 1, 1952, p. 318 ff.

2. Edward D. Gates, "Time Is Running Out"—Harold F. Harding, *The Age of Danger* (Random House, N. Y., 1952), p. 472 ff.

3. Henry W. Grady, "The New South"—W. N. Brigance, *Classified Speech Models* (Crofts, N. Y., 1928), p. 287 ff.

4. A. Whitney Griswold, "Man Thinking"—Harding, *The Age of Danger,* p. 376 ff.

5. Ernest Gruening, "Independence Day Address"—Lester A. Thonssen, *Representative American Speeches: 1959–1960* (H. W. Wilson Co., N. Y.), p. 31 ff.

6. Herbert Hoover, "Leadership for a Free World"—*Vital Speeches of the Day,* Vol. XIV, July 1, 1948, p. 548 ff.

7. Maurice G. Robinson, "The Eleventh Commandment"—Brigance, *Classified Speech Models,* p. 18 ff.

8. Lester A. Thonssen, "The Unrecorded Legacy"—A. Craig Baird, *Representative American Speeches: 1958–1959* (H. W. Wilson Co., N. Y.), p. 133 ff.

PROBLEMS

1. Be ready to discuss the following questions in class: For what situations are speeches to stimulate appropriate? Why does this type of speech require dynamic delivery? What are the types of imagery? How does their use help the speaker accomplish his purpose in the speech to stimulate? How is the motivated sequence developed for the speech to stimulate?

2. Examine Dr. Tittle's speech, printed at the end of this chapter, and note examples of his use of unusual or striking phrases, contrast, motive appeal. Does the speaker use a slogan? Is it repeated in a varied form?

3. Outline Dr. Tittle's speech and compare your outline with the method of organization suggested in this chapter.

4. What meetings have you recently attended where speeches to stimulate were presented? List the subjects discussed by the speakers. Were they appropriate to the audience and the occasion? What technics did the effective speakers use?

5. Analyze the speeches made at an athletic rally or celebration or at some other campus event at which a speech to stimulate was given.

6. Prepare to present orally brief descriptions developing each of the seven types of imagery. Here are a few suggestions:
   A. *Visual imagery:* fog at night; the city from atop a skyscraper; the countryside from a train window.
   B. *Auditory imagery:* in a sawmill; the Women's Guild meeting; in a night club.
   C. *Gustatory imagery:* a Winesap, Jonathan, or Delicious apple; a lemon; raw rhubarb.
   D. *Olfactory imagery:* a breeze from the stockyards; grandfather's pipe; harvest time.
   E. *Tactual imagery:* homespun woolens; inside a cold-storage plant.
   F. *Kinesthetic imagery:* stacking baled hay; shoveling sand; a stubborn olive-bottle top.
   G. *Organic imagery:* to the twentieth floor in a fast elevator; the last period before lunch.

7. Prepare a speech to stimulate to be given before your class. Consider campus traditions, American or state history, or commemorative events as sources for appropriate subjects.

The freedom to persuade and suggest is the essence of the democratic process.

Unsigned article in Freedom and Union

CHAPTER 22 / *The Speech to Convince*

(or to Actuate Through Conviction)

W e are living today in an organized society. No longer can a man do things of any magnitude alone; he must first secure the consent or the active support of others in order that the combined efforts of all may be converged upon a common objective. The preceding chapter explained how a speaker may sometimes secure support by stimulating emotions and arousing enthusiasm when his audience already agrees with him in principle. This chapter is concerned with conviction—with the necessity not only of arousing an audience but also of changing existing beliefs or instilling new ones.

SITUATIONS REQUIRING SPEECHES TO CONVINCE

Speakers are often faced with the problem of convincing an audience. Consider for a moment three typical examples: (*a*) *Busi-*

ness meetings. Whether the group is the board of directors of a large company or the executive committee of a small club, the members are confronted at every meeting with numerous decisions. Executive officers present reports for approval; committees make recommendations for future action; any individual of the group may express his convictions and make suggestions for changes and improvements. In each case, the speaker wants the group to agree with his conclusion or to authorize the course of action he recommends. (*b*) *Popular gatherings.* Speeches to convince are frequently given at political rallies or mass meetings. Here the speaker attempts to change political beliefs or to secure popular support for civic improvements. Even commercial policies are sometimes presented at public meetings; for example, a representative from a company may try to convince a group that they should vote for bond issues or public-utility plans. (*c*) *Debates.* In a debate, whether it is a formal intercollegiate contest or an argument in a legislative body or courtroom, the clash of opinion calls for the attempt to convince. These are only a few of the many situations in which speeches to secure belief are made. Church services, even meetings of a social committee or study group, often present similar problems.

THE PURPOSE: TO SECURE BELIEF OR ACTION BASED ON BELIEF

Although the ultimate goal of every speech to convince is to get your listeners to believe or to act as you wish, you must make them *want* to do what you propose rather than feel that they *have* to. For this reason, two subsidiary purposes should be kept in mind: (*a*) to impress your listeners with a motive for believing, such as self-preservation, power, profit, pleasure, pride, etc.; and (*b*) to convince them of the logic of your proposal—that is, the relation between the facts you present and the conclusion you draw. Sometimes, you will also have to create or strengthen an emotional attitude, such as anger or sympathy, that will encourage belief in your proposal. When this is necessary, your speech, while primarily to convince, should include some of the technics described in the preceding chapter.

Before you construct a speech to convince, you must be sure you thoroughly understand and believe in the proposition you are going to present. To achieve such complete understanding and belief, you must systematically analyze your proposition. This analysis should produce at least two results: it will give you more confidence in the proposition, and it will suggest ways in which you can convince your audience that they should believe in or act on your proposition. There are three general kinds of propositions which a speaker may present for approval or, on the other hand, may argue against: propositions of fact, of value, and of policy.

Propositions of fact or of value

If you are attempting to get an audience to believe that "the Russian revolution was inevitable" or that "large government expenditure for foreign aid tends to maintain high prices artificially," you would in each case be presenting a proposition asserting something to be a fact. Don't assume that your propositions of fact *are* facts; remember that they are simply statements which you are trying to prove to be facts. The analysis of such a proposition involves two steps:

Determine the criteria, or standards, upon which the judgment is to be based. If you were asked to determine a man's height, you would immediately look for a yardstick or some other standard of measure. A standard is often essential for judging the more complicated propositions about which you speak. In many arguments people disagree not on the evidence itself but on the standards by which that evidence is to be judged. Thus, in the propositions listed above, the first thing you would have to do is decide what standard to use in judging a thing to be "inevitable" or a cause that "tends to maintain high prices."

Apply your criteria one at a time to the evidence, measuring your proposition by each standard. Just as you would determine whether a man was tall or short by measuring him with a yardstick and comparing his height with the established average, so you must judge the validity of your proposition of fact by measuring it against the standards you have set. Later, when you speak, if you can first get your audience to agree on the standards for judgment and can then present evidence showing that your proposition measures up to each of these standards, you will find it much easier to secure their acceptance of your proposition.

Definite criteria are especially important when you are analyzing propositions of value, which assert that something is good or bad, desirable or undesirable, justifiable or unjustifiable. Are these propositions to be judged by economic or moral standards, or both, or by still other criteria? Often it is desirable to pick out two or three kinds of criteria which cover all the possible bases for judgment. For example, to determine the quality of a particular college, you might consider the distinction of its faculty, the adequacy of its physical plant, the success of its students in graduate and professional schools, the reputation it enjoys in its region, etc.

Propositions of policy

You would be dealing with questions of policy if you were urging your audience to approve of or act on the following propositions: "The United States *should increase* the size of its military forces." "Government expenditures for public works *should be cut in half*." "The football team *should be sent* to the Rose Bowl Game by airplane." In each instance you would be urging your audience to do something or to approve of having it done. You would be urging the adoption of a policy or course of action. To analyze such a proposition properly, you must answer four subsidiary questions, each of which involves a proposition of fact or value and must itself be individually analyzed:

1. *Is there a need for such a policy or course of action?* If an audience cannot be convinced that a change is needed, they will not approve a new policy.
2. *Will the proposed policy or plan work?* If you cannot show the audience that your proposed plan will be effective, they will have no reason for adopting or approving it.
3. *Are the benefits it will bring greater than the disadvantages?* People will not approve a proposal that seems likely to create conditions worse than the ones it promises to correct. The benefits and disadvantages of a plan must be carefully weighed along with its workability.
4. *Is it better than any other plan or policy?* Your listeners will not endorse your proposal if they believe some other way of

meeting the present need has fewer disadvantages or greater benefits.

In analyzing a policy or course of action, consider each of these four subsidiary questions (sometimes called "stock issues"). Determine the criteria upon which they are to be judged; examine the evidence you have collected; and see how the facts lead you to answer the questions. Observe how this was done in the speech on conservation in Chapter 17 (p. 309 ff.) and in the outline on filtering industrial waste at the end of this chapter (pp. 432–435).

Remember that you must later answer these four fundamental questions for your audience. Sometimes you will have to present proof for all four of them; sometimes your audience will already agree with you on the answer to one or two, and you can concentrate on answering the remaining questions.

From what has been said about the three types of propositions, you can readily see how important it is that you completely understand the proposition. Work out a concise statement of your proposition and be able to explain it clearly to your audience. Unless you can make your hearers understand exactly *what* you propose, there is very little reason for trying to get them to see *why*. Moreover, you will often find it important to have a thorough grasp of the historical background of your subject and particularly of any recent events which have made its consideration important.

ORGANIZATION

Speech seeking endorsement of a proposition of policy In Chapter 16 we saw how the motivated sequence could be applied to a speech to convince on a proposition of policy. In speeches of this sort, the speaker (*1*) secures the audience's *attention;* (*2*) shows that because of existing deficiencies or evils there is a *need* for some action; (*3*) provides *satisfaction* for this need by presenting a remedy which will remove the evils or deficiencies; (*4*) *visualizes* the benefits to be obtained from believing or acting as he proposes; and (*5*) requests the *action* or approval indicated.[1]

---

[1] At this point you should carefully review pages 293–301 of Chapter 16 where these steps are explained and illustrated.

*Speech opposing
endorsement of a
proposition of policy* On the other hand, the speaker who opposes a policy ("We should *not* deprive freshmen of the right to own and drive cars") will also try to capture attention, but he will then proceed by denying any or all of the contentions embodied in steps (*2*), (*3*), and (*4*). Thus he may argue:

(*a*) There is no need for a change; things are perfectly all right as they are.
(*b*) The proposed change is not practicable; it would not remove the alleged problem or deficiency.
(*c*) Instead of bringing benefits or advantages, the proposed policy would actually introduce new and worse evils; it would be costly, unfair, dangerous to our liberties, difficult to administer, etc.

Sometimes you will be able to use all three of these contentions in developing a speech to oppose a policy. On other occasions you will find that only one or two of them apply, and your speech must be limited to them. Proof beyond reasonable doubt on any of the three, however, will cause an earnest listener to reject a proposal, since obviously he will not want to adopt a policy that is unneeded or impracticable or productive of new problems and evils. Proof beyond reasonable doubt on all three contentions would, of course, constitute the strongest possible case against the endorsement of a proposed change.

Here is a partial skeleton outline of a speech in which a proposed action is opposed on the threefold ground that it is unneeded, impracticable, and undesirable. (For purposes of simplification, the attention step and supporting material have been omitted.)

THE PROPOSED TURNPIKE

Unneeded I. The turnpike from Ashton to Waterton proposed by the Governor's Committee on Highways is not needed.
A. The existing highway connecting the two cities is only three years old and in excellent condition.
B. Automobile traffic between Ashton and Waterton, instead of increasing, has actually decreased 6 percent during the last decade.

Impracticable II. Even if the proposed turnpike were needed, it would be impracticable.
  A. State funds for road construction are at an all-time low.
  B. Borrowing for road construction is difficult and costly in the present bond market.

Undesirable III. Finally, even if such a turnpike were both needed and practicable, its construction would be undesirable.
  A. It would impose a serious hardship on owners of motels, filling stations, restaurants, and other businesses along the present highway.
  B. The suggested route would spoil the Ashton State Park.

Speech seeking belief or disbelief in a proposition of fact Many speeches seek to prove that something is or is not so ("Good study habits result in good grades"). Questions of whether or not something is so may often be settled by personal observation, by conducting a controlled experiment, or by looking up the answer in a reliable printed source. Thus it would be absurd for men to argue whether it is raining outside, or whether the fruit in a certain basket is contaminated, or whether a particular train is the fastest one between Chicago and New York. The first of these questions of fact could be settled by glancing out the window, the second by making appropriate chemical tests, and the third by referring to a timetable.

But now consider these questions: Is Russia ahead of us in the space race? Do the countries of Latin America resent United States interference in their affairs? Is knowledge a virtue? Is Jones guilty of embezzlement as charged? Because they inquire whether something is or is not so, these too are questions of fact. But in answering them, none of the methods mentioned in the preceding paragraph would be conclusive. While observation or experimentation or printed data may help us arrive at a decision, in the end we must depend upon our own informed judgment—upon reasoning from the best facts available to what appears to be the most accurate or fairest answer; upon bringing together as much evidence as possible, establishing criteria by which to judge the evidence, and testing the evidence by the criteria. On factual questions of this sort, men can and do make speeches trying to convince others that the opinion they are presenting is a correct judgment and should therefore be adopted.

How should speeches on factual questions be organized and developed? As in the case of policy speeches, the motivated sequence furnishes the basic pattern, needing only to be adapted to meet the special requirements imposed by the nature of the subject.

1. Secure the *attention* and interest of the audience.
2. State clearly the question that is to be decided, and show your listeners why a decision is *needed*. Do this by pointing out either (*a*) why the question concerns them personally or (*b*) why it concerns the community, state, nation, or world of which they are a part. (With the need made clear, you may, if you wish, set forth the criteria upon which an acceptable answer to the question must rest.)
3. *Satisfy* the need developed in the preceding step by advancing what you believe to be the correct answer to the question under consideration and offering evidence and argument to support your view (and showing how this answer meets the criteria specified).[2]
4. *Visualize* for your listeners the advantages they will gain by accepting the answer you recommend or the evils and dangers they will incur by rejecting it.
5. Appeal for *action*—for acceptance of your proposed answer and a determination to adhere to it.

These steps are illustrated in the following skeleton outline:

OUR STUDENT GOVERNMENT

Attention   I. State University has one of the oldest and most widely imitated systems of student government in the entire nation.

---

[2] Sometimes a question of fact involves a term or set of terms which the audience may not immediately understand. In such cases, develop the satisfaction step in two separate steps. First define the crucial term or terms, and then show how the facts or circumstances peculiar to the present case fall within the definition thus established. For example, if a lawyer wished to prove to a jury that a certain person is mentally incompetent, he would first make clear the legal definition of *mental incompetence* and then demonstrate how this person's behavior justifies placing him within this category. Usually, however, the procedure outlined above (advancing your view and supporting it directly with evidence and argument) will be sufficient.

A. It was founded in 1883, when student government was almost entirely unknown.
B. Many of the leaders of our state and nation gained their first practical administrative experience as campus officers.
C. Representatives of many other colleges and universities have visited State to study how our student government is organized and to watch it in operation.

(Statement of question) II. Has our student government, once a free and powerful institution, become a mere tool of the dean of men and the university administration?

Need I. This is a question of vital importance to each of us.
A. The prestige of the university is at stake.
B. Our freedom as students to govern ourselves and conduct our own affairs is endangered.

Satisfaction (Answer to question) I. In recent years the dean of men and other administrative officers of the university have encroached upon the rights and powers of our student government.

(Supporting evidence)
A. All actions of the Student Senate must now have administrative approval.
B. The budgets of student organizations must be approved and their accounts audited by the university treasurer's office.
C. The election of class officers is conducted under the supervision of the dean.[3]

Visualization (Warning of future evils) I. Unless we are all aware of these serious encroachments upon our traditional rights as students and consider steps to oppose or counteract them, further encroachments will almost certainly occur.

Action I. Make these facts known to your fellow students.
II. Resolve that student government will once again be a strong and vital force on this campus.

---

[3] What criteria for judging the proposition of fact are implicit in these three points?

If your purpose is to uphold the negative position on a question of fact (in this case, to prove that the administration has *not* infringed upon student rights and privileges), proceed in exactly the same way, except offer a negative rather than an affirmative proposition at the beginning of the satisfaction step and present evidence and argument that justify this stand.

Speech seeking belief or disbelief in a proposition of value Whereas questions of fact ask whether something is so, questions of value, you will recall, inquire whether something is good or bad. Typical questions of value are: Is progressive education desirable? Are big-time athletics detrimental to the best interests of college students? Was Harry Truman one of our "great" presidents?

When speaking on a question of value, with a view to convincing your listeners that they should agree with your estimate of a man, practice, institution, or theory, you may adapt the basic pattern of the motivated sequence as follows:

1. Capture the audience's *attention* and interest.
2. Make clear that an estimate concerning the worth of the man, practice, or institution is *needed*. Do this by showing either (*a*) why an estimate is important to your listeners personally or (*b*) why it is important to the community, state, nation, or world of which they are a part. (With the *need* made clear, you may, as in the case of a speech on a proposition of fact, set forth the criteria upon which an appropriate estimate must rest.)
3. *Satisfy* the need developed in the preceding step by advancing what you believe to be the correct estimate (and showing how this estimate meets the criteria specified).
4. *Visualize* the advantages that will accrue from agreeing with the estimate you offer or the evils and dangers that will follow from endorsing an alternative estimate.
5. Appeal for *action*—for the acceptance of the proposed estimate and a determination to retain it.

Each of these basic steps is present in the following skeleton speech outline.

THE VALUES OF INTERCOLLEGIATE DEBATING

Attention   I. In recent years intercollegiate debating has come under strong attack from many quarters.
- A. Philosophers and social scientists charge that debate is a poor way to get at the truth concerning a disputable matter.
- B. Educators charge that debate teaches the student to approach a problem with an "either-or" attitude, thus causing him to develop habits of contentiousness and dogmatism rather than of fact-centered objectivity.

Need
(Evaluation
necessary)   I. How we evaluate debate is important to each of us for at least two reasons:
- A. As students we help support the debate program on this campus because a portion of our activity fee is allocated to the Debate Society.
- B. As citizens in a democratic society we are concerned because the method of decision-making employed in intercollegiate debating is essentially the same as that employed in the courtroom and the legislative assembly.

(Criteria)   II. As is true of any extracurricular activity, there are two important criteria by which debate can be evaluated:
- A. Does it develop abilities and traits of mind which will aid the student in his course work?
- B. Does it develop abilities and traits of mind which will be of value in later life?

Satisfaction
(Evaluation
provided)   I. The experience of many years has shown that debate is valuable.
- A. Debate helps the student do better work in his courses.
  1. It teaches him to study a subject thoroughly and systematically.
  2. It teaches him to analyze complex ideas quickly and logically.
  3. It teaches him to speak and write clearly and convincingly.
- B. Training in debate is of value in later life.
  1. It teaches courtesy and fair play.
  2. It develops self-confidence and poise.

Visualization	I. Picture the serious student of debate in the classroom and in his post-college career. A. As a student he will know how to study, analyze, and present material. B. As a business or professional man he will be better able to meet arguments and to express his views in a fair and effective manner.
Action	I. Remember these facts whenever you hear the value of intercollegiate debating questioned. A. The contribution debate training makes to business or professional success has been eloquently affirmed by many thousands of prominent men and women who were themselves debaters in college. B. We should encourage and support this worth-while activity in every way we can.

A negative speech on a question of value (for instance, a speech intended to prove that debating does *not* provide desirable and useful training) may be developed according to the same general pattern. But instead of showing that the practice or institution in question meets the criteria outlined in the need step, you will show that it *fails* to meet them. The visualization step would probably attempt to show that college debate experience was not merely useless to a person in his business or profession after college but even harmful.

THE MANNER OF SPEAKING

To recommend any uniform style of delivery for the speech to convince is impossible. Your delivery will depend upon the situation in which you find yourself—upon the occasion and the audience. Your manner in talking to a small group of businessmen in an executive meeting will, of course, be different from your manner in addressing a large audience at a public gathering. Moreover, your delivery before an apathetic audience will differ from your delivery before either an interested group or a hostile one. In general, however, a straightforward, energetic presentation that suggests enthusiasm without seeming overemotional is most effective in securing conviction.

Concrete facts and vivid illustrations

As in every other type of speech, you should avoid generalities and abstractions in a speech to convince. Use facts and figures that are within the experience of the audience. Incidents that are recent, common, or particularly striking are most powerful in securing conviction. No other single factor is so important in this type of speech as presenting facts, pertinent facts—and then more facts. Review the forms of support discussed in Chapter 12 and fill your speech with them.

Sound, logical reasoning

Regardless of how much detailed and concrete evidence you present, your speech will not carry strong conviction unless your reasoning is sound. A brief consideration of the three most frequently used forms of reasoning is therefore imperative.

Reasoning from example. This form of reasoning consists of drawing conclusions about a general class of objects by studying individual members of that class. For instance, if a housewife were in doubt about the flavor of the apples in a bushel basket, she would bite into one of them to test its flavor. If it tasted all right, she would reason that all the apples in the basket had a good flavor. Or perhaps, if she were a bit skeptical, she might dig down to the bottom to find out if all the apples seemed to be the same. This sort of reasoning is employed in most of our thinking, whether the point at issue is big or little. Scientific experiments, laboratory tests, the determination of social trends—all these employ the process of reasoning from example. Reasoning of this sort should be tested by answering the following questions:

1. Are there enough examples for a thorough sampling? One robin does not make a spring; nor do two or three examples prove that a general proposition is incontestably true.
2. Are the examples chosen fairly? To show that something is true in New York, Chicago, and Boston—all large cities— does not prove it true all over the country.
3. Are there any outstanding exceptions? One well-known instance which differs from the general conclusion you urge

will cause doubt unless you show that this instance is the result of unusual circumstances.

Reasoning from axiom. This form of reasoning consists of applying some accepted principle to a specific situation. For example, it is generally conceded that by buying in large quantities one may get merchandise more cheaply than by buying in small lots. When you argue that chain stores save money by purchasing goods in large quantities, therefore, you are merely applying this general rule to the specific instance—the chain store. Reasoning from axiom may be tested as follows:

1. Is the axiom, or rule, true? For many years people believed the world was flat. Many high-sounding assertions which pass for the truth are merely prejudices or superstitions. Before applying an axiom, make sure of its validity. But, no matter how true a principle may be, if your listeners do not believe it, you cannot base an argument upon it unless you can first convince them of its truth.

2. Does the axiom apply to the specific situation in question? There are too many loose applications of perfectly good rules. For instance, to argue, on the basis of the principle mentioned above, that chain stores buy goods more cheaply in large quantities, is perfectly valid; but to argue on this same basis that the customer can buy goods from the chain stores at a lower price is not valid. Some additional form of proof would be required to establish this further contention.

Reasoning from causal relation. When something happens, most of us believe that it must have a cause; and when we see a force in operation we realize that it will produce some definite effect. A great deal of our reasoning is based on this relationship between cause and effect. The rate of violent crime goes up, and we hasten to lay the blame on war, on bad housing, on public apathy, on inept public officials. We hear that the star on our football team is in the hospital with a broken ankle, and we immediately become apprehensive about the results of Saturday's game. We reason from known effects to inferred causes and from known causes to inferred effects. There is perhaps no other form of reasoning so often used by public speakers, nor is there any form of reasoning which may contain so many flaws. Test such reasoning for soundness by asking:

1. Has the cause been mistaken for the result? When two phenomena occur simultaneously, it is sometimes hard to tell which is the cause and which is the effect. Do higher wages cause higher prices, or is the reverse true?
2. Is the cause strong enough to produce the result? A small pebble on the track will not derail a passenger train, but a large boulder will. Be careful that you don't mistake a pebble for a boulder.
3. Has anything prevented the cause from operating? If a gun is not loaded, pulling the trigger will not make it shoot. Be certain that nothing has prevented the free operation of the cause which you assume has produced the situation.
4. Could any other cause have produced the same result? Four different possible causes were listed above for the increase in violent crime, each one urged by some persons as the sole cause. Be sure that you diagnose the situation correctly; don't put the blame on the wrong thing nor all the blame on one thing if the blame should be divided.
5. Does any causal connection exist at all? Sometimes people assume that merely because one thing happens immediately before another, they are causally connected. Developing a severe chest pain shortly after you have had a bad fall wouldn't necessarily mean that the pain was a result of the fall. Do not mistake a coincidence for a cause-effect relationship.

TECHNICS OF THE SPEECH TO CONVINCE

The most important characteristic of a speech to convince—indeed, more important than all the other characteristics put together—is that it is audience-oriented. In other words, you should always speak with the viewpoint of your audience in mind. You cannot sell a man an automobile just because you like it; you must approach him on the basis of his needs and desires. You cannot get a group of people to believe or act as you want them to unless you understand how they view your proposal. In no other type of speech is a thorough analysis of your listeners quite so important. You must find out all you can about them—their likes and dislikes, their attitude toward your proposition, and their habits of thought. Put yourself in their places and look at the problem as they look at it. With the viewpoint of the audience constantly in mind, utilize to the utmost the following technics.

Appeals to the dominant motives of the audience

Your speech must not only exhibit sound, logical reasoning and include many concrete facts and vivid illustrations, but it must also contain effective appeals to the motives for human action (see Chapter 10). You must convince your audience that their basic desires will be better satisfied if they do what you propose. You may prove that they are losing money under present conditions or that they will save money by approving your plan, but underlying all this proof is the appeal to the motive of saving.

Identifying your proposal with existing beliefs

Find out what your listeners' attitudes and beliefs are, and, if possible, show that your proposal embodies their values. For example, if your listeners believe that advertising is important, show how your proposal will act as advertising. If they believe in reciprocal trading in business, show that your plan embodies that idea. If they are opposed to communism, show how your proposal will serve to combat it. You will usually be able to find ways of linking your proposition with at least some of your audience's fixed opinions. Even when your plan is in exact opposition to some strong belief of your audience, you may be able to offset that disadvantage by balancing against that belief some equally strong belief in your favor.

The "yes-response" technic

Do not begin your speech with the idea your listeners will find most difficult to accept. Instead, begin with ideas you know they will approve of. If you get them into the habit of agreeing with you, you will lessen their resistance to your later arguments. Don't begin by saying, "I know you have a lot of objections to this plan, but you're all wrong about it," as did a man trying to persuade a group of stockholders to vote for a mining merger. A better beginning would have been, "You are interested in getting the greatest return on your investment consistent with safety." He could then have shown how the merger would produce this result.

The "this-or-nothing" technic — Show the impossibility of believing or doing anything other than what you propose. People often reject a proposition because they do not realize that it is the best one possible. By showing that there are only (let us say) three possible courses of action, two of which are undesirable, you will cut off all avenues of escape save the one you advocate. Thus, if you explain that the only alternatives to bankruptcy are heavy borrowing and curtailment of operating expense, you may, by showing the impossibility of further extension of credit, secure approval for your program of reduced expenses.

If you speak from the viewpoint of your listeners, present concrete facts and vivid illustrations which are within their experience, use sound reasoning, appeal to dominant motives, identify your proposal with their existing beliefs, employ the "yes-response," and use the "this-or-nothing" technic, you will be better able to secure the decision you seek.

While people are—or should be—convinced chiefly through logical reasoning and evidence, they often *act* largely because they *feel* as they do. Most of us, for example, are concerned for the safety of our families and ourselves, but we seldom take any active steps to insure safety until we experience and fear some actual threat to our well-being—epidemic, fire, flood, and so on. Together with logic and evidence, therefore, the speaker must employ vivid descriptions appealing to the basic desires and emotions which underlie his logic.

Appeals of this sort are particularly important in the visualization step; in fact, this step should always be descriptive and should usually contain a strong emotional appeal. Elsewhere in your speech, an occasional vivid example will add a dynamic quality to your argument which sound logic alone will not give. However, except in the visualization step, do not substitute emotional appeals for logic and evidence—use both. Make your logical argument vivid and compelling, and you will have the essence of an effective persuasive speech.

Earlier in this chapter we examined several of the more common forms of the speech to convince, and we saw that in each case the five-step structure of attention, need, satisfaction, visualization, and action was used. The detailed development of any particular speech to convince as it will actually be delivered, however, must be adapted to the audience's attitude toward the speaker's proposal. Let us, therefore, as a final step in our study of speaking to convince, consider some of the attitudes an audience may display toward a proposition and the adaptations which the speaker must make to each.[4]

Audience interested in the situation but undecided Some audiences are conscious that a problem or a need for decision exists, but they are uncertain as to what belief they should adopt or what course of action they should pursue. Therefore, your primary purpose is to get them to agree that your proposal is the best one possible.

Attention step. Since the audience is already interested in the situation, the attention step may be brief. Often it consists of a direct reference to the question or problem to be decided. At other times a brief example or story illustrating the problem is appropriate. When using this second method, however, take care to center your listeners' attention on the heart of the matter rather than on side issues or irrelevant details. Focus their thinking on fundamentals by excluding all but the central issue under consideration.

Need step. Review briefly the basic problem out of which the question or point for decision has grown. Summarize its causes and historical development if this will help your hearers understand the problem more clearly. Also, restate in a few words the scope and nature of the existing situation, and show why an immediate decision is imperative. Finally, you may set forth the standards or criteria which a sound decision must meet.

Satisfaction step. This will be the most important, and probably

---

[4] See chart on pages 612–613 of the Reference Manual where these methods of adaptation are summarized.

the longest, part of your speech. State the proposition or plan of action you wish your hearers to adopt, and define any vague or ambiguous terms. Show specifically how your proposal will satisfy the criteria outlined in the need step—why it will provide a practicable and desirable answer to the question under consideration. Proceed to demonstrate the benefits of your proposition and its superiority to any alternative proposal. Prove each of your contentions with an abundance of fact, figures, testimony, and examples.

Visualization step. Make this step rather brief in relation to the rest of the speech. Be vivid and persuasive, but don't exaggerate. Project the audience into the future by painting a realistic picture of the desirable conditions which will be brought about by approving your proposition or the evils that will result from rejecting it.

Action step. Restate in clear and forceful language your request for belief or for acceptance of the plan you advocate. Recapitulate briefly the principal arguments presented earlier in the speech.

Audience interested in the situation but hostile to the proposal   Other audiences are conscious that a problem exists or that a question must be decided but are opposed to the particular belief or plan of action you wish them to accept. Often this hostility is based either on a fear that some undesirable result will accompany the proposed action or on a positive preference for an alternative belief or policy. Sometimes the hostility is a reflection of deeply engrained prejudices. In any case, your goal must be to overcome existing objections and secure the acceptance of your ideas.

Attention step. This step is similar to that developed for the undecided audience. However, since you know there will be hostility toward your proposition or plan of action, you should try, first of all, to conciliate your audience and win a hearing. Approach your proposition indirectly and gradually. Concede whatever you can to your audience's point of view; establish common ground by emphasizing points of agreement; minimize or explain away differences. Make your listeners feel that you are genuinely interested in achieving the same results they are.[5]

---

[5] Review the discussion of common ground on page 161 of Chapter 9.

Need step. Secure agreement on some basic principle or belief and use this principle as the criterion by which to measure the soundness of the proposition you advance. Otherwise, develop this step as you would for an audience that is interested but undecided.

Satisfaction step. Show specifically how the proposed belief or plan of action meets the criterion established in the preceding step. Offer strong and extensive proof of the superiority of your proposal to any other proposition which you have reason to believe your listeners may favor. (But do not imply that you know they favor an alternative plan, or you may have to combat their embarrassment in admitting they have made a mistake.) Otherwise, develop this step in the same way you would if you were addressing an undecided audience.

Visualization and action steps. If you have been successful thus far, your audience should be in the same frame of mind as the audience discussed previously—that is, interested in the question but undecided about what to think or do. The development of your speech from this point on, therefore, will follow the pattern outlined above, with special emphasis on the visualization, or benefits, step.

Audience apathetic to the situation

In contrast to the two audience attitudes just discussed, hearers who are apathetic to the situation are not interested in the question at all. They say, "What's it to me?" "I should worry about that." "That's up to George." Obviously, with such persons your main object is to make them realize that the question *does* affect them—that they must assume a direct responsibility for arriving at a proper decision.

Attention step. Overcome apathy and inertia by touching briefly some vital spot of your listeners' self-interest. Present one or two striking facts or figures, and use vivid phraseology to show how their health, happiness, security, prosperity, chances for advancement, etc., are directly involved.

Need step. With interest thus aroused, proceed to demonstrate fully and systematically how the question under discussion affects each member of the audience. Relate the problem to the audience by showing: (*a*) its direct and immediate effect upon them; (*b*) its effects on their families, friends, business interests, the social and professional groups to which they belong, etc.; (c) its probable future effects.

In showing these effects, employ the strongest possible evidence —specific instances and illustrations, striking statistics, strong testimony—and emphasize little known or startling facts and conditions. This step will nearly always need to be longer in a speech to an apathetic audience than in a speech directed to either of the audiences already discussed. It will also require more impressive proof and more energetic delivery. From this point, however, you may develop your speech in the same manner as for an audience that is interested but undecided.

Audience hostile to belief in the existence of a problem   If an audience is hostile because they don't believe a problem exists, you must overcome their hostility at the outset, or your speech will have little chance of success. Your listeners favor things as they are and, therefore, stoutly resist any proposed change in belief or policy.

Attention step. Get on a common footing with the audience in the first few minutes by the use of the common ground or yes-response technics. Recognize their point of view, and admit whatever merits it may have, without in any way degrading your own. As early as possible secure agreement on an acceptable criterion by which to judge the belief or policy you intend to advance. Support this criterion by quoting the testimony of persons who are respected by members of the audience—if possible, persons from among their own number.

Need step. Show at some length exactly how your audience's present belief or the existing situation violates the criterion laid down in the preceding step and therefore must be corrected. Since this is the point concerning which your hearers are skeptical or uninformed, use powerful facts, figures, and especially testimony to establish your argument. Watch, however, that you do not exaggerate. Instead of stilling opposition, stretching the facts will create stronger opposition.

After convincing your hearers that the present belief or condition violates the criterion agreed upon, you may develop the rest of your speech as you would if you were addressing an audience that is interested in the question but hostile to the proposal.

Real-life audiences, obviously, are seldom as clear-cut and uniform in their attitudes as the foregoing discussion would seem to suggest. But if you can determine the attitude of the majority or of the more influential part of an audience, you can usually develop an effective speech by following one of the four plans outlined or by employing a combination of them.

Remember, too, that there are times when it will be helpful to develop the need and satisfaction steps of a speech in parallel order, as explained on pages 297–299 of Chapter 16. When this method is used, separate aspects of the need are discussed one at a time, together with that particular part of the plan or proposal which will satisfy it. The division of points may often be made according to the criteria advanced as a basis for judgment. Thus, you might first consider the "cost" criterion—that is, the desirability of adopting a proposal that will prove as economical as possible —and show how your proposition meets this test. Then present certain social or cultural criteria, and demonstrate that the proposal satisfies each of them. Finally, indicate the desirability of having a plan that would be flexible enough to meet changing conditions, and show that your proposed plan has this quality. In this way a complete case for your proposal would be developed in appropriate segments.

Whatever method of organization you employ, you must always keep in mind the attitude of your listeners toward your proposition; you must always talk from the point of view of the people who are sitting before you. Notice how the following student outline, supporting a proposed policy or course of action, is adapted to an interested but undecided audience. Notice also how Mrs. Luce skillfully adapts her arguments to a potentially hostile audience in the speech at the close of this chapter.

FILTERING OUR INDUSTRIAL WASTE

> *This is an outline of a student speech given by Howard Brown before an audience presumed to be the board of directors of the Central Fibre Products Company, presenting the recommendation of that company's production engineer.*

Attention step   I. The decision we reach today can mean greater profit for Central Fibre or a continuation of our practice of literally throwing money down the drain.

Need step   I. Our present waste disposal method is seriously inadequate.
    A. We need to diminish the amount of stream pollution caused by the waste water of our plant.
        1. Pressure has been brought under National Law #3972 and a corresponding state law by the State Board of Sanitation.
        2. The pollution we cause is equivalent to that of a city of 60,000 population.
    B. We are letting substantial profits drain into the Wabash River.
        1. Every minute we discharge water containing from three to twelve pounds of minute usable fiber.
        2. Every day we pump 15,500,000 gallons of water which we heat, use, and discharge into the river.
            a. This water carries with it countless B.T.U.'s we have added.

  II. In short, our disposal is both illegal and inefficient.

(*Criteria stated*) III. We need a practical solution of this problem that will meet the following requirements:
    A. The discharged water must be brought within the standards required by state and national laws.
    B. The system must be reliable in operation.
    C. It must be economical.
    D. It should reduce our present waste.
    E. If possible, it should help improve the quality of our product.

Satisfaction step   I. The installation of an Oliver Vacuum 8 x 10 Saveall in our mill will solve our problem.
    A. The Saveall would be conveniently located at the west end of the machine room in our mill.
        1. Here it would be close to the machines, screens, digestors, and beaters.
    B. Here is the way it operates:
        1. This oversize flow sheet shows the simplified operation of the Saveall in paper

mill use. (Show and explain chart.)

    2. These detailed working drawings and actual photographs of the Saveall show how it has been installed at other mills. (Show drawings and pictures.)

(Criteria satisfied)

C. The Saveall will meet the requirements of a practical solution:

    1. It will reduce our stream pollution below the legal limits allowed by statute. (Read specifications and guarantee.)

    2. The Oliver Filter Company is a very reliable firm of world-wide reputation.

        a. The Saveall was designed for paper mill use.

        b. Savealls are being used successfully by 1300 paper mills in all parts of the world.

    3. The plan is economical.

        a. The original cost of the Saveall will be $75,000.

        b. Since servicing is done by the Oliver Company, upkeep will be small.

        c. Added labor costs will be nil.

    4. Savealls in a short time will pay for themselves in the amount of fiber recovered.

        a. The Terre Haute Paper Company reports a saving of 660 tons of fiber last year.

        b. The Tama, Iowa, mill has shown a 900 ton saving per year.

    5. By reusing the "white" or clear water processed by the Saveall, higher grade products can be made.

        a. The Terre Haute mill has produced better products.

        b. The Tama mill also improved the quality of their products.

II. The Oliver Saveall is a practical and economical solution to our problem.

Visualization step

I. By installing an Oliver Saveall we can save an average of five pounds of fiber per minute—seven tons a day.

A. At $15 a ton, in one day our saving would be $105.

B. Inside of two and one-half years the Saveall will have paid for itself. (Show graph of cumulated savings vs. cost.)

II. The clear water we use will be free of river refuse.

A. This will speed up production.

B. It will give us a better grade product.

III. We shall be free from danger of legal action because of stream pollution.

Action step

I. I recommend we accept the Oliver Saveall and order it immediately.

A. The law demands action on our part.

B. An Oliver Saveall will meet that demand at the same time it ends the flow of thousands of our dollars down the Wabash.

SAMPLE SPEECHES

In the following two speeches, observe how the technics suggested in this chapter have been employed. The first speech ("What's Wrong with the American Press?" pp. 438–447) is provided with relatively full comments and analysis; the second ("Communications and Medicine," pp. 448–454) is provided with only brief comments and indications of the main divisions of the speech. Using the technics illustrated in the analysis of the first speech, you may wish to attempt a similar analysis of the second speech.

Preliminary comments on Mrs. Luce's speech

Few women have achieved distinction in so many different fields of endeavor as has Clare Boothe Luce. Author, editor, playwright, war correspondent, lecturer, congresswoman, and ambassadress, Mrs. Luce is perhaps even more widely known than her famous husband, Henry Luce, publisher of Time, Inc., publications.

Many of the talents which enabled Mrs. Luce to attain high rank in these varied pursuits are evident in the following speech which she delivered on April 21, 1960, to the Women's National Press Club at a dinner in honor of the American Society of Newspaper Editors. Defending a proposition of value before an interested but potentially hostile audience (see pp. 429–430), Mrs. Luce displayed not only a thorough command of her subject combined with sound reasoning and common sense but also the equally important qualities of tact, fairness, and courage. These qualities were all needed because Mrs. Luce attempted to frankly tell a group of journalists and editors what she believed was "wrong" with them and with the American press in general.

As you will see when you study her talk, Mrs. Luce approaches her central idea indirectly and gradually. During the first few moments she repeatedly uses the technics of concession, conciliation, and compliment to help her win a hearing and pave the way for her major contentions. Once she reaches these contentions, she states them boldly and explains and defends them at length.

Considered in terms of the motivated sequence, Mrs. Luce's speech falls into four major divisions. First comes a combined attention and need step some eighteen paragraphs in length. In this step, contact is made with the audience, the subject of the talk is disclosed and clarified, and an atmosphere of good will is established by Mrs. Luce's full recognition of what is admittedly "right" with the press. The step concludes with a clear statement of the abstract standard or criterion by which Mrs. Luce believes the quality of American journalism must ultimately be measured (last two sentences of paragraph 18).

The satisfaction step, beginning with paragraph 19, also works by indirection, employing examples and explanation to show how the press falls short of the ideal desired. Not until this step is well advanced are the speaker's two specific charges against the press openly stated (paragraph 28).

A relatively short visualization step is introduced by means of a humorous anecdote (paragraph 47) and developed by the method of contrast. An even shorter action step (paragraph 51), couched in the form of a challenge and containing an idealistic and patriotic appeal, concludes the talk.

While supporting material is present in considerable quantities throughout the speech, it is interesting to note that relatively little of it is concrete. Instead of massing incidents, cases, stories, and statistics to subtantiate her contentions, Mrs. Luce usually depends upon explanation or generalized references or examples to support her views. Moreover, she artfully employs her own prestige as a journalist and public figure to help underwrite her criticisms of the press and bolster her proposed remedies.

A second interesting feature of the speech is that, except in the action step, relatively little use is made of motivation or emotional appeal. Consequently, the total impression one receives is that of an intelligent and sensible woman presenting in a tactful, good-humored, and yet courageous way ideas that are the result of her own careful study and reflection on the problem.

The style of Mrs. Luce's talk is especially worthy of study. Not only is the expression consistently clear and facile, but, without at any time becoming obtrusive, it is often made vivid by striking phrases and figures of speech—especially rhetorical questions, used both as a means of emphasis and as transitions linking major ideas. From this point of view, the speech provides a good example of how a style may contribute to the general end of persuasion.

Mrs. Luce was born in New York City in 1903. She attended St. Mary's School in Garden City, Long Island, and graduated from Miss Mason's School, the Castle, in Tarrytown, New York. She has been granted honorary degrees by Colby College, Creighton University, and Georgetown University.

Following an unsuccessful first marriage to society sportsman George Tuttle Brokaw, Mrs. Luce was named an associate editor of *Vogue* in 1930. In 1931 she transferred to *Vanity Fair* and by 1933 had become managing editor of that magazine. After her marriage to Henry Luce in 1935, she expanded her journalistic and literary activities to include the writing of books and plays, and during World War II she served as a correspondent on both the European and Asiatic fronts. In 1942 Mrs. Luce was elected to Congress, where she remained until 1947. President Eisenhower appointed her ambassadress to Italy in 1953, a post which she filled until forced to retire four years later because of ill health.

As a playwright Mrs. Luce's most notable success was *The Women,* produced on Broadway in 1937 and later made into an extremely popular movie. Other plays for which she is remembered include *Kiss the Boys Goodbye* (1938), *Margin for Error* (1939), and *Child of the Morning* (1951). Among Mrs. Luce's several books perhaps the best known is *Europe in the Spring* (1940), a first-hand study of that continent on the eve of World War II.

WHAT'S WRONG WITH THE AMERICAN PRESS? [6]

Attention and need steps combined

Potential hostility of audience recognized

Conciliation through humor

I am happy and flattered to be a guest of honor on this always exciting and challenging occasion. But looking over this audience tonight I am less happy than you might think and more challenged than you could know. I stand here at this rostrum invited to throw rocks at you. You have asked *me* to tell *you* what's wrong with *you*—the American press. The subject not only is of great national significance but also has, one should say, infinite possibilities—and infinite perils to the rock thrower. /1

For the banquet speaker who criticizes the weaknesses and pretensions, or exposes the follies and sins of his listeners—even at their invitation—does not generally evoke an enthusiastic—no less a friendly—response. The delicate art of giving an audience hell is always one best left to the Billy Grahams and the Bishop Sheens. /2

Conciliation through compliment to audience

Appeal for a fair hearing

A basic truth or principle with which audience will probably agree readily

But you are an audience of journalists. There is no audience anywhere who should be more bored—indeed, more revolted—by a speaker who tried to fawn on it, butter it up, exaggerate its virtues, play down its faults, and who would more quickly see through any attempt to do so. I ask you only to remember that I am not a volunteer for this subject tonight. You asked for it! /3

For what is good journalism all about? On a working, finite level it is the effort to achieve illuminating candor in print and to strip away cant. It is the effort to do this not only in matters of state, diplomacy and politics but also in every smaller aspect of life that touches the public interest or engages proper public curiosity. It is the effort to explain everything from a summit conference to why the moon looks larger coming over the horizon than it does when it has fully risen in the heavens. It is the effort too to describe the lives of men—and women—big and small, close at hand or thousands of miles away, familiar in their behavior or unfamiliar in their idiosyncrasies. It is—to use the big word—the pursuit of and the effort to state the truth. /4

[6] From *Vital Speeches of the Day*, Vol. XXVI, June 15, 1960, pp. 538–541. Reprinted by permission of Mrs. Luce.

No audience knows better than an audience of journalists that the pursuit of the truth, and the articulation of it, is the most delicate, hazardous, exacting and *inexact* of tasks. Consequently, no audience is more forgiving (I hope) to the speaker who fails or stumbles in his own pursuit of it. The only failure this audience could never excuse in any speaker would be the failure to try to tell the truth, as he sees it, about his subject. /5

A second appeal for a fair hearing

In my perilous but earnest effort to do so here tonight, I must begin by saying that if there is much that is wrong with the American press, there is also much that is right with it. /6

I know then, that you will bear with me, much as it may go against your professional grain, if I ask you to accept some of the *good* with the bad—even though it may not make such good copy for your newspapers. /7

For the plain fact is that the U. S. daily press today is not inspiringly good; it is just far and away the best press in the world. /8

To begin with, its news gathering, news printing, news dissemination techniques and capacities are without rivals on the globe. /9

The deserving American journalist himself enjoys a far more elevated status than his foreign counterpart anywhere. And this, not only because Americans passionately believe that a free press is vital to the preservation of our form of democracy, but because the average American journalist has, on the record, shown himself to be less venal, less corrupt, and more responsible than the average journalist of many foreign lands. /10

No capital under the sun has a press corps that is better equipped, and more eager to get the news, the news behind the news, and the news ahead of the news, the inside—outside—topside—bottomside news, than the Washington press corps. /11

I must add only half-jokingly that if the nation's dailies are overwhelmingly pro-Republican in their editorial policy, then the Washington press corps is a large corrective for this political imbalance. Not because Washington reporters are *all* Democrats. Rather because they place on the administration in power their white-hot spotlight of curiosity and exposure. So that no one—Republican or Democrat—

The annotations in the left margin read:

Transition introducing the major idea of the combined attention-need step

Conciliation through humor

Explanation and support of proposition advanced in paragraph 8

Conciliation through compliment to audience

Conciliation through humor

can sit complacently in office in this capital unobserved by the men and women of the press who provide the news and information that can make or break an elected or appointed office-holder. /12

Ideas emphasized and style enlivened by use of rhetorical questions

Certainly no press corps contains more journalists of competence and distinction, zeal and dedication. What minds regularly tap more "reliable sources" in government, politics, diplomacy? What breasts guard and unguard more "high level" confidences more jealously? What hearts struggle more conscientiously and painfully to determine to what extent truth-telling, or shall we say "leaking," will serve or unserve the public interest? What typewriters send out more facts, figures, statistics, views, and opinions about great public questions and great public figures? /13

And in what other country of the world are there so many great newspapers? Who could seriously challenge the pre-eminence among the big-city quality press of the New York *Times?* Where in the world is there a "provincial" newpaper (I use the term only in its technical sense) greater than, to take only one outstanding example, the Milwaukee *Journal?* Even the biggest and splashiest of the foreign English-language press, the London *Daily Mirror,* cannot touch in popular journalism the New York *Daily News.* (And since we are talking in superlatives—good and bad—is there a worse paper in England, Japan, France or India than the New York Sunday *Enquirer?*) /14

While the range between the best and the worst is very wide, America's some 1800 newspapers nevertheless average out a higher quality, variety and volume of information than any other press in the world. /15

Emphasis by negation

Certainly no other press has greater freedom, more freely granted by the people, to find the news and to print it as it finds it. The American press need not be caught in the subtle toils of subsidies by groups or interests. It does not have to fight government newsprint allocations—that overt or covert censorship exercised in many so-called "free countries." Except as the American press is guided by the profit motive, which is in turn guided by the public demand for its papers, it is an unguided press. /16

Summary of
major idea of
attention-need
step

All this is what is right with the American press. And the result of this situation is that our people have more ways to be well informed about issues and events near and far than any people in the world. And they are, by and large, better informed. /17

Transition
introducing
central question
with which speech
is concerned

Criterion by
which this central
question must
be answered

But now let us come to the question of the evening: "What is wrong with the American press?" We cannot answer this question unless we will voluntarily abandon our relative measurement of it against the press of *other* countries. We must measure it, in absolute terms, against its own highest ideal of freedom, responsibility—and let us not forget, success. /18

Satisfaction step

It is easy to point to many instances in which the American press—especially its individual members —tend to abuse their freedom and shirk their responsibility. /19

For example, one could note that nowadays the banner of press freedom is more often raised in matters of printing crime, sex and scandal stories, than it is in matters of printing the truth about great national figures, policies and issues. Or that too many members of the working press uncritically pass on—even if they do not personally swallow— too much high level government and political cant, tripe, and public relations; or that there are too many journalists who seem willing to sell their birthright of candor and truth in order to become White House pets, party pets, corporation pets, Pentagon or State Department or trade union or Governor's Mansion pets; who wistfully yearn after Grey Eminency, or blatantly strive for publicity for themselves, on lecture platforms or political rostrums. /20

Supporting
material.
Examples and
explanation

While agreeing with most journalists that people are not as much interested in the issues as they should be, one could at the same time note that neither are many journalists. One could mention that such journalists seem to have forgotten that *men, not names* alone, make news, and that men are made by the clarity with which they state issues, and the resolution with which they face them. One could express the hope that more journalists would encourage rather than avoid controversy and argument, remembering that controversy and argument are not the enemies of democracy, but its friends. One could wish for fewer journalist prodigies of the well written factual story, and more gifted talents for drawing explanations from the facts, or that working pressmen would be more creative in reporting the news, or that they would reflect less in themselves of what in this decade they have so roundly condemned in American leadership: apathy, cynicism, luke-warmness, and acceptance of the *status quo* about everything, from juvenile delinquency to nuclear destruction. One could pray, above all, for journalists who cared less about ideologies, and more about ideas. /21

But such criticisms and complaints—important as they may be—cover only one area of the American press. It is, alas, a relatively small area. A large, unmeasurable percentage of the total editorial space in American newspapers is concerned not with public affairs or matters of stately importance. It is devoted instead to entertainment, titillation, amusement, voyeurism and tripe. /22

Criticisms in paragraphs above softened by declaration that public must share part of the blame

The average American newspaper reader wants news but he wants lots of things from his newspaper besides news: he wants the sports page, the comics, fashion, home-making, advice-to-the-lovelorn, do-it-yourself psychiatry, gossip columns, medical, cooking and decorating features, TV, movie and theater coverage, Hollywood personality stories, Broadway and society prattle, church columns, comics, bridge columns, cross-word puzzles, big-money contests. Above all, he wants news that concerns not a bit the public weal but that people just find "interesting" reading. /23

Concession on the part of the speaker

I confess to enjoying much of this myself. And I do not mean to suggest that every newspaper must read like the London *Times*. But the plain fact is that we are witnessing in America what Professor William Ernest Hocking and others have called the debasement of popular taste. /24

Rhetorical question used as transition

Is it necessary? An editor of my acquaintance was asked recently whether the new circulation rise of his increasingly wild-eyed newspaper was being achieved at the expense of good journalism. He replied: "But you don't understand; our first journalistic need is to survive." I submit that a survival achieved by horribly debasing the journalistic coin is short lived. The newspaper that engages in mindless, untalented sensationalism gets caught up in the headlong momentum it creates in its readers' appetites. It cannot continue satisfying the voracious appetites it is building. Such journalism may suddenly burn brightly with success; but it will surely burn briefly. /25

We have the familiar example of television closely at hand. The American press has rightly deplored the drivel, duplicity and demeaning programming that has marked much of television's commercial trust. A critic, of course, need not necessarily always have clean hands. The press is right to flail what is wrong in television just as it is obliged to recognize the great service television has provided in areas where its public affairs, news and good programs have succeeded in adding something new and enriching to American life. /26

But if the press criticizes what is wrong in television without recognizing the moral for itself, it will have missed a valuable and highly visible opportunity for self-improvement. /27

The double charge against the American press may thus be stated: its failure to inform the public better than it does is the evasion of its responsibility; its failure to educate and elevate the public taste rather than following that taste like a blind, wallowing dinosaur, is an abuse of its freedom. /28

In view of the river of information which flows daily from the typewriters of American correspondents at home and abroad, why are the American people not better informed? Whose fault is it? At first glance it would seem to be the fault of the publishers, and especially editors. But the publisher or editor who does not give his readers plenty of what they want is going to lose circulation to a competitor who does. Or if he has a news monopoly in his city, and feels too free to short change them on these things, he is going to lose circulation as his reader-slack is taken up by the radio, the TV, and the magazines. /29

Add that even the news the reader wants in most cities, especially the smaller cities throughout the United States, is primarily local news. He remains, even as you and I, more interested in the news of his neighbors, his community, and his city, than he is in the news out of Washington, Paris or Rome. /30

Rhetorical question used as transition

Can we quarrel with this? We cannot. The Declaration of Independence itself set the pattern of the American way, and with it American reading habits. Life, liberty and the pursuit of *happiness* were to be man's prime and legitimate goals. /31

Perhaps the history of our country would have been better—and happier—if "the pursuit of truth, information and enlightenment" had been his third great goal. But that was not the way our Founding Fathers saw things. And that is not the way the American public sees them now. /32

Emphasis by contrast

The fact is that while "man" is a rational animal, *all* men and *all* women are not pre-eminently rational, logical and thoughtful in their approach to life. They do not thirst, above all, for knowledge and information about the great domestic and international issues, even though these issues may profoundly affect not only their pocket-books, but their very lives. /33

Today, as yesterday, people are primarily moved in their choice of reading by their daily emotions, their personal, immediate, existential prejudices, biases, ambitions, desires, and—as we know too well in the Freudian age—by many subconscious yearnings and desires, and irrational hates and fears. /34

Very well then: let us accept the fact. /35

Should the American press bow to it? Accept it? Cater to it? Foster it? /36

Rhetorical questions used as transition

What else (the cynical and sophisticated will ask) is there to do? /37

Explanation

The American press, no less than the TV and radio, is Big Business. It is now, as never before, a mass medium. As Big Business it faces daily vast problems of costliness and competition. As a mass medium it cannot handle these problems without seeking to satisfy the public's feelings, desires and wants. It publishes in the noisiest and most distracted age in our history. It seems doomed to satisfy endlessly the tastes of the nation—pluralistic, pragmatic, emotional, sensuous, and predominately irrational. By its Big Business mass media nature it seems compelled to seek ever more and more to saturate the mass markets, to soak the common denominator reader-sponge with what it wants. /38

Certainly we must face this fact: if the American press, as a mass medium, has formed the minds of America, the mass has also formed the medium. There is action, re-action, and inter-action going on ceaselessly between the newspaper-buying public and the editors. What is wrong with the American press is what is in part wrong with American Society. /39

Concession

Rhetorical questions used as transition and for emphasis

Is this then to exonerate the American press for its failures to give the American people more tasteful and more illuminating reading matter? Can the American press seek to be excused from responsibility for public lack of information as TV and radio often do, on the grounds that after all, "We have to give the people what they want or we will go out of business"? /40

Despite earlier concessions, speaker courageously places blame primarily on press itself

No. Not without abdicating its own American birthright, it cannot. The responsibility *is* fixed on the American press. Falling directly and clearly on publisher and editor, this responsibility is inbuilt into the freedom of the press itself. The freedom guaranteed by the Constitution under the First Amendment, carries this responsibility with it. /41

"Freedom," as Clemenceau said, "is nothing in the world but the opportunity for self-discipline"; that is to say voluntarily to assume responsibility. /42

Concession and more specific assignment of blame (i.e., the criterion— responsibility— is not fully or well met at present)

There are many valiant publishers, editors and journalists in America who have made and are making courageous attempts to give readers a little more of what they *should* have, and a little less of what they want—or, as is more often true, what they only *think* they want, because they have no real knowledge of what is available to them. America owes these publishers and editors and journalists an incomparable debt of gratitude. /43

What is really wrong with the American press is that there are not enough *such publishers and editors*. There is hardly an editor in this room who could not—if he passionately would—give every day, every year, a little more honest, creative effort

to his readers on the great issues which face us—
the issues which, in the years to come, must spell
peace or disaster for our democracy. A beginning
would be to try courageously, which is to say *consistently*, to keep such news (however brief) on the
front page playing it in some proportion to its real
importance. For a newspaper which relegates to the
back pages news which is vital to the citizenry as
a whole, in favor of sensational "circulation-building" headlines about ephemeral stories of crime,
lust, sex and scandal, is *actively* participating in the
debasement of public taste and intelligence. Such
a newspaper, more especially its editor, is not only
breaking faith with the highest of democratic journalism, he is betraying his nation. And, you may be
surprised to hear me say, he may even be courting
commercial failure. /44

For there is enough in American life in these
exciting sixties to keep interested and absorbed
many of the readers who have been written off as
impossible to reach except through cheap sensationalism. The commercial challenge is not to
achieve success by reaching backward into cliché-ridden ideas, stories and situations. It is rather to
recognize that uniquely now in this country there
is natural and self-propelled drive toward a better
life, more sustaining and relevant interests. There
is, in sum, an infinity of new subjects that make
exciting, inviting and important exploration for
the American press. /45

There can be no doubt that honorable and patriotic publishers and devoted and dedicated editors
can increase little by little, in season and out, the
public's appetite for better information. There can
also be no doubt that they can also decrease, little
by little, in the rest of their papers the type of
stories which appeals to the worst in human nature
by catering to the lowest common denominator taste
in morals and ethics. /46

Teddy Roosevelt once said that a good journalist
should be part St. Paul and part St. Vitus. /47

A good editor today must be part Santa Claus,
part St. Valentine, part St. Thomas (the doubter),
part St. Paul, and certainly he must be part St.

Jude. St. Jude, as you know, is the patron saint of those who ask for the impossible. /48

*Visualization
step developed
by method
of contrast*

Negative phase

It is not impossible to ask that the American press begin to reverse its present trend, which Dean Ed Barrett of the Columbia School of Journalism calls "giving the public too much froth because too few want substance." If this trend is not reversed (which it can be only by your determined effort) the American press will increasingly become the creature, rather than the creator of man's tastes. It will become a passive, yielding and, curiously, an effeminate press. And twixt the ads for the newest gas range, and the firmest girdle, the cheapest vacuum cleaner, and the best buy in Easter bonnets; twixt the sports page, the fashion page, the teen-age columns, the children's comics; twixt the goo, glop and glamour hand-outs on Elvis Presley and Elizabeth Taylor, and above all twixt the headlines on the sexiest murders, and the type of political editorializing which sees the great presidential issues of the day as being between the case of the "boyish forelock" versus the "tricky ski-jump nose," the press will lose its masculine prerogative which is to educate, inform, engage the interest of and guide the minds of free men and women in a great democracy. /49

Positive phase

As I know that the American Society of Newspaper Editors holds hard to the belief in masculine superiority in the realm of the intellect, and could only view with horror the picture of the Fourth Estate as the "kept man" of the emotional masses, I—for one—am certain this will not happen. /50

Action step

*Challenge
in form of
idealistic and
patriotic appeal*

Let us watch then, with hope, for the signs of a new, vigorous, masculine leadership in the American press. For if you fail, must not America also fail in its great and unique mission, which is also yours: to lead the world towards life, liberty, and the pursuit of enlightenment—so that it may achieve happiness? It is that goal which the American press must seize afresh—creatively, purposefully, energetically, and with a zeal that holds a double promise: The promise of success and the promise of enlightenment. /51

COMMUNICATIONS AND MEDICINE [7]

The following speech by David Sarnoff, Chairman of the Board, Radio Corporation of America, was delivered at the National Health Forum in New York, March 16, 1961.

Attention It is a novel and challenging experience to at-
step tempt a layman's diagnosis of a subject relating to medicine, and to do so before a group of medical experts. In approaching it, I recall comment of a British nobleman, Lord Rochester. "Before I got married," he said, "I had six theories about bringing up children. Now I have six children and no theories."

Well, I have advanced from three children to eight grandchildren, and, being a less prudent man than Lord Rochester, I still have several theories left. Primarily, they relate to electronics, where the main function is the communication of information, and some bear on the subject assigned to me this morning—"Communications and Medicine."

Need I believe that electronics offers as many avenues for
step advance in medical communications as it has, over the years, for communications in other fields. The very theme of your National Health Forum, "Better Communication for Better Health," suggests that you, too, sense this need for rapport between your ancient art and science of medicine and our young one of electronics.

How do we meet this need?

First, I think, by an understanding of a problem that has become basic to almost every area of human endeavor. It is the problem of progress—the accelerated, diversified, omnibus type of Twentieth-Century progress.

Since 1900, there has been more scientific and technological progress than in all the previous centuries of recorded history. The present tempo of that progress is accelerating daily. Discoveries of science that once would have required several lifetimes to develop are now compressed into a few years—sometimes even months. It took half a century to move from mechanical office machines to modern computers; but it took less than a decade to increase the speed of these computers a thousandfold. It took forty years—from the Wright Brothers to the Second World War —to push flying speeds up to 500 miles an hour; but less than 15 years to go from 500 miles to 18,000 miles an hour at which man-made satellites now circle the globe.

How profoundly the world has altered in these 15 years! A hermit emerging today from a 1946 refuge would never have heard of earth and solar satellites or atomic reactors. Automation would be an alien word. He would never have flown in a jet plane, had his laundry washed with a

---

[7] From *Vital Speeches of the Day*, Vol. XXVII, May 1, 1961, pp. 446–448. Reprinted by permission of Mr. Sarnoff.

synthetic detergent, or seen the inside of a glass-walled building. He would never have watched color television or listened to stereophonic music.

This vast spawning of new products and services, and new information about them, has created a classic dilemma. Is a great quantity of new information truly useful if it does not reach those who are trained to use it? There was more than levity in the recent comment of a Harvard librarian that if new books continued to arrive at the present rate, it will not be long before the books crowd the students off the campus!

Even the weatherman suffers from an information surplus. The RCA-built Tiros weather satellite was designed to provide information that could lead to greater precision in the much maligned art of forecasting. It did just that! In the three months between its orbiting and the end of its operating life, Tiros I produced over 22,000 pictures of the earth's cloud cover. But the Weather Bureau—submerged in these informational riches—had to hire four new specialists just to index and classify the pictures.

Before the war, when anyone talked about electronics, he was talking about a single product, radio. With a good background in radio, a man could do his job with reasonable competence. Today, electronics encompasses a dozen different businesses, and the executive must have a working knowledge of each. It is not unusual at RCA to start the day with a meeting about space vehicles, shift to a study of the market potential for new automation devices, then move to a discussion of electroluminescent lighting for the home—and finally wind up with a chart report on the decibels of teen-age sound that greeted the latest Elvis Presley recording.

The thrust of invention and development has placed us all in an informational pressure cooker, and nowhere is this fact more clinically apparent than in the field of medicine. I am told by a doctor friend that seven out of ten prescriptions written today are for items unknown to medicine before World War II. The communications problems that result are more serious here than in any other area, since human health and life itself are involved.

Viewed statistically, information covering new medical developments is contained in an estimated 8,000 medical journals and bulletins that appear annually, about half of them in the United States alone. Stretched end-to-end, their 11 million pages would extend from New York to Denver.

To keep up with developments published in these journals, a physician would have to read the equivalent of one book every hour. If Harvard is threatened with a loss of students, you doctors are threatened with a loss of patients. Soon, you'll be too busy reading to see them.

This is a fundamental problem in the logistics of communications. On the one side, a mounting flow of fresh material on methods, techniques and drugs; on the other, the harried physician to whom this information must be funneled over and around the obstacle of his rapidly diminishing time.

The communications methods standard in the world of medicine—journal articles, conventions and symposiums, medical newspapers and house organs, and detailing—have served well in the past. But the past is not always an infallible guide to the future. Today, I find widespread agreement among my medical friends that your science moves ahead too rapidly for the older communications techniques to cope with its advances.

This was a key point in the report of the United States Senate's special Committee of Consultants on Medical Research, on which I was privileged to serve during the last session of Congress. The Committee's Report said in part: "The enormous problems of handling the rapidly increasing flow of new information in the literature, of codifying it and making it readily accessible, urgently cry out for solution . . ."

Satisfaction and Visualization steps in parallel　My theories on the solution of this formidable problem relate to the application of new electronic techniques in three broad areas.

The *first* is medical radio.

As some of you know, RCA has done exploratory work in this area. We are convinced, on the basis of intensive studies, that radio can be an effective method of keeping the doctor better informed about significant developments in medicine.

It is possible to set up a closed-circuit radio network that would link 100,000 to 200,000 doctors' offices, hospitals and medical schools in the principal metropolitan centers of the United States. At specified times during the day, this network could carry medical news, reports of scientific assemblies, discussions of medical economics and medico-legal topics, and reports on research activities.

In short, it could be a comprehensive medical journal of the air, with the scientific integrity of its program content insured by an Editorial Advisory Council serving as both a source of material and a critic of scripts.

Such a private network is possible through the imaginative use of what is known as FM multiplexing. This is a relatively new form of communications permitting two or more programs to be sent by the same transmitter along the same frequency. In principle, a multiplex system is not dissimilar to the message-carrying complex within the human being where trillions of interconnected cells coordinate messages traveling from one part of the body to another.

The multiplex signal could be heard only by those receivers designed for and tuned to the frequency of the network station. It is thus possible to cross-breed a mass communications technique with the privacy of a telephone line.

For the doctor, such a system would:

Sharply reduce lag-time between the scientist's laboratory discovery and its bedside application.

Provide post-graduate medical courses by a faculty of the nation's foremost specialists.

Provide up-to-the-minute news on significant developments across the entire spectrum of medical science.

Remove the specialist from the isolation to which the pressures of current medical practice drive him, and give him awareness of developments in all medical fields.

Above all, the radio network would give the doctor more information more quickly and more conveniently than any other means. In his own office, with no more than 50 or 60 minutes of daily listening, he could stay abreast of the unending march of medical advance.

A *second* way to enlist electronics in medicine is through television, particularly color television.

Since the first "on camera" surgery at Johns Hopkins in 1947, television has proven effective in training physicians, surgeons, dentists, and specialists in many other fields. Today, more than twenty-five medical schools find television indispensable for various aspects of their teaching programs.

As for the future, you can preview it today at the Walter Reed Army Medical Center in Washington. The most extensive color television system of its kind ever devised—a system comparable to that of a major commercial network—is in regular use.

A color TV microscope camera system allows for enlarged color reproduction on a television screen of minute biological material. It enables many doctors to observe simultaneously micro-organisms or tissue sections; it obsoletes the stand-in-line wait for the microscope.

At Walter Reed, a surgeon can send from the operating room to the pathology laboratory, through a pneumatic tube, tissues removed during surgery. The pathologist can examine and analyze the tissue and determine whether a malignancy exists. Then, through closed-circuit television, he can transmit to the operating room a microscope view of the tissue, in natural color, and discuss it with the surgeon.

This is a clinical and diagnostic use of television. A broader informational application comes through films made of "live" color programs and furnished to Army doctors stationed at remote posts around the world. Any military installation with a standard motion picture projector can take advantage of lectures, demonstrations and courses given by specialists at Walter Reed.

Eventually, lectures and demonstrations by front-rank specialists will be available to every physician in his own office. A compact, inexpensive television tape player, now under development, will reproduce television pictures and sound from magnetic tape over any television receiver. When the player reaches the market, taped versions of "refresher" courses will be mailed the physician to play through his own television set at his convenience.

In terms of international communications, electronic hardware is already available for man-made satellites that will serve as relays for world-wide medical television. Ultimately, such a system will permit round-table discussions between medical experts anywhere on the globe. It can bring together scientists, teachers, demonstrators and students into one vast audience—truly a "Medical School of the World."

World-wide television will permit thousands of physicians to sit in on diagnosis and consultation sessions among specialists of many nationalities. Heart specialists in London will be able to examine a patient, display on the television screen his x-rays and cardiograms, and discuss a diagnosis with specialists in New York, Berlin, Paris, Rome, Tokyo, or other parts of the world.

And through instantaneous electronic translation techniques, which are now in development, the barrier of language difference—as real to the doctor as to the statesman—will be finally surmounted.

A *third* way electronics can move against medical communications problems is with computing techniques.

Every physician, every medical researcher, every hospital struggles today with mountains of data requiring classification, analysis and storage for immediate retrieval. More and more of that burden can be shifted to modern electronic data processing equipment, with tremendous economies in time and gains in precision. Electronic performance provides in seconds the kind of statistical and probability findings that, with conventional methods, takes days or even weeks of onerous work.

No requirement is more fundamental to the research scientist than knowing what has been done in his immediate area and in related areas. Lacking this knowledge, he can grope aimlessly, duplicating the work of others to a wasteful extent. In industry, such duplication costs an estimated billion dollars a year, and the toll is comparable in other fields.

Medical knowledge is increasing so rapidly that it has far outstripped the storage capacity of any single human brain. But computers enable us to store accumulated knowledge compactly, update it continuously, recall it instantly.

Through a blend of electronic computation and communication techniques, it would be possible to establish a National Medical Clearing House which could serve as a central repository for all the latest medical information. By a combination of communications circuits, every major hospital and medical school in the country could be tied into this Clearing House.

If a doctor in a San Francisco hospital sought the source of information on a particular subject, he would simply dial a number. Instantly, a relevant bibliography would flash on a television-like screen before him. Then, when he made his choice of a particular article, he could dial again and get a microfilm version of the article on his screen.

Another service of great value to the physician would be rapid access to the medical history of any person seeking treatment. Now, the relevant data are so scattered in doctors' offices, hospitals, insurance company files and elsewhere that an individual's medical background has to be reestablished on every occasion through time-consuming questioning and examination. With a centralized electronic file of health records, the physician could simply dial the identifying code number of his patient and obtain an up-to-date report.

Action step In the presence of so many leaders of the medical profession, I should like to offer this suggestion: That the American Medical Association, in concert with representatives of the electronics industry, create a joint group to consider the feasibility of a National Medical Clearing House; and, if it is deemed feasible, to decide the soundest way of bringing it to fruition. In such a venture, I am certain that the electronics industry would cooperate wholeheartedly. Speaking for my own organization, I assure you that our experts, experienced in many fields of communications, would be pleased to assist such a group in its studies.

I realize, of course, that there are numerous details to be analyzed in any proposal of such magnitude. But I trust that the concept itself has sufficient promise to justify its careful pursuit. There is no technical reason why a Medical Clearing House, once established on a national scale, could not be expanded gradually to embrace the entire world.

At various times, centers like Rome, Berlin, Vienna, Edinburgh and London have claimed the distinction of being the "Medical Capital of the World." Today, few question that the center of medical learning has shifted from Europe to the United States.

To insure our continued pre-eminence, we must ceaselessly strive to increase our medical knowledge and to improve its dissemination. I believe that electronics can aid immeasurably by permitting the doctor to *hear* more—through radio; to *see* more—through television; to *find* information more quickly—through computing techniques.

It can also, as it has in the past, offer medical science a wide range of new tools for research, diagnosis and treatment. As an example, one of the newest developments is a transistorized low-frequency amplifier, sensitive enough to detect skin potentials due to cardiac action. The unit, developed by a research team under Dr. V. K. Zworykin, occupies less than one-half cubic inch of space. By variation of the light intensities, it can reproduce an electrocardiogram containing far more information than is provided today by conventional methods.

But in medicine, to a unique degree, your place on history's canvas is likely to be fixed primarily by your success in meeting the needs of other peoples. As Arnold Toynbee has said: "Our age will be well remembered . . . because it is the first generation since the dawn of history in which mankind dared to believe it practical to make the benefits of civilization available to the whole human race."

What high marks history would accord our two professions if we were to combine our medical knowledge and communications skills for the mastery of disease among the developing areas of Asia and Africa—and wherever such assistance may be needed! You in medicine have the necessary information; we in electronics have the necessary means for conveying it.

The more closely we work together, the more effectively we can contribute to "Better Health" for all mankind. This is our common objective, and its achievement would make this world a happier place in which to live.

SPEECHES FOR COLLATERAL STUDY

1. Adolf A. Berle, Jr., "The Irrepressible Issues of the 60's"—*The Speaker's Resource Book,* edited by Carroll C. Arnold, Douglas Ehninger, and John Gerber (Scott, Foresman, Chicago, 1961), p. 165 ff.

2. Pearl S. Buck, "Women's Place in a Democracy"—Jessie Haver Butler, *Time to Speak Up* (Harpers, N. Y., 1946), p. 212 ff.

3. Erwin D. Canham, "The Value of Self-Criticism for Business and Labor"—*The Speaker's Resource Book,* p. 187 ff.

4. Winston Churchill, "Their Finest Hour"—*Blood, Sweat, and Tears* (Putnam's, N. Y., 1941), p. 305 ff.

5. J. W. Fulbright, "The Synthesis of Both Liberty and Unity. Some Aspects of Our Foreign Policy"—*Vital Speeches of the Day,* Vol. XXVI, October 1, 1960, p. 739 ff.

6. Patrick Henry, "Against the Federal Constitution" and James Madison, "For the Federal Constitution"—*American Forum: Speeches on Historic Issues, 1788–1900,* edited by Ernest J. Wrage and Barnet Baskerville (Harpers, N. Y., 1960), p. 3 ff.

7. Millicent C. McIntosh, "The Goals of Education Are Not Sufficient Today"—*The Age of Danger,* edited by Harold F. Harding (Random House, N. Y., 1952), p. 382 ff.

8. William C. O'Neill, "Campaign Financing"—*Vital Speeches of the Day,* Vol. XXVI, April 15, 1960, p. 389 ff.

9. Adlai E. Stevenson, "World Tensions"—*Ibid.,* Vol. XXVI, July 1, 1960, p. 552 ff.

PROBLEMS

1. Be prepared to discuss the following questions in class: What is the central purpose of every speech to convince? How may the motivated sequence be adapted to a speech on a question of policy? A question of fact? A question of value? What is the most important characteristic of a speech to convince? How should a speech to convince be organized when the audience is interested but undecided? Interested but hostile? Apathetic? Hostile to belief in the existence of a problem?

2. Recall three speeches to convince that you have heard recently. Describe the situation in which each of these speeches was delivered. Was it at a business meeting? At a popular gathering? In a debate? On some other occasion? What was the speaker's purpose in each case? Was he attempting to support a proposition of policy? To oppose a proposition of fact? Etc.

3. Find in the Speeches for Collateral Study or elsewhere a speech dealing with a question of policy, a speech dealing with a question of fact, and a speech dealing with a question of value. Outline each of these speeches carefully. How do they compare in structure with the patterns of development recommended on pages 415–422?

4. Turn in to your instructor four questions of fact which cannot be settled by observation, experimentation, or direct recourse to data and which therefore would make suitable subjects for speeches to convince.

5. Make a list of five of your personal beliefs or convictions that might provide suitable subjects for speeches on questions of value. Compile a similar list for speeches on questions of policy.

6. Be ready to explain the function of each of the steps of the motivated sequence in a speech dealing with a question of fact, a speech dealing with a question of value, and a speech dealing with a question of policy.

7. Comment on the speaking manner or delivery used for a speech to convince that you have recently heard delivered in a face-to-face situation or over television. Did the speaker's delivery aid him in achieving conviction, or did it hinder him? Why?

8. Which of the two following methods do you think is more likely to result in full and lasting persuasion: (a) impressing your listeners with a motive for believing what you want them to believe or (b) convincing them of the logic of your proposal by presenting facts and reasoning?

9. Prepare a written or oral report on the ethics of persuasion. Consider such questions as these: What methods and appeals may legitimately be used in effecting persuasion? What methods and appeals should always be avoided? Are there any circumstances in which a man not only has the right but the obligation to undertake to persuade others?

10. Find in the Speeches for Collateral Study as many instances as possible of the special devices discussed on pages 425–427. Evaluate the effectiveness with which these devices are used.

11. Find in the Speeches for Collateral Study several instances of each of the forms of reasoning described on pages 423–425. How well does each piece of reasoning meet the tests listed on the same pages?

12. Study several newspaper editorials to determine the forms of reasoning used in them. In each case apply the appropriate test to deter-

mine how valid the reasoning is. Do the same for several advertisements clipped from magazines and for several television commercials.

13. Have your instructor help you locate a historically important speech that was delivered to an audience displaying one of the attitudes described on pages 428–431 (interested but undecided, interested but hostile to the proposal, etc.). Study the speech to determine the means the speaker employed to adapt his arguments and appeals to this audience attitude. How well would you say he succeeded? Speeches which you might study for this purpose include: Henry Ward Beecher, "Address Delivered at Liverpool, England, October 16, 1863," *Classified Speech Models*, W. N. Brigance (Appleton-Century-Crofts, N. Y., 1928), p. 40 ff.; Henry W. Grady, "The New South," *Select Orations Illustrating American Political History*, edited by Samuel Bannister Harding (Macmillan, N. Y., 1930), p. 489 ff.; Richard Nixon, "Address to the Russian People," *The Speaker's Resource Book*, edited by Carroll C. Arnold, Douglas Ehninger, and John Gerber (Scott, Foresman, Chicago, 1961), p. 240 ff.

14. Present in class a five-minute speech supporting or attacking one of the following propositions or a proposition suggested by one of these:

You are safer in an airplane than on the highway.

The Communist nations seek world domination through war and revolution.

Good employee relations increase production.

Americans are reading more and better books today than ever before.

Good grades in college are an indication of future success.

Extensive participation in intercollegiate athletics definitely benefits the college student.

Robert E. Lee is the greatest military commander America has produced.

A liberal education is to be preferred to professional or technical training.

Our facilities for treating the mentally ill are inadequate and outmoded.

The United States should adopt the British parliamentary system of government.

All states should require periodic reexaminations of persons holding drivers' licenses.

We should adopt a uniform system of marriage and divorce laws.

Intercollegiate athletics should be abolished.

We should have a nationwide system of compulsory health insurance.

He that nothing questioneth, nothing learneth.

Thomas Fuller

CHAPTER 23 / *Answering Questions and Objections*

When a speaker has finished giving his speech, he is often immediately confronted by questions or objections from his audience. The ability to adapt oneself with poise and certainty to a cross fire of interrogation, even when it interrupts the speech itself, is the real distinction between the speaker and the "deliverer of speeches." Rather than resenting such questions or taking them as evidence of failure, the speaker should welcome them as an indication of the interest he has aroused. In answering such questions, he can establish even closer contact with his audience than is otherwise possible and can meet directly those points which most vitally affect his listeners.

TYPICAL SITUATIONS

A speaker always faces the possibility of being questioned or heckled from the floor. A great deal of counterargument can be expected in any sort of business meeting, since the informality of the discussion encourages questions and the frank statement of objections. Audiences are most likely to question or object to proposals made in the speech to convince or to actuate, but no type of speech (save the introductory speech, the speech of tribute, and the speech for courtesy) is immune from this possibility. Of course, on more formal occasions the speaker is not likely to be interrupted or interrogated at the end of his speech; but some speakers, even on such occasions, call for questions after they have finished.

THE PURPOSE OF THE REPLY

When someone asks a question or raises an objection to something you have said, the *ultimate aim* of your answer will be to further the particular purpose of your speech. Thus, if the purpose of your speech is to get funds for a new building, getting funds will still be uppermost in your mind as you answer questions. The *immediate aim* of your answer, however, will be:

To satisfy your questioner. Questions are asked for one of two reasons—to secure additional information or to object to what has been said. To satisfy your questioner, therefore, you must either give him additional facts or convince him that his objection is invalid.

To satisfy others in the audience. Sometimes you may not care what the person who questioned you thinks, but the point he has raised may be important to other members of your audience. Therefore, your answer must be directed not only to the questioner but also to the others in the audience whose objection he has voiced.

To retain your own prestige. Sometimes a question is asked or an objection raised merely to put you on the spot, to place you on the defensive, or to grab the spotlight. When this happens, your answer will have as its immediate object the retention of your own prestige; your attempt will be to keep control of the situation.

Although one of those purposes will usually predominate, you should keep them all in mind as you phrase your answer to a question.

METHODS OF ANSWERING

Your method of answering questions or objections must depend upon the real motives of those who raise them. You will answer the mere troublemaker in one way and the sincerely interested questioner in another. Let us consider some of the methods which speakers have found useful.

Information

Very frequently objections are raised because people do not know enough about your subject. When this is the case, present additional information on the point in dispute. The added facts will not only answer the question raised but will also add weight to what you have already said. Do not present the bare facts alone, however; connect the unknown with the known. (See p. 360.) Make sure that the audience understands the significance of your information. In general, organize your facts in the following way:

1. Repeat the question (so that everyone can hear it).
2. Present the additional information.
   A. Use time order, space order, etc.
   B. Connect what you now say with what you have already explained.
3. Draw a conclusion from this information.
4. Show how this conclusion answers the question and, if you can, how it supports some point in your original speech.

Comparison

Sometimes a valid objection to your proposal is raised. When this occurs, two courses are open to you: either you may modify your proposal to meet the objection, or, if this is impossible, you may weigh the objection against the benefits you have shown. In the latter case, make your reply somewhat as follows:

1. Repeat the objection.
2. Admit its validity, but minimize its importance.
3. Remind the audience of the benefits of your proposal by restating them in summary form.
4. Point out that the benefits outweigh the disadvantages.

Sometimes a listener will ask a question, not because he seeks more information or wishes to voice a valid objection, but because he has not reasoned soundly or has some personal prejudice about the subject. In this event you must deal with either (*a*) a train of reasoning at variance with your own or (*b*) a strong personal motive or established belief. These may be handled thus:

To attack a train of reasoning at variance with your own:
1. Repeat the question or objection.
2. Point out its underlying logic or assumption.
3. Show the fallacy in reasoning or the invalidity of the assumption. (Cite facts, figures, testimony.)
4. Deny or definitely modify the questioner's point on the basis of what you have just shown.
5. State the correct conclusion and, if possible, connect it with some point in your speech.

To meet a personal motive or established belief:
1. Repeat the question or objection.
2. Point out the underlying belief or motive for this objection, and show, if you can, that your proposal is really in line with it, or at least does not oppose it. Present some new aspect of the situation which will identify your proposition with the questioner's belief or motive.
3. Emphasize some stronger motive or established belief than that on which the objection is based, and show that your proposal is in line with this stronger motive or established belief. (Step 2 is sometimes omitted and Step 3 relied upon entirely.)
4. Draw a definite conclusion and, if possible, connect it with some point in your speech.

You will notice that the fundamental technic used in both methods outlined above is that of securing agreement upon some point of logic, motivation, or belief and then putting the objection in opposition to this point and your proposal in agreement with it.

Question　　　　　Sometimes one question can best be answered by another. Such a counterquestion often puts the questioner on the defensive, and he must either answer your question or admit defeat. Frequently his answer to your question will give you the cue for answering his original question. Even if he is not completely appeased, he may be quieted and the rest of the audience satisfied. Be careful, however, to be tactful when you reply in this way.

One example will illustrate this method. A speaker who was advocating home rule for one of the British dependencies was interrupted by a listener who asked whether he didn't think "these people are too illiterate to govern themselves." The speaker rejoined by asking, "Do you know what the percentage of literacy was in the United States when we declared our independence?" The questioner did not, and sat down. The point was so obvious that it was almost needless for the speaker to proceed, as he did, to compare the figures between the dependency of which he spoke and the American Colonies in 1776.

Humor　　　　　Sometimes, when the speaker considers the point raised by a question or objection to be unimportant, he may meet the difficulty by using humor. Be careful, however, that the point you consider unimportant is not considered important by your audience. Handle the situation thus:

1. Sidetrack the point with genial humor. Show the funny side of the objection, but beware of sarcasm.
2. Shift the attention of the audience to another point by taking up some more serious objection that has already been raised or re-emphasizing some important point made in your original speech.

Sometimes it is allowable to take an ironical dig at the person asking the question or making the objection. By poking fun at him, you please the sporting tendency in men and reduce the effect of his objection. This is particularly true if the questioner is a bombastic, self-important individual who is known as a chronic objector. Be careful, however, not to use sarcasm on someone who is respected by the audience, or your attack will boomerang.

Prestige Sometimes you can rely upon your own word to answer the objection. A simple statement that "I have not found it so in my experience" will occasionally be sufficient. This is particularly true if the audience regards you as an authority upon the subject. Your own prestige will outweigh that of the person raising the question. However, do not overestimate your own reputation. Usually a far better plan is to take the extra time for presenting the information or argument upon which your conclusion is based.

Admission of ignorance Far from reducing your prestige, your admission that you do not know the answer to a question will often raise you in the audience's esteem. Such an admission labels you as a conscientious person who sticks to the facts and refuses to go beyond them. You avoid being thought a bluffer or a know-it-all. This does not mean that you never need to know the answer to what is asked. Before speaking, you should be thoroughly informed upon your subject, but you cannot be expected to be able to answer everything that may be asked. However, if you cannot answer a question, combine your admission of ignorance with a valid reason for it.

1. Restate the question.
2. Admit your ignorance.
3. State definitely where the information can be found, or demonstrate why it is inaccessible.
4. Direct attention to some other point in your speech.

ORGANIZATION

The methods for organizing your answers have already been discussed in the preceding pages. Note that every method includes these three essentials:

1. Restatement of the question or objection.
2. Statement of your conclusion on the matter.
3. Some connection with your original speech.

The first of these is important to show the audience just what you are talking about; the second, to make your position clear;

and the third, to keep your original purpose in the foreground and to prevent wandering. Inserted between these three steps in the manner outlined above will be your information, argument, humor, etc.

As you frame your replies, remember above all that you are not conducting a tea-table conversation—that you have spoken for a purpose and that the discussion must not be allowed to wander away from that purpose.

EXAMPLES

The first example is taken from the television debate on "The Relationship of the Federal Government to the Arts," in which John K. Galbraith, Professor of Economics at Harvard University, supported federal assistance for nonprofit performing arts groups and Russell Lynes, Managing Editor of *Harper's* magazine, opposed the proposal. After opening statements by each speaker, John K. M. McCaffery, moderator of the program, asked the following question:

Mr. McCaffery: Gentlemen, there is another contemporary example of government in art and that is in the Soviet Union, and a good deal is made of the propaganda effect of the cultural state of the Soviet Union, their export of culture and its effect on the rest of the world. Do either one of you want to make a comment on the kind of art that is produced under complete government subsidy and direction? [An aside by Lynes is deleted.]

Professor Galbraith: Yes. I would not want to make any case for Soviet painting, Soviet art. The wheat fields and the strong maidens do not particularly appeal to me, I must say. But this would not, I think, be a fair parallel to anything, with anything we are talking about here. This is complete and total domination. What we are talking about here is encouragement in a free society, which encouragement is without any thought of repression.

Mr. McCaffery: Mr. Lynes feels that this is inevitable, do you?

Mr. Lynes: Well, I do not think this is necessarily going to be political repression at all. I think this is committee repression. This is the kind of thing that happens when you get an organization together saying, we will support these arts; we will support these arts more than we will support these arts. Who is to decide whether the theater ought to be supported less or more than sculptors or architecture. You get a committee with so much funds; they are going to have to sit down and decide which of these arts is going to get more money. You find yourself in the position which the individual sponsor is not in. He supports what he loves. The foundation can support what it thinks is most important. This foundation supports this, and that foundation supports that. And this spreads the interest and it spreads the subsidy over the widest possible base. And where you are not putting art against art, or in competitive terms for the government dollar.[1]

The following questions were asked of Mr. James M. Landis, Special Assistant to the President, shortly after he presented his conclusions about needed reforms in federal regulatory agencies. Observe how Mr. Landis answers each question directly and then adds explanation to make his viewpoint clear.

QUESTION: Does a federal agency have any role in trying to improve the quality of an industry, such as radio and TV?

Mr. Landis: I think it does. It certainly should.

There, incidentally, is another slight advance that's been made by the Federal Communications Commission. I think I criticized the Commission for not doing a job on the renewal of its licenses.

When a licensee seeks a license, one of the criteria in determining who should be the licensee with regard to a particular frequency is the nature of the programs he says he's going to put on. And an element in evaluating the quality of the programs is the emphasis that it places on, let's say, the public-interest aspect of its programs.

If that is a true criterion, when that licensee comes up for renewal in three years' time, he ought to be asked, "Have you done what you promised you'd do, or what you said you'd do?"

QUESTION: Does that amount to censorship?

Mr. Landis: That is not censorship. It isn't censorship in any sense.

Censorship is really preventing somebody from saying or speaking what they want to say. Now here, because of the "nature of the beast," there is only one frequency available. You have to award that to some applicant who comes along.

Now, obviously, you have to have criteria as to whether you pick A, B or C. You pick A, rather than B, because A promises to do so-and-so. I don't think it's a matter of censorship. I think it's a matter of how that frequency can be used best in the public interest.[2]

Soon after he took office as Secretary of State in 1961, Dean Rusk was interviewed on the "Today" show over NBC-TV. Martin

---

[1] From *The Nation's Future*, NBC Television, February 11, 1961.
[2] From *U. S. News and World Report*, Vol. 50, March 27, 1961, pp. 85–86.

Agronsky of NBC asked Mr. Rusk for his interpretation of the role the Secretary of State should have in formulating foreign policy.

Mr. Agronsky: Mr. Secretary, you noted once that Harry Truman had defined the President's relation to foreign policy in five words. He said, "The President makes foreign policy." What does the Secretary of State make? What is the function of your job? How do you see it?

Mr. Rusk: The primary responsibility of the Secretary of State is to help the President carry one of the most awesome responsibilities that is known to man. That means that the Secretary of State must be a principal, perhaps the primary, adviser to the President on foreign policy, but it also means that the Secretary must administer and lead the Department of State so that a great department can be of maximum help to the President. It means that the Secretary must help to represent the administration's point of view with the Congress and with congressional leaders and also help explain to the country what we are trying to do in foreign policy. Because, although the Constitution gives very heavy responsibilities to the President, our Constitution also gives the President a license to lead, and, in exercising that leadership in a country which moves by consent, the President must have the help of a great many others, including his principal Cabinet officers. The Secretary of State's role is to help in every way possible the President carry out his far-reaching and extremely complicated and difficult responsibilities in the foreign policy field.[3]

PROBLEMS

1. Be prepared to discuss the following questions in class: For what reasons are questions or objections raised? What is the ultimate purpose of a speaker's response? The immediate purposes? By what methods may a speaker reply to questions and objections? What points should be included in every method?

2. Phrase an objection to one of the arguments presented in one of the speeches printed at the end of the preceding chapter, and then write out answers to this objection, using several of the methods explained in this chapter.

3. Analyze a speaker's answers to questions and objections made at a student government meeting, a house meeting, or a convocation lecture. Identify the methods used by the speaker. What other methods do you believe would have been more effective?

[3] From *The Department of State Bulletin*, Vol. 44, February 27, 1961, p. 306.

4. In the *Congressional Record*, examine the reported proceedings of the United States Senate for one day during which there is debate. List the methods used by the speakers to handle questions and objections.

5. Make a short argumentative speech during and after which the audience is urged to ask questions or raise objections. In answering them employ the various methods discussed in this chapter.

part five

Special
Types of
Public
Speech

How to preside at a meeting and introduce speakers • Speeches for courtesy • Speeches
to secure goodwill • Speeches of tribute • Adapting speech to radio and television

Reason and judgment are the qualities of a leader.

Tacitus

―――――――――――――――

CHAPTER *24/How to Preside at a Meeting and Introduce Speakers*

The success of many a program—whether it is a public lecture, the planned entertainment for a dinner meeting of a business or professional group, or a series of speeches at a conference— is often largely determined by the effectiveness with which the chairman or toastmaster presides. A good presiding officer does not say much and does not parade himself, yet his presence is felt. The audience feels his unobtrusive control in the smooth running of the program. Sincerity, energy, and decisiveness —these are the personal qualities which mark him.

COMMANDING THE SITUATION

The first duty of the presiding officer is to command the situation, to be boss without being bossy. And why must he do this?

For three important reasons: (*a*) *To make the audience feel that all is going well.* People like to see that things are organized and running efficiently and to know that someone is in control. (*b*) *To hold the audience's attention by keeping the program moving.* If the chairman is uncertain or hesitant, the audience becomes fidgety, and the meeting invariably drags. But if the chairman is decisive and keeps things moving, the audience will be attentive and orderly. (*c*) *To discourage opposition.* People occasionally come to a meeting with the purpose of creating trouble or of opposing the plans to be presented. If they feel that the presiding officer really is in command and if there is no hesitation in the program, they may be discouraged from carrying out their plans.

To command a situation, you must prepare yourself beforehand. Do not trust to the inspiration of the moment merely because you are not the principal speaker. The chairman's preparation must often be just as thorough as that of the main speaker. Prepare yourself as follows:

1. Determine the purpose of the meeting.
2. Acquaint yourself with the program. Know who is going to speak or sing or play; know the title of each speaker's talk and the name of each artist's number; understand the function of each part of the program in advancing the purpose of the meeting.
3. Make a time schedule. Determine how long the meeting should last; apportion the time among the various persons on the program; and before the meeting begins, tell each participant tactfully how much time he will have at his disposal.
4. Prepare your own remarks. Know what you are going to say in your opening speech and in your later remarks. You may modify these remarks later, according to the turn of events, but you must always be ready with something.
5. Start the meeting on time. Be on time yourself and see that the others on the program are, too; then keep things moving as nearly on schedule as possible.

If you prepare yourself in this way, the meeting will not be assured of success, but its chances of success will be greatly improved.

In addition to commanding the situation, the presiding officer frequently has three incidental duties: (*a*) setting the keynote, (*b*) performing duties of courtesy, and (*c*) preserving order.

Setting the keynote At the beginning of a program, the audience will be either in a state of confusion and distraction or in a condition of expectant curiosity. When there is confusion, your first duty is to quiet the audience and direct its attention to the platform. After order has been established, you are ready to set the keynote of the meeting. What you say in your first minute on the platform will do much toward making the meeting a success or a failure. If the occasion is to be one of fun and good humor, your opening remarks should prepare the way. Speak as though you expected to have a good time and expected everyone else to. But if the occasion is one with a serious, businesslike purpose, your remarks should be serious and to the point. Remember that your duty here is not to make a great name for yourself but to get the audience in the proper frame of mind for what is to follow. In general, follow the technic described in Chapter 21, modified to suit the occasion. When the purpose of the occasion is essentially informative, set the keynote with a one-point speech (as explained in Chapter 12, p. 212) that stresses the need for the information which will follow. Let the audience know the purpose of the meeting, either by direct statement or by suggestion. Refer to the place of the meeting, or to the occasion for it, or to the organization under whose auspices it is held. Make reference to the background of events which has led up to the meeting or to previous occasions similar to this one. Be careful, however, not to steal the thunder of those who follow you by saying too much yourself.

Your duty of setting the keynote does not end with your opening remarks. Each time you introduce a new speaker or make any comment at all, you should keep in mind the mood of the meeting. Don't destroy the high level attained by a preceding speaker by injecting facetious comments, and don't mar the good humor which a speaker has created by a dry and laborious analysis of what he has said. However, if one of the speakers falls down on his job, then you must attempt to bring the meeting back to its intended level. A chairman must be wise enough to know when to speak and when not to speak. Experience alone will enable you to judge the mood of the audience and the probable effect of your incidental remarks.

Performing duties of courtesy

The presiding officer is frequently expected to perform certain acts of courtesy. There may be visitors to welcome; or, if the chairman is himself a visitor, he may wish to express appreciation of his hosts' welcome. Many times at the close of a convention the presiding officer may appropriately express the thanks of the group he represents for the courtesies extended by those responsible for entertaining his organization. Moreover, the chairman must sometimes act as spokesman for his organization in expressing appreciation for the services of a visiting speaker or entertainer. (A more complete discussion of this problem will be found in the following chapter.)

Such acts of courtesy should never become long and elaborate speeches. They may often be incorporated in the chairman's opening remarks or in a brief comment at the close of the meeting. Above all, such remarks should be sincere. Do not try to exhibit your vocabulary or the flourish of your imagination. Express a genuine welcome or a sincere appreciation in simple language, mention one or two pertinent facts, and proceed with the program. In such situations, the way you look and the tone of your voice will express your feeling more fully than anything you can say.

Preserving order

If the chairman sets the keynote at the beginning of the meeting and keeps the program moving rapidly and smoothly, he will seldom have trouble preserving order. Disorder is more often the result of restlessness than of bad intentions. Therefore, if you notice disorder in the audience, do not immediately bark at the offenders; instead, increase the tempo of the program and make your own remarks more lively. You will find in most cases that the commotion will cease.

Occasionally, however, some individual in the audience will attempt to interrupt the speaker or to heckle him. Most speakers can handle such matters themselves; but if you see that the speaker is becoming annoyed, you may have to intervene. Suggest to the individual that he wait till the speaker has finished and that he will then be given an opportunity to ask questions. This will usually stop the disturbance, and frequently the heckler's question will be answered in the course of the speech. If during the question period several people start objecting and questioning at the same time, ask them to wait their turn and to state their questions simply. When the speaker has answered one person, call on another before the first objector has a chance to grab control of the situation by making a long speech or asking a protracted series of questions.

Such action on the part of the chairman should be prompt and decisive but exceedingly tactful. Coercion usually results in greater disorder or in sullen hostility. Firmness combined with dignified courtesy will usually quell any unruly element in the audience and at the same time keep the respect of the rest of the audience.

Once in a great while the chairman must administer a reprimand to the entire audience or to someone in it. You should do this only as a last resort; but if you are forced to this extremity, don't be half-hearted about it. Let the person know in no uncertain terms that he is disturbing the meeting by his actions; then if he persists, have him ejected by the ushers or the police. It is much better to go through with this unpleasantness than to lose your command of the situation. After such an incident has occurred, however, do or say something which will quickly and forcibly call the attention of the audience back to the program. Never prolong the agony by discussing the incident with the audience.

INTRODUCING SPEAKERS

In addition to controlling the situation and performing the incidental duties outlined above, the chairman must introduce the speakers. Performing this duty effectively is not so simple as it may seem. Too often the introduction is long and rambling and only bores the listeners. Although extremely important, the speech of introduction should be brief and to the point.

If someone else is better acquainted with the main speaker than you are, you may well request that person to introduce him. But be sure that he understands he is to introduce the speaker and not to tell a long series of anecdotes about their acquaintanceship. And make your request before the meeting—don't call upon him without warning.

The purpose of the introductory speech Remember that your main object is to arouse the audience's desire to hear the speaker; everything else must be subordinated to this aim. Your duty is to introduce, not to make a speech. Do not take this as an opportunity to air your own views on the subject. You are only the advance agent; your job is to sell the speaker to your audience.

This implies two things: (*a*) You must arouse curiosity about the speaker or his subject; by doing this, you will make it easier for him to get the attention of the audience. And (*b*) you must make the audience either like him or respect him—or both; in this way you will make his listeners more likely to believe what he says and to do what he asks.

The manner of speaking The dignity or informality of your manner will depend entirely upon the type of occasion, upon the closeness of your acquaintance with the speaker, and upon the prestige of the speaker himself. If you were introducing the Chief Justice of the United States Supreme Court, for instance, it would hardly be appropriate to poke fun at him. Nor would such a thing be tactful if the speaker were a stranger to you or if the occasion were serious and dignified. On the other hand, if you were to present an old friend to a group of your associates at an informal occasion, a solemn, dignified manner would be just as out of place. The difficulty with most people is that they know only *one* method: either they introduce every speaker with ponderous dignity regardless of the occasion, or they start every speaker off by telling a joke about him. Neither of these methods is bad in itself, but you should be able to use each in its proper place.

Regardless of the formality or informality of the occasion, you must talk with sincere enthusiasm. Suggest by the way you talk about a speaker that you yourself are enthusiastic about him. Be careful, however, not to overdo your enthusiasm. Your audience will quickly catch on if your enthusiasm is forced. One chairman's introductions were so enthusiastic that his audience got the impression that the poorer the speaker the more enthusiastic the introduction for him would be. If you have no real interest in the speaker, ask someone to introduce him who has.

Characteristics of content

As the chairman of a meeting, you should follow these principles in your introduction:

Be brief. To say too much is worse than to say too little. Many people think that Shailer Matthews' introduction of President Wilson was the best introductory speech ever made; he said, "Ladies and Gentlemen: the President." The prestige of the man you introduce will not always be great enough for you to be this brief, but it is better to err in this direction than to speak too long.

Don't talk about yourself. There is a great temptation to present your own views on the subject or to tell anecdotes about your own experiences as a speaker. This is strictly taboo, for it calls attention to you when your object is to call attention to the speaker.

Tell about the speaker. Who is he? What is his position in business or government? What experiences has he had that qualify him to speak on this subject? Caution: beware of emphasizing what a good *speaker* he is. Such comment may embarrass him. Let him demonstrate his own speaking ability; you tell who he is and what he knows. Never introduce a man as "a distinguished orator."

Emphasize the importance of his subject unless the audience already realizes its importance. This does not mean that you should give a great deal of information about the subject. Don't make the speaker's speech for him. Merely point out to the audience the value of the information the speaker is about to offer. For example, "All of us drive automobiles in which we use the products made from petroleum. A knowledge of the way these products are manufactured and marketed is therefore certain to be interesting and valuable to us. . . ."

Mention the appropriateness of the subject or speaker if possible. If a golf club is considering the construction of a new course, a speech on types of grass is very timely. Or if the occasion is the anniversary of a firm, it is appropriate that the founder should be one of the speakers. Statements of such facts serve to connect the speaker more closely with the audience.

Use humor if it suits the occasion. Nothing puts an audience at its ease and creates a friendly feeling better than congenial laughter. Take care, however, that your humor is in good taste. Do not destroy the prestige of the speaker or run the risk of offending him.

Organization
The speech of introduction rarely employs all five of the steps in the motivated sequence. Only fairly long introductions do so; more often, brevity requires that only one or two of the steps be definitely stated—the others are merely implied. To make this point clear, we shall first set down the complete sequence as used in longer introductions and then indicate the more frequent abbreviations of it.

Attention step. The introductory speech may be opened by a brief reference to the occasion for the meeting, a reference to the introducer's personal acquaintance with the speaker, a humorous quip at the expense of the speaker if it is in good taste, or a curiosity-provoking statement. More often, however, attention is obtained by beginning with the need step or the satisfaction step, using the facts presented there to attract attention.

Need step. The audience may be shown a need for information on the subject which the speaker is going to discuss. Arouse curiosity about the subject or make the audience aware of the personal value to them of the information they are about to hear.

Satisfaction step. Demonstrate that the speaker is well qualified to speak on the chosen subject because of his position or experience. Tell who he is, where he comes from, and what he has done; include any unusual facts about him that may be appropriate. Build up his prestige to whatever extent necessary, but don't extend your remarks into a complete biographical sketch—

remember the requirement of brevity. The better known a speaker is, the shorter this step can be.

Visualization step. Rarely is the visualization step an extended part of the speech, and frequently it is omitted entirely. The manner of your speaking will do more to arouse pleasurable anticipation of the speaker's remarks than anything you can say. A sincere statement that "I am happy to present Mr. ———" will often be adequate.

Action step. Your purpose is to get the audience to listen to the speaker. This action is suggested by turning and calling upon the speaker to come forward. By so doing you imply, "Here is the person about whom I have been talking; listen to him." If you have not mentioned the speaker's subject previously, briefly announce it at this time.

As was indicated earlier, the entire sequence will rarely be needed. In most instances, you can use one of the following abbreviated sequences.

When the subject is important, secure attention by plunging directly into the:

1. *Need step:* a statement of the importance of the subject to the audience.
2. *Satisfaction step:* a sharply abbreviated statement of the speaker's special qualifications to talk on this subject.
3. *Action step:* the presentation of the speaker.

When the speaker may be considered more important than his subject, secure attention by plunging directly into the:

1. *Satisfaction step:* a statement of facts about the speaker, especially facts that are not ordinarily known or those that are of particular significance to the occasion.
2. *Action step:* the presentation of the speaker and a brief announcement of his subject.

When time is short or the speaker is so well known that extreme brevity is desirable, secure attention by your salutation— "Ladies and Gentlemen," "Members of the Izaak Walton League," etc.—and proceed at once to the:

1. *Action step:* a brief announcement of the speaker's name, position, and subject.

Usually, the better known and respected the speaker is, the more abbreviated should be your introduction; the more completely unknown he is, the more you will need to arouse interest in his subject and build up his prestige. But always remember the four primary virtues of the speech of introduction: tact, brevity, sincerity, and enthusiasm.

EXAMPLES

The examples printed below are of different types. The first places emphasis on the speaker and his importance to the audience; the second gives greater attention to the subject to be considered.

CLARICE KLINE, INTRODUCING JOHN S. COOPER [1]

Satisfaction step   It is altogether fitting and proper that the Honorable John Sherman Cooper, Senator from Kentucky, is our speaker for this evening. As you know, Senator Cooper was a cosponsor of the Murray-Metcalf bill for broad federal support of public education. In the years he has served in the Senate since 1946, he has faithfully supported bills which authorized federal assistance to the states for educational purposes. In fact, the Republican senator was coauthor of the Taft bill in 1947 which passed the Senate but was not acted on by the House.

In 1954 he introduced and reported to the Senate a school construction aid bill which did not come to a vote. In 1958 he was a cosponsor of the National Defense Education Act which provides loans for high-school graduates attending college, fellowships for graduate students, grants for teachers attending training institutes, and assistance for vocational training and the purchase of specialized school equipment. This past year, the senator was a member of the Education Subcommittee of the Senate Committee on Labor and Public Welfare which reported the school construction bill, S. 8, to the Senate. He also supported the Clark-Monroney amendments to this bill, which authorize grants to the states to be used either for classroom construction or to increase teachers' salaries.

A June poll conducted by *Newsweek* magazine of 50 top Washington correspondents rated Senator Cooper among the four "ablest men in Congress." As a matter of fact, he was named the leading Senate Republican out of the quartet of winners in the survey.

---

[1] From *National Education Association, Addresses and Proceedings of the Ninety-Eighth Annual Meeting, June 26–July 1, 1960,* Vol. 98, p. 140.

Action step In these and many other matters, Senator Cooper has worked gladly with the National Education Association in the interests of our schools. It is a pleasure to present to you Senator John Sherman Cooper of Kentucky, who will speak on "Imperatives of Our Times."

JOHN K. M. MCCAFFERY, INTRODUCING JOSEPH S. CLARK [2]

Attention step Ladies and gentlemen, welcome to this special half-hour edition of *The Nation's Future*. Now every third week we concentrate on issues of national impact which have special local application, and our subject tonight is "Should Federal Aid to Education Include Teachers' Salaries?"

Need step Now this evening of course we are talking not only about the nation's future but the future of our children, which is bound up in it. And we meet the questions: Can we afford a teacher shortage numbering almost 200,000? Can we afford to have half a million children going to school part-time? Can we get good teachers for our children when the national average of teacher salaries is less than $5,000?

To fulfill the potential of every youngster and to insure the maximum strength and capability of our democratic society it is clearly recognized that we need more teachers, and that we need better teachers, and we need more schools. Now there is little argument over our goals but what is at issue is the best means to provide or to obtain these goals. Now who should pay for the school system that we need and that we want and to what degree? Now that is what our two distinguished speakers are prepared to debate this evening.

Satisfaction step Our first speaker, Senator Joseph S. Clark, is the senior Senator from Pennsylvania. After obtaining his law degree from the University of Pennsylvania he subsequently became city controller and then mayor of Philadelphia. He was elected to the United States Senate in 1956 for the term expiring January, 1963.

Action step And may we hear your position, please, Senator Clark?

SPEECHES FOR COLLATERAL STUDY

1. James Brown, introducing Julius H. Barnes—Homer D. Lindgren, *Modern Speeches* (Crofts, N. Y., 1930), p. 392.

---

[2] From *The Nation's Future*, NBC Television, December 17, 1960.

2. William Green, introducing James J. Davis—James M. O'Neill and F. K. Riley, *Contemporary Speeches* (Century, N. Y., 1930), p. 71.

3. Robert Morss Lovett, introducing Sam A. Lewisohn—*Ibid.*, p. 68.

4. George Barr McCutcheon, introducing Meredith Nicholson—W. N. Brigance, *Classified Speech Models* (Crofts, N. Y., 1928), p. 236.

5. Mary McSkimmon, introducing Francis G. Blair—*Ibid.*, p. 239.

6. Frank S. Streeter, introducing Dean Jones of Yale—James M. O'Neill, *Modern Short Speeches* (Century, N. Y., 1923), p. 5.

7. See also Guy R. Lyle and Kevin Guinagh, *I Am Happy to Present* (H. W. Wilson Co., N. Y., 1953).

PROBLEMS

1. Be ready to discuss the following questions in class: How can the chairman of a program command the situation? What are his incidental, but essential, duties? What principles of delivery and content will help him accomplish the purpose of his introduction? What conditions affect the organization of the speech of introduction?

2. Assuming that you are to be the presiding officer, outline a program for each of the following occasions: (*a*) a banquet celebrating a successful football season, (*b*) the opening convention session of some organization with which you are familiar, (*c*) a program meeting of some club to which you belong. Arrange the items of the program in order, indicate the function of each item with reference to the purpose of the meeting, allocate the amount of time for each item, and indicate what incidental duties you must perform.

3. Analyze five printed speeches of introduction. Outline each and determine whether the long or short type of organization was used. Upon which was greater emphasis laid: the importance of the subject or the qualifications of the speaker? Why?

4. Attend some meeting where several speakers are to be introduced. Analyze the introductions in the manner indicated in Problem 3.

5. Assume that you are to introduce one of the speakers whose speeches are printed at the end of Chapter 19, 20, 21, or 22. Prepare an appropriate introduction using one of the shorter forms.

6. Preside for one day during the next series of class speeches. See that the program runs on schedule; maintain a lively atmosphere in the meeting; and introduce each speaker in an appropriate manner.

True politeness consists in being easy one's self, and in making every one about one as easy as one can.

Alexander Pope

CHAPTER **25**/*Speeches for Courtesy*

M ost speakers, at one time or another, will have occasion to give a speech for courtesy either on behalf of themselves or on behalf of an organization they represent. The ability to say the appropriate and effective thing on such an occasion is a valuable asset.

TYPICAL SITUATIONS REQUIRING SPEECHES FOR COURTESY

Speeches for courtesy are given most frequently to fulfill one of three obligations: (*a*) *To welcome visitors or new members.* Some organizations have a standardized ritual for welcoming guests or initiating new members, but the more usual method is a greeting by the presiding officer or some prominent member. For example, at a convention, the mayor of the city where it is held or the president of the local branch of the organization usually welcomes the visiting delegates; or at a local meeting, the presiding officer is usually expected to extend greetings to any guests present. (*b*) *To respond to a welcome or greeting.* An individual or organization thus welcomed is often expected to express appreciation of that greeting. (*c*) *To accept a gift or an office.* Occasionally an individual may be presented with a gift or a prize for some special accomplishment, or he may be elected to an office of responsibility or given some honor. In such cases, the recipient of the gift, prize, office, or honor may be expected to express his appreciation. If an organization is the recipient, a spokesman for the group acknowledges the gift or honor.

THE PURPOSE

The speech for courtesy has a double purpose. It enables the speaker not only to express a genuine sentiment of gratitude or hospitality but also to create good feeling in the audience. The success of the speech for courtesy often depends upon whether the audience feels that the appropriate thing has been said. When guests are present or acknowledgments are due, the audience expects the proper courtesies to be extended. Just as the courtesies of private life put people at ease, so the public acts of courtesy create good feeling in an audience.

THE MANNER OF SPEAKING

In no other type of speech is the temptation so great to repeat with oratorical flourish a series of flowery platitudes. Above all, speak sincerely in a speech for courtesy. Do not try to overdo yourself in graciousness. Speak straightforwardly and honestly. Moreover, let your manner—serious or jovial, brisk or tranquil—fit the spirit of the situation. Usually a note of optimism is appropriate. Suggest by your manner that you are pleased by the presence of the guest, that you will enjoy the gift, or that you are glad to be present.

CHARACTERISTICS OF CONTENT

Remember that your duty is to perform tactfully an act of courtesy. With respect to the content of your speech, therefore, keep in mind the following points.

Indicate for whom you are speaking. If you are the spokesman for a group, be sure to make clear that the greeting or acknowledgment comes from the whole group, not from you alone. For example, "It is a privilege to be here this afternoon to accept in the name of the Markham Hospital Board the ambulance your organization has so generously contributed to our community hospital." References to yourself or to the group you represent should, of course, be modest.

Present complimentary facts about the person or group to which you are extending the courtesy. Your emphasis should be on the achievements or good qualities of the person or group you are greeting or whose gift or welcome you are acknowledging, rather than on yourself or the group you represent.

Avoid points of disagreement. In giving a speech for courtesy, you should of course beware of saying anything that might offend your hosts or guests. Avoid, as far as possible, any points of disagreement. Let the incidents and facts which you present serve to illuminate and develop the importance of the occasion or the group you are addressing or the guest you are welcoming. Suppose, for example, that a prominent judge were a guest at your local club. In welcoming him, it would be bad taste to talk about the red tape in legal procedure or the organized strength of criminal gangs. Present, rather, incidents concerning the judge or his accomplishments which will show you appreciate his prestige and personality and are glad to have him with you.

ORGANIZATION

The speech for courtesy should seldom include more than three of the steps in the motivated sequence. At times only the satisfaction step—the actual greeting—is required. Quite obviously no need step is used, for the situation implies the audience's consciousness of the need for an act of courtesy; and just as obviously no action is required. If all three remaining steps are included, they are arranged in somewhat the following fashion.

Attention step   A speech for courtesy may be opened by a reference to the occasion, to the person or group addressed, or to the group for which you are spokesman. If you are accepting a gift or an office, you may appropriately begin by referring to the donor of that gift or to the group which has elected you. Such references at the beginning of your speech should be brief and lead directly into the satisfaction step.

Satisfaction step The bulk of the speech is the satisfaction step—the performance of the act of courtesy. The actual greeting or acknowledgment is illuminated and amplified by one or more of the following points:

(*a*) Complimentary facts about the host, or guest, or donor.

(*b*) Facts about the group you represent, indicating the warmth or extent of your greeting—for example, the number of people who join with you in this greeting.

(*c*) Plans for the future, giving tangible evidence of the practical nature of your hospitality or appreciation—for example, plans made for the accommodation or entertainment of the guests welcomed, plans you as a guest have for the period of your stay, plans you have for the use of the gift being accepted, or plans for the performance of the duties of the office you are accepting. (Note here that the speech made in accepting a nomination for a political office is not properly a speech for courtesy but a speech for action urging people to vote; hence, the technic employed should be that explained in Chapter 21 or 22, although some elements of courtesy would be included.)

Visualization step The function of the visualization step in the speech for courtesy is to suggest anticipated pleasure in having the guests present, in being present as a guest, in using the gift and remembering the donors of it, or in performing the duties of the office. Many times, instead of forming a separate section of the speech, visualization is included in the discussion of the various points of the satisfaction step. Whether treated separately or combined with the satisfaction step, an expression of anticipated pleasure should always be included. (One caution: It is always bad taste to refer to the monetary value of a gift.) At the end of the visualization step close with an emphatic, sincere reiteration of the greeting or acknowledgment.

The organization suggested above is rather complete; not all the items listed will be used in every speech of courtesy. Instead, the steps included will vary with each situation. For example, a student to whom a prize is awarded is frequently not expected to say more than "Thank you" or to show his appreciation by smiling. The following examples suggest various ways of developing the speech for courtesy.

CALIFORNIA WELCOMES THE UNITED NATIONS [1]

> *The following address was delivered by Earl Warren, then Governor of California, to the delegates assembled at the United Nations Conference on International Organization, held in San Francisco in the spring of 1945.*

Attention step   Mr. President, Ladies and Gentlemen: The people of California are highly honored by your presence. We are profoundly grateful to the United Nations for the unity which has pushed the war to a stage that makes timely such a Conference as is now being opened. We share with you the full realization of the importance and the solemnity of the occasion.

Satisfaction and visualization steps   You are meeting in a State where the people have unshakeable faith in the great purposes which have inspired your gathering. We look upon your presence as a great and necessary step toward world peace. It is our daily prayer that the bonds of understanding forged here will serve to benefit all humanity for generations to come.

We here on the Pacific Coast of the United States of America are fully aware of the special recognition you have given us. Ours is a young civilization, a civilization that has made its greatest development during the life-times of men now living. Many of you represent nations which are not only ages old, but which have for centuries been making the struggle for a better world, the struggle in which we are now all joined. It is a double compliment to us, therefore, to have our young and hopeful segment of the world chosen as the drafting room for a new era in international good will.

We recognize that our future is linked with a world future in which the term "Good Neighbor" has become a global consideration. We have learned that understanding of one another's problems is the greatest

---

[1] From the verbatim record of the Plenary Sessions of the United Nations Conference on International Organization in San Francisco, April to June, 1945. Printed on page 30-A of the copy published by the *United States News.*

assurance of peace and that true understanding comes only as a product of free consultation.

This Conference is proof in itself of the new conception of neighborliness and unity which must be recognized in world affairs. The plan to hold this Conference was announced at Yalta—half way around the world—only two and a half months ago. Yet, in spite of all the tragic events of the war, including the sad and untimely death of our own President, it opens today here in San Francisco on schedule and without the slightest interference with the greatest military undertakings in all history.

Unity has created the strength to win the war. It is bringing us ever closer to the end of world conflict. This same strength of unity, continued and cultivated here, can be made to develop a sound pattern of world affairs with a new measure of security for all nations.

It is in the spirit of neighborliness that we join you in advancing tolerance and understanding, the tools with which we are confident a better and happier world can be built.

Formal It is in expression of this spirit that I, as Governor
restatement of California, welcome you.

RESPONSE TO WELCOME [2]

> *This is the response made by Anthony Eden, Chairman of the United Kingdom Delegation to the United Nations Conference on International Organization. Note how Mr. Eden used his opening salutation to gain attention and then immediately plunged into the response required to satisfy the implied need for courtesy. Observe, too, how he compressed into three sentences the characteristics of such a speech.*

M r. Chairman, Fellow Delegates, Ladies and Gentlemen: No more suitable setting could have been found anywhere for this assembly than the splendid city of San Francisco, one of the main centers of the United Nations war effort—San Francisco, whose confidence in the future is only equalled by its sense of comradeship today. Our deep gratitude, Sir, is due to the city itself and to the whole State of California, which with traditional hospitality has opened its gates to us, and also to the Government and the people of the United States who in a wider sense are our hosts at this momentous function. We thank you, Sir, and through you all those who have helped to organize this Conference, for the labor which they have given so generously in the common cause.

---

[2] *Ibid.*, p. 31-A.

ACCEPTANCE OF HONORARY MEMBERSHIP [3]

> *The following remarks were made by Dwight D. Eisenhower, then the newly appointed President of Columbia University, in accepting an honorary membership in the Chamber of Commerce of the State of New York. These remarks served also as the opening for his prepared address on "Support for Western Europe" to that group.*

Mr. President, Mr. Grimm, Gentlemen: I am keenly sensible of the great honor this Chamber has done me. And it is doubly welcome because this award—the priceless token of your honorary membership—comes to me so quickly after my own transfer to this city. It is a distinction I shall always treasure.

I could only have wished as I listened to the overgenerous remarks of Mr. Grimm that the people really responsible for the achievements for which I am honored today—for which I have often been so honored —could be here to hear them: The GI's, the officers, the Brass Hats— indeed, every single citizen of the United States, that each in his own sphere attempted to do his job in the late war.

SPEECHES FOR COLLATERAL STUDY

1. Celal Bayar, "Our Common Convictions"—*Vital Speeches of the Day*, Vol. XX, March 1, 1954, p. 290 ff.

2. Dwight D. Eisenhower, "This Continent a Single Entity"—*Ibid.*, Vol. XX, December 1, 1953, p. 98 ff.

3. William Faulkner, Speech of Acceptance—Harold F. Harding, *The Age of Danger* (Random House, N. Y., 1952), p. 397 ff.

4. William Green, Response to Toronto's welcome—James M. O'Neill and F. K. Riley, *Contemporary Speeches* (Century, N. Y., 1930), p. 25 ff.

5. Theodore Roosevelt, Accepting a horse and saddle—James M. O'Neill, *Modern Short Speeches* (Century, N. Y., 1923), p. 66.

6. John F. Stevens, Response to presentation of the John Fritz Medal —William P. Sandford and W. H. Yeager, *Business Speeches by Business Men* (McGraw-Hill, N. Y., 1930), p. 704 ff.

7. Adlai E. Stevenson, Address of Welcome—Adlai E. Stevenson, *Major Campaign Speeches of Adlai E. Stevenson* (Random House, N. Y., 1953), p. 3 ff.

PROBLEMS

1. Be prepared to discuss the following questions in class: What are speeches for courtesy? What characteristics of delivery and content are

---

[3] From *Vital Speeches of the Day*, Vol. XIV, May 15, 1948, p. 461.

common to each of the purposes? How is the motivated sequence adapted to speeches for courtesy?

2. Find printed copies of at least one speech of welcome, one speech of response, and one speech of acceptance. Outline each. Note in what way each employed the characteristic elements of content, and compare the organization of each with the plan proposed in this chapter.

3. Prepare a speech suitable for one of the following situations:
  A. Welcoming a distinguished alumnus.
  B. Welcoming the newly initiated members to an honorary society.
  C. Responding to one of the welcoming speeches listed above.
  D. Accepting an award for an athletic or scholastic achievement.
  E. Accepting an office to which you have been elected.

Good Will is the mightiest practical force in the world. . . .
Charles Fletcher Dole

CHAPTER *26*/ *Speeches*
to Secure
Goodwill

E very speech, of course, seeks the goodwill of the audience,
but the type of speech considered in this chapter has the securing of the audience's goodwill as its primary aim. In a sense,
the purpose of the goodwill speech is to inform, since it tells about
the organization for which goodwill is sought; in another sense,
its purpose is to convince or actuate, yet it must not be too argumentative—the appeal for direct support must be subordinated
or even hidden. The goodwill speech is, then, a sort of hybrid,
combining the characteristics of two basic types of speech considered in Part Five: it is an informative speech which attempts
to stimulate or convince. Within recent years goodwill speeches
have begun to play an important part in the public relations of
many business firms. For example, more than eighteen hundred
speeches of this type were made in one year by the representatives
of one large Chicago corporation. But business firms are not

alone in this practice; schools, churches, clubs, and public institutions—all employ this technic for obtaining public support.

TYPICAL SITUATIONS

Four of the most common situations in which goodwill speeches are given are luncheon club meetings, educational programs, special demonstration programs, and conventions. *Luncheon club meetings* present an excellent opportunity for such talks because the typical audience, composed of leading men and women from all types of businesses and professions, is usually interested in civic affairs and in the way other businesses operate. Since such meetings are semisocial in nature, the good feeling of the audience is practically guaranteed. Gaining the goodwill and support of such an audience is not only relatively easy but also extremely valuable. *Educational programs* are often arranged by schools, clubs, and church groups in order to have the young people hear a speaker tell about his business or profession and explain the opportunities it affords and the training it requires. By tactful reference, a speaker may secure goodwill for the particular organization he represents. *Special demonstration programs* are frequently presented by corporations and by university extension departments. For example, the county farm agent, referring to experiments conducted at the state university, may show better methods of grading butter or of feeding poultry. Although the speech is primarily informative, the speaker does not allow the point to be lost that the experimental work was done by the university for the benefit of farmers such as those who make up the audience. *Conventions* sometimes offer opportunities for goodwill talks, particularly at their banquets and luncheons. A typical goodwill speech was given at a recent convention of bankers by an official from an airplane manufacturing concern who spoke on commercial aviation, showing its relation to banking.

THE PURPOSE

Although the *real* purpose of the speech is to secure goodwill, this must not be *apparent*. As far as the audience is concerned, the purpose must appear to be primarily informative (or sometimes persuasive: urging joint action toward a common goal). Moreover, to secure his listeners' goodwill, the speaker must present his information so that they will understand and appreciate his organization. In short, the purpose of the speech is to present information about the speaker's profession or organization in such a way that he will unobtrusively gain goodwill and support for it.

THE MANNER OF SPEAKING

Three qualities—modesty, tolerance, and good humor—characterize the manner of speaking required for goodwill speeches. Although the speaker will be talking about his own vocation and trying to make it seem important to his audience, he should beware of bragging. In giving a goodwill speech, you should let the facts speak for themselves. Moreover, show a tolerant attitude toward others, especially competitors. The railroad representative who violently attacked the truck companies and bus lines gained more ill will than good. A courteous attitude accompanied by a tactful presentation of the good things his company had done would have been much more effective. Finally, exercise good humor. The goodwill speech is not for the crusader. Take the task more genially. Don't try to cram your talk down people's throats; instead, show so much good feeling toward your listeners that they will spontaneously respond to your manner of speaking.

CHARACTERISTICS OF CONTENT

Four things should characterize the content of your goodwill speech:

Present novel, interesting facts about your organization or profession. In one sense, a speech of this kind implies indulgence in a little gossip. Make your listeners feel that you are letting them in on the inside; give them first-hand information about things that are not generally known. But avoid talking about what is common knowledge.

Show some definite relation between your organization or profession and the lives of your listeners. Make them see how your organization or profession is related to their prosperity or happiness. (For example, the official from the airplane manufacturer who spoke to a convention of bankers showed how the rapid transfer of commercial paper resulted in a great saving to banks.)

Avoid too definite a request for approval; assume that you already have it. Don't make the mistake of telling your listeners that they don't know anything about your organization and that you are trying to get their goodwill. Instead, suggest that they already know a good deal about it (if they don't, they will probably think they ought to) and then proceed as suggested above.

Offer some definite service. This may be in the form of an invitation to visit your plant or office, the distribution of samples or souvenirs, the offer of some special service to the members of this particular audience, or the suggestion that your organization will join theirs in attacking a common problem. The important thing is not *what* you offer them but the impression that you are at their service.

ORGANIZATION

Let us see how these things can be organized into a well-rounded goodwill speech.

Attention step   The purpose of the beginning of your speech is to establish a friendly feeling and to arouse the audience's curiosity about your profession or the institution you represent. You may gain the first objective by a tactful compliment to the group or a reference to the occasion that has brought you together. Follow this with one or two unusual facts or illustrations concerning your organization. For instance, "Before we began manufacturing automobile parts, the Lash Company confined its business to the making of carpenter tools. We succeeded so well that we almost went bankrupt! That was only thirty years ago. Today our export trade to foreign countries is over one hundred times as large as our total annual business in those days. It may interest you to know how this change took place." In some such way you may arouse the audience's curiosity about your organization.

	Point out certain problems facing
Need step	your audience with which your in-
	stitution or profession is vitally

concerned. For instance, if you represent a railroad, show the relation of transportation to community business. By so doing, you can establish common ground with your audience. Ordinarily the need step will be relatively brief and will consist largely of suggestions without much development except for an occasional illustration. However, if you intend to suggest joint action in meeting a common problem, the need step will require full development.

	The meat of your speech will be in
Satisfaction step	the satisfaction step. Here is the
	place to tell the audience about

your institution, profession, or business and what it does. You can do this in three ways.

Relate interesting events in the history of the institution. Pick those events which will demonstrate its humanity, its reliability, and its importance to the community.

Explain its organization and operation. Pick out those things that are unusual or that may contain helpful suggestions for your audience. This method often helps impress upon them the size and efficiency of your organization.

Tell what your organization does. Explain its products; point out how widely they are used; discuss the policies upon which it is run (especially those which you think your audience will agree with or admire); point out what your company has done for this particular community—people employed, local purchases made, assistance in community enterprises, improvement of real estate. Don't boast, but see that your listeners realize the value of your work *to them.*

	Your object here is to crystallize
Visualization step	the goodwill that your presentation
	of information has created. Do this

by giving your hearers a bird's-eye view of the importance of your work to them. Make a rapid survey of the points you have covered in your satisfaction step, or combine them in a single story or illustration. Or, to approach this step in the opposite direction, picture for them the vacancy or loss that would result if the organization you represent should leave the community or go bankrupt. If you use the latter method, be careful not to leave the impression that there is any real danger that this will occur.

Action step It is here that you make your offer of service to the audience—for example, invite the group to visit your plant or point out the willingness of your organization to assist in some community enterprise.

SAMPLE SPEECH

The plan outlined above will have to be modified to suit the needs of your organization or profession and the occasion at which you speak. But never lose sight of one fact: you must indirectly demonstrate to your listeners that your work is of value to them. See how this is done in the following sample speech.

PERPETUAL PROSPERITY [1]

> *The following address by Owen R. Cheatham, Chairman, Georgia-Pacific Corporation, was delivered to the Forum of The Portland Chamber of Commerce, Portland, Oregon, on October 17, 1960, during National Forest Products Week.*

Attention step Mr. Chairman, honored guests, ladies and gentlemen, it is a great honor to have been asked to speak to you here today on the occasion of the first day of National Forest Products Week. And I appreciate it.

The famous industrial genius, Charles Kettering, once told an inquiring reporter: "I am only interested in the future because I expect to spend the balance of my life there." I believe it safe to assume that we all share this notion.

A future that is planned and managed for growth is the most exciting and rewarding kind. In fact, a future spent in calmly admiring something that has stopped growing *is really no future at all.*

This is a fact to keep in sharp focus as we discuss the timberlands of America, and the Pacific Northwest and Oregon in particular. As

---

[1] From *Vital Speeches of the Day*, Vol. XXVII, January 1, 1961, pp. 183–186. Reprinted by permission of Owen R. Cheatham.

you know, the official tree of Oregon—the Douglas Fir—grows rapidly for 70 years then begins to slow down. It slows down even more after 80 and grows at a snail's pace after 100 until ultimately it quits entirely. But, a whole *forest* of trees—properly managed, nurtured, and harvested—will *never* stop growing!

Need and satisfaction steps combined — Timber is the only natural resource that continuously replaces itself. To this wonderful fact, let us harness a couple of sciences—*first, research* which steadily enlarges the use of each harvested tree; second, *scientific* forestry which steadily accelerates regrowth. *Now* we have as close to a guaranteed formula for *economic growth* as can be compounded. The formula works particularly well in the Pacific Northwest, and perhaps better in Western Oregon than anywhere. For, in the raw materials which make up the formula, Oregon is richly endowed.

We are richly endowed by *nature*. Oregon has more than 20 per cent of all the saw timber in America. It has adequate fresh water, ideal river and harbor facilities, and ample supplies of low-cost power. But more important, Oregon has the finest timber-growing land in the world, *capable* of ultimately producing an annual growth of over *15 billion board feet* perpetually. Indeed, with foresighted management, Oregon will have more timber—more cubic inches of wood fiber—50 years, 100 years hence—and on up—than it has today!

Many fine and nationally known forest products companies are operating in Oregon and the Northwest and are a vital part of the future of this region. Among them: Crown-Zellerbach, Simpson, U. S. Plywood, Weyerhaeuser, and dozens of others. This area and the nation can be justly proud of them, and I do not believe you will think me immodest if I add my own company, Georgia-Pacific, to this group.

To play our role in the over-all growth picture to the best of our ability, we shall continue to employ a timber philosophy which will assure continual success. Some people call it perpetual growth; some call it sustained yield. But, I would like to coin a new term which seems to more vividly and fully describe the process. I would like to call it *dynamic conservation.*

We should all believe in conservation and we should all practice it. We must be insistent that America's greatest natural resource will not be burned, eroded, or dissipated. But *neither* do we want to see the valuable timberlands wasted through lack of use nor stunted through lack of scientific forest management. So conservation alone isn't an active enough word to describe our mission. *Negative* conservation eventually destroys its own objective. *Dynamic* conservation, on the other hand, increases the timber by growing *more of it* while getting *more out of it* as each year goes by.

To illustrate dynamic conservation, I must of necessity use Georgia-Pacific as an example, because that is the company I am supposed to know most about. Now what I have said thus far is the central idea behind Georgia-Pacific Corporation. The idea isn't new. It was there in the beginning and it's been there all along, and it will always be there. And it has been outstandingly successful, too. For in the over three decades of Georgia-Pacific's existence, each decade has shown about the same rate of growth, in relationship to invested capital, compounded.

This, too, is the same underlying idea and propelling force that can assure the future growth and success of the whole forest products industry. An examination of the facts will disclose that the great potential of Oregon and its timber industries has not yet been realized— that its fulfillment lies in the future.

From time to time we have all heard stories implying that the forest products industries in Oregon might possibly be on the decline. I vigorously dissent from any such woeful conclusions. I disagree that the timber industry is "gradually withdrawing from the Oregon scene." Indeed, we of Georgia-Pacific Corporation believe that Oregon—and Portland—because of important over-all trends, are emerging as a greater factor than ever in the timber using industries of today and tomorrow, and perpetually.

Many basic changes have taken place in the past decade and many are continuing—changes which, while they may be altering the complexion of the sawmill industry as such in Oregon, are serving at the same time to confirm Oregon as the forest products capital of the world —and thus a center of the timber products industry for the perpetual future.

There's an old Chinese proverb that goes something like this: "If you want a crop for one year, grow millet. If you want a crop for 50 years, grow trees. If you want a crop for 100 years, grow men." With your permission I would like to amend this bit of ancient wisdom by adding just one more sentence—"If you want a crop forever, grow men who know how to use and re-grow trees."

Modern forest management has shown us how to grow as much new timber as we use. Modern industrial genius has shown us how to produce a whole host of products from trees of all ages.

Because of these developments there have been and will continue to be realignments within the industry. As the old segments based entirely upon mature, old-growth, overripe timber decline, other and more profitable segments of the industry emerge. As companies find ways to make newer, better and more products from the growing timber crop, new services, new material requirements, all serve to bring additional strength and diversity and added employment, payrolls and perpetual prosperity to Oregon. Everyone knows that in the case of the entire industry, the mature, old-growth, overripe timber cannot be with us forever. It must be harvested or it will deteriorate and die as the years go along. It must be harvested to make way for new growth—perpetual new growth, and out of it all is coming an orderly transition to a stronger, bigger and better forest products industry—and more growth of the crop we call timber.

Consider, for example, what used to be known as the Boeing tracts in Lincoln County, Oregon, with which many of you are familiar. The North Boeing tract consists of old-growth Douglas Fir, that is upwards of 420 years old, whereas the South Boeing tract is about 80 to 100 years old because the original stand was burned out by the Indians. We have made an intensive study of the growth of these two tracts. It is enlightening to know that over their respective lives, the younger timber in the South Boeing tract has produced five times more growth per acre per year than the older timber in the North tract. And the industry is aware that ways have now been found to get as much dollar return from this young growth as from the old. Food for thought, isn't it?

Or, more amazing—take Georgia-Pacific's Redwood reserves in northern California. There the second growth timber is showing more growth in 50 years than the old-growth has added in the last 1000 years!

Emanating as some of us have from another great timber center of the nation—the Southeast—and with substantial operations in the South, we of Georgia-Pacific may realize better than some the great value and future of growing timber as a crop. Back in the twenties, one heard many tales of woe in the South that the old-growth timber would be gone in a few years. Little did people then realize that today, with the old growth virtually gone, the second crop would be worth many times the value of the old growth of the past.

When I was a small boy, my grandfather told me that when he was released from the army at the end of the Civil War in 1865, he gave some thought into going into the lumber business. However, he was advised that "in 20 years all of the timber would be cut out," so instead he went into tobacco farming in Virginia.

Productivity, progress and prosperity—all are greater from the new Southern timber resources than ever before, thanks to research, new uses, and scientific forest management.

These are some of the reasons why we of Georgia-Pacific have great faith in the future of Oregon and the Northwest as a perpetual forest products center. Indeed, we have proved our faith by deeds. In the past decade our Company has paid out more than $300 million in cash in the process of acquiring West Coast timberlands—and has spent over $60 million in the last five years in new plant construction, the major share in Oregon. Moreover, we are completing this year some $18 million additional investment in new plants. The results of these investments are a matter of public record.

Research is the lubricant of dynamic conservation. It results in more and more profitable use of each harvest, integrates production facilities with the forests, and accelerates the growing of new trees.

A good example is the Georgia-Pacific integrated operations at Toledo, Oregon. In 1951, about nine years ago, we purchased a sawmill and related timberlands there. The operation did not own anything like enough timberlands for a perpetual operation. There was only enough timber at the then rate of production to last until 1960. This is the year the economy of Toledo was supposed to wither. Our first step was the acquisition of adjacent timber and timberlands through several large purchases to make practical a long-range, perpetual harvesting and re-growing schedule and the placing of all the timber under a perpetual-yield plan. Next was the construction and engineering program which called for the best possible utilization of this timber harvest—to reduce the log requirements of the sawmill—a program which required a new plywood mill, a new paper and containerboard mill, and other new facilities, with an expenditure for new plants of over $40 million. Under this program the best of the logs go for the manufacture of plywood and veneers; the logs that are not suitable for that go to the sawmill; and the waste material from both these operations, which was formerly burned, goes into the paper mill. Moreover, supporting salvage opera-tions are conducted to utilize low quality logs and tops that were formerly left in the woods.

Well, what's the score after nine years of this at Toledo?

1. The timber supply is on a perpetual yield basis.
2. Employment has increased 50 per cent.
3. Payrolls are up 100 per cent.
4. The amount paid out for services and supplies is up 65 per cent.
5. The area population has increased by 33 per cent.
6. Sales from the Toledo operations have increased by 100 per cent.
7. *And,* the annual rate of timber harvested is *less* than it was nine years ago. In other words, through research and scientific forestry management, the rate of timber harvest has actually decreased, and all these other developments are on the record, measurable in com-munity well-being, increased productivity for a growing economy, and increased profits for the stockholders.

Not only has this procedure created a sustained and perpetual economy, but it has also added substantially to the tax base, and to the ability of Oregon to provide for the needs of its people. In the Toledo area, for ex-ample, the annual taxes paid on our new paper mill alone are nearly 40 times the annual revenue lost each year through the removal of the harvested old-growth timber from the tax rolls.

While Toledo is a classic example of dynamic conservation, we can cite similar examples of perpetual yield and maximum utilization, either completed or under way, at our other major operations, including Coos Bay, Springfield and Pilot Rock in Oregon—and Eureka-Samoa and Feather Falls in California.

The ownership of a perpetual and everlasting supply of good, well located, well-managed timber and timberland, is not only important to guarantee perpetual and growing operations, but it is just plain good economics.

Several years ago, the late Dr. Charles Roos, of the Econometric Institute, conducted a study on timber values. Digging back into all available records, he found data going back as far as 200 years. He brought his studies up to date by 20-year periods. He could not use the dollar as a basis of comparison because the dollar has fluctuated in purchasing power. Instead, he used as a measuring stick twelve other commodities, such as wheat, corn, cotton, iron ore, and coal. His study disclosed that, in each successive 20-year period over the 200-year record, timber was worth more than it was the preceding 20 years. In other words, it took more bushels of wheat or more tons of coal to buy a thousand feet of standing timber in any given 20-year period than it did in the preceding 20-year period.

This is not difficult to understand when you examine the underlying facts. A host of new products made from wood fibre has come into our way of life in constantly increasing quantities. As late as the 1920's, when we thought of timber we all thought of lumber as the end product. Today, when we think of things made from timber, we think of plywood, paper and paper products, hardboards, particle board, plastics, synthetic textiles, chemicals and many other items, as well as basic lumber. In the United States, the per capita consumption of plywood and of paper and paper products is increasing at as fast a rate as any basic industry.

One of the toughest jobs the engineers of the future are going to be confronted with will be that of supplying the raw materials for our industries. And here again it must be borne in mind that timber is the only natural resource which can replace itself—and in less than one man's lifetime.

Of the approximately one million acres of timber and timberlands which Georgia-Pacific owns outright in the United States, more than 50 per cent is in Oregon. This reserve consists not only of mature old-growth timber but of second growth in all age groups, ranging up to 75 to 100 years of age. And it is being managed on a long-term plan that will furnish a perpetual supply of raw materials for our mills. Timber grows 24 hours a day and it not only guarantees perpetual operations but it places a sound floor under earnings. Moreover, as the mineral rights are owned on nearly all of this acreage, the royalties from proven reserves of natural gas, metallurgical coal and other minerals, all increase the potential.

A successful long-range program requires carefully planned harvesting, followed by scientific regrowing. Yes, nature will take care of regrowth after a fashion but nature alone isn't enough. As we harvest old-growth, mature timber, we must plant and grow more timber. We sow tons of seeds by helicopter. We must make sure that the harvested land is properly reseeded, so we follow up seeding by manual planting of millions of nursery seedling trees to fill in the gaps. Each year, in Oregon alone, Georgia-Pacific is planting more than 2½ million of these new trees.

Dynamic conservation equates with public responsibility—but it is good economics too. It works. In the case of Georgia-Pacific, it has consistently accelerated regrowth, improved the recovery from timber harvested and sharply increased profit margins.

The forest products industry makes a great contribution to the economy and prosperity of the nation. We of Georgia-Pacific are glad to be playing our part. Of interest wherever we operate, and particularly in Oregon, I would like to note for your information:

1. Our total payrolls are about $50 million annually, of which 56 per cent is in Oregon.
2. Our total employees number over 11,000. 6,500 are in Oregon . . . I am told this is the largest group of employees in the state.
3. We pay out annually for goods and services about $26 million, of which 46 per cent is in Oregon.

We operate 46 plants in 33 localities in the United States. But we must never forget that sales and distribution are important, and to accomplish this we have 70 branch sales offices and distribution warehouses located in major cities from coast to coast, and to serve the export trade we have outlets in more than 36 countries abroad.

But above all, to implement dynamic conservation nothing is as important as people, and we are proud of the Georgia-Pacific people, their integrity and their record. A wise man once said, "The owner's eye is the best fertilizer." And Georgia-Pacific management and employees are substantial stockholders. Through its stock bonus plan all salaried employees participate in such ownership. Also, as the result of cordial management-labor relationships our A. F. of L. hourly employees have recently adopted a plan whereby they, too, participate in ownership of the company through a continuous investment fund administered by trustees jointly appointed by management and labor.

We endeavor to be constantly mindful of our civic responsibilities and try to be good citizens wherever we operate. We are grateful for our opportunities to aid civic improvement, to provide scholarships, to support charity and welfare, to work in our individual churches, and to help forestry research at various colleges and universities. Our forests are operated on a multiple use basis and are open to the public for hunting, fishing, and other types of recreation.

Visualization and action steps combined

I cannot let this opportunity pass without saying to you, so large and illustrious a group of Portland's citizens, on the occasion of this National Forest Products Week, that we are tremendously proud to have Portland as the location of our General Offices and the base from which all of our operations emanate. It is an appropriate, logical and natural location, for Portland is the timber capital of the world and the metropolis of Oregon, where some 60 per cent of the economy comes from the forest. No other section is so endowed with natural resources.

We foresee growth far and beyond the 800-thousand population of metropolitan Portland. Certainly there is every warrant for an optimistic outlook for the forest products industry and for over-all industry, and the obvious great growth and expansion which lies ahead for this great area. The recent civic improvements that have been made; one of the nation's largest and most modern airports, a new modern hotel recently completed and another, under construction, to be one of the largest in the Northwest, the new Memorial Coliseum, which will attract great meetings and conventions of national importance—all speak well for the spirit of Portland and of Oregon and its citizens.

The history of Oregon and, indeed, of the great Northwest, is rooted in its endless boundaries of rich, green, growing timberlands, unexcelled in the world. There was its strength in decades past. There lies the foundation for its unceasing growth in the future.

I never fail to get a thrill in coming into Portland—in seeing its surroundings; beautifully cultivated farm lands, perhaps the most fertile in the world; its great forest lands; its breathtaking scenery accented by snow-capped Mt. Hood, Mt. Adams and Mt. St. Helens; its great rivers flowing to the nearby Pacific.

And may I share with you another thrill relating to "home country." About two weeks ago I went down to Virginia, my native state, to visit my mother who has always resided there. We drove over to nearby Lexington and attended a football game at historic Virginia Military Institute. We walked through the campus of Washington and Lee University which adjoins VMI. We passed the Chapel which is the last resting place of Robert E. Lee. I saw one of his quotations, "The education of a man is never completed until he dies." I could not help but think that this is basic to research and indeed to all progress. While the ingenuity of man has contributed much to past progress, there remains a great deal more to learn and the future is unlimited. The past is truly prologue. After the game we visited some of the historic VMI buildings. Engraved in the stone of Stonewall Jackson Arch I saw another quotation from that great military genius, "You may be whatever you resolve to be." And so it is with this great city and state, backed by unexcelled resources. "You may be whatever you resolve to be."

In closing, may I say that I am grateful for this invitation today. My associates and I join you in this high resolve.

SPEECHES FOR COLLATERAL STUDY

1. Richard J. Babcock, "The Dynamic Future of Agriculture"—*Vital Speeches of the Day,* Vol. XXVII, February 15, 1961, p. 269 ff.

2. Winston Churchill, Address to the American Congress—*Congressional Record,* Vol. 87, Proceedings for December 26, 1941. Printed also in *Representative American Speeches: 1941–1942,* edited by A. Craig Baird (H. W. Wilson Co., N. Y.), p. 19 ff.

3. Leroy Collins, "Industrialization of the South"—*Vital Speeches of the Day,* Vol. XXVI, July 1, 1960, p. 564 ff.

4. S. F. Ferguson, "Clocks and the American Clock Industry"— William P. Sandford and W. H. Yeager, *Business Speeches by Business Men* (McGraw-Hill, N. Y., 1930), p. 364 ff.

5. Haley Fiske, "Common Aims of the Light and Power Industry and Life Insurance"—*Ibid.,* p. 341 ff.

6. Liaquat Ali Khan, "A Century of Great Awakenings"—Liaquat Ali Khan, *Pakistan, The Heart of Asia* (Harvard University Press, Cambridge, 1950), p. 227 ff.

7. David J. McDonald, "Labor's Responsibility for Human Rights"— *Representative American Speeches: 1958–1959,* edited by Baird, p. 92 ff.

8. Margaret Hayden Rorke, "Color in Industry"—Sandford and Yeager, *Business Speeches by Business Men,* p. 356 ff.

9. See also current issues of *Vital Speeches of the Day.*

PROBLEMS

1. Be ready to discuss the following questions in class: How do speeches of goodwill combine the characteristics of informative and persuasive speeches? What qualities of delivery and content will contribute to realizing the objectives of the speech of goodwill? What is the purpose of each of the steps of the motivated sequence in a speech of goodwill?

2. Make a list of twenty specific occasions at which goodwill speeches might be made.

3. Prepare a speech for your class to secure goodwill for a campus organization to which you belong. Be sure to incorporate each of the four special characteristics of content for a speech of this type.

4. How might the above speech (Problem 3) be varied for presentation before:
   A. A convocation of all students on campus.
   B. A convocation of high school students.
   C. A meeting of the faculty of your school.
   D. A regular meeting of a local service club.

5. Prepare a speech to secure goodwill for some firm, institution, or organization with which you are familiar. How would it be varied for presentation before:
   A. The county farmers' institute.
   B. One of the local luncheon clubs.
   C. The parent-teacher association.
   D. A convention of dentists, doctors, or other professional group.

6. Survey the last few issues of *Vital Speeches of the Day* and list the speeches which you believe were presented to secure goodwill. Compare and discuss your conclusions with others in your class.

*The noblest deeds can be adequately stated in simple lan-
guage; they are spoiled by emphasis. It is insignificant
matters that stand in need of high-flown words, because
it is the expression, the tone, and the manner that alone
give them effect.*

Jean de la Bruyère

CHAPTER *27* / *Speeches
of
Tribute*

O n many occasions an individual wishes to pay public tribute to
another's personal qualities or achievements. Such occasions
range all the way from the award of a contest trophy to the eulogy
given for one who has died.

TYPICAL SITUATIONS

The eulogy. Memorial services to pay public honor to one who
is dead usually include a speech of tribute. Occasionally a speech
of this kind is given years after the person's death—witness the
many speeches given in honor of Lincoln. More often, however,
the speech concerns a contemporary of the audience.

Dedication. Memorials, in the form of art museums, monuments,
libraries, etc., are sometimes set up to commemorate the life of
some outstanding personality. At the dedication it is appropriate

that a speech be given in honor of the person to whom the memorial is dedicated.

Farewell. When an executive with whom a group of men have long been associated retires or leaves to enter another field or when anyone generally admired is about to leave the community or the office which he has held, public appreciation is often expressed for his fellowship and work.

Presentation. Sometimes a person who is leaving or being honored for some other reason is presented with a gift. Here again, the speech made in presenting the gift expresses the group's admiration of the man.[1] Or if an award is given to the winner of some competitive activity, a tribute may be paid to his success in this particular endeavor. Awards are usually made by superiors to their subordinates, whereas gifts are most frequently given by subordinates or associates to those above them or in similar positions.

Nomination. When a man is nominated for office, it is customary to pay tribute to him in order to show his fitness for the position. In most respects, a nominating speech is similar to other speeches of tribute; but since there are some fundamental differences, its organization will be taken up separately at the end of this chapter.

THE PURPOSE

The basic purpose of a speech of tribute is to secure appreciation of the commendable traits or accomplishments of the person being honored. If you can get your audience to feel deeply the essential worth or importance of the man, you have succeeded. But you may go further than this. (*a*) You may, by honoring him, arouse deeper devotion to the cause he represents. Did he give all he had for his company? Then strive to make your audience feel a deeper loyalty to the company for which he worked. Was he noted as a friend of boys? Then try to arouse a feeling that boys' work deserves your audience's support. But in addition to all this, (*b*) you may create a desire in your listeners to emulate the person

---

[1] Some writers refer to speeches made in presenting gifts or awards as speeches for courtesy. Since such gifts are usually given because of the merit of the recipient, this type of speech is in reality a speech of tribute.

being honored—to follow in his footsteps, to develop the same virtues, to achieve the same renown.

THE MANNER OF SPEAKING

A farewell banquet usually mingles an atmosphere of merriment with a spirit of sincere regret. Memorial services, the unveiling of monuments, and the like are on the whole quite dignified and formal, while enthusiasm is usually the keynote when awards are made. Regardless of the general tone of the occasion, however, avoid high-sounding phrases, bombastic oratory, obvious "oiliness"; these things will kill the effect of a speech of tribute more quickly than anything else. A simple, honest expression of admiration is best.

CHARACTERISTICS OF CONTENT

Too often speeches of tribute are mere enumerations. Many speakers do nothing but recite the facts concerning a man's life, accomplishments, or club membership. Such a speech is little better than an obituary. Remember the impossibility of telling everything about a man in the brief time during which you are to speak. Pick out a few things and emphasize them. Focus the content of your speech on one of three things:

Dominant personal traits. Select the aspects of the man's personality which are the most worthy of admiration and then relate incidents from his life or work which will illustrate those traits. Show how they affected his decisions, enabled him to overcome obstacles, or influenced others.

Outstanding achievements. Pick out a few of his most successful accomplishments. Tell about them in detail to show how valuable they were and how influential he was in securing results. Let your speech say, "Here is what this man has done; see how important it is."

Influence on his associates. The importance of many men lies not so much in any material personal accomplishments as in the influence they have had on the lives of their fellow men or on the course of events. Since you will quite naturally mention an individual's personal traits and achievements in showing what his influence has been, this method differs from the other two mainly in emphasis—in the point of view taken.

Keep in mind, then, that these three methods are not mutually exclusive. Every speech of tribute will contain each of these characteristics to some extent. In the interest of unity and effect upon the audience, however, emphasize only one and subordinate the other two.

In developing your points, beware of complicated statistics and long enumerations. Do not name organization after organization to which the man belongs. What few things you do tell about, narrate in an interesting, human way. After all, you are telling about a man, not a machine. You are not engaged in giving a technical report on his output, but in relating characteristic events in his life. Let each event become a story, living and personal. Only in this way will you get your audience to admire the *man*.

ORGANIZATION

Ordinarily you will have little trouble in getting people to listen to a speech of tribute. The audience probably already admires the man about whom you are to speak and is curious to know what you are going to say about him.

Attention step

Your task, therefore, is to *direct* the attention of the audience toward what you consider important about the man being honored. There are three ways to do this:

1. Make a straightforward, sincere statement of the commendable traits, achievements, or influence which make this man worthy of tribute.
2. Tell about some incident from his life which vividly illustrates these dominant traits, etc.
3. Relate an incident showing the problems he has faced, thus leading directly into the need step.

Need step

The speech of tribute contains no real need step in the sense of demonstrating a problem confronting the audience. The tribute paid in the satisfaction step may be heightened, however, by pointing out here the obstacles which confronted the person to whom tribute is being paid. In a sense you thus help your listeners identify with him and feel sympathy for his needs and problems. Point out in this step, therefore, the difficulties he faced, the opposition he had, the handicaps he had to overcome. This serves to throw into sharp relief his traits or achievements. Theodore Roosevelt's energetic career, for example, becomes the more noteworthy when contrasted with his sickly physical condition in childhood.

A slightly different method is that of pointing out, not the personal problems of the one to whom tribute is paid, but the problems of the organization which were his official responsibility to meet or, in a still larger sense, the problems of society which his accomplishments helped solve. Thus, an account of the former seriousness of diabetes might precede a tribute to the men who isolated insulin.

Satisfaction step   The largest part of your speech will be contained in the satisfaction step. Here the tribute is actually paid. Relate incidents which show how this man or woman met the problems, personal or public, which you have outlined in the need step. In doing this, be sure to demonstrate one of three things:

1. How his personal traits made it possible for him to deal successfully with these problems.
2. How remarkable his achievements were in spite of the obstacles that confronted him.
3. How great his influence on others was.

Visualization step   In the preceding steps you will have enumerated the individual traits or achievements of the person being honored. In this step try to bring all these together so that your audience may get a vivid portrait of *the whole man.*

Introduce an apt quotation. If you can find some bit of poetry or literary description which just fits the man or woman to whom you are paying tribute, introduce it here. If you use this method, however, commit the passage to memory so that you do not falter, and be sure the quotation is not too flowery.

Draw a picture of a world (community, business, etc.) of such persons. Suggest how much better things would be if there were more persons with similar qualities.

Suggest the loss which the absence of this person will bring. Show vividly how he will be missed. Be specific: "It's going to seem mighty strange to walk into Bob's office and not find him there ready to listen, ready to advise, ready to help."

Action step

Frequently, no action step is used in a speech of tribute. When it is, the close of your speech will vary with the occasion somewhat as follows:

Eulogy. Suggest that the best tribute the audience can pay this person is to live as he did or to carry on what he started.

Dedication. Suggest the appropriateness of dedicating this monument, building, etc., to this person, and express the hope that it will inspire others to emulate his accomplishments.

Farewell. Extend the best wishes of those you represent to the person who is going away, and express a determination to carry on what he has begun.

Presentation. Present the gift as a token of your appreciation. (Don't talk about the gift—talk about the loyalty and admiration it represents. It's the thought that counts on such occasions.)

Award. Congratulate the winner, present the prize, and express the hope that he will continue in his achievements.

Remember that what has been said above is not a speech of tribute but merely a skeleton of it. Fill it in with living, illustrative material, and develop it to suit the mood of the occasion.

NOMINATION: A SPECIAL FORM

The nomination is a special type of speech of tribute. Here your primary purpose will be to get the man nominated or elected; the tribute will be secondary, used as a means of securing approval of him. Your manner of speaking will generally be less formal and dignified than when giving other speeches of tribute. It should be businesslike and energetic. In general, the content of your speech will follow what has already been said, though the illustrations should be chosen to show the nominee's qualifications for this particular office. Fundamentally, this is a speech to actuate through conviction, but it has special requirements. Organize the speech as follows:

Attention step. Announce that you are going to nominate a man for this office.

Need step. Point out the qualifications the nominee will need. Enumerate the problems that will face him or those problems facing the organization which he will have to handle.

Satisfaction step. Present evidence that your nominee has the necessary qualifications. Emphasize especially his past experience and the policies to which he has adhered.

Visualization step. Picture the probable success of his term in office and the value the organization will derive from it.

Action step. Formally place his name in nomination and urge your audience to vote for him.

Obviously not all nominations need to be supported by a speech. More often than not, the person nominated is well known by the audience, and his qualifications appreciated. The mere statement "Mr. Chairman, I nominate John Citizen for the office of treasurer" is all that such a situation requires. The organization outlined above is recommended not for purely routine nomination, but for those special occasions when more definite tribute is needed to support the nomination.

In political conventions a man's name is often withheld until the very end of the nominating speech to avoid premature demonstrations. This practice should not be used elsewhere. Everyone guesses who the man is before the end of the speech, and the device is too obviously a mere trick of rhetoric. Frequently, the man is named at the very beginning of the speech in the attention step. This is good practice if the audience is already favorable toward this man's nomination. But if there is some doubt about the attitude of the audience, wait until the satisfaction step to reveal his name. In this way unnecessary hostility may be avoided by showing the particular fitness of the man before he is actually named.

SAMPLE SPEECHES

In the speeches which follow you will find illustrated many of the ideas presented in this chapter.

WORLD BROTHERHOOD IN A SPACE AGE [2]

> *The following address was given by Adlai E. Stevenson at the World Brotherhood Dinner of the National Conference of Christians and Jews, in New York City, on Monday, November 11, 1957. Note how the speaker pays tribute to one who has made significant and numerous contributions to the goal of world brotherhood.*

Attention step　　I have here, if I may play just a little on a word, what I consider the perfect address for a meeting in behalf of World Brotherhood. It is the address on a letter that figured in Thornton Wilder's play *Our Town*. This is the address: "Jane Crofeet, the Crofeet Farm, Grover's Corners, Sutton County, New Hampshire, United States of America, Continent of North America, the Earth, the Solar System, the Universe, the Mind of God."

The address contains some truths the postman probably didn't appreciate. They are the truths we mark by our meeting here tonight: that we are all part of the one great company of mankind; that we are all residents in the one realm which knows no boundaries, no capitals, no foreign policy—for there are no foreigners; that we are all believers together in different prophets but in a single faith.

Need step　　A hundred years ago, even fifty, perhaps even fifteen, to speak of World Brotherhood was, I suspect, to adorn with rhetoric what was at most a remote ideal. Today, however, it has become an insistent, demanding reality, thrust upon us whether we accept it or not by a science that has broken down the fences which had before separated the peoples of the world.

Last month a new star flashed across the skies. I wish it had been we who lighted that new star. It disturbs me greatly, as an American, that it was not. Yet I know, as a citizen of the world and as a member of tomorrow, that the basic issue is no longer the supremacy of nations. It is the supremacy of man for good or for evil, for survival or suicide. The significance of what has happened lies not in which nation has first reached into outer space but in the fact that man has now obliterated, for better or for worse, what we used to call time and distance.

I deny that the satellite is a portent of disaster. I think rather of John Donne's marking of the times in history that "are pregnant with those old twins, Hope and Fear." Surely this is such a time, a time not of catastrophe but of choice, not of disaster but of decision, a time when the preferment of our aspirations over our fears becomes the duty of citizenship in civilization.

---

[2] From *Representative American Speeches: 1957–1958*, edited by A. Craig Baird (H. W. Wilson Co., N. Y.), pp. 58–63. Reprinted by permission of Adlai E. Stevenson.

A very large part, I suspect, of the maturing of mankind to its present estate has come from adversity, or the threat of adversity. More frontiers of what we call progress have probably been crossed under the pressure of necessity than by the power of reason. Prophets have appeared all through history to proclaim an ethic, but humanity has not heeded them, and the world has wandered its way—until the hard steel of survival itself has been pulled against our too soft mouths.

Now, once again, science has forced humanity to a crossroad from which there is no turning back, no escape—and just one road that leads upward. The choice is either extinction—or the human brotherhood that has been the vision of visionaries since the beginning of time.

I deny that human fulfillment cannot keep pace with material advance. We know and must insist rather that what was heralded by the splitting of the atom, what is now proclaimed by the earth satellite, is nothing narrower than man's complete genius—not to exterminate himself, but to control himself.

What that "bleep-bleep" is saying is that now the world has no option, that it must turn from narrow nationalism, sectarianism, racialism, that the only conceivable relationship among men is one based on men's full respect—yes, their love, if you please—for each other.

There is no cause for despair. There is only now a new imperative for peace—that we find that "great beat that is the heart of all human circumstances and of all human feeling."

Yet, to say, in effect, that now once again we have been driven forward by the pressure of crucial circumstances is no cause surely for satisfaction, no counsel of wisdom. If we have in the past been successful we have also been lucky. And surely the achievement of the brotherhood of man is not something to be left to the vagaries of chance or to the complacent, trusting hope that every new crisis may by some alchemy of fate be turned to humanity's good fortune.

Satisfaction step It is my very great privilege and personal pleasure to represent you tonight in saluting a man whose precept it is that we cannot afford just to wait and to hope that everything will work out all right. By his deeds he has rejected the counsel that world brotherhood can win by a policy of brinksmanship, or that mankind can be safely merged by a series of shotgun—or shall we say, missile—marriages. This man's view is rather that world brotherhood must be worked for, prepared for, lived for and sought after with every resource at man's command.

Mr. Chairman, I have, in the discharge of my appointed duties on this occasion, made what we lawyers (you will pardon this brief "commercial") call a title search.

I find, and hereby certify to you, that Albert M. Greenfield is the holder of clear title to the status of rugged pioneer and devoted patron of world brotherhood. I find that he has, without regard to race, creed, color, or any other discernible line or distinction, taken active part in the most extraordinary variety of functions ever to come to my humble attention. I find that he has lent his name and services (and I suspect frequently something even more tangible) to the United Fund and the Community Chest, to the Philadelphia Symphony and to the Connie Mack Golden Jubilee Committee, to the Chapel of Four Chaplains and to the Army and Navy football games.

I can tell this group nothing of Albert Greenfield's contributions of mind and spirit and substance to the work of literally scores of organizations dedicated to the special service of what we call minority groups, and to the elimination of the false lines which mark minorities where there should be no divisions at all.

It is perhaps less well known that our guest of honor has been previously saluted by such various bodies as the Pen and Pencil Club and the Golden Slipper Square Club, the Veterans of Foreign Wars and the Chestnut Street Association, that the Keneseth Israel Men's Club has made him its "Man of the Year" and that he has been decorated by Pope Pius XI as a Commander in the Order of Pius IX.

My research, Mr. Chairman, has gone even to statistics. I am in a position to report, what I am sure Mr. Greenfield does not himself know —except perhaps with a kind of numbness—that there is record evidence of his participation, usually as chairman, in sixty-one committees, commissions, campaigns, chambers or celebrations; and of his previous receipt of twenty-nine honorary awards. The common denominator of most of this activity has been its reflection of this man's consuming belief in the dignity of man.

I note, Mr. Chairman, one lighter point. We speak of brotherhood as an all pervasive thing. Yet we appreciate its respect for one line. It asks of us that we bury all prejudice, every bias—except one. A Republican can in good conscience (I guess) be a Republican and (except in the suburbs) a Democrat. Mr. Chairman, I have said that there is *no* flaw in the brotherhood title of our honored guest. I advise you now that in 1928 he was a delegate from Pennsylvania to the National Convention of the Republican party. I advise you further that in 1948, 1952 and 1956 he was a delegate-at-large from Pennsylvania to the National Convention of the Democratic party. *This* is Brotherhood! And this is also *progress!*

(I might add that not only was Albert Greenfield a delegate to the 1956 convention. He was also a Democratic presidential elector. I claim the personal distinction of being the only living man who ever put Albert Greenfield out of a job.)

Visualization step My friends, you will know that this indulgence of pleasantry only reflects the realization that virtually everything a grateful people can say to Albert Greenfield has been said before.

Yet we mark particularly tonight his most recent and perhaps most enduring contribution to the proposition that men are not only born equal but are entitled to live equal.

The Albert M. Greenfield Center for Human Relations at the University of Pennsylvania is living testament to the fact that today, more than ever before, the price of living is knowing. We cannot count, in the realm of human welfare, on being always the beneficiaries of scientific accomplishment. Nature is no longer man's master. It has become now man's servant. Because we have learned now to control some of the physical world we *must* hasten to learn to control ourselves. This Center for Human Relations is a pioneering step toward our studying now the ways of man and the laws of practical morality as deeply and as urgently as we have studied the ways of matter and the laws of nature.

By building this Center, Albert Greenfield has marked his faithfulness to what is written in the Talmud: "I did not find the world desolate when I entered it, and as my fathers planted for me, so do I plant for my children."

Action step Ladies and gentlemen, acting for you, I confer the World Brotherhood Award Citation upon Albert M. Greenfield, Sugar Loaf, Chestnut Hill, Philadelphia, Pennsylvania, United States of America, Continent of North America, the Earth, the Solar System, the Universe, the Mind of God.

ADDRESS AT THE UNVEILING OF THE STATUE OF LINCOLN [3]

> *The following address by David Lloyd George was given at the ceremonies in Westminster Abbey upon the unveiling of the Saint-Gaudens statue of Lincoln, July 28, 1920. This is a fine example of the lofty and dignified type of tribute expressed at ceremonial occasions. The preceding speaker had described Lincoln's lowly origin and the grave problems he had been required to face. The speech below is in contrast, showing the great character and accomplishments which developed to meet those conditions.*

Attention step I have only a very few words to add to the extremely fine and eloquent address with which our distinguished visitor has fascinated and thrilled us. In a few moments we shall see unveiled before our eyes a presentment in bronze of the best-known historical face in the Anglo-Saxon world—in fact, one of the few best-known faces in the whole world. On behalf of the people of

---

[3] From *International Conciliation*, November 1920 (No. 156), p. 497 ff. Reprinted by special permission of the Carnegie Endowment for International Peace.

this country—and I think I may also say on behalf of the people of the British Empire—I accept with gratitude this fine statue, by a brilliant American sculptor, of a great leader of men. I doubt whether any statesman who ever lived sank so deeply into the hearts of the people of many lands as Abraham Lincoln did. I am not sure that you in America realize the extent to which he is also our possession and our pride. He was in many respects the most remarkable man of his day. If you look at his portraits, they always give you an indelible impression of his great height. So does his life. Height of purpose, height of ideal, height of character, height of intelligence. Amongst many notable men who filled the stage in that day, he was the tallest of them all. His figure stands out now, towering above his tallest contemporaries.

Satisfaction step   In many respects he was taller than even the great events in which he took a directing part. The preservation of the American Union, the emancipation of the slaves, are notable events in the world's history, and any man who took the leading part in those events, as he did, would have won for himself enduring fame; but, reading the story, I feel that the personality of Abraham Lincoln and his statesmanship are in some respects even greater than those colossal events. His courage, his fortitude, his patience, his humanity, his clemency, his trust in the people, his belief in democracy—and, may I add, some of the very phrases in which he gave expression to those attributes—will stand out forever as beacons to guide troubled nations and their perplexed leaders. Resolute in war, he was moderate in victory. Misrepresented, misunderstood, underestimated, he was patient to the last. I know why his face appeared to become sadder as the years of the war rolled past. There were those who thought he ought to have shown his abhorrence of war by waging it half-heartedly, and there were those who thought he ought to have displayed his appreciation of victory by using it hard-heartedly. He disdained both those counsels and he was often reviled by both those counselors. His tenderness was counted as weakness of character, his simplicity as proof of shallowness of mind; but the people believed in him all the time, they believed in him to the end, and they still believe in him now.

Visualization and   In his life he was a great American. He is no longer *action steps*   so. He is one of those giant figures, of whom there are very few in history, who lose their nationality in death. They are no longer Greek or Hebrew, English or American; they belong to mankind. Those eminent men whose statues are in that square are great Englishmen. I wonder whether I will be forgiven for saying that George Washington was a great American, but Abraham Lincoln belongs to the common people in every land. He is of their race, of their kin, of their blood, of their nation—the race of the common people. That is the nationality of Abraham Lincoln today. Everywhere they love that haggard face with the sad but tender eyes gleaming through it. There is a worship in their regard; there is a faith and a hope in that worship. The people—the great people—who could produce men like Lincoln and Lee for their emergencies are sound to the core. The qualities that enabled the American nation to bring forth, to discern, to appreciate, and to follow as leaders such men are needed now more than ever in the settlement of the world. May I respectfully but earnestly say one word from this platform to the great people of America? This torn and bleeding earth is calling today for the help of the America of Abraham Lincoln.

SPEECHES FOR COLLATERAL STUDY

1. Bernard Baruch, "Woodrow Wilson"—*Representative American Speeches: 1956–1957*, edited by A. Craig Baird (H. W. Wilson Co., N. Y.), p. 141 ff.

2. James M. Beck, "John Marshall, Jurist and Statesman"—Lew R. Sarett and W. T. Foster, *Modern Speeches on Basic Issues* (Houghton Mifflin Co., Boston, 1939), p. 211 ff.

3. William E. Borah, Nominating Charles Curtis for the Vice-Presidency—James M. O'Neill and F. K. Riley, *Contemporary Speeches* (Century, N. Y., 1930), p. 496 ff.

4. Winston Churchill, "King George VI"—*Vital Speeches of the Day*, Vol. XVIII, March 1, 1952, p. 290 ff.

5. Eugene C. Elliot, "Horace Mann"—Willard Hayes Yeager, *Effective Speaking for Every Occasion* (Prentice-Hall, N. Y., 1940), p. 138.

6. Irving M. Ives, Tribute to the late Senator Robert Taft, *Congressional Record*, Vol. 99, Proceedings for August 3, 1953.

7. John F. Kennedy, "Portraits of Five Senators in the Senate Reception Room"—*Representative American Speeches: 1957–1958*, edited by Baird, p. 83 ff.

8. William McKinley, "Characteristics of Washington"—James M. O'Neill, *Modern Short Speeches* (Century, N. Y., 1923), p. 162 ff.

9. Wendell Phillips, Eulogy on Daniel O'Connell—W. N. Brigance, *Classified Speech Models* (Crofts, N. Y., 1928), p. 373 ff.

10. Franklin D. Roosevelt, Nominating Alfred E. Smith for the Presidency—Homer D. Lindgren, *Modern Speeches* (Crofts, N. Y., 1930), p. 203 ff.

11. See current issues of *Vital Speeches of the Day*.

12. See the annual volumes of *Representative American Speeches*, edited by Baird and Thonnsen.

PROBLEMS

1. Be ready to discuss the following questions in class: When is a speech of tribute appropriate? What points should be emphasized to

accomplish the purpose of the speech? How may the speech of tribute be organized?

2. Select three of the speeches suggested for collateral study. For each one determine what is used as the focal point of the tribute; outline and compare the organization with that suggested in this chapter; and determine to what extent the speaker encouraged the audience to identify with or emulate the person being praised.

3. Prepare a speech paying tribute to some person on the campus or in the community, such as:
   A. A faculty member who is retiring.
   B. A faculty member who has served for a long term as a fraternity or campus activity advisor.
   C. A member of the secretarial or service staff who has helped many students.
   D. The student who ranks first scholastically in your class.
   E. An outstanding athlete who has received state or national recognition.
   F. An officer of a student organization who has served faithfully and well.

4. For each of the persons suggested above, determine which of the three—personal traits, achievements, or influence upon others—would form the most effective focal point for a speech of tribute.

The microphone is the most tell-tale instrument in the world.

César Saerchinger

CHAPTER 28 / *Adapting Speech to Radio and Television*

A thorough discussion of all the various ways in which speech is broadcast—newscasts, sports broadcasts, market reports, commercials, travelogues, dramatic productions, and many others —would be far beyond the scope of this book. Several excellent books devoted entirely to this subject are available; you should read them if you expect to do specialized work in radio or television.[1] But every speaker today needs at least a general knowledge of broadcasting technics. Any man or woman in business or in a profession or in a position of community leadership can expect to be called upon at times to speak from the local radio or television station. The aim of this chapter, therefore, is to point out the most important differences between face-to-face speaking and speaking over the air and to suggest briefly how the principles and proce-

---

[1] A number of these books are listed at the end of this chapter.

dures already presented in this book may be adapted to meet the broadcasting situation. You will observe that, although important differences do exist, the fundamental principles still apply for the most part and that more often than not what is good speech before a visible audience is good speech over the air.

THE PURPOSE OF A BROADCAST SPEECH

Except for attempting to reach a larger audience than could be gathered together in person at one place, there is no great difference between the purposes of broadcast speeches and of the types of speeches discussed in the preceding chapters. Like other speakers, speakers who broadcast attempt to convince, to stimulate, to entertain, to inform, and to actuate; they introduce speakers, express welcomes, debate public issues, pay tributes, and attempt to gain goodwill. Whatever might be your purpose in talking before a visible audience may also be your purpose when you broadcast. And with some modifications, the same characteristics of speech content and delivery and the same methods of speech organization are used.

THE RADIO AND TELEVISION AUDIENCE

To understand the basis for the modifications necessary in broadcast speaking, you must appreciate the nature of radio and television audiences. First of all, since anyone who has a receiving set within the power range of the broadcasting station can tune in, your listeners are likely to be of both sexes and of all ages, creeds, occupations, interests, and degrees of intelligence. There is no such thing as a radio or television audience composed entirely of young men, or of Democrats, or of Baptists, or of union members. This fact puts an additional premium upon tact and upon the ability to give a subject universal interest.

The hour of the broadcast and the location of the station may modify the nature of the broadcast audience somewhat. Surveys have shown that women listeners predominate during the morning and early afternoon hours when husbands are away at work and children are at school. Children listen mainly in the late afternoon and early evening and only rarely in the late evening. Men are more likely to listen during the evenings and on Sundays and holidays, since they are usually not working then. At mealtimes anyone is likely to listen, but the audience may be small since most people prefer musical programs or brief announcements (markets, news, weather, etc.) at this time. The location of the station sometimes modifies the nature of the audience. On the whole, a metropolitan station tends to draw a larger urban audience and a station in a smaller city, a larger rural audience. This is less true, however, of large powerful stations and network broadcasts, which usually reach every kind of community. Moreover, some stations cater to certain types of listeners, and some program series are frankly pointed to specialized groups. If you speak from such a station or on such a program, many of your listeners are likely to be those whose special interest in that sort of program has led them to tune in. College and university stations, for example, are very apt to specialize in various types of educational programs.

A very important characteristic of radio and television audiences is that the listeners are usually by themselves or in small, intimate groups. In spite of the fact that the audience in general is quite large, the individuals will not be gathered in a large mass but will be scattered about in living rooms, offices, hotel rooms, automobiles, and the like. Thus, while the listener is no doubt aware that others are also listening to the same program, he is primarily influenced by his own intimate environment and expects the speaker to talk to him in an informal, conversational manner suited to that environment, unless he knows that the speech is being made before an actual audience.

Two further facts need to be remembered: listeners can easily turn off a broadcast at any time, and they are apt to have many distractions. People hesitate to make themselves conspicuous by getting up and leaving an audience which a speaker is addressing in person; but the radio or television listener feels no hesitation at all about tuning you out by a twist of the dial. In addition, he is likely to be surrounded by household noises—the baby's crying, the clatter of dishes, a conversation at the other end of the room—which compete with the broadcast for his attention. Both of these facts require that the broadcast speech have a high degree of interest value.

TWO TYPES OF SPEECH BROADCAST

There are two principal types of broadcast speeches: those which are made in the studio without an audience and those which are presented before actual audiences in the studio or broadcast from the speaker's stand in an auditorium.

Broadcasts without an audience present When you speak directly from the studio for the broadcast audience alone, your style of speaking should be very informal and conversational. The novice is apt to think of the "millions" of listeners in his audience and to make an oration to them, forgetting that he is talking directly to only one, two, or three persons in each place. A better plan is to imagine that you are talking with someone over a very clear-toned telephone or that you are conversing with someone sitting across the room from you. Indeed, some speakers bring a friend into the studio with them and direct their remarks to him or to the announcer if he is in the same room. You needn't shout; the transmitter is sufficiently powerful to carry your voice miles away. Do not strain for over-dramatic effects; remember that your radio listeners will be gathered in very small groups and that your talking should therefore be very natural and informal. Now and then you should glance at the engineer in the control room; he hears how your voice sounds over the air and can use hand signals to tell you if you are doing anything wrong.

At first, perhaps, talking in a soundproof room may seem strange to you. Do not be alarmed if your voice sounds a little flat or the pauses between phrases seem a little long—these things are natural results of studio acoustics. Nor is the microphone a deadly instrument as some novices seem to believe; it is simply a substitute for the ears of your listeners—a sort of mouthpiece for a multiple telephone circuit. Talk to it naturally as you would in talking over the telephone to a friend.

Broadcasts with an audience present Sometimes a speech for a particular audience or occasion (such as an anniversary banquet, a dedication, etc.) is of sufficient general interest to justify broadcasting it. On nearly all such occasions the speaker's primary duty is to the audience before him; radio and television listeners are allowed, as it were, to listen in through the window. When your broadcast audience knows that an actual audience is before you, they do not mind your talking in a manner appropriate for formal public speaking rather than for intimate conversation. They use their imaginations to project themselves into your presence and in a sense become a part of the crowd at the dinner or in the auditorium. If the broadcast is over radio only, you can help the imaginations of your radio listeners by occasionally referring pointedly to the specific audience before you or to the occasion which has brought the group together. Of course an occasional ripple of laughter, applause or questions from the audience will help remind the radio listener of the audience before you. Although your primary duty is to your immediate audience, you must not forget the broadcast audience entirely; even in this situation the content and structure of your speech, and to some extent your manner of speaking, should be somewhat modified in the interest of your radio listeners.

A great many programs are broadcast from a studio with an audience present. Quite often a group of twenty or thirty people (in large stations, even more) are invited to participate as a special audience. Then, after the scheduled speech or discussion is concluded, they participate by asking questions or engaging in the discussion. Even when no such studio audience is present, a speaker on a panel will use the other panel members as his audience and will join them in discussion after the prepared speeches. Such broadcasts differ from those discussed in the preceding paragraph because the primary consideration here is for the broadcast audience; the studio audience is present only to represent this larger audience and to give a greater sense of reality to the situation. Hence, although the speaker must talk directly to the actual audience and seek responses from it, he must remember that his primary purpose is to reach the outside listener. He must beware of letting the studio audience run away with the show; he must spend more time answering questions of general interest and cut short his replies to unrepresentative questions. His manner of speaking, however, will be governed by the presence of an actual audience.

In presenting a radio talk, remember that your audience cannot see you and is therefore robbed of all the visual cues so meaningful to the ordinary audience. Gestures, for example, may help you get rid of excess energy or emphasize points in your own mind (and many radio speakers use them unconsciously for these reasons), but your radio listener cannot see them, and their visual emphasis will be lost on him. A great deal of meaning is also conveyed by facial expression, but again, your listener cannot see it. You must make up for this loss of visual clues in some other way. Furthermore, you will be unable to use visual aids in trying to explain a point in a radio speech. All meaning must be conveyed by sound alone: attention must be secured and held, ideas made clear, and action impelled by your voice alone.

In both television and radio speaking, your voice passes through the microphone, transmitting set, and receiver before reaching your listener. Regardless of the perfection of the equipment, some distortion will occur. Frequently this distortion is beneficial, making one's voice sound better than it is naturally; but many little faults may be exaggerated with ruinous effect. Moreover, failure to use the proper microphone technic may result in indistinctness or even in disagreeable noises. Let us see what can be done to use the microphone properly and to compensate for the lack of visual cues in radio speaking.

Microphone technic Many different types of microphones are used in broadcasting. Some pick up sound equally well from all directions; others pick up sound made directly in front of them with much greater volume than that made at the side or above or behind. Ask the announcer or the technician in the studio how far from the microphone you should stand or sit, and at what angle to it you should speak. Ask also how loud you should speak, because microphones differ in their sensitivity.

With most microphones the loudness of the sound picked up varies in approximate geometric ratio to its distance from the source of the sound. That is, if you move about but speak with the same degree of force, the sound picked up by the microphone at a distance of one foot will be four times as loud as at a distance of two feet. Therefore, to avoid fading or an undesired increase in volume, you should always stay at approximately the same distance from the microphone. Especially when you have an actual audience as well as a microphone in front of you, remember not to move too far from the microphone. Hand, lapel, and chest microphones have been developed in order to give the speaker more mobility in such circumstances, but you may still have uneven volume if you turn your head too often or too far to one side from the microphone. In the studio the temptation to move is not so great; if you are seated or standing comfortably, you are likely to stay still. However, if you are reading your material from manuscript, you must be careful not to move your head in looking up at the microphone and down at the script, because this movement may sharply change the volume.

Most radio equipment is very sensitive, and for this reason sudden increases in volume are apt to produce "blasting," an effect similar to what would happen if you hit the keyboard of a piano with a sledge hammer—a crash of sound rather than a clear tone. For this reason, don't shout, and avoid any sudden increase of volume. The man in the control room can modify the volume of your voice, building it up or toning it down, within reason; but he cannot anticipate every sudden change you may make. Seek your vocal variety in differences of rate or pitch, therefore, and keep the degree of force reasonably constant.

Two mistakes amateurs commonly make are intensified in their effect by this same sensitivity in broadcasting equipment. The first is rattling or rustling papers close to the microphone. The actual noise in the studio is slight, but as amplified over the air, it is very noticeable to the listener. At its worst, it may sound like the rapid firing of a gun, the flapping of an awning in an angry wind, or the crushing of an orange crate into kindling. At the very least, it will make your listener keenly aware that you are reading and will destroy the illusion of direct spoken communication. The second mistake is tapping the microphone or table. Like rustling papers, this is a slight noise in the studio but a loud one over the air. Take care, then, to avoid nervous drumming on the table or thumping it for emphasis; let your gestures be noiseless ones. If you use manuscript, choose soft paper, unclip it before you approach the microphone, and lay each sheet aside carefully and quietly when you have finished reading it. In general, you will make less noise if you leave your manuscript on the table or speaker's stand rather than hold it in your hand. A note of caution: check the pages of your manuscript before the broadcast to make sure they are in the correct order. No pause seems as long as when you turn to page three and find page four instead.

Both because the microphone is so sensitive and because your listeners focus their attention entirely upon your voice, the distinctness of your speech and the accuracy of your pronunciation are especially important. Errors and crudities that might pass unnoticed on the platform will stand out over the air. A little care on your part will enable you to avoid such faults. (Refer again to the suggestions made in Chapter 6 on this point.) Many persons, in attempting to avoid indistinctness, speak so carefully that their speech sounds stilted and artificial. To speak overprecisely is almost as bad as to speak indistinctly, for it calls attention to the utterance rather than to the thought. Try, therefore, to avoid both extremes. Special comment should be made about the sibilants— sounds such as *s, z, th, sh*. While some microphones minimize the problem, the high frequencies characteristic of these sounds tend to produce a whistling or hissing sound if they are given too much emphasis. If you have trouble with sibilants, use sparingly words in which these sounds occur in stressed positions—or better, learn to subdue your production of them.

There is no question that the quality of the speaker's voice is changed in transmission. In general, high-pitched voices are less pleasant over the radio, while those of moderately low pitch are sometimes improved in the process of broadcasting. The only way to check the effect of transmission on your own voice is to have an audition or a comparable recording made so that you can listen to yourself talk. In general, speak in the lower part of your pitch range. The fact that you can talk conversationally before the microphone and do not have to project to an audience should improve the quality of your voice, since most people use better quality when they speak quietly than when they apply force. Keep the resonating passages open, however, and use them. Do not allow the quietness of the studio to deceive you into allowing your voice to become flat and colorless.

Compensating for the lack of visual cues Since your listeners cannot see you, you must use your voice to fill in the gaps that would otherwise be filled by visible cues. You must, therefore, speak at a fairly rapid rate. This does not mean that you have to rush, but it does mean that you cannot allow yourself to drag. Long pauses are bad. On a platform where the audience can see you, you can sometimes emphasize a point by standing silent, holding your listeners attention by the earnestness of your facial expression and the apparent tension of your body; all this is lost to the radio listener—he gets only the silence. Pauses can, of course, sometimes be used effectively in radio speaking, but they must be used sparingly and with shorter duration. Again, on the platform a speaker may pause to search for the exact word to express his thought; he is thinking it out with his audience, and they see him doing it. On the air, however, such pauses are empty and may suggest that the speaker is ill at ease and unprepared.

The visual cues a speaker gives his audience do more than fill in the gaps left by pauses in his voice, however. They serve to give emphasis, to convey additional meaning, and to hold the attention of the audience. When (as in a radio speech) this burden is thrown entirely on the voice, variety of vocal expression is more than a valuable asset—it is a primary essential. Monotony is the very antithesis of effective radio speech. However, since sudden changes of force produce blasting, you must rely on variety of rate and of pitch to communicate effectively by radio. Refer to Chapter 5 and study the sections on rate and pitch again; practice the exercises given there; develop your vocal flexibility to the utmost.

Groping for words is a major sin in radio broadcasting. Since the audience cannot see the speaker, most people write out radio speeches word for word and read them from manuscript. This procedure also insures that you will be able to finish your speech within the allotted time. There is one disadvantage: some persons cannot write with the informality of oral style, and, even when they can, they have difficulty in reading aloud in a natural, easy, conversational manner. This disadvantage, however, can be overcome with a little practice. The almost unanimous advice of experts is to use manuscript for a radio speech and to learn how to read from it naturally.

This procedure requires, first of all, that you write your manuscript in an informal, direct style. Avoid sentences with complex subordinate clauses and stilted or inverted expressions. Instead of writing "Only two runs did the team score," write "The team scored only two runs." Insert connective phrases and summary sentences that sound the way you talk. A helpful procedure is to make a recording of your speech using notes; transcribe the recording; edit the resulting manuscript for errors of fact or wording, and then cut it down in length if necessary, being careful not to lose its spoken style.

When you have prepared the manuscript, practice reading it aloud. Don't read it for the first time before the studio microphone. Become familiar enough with it so that you can ad lib if you happen to lose your place or misplace a page. Above all, practice reading it with a mental image of your listener before you—make it sound like talk. Don't overstress the unimportant words like *the* and *of* and *to*. Use a normal, conversational manner, avoiding equally a droning monotone and an artificial overemphasis or stagy inflection. Read again the comments in Chapter 1 about the conversational mode and strive for sincere and natural communication even in your practice reading.

THE MANNER OF SPEAKING FOR TELEVISION

Unlike radio broadcasting, television broadcasting permits your audience to see you while you talk. Thus your physical behavior —your appearance, facial expression, and movement—may help convey your thought just as they do when you are speaking to an audience in person. At the same time, irritating mannerisms will annoy your listeners, and a monotonous dead-pan expression or slavish dependence on a manuscript will cause them to lose interest. Indeed, the way in which the television camera picks up your image (especially in close-ups) and the intimacy with which your audience views that image on the receiving set make your appearance and movement even more important than when your audience sees you in person.

Thus you cannot concentrate on voice alone as you do in radio broadcasting. Neither can you talk as you would if you were only facing an immediate audience. Your voice and action must conform to the limitations imposed by the microphone and the television camera. Thus the suggestions offered earlier in this chapter regarding microphone technic and the avoidance of distracting noise are equally pertinent to television broadcasts. In addition, you must adapt yourself to the distractions of the dazzling lights and their heat and the movement of cameras on their booms or dollies and to the restriction of your movement within the area upon which the lights and cameras are focused. And yet this adaptation must seem natural, avoiding equally a stunned or disconcerted appearance and the tendency to overact, to play the gallery.

The technical aspects of television are changing rapidly, and the facilities at different stations vary considerably. Hence, each time you broadcast you will need special advice from the directors and technicians in charge in order to adapt your presentation to the prevailing conditions. For this reason, detailed instructions would be inappropriate here and the following suggestions are limited to matters which are fairly universal in their application.

Adapting to the television camera Like the ordinary camera, the television camera takes a picture. And, like the ordinary camera, its lens adjustment and its distance determine what view of the speaker (face only, waist up, full view, etc.) and how much background scenery, demonstration materials, and the like are shown. Moreover, the angle from which the picture is taken can be varied— front, side, above, or below. Usually the camera angles and distances are changed during the broadcast to provide variety. Often more than one camera is used, the broadcast pick-up shifting from one to another so that the picture changes from a distance view to a close-up or from a front view to an angle shot, or the camera may be moved on a boom or dolly so that the angle is shifted gradually. If an actual audience is present, the camera may go from speaker to audience and back again. Find out ahead of time, therefore, where you are to stand or sit, how far you may safely move without getting beyond the focal depth or angle of the camera or outside of the lighted area; and if you intend to use visual aids, such as maps and models, arrange for their proper placement.

A further adaptation is necessary because of the reaction of the television camera to various colors. For instance, the normal reddish color of the lips fades out and the natural shadows of the face may disappear under the bright lights so that the face will appear flattened. Hence, special facial make-up must be used to make the picture appear natural. Shiny objects (or even beads of perspiration on the face or a bald head) may glitter or glare in the brilliant light unless toned down with dull paint or panchromatic powder; and without basic make-up, a man's shaven face may appear dirty and unkempt. Also, clothes must be properly chosen for pattern and color to give life to the image without creating bizarre effects. Technical developments may reduce the necessity for some of these adaptations, but you should inquire what the local situation demands.

Adapting appearance and movement to the type of broadcast An earlier part of this chapter discussed the difference between broadcasts in the studio without an audience and broadcasts before an actual audience. In television, this difference is particularly important. If you are speaking to an actual audience, you will be expected to talk to the real audience, not to the camera. Your posture, movement, and gesture must fit the real audience before you. Use enough movement and gesture to keep the scene alive but avoid overdramatic gestures, for these will amuse rather than impress your television audience.

The studio telecast without an audience, however, is a much more intimate thing. Here you must think of yourself as if you were talking to your listener in his living room. You may stand up to speak, especially if you have something to point out or demonstrate. Quite as often you will be seated, at a desk or even in an easy chair. Your movements should be those natural to easy, informal, animated conversation. Do not sit stiffly, but change your position occasionally, and use your hands to emphasize and clarify your points. You may lean forward to emphasize important statements or move your head to bring out a transition. The sweep of your gestures, however, should be somewhat restrained, involving movement of the hand and forearm in a relatively small arc; avoid declamatory gestures as you would the plague. To give the impression of direct eye contact with your listener, look directly at the camera frequently, but don't glare at it continuously or you will seem unnatural. Look away at not too great an angle and then look back again. Above all, don't rely too heavily on a manuscript or notes. If you must read all or part of your speech, arrange for the use of a teleprompter. This device puts a copy of your speech, in large type, on or near the camera. Thus, even though you are reading, you can maintain fairly good eye contact.

The use of visual aids Television makes possible the use of all sorts of visual aids to illustrate and substantiate the content of a speech. Indeed, the use of maps, charts, pictures, models, and even short sequences from motion pictures adds variety and life to the television speech. After all, people may tire of looking only at a picture of the speaker for very long at a time. Sometimes large-scale visual aids are placed beside or behind the speaker so that he can point to them as he talks. Frequently, small pictures or miniature models are picked up by a separate camera. When talking before a large face-to-face audience, you will be unable to use these devices very often, but in the intimate studio broadcast, you should use them. In fact, you may best organize such a talk around a series of visual aids devised to portray your ideas.

Adapting vocal delivery While most of the vocal requirements of radio broadcasting apply equally to television broadcasting, there are a few variations. Since the audience sees as well as hears the speaker, he can speak more slowly and can pause longer for transitions or emphasis. In fact, fairly long pauses accompanied by the speaker's pointing out of pertinent details on maps or charts are perfectly natural. When the same program is broadcast over radio and television, the speaker must not pause too long or slow down his rate of speaking too much.

In telecasts, the speaker should be particularly careful to avoid overemphatic vocal delivery; he should maintain a quiet, conversational delivery. Variety and emphasis are needed, but too excited a tone, too fast a rate, or too assertive an inflection is likely to be in bad taste. Especially in the intimate studio telecast, you must remember that you are conversing with your listeners as a guest in their homes and should therefore keep your voice within reasonably animated conversational limits.

CHARACTERISTICS OF CONTENT
AND ORGANIZATION

Although the principles of speech development presented in previous chapters apply to broadcast speech as well, some of them deserve special emphasis. In particular, bear the following suggestions in mind.

Remember that the time limit is exact. Most broadcasting stations operate on a schedule that is adhered to within thirty seconds leeway; if the program runs overtime, it will be cut off. Moreover, programs start on time too; if the studio is up several flights of stairs, allow yourself time to get there and catch your breath before you have to begin speaking. If you are to speak on a fifteen-minute program, you will not have a full fifteen minutes to speak; you must make allowances for announcements and introduction. Ask how much time is actually yours, and find out what sort of signal you will be given to indicate how the time is going. Without realizing it, many people find that they talk much faster in a studio than elsewhere; allow for this possibility by having an additional illustration or story prepared, which can be conveniently inserted near the end if you see that you are getting through too early. Be prepared also to cut part of your speech if necessary. To do this smoothly, "back time" your speech by noting on the manuscript or teleprompter copy at what point you have one or two minutes of material remaining to deliver. If, near the end of the broadcast, the clock shows that you have too much or too little time, you can easily add to or cut your speech.

Make your appeal as universal as possible. Remember that all sorts of people may be listening; try to interest as many as you can by making your illustrations, comments, and applications as varied as possible.

Use animated, lively, concrete material. Avoid abstract theorizing; listeners will turn you off. Use a wealth of stories, illustrations, comparisons, and the like, especially those which are "believe it or not" in type, those which contain plenty of action, and those which relate to the everyday experiences of your listeners.

Apply as many of the factors of attention as possible. Review the principles of attention in Chapter 13. Give special emphasis to the *vital*—relate your material to the important needs and desires of as many types of people as you can; to *activity and reality*—keep your speech concrete and full of movement; to *suspense*—early in your speech arouse curiosity or promise that some valuable information will be presented later.

Use simple (but not childish) wording and sentence structure. Avoid technical terms where common terms will do; if you must use such terms, explain them. In general, avoid flowery, over-elegant diction, and use relatively simple sentences. Do not, on the other hand, talk down to the audience; even children like to be talked to as if they were grown up.

Use a simple type of speech organization. Avoid complex reasoning. Rarely will you have time to make such reasoning clear, and without being able to see your listener, you cannot tell whether he is understanding it or not. A few main ideas, clearly related and moving definitely in a straightforward direction, should serve as the main structure of your speech.

Mark your transitions clearly. When you move from one idea to another, be sure to indicate this fact by a word or two or by a distinct change of rate or pitch. On the platform or in a television broadcast you can indicate such transitions by movement or gesture, but over the radio your voice alone must do this work. Such transitions should not become stereotyped, however; vary them and keep them informal. Such phrases as "In the first place" and "Secondly" sound a bit stilted for the conversational type of speaking called for in the studio. It is much better to say, "Now I want to tell you" or "But let's look at something else for a minute."

Give a sense of continuous movement and development. Don't let your speech bog down or ramble around. Keep your listeners aware that you are getting somewhere, that you have an objective and are moving steadily toward it.

Avoid profanity and remarks offensive to special groups. You must be extremely careful to avoid remarks that could be interpreted as slurs upon any religious, racial, or occupational group. Remember that the air is public property and that all types of people may be listening. Profanity or risqué stories are never necessary to a good speaker; on the air they are absolutely taboo—to protect its license, the station will shut you off if you try to use them.

These are a few of the considerations you should keep in mind when you prepare a speech for broadcasting. You can observe their application every day by listening to speakers on the radio or television.

THE AUDITION OR REHEARSAL

Many stations require an audition or rehearsal before a broadcast; whether or not an audition is required, you would be wise to arrange for one if possible, particularly if you have not had much experience in broadcasting. In such an audition you proceed with your speech before the microphone just as if the program were on the air; the difference lies in the fact that the speech is recorded or is transmitted directly to a loud-speaker in an adjoining room. In a similar way, television broadcasts may be rehearsed to check the lighting, camera locations, and movements of the speaker.

The audition serves to test your delivery—the rate, modulation, and quality of your voice, the proper use of microphone technic, and the like. Furthermore, an audition serves as an excellent check on the timing of your speech; if you find that your speech is too long or too short as given in the actual studio situation, you still have time to revise it. Moreover, an audition will accustom you to the studio, to the deadened sound resulting from acoustically treated walls and ceiling, to the quiet movement of people, and to the sense of mystery with which broadcasting even yet affects so many people.

SAMPLE SPEECHES

Examine the speeches which follow and observe how their content and organization were adapted to the broadcast audience.

THE FIRST "FIRESIDE CHAT"—ON BANKING [2]

> *This was the first broadcast from the White House given by Franklin D. Roosevelt on March 12, 1933, eight days after his inauguration as President of the United States.*

---

[2] From *The Public Papers and Addresses of Franklin D. Roosevelt*, Vol. II, 1933, Item No. 16. By courtesy of Random House, Inc.

Attention step I want to talk for a few minutes with the people of the United States about banking—with the comparatively few who understand the mechanics of banking but more particularly with the overwhelming majority who use banks for the making of deposits and the drawing of checks. I want to tell you what has been done in the last few days, why it was done, and what the next steps are going to be. I recognize that the many proclamations from State capitols and from Washington, the legislation, the Treasury regulations, etc., couched for the most part in banking and legal terms, should be explained for the benefit of the average citizen. I owe this in particular because of the fortitude and good temper with which everybody has accepted the inconvenience and hardships of the banking holiday. I know that when you understand what we in Washington have been about I shall continue to have your cooperation as fully as I have had your sympathy and help during the past week.

Need step First of all, let me state the simple fact that when you deposit money in a bank the bank does not put the money into a safe deposit vault. It invests your money in many different forms of credit—bonds, commercial paper, mortgages, and many other kinds of loans. In other words, the bank puts your money to work to keep the wheels of industry and of agriculture turning around. A comparatively small part of the money you put into the bank is kept in currency—an amount which in normal times is wholly sufficient to cover the cash needs of the average citizen. In other words, the total amount of all the currency in the country is only a small fraction of the total deposits in all the banks.

What, then, happened during the last few days of February and the first few days of March? Because of undermined confidence on the part of the public, there was a general rush by a large portion of our population to turn bank deposits into currency or gold—a rush so great that the soundest banks could not get enough currency to meet the demand. The reason for this was that on the spur of the moment it was, of course, impossible to sell perfectly sound assets of a bank and convert them into cash except at panic prices far below their real value.

By the afternoon of March 3rd scarcely a bank in the country was open to do business. Proclamations temporarily closing them in whole or in part had been issued by the Governors in almost all the States.

Satisfaction step It was then that I issued the proclamation providing for the nationwide bank holiday, and this was the first step in the Government's reconstruction of our financial and economic fabric.

The second step was the legislation promptly and patriotically passed by the Congress confirming my proclamation and broadening my powers so that it became possible in view of the requirement of time to extend the holiday and lift the ban of that holiday gradually. This law also gave authority to develop a program of rehabilitation of our banking facilities. I want to tell our citizens in every part of the Nation that the national Congress—Republicans and Democrats alike—showed by this action a devotion to public welfare and a realization of the emergency and the necessity for speed that it is difficult to match in our history.

The third stage has been the series of regulations permitting the banks to continue their functions to take care of the distribution of food and household necessities and the payment of payrolls.

This bank holiday, while resulting in many cases in great inconvenience, is affording us the opportunity to supply the currency necessary to meet the situation. No sound bank is a dollar worse off than it was when it closed its doors last Monday. Neither is any bank which may turn out not to be in a position for immediate opening. The new law allows the twelve Federal Reserve Banks to issue additional currency on good assets, and thus the banks which reopen will be able to meet every legitimate call. The new currency is being sent out by the Bureau of Engraving and Printing in large volume to every part of the country. It is sound currency because it is backed by actual, good assets.

A question you will ask is this: why are all the banks not to be reopened at the same time? The answer is simple. Your Government does not intend that the history of the past few years shall be repeated. We do not want and will not have another epidemic of bank failures.

As a result, we start tomorrow, Monday, with the opening of banks in the twelve Federal Reserve Bank cities—those banks which on first examination by the Treasury have already been found to be all right. This will be followed on Tuesday by the resumption of all their functions by banks already found to be sound in cities where there are recognized clearing houses. That means about 250 cities of the United States.

On Wednesday and succeeding days banks in smaller places all through the country will resume business, subject, of course, to the Government's physical ability to complete its survey. It is necessary that the reopening of banks be extended over a period in order to permit the banks to make applications for necessary loans, to obtain currency needed to meet their requirements, and to enable the Government to make common sense check-ups.

Let me make it clear to you that if your bank does not open the first day you are by no means justified in believing that it will not open. A bank that opens on one of the subsequent days is in exactly the same status as the bank that opens tomorrow.

I know that many people are worrying about State banks not members of the Federal Reserve System. These banks can and will receive assistance from member banks and from the Reconstruction Finance Corporation. These State banks are following the same course as the National banks except that they get their licenses to resume business from the State authorities, and these authorities have been asked by the Secretary of the Treasury to permit their good banks to open up on the same schedule as the national banks. I am confident that the State Banking Departments will be as careful as the national Government in the policy relating to the opening of banks and will follow the same broad policy.

It is possible that when the banks resume, a very few people who have not recovered from their fear may again begin withdrawals. Let me make it clear that the banks will take care of all needs—and it is my belief that hoarding during the past week has become an exceedingly unfashionable pastime. It needs no prophet to tell you that when the people find that they can get their money—that they can get it when they want it for all legitimate purposes—the phantom of fear will soon be laid. People will again be glad to have their money where it will be safely taken care of and where they can use it conveniently at any time. I can assure you that it is safer to keep your money in a reopened bank than under the mattress.

The success of our whole great national program depends, of course, upon the cooperation of the public—on its intelligent support and use of a reliable system.

Remember that the essential accomplishment of the new legislation is that it makes it possible for banks more readily to convert their assets into cash than was the case before. More liberal provision has been made for banks to borrow on these assets at the Reserve Banks, and more liberal provision has also been made for issuing currency on the security of these good assets. This currency is not fiat currency. It is issued only on adequate security, and every good bank has an abundance of such security.

One more point before I close. There will be, of course, some banks unable to reopen without being reorganized. The new law allows the Government to assist in making these reorganizations quickly and effectively and even allows the Government to subscribe to at least a part of new capital which may be required.

I hope you can see from this elemental recital of what your Government is doing that there is nothing complex, or radical, in the process.

We had a bad banking situation. Some of our bankers had shown themselves either incompetent or dishonest in their handling of the people's funds. They had used the money entrusted to them in speculations and unwise loans. This was, of course, not true in the vast majority of our banks, but it was true in enough of them to shock the people for a time into a sense of insecurity and to put them into a frame of mind where they did not differentiate but seemed to assume that the acts of a comparative few had tainted them all. It was the Government's job to straighten out this situation and do it as quickly as possible. And the job is being performed.

Visualization step   I do not promise you that every bank will be reopened or that individual losses will not be suffered, but there will be no losses that possibly could be avoided; and there would have been more and greater losses had we continued to drift. I can even promise you salvation for some at least of the sorely pressed banks. We shall be engaged not merely in reopening sound banks but in the creation of sound banks through reorganization.

It has been wonderful to me to catch the note of confidence from all over the country. I can never be sufficiently grateful to the people for the loyal support they have given me in their acceptance of the judgment that has dictated our course, even though all our processes may not have seemed clear to them.

Action step   After all, there is an element in the readjustment of our financial system more important than currency, more important than gold, and that is the confidence of the people. Confidence and courage are the essentials of success in carrying out our plan. You people must have faith; you must not be stampeded by rumors or guesses. Let us unite in banishing fear. We have provided the machinery to restore our financial system; it is up to you to support and make it work.

It is your problem no less than it is mine. Together we cannot fail.

ALIANZA PARA PROGRESO [3]

> *The following address by John F. Kennedy, President of the United States, was broadcast on March 13, 1961, from Washington, D.C., to the people of South America over Voice of America radio. The speech was later presented in some parts of the United States by recording or video tape. Diplomats from South American countries and Congressmen from the United States were present as the speech was delivered. Note the frequent references to past and present leaders and events in the Western Hemisphere, especially those of South America.*

Attention step   It is a great pleasure for Mrs. Kennedy and for me, for the Vice President and Mrs. Johnson, and for the Members of Congress, to welcome the ambassadorial corps of the hemisphere, our long-time friends, to the White House today. One hundred and thirty-nine years ago this week the United States, stirred by the heroic struggles of its fellow Americans, urged the independence and recognition of the new Latin American Republics. It was then, at the dawn of freedom throughout this hemisphere, that Bolívar spoke of his desire to see the Americas fashioned into the greatest region in the world, "greatest," he said, "not so much by virtue of her area and her wealth, as by her freedom and her glory."

---

[3] From *Department of State Bulletin*, Vol. XLIV, April 3, 1961, pp. 471–474.

Never, in the long history of our hemisphere, has this dream been nearer to fulfillment, and never has it been in greater danger.

The genius of our scientists has given us the tools to bring abundance to our land, strength to our industry, and knowledge to our people. For the first time we have the capacity to strike off the remaining bonds of poverty and ignorance—to free our people for the spiritual and intellectual fulfillment which has always been the goal of our civilization.

Yet at this very moment of maximum opportunity, we confront the same forces which have imperiled America throughout its history—the alien forces which once again seek to impose the despotisms of the Old World on the people of the New.

I have asked you to come here today so that I might discuss these challenges and these dangers.

Need step We meet together as firm and ancient friends, united by history and experience and by our determination to advance the values of American civilization. For this new world of ours is not merely an accident of geography. Our continents are bound together by a common history—the endless exploration of new frontiers. Our nations are the product of a common struggle—the revolt from colonial rule. And our people share a common heritage—the quest for the dignity and the freedom of man.

The revolutions which gave us birth ignited, in the words of Thomas Paine, "a spark never to be extinguished." And across vast, turbulent continents these American ideals still stir man's struggle for national independence and individual freedom. But as we welcome the spread of the American Revolution to other lands, we must also remember that our own struggle—the revolution which began in Philadelphia in 1776 and in Caracas in 1811—is not yet finished. Our hemisphere's mission is not yet completed. *For our unfulfilled task is to demonstrate to the entire world that man's unsatisfied aspiration for economic progress and social justice can best be achieved by free men working within a framework of democratic institutions.* If we can do this in our own hemisphere, and for our own people, we may yet realize the prophecy of the great Mexican patriot, Benito Juarez, that "democracy is the destiny of future humanity."

As a citizen of the United States let me be the first to admit that we North Americans have not always grasped the significance of this common mission, just as it is also true that many in your own countries have not fully understood the urgency of the need to lift people from poverty and ignorance and despair. But we must turn from these mistakes—from the failures and the misunderstandings of the past—to a future full of peril but bright with hope.

Throughout Latin America—a continent rich in resources and in the spiritual and cultural achievements of its people—millions of men and women suffer the daily degradations of hunger and poverty. They lack decent shelter or protection from disease. Their children are deprived of the education or the jobs which are the gateway to a better life. And each day the problems grow more urgent. Population growth is outpacing economic growth, low living standards are even further endangered, and discontent—the discontent of a people who know the abundance and the tools of progress are at last within their reach—that discontent is growing. In the words of José Figueres, "once dormant peoples are struggling upward toward the sun, toward a better life."

Satisfaction step   If we are to meet a problem so staggering in its dimensions, our approach must itself be equally bold, an approach consistent with the majestic concept of Operation Pan America. Therefore I have called on all the people of the hemisphere to join in a new Alliance for Progress—*Alianza para Progreso*—a vast cooperative effort, unparalleled in magnitude and nobility of purpose, to satisfy the basic needs of the American people for homes, work and land, health and schools—*techo, trabajo y tierra, salud y escuela.*

First, I propose that the American Republics begin on a vast new 10-year plan for the Americas, a plan to transform the 1960's into an historic decade of democratic progress. These 10 years will be the years of maximum progress, maximum effort—the years when the greatest obstacles must be overcome, the years when the need for assistance will be the greatest.

And if we are successful, if our effort is bold enough and determined enough, then the close of this decade will mark the beginning of a new era in the American experience. The living standards of every American family will be on the rise, basic education will be available to all, hunger will be a forgotten experience, the need for massive outside help will have passed, most nations will have entered a period of self-sustaining growth, and, although there will be still much to do, every American Republic will be the master of its own revolution and its own hope and progress.

Let me stress that only the most determined efforts of the American nations themselves can bring success to this effort. They, and they alone, can mobilize their resources, enlist the energies of their people, and modify their social patterns so that all, and not just a privileged few, share in the fruits of growth. If this effort is made, then outside assistance will give a vital impetus to progress; without it, no amount of help will advance the welfare of the people. •

Thus if the countries of Latin America are ready to do their part—and I am sure they are—then I believe the United States, for its part, should help provide resources of a scope and magnitude sufficient to make this bold development plan a success, just as we helped to provide, against nearly equal odds, the resources adequate to help rebuild the economies of Western Europe. For only an effort of towering dimensions can insure fulfillment of our plan for a decade of progress.

Secondly, I will shortly request a ministerial meeting of the Inter-American Economic and Social Council, a meeting at which we can begin the massive planning effort which will be at the heart of the Alliance for Progress.

For if our alliance is to succeed, each Latin nation must formulate long-range plans for its own development—plans which establish targets and priorities, insure monetary stability, establish the machinery for vital social change, stimulate private activity and initiative, and provide for a maximum national effort. These plans will be the foundation of our development effort and the basis for the allocation of outside resources.

A greatly strengthened IA-ECOSOC, working with the Economic Commission for Latin America and the Inter-American Development Bank, can assemble the leading economists and experts of the hemisphere to help each country develop its own development plan and provide a continuing review of economic progress in this hemisphere.

Third, I have this evening signed a request to the Congress for $500 million as a first step in fulfilling the Act of Bogotá. This is the first large-scale inter-American effort—instituted by my predecessor President Eisenhower—to attack the social barriers which block economic progress. The money will be used to combat illiteracy, improve the productivity and use of their land, wipe out disease, attack archaic tax and land-tenure structures, provide educational opportunities, and offer a broad range of projects designed to make the benefits of increasing abundance available to all. We will begin to commit these funds as soon as they are appropriated.

Fourth, we must support all economic integration which is a genuine step toward larger markets and greater competitive opportunity. The fragmentation of Latin American economies is a serious barrier to industrial growth. Projects such as the Central American common market and free-trade areas in South America can help to remove these obstacles.

Fifth, the United States is ready to cooperate in serious, case-by-case examinations of commodity market problems. Frequent violent changes in commodity prices seriously injure the economies of many Latin American countries, draining their resources and stultifying their growth. Together we must find practical methods of bringing an end to this pattern.

Sixth, we will immediately step up our food-for-peace emergency program, help to establish food reserves in areas of recurrent drought, and help provide school lunches for children and offer feed grains for use in rural development. For hungry men and women cannot wait for economic discussions or diplomatic meetings; their need is urgent, and their hunger rests heavily on the conscience of their fellow men.

Seventh, all the people of the hemisphere must be allowed to share in the expanding wonders of science—wonders which have captured man's imagination, challenged the powers of his mind, and given him the tools for rapid progress. I invite Latin American scientists to work with us in new projects in fields such as medicine and agriculture, physics and astronomy, and desalinization, and to help plan for regional research laboratories in these and other fields, and to strengthen cooperation between American universities and laboratories.

We also intend to expand our science-teacher training programs to include Latin American instructors, to assist in establishing such programs in other American countries, and translate and make available revolutionary new teaching materials in physics, chemistry, biology, and mathematics so that the young of all nations may contribute their skills to the advance of science.

Eighth, we must rapidly expand the training of those needed to man the economies of rapidly developing countries. This means expanded technical training programs, for which the Peace Corps, for example, will be available when needed. It also means assistance to Latin American universities, graduate schools, and research institutes.

We welcome proposals in Central America for intimate cooperation in higher education, cooperation which can achieve a regional effort of increased effectiveness and excellence. We are ready to help fill the gap in trained manpower, realizing that our ultimate goal must be a basic education for all who wish to learn.

Ninth, we reaffirm our pledge to come to the defense of any American nation whose independence is endangered. As confidence in the collective security system of the OAS [Organization of American States] spreads, it will be possible to devote to constructive use a major share of those resources now spent on the instruments of war. Even now, as the Government of Chile has said, the time has come to take the first steps toward sensible limitations of arms. And the new generation of military leaders has shown an increasing awareness that armies can not only defend their countries—they can, as we have learned through our own Corps of Engineers, help to build them.

Tenth, we invite our friends in Latin America to contribute to the enrichment of life and culture in the United States. We need teachers of your literature and history and tradition, opportunities for our young people to study in your universities, access to your music, your art, and the thought of your great philosophers. For we know we have much to learn.

Visualization step In this way you can help bring a fuller spiritual and intellectual life to the people of the United States and contribute to understanding and mutual respect among the nations of the hemisphere.

With steps such as these we propose to complete the revolution of the Americas, to build a hemisphere where all men can hope for a suitable standard of living and all can live out their lives in dignity and in freedom.

To achieve this goal political freedom must accompany material progress. Our Alliance for Progress is an alliance of free governments—and it must work to eliminate tyranny from a hemisphere in which it has no rightful place. Therefore let us express our special friendship to the people of Cuba and the Dominican Republic—and the hope they will soon rejoin the society of free men, uniting with us in our common effort.

This political freedom must be accompanied by social change. For unless necessary social reforms, including land and tax reform, are freely made, unless we broaden the opportunity of all of our people, unless the great mass of Americans share in increasing prosperity, then our alliance, our revolution, our dream, and our freedom will fail. But we call for social change by free men—change in the spirit of Washington and Jefferson, of Bolívar and San Martín and Martí—not change which seeks to impose on men tyrannies which we cast out a century and a half ago. Our motto is what it has always been—progress yes, tyranny no—*progreso sí, tiranía no!*

But our greatest challenge comes from within—the task of creating an American civilization where spiritual and cultural values are strengthened by an ever-broadening base of material advance, where, within the rich diversity of its own traditions, each nation is free to follow its own path toward progress.

The completion of our task will, of course, require the efforts of all the governments of our hemisphere. But the efforts of governments alone will never be enough. In the end the people must choose and the people must help themselves.

Action step   And so I say to the men and women of the Americas —to the *campesino* in the fields, to the *obrero* in the cities, to the *estudiante* in the schools—prepare your mind and heart for the task ahead, call forth your strength, and let each devote his energies to the betterment of all so that your children and our children in this hemisphere can find an ever richer and a freer life.

Let us once again transform the American Continent into a vast crucible of revolutionary ideas and efforts, a tribute to the power of the creative energies of free men and women, an example to all the world that liberty and progress walk hand in hand. Let us once again awaken our American revolution until it guides the struggles of people everywhere—not with an imperialism of force or fear but the rule of courage and freedom and hope for the future of man.

BOOKS FOR COLLATERAL STUDY

1. Waldo Abbott and Richard L. Rider, *Handbook of Broadcasting,* 4th ed. (McGraw-Hill, N. Y., 1957).

2. Samuel L. Becker and H. Clay Harshbarger, *Television: Techniques for Planning and Performance* (Henry Holt, N. Y., 1958).

3. Hadley Cantril and G. W. Allport, *Psychology of Radio* (Harper and Bros., N. Y., 1935).

4. Giraud Chester and Garnet R. Garrison, *Television and Radio*, 2nd ed. (Appleton-Century-Crofts, N. Y., 1956).

5. Edward Stasheff and Rudy Bretz, *The Television Program* (Hill and Wang, N. Y., 1956).

6. Max Wylie, *Radio and Television Writing*, rev. ed. (Rinehart, N. Y., 1952).

PROBLEMS

1. Be prepared to answer the following questions in class: Do broadcast speeches differ in purpose from other speeches? What are the special characteristics of radio and television audiences? How do broadcast speeches differ when delivered with a studio audience and without a studio audience? What manner of speaking is recommended for radio broadcasts? What special problems are created by television? What principles of speech development are especially important for broadcast speeches?

2. Analyze the speech by President Kennedy printed at the end of this chapter. Determine its purpose and type. Review the chapter which deals with speeches of this type, and then examine the speech critically as to its organization and content. Note in what ways the speech applies the suggestions made in this chapter for adapting organization and content to broadcasting. (Remember that an actual audience was present as the speech was delivered.) In a similar way, analyze the speech by Franklin D. Roosevelt.

3. Listen to some skilled speaker broadcast over radio or television and report to the class what you think are the factors of his effectiveness; comment both on his manner of speaking and on the organization and content of his speech.

4. Acting as an announcer, introduce some famous person to the radio audience.[4] Adapt the content and delivery of this introduction for use on television.

5. Select one of the longer speeches listed in the Speeches for Collateral Study for Chapters 19 to 27 and prepare a revised draft of it in your own words that will, so far as possible, achieve the same purpose as the

---

[4] If a loud-speaker system is available with the microphone in an adjoining room, its use will make these exercises more realistic and valuable. A workable substitute consists in having the speaker talk from behind a screen or from the rear of the room so that he will be heard but not seen.

original speech, be suited in organization and content to radio presentation, and fit exactly a time limit of five minutes ("Back time" the speech so you can modify your closing statements and finish exactly on time). Present your version of the speech to the class as if over the radio.

6. Adapt the speech you have prepared for Problem 5 for television broadcast. Indicate with marginal notes what visual aids you would use and what special adaptations of movement and gesture would be appropriate. Deliver the speech from manuscript first, attempting to maintain good eye-contact with the camera. Then present the speech by reading the manuscript from a teleprompter which you have constructed and which someone else operates during the broadcast.

7. Give a five-minute survey of the day's campus news (or a coverage of the week's news in ten minutes). Write out the opening and closing statements verbatim and outline the intervening material. Set a clock on the table before you and adjust your remarks so that you close exactly on time.

part six

Discussion

Preparing for discussion ● Outlining the discussion plan ● Taking part in discussion ● Parliamentary law for informal groups

It is not the facts which guide the conduct of men, but their opinions about facts; which may be entirely wrong. We can only make them right by discussion.

Sir Norman Angell

CHAPTER 29 / *Preparing for Discussion*

In our society more and more of the daily operations of business, education, and government are being directed by groups of people—committees, boards, councils, and conferences. Certainly any business or professional man spends much of his time participating in discussions; in fact, his effectiveness in his job may be largely determined by his skill in discussion. What do we mean by *discussion?* Although discussion varies in method from group to group, the following is a good working definition: Discussion is a cooperative process in which a group of persons exchange and evaluate ideas and information about a mutual problem in order to understand or solve that problem.

From taking part in discussions in the classroom and in campus, social, and church groups, you have undoubtedly discovered that merely having a group of people talk over a problem does not necessarily insure an effective solution. Nor will group discussions guarantee good results when you enter your business or profession. Too frequently discussion is justifiably criticized for wasting time and getting nowhere. It is true that a wise individual can often think through and solve a problem more rapidly and efficiently than can a group. Many times, however, an individual fails to give sufficient consideration to some phase of the problem—to a phase that is not important to him but is very important to those whom his decision affects. A group is more likely than an individual to be aware of and give attention to all sides of a question. Moreover, a group decision is more democratic than an individual decision and, since people tend to support the decisions they have helped make, more likely to produce satisfaction and permanent results. And, although group discussions do take time, their efficiency can be increased if the participants plan for the discussion and are familiar with effective methods of participation and leadership. The purpose of this chapter and the next three is to help you gain an understanding of the principles and methods of discussion.

In this chapter some basic questions about discussion will be considered: What are its purposes? What are the types of discussion groups? What are the characteristics of effective discussion? How should an individual prepare for a discussion?

PURPOSES OF DISCUSSION

Although the specific purpose of a discussion depends on the situation, the general purpose usually includes one or both of the following objectives: to exchange ideas or opinions or to reach an agreement or decision.

To exchange ideas or opinions

The least a discussion can do is to inform each participant of the other members' knowledge and opinions about the subject under consideration. Sometimes, as in the classroom, this is the only purpose of the discussion, but often the exchange of ideas is merely a preliminary to making a decision. In either case, the pooling of information and the expression of divergent opinions are valuable methods of gaining a broad understanding of the problem and of providing a sound basis for making a decision.

2) To reach an agreement or make a decision In many discussions the purpose is not just to exchange and to examine ideas but to arrive at some agreement. Differences of opinion are evaluated in an attempt to bring opposing points of view together on some common basis. Through the give-and-take of discussion, individual beliefs are often modified and a consensus reached. If a consensus proves impossible, at least the range of disagreement may be narrowed and a clear understanding of the remaining basic differences arrived at. Usually agreements are reached quite informally, although at business meetings decisions may be determined by balloting.

TYPES OF DISCUSSION GROUPS

Discussion groups may be classified according to their purposes, members, and methods. The four most common forms are study groups, committee or executive meetings, panel discussions, and symposium discussions. The last two are discussions before audiences, or "public" discussions, and may be adapted to radio and television broadcasting.

1) Study groups A study group is usually quite informal. A speech or lecture is often given at the beginning, but the bulk of the time is devoted to the mutual exchange of information and ideas. The purpose is to learn something from the others present. A common type of study group is the college class. Conventions, where men and women in the same business or profession tell each other of experiences or the results of their research or methods of dealing with common problems, are another example of study groups. Women's clubs and religious organizations conduct classes or hold study sections on various matters of interest to their members. These are but a few of the innumerable occasions upon which people get together to exchange ideas.

2) Committee or executive meetings When the president of an organization calls a meeting of the executive committee, the members hear reports on the latest activities and developments and discuss and decide on what policies to follow in the future. The chairman of the fraternity dance committee calls the members together to discuss plans for the spring dance. The business manager of the student dramatic organization calls his assistants together to discuss the budget for the next play or the details of the coming ticket-selling campaign. The rules committee of the women's self-government association meets to consider problems of social regulation among the women students. These are only samples selected from the many discussions which take place daily on every campus; they are counterparts of similar meetings occurring in any modern community.

The rules of parliamentary procedure are occasionally followed in these less formal types of discussions, and they are indispensable for the proper conduct of business meetings. Parliamentary law for informal groups and for business meetings will be considered in Chapter 32.

3) *Panel discussions*

When a group is too large to engage in effective discussion or its members are too uninformed for such discussion to be profitable, a small group—five to ten individuals, usually seated on a platform—often discusses the topic before the larger group. The individuals in this small group, or panel, as it is called, are chosen either because they are well informed on the subject and can supply the facts needed for intelligent discussion or because they are known to represent points of view held by a considerable part of the larger group and can act as spokesmen to express these viewpoints. The members of the panel discuss the subject among themselves, asking questions of one another and agreeing and disagreeing as the occasion arises, as if they were in a study group or on a committee. In this public type of discussion, however, they speak for the audience and before the audience.

4) *Symposium discussions*

In another type of public discussion, several people—usually three to five —give a series of short speeches, each presenting a different viewpoint or facet of the subject. The symposium is a common procedure at large conventions or conferences, where experts are asked to speak on different aspects of a general topic, and is also a method used to report the findings or decisions of a committee.

The symposium or the panel discussion is often followed by an open forum in which the participants answer questions asked by members of the audience. Various combinations and modifications of the panel and symposium procedures are used, but the essential characteristic is that a group of experts or spokesmen do most of the talking while the larger group listens.

(5) Radio and television broadcasts of discussion Of all the types of discussion, the panel discussion is the most frequently broadcast. Local radio stations present high school students, civic leaders, and others in panel shows each week; radio and television networks give time to the discussion of current events by groups of government officials or news commentators. "The Northwestern University Reviewing Stand" exemplifies the panel discussion on a radio network. (See page 582.) This is an informal type of discussion at which no audience is present. Although the participants are experts on the subject under consideration, they rarely make a formal or extended statement of their individual opinions. Instead, they discuss the topic conversationally under the direction of the chairman who seeks by careful questions to bring out the views of the participants and to lead them to a clear statement of those points upon which they agree. Although more formal than panel discussions, symposium discussions are convenient for broadcasting because the speeches can be more carefully timed. In broadcasting a symposium, speakers with sharply differing points of view are often asked to present their opinions in short, uninterrupted statements, after which they engage in an informal question and answer period.

In all broadcasts of discussions, two things are characteristic: first, the discussion is carried on for the benefit of the listening audience whose background of information, or lack of it, and whose attitudes and interests must be constantly kept in mind (see Chapter 28) ; and second, the discussion centers on a single theme or problem of general interest to which the speakers attempt to contribute from their background of special information.

Thus, such broadcasts as conversations with celebrities do not constitute discussions in the sense in which the term is used here but are really forms of entertainment; on such programs the conversation usually rambles from one topic to another and varies in wit and elevation depending on the caliber of the participants. Radio and television discussions, whether informative or argumentative or conducted as panels or symposiums, should be like any other discussions. They differ from other discussions chiefly in their adaptation to the nature of the listening audience and to the strict time limits which broadcast schedules impose. In televised programs, of course, the discussion group must be seated on only one side of the table or, depending upon the number and position of cameras employed, in some other manner so that the speakers' faces instead of their backs will be visible during the discussion. Within these limits, what is good discussion elsewhere is good on radio or television.

ESSENTIALS FOR EFFECTIVE DISCUSSION

If the discussion is to be effective, the individuals taking part in it must be capable of contributing to it, and the conduct of the group as a whole must be such that worth-while discussion is possible.

Essentials for the group as a whole   The first essential in discussion is order. This does not imply great formality; indeed, formality is often undesirable. Order does require, however, that only one person talk at a time, that the members be consistently courteous, and that some rather definite procedure be followed to prevent the discussion from wandering too far afield. A discussion plan (see Chapter 30) will help achieve this last requirement. In the second place, every member must cooperate. If each person insists on having his own way, the discussion will get nowhere. Members of the group must be willing to discuss points of view other than their own and, instead of criticizing a member for the mistakes he makes, should try to understand and assist him. Moreover, there must be a willingness to compromise. There are times, of course, when compromise is not desirable; but reasonable compromise hurts no one and is sometimes the only way of reaching an agreement or making a decision. If a general desire to "meet the other fellow halfway" prevails, there is likely to be a better feeling in the group and a more fruitful discussion. Finally, the group should have a feeling of accomplishment. Unless a group feels it is getting somewhere, its interest and enthusiasm will diminish. A definite goal should be set and the field of discussion limited before the conference actually begins. This can best be achieved by putting the topic into the form of a question, phrased as specifically and impartially as possible. The topic "The Road to Peace," for example, would probably result in a vague and rambling discussion, but the question "How can the United States protect the security of the free world?" would give the group a definite goal.

Essentials for the individual

Without doubt, the most important single thing for the individual is a knowledge of the subject being considered. If you know what you are talking about, other faults will sometimes be forgiven. The second essential is an acquaintance with the other members of the group. The more you know about them, the better able you will be to judge the value of their remarks and to secure approval of your own. Equally important is close attention to the discussion as it progresses. Unless you listen to what is going on, you may lose track of the direction the discussion has taken and will be likely to make foolish comments, to require repetition, or to entertain mistaken ideas of the positions taken by the other participants. Finally, meaningful contributions to the discussion itself are desirable. If you keep quiet, you may learn a good deal, but you will not help solve the problem. Develop the ability to present your ideas clearly and tactfully and learn to bring them in at the most strategic time.

Qualities required of the leader

The fruitfulness of a discussion depends a great deal on the leader's capacity for rapid analysis. He must be able to see in what direction the discussion is turning, to catch significant points even when they are buried in superfluous detail, to note essential agreements between points of view even when they are expressed so that they seem divergent, to strip controversial points of unnecessary complexity and thus narrow the discussion to the basic issues. In short, he needs to be alert, quick-witted, and clear-thinking. Moreover, a good discussion leader must be able to state the results of his analysis clearly and briefly, to make the essential point stand out before the group as clearly as it does in his own mind. Just as important for the leader is the quality of fearless impartiality. By seeing that minority points of view are allowed expression and by phrasing questions and summarizing discussions fairly, he can help maintain a spirit of cooperation and conciliation among members of the group who may differ from one another vigorously. By fearlessness in maintaining this impartiality, even under pressure from the majority, he is likely to gain respect and support for his leadership. Discussion groups are no different from other groups in preferring leaders who are fair, firm, and decisive. But the keenness of his analysis and the fearless impartiality of his leadership must be tempered with tact both in words and in manner. There is no place in discussion for a leader who is easily irritated or who says things in a way that irritates others. A good rule is always to accept comments and to state them with the most generous interpretation possible; given a comment containing a reasonable argument and a sarcastic connotation, focus the discussion on the reason, and ignore the sarcasm. And finally, there are times when the leader needs to be stimulating in order to encourage people to participate. Often, especially at the beginning of a discussion, people are hesitant and cautious about entering the discussion. Provocative questions may help, but even more important is an encouraging and stimulating manner in the leader, a manner which suggests the importance of the subject and confidence that the group does have important things to say about it.

What we have said thus far, about the purpose and function of discussion and the essentials for effective discussion, should have made clear the objectives of your preparation. Now let us turn our attention to the process of preparation itself.

GENERAL PREPARATION

Just how should the individual who expects to participate in or to lead a discussion prepare? What should he do to assure his contributing to the best of his ability? Two fundamental steps are required: he must study the group, and he must study the problems which are to be considered.

Even though you are thoroughly fa-
Analysis of the group   miliar with the subject to be discussed, you will be handicapped
unless you appreciate the relation between the subject and the objectives of your group. At the very beginning, then, determine the function of the group. Find out whether it has any official origin or power. Is it brought together merely to investigate, or does it have power to make decisions? What resources are at its command? Next, analyze the larger unit of which this group is a part. If you are a member of the student council, you must know not only the function of that council but also the policies and traditions of the college or university of which it is a part. Finally, make a detailed analysis of the individuals who compose the group. By doing so, you will know that Mr. X's comments are likely to be exaggerated and must be taken with a grain of salt but that what Mr. W says will bear serious consideration. Furthermore, you will know that the best way of getting Mr. X to agree with you will be to use vivid illustrations but that substantial facts will be needed to convince Mr. W. In particular, answer for yourself as well as you can the following questions: What is the official position of each member of the group? What are each one's personal traits? What knowledge does each one have of the questions to be discussed? What attitude will each individual have toward the proposals we expect to discuss?

Although knowledge about the group is important for every member, it is doubly so for the leader; his analysis must go even deeper. For example, as the discussion leader you should determine each person's special field of knowledge so that when questions arise which require a special type of information, you can immediately call upon the person who can supply it. Take note also of each person's prestige with the other members of the group. If one person is considered an extremist, plan to limit that person's participation. An extremist often has good ideas, but they may be rejected merely because he advocates them. Let someone else follow up the points such a person raises so that a more moderate point of view may save the essential idea. See to it that other persons do not become disgusted because some crank monopolizes the time. Finally, find out about each person's administrative abilities and special capacities. Groups often make decisions and determine policies but leave them to be carried out by individual members or a committee appointed by the chairman. The chairman's appointment of persons to administer the work can often cause a project to succeed or fail, and even when he has no such official power, his suggestions usually have considerable weight.

Analysis of the specific subjects to be discussed The more you know about the subject under discussion, the better. Don't rely just on old knowledge, however; make sure that your facts are up-to-date. The more specific and ready the information at your command, the better able you will be to take part in the discussion. (Review Chapter 11 for suggestions on sources and methods of gathering and recording material.) Unfortunately, many persons believe they do not need to prepare as carefully for a discussion as for a speech. In a discussion, however, you cannot narrow the subject or determine the specific purpose by yourself, nor can you be sure of the exact direction the discussion will take. Since you must therefore be ready for any turn the discussion may take, preparing for a discussion is often a greater challenge than preparing for a speech.

For each problem you think will be discussed, make the following analysis. First, review the facts you already know. Go over the information you have acquired on the subject and organize it in your mind. Prepare as if you were going to present a speech on every phase of the entire subject; you will then be better able to discuss any part of it on short notice.

Second, find out what recent changes have occurred that might affect the problem. Bring your knowledge up-to-date. Fit the new information you acquire into the outline of what you already have. At this stage the leader should turn his attention to the preparation of a discussion plan, described in the next chapter (p. 557 ff.), so that he will give impartial consideration to each point of view; the participant, on the other hand, will be concerned with the preparation and evaluation of his own proposal and should continue with the last two steps in this analysis.

Third, determine a tentative point of view on the question. Make up your mind as to what your attitude will be. Are you in favor of limiting membership or of increasing its size? Is $60,000 too much to spend in building a new clubhouse? Do you believe dues should be paid annually or monthly? Stake out rather definitely your position on each question that is to come before the group and have clearly in mind the reasons for your point of view. However, keep your decision tentative; be willing to change your mind if additional facts disclosed in the discussion prove you wrong.

Finally, examine the effect your idea or proposal will have upon the other members of the group. If you ask yourself what the effect will be on the organization as a whole and on the individuals in it, you will be prepared to deal with any objections which may arise or to modify your proposal to meet them. Possibly what you propose will cause someone to lose money or to retract a promise he has made; forethought will prepare you to meet his opposition. If an audience will be present to hear and participate in the discussion, or if radio and television listeners are involved, extend your analysis to include an estimate of their probable knowledge and attitude toward the subject. The more thoroughly you organize your facts and relate them to the problem involved and to the people who are to discuss them, the more successful and influential will be your contribution to the discussion.

PREPARING FOR DISCUSSION BEFORE AN AUDIENCE OR FOR BROADCASTING

When the discussion is to be held before an audience or is to be broadcast, a preliminary warm-up period or even a complete practice discussion is in order. The former method consists of a preliminary discussion by the panel in private (or for broadcasting, with the microphone off) immediately before the program begins. The ice is thus broken, and the participants will more quickly join in a vigorous discussion before the audience and, since they have a chance to verify each other's point of view, are apt to make their comments more pointed. Moreover, the leader is enabled to gauge the temper of his group so that he can adapt his method of handling the participants, and he has an opportunity in this preliminary period to explain any special details of procedure and the like.

A complete practice discussion may be held immediately before the program, but more often this practice takes place some time in advance. In a practice session the participants discuss the topic at some length and agree on what points are most important to include when the group appears before the audience. Sometimes, the entire agenda and discussion plan are worked out, even to the detail of deciding which participant is to introduce each phase of the problem and when. Sometimes these practice discussions are recorded so that the participants may analyze their remarks and improve the manner in which they are to be presented.

Even for broadcasting, however, discussions of this type are rarely written out and read from a script, since this tends to rob discussion of its spontaneity and liveliness. Instead, for radio or television presentation, the discussion plan is carefully outlined, the names of the participants who are to introduce each point are noted on this outline, and the principal points that are to be brought out during each phase of the discussion are itemized at the proper place. Then, on the basis of the practice discussion, the leader notes the amount of time which can be spent on each point so that he can lead the group to a conclusion within the broadcast time allotted.

Care must be taken not to continue preliminary discussions to the point where the participants become stale. Mere rehearsals in which the same things are said in the same way soon become boring and lead to a final presentation that sounds cut and dried. Instead, limit the length and number of such practice periods, or see to it that new material or fresh points of view are brought in at each succeeding period. Of course, be sure that the final selection of points to be covered is made on the basis of importance, not merely of recency.

Preliminary practice of this sort is possible only for discussions before an audience or for broadcasting. The other aspects of preparation, however, both for the leader and for the individual participants, are not only possible but necessary if intelligent and fruitful discussion is to follow. We shall see in the following chapters how careful preparation can lead to an orderly consideration of the subject and to effective participation in the discussion itself.

PROBLEMS

1. Be ready to discuss the following questions in class: For what general purposes are discussions held? What are the common types of discussion groups? What does effective discussion require of the group? Of the individual participant? Of the leader? What procedure is suggested for analyzing the group? The subject? What additional preparation is needed for a discussion before a group or for broadcasting?

2. Compare *discussion*, as defined in this chapter, with your concept of *social conversation, interview,* and *debate.* What are the similarities? The differences?

3. From your own experience, list two or three examples of each of the four types of discussion groups. What differences did you note in them other than those pointed out in this chapter?

4. What was the purpose of each of the groups listed in Problem 3? Would the discussions have been more successful if the purpose had been clearly understood by all the participants?

5. Listen to a broadcast discussion and determine what type of discussion was employed. What special adaptation to the radio or television situation did you note?

6. Analyze the discussion carried on in one of your classes. To what extent did the group as a whole conduct itself in a way consistent with the essentials (laid down on pp. 549–550) for effective discussion? Criticize two or three individuals in the group with reference to the essentials (see p. 550) for individual effectiveness. To what extent did the leader possess the special qualities (see pp. 550–551) required?

7. Make an analysis of the class in Problem 6 as a group (see pp. 552–553) for the discussion of some subject which you select.

8. Analyze similarly three or four other groups to which you belong where discussion is held. Observe the differences and note the problems that participants and leader should anticipate.

9. Compare the preparation you made for your most recent speech and for your most recent discussion. What were the similarities? The differences? How do you account for the similarities and differences?

10. Assume that you have been selected to arrange for a panel discussion on your campus. Select a subject that would be of interest to the entire student body. Indicate whom you would invite to sit on the panel and why. What sort of preliminary or practice discussion, if any, would you plan?

Discussion should be one of the most important things in the world, for it is almost our only arena of thinking. . . . Without discussion intellectual experience is only an exercise in a private gymnasium.

Randolph Bourne

CHAPTER 30 / *Outlining the Discussion Plan*

In discussion, much time is often lost because of needless repetition and aimless wandering from point to point. A carefully developed discussion plan will do much to eliminate this difficulty.

Ideally, the entire group should work out the discussion plan; but if this is impossible, the leader must take the responsibility for developing one. Whether or not you are to serve as leader, you should understand the basic types of discussion plans: as a participant, you will be able to follow the discussion more intelligently, and if the leader fails to prepare a plan, you can help speed the discussion by "leading from the floor" with appropriately timed questions and comments.

Since there are several distinct types of discussion, this chapter will present separate plans for study groups and for deliberative (decision-making) groups and will give suggestions for the discussion of a series of problems and for panel and symposium discussions. These plans can be used in most situations, although some modifications may be required because of variations in group membership and discussion topics. No separate plan for radio or television discussion has been included since broadcasting does not change the basic sequence of discussion but merely applies one of these plans to the broadcast situation.

A PLAN FOR STUDY GROUPS

Often a study group discusses a book, or parts of it, and occasionally uses a study outline or syllabus, prepared by some authority in a given field. If the group is discussing a book or using a syllabus, your discussion should follow a sequence similar to the outline of the material studied. Your main task will be to relate the points in that outline to the experience of individuals in the group and to see that the more important facts and principles receive proper emphasis and consideration. Sometimes prepared outlines are out of date or incomplete; if you feel this to be true, your discussion plan should provide questions that will bring the missing information or points of view into the discussion.

Usually, however, no prepared outline is available; or if it is, it is not suited to the needs of the particular group. In that case, the leader or the group should word the objective of their discussion as a question—usually a question of fact or a question of value. (See p. 413.) Questions of fact, such as "What are the essentials for effective discussion?" or "What is our community doing to combat the increasing crime rate?" attempt to increase and clarify knowledge within the group; questions of value, such as "How successful is our community recreation program?" or "Is the United Nations the best means to world peace?" seek judgments, appraisals, or preferences. The following suggestions should help you prepare a satisfactory discussion plan for such questions.

Introduction   The introduction consists of a statement of the discussion question by the leader, together with one or two illustrative examples showing its general importance or its relation to the individuals in the group.

After the leader's introduction, the
Analysis group determines the importance of
the subject and narrows the scope of
the discussion to those phases which seem most important. The
following questions should be answered:
1. What importance does the subject have for the group? Why?
2. Into what major topical divisions may this subject be conveniently divided? (See pp. 192 and 235–239 for some suggestions.)
3. To which of these phases should the discussion be narrowed?
   A. Which topics are of the greatest interest and importance to the group?
   B. Upon which topics are the members of the group already informed so fully that further discussion would be fruitless?
4. Summary. A summary, by the leader, of the discussion thus far includes a list of the topics to which the general subject has now been narrowed and an arrangement of these topics in logical sequence for further discussion. (The suggestions on pp. 235–239 also apply here.)

In the investigation, the members
Investigation consider each topic chosen in (3)
above in the order determined by
the group. The discussion of *each topic* should cover at least the
following points:
1. What terms need definition? Is there disagreement as to what is the generally accepted meaning? What definition does the group prefer?
2. What background material needs to be considered: historical, social, geographic, etc.?
3. What personal experiences of members of the group might illuminate and clarify the discussion?
4. What basic principles or causal relationships seem to underlie this information and these experiences?
5. Summary. The leader should point out what seem to be the essential facts or principles upon which there is general agreement and indicate upon which points information is still lacking or conflicting.

Final summary   The chairman should make a compressed restatement at the close of the discussion pointing out (*a*) the reasons disclosed in the discussion for considering the subject important and (*b*) the essential points brought out under each of the main topics discussed. Do not attempt to make this summary exhaustive; its purpose is rather to bring together the more important points in such a way that they will be easily remembered and their relationship to each other and to the general subject clearly recognized.

Obviously this plan is only a general outline; as the leader, you will need to develop it in more detail for a specific subject. You should be sufficiently familiar with the subject so that you can anticipate the probable answers, or the type of answers, to the questions and so that you will know what facts or principles should be brought out. By thinking through this general plan in the light of your own knowledge of the subject, you will be able to prepare specific questions that will bring out information from the group members; and by properly analyzing the people in the group, you will often be able to estimate in advance in what direction their interests will lead them during the discussion. A good method is to write out a detailed outline of your plan, phrased as a series of questions rather than statements. Remember, however, that your function is to steer rather than to dominate the group; you should be sufficiently familiar with your discussion plan so that you can keep it flexible and can modify it, if necessary, as the discussion proceeds.

A PLAN FOR DELIBERATIVE GROUPS

Deliberative groups are concerned with more than the exchange of opinions and information; they are faced with situations requiring agreement on courses of action to be pursued. If the group is one which meets regularly, such as an executive committee, the members may not be aware of the problem prior to the meeting at which it is to be discussed. More frequently the problem is known in advance, and at times a serious difficulty or conflict of interests may be the very reason for calling the group together. At any rate, the principal function of this sort of group discussion is to solve a problem; the object is to reach a consensus on what to do about it and how to do it. Discussions with this purpose deal with questions of policy. (See p. 414.) Two examples of such questions are: "What can be done to increase the number of participants in our activity?" and "How can our company meet the competition from foreign imports?" Of course, as we shall see in the following suggested procedure, answers to such questions also require the consideration of questions of fact and value.

The steps in the following plan are an adaptation of John Dewey's analysis of how we think reflectively when we are confronted with a problem.[1] Although presented in some detail, this plan should be viewed as only one of several possible ways for discussing a single problem; later we shall suggest ways for planning a discussion involving a series of problems. As you develop your own plan, you should phrase most of the points in the form of questions, as is done in the following outline.

Defining the problem   The first step in the discussion should include:

1. Brief introductory remarks by the chairman touching on the general purpose of the discussion and its importance to the group.
2. How can the purpose of the discussion be phrased as a question? (Note: Usually the question has been phrased by the leader or the group before the discussion begins. If not, it should be phrased at this time.)
3. What terms need defining?
   A. What do the terms in the question mean?
   B. What other terms or concepts will be encountered in this discussion that should be defined at this time?

Analyzing the problem   The analysis of the problem consists of evaluating its scope and importance, discovering its causes, determining the essential matters that need correction, and setting up the basic requirements for an effective solution. The following sequence of questions is suggested:

---

[1] See *How We Think* by John Dewey (D. C. Heath & Co., Boston, 1933), pp. 102–118.

1. What is the evidence that an unsatisfactory situation exists?
   A. In what way have members of the group noticed the problem; how have they been affected by it, or how are they likely to be affected?
   B. What other persons or groups does the situation affect, and in what way?
   C. Is the situation likely to improve by itself, or will it become worse if nothing is done about it?
   D. Is the problem sufficiently serious to warrant discussion and action at this time? (If the answer to this question is negative, further discussion is obviously pointless.)
2. What caused this difficulty?
   A. Are its causes primarily financial, political, social, etc.?
   B. To what extent is this difficulty the result of misunderstandings or emotional conflicts between individuals or groups?
3. What conditions in the present situation must be corrected? What demands must be met; what desires satisfied?
   A. On what points is the entire group, or a large part of it, agreed?
   B. What additional changes are desired by a substantial or important minority?
4. What satisfactory elements in the present situation must be retained?
5. In the light of the answers to questions (3) and (4) above, what are the essential criteria by which any proposed plan is to be judged? (See p. 413.)
   A. What must the plan do?
   B. What must the plan avoid?
   C. What limits of time, money, etc., must be considered?
6. In addition to the above requirements, what supplementary qualities would be desirable though not absolutely essential?
7. Summary. The leader should summarize the points agreed upon thus far. Particularly important is a clear statement of the agreements reached on questions (5) and (6), since these requirements will serve as the basic criteria for evaluating the proposals which will be considered. Moreover, a clear understanding and agreement regarding these requirements will tend to make further discussion more logical and will

minimize the tendency to attack and defend proposals because of personal prejudices.

Suggesting solutions In this step, every possible solution should be presented. The group should:

1. Discover all proposed solutions for the difficulty. If the group has met primarily to discuss the merits of a previously proposed plan, they should now consider various alternatives for comparison.
   A. Be sure that each proposal is defined or explained briefly but clearly.
   B. If the list of proposals is long, group them according to type for initial consideration.
2. Be sure that all the proposals are listed, preferably on a blackboard, so that the subsequent evaluations and comparisons can be complete.

Evaluating the solutions The various proposals suggested for meeting the problem should be examined and compared in an attempt to agree on a satisfactory plan. The following procedure is suggested:

1. Note what elements are common to all the proposals and secure agreement for their retention.
2. Examine the differences in the proposals in the light of the criteria set up in (5) of the analysis step. This may be done in either of two ways:
   A. Consider each plan (or type of plan) separately; examine it in the light of all the criteria; determine in what respects it is acceptable and unacceptable.
   B. Consider each criterion separately; determine which proposals best satisfy it.
3. On the basis of this examination, eliminate the less desirable proposals and narrow the discussion to those which remain.
4. Examine the remaining proposals to see whether one of them can be revised to eliminate objectionable features or to add desirable ones or whether the better parts of two or more plans can be combined into a new and more satisfactory one.

(If there are strong differences of opinion within the group, unimportant points—at times, even important ones—will often need to be compromised.)

5. Summary. As soon as an agreement has been reached, the chairman should sum up the principal features of the accepted plan. In groups which have no power or authority to act, this statement will normally end the discussion.

Putting the solution into effect

When a group is able to put its proposal into operation, the following points should be considered:

1. Selection of persons or committees to be responsible for taking action.
2. Determination of the time, place, etc., when the proposal should go into effect.
3. Taking official action, such as appropriating money, etc., whenever such action is necessary. (Note: If several divergent methods of putting the solution into effect are suggested, the group may need to evaluate these various methods briefly in order to decide on the most satisfactory method.)
4. Summary. The chairman should briefly restate the action agreed on to be sure it is clear to the group. This statement normally ends the discussion.

Although preparation and participation are not the same for group discussions and for speeches, the similarities between the motivated sequence for the complete speech presented in Chapter 16 and the plan for deliberative groups offered here are striking. You may find the motivated sequence or its principles useful as a guide in preparing for a deliberative group meeting. The two methods may be compared as follows:

Deliberative plan	*Motivated sequence*
Defining the problem	Attention step
Analyzing the problem	Need step
Suggesting solutions	Satisfaction step
Evaluating the solutions	Satisfaction step
	Visualization step
Putting the solution into effect	Action step

ADAPTING THE DELIBERATIVE PLAN
TO THE QUESTION

The discussion plan suggested above covers the entire process of deliberation from the first analysis of existing conditions to the taking of final action. This entire process is not always required. As H. S. Elliott points out in his book, *The Process of Group Thinking*, "A group may face a question in any one of five stages: (1) a baffling or confused situation; (2) a problem definitely defined; (3) alternatives specifically suggested; (4) a single definite proposal; (5) ways and means of carrying out a conclusion" (p. 89 ff.). How much of the deliberative process will need to be included in the discussion plan will depend, then, upon the stage at which the question comes before the group. If a proposal has already been approved at a previous meeting, or if the group finds itself in immediate agreement on it, all that needs to be discussed is the method of putting the proposal into effect—only the last section of the deliberative discussion plan described above will need to be included in this particular plan. Similarly, if the group meets to consider the merits of a single definite proposal to a generally recognized problem, the analysis of the problem in the outline above can be condensed to a brief discussion of the essential requirements for a satisfactory plan, or merely to a summary of those criteria by the chairman, followed immediately by an examination of the proposal in the light of those requirements. The first step in preparing a discussion plan, therefore, is to determine at what stage the question is likely to come before the group; you can then prepare your outline to pick up the discussion at that stage without needless reconsideration of already settled points. The chairman, however, should study the entire outline so that he will be able to adapt his outline if something he thought was settled turns out not to be.

A situation requiring a modified discussion plan of the type indicated above occurred on a university campus. Three student organizations had made preliminary plans to produce musical comedies on the campus during the same week. Obviously three such shows would conflict with one another, yet none of the organizations wanted to give up its plans entirely. All agreed that the best solution would be for the three groups to combine their efforts in a joint production, but differences in membership requirements, financial policies, and standards of skill required of the participants made it difficult for the organizations to agree on a definite plan. A preliminary meeting of representatives from the student organizations together with representatives of the faculty had disclosed that the final plan, to be acceptable, must provide for (a) skilled professional direction; (b) opportunity for all students, regardless of organization membership, to try out for places in the cast or chorus or to work on the stage crew; (c) equal representation of the three student groups on the managing board; and (d) provision for an adequate financial guarantee. Prior to the second meeting the chairman had secured from members of the joint committee several definitely outlined proposals; copies of these proposals, with the names of the authors omitted, were placed before each member of the committee at the beginning of the meeting. The chairman opened the discussion by recalling the four general requirements listed above and securing their confirmation by the group. From this point on the discussion focused upon the typewritten proposals before the group. It was found that the three plans had a number of common features; the differences were ironed out; some details were added and some dropped; a revised plan was found to be acceptable and was adopted; and provisions were made to put it into operation. Thus, beginning with the suggestion and evaluation of solutions, the procedure indicated in the preceding section of this chapter was followed almost exactly. Similar abridgments of the complete discussion plan can often be adapted to the actual stage at which the question comes before the group.

PLANNING FOR THE DISCUSSION OF A SERIES OF PROBLEMS

Groups such as executive committees, governing boards, and the like are often faced with the necessity of discussing several problems during the same meeting. Some of these problems may be related to one another, while others are quite distinct. Obviously, related questions should be discussed together or in immediate sequence, but the order in which unrelated questions should be considered requires some thought by the chairman. The following procedure, or a similar one, may be helpful for arranging the agenda for such a meeting.

Make a list of all the items to come up for consideration. Include both important and less important matters, those which need immediate attention and those which can be postponed.

Reduce this list to fit the time limit. Determine how much time is available for the discussion, and cross off enough of the less important items to bring the list within reason. The deleted items can be put into a supplementary list which can be used in case the primary items are disposed of in less time than expected.

Arrange the items to be discussed in an orderly sequence. Some matters are dependent upon others. Suppose, for example, that the managing board of the college newspaper is meeting to decide upon the size of the editorial staff but that a proposal is also under consideration for issuing the paper daily instead of weekly. Obviously the second item would have to be settled before the first. If you are to lead the discussion efficiently, you must arrange the items for consideration so that there will be no need to double back.

Outline the subsidiary questions involved in each major problem to be discussed. In the proposal to issue the college paper daily, a number of subordinate points will need to be considered: What will be the added cost of printing and distributing? Can enough advertising space be sold to meet this added expense? What will be done about existing advertising contracts based on the weekly plan? Is there enough local news to provide copy for a daily paper? Should an attempt be made to carry national as well as local news? The leader must have such points as these well in mind so that none of them will be overlooked. A mimeographed or blackboard outline of these points will often help keep the discussion centered on the problem and moving in an orderly fashion.

Finally, determine the questions which will arise from each decision that is made. If it is decided to publish the paper daily, a procedure must be agreed upon for getting the approval of the college authorities; a date must be set for instituting the change; and plans must be laid for putting the proposal into effect. The leader must be ready as each decision is reached to lead the discussion on to the next one. Leadership of this sort will make the discussion orderly and productive.

These suggestions should help the leader decide on the sequence in which the problems should be discussed. The final outline, then, will consist of a series of deliberative discussion plans, modified to suit the stage at which the respective questions arise and arranged as logically as possible.

PLANNING FOR PANEL AND SYMPOSIUM DISCUSSIONS

When a panel discussion before an audience is to be given, the discussion plan should be prepared in great detail. The plan may be similar to those presented earlier in the chapter. If the purpose is to be informative only, the study-group type of plan can be used; if a problem or a proposed course of action is to be discussed, the deliberative type of plan will be more suitable. As explained in the preceding chapter, it is often desirable that the speakers run through the discussion in private before their public appearance; this preliminary practice often suggests how the discussion can be compressed, what less important points can be omitted, and how the whole plan can be made more coherent.

Whatever type of discussion plan is used, it should provide for utilizing the specialized information of all the panel members. Although no one should limit his remarks to his special field of knowledge, he should at least be given the first opportunity to discuss questions relating to that field. Unless something of this sort is done, the very purpose of selecting a panel to conduct the discussion for the audience is likely to be defeated.

If the discussion is to be a symposium (a series of speeches followed by an open forum), the plan will normally be a simple partition of the topic among the speakers, a different phase being assigned to each. The number of speakers will often determine the divisions of the subject. One person, for example, may present the problem, and each of the other speakers may suggest and evaluate a different type of solution; or different persons may discuss the political, economic, religious, and educational aspects of the topic. After the speakers have completed these rather formal remarks, the meeting may be opened for questions from the audience, the chairman referring the questions to the various symposium speakers for reply.

Any type of discussion plan must conform to the personnel of the group. The discussion leader must not assume that everyone will be logical, clear-thinking, and unemotional. He should be aware of prejudices and strong feelings and plan how to modify their firmness or violence. Or if certain points are not vital to the issue and are likely to cause bitterness or unnecessary controversy, the leader must plan a tactful method of excluding these points from the discussion. If a certain person is known to have considerable prestige with the other members of the group, the discussion plan must be arranged to include the consideration of beliefs other than his in order to avoid too hasty an acceptance of his point of view. In short, the plan must be developed not only to cover the subject but also to direct people in their discussion of it.

None of the suggestions presented in this chapter will take the place of the discussion leader's good sense or experience in planning discussion. The better informed you are on the subject or problem to be discussed and the better you know the members of the group, the better able you will be to outline a discussion plan. When good sense or experience or special knowledge indicates that a procedure different from that suggested in this chapter would lead to more rapid progress and more fruitful results, do not hesitate to devise a completely different type of plan. In the beginning, however, you will be wise to follow rather closely the procedures suggested in this chapter, which are based on the advice of experienced discussion leaders.

SUGGESTED DISCUSSION QUESTIONS

The first list includes both questions of fact and questions of value, suitable for use with the study-group plan. The second list contains questions of policy for deliberative groups (usually committees and executive groups). Panels and symposiums, of course, may direct themselves to any of these goals.

For study groups:
1. How effective is our freshmen orientation program?
2. What benefits does the undergraduate gain from participating in extracurricular activities?
3. What are the greatest opportunities for religion today?
4. How well are high school students prepared for college?
5. How do democracy and communism differ in philosophy?

6. What was Shakespeare's greatest play?
7. How have expressways affected the growth of American cities?
8. What are the present forms of federal aid to education?
9. What is the present foreign policy of the United States?
10. What countries have best utilized economic assistance from the United States?

For deliberative groups:

1. What can be done to increase the effectiveness of student government in our college?
2. How can the colleges and universities more effectively meet the problem of increased enrollments?
3. What can be done to increase the number of qualified teachers in our public schools?
4. What tax program would provide the best support for the public schools of our state?
5. What system would provide the best medical care for the people of the United States?
6. How can labor and management increase their understanding of the other's problems?
7. How can the quality of television programs be improved?
8. How can the United States get more for its foreign-aid dollars?
9. How can the United States improve its relations with the Latin American nations?
10. How can the United Nations help maintain peace among the nations of the world?

PROBLEMS

1. Be ready to discuss the following questions in class: What general outline can the study group usually follow for its discussions? What are the five steps in the complete plan for deliberative groups? Under what conditions will one or more of these steps be unnecessary? How may a series of problems be effectively discussed at the same meeting? In what ways should the discussion plan be modified for panel and symposium discussions?

2. Outline a discussion plan to use if you were to lead a discussion by members of your speech class on any of the questions listed above for study groups.

3. Meet with five or six persons in your speech class and select a leader; choose a question from the list for deliberative groups or frame a question of your own choice; gather information and prepare a discussion plan; present a panel discussion before the class.

4. Select a topic suitable for discussion by persons engaged in the vocation or profession you intend to enter and state it as a question. Then prepare the appropriate discussion plan for a study or deliberative group.

5. Recall a committee meeting you have attended and indicate the different problems which were discussed and whether each question arose as an undefined difficulty, a definite problem, a proposal for consideration, or a question only of ways and means.

6. Make a list of problems likely to arise at the next meeting of some organization to which you belong, and, assuming you are to act as chairman, arrange these problems in the most effective sequence for discussion and prepare an appropriately abridged discussion plan for each of them.

7. Taking the subject and panel members chosen in working out Problem 10 in the preceding chapter, prepare a suitable discussion plan. How would you partition the subject for a symposium? What changes, if any, would be required if these discussions were to be broadcast?

Men are never so likely to settle a question rightly as when they discuss it freely.

Thomas Babington Macaulay

CHAPTER 31 / *Taking Part in Discussion*

To be an effective participant in discussion, either as a leader or as an ordinary member of the group, requires effective speaking, knowing when to speak and when to remain silent, and the ability to judge the importance of other people's remarks. This chapter, therefore, will consider briefly five things: how to stimulate and direct the discussion when you are the leader; how to evaluate the opinions of others; when to take part in the discussion and when to remain silent; how to act when you do participate; and what special devices of persuasion you may use.

STIMULATING AND DIRECTING DISCUSSION

Even though he has carefully outlined a suitable discussion plan, the leader still faces the task of stimulating and directing the actual discussion so that the group will feel free to talk, will focus its attention on the most important problems, and will reach a profitable conclusion. To these ends, experienced leaders have offered the following suggestions.

Getting the discussion started — Begin, as suggested in Chapter 30, by making a brief statement of the question to be discussed and pointing out its importance, especially as it is related to the group members. This statement should be made with vigor and earnestness, suggesting the vital nature of the subject, and should be expressed in concrete terms supported by specific instances; but it should not be so long that it seems to exhaust the subject matter. It should, moreover, lead into a series of provocative questions designed to pull members of the group into the discussion. The questions ought not to be too general; they should call for specific answers based on the experiences of individuals in the group. You might ask, for example, "In what way have you, personally, met this problem recently?" Or better, "Mr. Knowles told me that he ran into this problem in the following way. . . . (Briefly describe.) Have any of you had a similar experience, or if not, how did your experience differ?" If such questions fail to provoke sufficient discussion, call on certain individuals by name to relate their experiences or to express their opinions on the problem. Ask someone for specific information that you know he has—ask the treasurer for a statement of the cash on hand, or the secretary for the size of membership, or a fraternity man for the attitude of the members of his chapter; be sure, of course, that such questions are germane to the subject under discussion. Or go to the board and start a list—of causes of the problem, of types of people or groups whom it affects, of terms needing definition, of proposed courses of action, of anything which fits into your discussion outline and calls for enumeration; curiously enough, people who hesitate to begin a discussion seldom hesitate to add to a list which has been started.

Still another method is to bring out, at the beginning, one or more extreme points of view on the question. You can relay these viewpoints yourself or, better, call on members of the group who have them. Nothing seems to stir a group into active discussion so much as an extreme statement with which to disagree; the danger of this method is that it may start a verbal battle which consumes too much time or stirs up personal animosity. Usually the problem which brought the group together is sufficiently provocative to start the discussion; but if the group lags at the beginning or hits a "dead spot" later in the discussion, the methods described above will prove helpful.

Keeping the discussion from wandering The tendency of the group to stray from the central issue can be greatly diminished if the leader writes a skeleton outline of the discussion plan on a blackboard. When people can see what points are to be taken up and in what order, they are likely to focus their attention on those points and in that order. Unless something really important has been omitted from the outline, the leader can direct attention to the points in it, one after another, and thus keep the discussion progressing steadily. Using the outline as a skeleton, many leaders fill in the details on the blackboard as they are brought up in the discussion, thus providing the group with a visual record of what has been said. If, in spite of this, the discussion takes an irrelevant turn, all the leader usually needs to do is call attention to the irrelevancy and refer to the outline. The same is true when someone doubles back to a point already discussed or jumps ahead to a point not yet reached. Of course, the leader must be sensible and fair in this matter: sometimes the fault is in his outline rather than in the speaker who moves away from it. For example, something important may have been omitted from the outline. In general, however, the leader will do well to hold the group pretty closely to the outlined discussion plan.

There will be times when one or two persons in the group begin to monopolize the discussion. Not infrequently such persons really have a great deal to contribute, but just as often they tend to repeat or overexpand some point. When this occurs, the leader should call on other members of the group, by name if necessary, asking them definite questions which will lead the discussion forward and away from the overworked point and the overtalkative person. In extreme cases, a time limit may be invoked, or the number of times any one person may talk may be limited. If the time for closing the discussion is drawing near, a statement of that fact usually has a marked effect in keeping talk from wandering or becoming repetitive. Remember that while the discussion leader does not usually have the right to direct what conclusion is to be reached, he does have the right and the duty to control the direction of the discussion and to keep it centered on the important issues. A good leader is one who can do this with tact and firmness.

Bringing out the facts

Normally, if you follow the preceding suggestions, you will bring out the facts needed to solve the problem or cover the subject of the discussion. If the participants are fair-minded and well-informed and the discussion plan is complete, no special effort beyond that already indicated will be required. Unfortunately, discussion groups do not always behave so perfectly, and the leader sometimes needs to see that important facts or viewpoints are not ignored and that opinions are not mistaken for proven facts.

When he feels that something important has been ignored, the leader may tactfully inquire, "Has anyone noticed that . . . ," adding the missing fact himself. Or he may say, "Mr. Smith called my attention yesterday to the fact that. . . . Has anyone else noticed this to be true?" It is even better, of course, to ask some individual in the group a direct question designed to bring out this fact. Similarly, if there seems to be a tendency to dwell on one point of view to the exclusion of an equally important one, the leader may call attention to the neglect by suggesting, "Perhaps we should ask Mr. Johnson to express his view of this," or, "I have heard this other point of view expressed too. . . . What do you think of it?"

The leader should never directly accuse a member of his group of twisting facts or making unsupported statements, but he should see that such remarks do not pass unchallenged. He may handle instances of this sort tactfully by asking the speaker for further detail or for the evidence on which the statement is based. Thus he may say, "I wonder if you would tell us, Mr. Pike, what has led to this conclusion?" or, "Is that a statement of your own opinion, Mr. Stout, or have you observed it to be true in actual practice?" By skillful questioning, a good discussion leader can insure the inclusion of all sides of the argument in the discussion, see that the important facts are carefully considered, and prevent the group from uncritically accepting assertions without supporting evidence. He must, however, seem to draw these facts out of the group and avoid appearing to dominate the argument.

Arriving at profitable conclusions   If a good plan has been outlined and adhered to without too many digressions, the group will have come a long way toward concluding the discussion profitably. The leader may increase the likelihood of this result in two or three ways. As the discussion proceeds, he will notice a number of things upon which most of those in the group agree, and he can bring these together in brief summaries at appropriate intervals. In this way he can narrow the discussion to the points not yet agreed to and attempt to secure agreement on them. Summaries of this sort lend a sense of accomplishment and encourage the group to reach a final settlement of the problem. As already indicated, the leader may also add to the value of the discussion by calling forth factual information. Since many disagreements disappear when the facts are known, the leader can often thus eliminate needless argument. By this same method, he can also minimize personal antipathies and keep the discussion on a more rational basis. Finally, at the close of the discussion, the leader should summarize the results, emphasizing the points of agreement but indicating any important minority viewpoint. If some things remain unsettled, he should point them out, especially if there is to be a later meeting. The tone of this final summary should be judicious and, if it is at all justified, should suggest satisfaction with the outcome.

EVALUATING THE OPINIONS OF OTHERS

One of the greatest differences between a public speech and a group discussion lies in the obvious fact that in the latter, one person does not do all the talking. Each member will do some speaking, but during the greater part of the time he will be listening. This is true of the discussion leader as well as the other members of the group. While you are listening, your principal task will be to evaluate what the speaker is saying so that you may weigh his opinions against your own and against those expressed by other members of the group. By asking yourself the following questions, you will be able to make your judgment both thorough and systematic:

1. Does the training and experience of the speaker qualify him to express an authoritative opinion? Is he an expert in the particular field of knowledge under discussion?
2. Is his statement based on first-hand knowledge? Did he observe the evidence, or is he merely reporting a rumor?
3. Is his opinion prejudiced? Is it influenced by personal interest? Does he stand to profit personally from some decision the group may reach?
4. Does he usually state his opinions frankly? Does he reveal all the facts known to him, or is he in the habit of concealing facts unfavorable to his cause?
5. Are the facts or opinions presented consistent with human experience? Do they sound plausible? Could they reasonably be true?
6. Are the facts or opinions presented consistent with one another? If two reports contradict each other, which seems more substantial and trustworthy?
7. What weight will other members of the group give to this person's opinion? Is his prestige so great that the group will agree with him in the face of conflicting evidence, or is he so little respected that he will not be believed unless someone else supports his opinion?

If you ask yourself these questions about each participant and his contribution, you will be able to evaluate his remarks more accurately. (Observe, moreover, that these questions will serve in passing judgment not only on the opinions of speakers in group discussions but also on those opinions expressed from the public platform or on the printed page.) If you make a running evaluation of the comments made by others in the discussion, you can make a decision more easily and justly and can predict the reaction of the group to whatever remarks you may make.

WHEN TO TAKE PART IN THE DISCUSSION

There is no dogmatic answer to the often asked question, "When should I talk and when should I keep quiet?" In general, the longer you have been a member of a group, the freer you may be with your comments. Newcomers do well to speak rarely and only when they have something important to say. In most cases, however, the following suggestions will apply:

Do not speak beside the point. If what you have to say does not bear directly on the point at issue, keep quiet. Too often someone wanders far off the point to discuss another far removed and thus drags out the settlement of the main point interminably. No matter how important your point, wait until the point under discussion is settled before you shift to a different one. Remember that one point must be settled at a time.

Speak when you have a report to present. Frequently reports are made to a group by officials or committee chairmen. The treasurer's report, for instance, is an important part of a business meeting. The purpose of such reports usually is either to present information or to suggest some action; sometimes, of course, these purposes are combined. In any case, the report should be brief and to the point and should emphasize at the end, in summary fashion, those facts or conclusions which are important to the group.

Speak, of course, when you are asked a direct question. Do not, however, give a long-winded reply. Unless you can contribute a new point of view or additional information, cut your answer short.

Speak when you have an intelligent comment or suggestion to make. Frequently some aspect of the subject has been neglected, or some important point has slipped by unnoticed. Even when you have no tangible information upon this particular point, a brief comment or question may stimulate others to contribute the needed information.

Speak when you can make clear a point another person has badly muddled. Quite often someone else may make an important point but express it so vaguely that no one else appreciates its significance. If you can tactfully make the point clear, you will have performed a valuable service.

Speak when you can correct an error. In doing this you must exercise a great deal of tact to avoid starting a fruitless argument. If the point is important, however, and you know the other man is wrong, by all means make the correction. If you are courteous and modest, avoiding any suggestion of officiousness, you should be able to correct the error without offense.

Speak when you can offer added information upon the question. No one person knows everything. Only by the combined information of the entire group can a sound judgment be made. If, therefore, you can illuminate the problem by an apt illustration, if you can cite accurate figures bearing upon it, or if you can relay the testimony of someone outside the group, by all means do so. Be sure of only one thing: that what you say has a direct bearing upon the point at issue. Remember that nothing is so disconcerting as to have someone inject discussion which is entirely beside the point.

Speak when you can ask an intelligent question. If you are in doubt about something and are fairly sure that others are also in doubt, find out about the matter at once; do not allow the decision to be made until your doubt is resolved. Obviously, you should not ask questions continually, but a question asked at the proper moment will often save a great deal of muddled thinking and discussion. Moreover, when the discussion has wandered, a question will frequently bring it back to the main issue. Finally, whether you are the leader or only a member, ask questions to bring out the facts behind unsupported opinions.

Speak when you can inject humor into an otherwise dry discussion. This suggestion needs to be followed with extreme caution. Once in a while, however, a little humor will liven up a tired group and quicken the pace of the discussion. Moreover, if strong disagreement should reach the point of personal animosity, a little good-natured humor will often serve to relieve the tension that has built up.

PROPER PARTICIPATION

The manner of speaking varies considerably with the type of discussion being conducted. Informal groups permit an easier and more familiar manner than does a formal business meeting. Members of a panel or a symposium must talk loudly enough to be heard by the audience as well as by the other members of the group. In radio and television discussion, the members of the group should be seated equally distant from the microphone so that there will not seem to be a difference in the loudness of their speech. The comments made in Chapter 28 about microphone technic, especially those about rustling paper and tapping the table, apply even more to discussion than to single speeches since the more people there are, the more chance there is for noisy movement.

Regardless of these differences, however, the manner of participating in discussion has one basic common characteristic: consideration for the other members of the group. Discussion is a joint enterprise and not the place for prima donnas. Remember these suggestions: Do not show off, yet avoid false modesty when you have something worth while to say. Talk loudly enough to be heard. Speak to the point and avoid vague, unsupported statements. Accept criticism with dignity, and treat disagreement with both critical judgment and an open mind. To remember all this in the midst of vigorous discussion is not easy; but if you develop the habit of participating with these ideas in mind, your comments will be more useful and more persuasive.

SPECIAL TECHNICS

In addition to these general technics for participating in discussion, there are some special devices you can use when you wish to secure agreement to a proposal. Too often people try to swing a group around to their point of view merely by argument, forgetting that argument quite often only makes the other person more decided in his own opinion.

All the technics for securing belief mentioned in Chapters 22 and 23, especially the "yes-response" technic, have a continual application in group discussion. The more often you can get the members of the group to agree with you, the more likely they will be to continue agreeing, even upon doubtful points. Do not present the most disagreeable proposition first; present it last, and then only after you have secured agreement upon several other points.

In addition, consider the following six technics:

Pull your proposal from another person by suggestion. Instead of making the proposal yourself, lead the discussion to a position where the actual point is quite obvious and someone else will be likely to make it for you. Suppose, for example, that you are in favor of spending more money for advertising but do not want to make the proposal yourself. Maneuver the discussion to the point of considering ways and means of expanding the business. Then suggest that the group should catalog (on the blackboard or on paper) all the possible ways in which expansion can be brought about. Someone will be sure to suggest advertising as one of the means. Then, when all the methods have been set down, side with the person who proposed increased advertising. Since you will now be supporting someone else's proposal rather than putting forward your own, you can be much more outspoken. This technic is particularly valuable when you have a number of proposals to present. A group becomes annoyed if one person brings up all the ideas.

Ask the opinion of another who you know will agree. Quite often the first few opinions expressed about a proposal will set the tone for subsequent statements. If the first few persons to speak are quite definite in favoring or opposing a proposition, there is likely to be a tendency for others to voice different opinions more temperately. It is a case of getting off on the right foot. As soon as you have made a proposal, therefore, ask someone who you think will agree with you, "What do you think about it, Mr. Jones?"

Compromise on small points to secure agreement on big ones. The attitude of dogmatism tends to breed dogmatic opposition. If by giving in on smaller points you can demonstrate that you are willing to be reasonable, you will tend to strengthen your prestige with the group and to reduce its resistance. The principle of reciprocity is quite as applicable here as elsewhere. By supporting another's proposal, or by giving in to it, you tend to create an obligation in him to support you.

Eliminate doubtful points from your proposal. Frequently opposition to a proposal arises not from any objection to its central idea but only to some part of it, such as the date or method of application. If it is impossible to secure a compromise on points of this sort, they may sometimes be eliminated from the proposal entirely and left for later decision by the chairman or president. Frequently such points can be dropped without sacrificing the strength of the plan. Shrewd persons have been known to include points of this kind purposely in order to draw the fire of opposition away from the central plan.

On rare occasions, deliver an ultimatum. When nothing else succeeds and you are determined to force the adoption or rejection of some proposal, you may find the use of a threat effective. The ultimatum is by nature a weapon of force rather than of persuasion, however. It should be employed only when you are prepared to apply force—either the force of your personal prestige or some concrete action undesirable to the group—if your ultimatum is not heeded. Remember, however, that force breeds force and that no friends are made by presenting ultimatums.

Postpone decision to avoid negative action. If you see that there is no possibility of securing agreement on a proposal that you favor, or if the opposition to it seems so strong that there is a chance of definite rejection, you should try to postpone decision to a later date. Conditions may change before the next consideration of your proposal, or the opposition may become less active. A proposal can be put through more easily if it does not have the stigma of a previous rejection. As far as possible, therefore, postpone a decision until you are relatively sure it will be accepted.

Throughout the entire discussion, however, remember that the fundamental object should be to arrive at the best possible decision or to secure the most accurate information. Do not engage in discussion merely to win points or to prove the other fellow wrong.

SAMPLE DISCUSSION

The following discussion illustrates many of the technics discussed in Chapters 29 through 31. Problems 2, 3, and 4, pages 589 to 590, suggest some ways of analyzing this discussion.

HOW IMPORTANT ARE TESTS IN EDUCATING YOUR CHILD? [1]

The following discussion was presented by the Northwestern University Reviewing Stand over radio station WGN, Chicago, on September 4, 1960.

D*ean McBurney:* Today we ask the question: "How important are tests in educating your child?" This is your moderator, James H. McBurney, Dean of the School of Speech, Northwestern University. We are pleased to welcome our guests for today: Kenneth W. Lund, Superintendent of the Oak Park–River Forest High School, Oak Park, Illinois; Arthur H. Oestreich, Superintendent of Schools in Kenilworth, Illinois; and Mrs. Blanche B. Paulson, Director of the Bureau of Pupil Personnel Services in the Chicago Public Schools.

[1] Reprinted by permission of Dean James H. McBurney and the participants.

Educators seem to have devised tests in almost every area of human experiences. How useful are these tests in the educational process; how reliable are they; what are their advantages and limitations? I am sure these are some of the things we will want to consider. To start us off, Mrs. Paulson, I wonder if you could identify what we are talking about. What is a standardized test; how many of them are there; how many people take them? Would you do that for us?

Mrs. Paulson: Those are very good questions and certainly fundamental to any discussion that we would have. To take the easiest part first. In 1958 about 122 million standardized tests were used throughout the United States. In 1956 a hundred million were used. So you see we have quite an increase there.

Dean McBurney: You mean by that, that at least this number of tests were sold—

Mrs. Paulson: That's right.

Dean McBurney: . . . and evidently taken by somebody.

Mrs. Paulson: This wouldn't be 122 million different titles of tests, but this shows the quantity of testing in the United States—most of it, of course, in our school systems. Well now, as a sort of easy distinction, a standardized test can be distinguished from the teacher-made test or the homemade test in that the standardized test is a printed test put out by a publisher and a great deal of work has gone into the creation of this test. Usually test publishers employ research people and curriculum people; they go over an area that is to be used for the testing; the selections of questions are made; and then before the test ever appears on the market, it is given to hundreds or maybe thousands of students. On the basis of the performance of these youngsters, standards are set up for the performance of any youngster who may take it. This is essentially what a standardized test is.

Dean McBurney: So, presumably, someone who takes one of these standardized tests can come out with a score that is relatively, at least, meaningful.

Mr. Lund: And, of course, can know so much more than if your only group reference is the class in which the child is. All of a sudden he's now compared to 10,000, 100,000, other youngsters who are perhaps in fifth grade nationally. Now his reading ability as contrasted or achievement as contrasted with other reading performances of other children can be measured much more accurately.

Dean McBurney: In what areas are these tests prepared, Mr. Oestreich? What types of tests are available?

Mr. Oestreich: There are many groups. I should say there are probably five that we might consider in our discussion. First of all, mental ability, which would include the so-called IQ test, probably better named the scholastic aptitude test. Then there are all sorts of special aptitudes which have reference in the academic field. I am speaking now of reading aptitude, for instance. There are vocational aptitude tests and there are certain tests devised for the creative field—art, music, etc. There is a third category of interest type tests and a fourth category of personality type tests. Then, in a general way, we can lock together the clinical type tests which are not used, generally speaking, for all pupils of a school but are designed more for special cases and for special needs of children.

Dean McBurney: Before we explore these different kinds of tests and their usefulness, I would like to ask some one of you—maybe you would speak to this, Mr. Lund—how you explain what appears to be an enormous increase in the number of these tests given over the country?

Mr. Lund: Of course, this has been a steady increase. If you really want to date our concern for individual differences—usually the father of all this is thought of as the Frenchman, Binet, as of the turn of the century—1900. Then with the war we began to test people to place them in the military. For instance, 18 million took tests so that they would be placed during World War II, and this had an impetus for the whole testing movement. Then I should say, of course, America is excited about education, certainly has been in the postwar years, and Sputnik as of 1957 helped this along. We are really now, I think, in American education, ready to come to grips with the reality of individual differences. We want to make differential programs for youngsters who have differing levels of abilities and interests. Obviously you begin by first of all identifying those factors through tests, through performance in school, through counseling conferences, and many other techniques. So testing is part of what I would call the general excitement in education today, and I would certainly expect this trend that was described by Mrs. Paulson to go on. We're going to have more testing.

Dean McBurney: Let's talk about the so-called intelligence test that Mr. Oestreich mentioned. Most people are vaguely familiar with the IQ, the intelligence quotient. What are we trying to get at with such intelligence tests anyway, Mr. Oestreich?

Mr. Oestreich: Well, in the frame of reference of the school picture— and this is where most of this testing takes place—I think probably we'd better redefine what we mean by this intelligence. I think that "scholastic aptitude" is a far better name since it refers to that kind of mental or intellectual ability which has direct application to work in school. If we use it in this context, we are not talking about a very broad general base of intellectual capacity so much as we are talking about a particular kind of aptitude for school work. In that context then we had better talk about, not IQ, but rather scholastic aptitude. I don't know whether Ken or Blanche would agree with me on this, but certainly this is the interpretation that I would put on it.

Mr. Lund: If you would examine the instruments that are used for these purposes, you'll find they're loaded with verbal type questions and quantitative arithmetic-type questions—all to the end that the child's performance on these items will help us predict how well he's going, later, to do English, mathematics, language, history, and science in school. So they are school predicting type tests. We do have other kinds of intelligence tests that are used in nonschool settings which include what we call nonverbal or performance-type items. They're often used quite commonly with younger children where the reading skills and arithmetic skills are not well developed. They're also used when you want to predict, for instance, performance. In the army it was very customary to use almost a 33⅓ up to a 50 percent loading factor of nonscholastic items because, after all, they were not then testing for how well the recruit was going to learn in school; they were testing for how well he was going to perform in the military situation.

Mrs. Paulson: Of course, for the next few years for any youngster in school, his performance in school is his main endeavor and the main concern of the people who are around him.

Dean McBurney: Well now, Mrs. Paulson, let's say that I am the parent of a child—matter of fact, I'm the parent of three of them, but this child will be completely hypothetical—and I go to his counselor or teacher and I am told that this child of mine has an IQ of 90. Am I to be proud of this; am I to be in deep despair? What does this mean anyway; what should I make of this?

Mrs. Paulson: I would hope that the counselor would not approach the problem of helping you to understand your youngster's ability in quite this fashion. But if this did happen, then there should be an explanation to you of the meaning of the numeral 90, as being part of a band that defines an average intelligence performance at the average point. I think we are often controlled in our thinking with these terms by the idea that we used to have in education that a hundred was perfect. Nowadays in connection with testing and standardized testing, 100 becomes the average. It indicates that for every year of normal growth there has been a year of intellectual growth at the same time so that a youngster who has an IQ of 90 would be at the lower level of the average ability.

Dean McBurney: What is the average IQ in the schools?

Mrs. Paulson: The average, I suppose, is this band of between, let us say, 90 and 110, rather than saying any one point is an average, such as a hundred or any other figure you would want to take. You can't pinpoint any one specific number and say this is the average and no other number close to it is part of the average.

Mr. Lund: I wonder if I could suggest that I wish we could start over counseling you about your child's intelligence and not begin with the 90 score. I think, rather, you should know in conferring with the counselor that the tests show that about seven out of ten of the other children the same age as your child have evidently a higher intelligence or higher intellectual ability than your child, using the score you have given. Now this helps you to set standards for the child, and expectations. It is unwise, of course, for all parents to expect their children to all be, we'll say, "A" students or honor scholarship students; it is right for every parent to expect their children to perform up to their level of ability.

The trouble with just giving you a score of 90 is, I would guess, that we didn't communicate to you something that you could use. What do I do now with this score is really your problem and I think schools more commonly say, your child is more capable than three out of five of his classmates, four out of five, seven out of ten, some other value like this. This is more meaningful really than any precise IQ score.

Dean McBurney: Once I get this value or this band, how much confidence can I place in it, as a parent?

Mr. Oestreich: Well, I would like to follow through in what Ken said, that certainly in this counseling situation I would be very careful to point out to you that this is but one and perhaps a very small facet of the total picture of your youngster. We've said nothing about his industry; we've said nothing about his application; we do not know what his goals, his aspirations and his hopes are. In the last analysis, these parts of the total personality which are not amenable to tests, perhaps are much, much more important than this band score or specific IQ score.

Dean McBurney: Now, are you, Mr. Oestreich, just trying to be encouraging to me when I have a child on my hands that is a little dull and you're trying to make me feel happy about it? At least he'll work hard?

Mr. Lund: I'll use an illustration from our own experience. In recent months I've had a questionnaire come to our school asking for information about eleven of our graduates, who in 1957 earned Ph.D. degrees in Science and were registered with the Office of Scientific Manpower. They're trying to do a follow-up study on what kind of young people these were. We went back to their records, and it was interesting to us to discover that, out of these eleven, four did not graduate in the upper quarter of their high school class and one of them graduated just slightly above the middle of his class. On intelligence measures they came down below even the average of the class in some tests. Now all this said was that these youngsters may not have outstanding ability but they have other outstanding characteristics—the ones Mr. Oestreich mentioned, diligence, and a narrower more specific type of talent. Some of them went on and gave great performances in specialized areas of science even though they perhaps would not have done well in your area of speech, or someone else's area of English, or history, or something such as that. They had a narrower and a greater specific talent that did not really show up on the test. So the test by no means should close doors, as I've heard it often said, to people who have specialized ability.

Mrs. Paulson: Don't you think we ought to bring your point that you just made together with Art's that he made just now, that we can't really place too much emphasis on just one test? You might want to go back to the date when these youngsters took these tests and ask some questions about that, too.

Mr. Lund: True.

Dean McBurney: If I may ask a specific question, Mr. Oestreich. Now you preside over an elementary school?

Mr. Oestreich: That's right.

Dean McBurney: If I may say so, a very good one. What kinds of tests do you give to these youngsters in the early grades?

Mr. Oestreich: Well, we are concentrating primarily on three different types of tests. One, surely we want to know what their intellectual capacities are, and number two, we—

Dean McBurney: And this is the IQ that we've been talking about?

Mr. Oestreich: Yes, but we don't use the term IQ in our school.

Dean McBurney: You don't?

Mr. Oestreich: No, we do not. But mental ability or scholastic aptitude, fine. Then we try to get some measure of their achievement. This is all slanted at education, let me say, because we know that in our particular school the vast majority of youngsters are college bound and therefore our emphasis logically must be placed on the academic field. So we test mental ability, or scholastic aptitude, achievement. Then, in special fields such as reading, readiness at the very low grades, reading achievement, or, in some instances, diagnostic types of reading tests to find out what kind of difficulties the youngsters are having. And that's about all that we do at this moment.

Dean McBurney: And once you get these data, what do you do with them?

Mr. Oestreich: We try to encourage parents to come in and see for themselves what their youngsters have done. We try to do a good job—I hope as well as Mr. Lund has suggested in his interview with your hypothetical child—we try to point out to them their potential. The theory is that if the youngster has the capability of doing exceptional work he should be encouraged to do exceptional work and if the best he can do is average work, well that is about all that you can expect. In other words, we try to interpret to them the potential of the youngster and then what he is doing to live up to that potential.

Dean McBurney: Well now, I imagine that through these tests you would identify for certain people certain youngsters—our highly talented.

Mr. Oestreich: That's right.

Dean McBurney: Now do you try to do anything special for this gifted group?

Mr. Oestreich: No, I don't think that this is quite the place, at the elementary school level, because we're trying to lay foundations. I would lean more in the direction of special programs for special talents at the secondary level. I am sure that Dr. Lund would agree with me on this.

Dean McBurney: Do you agree with that?

Mr. Lund: Oh yes, and we have many such special programs. I think, however, in the elementary school they often give specialized reading programs and they encourage development of interests, science hobbies, music hobbies, special areas, but not with the end in view of a special school or even a special class. However, at the high school then you really lay out a four-year plan to make use of their talents, as we do and many schools do, to help them go all the way through, even to taking college level work. In their senior year we ask them both to use their talents and to hurry because there's so much to learn in this world and they who are most capable should be about it. There are many other aspects, of course. You plan this in relation to vocational goals, adjustment goals. These certainly come in here too.

Dean McBurney: Is this kind of thing going on in the Chicago schools?

Mrs. Paulson: Oh yes, it is. We think in terms of having differentiated programs at the high school level to accommodate youngsters of different ability levels and different achievement levels, so that the youngsters who are in this top percent that we've been talking about here have the opportunity of moving ahead rapidly. The other youngsters have the opportunity of having good solid programs for themselves where they're challenged and where they can find achievement.

Dean McBurney: You think there's any danger in carrying this kind of identification too far, Mr. Lund, of setting up special groups for superior students, of grouping them in homogeneous ways in such a way as to deny the superior student the experience of living with people who are somewhat less gifted?

Mr. Lund: I really think that's a sort of armchair comment that my actual on-the-scene experience doesn't fulfill. We group youngsters, for instance, in areas where they have special talents, which might be mathematics or science or English, and then in other courses they commonly will be in with the regular groups. They will also be in with them in many other types of activities. This really means they go apart for special study from their classmates once a day, twice a day, something of that kind, but they come together in the morning and they are in many classes together throughout the day and leave together in the evening. There's no real separation. It's no more separate than if one youngster elects physics, and another industrial arts, and another takes Spanish, or something like this. There's no feeling of stigma.

Mrs. Paulson: I think there's another variation of what he's just said that I would like to point out and that is that a youngster may be very gifted in, let's say, mathematics and belong in and be enrolled in an accelerated group in mathematics. Yet, in some other subject, foreign language or English or something like this, might not be performing at that same level and he wouldn't be with the same group of youngsters all day long. I think this concept of, you might even say, the unevenness of intelligence is an important one.

Dean McBurney: What do you think, Mr. Lund, of the test given by the college entrance examination board?

Mr. Lund: Well that's a big order in one minute, but it of course is one of the fastest growing programs in America and it has had great value to us in high schools. For a while we were in the position, you know, where every college gave a different entrance examination. We send our students to about 145 colleges in a year, and if you one day had the test for the University of Tulsa and the next day for Indiana and the next day for another one, this was a bad idea. Now, of course, we give these examinations several times a year. They measure, again, scholastic aptitude, the likelihood that he will succeed in college, and they do a good job of predicting that. However, I would urge that they be used in conjunction with his academic performance in high school, his goals and plans— in other words, a full picture. It's like any other single score, it's an indicator, but it isn't in any sense the complete answer on how well this person will do.

Dean McBurney: How generally should the results of these tests be made available, do you think, to students themselves and to their parents and other interested parties, Mr. Oestreich?

Mr. Oestreich: I believe they should be made available both to parents and to the students at whatever level of understanding they possess, and this is the key to the whole thing. If they do not understand what the tests mean in terms of their own capacities, then they're meaningless and they're just statistics. And I just want to mention one more thing. I hope we will never use tests to help shape round pegs to fit round holes, and I'm afraid that there is too much of that in this whole testing field.

Dean McBurney: Do you share that view at all?

Mrs. Paulson: Yes I do, I would agree with it wholeheartedly.

Dean McBurney: I'm sorry I'm going to have to interrupt you—our time is up. I don't know when I've conducted a program where the time has gone as rapidly as here. We've been discussing, "How important are tests in educating your child?" I wish to thank our guests for today. This is your moderator, James H. McBurney, Dean of the School of Speech at Northwestern University.

PROBLEMS

1. Be ready to discuss the following questions in class: What can the discussion leader do to get the discussion started? To keep the discussion from wandering? To bring out the facts? To help the group arrive at profitable conclusions? What tests can be applied to opinions expressed by the participants in a discussion? At what times can your participation help the discussion? How can you secure agreement in a discussion group?

2. Compare the methods of stimulating and directing discussion used by Dean McBurney in the Northwestern University Reviewing Stand discussion printed above to those used by the leader of some discussion in which you recently participated. In what ways do you believe the size, the personnel, or the purposes of the groups affected the methods used by the leaders?

3. Select a point about halfway through the discussion printed above and prepare a short statement which summarizes the discussion up to that point.

4. Select several statements of opinion made in the Northwestern University Reviewing Stand discussion and evaluate each of them by applying the tests listed in the seven questions listed on page 577.

5. Apply the same tests (Problem 4) to the opinions expressed by five different people in the next discussion in which you participate.

6. Assuming that you were to lead the discussion of a student group on some current problem, phrase questions which you could use in dealing with participants who were: (a) monopolizing the discussion, (b) not participating, (c) wandering from the subject, and (d) confusing opinions and facts.

7. In a discussion at which you are present, tabulate the reasons for the first twenty remarks that are made. As a basis for this tabulation, use the list given in this chapter under the heading, "When to take part in the discussion," pages 577–579.

8. In the next discussion in which you participate, plan beforehand to use one or more of the special technics explained in this chapter to secure acceptance of some point of view or plan of action. Report how well this technic succeeded, or, if it did not succeed, tell why.

Law is a form of order, and good law must necessarily mean good order.

Aristotle

CHAPTER *32 / Parliamentary Law for Informal Groups*

The degree of formality with which discussion is carried on depends largely upon the group involved. Legislative assemblies follow detailed and somewhat complicated rules, while many informal study groups employ very few if any rules. To insure an orderly discussion, however, most groups follow, either by formal regulation or by tacit consent, certain rules of order which are known as parliamentary law, because they originated in parliamentary bodies. For a detailed list of these rules, consult a complete manual such as *Robert's Rules of Order*. For the average group, however, less detailed procedure is required. This chapter contains only a brief outline of rules for conducting business meetings—rules that are followed almost universally, even in less formal groups. To participate properly in discussion where parliamentary procedure is followed, you should know these basic rules. The presiding officers of such groups must master these rules particularly well, for they are responsible for seeing that the rules are observed. If the procedure outlined in this chapter is followed, business will be disposed of with more dispatch and with less confusion, and meetings which previously dragged will proceed with greater rapidity and order.

THE CHAIRMAN

If the president of the organization or the chairman of the committee has already been chosen, he automatically becomes the presiding officer. When no such officer has been selected, the first duty of the group is to nominate and elect by a majority vote a chairman from among its members.

The most important duty of the chairman is to preserve order. To avoid a general hubbub, speakers are required to address the chairman and be recognized by him before speaking. The chairman must see that only one person speaks at a time. In addition, he has certain appointive powers, such as the naming of subcommittees and minor officers. In informal groups the chairman is allowed to enter the argument and to vote on proposals which are presented; in fact, as explained in the preceding chapters, he often exercises a vigorous leadership in the discussion. In formal bodies, however, he is limited to the duties of presiding.

ORDER OF BUSINESS

Nearly every organization has a regular order of business which is followed at each meeting. When no such predetermined order exists, the following one, or such parts of it as fit the business of the group, may be used.
1. Roll call.
2. Minutes of the last meeting—to be read, corrected, approved.
3. Settlement of business left over from the last meeting as indicated in the minutes.
4. Committee reports; action upon their recommendations.
5. Consideration of new items of business.
6. Determination of the time and place of the next meeting, unless this is regularly established.
7. Adjournment.

Special order determined in advance   Sometimes a problem arises which is so important that it is made the special order of business for the next meeting. When this is done, the regular order of the next meeting is modified to give this special problem precedence, and all other matters are omitted or postponed.

Changing the order   Occasionally an important question comes up unexpectedly. When it requires immediate attention, it may be considered in advance of its regular place in the order of business by the vote of two thirds of the group.

THE SUBJECT FOR DISCUSSION

At times the subject or subjects for the discussion have been determined in advance; the group may be a committee whose duty was specified by the authority which created it, or the subject may be introduced by the recommendation of a subcommittee. Usually, however, the specific proposal is introduced by a motion made by some member of the group.

How the subject is introduced by a motion   The proper form for introducing a motion is to say, "Mr. Chairman, I move that. . . ." Before the motion can be discussed, a second person must usually support it in order to prevent considering matters which interest only one person. To second a motion, you should say, "Mr. Chairman, I second the motion."

Until a motion is made and seconded, no one is allowed to discuss it. After a motion has been made and seconded, no other subject may be discussed until the motion has been disposed of.[1] Too much emphasis cannot be placed on this latter point, for unless this rule is followed, the discussion is likely to wander about, and no decision will be reached.

---

[1] For a discussion of privileged, subsidiary, and incidental motions, some of which may be injected into a discussion at any time, see *Robert's Rules of Order* (Scott, Foresman and Company, Chicago, 1951). See also the table of motions on pages 598–599.

How the subject may be limited   The motion may be limited or modified in two principal ways: the first is by a division of the question and the second is by amendment of the motion.

Division of the question. Sometimes a motion contains two questions. For example, the motion that "this organization rent an office in the Union Building for six months beginning tomorrow" contains the question of the *place* of the proposed office and the *duration of time* for which the office is to be rented, as well as the question of renting an office at all. When such a motion is made, any member of the group may ask the chairman to divide the motion into two or more parts so that each part can be discussed separately. The chairman has the authority to do this if no one objects; if someone does object or the chairman refuses to divide the question, "a motion for division" may be made and passed by a majority vote.

Amendment of the motion. At times the general idea of the motion is satisfactory, but some part of it is undesirable or not clearly stated. The motion can then be changed by striking out or adding certain words. In order to do this, a "motion to amend" is required, which must itself be seconded and passed by a majority vote before it may become part of the original motion. The proper form for proposing an amendment is the following: "Mr. Chairman, I move that the motion be amended by striking out the words ['six months'] and inserting the words ['one year'] so that the motion will read ['this organization shall rent an office in the Union Building for one year']." The motion to amend may itself be amended or discussed, but it must be voted upon before the main question is decided. If the motion to amend is approved, the discussion returns to the original motion *as amended;* if the amending motion fails, the discussion returns to the original form of the main motion.

A motion to amend must meet two requirements in order for the chairman to accept it for consideration. First, it must be germane; that is, the amending motion may modify the original motion but must not change its meaning entirely. To strike out the whole motion and substitute an entirely different proposition is not allowed by the method of amendment. Second, it must embody a real change. Merely to change the motion from an affirmative to a negative statement of the same thing is not permissible. The following example will indicate a proper use of amendment:

1. *Original motion*—"that an expenditure of $500 be authorized for repairing the clubhouse roof."
2. *Amendment*—"that the sum of '$1000 be' substituted for '$500'; and that the words 'and completely re-covering' be inserted after the word 'repairing' in the motion."
3. *Motion as amended*—"that an expenditure of $1000 be authorized for repairing and completely re-covering the clubhouse roof."

The discussion of the subject

Any member may discuss the motion before the group, but he must limit his discussion to that motion until it is disposed of in some way. The chairman has the right to stop any member who violates this rule and to give the floor to someone else. As soon as the motion has been settled or disposed of, discussion on it must cease unless a formal motion to reconsider it is made and approved. A motion "to reconsider" must be presented by someone who voted with the majority but who wishes to change his vote, and a majority must favor reconsideration. Except in this special case, disposal of a motion automatically ends the discussion on it.

Certain types of motions cannot be discussed at all but must be put to a vote at once. The most important of these are the following:

1. Motions to call for the regular order of business.
2. Motions for the "previous question."
3. Motions to "lay on the table."
4. Motions for adjournment.

How motions may be disposed of

There are three principal ways by which motions may be disposed of: a vote on the motion, a motion to postpone or to lay on the table, and reference to a committee.

Vote on the motion. Usually the vote on the main motion comes about naturally. When the important points have been discussed, the group automatically seems to become ready for a vote. As soon as the chairman senses this attitude, he may suggest a vote, and if there is no objection, the vote is taken. There are times, however, when the attitude of the group toward the proposal is sharply divided, and the discussion continues vigorously even after all the important points have been made. At such times, it is necessary to make a motion to end the discussion and to take a vote. Such a motion is called a motion for the "previous question," and is made as follows: "Mr. Chairman, I move the previous question." (In less formal groups, this motion is sometimes made by merely calling out, "Question!") The motion for the previous question cannot be discussed but must be voted on at once, and it must receive a two-thirds vote for adoption. If it is adopted, the discussion on the main motion must cease and a vote on the main motion be taken at once.

Motion to postpone or to lay on the table. The principal effect of a motion to postpone or to lay the proposition on the table is to remove the proposal from discussion for the time being in order to allow a consideration of more important matters. A motion which has been postponed or laid on the table may then be called up for discussion at a more convenient time and disposed of then. The motion to postpone is made by saying, "Mr. Chairman, I move the question be postponed indefinitely," or ". . . postponed until . . . [a definite time]." To lay a proposal on the table, simply say, "Mr. Chairman, I move the question be laid on the table." The effect of either motion is practically the same. The motion to postpone or to lay on the table may be made at any time during the discussion and may be adopted by a majority vote.

Note that unless a definite time is set for reconsidering a motion which is postponed or laid on the table, the chances are that it will be forgotten or that the pressure of other matters will prevent its being brought up again and voted on. In fact, the motion to postpone indefinitely is often used to defeat a proposal politely without making the members of the group commit themselves upon it definitely. Moreover, this motion is often used to test the strength of the support for or opposition to the proposal; each person's vote on postponement tends to show his attitude toward the proposal itself.

Reference to a committee. A motion to refer the proposal to a committee may be made at any time during the discussion and, if adopted by a majority vote, has the effect of removing the main motion from discussion and passing it on to the committee indicated. There are sometimes standing committees to which the motion may be referred; if not, the chairman may be authorized to appoint a special committee or a special group may be named in the motion itself. The proposal may be passed on to a committee without instructions, or the committee may be instructed to investigate and report back, or it may be authorized to take final action on the proposal.

This means of disposing of motions is especially valuable for handling proposals on which the group does not wish to spend time for detailed consideration. Sometimes, moreover, no one in the group at the time has adequate information on the subject to justify a final decision, and by instructing a committee to investigate and report, that information can be assured for future consideration.

The form for stating a motion to refer to committee varies with its detailed intent. A few of the forms frequently used are: "Mr. Chairman, I move that the question be referred to the —— committee," or "to the —— committee, with instructions to report at . . . [a definite time]," or "—— committee, with power to act." When a special committee must be set up to consider the proposal, provision for creating that committee must be included in the proposal as follows: "Mr. Chairman, I move that this question be referred to a committee of —— members to be appointed by the chair," or "committee of —— members, namely, Mr. ——, Miss ——, Mrs. —— [etc.]," the remainder of the motion continuing as indicated above.

ADJOURNMENT

When the business of the meeting is concluded and no one addresses the chairman for further discussion, the chairman may close the meeting by simply declaring it adjourned. Sometimes a fixed time for adjournment has been determined before the group meets; in this event, when the time arrives, the chairman is required to declare the meeting adjourned unless a motion is passed definitely extending the discussion beyond that limit. At any time during the discussion, a motion fixing the time for adjournment may be adopted by majority vote. When the time decided on

PARLIAMENTARY PROCEDURE FOR HANDLING MOTIONS

CLASSIFICATIONS	TYPES OF MOTIONS	ORDER OF HANDLING	MUST BE SECONDED	CAN BE DISCUSSED	CAN BE AMENDED	VOTE REQUIRED	CAN BE RE-CONSIDERED
Main motion	To present a proposal to assembly	Cannot be made if any other motion is pending	Yes	Yes	Yes	Majority [1]	Yes
Subsidiary motions [2]	To postpone indefinitely action on a motion	Has precedence over above motion	Yes	Yes	No	Majority	Affirmative vote only
	To amend (modify) a main motion	Has precedence over above motion	Yes	When motion is debatable	Yes, but only once	Majority	Yes
	To refer motion to committee	Has precedence over above motions	Yes	Yes	Yes	Majority	Yes
	To postpone action on a motion to a certain time	Has precedence over above motions	Yes	Yes	Yes	Majority	Yes
	To limit discussion to a certain time	Has precedence over above motions	Yes	No	Yes	Two-thirds	Yes
	Previous question (to call for vote)	Has precedence over above motions	Yes	No	No	Two-thirds	No
	To table a motion (to lay it aside until later)	Has precedence over above motions	Yes	No	No	Majority	No
Incidental motions [3]	To suspend a rule temporarily (e.g., to change order of business)	No definite precedence rule	Yes	No	No	Two-thirds	No
	To close nominations [4]		Yes	No	Yes	Two-thirds	No
	To reopen nominations		Yes	No	Yes, only as to time	Majority	Negative vote only
	To withdraw or modify a motion (to prevent vote or inclusion in minutes) [5]	These motions have precedence over motion to which they pertain	No	No	No	Majority	Negative vote only
	To rise to a point of order (to enforce rules) [6]		No	No	No	No vote; chairman rules	No
	To appeal from decision of the chair (must be made immediately) [6]		Yes	When motion is debatable	No	Majority	Yes
	To divide a question (consider by parts)	Takes precedence only over motions to postpone indefinitely	[7]	No	Yes	[7]	No

	Motion	Precedence				Two-thirds	Negative vote only
	To object to consideration of a question [8]	Takes precedence over main motion	No	No	No	Majority	No
	To secure a division of the assembly (standing vote)	Has precedence after question has been put	No	No	No	No vote required [5]	No
Privileged motions	To call for orders of the day (to keep meeting to order of business) [9]	Has precedence over above motions	No	No	No	Majority	No
	Questions of privilege (to point out noise, etc.) [6]	Has precedence over above motions	Yes	No	No	Majority	No
	To take a recess	Has precedence over above motions	Yes	If no motion is pending	Yes	Majority	No
	To adjourn	Has precedence over above motions	Yes	No	No	Majority	No
	To set next meeting time	Has precedence over above motions	Yes	If no motion is pending	As to time and place	Majority	Yes
Unclassified motions	To take motion from table (to bring up tabled motion for consideration) [10]	Cannot be made if any other motion is pending	Yes	No	No	Majority	No
	To reconsider (to discuss and vote on previously decided motion) [11]	Can be made if another motion is pending [11]	Yes	When motion is debatable	No	Majority	No
	To rescind (repeal) decision on a motion [12]	Cannot be made if any other motion is pending	Yes	Yes	Yes	Majority or two-thirds	Yes

[1] A tied vote is always lost except on an appeal from the decision of the chair (see "Incidental motions") when a tied vote sustains the chair.

[2] Subsidiary motions are motions that pertain to a main motion while it is pending.

[3] Most incidental motions arise out of a pending question and must be decided before the question out of which they arise is decided.

[4] The chair opens nominations with "Nominations are now in order." Nominations may be made by a nominating committee, by a nominating ballot, or from the floor. A member may make a motion to close nominations or the chair may declare nominations closed.

[5] The mover may request to withdraw or modify his motion without consent of anyone before the motion has been put to the assembly for consideration. When the motion is before the assembly and if there is no objection from anyone in the assembly, the chairman announces that the motion is withdrawn or modified. If anyone objects, the request is put to a vote.

[6] A member may interrupt a speaker to rise to a point of order or of appeal, call for orders of the day, or raise a question of privilege.

[7] If propositions relate to independent subjects, they must be divided on the request of a single member. The request may be made when another has the floor. If the resolutions relate to the same subject but each can stand alone, they may be divided only on a regular motion and vote.

[8] The objection can be made only when the question is first introduced before debate.

[9] Orders of the day may be changed by a motion to suspend the rules. (See "Incidental motions.")

[10] A motion can be taken from the table during the meeting when it was tabled or at the next meeting.

[11] A motion to reconsider may be made only by one who voted on the prevailing side. A motion to reconsider must be made during the meeting when it was decided or on the next succeeding day of the same session. If it is made while other business is pending, consideration is delayed until the current subject is finished, at which time it has precedence over all new motions of equal rank.

[12] It is impossible to rescind any action that has been taken as a result of a motion, but the unexecuted part may be rescinded. Notice must be given one meeting before the vote is taken, or if voted on immediately, a two-thirds vote to rescind is necessary.

arrives, the chairman merely announces, "I declare the meeting adjourned."

Motion to adjourn

If no fixed time has been set, the meeting may be ended at any time by adopting a motion to adjourn. This motion may be introduced at any time during the discussion and adopted by a majority vote. No discussion upon it is allowed; it must be voted upon at once—unless adjournment would have the effect of disbanding the group entirely with no provision for reassembling, in which case the motion to adjourn loses its privileged character and becomes debatable and subject to amendment.

Setting the time for the next meeting

When no definite provision has been made for a future meeting of the group, the motion to adjourn may be amended to fix the time for reconvening. Such an amendment is called a motion "to fix the time to which to adjourn." This motion may be discussed or amended and must be decided by a majority vote before the motion to adjourn is itself put to a vote. Unless such an amendment is made, business is often left unfinished with no provision for ultimate settlement.

MODIFYING THE RULES OF ORDER

All of the rules listed above may not be necessary when the group is small or informal. The purpose of parliamentary procedure is to speed up the orderly conduct of business; it must never be employed with such unnecessary detail and dogmatism that it merely formalizes and complicates the discussion. To follow the rules slavishly in small groups is frequently a waste of time rather than a help. On the other hand, larger meetings frequently require the application of parliamentary rules in all their detail—much greater detail than that presented in this chapter. Sometimes the situation requires the adoption of special rules which are not listed even in manuals of parliamentary procedure but which are fitted to the peculiar needs of a particular group. Apply the rules of parliamentary law as fully as required to preserve order, insure fair play, and expedite business—but only to that degree.

Although the primary object of parliamentary law is to secure an orderly conduct of business, a skillful use of these rules may often be used to strengthen materially the position of majority or minority groups within the organization. With the ethics of such tactics we are not here concerned. Logrolling may or may not be justified, depending largely upon personal points of view, but the fact remains that such tactics are often used. It is therefore important—for defensive purposes, if for no other—to understand a few of the basic stratagems employed.

Selection of officers and committees

The ultimate disposal of a proposition often depends as much upon the attitude of officials or committees as upon the attitude of the whole group. A chairman who is partial to one side or the other can very skillfully give the floor only to those whose opinions agree with his own, or he may call upon the best speakers on his own side and the worst on the opposing side. The effect of this upon those who are undecided is obvious. The secretary may phrase his reports and minutes in such a way that they are technically accurate and yet give a decidedly biased impression. Committees are often more important than the entire organization as a whole; complicated problems are generally referred to them for study and report. This practice saves a good deal of time, but if the committee happens to be biased, the report will be prejudiced, and its influence upon the whole group will therefore be one-sided. For these reasons, scrutinize the selection of officers and committees very carefully.

Order of business

A change from the regular order of business may often be used strategically. In this manner, certain items are withheld from discussion until a time when absence has depleted the ranks of the opposition; then, while those who support the measure are in the majority, the order of business is changed, the item in question is introduced, and its approval is pushed through. Similarly, approval of a measure may be defeated by injecting another item ahead of it. Thus, consideration of the first measure can be delayed until greater opposition to it can be marshaled. This particular type of strategy is often applied so subtly that it is detected only with difficulty.

Amendment

The most frequent strategic use of amendments is for the purpose of dividing the majority. The idea beneath this stratagem is the same as that often used in politics. Party A is in the majority; Party B is in the minority. Party B therefore induces one of the members of Party A to run on an independent ticket. The result is that Party A is divided between its regular nominee and the independent candidate, thus giving Party B a plurality in the election.

This same technic may be applied to motions. Suppose that those who favor the proposal are in the minority. An amendment may be offered to the motion which will please some of those who were originally opposed to it. When the motion is so amended, the opposition to it is split, and the motion is passed.

Now reverse the situation. Suppose those who oppose the motion are in the minority. They may offer an amendment which will split the majority and draw support away from the original proposal. Enough votes are gained from the majority to help the minority group pass the amendment. Then when the motion *as amended* is put to a vote, the minority is helped in defeating it by the votes of those who violently opposed the amendment and who prefer to see the whole proposal fail rather than have it approved in its amended form.

Of course, the strategy of using amendments to divide the opposition is seldom as simple as indicated above. Amendments cause shifts in both directions—from the minority to the majority as well as from the majority to the minority. The resulting balance of power must be neatly calculated if this method is to be successful. Moreover, it must not be obvious that the amendment is made for strategic purposes, or suspicion will be aroused and the plan will fail. Nevertheless, dangerous and doubtful as it is, this type of strategy is often employed with success. Be careful, however, that your proposal doesn't become a victim of this strategy of dividing by amendment.

Frequently, a proposal requiring *Reference to committee* further study is referred to a committee. But there are committees and committees. In the Federal Congress, for example, there is a committee "For the Care of Old Documents." Many a bill referred to this committee is carefully filed away and nevermore brought to light. Thus, if a proposal is referred to a committee composed of members known to favor it, the chances of ultimate adoption are greater than if it is referred to a committee known to oppose it. Usually the subject matter of a proposal determines the committee to which it is referred; but many proposals extend within the possible jurisdiction of more than one committee so that a choice between them is possible. For instance, the proposal for roofing a clubhouse, mentioned on page 595, might be referred either to the house committee or to the finance committee. Sometimes an entirely new (special) committee is elected or appointed to deal with the proposal. When this is done, the make-up of this committee is exceedingly important.

Sometimes after the fatigue of a *Adjournment* long session the proposal for adjournment is welcomed. When such is the case, minorities can prevent unfavorable action upon a proposal by cutting short the discussion on it. This method is most often used when there are many absentees whose vote would add weight to the minority side or when there is a probability that subsequent events will afford additional arguments.

There are, of course, many other stratagems of parliamentary procedure which are employed. These few, however, are the most frequently used and form the foundation for many of the others. The employment of such tactics requires the utmost care. Unless there is a seeming innocence in the strategy used, it may boomerang. There must be an obvious and plausible reason for each move made so that the real reason will not become evident. Conversely, to protect oneself from such tactics, it is not enough to examine the *obvious* reason for some move; the scrutiny must extend to the motive itself.

In the long run, the best strategy to employ is that of absolute fairness and frankness. A reputation for being aboveboard usually adds more weight to one's opinions and secures more permanent support than any stratagem of parliamentary law. Remember that the real purpose of parliamentary procedure is to make sure that the majority's judgment prevails and at the same time to protect any reasonable attempt of the minority to modify that judgment.

PROBLEMS

1. Be ready to discuss the following questions in class: What is the purpose of parliamentary law for informal groups? What is a typical order of business of such a group? How are subjects for discussion presented, considered, and disposed of? How do stratagems affect the operation of parliamentary law?

2. Outline a suitable order of business for (a) a special meeting of the senior class called to select an appropriate class gift and (b) a regular business meeting of some specified club.

3. Phrase five proposals as main motions.

4. Give an example of a motion that contains more than one proposition. If you were chairman, how would you divide it, and in what order would you allow the parts to be discussed?

5. Phrase amendments to each of the five main motions prepared for Problem 3. Be sure that your amendments are germane and that they embody a real change.

6. Taking one of the main motions stated for Problem 3, phrase correctly a motion (a) for the previous question, (b) to postpone, (c) to lay on the table, (d) to refer to committee.

7. Phrase correctly a motion to fix the period for which to adjourn. Would such a motion be in order for situations (a) and (b) of Problem 2?

8. Organize the class into a hypothetical meeting of some organization—for example, the student council, the sophomore class, the dramatics board, or the city council—and proceed to conduct business. Be careful to follow correct parliamentary procedure and not to allow others to violate it. Employ whatever parliamentary strategy seems justifiable, and watch to detect its unscrupulous use.

Student's
Reference
Manual

A GUIDE TO EFFECTIVE LISTENING

The ability to listen well is quite as important as the ability to speak well, since effective oral communication depends on both. This point was emphasized in Chapter 2 (pp. 28–30), where speech was described as a circular response. Throughout the book the importance of adapting speech to the listener has been stressed. The primary emphasis has been on learning to *speak*, but many of the principles discussed can also help you become a more alert and intelligent *listener*.

Some improvement in your listening ability may occur as a matter of course, but you will progress more rapidly and make greater improvement if you exert conscious effort. The value of such effort is obvious. You will learn more accurately and easily from lectures and discussions in your college classes. You will listen more critically to arguments about community and national affairs. And as a student of speech, you will learn to analyze the effectiveness of methods and technics used by other speakers in class and out.

This section of the Reference Manual is designed to point out some of the special problems involved in good listening and to suggest how some of the principles discussed in the main parts of the book can be applied to improve your listening ability.

Hearing

The first problem, of course, is simply to hear what the speaker is saying. This involves:

1. *The ear.* A diagram of this organ is shown on page 607. Sound waves (vibrations of air) are transmitted through the pinna into the auditory canal, where they strike the eardrum. This sets in motion three hinged bones—the hammer, anvil, and stirrup—in the air cavity of the middle ear. This cavity is supplied with air by the Eustachian tube, leading in from the throat. The movements of the stirrup are transmitted to the oval window and, in turn, to the fluid of the inner ear, where tiny hair cells and nerve endings in the cochlea carry the impulses to the auditory nerve. From there they travel finally to the auditory areas of the brain. Any slip-up in this total process results in faulty hearing and, if possible, should be corrected with professional aid.

THE HUMAN EAR

1. Pinna
2. Auditory canal
3. Eardrum
4. Hammer, anvil, and stirrup
5. Eustachian tube
6. Oval window
7. Cochlea
8. Auditory nerve
9. Semicircular canal

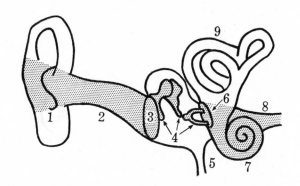

2. *External acoustic disturbances.* A review of Chapter 6 is useful here, especially the discussion of loudness, pages 113–116. Usually the listener can do little to reduce outside noise—except to close an open door near his seat—nor can he improve the speaker's distinctness or the loud-speaker adjustment. But the listener *can* arrive early enough to get a seat close to the speaker and with a clear view of him. In addition, he can avoid making disturbing noises himself and to some extent discourage others around him from doing so.

3. *Concentration of attention.* Disturbing noises will interfere less with your ability to hear what the speaker says if you concentrate your attention on him. Your mind tends to sort out the sounds received by the ear, discarding the meaningless ones. Some of the intelligibility word lists on pages 122–127 can be used for listening practice of this sort, with classmates providing the disturbing noise.

Comprehension   Good listening requires more than merely hearing the speaker; it means grasping and understanding what he says. To do this, you must:

1. *Concentrate on the speaker's ideas.* Just as concentrating on the speaker's words helps you to hear them above the noise, focusing your thought on his expressed ideas helps you to grasp them clearly. If your mind is occupied with worries about an impending draft notice or your acceptance into graduate school, you may

hear what the speaker says but fail entirely to grasp his *meaning.* For effective listening, try to concentrate on the speaker's subject.

2. *Recognize the speaker's organization.* In Chapter 14 on outlining, a thorough discussion of arranging main ideas and subordinate points was presented. Your comprehension of someone else's speech will be increased if you learn to recognize the arrangement of his ideas: What is the central thesis? What are the main points, and how are they arranged—in time sequence, space, problem-solution, topical? What are the minor points, and to which main point do they relate? It is helpful to practice taking notes in a *structured* manner as the speaker proceeds.

3. *Note the supporting details and proof.* As you learn to listen for the idea structure, note the relationship of illustrative detail to the main points. Listen carefully as the main points are filled in so that you can grasp their full significance clearly, perhaps jotting down some of the more important details. But learn not to mistake vivid details for the main ideas they support. Review Chapter 12 on this point.

4. *Relate the ideas to your own knowledge.* Your comprehension will be increased in most instances by an active effort to relate what you hear to what you already know. If you know little about the subject, some advance study will help. But avoid letting your prior opinions prevent your listening to new ideas. Usually a receptive, open-minded attitude is most conducive to understanding; listen to *all* the speaker has to say before deciding whether or not to agree.

Appreciation   Speeches to entertain are for enjoyment and require only an appreciative attitude from the audience. Appreciation, in turn, requires a relaxed, receptive, and imaginative attitude on the listener's part. This type of listening, of course, should not be used where critical analysis is required to reach logical decision, lest the listener's emotions, fed by a vivid imagination, lead him to faulty judgments. But where critical judgment is not required, receptive and imaginative listening will increase the listener's pleasure and enrich his perception. Appreciative listening requires:

1. *Physical and mental relaxation.* Sit in a comfortable, relaxed position. So far as possible, free your mind of other interests and vexing problems and worries.

2. *Receptive attitude.* For the time being, put aside critical attitudes. Open your mind as well as your ears; let the speaker, for the moment, direct your train of thought.

3. *Imaginative projection and empathy.* Instead of holding back, let go. Give your imagination free play so that you join with the speaker in vividly picturing what he describes. Permit yourself to respond freely; allow your enthusiasm and emotion to reflect that of the speaker.

Evaluation

Critical and analytical listening is necessary for evaluation. Appreciative listening, although not ruled out, is carefully controlled. Thorough comprehension forms the basis of evaluation, but the listener must do more than merely comprehend. He must analyze the speaker's reasoning and judge the value of his evidence; he must recognize emotional appeal for what it is and accept or reject it knowingly; and he must not let vivid phraseology influence his judgment more than solid fact.

1. *Analysis of problems.* (See pp. 413–415, 560–566.) As you listen, ask yourself whether the speaker has properly analyzed the problem and whether the proposal he advocates is the best way of meeting it.

2. *Reasoning.* (See pp. 31–35, 423–425.) Note the type of reasoning used by the speaker. Does he reason from example, axiom, or causal relation? Is his reasoning sound, or does it contain flaws in logic?

3. *Evidence.* (See pp. 194–207, 576–577.) Note both the amount of supporting material and its reliability. Does the speaker use unsupported assertions reinforced only by vivid phrasing or his own positive manner? Does he present the facts fairly, or does he seem to be biased in selecting which facts to present or which to withhold?

4. *Motivation.* (See pp. 168–183.) Recognize the motive appeals the speaker employs and their relation to his reasoning. Accept or reject such appeals judiciously; avoid being swayed by emo-

tion and appeal to prejudice when they are contrary to logic and fact.

5. *Wording.* (See pp. 358–365.) Pay close attention to the wording used. Is it accurate or vague? Are false conclusions suggested by loose phraseology? Does the speaker rely on loaded words, name-calling, and generalities instead of reasoning and evidence?

Listening as a Critical Speech Student

As a student of speech, you should also observe and analyze the speaker's qualities as a speaker. In addition to the problems of hearing, comprehension, appreciation, and evaluation common to all listeners, you have the special task of studying the speaker's manner and method. By doing so you can develop your ability as a judge of good speaking and at the same time improve your own speech by observing that of others.

A thorough critical analysis would include nearly all the topics covered in this book. In the beginning, center your analysis on a few related points. The chart of "Common Errors" inside the back cover of this book can be used as a guide. Later you will be able to judge more points at a time. In listening to class speeches, the points you should center on are those which the particular assignment emphasizes.

INTERNATIONAL PHONETIC ALPHABET

On the following page is an abridged version of the International Phonetic Alphabet. The symbols are divided into vowels, diphthongs, and consonants. The phonetic symbols are in the left-hand column. In the center column are words containing the sound represented by the symbol. These illustrative words are translated into phonetic symbols in the right-hand column. In words of more than one syllable, the accent mark always *precedes* the accented syllable.[1]

---

[1] For a more complete explanation of the phonetic alphabet, see John S. Kenyon and Thomas A. Knott, "Introduction," *A Pronouncing Dictionary of American English* (G. and C. Merriam Co., Springfield, Mass., 1951).

Sym-bol	Key Word	Pronunciation	Sym-bol	Key Word	Pronunciation

VOWELS

Sym-bol	Key Word	Pronunciation	Sym-bol	Key Word	Pronunciation
i	flee	fli	o	no	no
ɪ	sit	sɪt	ʊ	good	gʊd
e	mate	met	u	suit	sut
ɛ	fed	fɛd	ɝ³	mercy	'mɝsɪ (r sounded)
æ	hat	hæt	ɜ³	mercy	'mɜsɪ (r silent)
a¹	ask	ask	ɚ³	mother	'mʌðɚ (r sounded)'
ɑ	part	pɑrt	ə³	rather	'ræðə (r silent)
ɒ²	wad	wɒd		attack	ə'tæk
ɔ	thaw	θɔ	ʌ³	annul	ə'nʌl

DIPHTHONGS [4]

Sym-bol	Key Word	Pronunciation	Sym-bol	Key Word	Pronunciation
aɪ	mile	maɪl	ju⁵	union	'junjən
aʊ	cow	kaʊ		mute	mjut
ɔɪ	employ	ɪm'plɔɪ	ɪu⁵	mute	mɪut

CONSONANTS

Sym-bol	Key Word	Pronunciation	Sym-bol	Key Word	Pronunciation
p	post	post	h	hat	hæt
b	bat	bæt	tʃ	chat	tʃæt
t	tale	tel	dʒ	jest	dʒɛst
d	duty	'djutɪ	m	mute	mjut
k	cow	kaʊ	m̩	keep 'em	'kipm̩
g	gap	gæp	n	union	'junjən
f	face	fes	n̩	mutton	'mʌtn̩
v	vine	vaɪn	ŋ	bang	bæŋ
θ	both	boθ	l	mile	maɪl
ð	then	ðɛn	l̩	handle	'hændl̩
s	sit	sɪt	w	wet	wɛt
z	zero	'zɪro	hw	when	hwɛn
ʃ	push	pʊʃ	j	yellow	'jɛlo
ʒ	measure	'mɛʒɚ	r	red	rɛd

[1] The vowel in *ask* as it is heard in the East, between "hæt" and "pɑrt."

[2] The vowel in *wad* as it is heard in New England, between "pɑrt" and "θɔ."

[3] In this phonetic alphabet the sounds ɝ, ɜ, and ʌ are used only in accented syllables, being regarded as separate speech sounds from ɚ and ə which appear only in unaccented syllables.

[4] Diphthongs are here considered single speech sounds. Diphthong symbols, and such consonant symbols as tʃ and dʒ, are regarded as single phonetic symbols.

[5] The diphthongs ju and ɪu often alternate (as in "mjut," "mɪut"), with the same speaker sometimes using both forms. The symbol ju is a rising diphthong (the second element stressed more than the first), whereas ɪu is either a falling diphthong (first element stressed) or a level-stress diphthong.

GEN-ERAL END	AUDIENCE ATTITUDE	ATTENTION STEP	NEED STEP
To Enter-tain	(A) Interested	1. Mention subject. 2. Use series of anecdotes and illustrations to amplify your viewpoint. 3. Use humor. (Normal End of the Speech)	*Sometimes:* Burlesque the development of the entire motivated sequence as if for one of the other general ends. Exaggerate obviously if you use this method.
	(B) Apathetic	1. Relate subject to the experience and interests of the audience. 2. Proceed as above.	Proceed as above.
To In-form	(C) Interested in Subject	1. Reference to subject. 2. Narrow scope of subject to limits of the speech.	Briefly mention its importance to the listeners—why they need to know.
	(D) Apathetic to Subject	Overcome inertia; arouse curiosity by the use of: 1. Unusual illustration. 2. Striking facts.	Demonstrate the importance of the subject to the audience by: 1. Explanation of its importance. 2. Illustrations.
To Stim-ulate	(E) Favorable but not Aroused	Intensify interest: 1. New angles of situation. 2. Vivid illustrations. 3. Personal challenge.	Make the need *impressive:* 1. Vivid illustrations; imagery. 2. Unusual comparisons and contrasts. 3. Striking factual disclosures. 4. Point out effect on audience.
	(F) Apathetic to Situation	Same as above, but *more striking.* Especial emphasis of *vital* attention factor.	Same as above with special stress on the vital effect of problem on the audience. Apply strong personal motive appeals.
To Con-vince	Same as above.	Same as above.	1. Same as above, with particular emphasis of powerful factual evidence: *Specific instances, striking statistics, testimony.* 2. State requirements as below.
	(G) Interested in the Situation but Undecided	1. Reference to need (or) 2. Brief illustration of some unusual aspect of it. 3. Narrow attention toward basic aspect of the problem which underlies the need.	1. Point out basic nature of problem: (a) Historical background. (b) Basic causes. 2. Ramifications of present bad effects. 3. Point out what *requirements* an effective solution must meet to satisfy this need.
	(H) Interested in the Situation; Hostile to Proposal	1. Establish common ground by emphasizing point of agreement with audience: (a) Attitudes. (b) Beliefs. (c) Common experiences. 2. Continue as above.	1. Secure agreement on some basic principle or belief. 2. Continue as above, relating entire discussion to this principle. 3. Establish requirements of the solution on this basic principle.
	(I) Hostile to Belief in Existence of Problem	1. Begin as above. 2. Establish agreement as soon as possible on an acceptable principle to use in basing judgment of present situation: (a) Quote persons respected by audience.	1. Show that present conditions violate this principle. (a) Use facts, figures, and especially acceptable testimony. (b) Beware of exaggeration. 2. Continue as above.
To Ac-tuate	(E) to (I) Same as above.	Develop as above depending on attitude of the audience. Follow methods in proper row (E) to (I) as indicated.	Develop as above using methods as indicated in rows (E) to (I) depending on the attitude of the audience.

AUDIENCE ATTITUDES TOWARD THE SUBJECT OR PURPOSE

SATISFACTION STEP	VISUALIZATION STEP	ACTION STEP
Sometimes: Continue burlesque as suggested.	*Sometimes:* Continue burlesque as before.	*Sometimes:* Continue burlesque as before.
Proceed as above.	Proceed as above.	Proceed as above.

1. Begin with initial summary.
  (*a*) Define terms if necessary.
2. Present details of information.
  (*a*) Be concrete and specific.
  (*b*) Retain interest with factors of attention.
  (*c*) Follow: time order, space, etc.
3. Close with final summary.
	Sometimes: Suggest pleasure to be had from knowledge of this information.	*Sometimes:* Suggest places for a further study or application of this information.

Make a brief statement of the attitude or future action desired. 1. Make it short. 2. Use dynamic phrasing.	Use *Positive* method. 1. Project audience into future. 2. Picture desirable conditions. 3. *Mild* exaggeration. 4. Use vivid imagery.	1. Use challenge to commit listeners to proposal (or) 2. Use suggestion to assume they are already so committed.

1. State the proposed belief or plan of action to be approved.
2. Explain it clearly.
3. Show logically how it will meet the requirements laid down in the need step.
4. Offer proof that the proposition will work:
  (*a*) Facts.
  (*b*) Figures.
  (*c*) Testimony of experts.
  (*d*) Examples of successful operation.
5. Demonstrate its benefits.
	Use *Positive, Negative,* or method of *Contrast.*
	1. Project audience into the future.
	2. Picture desirable (or undesirable) conditions.
	3. Use vivid imagery.
	4. *Be brief.*
	5. *Don't exaggerate!*
		1. Restate request for belief or approval of plan of action.
		2. Recapitulate reasons for its adoption:
		  (*a*) Summary.
		  (*b*) Illustration.
		  (*c*) Quotation.
		  (*d*) Personal intention.

1. Show relation of the proposal to the basic principle laid down in the need step. 2. Show its superiority on this basis to any other proposal. 3. Otherwise, proceed as above.	Proceed as above.	Proceed as above.
Proceed as above.	Proceed as above.	Proceed as above.
Develop as above using methods as indicated in rows (*E*) to (*I*) depending on the attitude of the audience. Stress importance of *definite action by the audience.*	Develop as indicated in appropriate row above.	Develop as indicated in appropriate row above. Place responsibility for action on the individual members of the audience.

Index

Titles of sample speeches appear in SMALL CAPITALS.
Titles of selections for vocal practice appear in *italics*.

3 4 5 6 7 8 9 10 11 12 13 14 15 16   68 67 66 65 64

Common errors in speech construction, delivery, and outlining

This chart is useful for indicating criticisms of outlines, manuscripts, or speeches. The abbreviations (**ANAL., DEV., QUES.**), numbers (**17, 25, 34**), or number-letter combinations (**15D, 27A, 28E**), when placed at the *top* of the sheet, indicate that the fault is general; when placed in the *margin*, they refer to the section immediately opposite. The instructor can also record the criticisms on a card when listening to a speech. (The numbers in parentheses after the entries refer to pages where the problem is discussed.)

ANAL.—Faults in analysis

1 Audience not specified
2 Audience diagnosis incomplete (157–165)
3 Primary interests and fixed ideas of audience not indicated, or incorrectly stated (160–161)
4 Audience attitude not correctly analyzed (161–165)
5 Occasion not well analyzed (156–157)
6 Subject too broad (143–144)
7 Subject not appropriate (143)
8 Wrong general end (145–150)
9 Purpose not specific, or impossible to attain (150–154)

CONT.—Faults in content

10 Inadequate support for proof or illumination of ideas
  A Needs explanation (196–197)
  B Needs analogy (197–199)
  C Needs illustration (199–202)
  D Needs instances (202–203)
  E Needs statistics (203–204)
  F Needs testimony (205–207)
  G Needs restatement (207)
  H Needs visual aids (207–212, 360)
11 Reasoning weak or illogical (423–425)
12 Requires special technics
  A Use "yes-response" (426–427)
  B Use "this-or-nothing" (427)
  C Establish principle of agreement (426)
13 Inadequate motive appeal
  A Wrong motive for audience (170–183)
  B Weak appeal (181–182)
  C Tactless appeal (182)
14 Attention factors weak or lacking (226–231)
15 Poor wording (330–339)
  A Meaning not adequately expressed (330–332)
  B Lacks imagery; not vivid enough (332–334, 393–397)
  C Language too flowery (334–335)
  D Faulty grammar
  E Poor diction (117–121)
  F Vague or clumsy wording of main points (240–242)